The Century
IN REVIEW

As compiled by Kyle Anderson and Jo Ann Reynolds
for the Okanagan Valley Newspaper Group

There is a magic to producing a newspaper seven days a week. When all goes well, the blend of well told stories, lively opinions, strong art and deft design results in a compelling mix for readers.

You can only imagine the task of retelling the events of the past 100 years. The Okanagan Valley Newspaper Group has spent the better part of 1999 shepherding along The Century In Review, although the project has truly been 100 years in the making. Our newspapers have been chronicling the Valley's affairs since the earliest part of this century.

It was early in the new year when the Valley's newspapers began pondering special projects to mark the end of the millennium. Some ideas were downright silly - others seemingly too ambitious. The Century In Review falls into the second category, but editors, researchers and sales staff soldiered on, steeled by belief the project was worth doing well.

Sure, there will be other tributes. The deafening roar of presses from Eastern Canada and the United States can almost be heard here in the Okanagan as publishers race to produce salutes to the 1900s.

At the very outset, everyone involved in The Century in Review agreed it was important to relive the events from an Okanagan perspective. A first class publication would naturally have to include man's first footsteps on the moon, the tragic death of JFK and the all-too-many rifle shots of all-too-many conflicts. Just as importantly, a tribute to the past – one rooted in the Okanagan - would have to contain the tragedies and triumphs experienced closer to home. It is here where our book will make its mark.

As project editor Kyle Anderson will tell you, The Century in Review is not a linear listing of the events from the past 100 years. It's not a reference guide which can be counted on for quickly solving family spats or getting higher grades on school tests. Better than that, The Century in Review is a series of snapshots gleaned from the Okanagan's daily newspapers. Using actual news stories and photos plucked from the archives, The Century in Review is a lively look at the past and is filled with surprises.

And, perhaps, the book is also a modest celebration of the Okanagan's newspapers and the duty they share to chronicle the passing of another day.

David Marsden

Executive Editor

Okanagan Valley Newspaper Group

The Century In Review
COMPILED BY
Kyle Anderson & Jo Ann Reynolds
for the Okanagan Valley Newspaper Group

RESEARCH
Jo Ann Reynolds
Lenore Schur
Sandra Shwaykosky
Chris Hendricks

TYPESETTING
Leanne Clare
Kim Chadwick
Erin Senger

PAGE LAYOUT
Rob Biron
Leanne Clare
Kyle Anderson

EDITING
Jo Ann Reynolds
Kyle Anderson

DESIGN CONCEPT AND COVER
Carole Humphreys

OKANAGAN VALLEY NEWSPAPER GROUP
David Marsden - Executive Editor - OVNG
Michael Turner - Managing Editor - Penticton Herald
Terry Armstrong   Willy Kerntopf   André Martin   Jack & Marion Morrison

ACKNOWLEDGEMENTS
Larry Little & Staff - Penticton Public Library
Annie Pope & Staff - Kelowna Public Library
Randy Manuel & Staff - Penticton Museum
Wayne Wilson - Kelowna Museum
Okanagan University College Libraries - Penticton & Vernon
Stuart Bish - Cover Photograph

ISBN 1-55056-735-7
Printed in Canada

Acknowledgements

Now it's time for my personal thanks.

When I was approached about compiling a book of this magnitude I was, needless to say, intimidated by the potential size of the project. I started looking for people who could realize my rather vague vision as to this book's direction.

It wasn't until my team started to take shape through these talented people that the vision did too.

First, my thanks go to Mike Turner, who had enough faith in my abilities to give his personal endorsement for me to create this project.

Carole Humphreys, one of the premier designers in the valley, created the "look" - a look that makes all that newspaper copy so readable and easy on the eye. Her cover design says so much in its own simplicity.

Leanne Clare is that ever so special person who creates magic with whatever she touches. She can be left with a pile of stories to typeset, photos to scan and a blank page to act as her palate, and effortlessly put it all together and paint a magic that is hers alone.

Rob Biron is man of many exceptional talents. He is a professional photographer and superb page editor. But most of all, to me, he is a man who heard that I was looking for help with layout and came to my rescue. His many early mornings and late evenings working at home made this book possible.

Lenore Schur is a very special friend who jumped in feet first to scan through hours and hours of microfilm in the Kelowna Library. Even when she gave birth to a baby son she wouldn't quit. Her teen-aged step-son, Chris Hendricks, immediately picked up where Lenore left off and he became yet another appreciated member of our little team.

Sandra Shwaykosky was also an invaluable part of this group. This woman also spent days looking through a mind-numbing amount of microfilm at the Penticton Public Library, finding and fleshing out stories for use in this book.

Kim Chadwick is an amazing person. As the person who retyped the photocopied stories provided from the researchers, Kim spent many an hour deciphering hundreds of pages of text with so much speed and precision, you could feel the breeze off the keyboard as she typed!

No research project could be accomplished without libraries and museums. My heartfelt thanks to Larry Little and his wonderful staff of the Penticton Public Library for allowing my team to take over the reference area all summer long. Ditto to Annie Pope and crew at the Kelowna Library. Thanks to all for not getting tired of looking at us staring into the microfilm readers.

Randy Manuel, curator of the Penticton Museum, did more than just supply us with photographs of early Penticton. His wealth of historical knowledge and his enthusiasm to share that knowledge created a desire in us to find out more about this great valley's people and history. Wayne Wilson's help at the Kelowna Museum also proved invaluable to us. His ability to know exactly what we were looking for helped create some very exciting pages about Kelowna's past.

My warmest appreciation goes to Jo Ann Reynolds. My lifelong friend is, in many ways, responsible for this book happening at all! Her organizational skills kept all the many facets of the book running on track. Her researching abilities, based around her journalism background, proved incredibly intuitive. Her people skills kept stress levels low and most of all, her constant support at my side kept the project pointed in an ever forward direction. In many ways this book is yours, Jo.

And finally, my thanks to you, who have purchased this book. I hope our group of dedicated people has done its job to give you an entertaining and informative look at the last 100 years of the world around you through the words of your own newspapers.

Kyle Anderson

Forward

Welcome to "The Century in Review."

And what a century it has been!

100 years ago the Okanagan was little more than a sparsely populated valley, with the orchard industry and small town commerce being pioneered by its residents.

We collectively crawled through the early years... From boardwalks to sidewalks, from telegraph to telephones, from stagecoach to automobiles, from war to peace to war to...

Then we took our first steps, tentatively, into space, into resolving racism, the self-destructive arms race and the population explosion.

Until finally... we began to run, at break neck speed, towards an era of instant communication, liberation and wealth.

Those rapid technological advancements brought us out of our insular world into the big one, where news from around the globe could enter our homes and our lives moments after it had occurred.

This book is a chronicle of the growth of our world and our access to it. From early stories about daily life in the orchards of the Okanagan to international coverage of major events from around the world and beyond, our newspapers have always acted as our window looking outward.

The words in this book come directly from the Kelowna Clarion (later the Courier), The Penticton Free Press (later the Herald) and the Vernon News, the oldest of the valley newspapers. Only a few photo descriptions and headlines have been modified for clarity and flow.

Journalistic styles and presentation have changed over the decades. Writing and spelling have evolved through the years and we have kept those idioms, editing the stories only for length so they could take their place in our valley's history.

In the world of ever-changing political correctness, we must emphasize that some stories written in their day might offend current-day sensibilities. We believe that by presenting the stories the way they were written at the time, we can now, in hindsight, recognize the folly in our prejudices.

Everyone who reads The Century in Review will have a different perspective on its contents. 100 years is a vast time period in the "world of news" to try and encapsulate in 400 pages. This is not a chronological encyclopedia of events nor does it include everything that happened everywhere. It is an account of what happened in the Okanagan and in the world... as reported in the newspapers of the day. We have given stories, in some cases, as much attention as the reporters gave it ten, twenty, fifty years ago. In others we have expanded the scope, taking a topic and completing it from start to finish, taking creative license with the chronological order of other articles to improve thought flow. As an example, let's look at the world wars. Each war is presented from its declaration to its armistice. The daily stories that happened during that time frame pick up again after the war years to maintain the pace of the book.

We hope that we have highlighted some of the events that were important to you and your family over the last century. If we have missed some of those, we are sorry. If we placed an emphasis on stories others would deem less important, we do so to create a balance for all.

Have a read and decide for yourself. We sincerely hope you will enjoy what is there.

This book is for the people of the Okanagan, written (for the most part) by the people of the Okanagan. It marks our past successes, discoveries and tragedies so we can open the door on the new millennium with a sense of where we've come from.

Table of Contents

A DECADE
IN REVIEW

1900 ~ 1909

Happy New Year
1900

LONDON, AUG. 19, 1899. — Though many signs point to the extreme likelihood of war between Great Britain and the Boers, and though troops are pouring in the direction of the Cape, and the British army chiefs are deep in problems of preparation for probable hostilities, the English people as a whole scarce heed the course of events. The nation seems completely absorbed in the Dreyfus case. As each day passes without an answer from the Boers to the proposition of Great Britain for a joint commission to investigate the effect which the franchise reform legislation will have on the Uitlanders, the probability of a pacific settlement of the difficulty decreases, yet national interest, tired of delay, flags as the tension at the war and colonial offices grows. If war comes Great Britain will awake with a tremendous start. If the Boers surrender to the British demands, scarcely more than a ripple of interest will be excited as long as the Rennes court-martial holds the world under the spell of its dramatic recital.

Boers Preparing For War

Forces are Rapidly Moving to the Front. Forts Being Strengthened

OCT. 5, 1899 — British Troops Moving Towards the Border and Taking Up Strong Positions on the Way.

NATAL, SEPT. 30. — It is asserted that the Boers have mobilized at Utrecht and at the railway bridge on the Transvaal side of Buffalo river. There are 6,000 men at each place. The Boers have cut a route through the high bank and are ready to cross to Natal.

LONDON, SEPT. 30. — A despatch received this evening from Johannesburg says:

The Transvaal government officials today requisitioning 700 horses, provisions and general equipment for the burghers. Horses were even requisitioned from the streets and the stables, and the town was depleted.

The first raid command of 6,000 men started for the front this morning and the Johannesburg corps of 750 men is following.

The blaze of battle

JOHANNESBURG, OCT. 12. — War was declared yesterday. The formal declaration occurred at 10 o'clock this morning.

LONDON, OCT. 12. — The following is the text of the British reply to the Boer ultimatum:

"Right Hon. Joseph Chamberlain to Sir Alfred Milner, High Commissioner, sent 10:45 p.m. Oct. 10, 1899:

"Her Majesty's government received tonight with great regret the peremptory demands of the South African Republic, conveyed in your telegram of October 9th. You will inform the Government of the South African Republic in reply that the conditions demanded by the Government of the South African Republic are such as her Majesty's Government deem it impossible to discuss."

LONDON, OCT. 14. — War, so often predicted in these dispatches as being the inevitable climax to hopeless negotiation, has come at last and is now in full swing for the subjection of the little republic, whose military sun sets and rises at Majuba Hill. Great Britain has set going machinery more powerful than that which crushed Napoleon and twice as strong as that which gave her Egypt and the Sudan. Gen. Sir Redvers Buller has gone, and already the Boer bullets have sung the song of desperate defence.

That the next few weeks will be marked by sharp fighting can almost be taken for granted. That the result will probably be for a time not too favorable to the British is also to be admitted. The main question is, how long are hostilities to last? Ultimate English victory is assured by virtue of overwhelming strength. A forecast of the length and nature of the campaign should not be ventured without knowledge of an extraordinary circumstance communicated to the Associated Press on most reliable authority, namely that Gen. Buller has gone to take entire command of the South African situation.

War's Grim Visage Shadows South Africa. Boers Capture an Armoured Train.

NEWCASTLE INVESTED, KIMBERLY BESIEGED

Reported Engagement in Which 300 Boers are Said to Have Been Killed—Despatches of the Week Give But Meagre Information—Hot Engagement Daily Expected.

Canadians For Africa

OTTAWA — It was officially given out that the Dominion Government was going to send troops to the number of 1,000 men to South Africa, a larger number than any of the other colonies, and larger than the British Government suggested. The only difficulty which met the Government was as to whether Parliament should be called on for so heavy an expenditure. This was got over by the form of enlistment, and the fact that Britain only wanted units of 125 men each, to be attached to the Imperial corps.

The Canadian Government will equip the contingent, and pay the cost of transport to the point of debarkation in South Africa. In the Militia Department, everything is ready to send the troops, and they will be dispatched from here not later than Oct. 30th. Enrollment begins at once. Good marksmen are preferred.

GEN. LORD KRUGER,
The Man Who Was Primarily Responsible for the War.

EX-PRESIDENT STEYN,
In Whose Hands Rested the Termination of the War.

GEN. LORD KITCHENER,
The Commander-in-Chief Through Whom the Peace Proposals Were Forwarded.

FIELD MARSHAL LORD ROBERTS,
Who Changed the Whole Complexion of the Campaign.

Peace Reigns At Last. End Of The Boer War

Unconditional Surrender Agreed to Last Saturday.

The Ontario Election Results in a Liberal Victory - Premier Ross Probably has Majority of Four - Several Changes and Surprises in Various Constituencies - None of the Ministers Meet With Defeat.

London, June 2. - Peace has been declared after nearly two years and eight months of a war that tried the British army to the utmost, and has wiped out the Boers from the list of nations. The war has come to an end with Lord Kitchener's announcement from Pretoria, that Lord Milner and the Boer delegates had signed the terms of surrender.

This announcement had been anticipated for several days and it was definitely forecasted in these dispatches but its receipt on Sunday afternoon took the nation by surprise as everybody had confidently believed that the House of Commons would hold the first

news today.

According to a despatch the "Daily Express" from Utrecht, Holland, Mr. Kruger was informed that peace had been declared shortly after 9 o'clock last night. Mr. Kruger had been asleep.

"My God!" he said; "it is impossible!"

Mr. Kruger and his entourage, the despatch continues, hope to be permitted to return to the Transvaal. This, however, is quite unlikely.

The King's Message.

LONDON, JUNE 2.— The following message from King Edward to his people was issued after midnight:

"The King received the welcome news of the cessation of hostilities in South Africa with infinite satisfaction, and His Majesty trusts that peace may speedily be followed by the restoration of prosperity on his new domains, and that the feelings necessarily engendered by the war will give place to earnest co-operation on

the part of His Majesty's South African subjects, in promoting the progress of the country."

Some of the Conditions.

LONDON, JUNE 2.— In the House of Commons today the government leader, A.J. Balfour, announced the terms of peace in South Africa as follows: The Burgher forces lay down their arms and hand over rifles and munitions of war in their possession or under their control. All prisoners are to be brought back as soon as possible to South Africa, without loss or liberty or property. No action is to be taken against prisoners, except where they are guilty of breaches of the rules of war. Dutch is to be taught in the schools, if desired by the parents, and used in the courts if necessary. Rifles are allowed for protection. Military occupation is to be withdrawn as soon as possible, and self-government substituted. There is to be no tax on the Transvaal to pay the cost of the war. The sum of three million ster-

ling ($15,000,000) is to be provided for re-stocking the Boer farms. Rebels are liable to trial, according to the law of the colony to which they belong. The ranks and file will be disfranchised for life. The death penalty will not be inflicted.

THE VERNON NEWS

The Okanagan Farm, Live Stock, and Mining Journal.

No. 4. WHOLE NUMBER 577.   VERNON, B. C., THURSDAY, JUNE 5, 1902. $2.00 IF

SOLICITOR, PUBLIC, CONVEYANCER, ETC.

PROVINCIAL ND SURVEYOR. EIG. ENGS. B. C.

VALLEY LODGE 18, I.O.O.F. every Wednesday the Odd Fellows' Barnard Avenue, at 8 o'clock. So- r brethren are

PEACE REIGNS AT LAST. END OF THE BOER WAR

Unconditional Surrender Agreed to Last Saturday.

Cardwell, Little, con., 384 maj.
Carleton, Kidd, con., 284 maj.
Dufferin, Barr, con., 600 maj
Dundas, Whitney, con.
Durham, E.
Durham, W., Richard, lib., 30 maj liberal gain.
Elgin, E., Brower, con.
Elgin, W., Macdiarmid, con.
Essex, N., Reaume, con., 879 maj., conservative gain.
Essex, S., Auld, lib., 400 maj.
Fort William and Lake of the Woods, Cameron, lib., new constituency.
Frontenac, Gallaher, con., 100 maj.
Glengarry.
Grenville, Joint, con., 863 maj.
Grey, C., Lucas, con., acclamation.
Grey, N., Boyd, con., 8 maj.
Grey, S., Dr. Jamieson, con.
Haldimand, Holmes, lib., 152 maj.

standing of the parties : Liberals 49, Conservatives 49, the same estimate as is made by the Toronto *Mail and Empire.* The *Globe* claims a majority of four for the Liberals.

ANOTHER ESTIMATE.

Toronto, May 31.—Mr. J. W. Munroe, Liberal member-elect for North Renfrew, died this morning of blood-poisoning. This reduces the election results to Liberals, 50 ; Conservatives 47, with one seat vacant. The "Mail" claims that North Grey will be Conservatives, but in this estimate it is given to the Liberals.

Prov The follow too late for Victoria, got a surpri when the o McInnes me do not spea an appeal fr and Mr. Cl position. M prise to mar have known ment's cou ment had a c is stated an

Queen Victoria is dead

Her Most Gracious Majesty Succumbs to the Grim Reaper

THE NATION OVERWHELMED WITH GRIEF

The World Sorrows over the Decease of Its Most Respected Sovereign–

The End Came on Monday, at 6:55 London Time– The Prince of Wales Now King Edward VII

QUEEN VICTORIA

LONDON, JAN. 18 —

Alarming rumors were in circulation to-day to the effect that Queen Victoria was seriously ill and that her family had been summoned to Osborne. Inquiries of the Associated Press at Osborne at three o'clock this afternoon elicited a flat denial of the report. The Prince of Wales is not at Marlborough House, where no news had been received indicating that Her Majesty is not enjoying her usual health. The Duke of York went to Sandringham this afternoon.

THE NATION STARTLED

LONDON, JAN. 19. —

Although it is fully understood that there is no cause for alarm, beyond what would naturally be felt at the indisposition of any one of the Queen's age, the official announcement issued last evening, has caused a shock to the country, the effect of which would be difficult to exaggerate. Her Majesty's absolute freedom from illness during the longest reign in English history, has led her people to regard her almost as more than mortal; and the mere novelty of having to face the possibility of a Regency, alone suffices to create unnecessary apprehension.

PRECIPITATED BY WORRY

In the opinion of those best qualified to judge, the queen's present serious condition was precipitated by intense worry over the losses and hardships suffered by the British troops in South Africa. Frequently she has remarked to the court attaches that another war would kill her.

THE PONTIFF'S BLESSING

ROME, JAN. 21. — The Pope yesterday telegraphed Cardinal Vaughan to London, to express to the British Royal Family, the feeling of sorrow which all Christendom shared with England, regarding the illness of Queen Victoria, adding: "The liberal reign of the Queen, which has permitted the Roman Catholic Church to increase in the United Kingdom, will leave an indelible trace upon all Christian hearts."

LONDON, JAN 22. — 1:35 P.M. — A bulletin posted at the Mansion House reads as follows: "Osborne, 4 p.m. — My painful duty obliges me to inform you that the life of our beloved Queen is in the greatest danger, signed Albert Edward."

VANCOUVER, JAN. 22 —11:40 a.m.—The official notice of the Queen's death has been received. Her Majesty died at 6:55 p.m. London time.

VANCOUVER, JAN. 22.—The Prince of Wales has been sworn in as King Edward VII. Mayor Townley has sent a message of condolence to the King and has proclaimed the next twenty-four hours as a period of mourning. Business has been suspended in Vancouver.

THE VERNON NEWS

The Okanagan Farm, Live Stock, and Mining Journal.

VERNON, B.C., THURSDAY, JANUARY 24, 1901.

QUEEN VICTORIA IS DEAD

Her Most Gracious Majesty Succumbs to the Grim Reaper.

THE NATION OVERWHELMED WITH GRIEF

The World Sorrows over the Decease of Its Most Respected Sovereign—The End Came on Monday, at 6:55 London Time—The Prince of Wales Now King Edward VII.

Vernon mourns the Queen

The City United in Manifesting its Respect to Her Memory.

THE PROCESSION AND SERVICES

A Very Large Attendance at the Hall—Impressive Addresses From the Clergymen of the City.

Among all the myriad towns dotting the vast empire so long ruled over by Her late Majesty, Queen Victoria, it is doubtful if any single place manifested in a more united manner its sorrow during the solemn day upon which the funeral services were carried out. All classes, conditions and creeds joined together to do reverence to the memory of a sovereign whom from their earliest days they had loved and revered. It is improbable that such an event will ever occur again during the lives of those who participated in Saturday's exercises, and it will long remain prominent in the memory of our citizens.

The Funeral of the Queen.

LONDON, FEB. 2.—Half a million of the late Queen Victoria's devoted subjects lining the shores of the Solent yesterday witnessed a majestic and awe inspiring pageant and bade a last farewell to their beloved ruler, happy in the circumstances of her death, sovereign of the greatest naval power in the world and fortunate in the manner of her obsequies. The ceremony was a fitting tribute from a nation owing Nelson for its hero to its dead monarch. All who were witnesses of the function testify to the profound emotion it inspired, and agreed that the spectacle could not have been surpassed for splendor and solemn effect.

WINDSOR, FEB. 4.—The last honors have been paid to Queen Victoria. Her body now rests peacefully near that of her husband in the mausoleum at Frogmore.

OUR KING, EDWARD VII.

The King's Speech

The following is the full text of His Majesty's accession speech:

"Your Royal Highnesses, my Lords and Gentlemen:

"This is the most painful occasion on which I shall ever be called upon to address you. My first melancholy duty is to announce to you the death of my beloved mother, the Queen; and I know how deeply you and the whole world sympathize with me in the irreparable loss we have all sustained.

"I need hardly say that my constant endeavor will be always to walk in her footsteps.

"In undertaking the heavy load which now devolves upon me, I am fully determined to a constitutional sovereign to the strictest sense of the word, and, so long as there is breadth in my body, to work for the good and amelioration of my people.

"I have resolved to be known by the name of Edward, which has been borne by six of my ancestors. In doing so, I do not undervalue the name of Albert, which I inherit from my ever to be lamented, great and wise father, who, by universal consent is, I think deservedly, known by the name of Albert the Good, and I desire that his name should stand alone.

"In conclusion, I trust to parliament and the nation to support me in the arduous duties which now devolve upon me by inheritance."

Most Fearful Calamity Modern History Records

Forty Thousand people Engulfed in Fire From a Volcanic Eruption.

THE ISLAND OF MARTINIQUE DEVASTATED

PARIS —

The commander of the French cruiser Suchet has telegraphed to the minister of marine, M. deLanessan, from Fort de France, Island of Martinique, under the date of Thursday, May 8th, at 10 p.m. as follows:

"I have just returned from St. Pierre, which has been completely destroyed by a mass fire, which fell on the town at about 8 o'clock in the morning. The entire population (about 25,000) is supposed to have perished. I have brought back the few survivors, about 30. All the shipping in the harbor has been destroyed by fire. The eruption continues.

LONDON, MAY 10. — A despatch to the Daily Mail, from Point a Prite, island of Guadeloupe, dated yesterday, says: "The Mount Pelee crater ejected yesterday morning molten rocks and ashes during three minutes, and completely destroyed St. Pierre and the districts within a four mile radius. All the inhabitants were burned.

ST. THOMAS, MAY 9 —

It is now estimated that forty thousand persons perished as a result of the volcano eruption in the island of Martinique.

The British schooner Ocean Traveller, of St. John, N.B., arrived at the Island of Dominica, B.W.I., at 3 o'clock this p.m. She reported having been obliged to flee from the island of St. Vincent on May 7th, owing to a heavy fall of sand from a volcano which was in eruption there. She tried to reach the island of St. Lucia, but

adverse currents prevented her from so doing. The schooner arrived opposite St. Pierre, May 8th. While about a mile off shore, the volcano of Mount Pelee exploded, and the fire from it swept the whole town of St. Pierre out of existence, destroying the shipping there including the cableship Grappler which was engaged in repairing the cable near the Guerin factory. The Ocean Traveller, while on her way to Dominica encountered a quantity of wreckage.

WASHINGTON, MAY 12. — Secretary Hay, has received the following cable, dated May 11, from United States Consul Ayme at Guadeloupe, who went to Port de France, Martinique, by instructions from this government:

"The disaster is complete. The city wiped out. Consul Prentiss and his family are dead. The Governor says 30,000 have perished; 5,000 are homeless and hungry. He suggests that the Red Cross be asked to send codfish, flour, beans, rice, salt meats and biscuits as quickly as possible. The visits of war vessels will be valuable."

VALPARAISO IN RUINS

Santiago and Other Cities, also Badly Shaken.

On August 16 and 17 the western coast of South America was visited by a series of earthquakes with most disastrous results to many of its most important cities. The reports received so far have been meagre and conflicting, but it is feared that the situation may prove as serious as that of San Francisco.

Valparaiso is a fortified seaport of Chile and the most important commercial city of the western coast of South America. It has a population of 150,000.

As reported, practically every building in Valparaiso is damaged, and there are fires in different parts of the city. The earthquake has interrupted cable facilities, and communication is now confined to the route via Lisbon. The first shock lasted four minutes and fifty seconds.

SANTIAGO, AUG. 20 — Five hundred persons are dead at Valparaiso as a result of the earthquake shocks, according to the latest advices based on the reports of refugees who reached this city this morning. Six or eight other cities have been destroyed. The railroad, street railway, telegraph and telephone systems are thoroughly demoralized.

Santiago also suffered severely. The deaths number thirty, while the property loss is placed at $2,000,000. The majority of the houses are unsafe for habitation, and the authorities have organized a special corps to guard the tottering buildings. It is not safe to walk in the streets owing to the falling debris. The place resembles a camp. The public squares and principal avenues are crowded with people sleeping in the open.

The night of Aug. 16 was rendered dreadful by lightning and pouring rain, the electric cables and wires snapping as a result of the constant movement of the earth, causing the greatest consternation, which was heightened by the tolling of the firebells announcing the breaking out of fires in various places in the city.

Experts say that the only thing which saved Santiago from complete ruin was that the motion was circular. The principal shock was from Valparaiso to Santiago and Maripella, with its centre at Limache. The two last-mentioned towns were destroyed, as also were Quillota and Liaillai.

What About Lent ?

We can supply your demands in the Grocery line no matter what they may be. In the Fish line we have just received a nice stock of Labrador Salt and Smoked Herrings Salmon Bellies, Oolichans, canned B. C. Salmon, etc. Our Hams and Bacon are the best. We also carry all brands of Flour. Our Buckwheat Flour in packages, for making pancakes, and pure Maple Syrup, are daily requisites at this time of the year. You will find all of these at the

VERNON PRODUCE Co.
G. H. GILLESPIE.

Terrible Loss of Life

Earthquake and Flames Destroy Half of San Francisco - 1000 People Killed.

(Special to the Vernon News)
VANCOUVER, APRIL 18. — By an earthquake and resulting fires in San Francisco at 5 o'clock this morning, half the city was destroyed. The loss of life is estimated at over one thousand. The railway and telegraph service is altogether disorganized. The water system is paralyzed and the flames are spreading. Buildings are being blown up with dynamite to confine the fire region.

LATER — Fires are raging within one block of the Palace Hotel. Ten blocks of the main wholesale district have been destroyed. The Call and Examiner buildings have been totally destroyed. Three miles of the railway between Suisun and Benecia have sunk out of sight.

STOCKTON, CAL., APR. 18 — The most terrible disaster in the history of San Francisco occurred at 5:13 this morning. An earthquake shock so violent and prolonged that it damaged every building on the peninsula in some degree, the damage being from cracks in the walls, toppled chimneys and cornices, to complete collapse of hundreds of buildings, rocked the earth for fully two minutes. It was like a cataclysm. The oscillation was north and south in a succession of increasing and apparently renewed shocks, with a twisting movement that threw sleeping people out of their beds. In those two minutes the great city was ruined. Many were killed, perhaps hundreds, perhaps thousands, for in the shattering, followed by confusion and fire, no one may estimate the number of dead. No part of the city escaped from wreck, fire and death. Gas, water and electric power were suddenly cut off. The business section of the waterfront to Tenth Street suffered most appallingly from the disaster. It lies devastated by the trembler and by fire.

Fire Chief Sullivan, who served in the fire department for over a quarter of a century, was killed in his engine house, adjoining the California Hotel. The corner tower of the hotel fell, crashing in the roof of the engine house, cutting off the means of exit, burying even the horses in the debris and killing the veteran chief when he was needed most. Fires broke out everywhere.

The suddenness and the awfulness of the disaster left the police as powerless as the fire department. General Funston at once offered Chief of Police Dinan aid. He detailed a regiment of soldiers to work with the police in the rescuing of the wounded and the protection of property.

Chief Dinan in an interview said: "The police are absolutely unable to cope with a disaster of this extent, and the soldiers are a godsend. Ghouls are already at work."

Still Burning.

SAN FRANCISCO, APR. 18. 4 P.M. — The fire is still burning and buildings in the heart of the business section are being destroyed to stop the spread of the flames. The number killed will probably reach 200 and the injured ten times that number. Experts estimate the financial loss from fire at more than $100,000,000. The city is under martial law and precautions have been taken to prevent disorder and looting tonight. Four thieves were shot by soldiers this afternoon for looting. The soldiers have orders to shoot without warning any person acting in a suspicious manner. The city hall has been burnt, also many of the principal business blocks and the hall of justice is threatened.

The fire swept down the streets so rapidly that it was practically impossible to save anything in its way.

Nearby Cities Suffered.

SAN FRANCISCO, APR. 19 — Reports from cities near San Francisco show the destruction is general. Santa Rosa, 60 miles north, is in flames and the damage there is over one million dollars. The loss of life is not known.

At Napa many buildings were shattered and the loss will amount to $300,000. No loss of life is reported.

At Vallejo the damage was slight in comparison with that suffered in other cities. The loss will be about $10,000.

Fruitless Efforts

SAN FRANCISCO, APR. 19 — All efforts to check the flames at Van Ness Avenue by blowing up a mile of buildings on the east side of the avenue have proved fruitless. The fire has spread across the broad thoroughfare and from present indications the entire western addition, which contains the homes of San Francisco's millionaires and people of the wealthier class, is now doomed. The destruction of the western addition of the city practically completes the work of the ravaging flames and marks the devastation of the entire city.

Relief for San Francisco

Generous Contributions from the Civilized World.

SAN FRANCISCO, CAL., APRIL 20 —

The problem now confronting the city government and Federal authorities, is how to feed the multitudes of destitute. Supplies are coming in by the load, but as yet the system of distribution is not in complete working order. At the Presidio, where 50,000 people are camped, affairs are conducted with military precision. Water is plentiful and rations are dealt out

all day long. The refugees stand patiently in line, and there is not a murmur. This characteristic is observed all over the city. The people are brave and patient and the wonderful order preserved by them has been of great assistance. In Golden Gate Park are encamped 200,000 people. They are being taken care of. A huge supply station has been established there, and provisions are being dealt out. Probably 100,000 more people are camped in vacant

lots and squares scattered about the city and these are the unfortunates that are hard to reach.

Generous Contributions.

NEW YORK, APRIL 21. — The appeal of San Francisco has been heard throughout the civilized world. From every city and town in the country, from European capitals and from far East communities, comes news that all humanity, in expressing its sympathy, is also offering enormous material assistance. It is estimated tonight that the San Francisco fund is rapidly nearing the total of $10,000,000, and will have passed that figure by Monday, when the United States Congress, it is announced, will add $1,500,000 to the $1,000,000 already appropriated.

VANCOUVER, APRIL 20. — The Government has made arrangements to send $10,000 to the Governor of California, as the Provincial contribution to relieve the pressing necessity at San Francisco.

Ottawa Contributes.

OTTAWA, APRIL 20. — The Dominion Government has

decided to give $100,000 to San Francisco sufferers, and an estimate for this amount was presented to Parliament today.

Confidence Restored

SAN FRANCISCO, APRIL 24 — The city is now in the first stage of rebuilding.

After six days confusion and almost superhuman effort on the part of the citizens of California's metropolis in the great task of sheltering, feeding and otherwise caring for the homeless thousands, complete order has been re-established and attention turned to the future. Throughout the great business district, where the devastation of the flames was most complete, walls are being raised, buildings not disintegrated before the intense heat are being inspected with the view of re-occupancy, and even the ground is being cleared for the immediate construction of some sort of buildings in which to resume business at the earliest possible opportunity; in short, confidence has been restored.

The Earthquake

THE KELOWNA COURIER

As it is not within the province of a weekly local paper to repeat the news already published in the provincial dailies, we do not attempt to give an account of the fearful disaster at San Francisco, but we would like to draw the attention of our readers to the fact that the zone of greatest volcanic activity is largely within the tropics and near the seacoast, and that we may regard ourselves as fortunate in possessing a beautiful climate and yet outside the sphere of nature's convulsions. The places most attractive in some respects hide lurking dangers ready at any time, when least suspected, to overwhelm all. New Zealand, Hawaii, Southern Italy, Sicily, Japan and California are famous for their climate and scenery, but all are subject to volcanic or seismic action, and their residents may dwell in a peaceful paradise with death and destruction beneath their feet. The effect of the disasters that have occurred in recent years, including Mont Pelee and eruptions in Guatemala, should lead people to seriously

consider whether desirable places of residence cannot be found in more northern latitudes, and there may be less migration south than has been. The natives of a country subject to earthquake shock seem to regard those upheavals with a kind of fatalism and rebuild on the ruins of their destroyed cities, content to let the future rest in the lap of Destiny. The volcanic ash of Vesuvius makes a fertile soil after the disintegration of a few years' exposure to the weather, and it will not be long until the slopes of the mountain are again clad with vines and dotted with villages. Similarly San Francisco will rebuild, as did Galveston after its ruin by flood and fire. It is impossible not to admire the courage with which the American people face such emergencies, but the dweller in the interior will feel inclined to use the homely phrase, "back to the cactus for me."

Kelowna's Successful Growth

The past year has undoubtedly been the most successful in the history of Kelowna. Not only has the town and district come before the public as never before, but its material prosperity has been unprecedented. Two large ranches in the hands of the Kelowna Land and Orchard Co. and the Okanagan Fruit and Land Co. have been split up and placed on the market, with the result that large numbers of settlers have been attracted from the east and have located either in town or in the vicinity. Over forty buildings, exclusive of stables and other out houses, have been added during the year, while the character of the dwellings and business houses, built and under construction is superior to that of former years. The old one roomed school house has given place to a fine large four roomed modernly equipped building capable of accommodating over two hundred pupils. The Kelowna Land and Orchard Co. have at a large expense opened up excellent roads and streets through their property and are now engaged in clearing a large area of excellent land adjacent to town prior to placing it on the market. The Okanagan Fruit and Land Co. have disposed of a large amount of town property to actual settlers. Doubtless next year will be even more prosperous than the past, and a lively time is anticipated by local builders. The spirit that has animated Kelowna is taking possession of every part of the Okanagan, with the result that a united effort is being put forth to place our resources before the public. We may well look to the coming summer as the most prosperous period heretofore experienced by the whole Okanagan, and with it an increased prosperity for our own town and district.

The City Elections

The preliminary work incident to the incorporation of Kelowna as a city has at last been brought to a successful termination, the date of nomination being fixed for the 15th, and that of polling on the 22nd. The requirements of the election act will, unfortunately, debar a great many of the more recent arrivals from either standing for election or exercising their franchise. The list of those entitled to vote at this, the first election, will also be very small, but there should be no difficulty in securing the required number to fill the offices. At the first election there will be no division into wards and only five aldermen are required.

Looking east along Bernard Avenue circa 1905. Kelowna was a typical pioneer town with wooden sidewalks, false front buildings, hitching posts etc.

Photo courtesy of Kelowna Museum

The Ferry

The granting of a subsidy of $1000.00 at the recent session of the Legislature, for the placing of a ferry on Okanagan Lake, although inadequate to defray the total cost of such an institution, and thereby make a government owned ferry possible, may yet be sufficient to secure its construction by private enterprise. In making the appropriation, this is doubtless what the government had in view, and it will probably advertise for applications for a charter to ply a ferry across the lake, in accordance with certain conditions of service and tolls. If this plan is adopted, there is good reason to hope that the coming summer may see an efficient ferry in operation. The pressing needs of such communication have heretofore been set forth in these columns and need not be rehearsed here, and it is hoped that the government will see the advisability of expediating matters as much as possible. Probably, under the circumstances, a privately owned ferry, under proper restrictions, would be as acceptable as if owned and operated by the Government and could certainly be established and maintained at less cost to the province. There should be no difficulty in finding some person with sufficient enterprise to take the matter in hand, as the rapid advance in the settlement of both sides of the lake warrant success if a nominal fee were charged. We hope, therefore, to see this long felt want remedied in course of a few months, and will await with interest the announcement of a definite plan in the matter.

Incorporation of City of Kelowna Complete

Kelowna has recently made a little bit of history by a process which can never be repeated. The first Council of our embryo city has been elected and organized. An epoch, this, in our civic life. Most folk are familiar with the main purposes for which municipal machinery is set up and operated. Street construction; the grading, draining and maintenance of good roads, that the tides of our industrial and social life may flow freely through their channels day by day; provision for the public health by the prompt removal of waste matter, solid or liquid, hence a system of drainage or deportation, or both; the preservation of order, that citizens may attend to their own affairs untroubled by the idle or lawless; protection from fire, which wastes in an hour the material gains from the labor of years.

Mitchell Collection Courtesy of Penticton Museum

WAYS IN WHICH WOMEN CAN EARN MONEY

By Cynthia Westover Alden

MAY 3, 1906 — Many women would not be so helpless if they had the courage to take up the business of the loved one who has been taken away from them by death. Just to give you courage to pick up the lines of support where they have been dropped by the one who has heretofore been your protector, I give some instances where the women, by their strength of determination, not by their knowledge at first, have succeeded.

The owner of a mine fell ill. His wife did not allow the mine to shut down, as everybody thought it must. She, aided by the employees, conducted the entire business, even to the shipment of the ore.

A long time ago, when editor on a New York Newspaper, I suggested to a woman who came to me, stranded, that she make "flies" for catching fish. I did not know of any one doing it then, but I did know that my father, who was fishing everywhere there was a fish to be caught, said that he knew he could make a living that way if he had to. She went direct to the sporting goods house nearby, got all the information she could there, got a promise of an order if her "flies" were good, and she still fills orders for this firm, so I understand. Her orders give her a good income. Should any one want to try this - I am told it is hard to do unless one is particularly apt with the fingers - there are books devoted to directions for fly making. Samples of materials are given with books. Any sporting goods house can tell you the best works on the making of all fishing tackle.

Card playing is growing in favor. Whist and euchre clubs have made their way from the cities into the smaller towns, and classes in whist, euchre and cribbage, and even chess, are often heard of nowadays. If you are a successful card player there is pin money in store for you if you succeed in forming classes in three or four neighboring towns. Much amusement and great interest can be brought into the classes by having one town play against the other at the end of so many lessons. To get these classes one must be introduced into the best circles of these towns, as it is generally the women of such circles who would have or could have the time to attend "card clubs" (as these classes would naturally be called.)

Prosperous Okanagan

A great wave of prosperity has at last struck the Okanagan. We notice in an exchange that the real estate sales during the past six months between Vernon and Kelowna are computed at half a million dollars. We have not the figures at our disposal, but are of opinion that the sales during the same period between Kelowna and Penticton, including of course the property in and adjacent to the latter place, would be quite equal if not in advance of the figures given above. In Peachland and Summerland a number of good turnovers have been made. At Woodlands some three or four hundred acres formerly owned by Duncan Woods has been sold in fruit and town lots, largely to actual settlers. The fifty acres of George Gartrell in the same vicinity is being scooped up at the present time. The Dunsdon property at the back of Summerland has been nearly all sold. At Nine Mile Point, now East Summerland, the property, in fruit and residential lots, is being disposed of readily in Winnipeg and to residents of Summerland. The same is true of Penticton, not a week passes without the Land Company making important sales, while fruit lots and town property

are being continually turned over at good advances. People are only beginning to realize the actual value of property in the Okanagan. The marvelous productiveness of the soil, the unsurpassed climate, and the scenic attractions make up a combination that cannot be beat in any other part of Canada. We venture to predict that land which may now be procured for one hundred and fifty dollars per acre in five year's time will be worth one thousand dollars per acre. Neither will this be an inflated value, as from the business standpoint of interest on capital, land in bearing orchard is cheap at that price. There are hundreds of acres of the very best bench land with excellent irrigation facilities in close proximity to the lake still for sale at Penticton. The geographical situation of Penticton ensures its being one of the most important towns in the interior, hence an additional inducement for people to settle here. We are glad to observe that the prosperity is not confined to any particular section, but that when one portion of the valley prospers all others prosper along with it. Let the people of the entire valley unite in forwarding the interests of the whole, and the greatest success is assured.

People like Jim & Norma Mitchell of Naramata recognized the potential of the Okanagan and settled in the valley in the early 1900's.

Telephone service in sad repair

The Dominion Government telephone line to the south of Penticton is in a shameful condition. At one point about eight miles out where the wire crosses the road a post is down and the wire hangs so low that a rider or driver is obliged to stoop in order to pass under. This is likely to occasion some serious accident, if not repaired at once. A person running against the wire in the dark could not fail to be badly hurt. A little farther on a large tree has fallen across the wire bringing it to the ground. This is a common occurrence, and the system is in such bad working order that it is often difficult, or even impossible, to get a message through. That a telephone line, extending for considerable over two hundred miles, should be left to care for itself seems absurd. If the line were owned by a private company, there would be a man employed to look after it and make necessary repairs. The government, however, seems to regard its duty done with the installation of the system, and is content to derive a revenue without sufficient expenditure to keep it in decent operation. No effort whatever, has been made to preserve secrecy in communication. Consequently, in all cases where velocity is not desired, business men make sure of the mails in preference to the telephone. This, as previously pointed out by the Press, could be overcome by the establishment of a telegraph system by the same wire; but to be supplied with merely a poor telephone system, is hard lines for one of the most important and wealthy sections of the province. This is the first public work the Dominion government has ever done in the Okanagan, and even the most moderate minded must concede that it has been done badly.

There is no reason why a government service should not be as efficient as one operated by a company if merely the commonest business principles were adhered to. The very least that should be done would be the employment of an overseer to keep poles erected and the line in good working order.

Penticton Building Review For 1906

The year of 1906, Penticton's first building year, has left substantial evidence of confidence in Penticton's bright futures.

From a settlement of a few buildings at the beginning of the past year the building total of the year amounted to over forty thousand dollars, many of the buildings being substantial and artistic structures. Over fifty buildings were erected, several at a cost of over two thousand dollars, and about twenty-five at a cost approximating between one thousand to two thousand dollars, while the majority, though but the nucleus of larger and better residences in the coming year, are designed to conform with the natural surroundings.

In the townsite of Penticton, Messrs. Shepherd and Hatch have erected buildings, which compare with any in the Okanagan as masterpieces of architecture. Main and Smith St's., the business streets of Penticton, are being rapidly built with stores, offices etc. necessary to accommodate the increasing mercantile business of the town. The B.C. Hotel has completed an addition to the former premises making one of the most commodious hotels in the Southern Okanagan.

Main St., the principal business St., boasts many substantial commercial buildings, among which erected in 1906 are a business block of two stories for E. Lee, now occupied by C.A.C. Steward with a large assortment of furniture, etc. The Penticton Press building, where Penticton's Pioneer newspaper is turned out, and where an extensive job printing business is done.

Looking north on Main Street downtown Penticton in 1907

Stocks Collection · Hudson photo courtesy of Penticton Museum

Canada's Sunday Law

Full Text of the Lord's Day Act, Which Comes Into Force March 1, 1907.

His Majesty, by and with the advice and consent of the Senate and House of Commons of Canada, enacts as follows:

1. In this Act, unless the context otherwise requires, -

(a) "The Lord's Day" means the period of time which begins at twelve o'clock on Saturday afternoon and ends at twelve o'clock on the following afternoon;

(b) "Person" has the meaning which it has in the Criminal Code 1892;

(c) "Vessel" includes any kind of vessel or boat used for conveying passengers or freight by water;

(d) "Railway" includes steam railway, electric railway, street railway and tramway;

(e) "Performance" includes any game, match, sport, sport contest, exhibition or entertainment;

(f) "Employer" includes every person to whose orders or direction any other person is by his employment bound to conform.

(g) "Provincial Act" means the charter of any Municipality or any Public Act of any province whether passed before or since Confederation.

2. It shall not be lawful for any person on the Lord's Day, except as provided herein or in any Provincial Act or law now or hereafter in force, to sell of offer for sale or purchase any goods, chattels, or other personal property, or any real estate, or to carry on or transact any business of his ordinary calling, or in connection with such calling, or for gain, to do or employ any other person to do, on that day, any work, business or labor.

3. Notwithstanding anything herein contained, any person may on the Lord's Day do any work of necessity or mercy, and for greater certainty, but not so as to restrict the ordinary meaning of the expression "work of necessity or mercy," it is hereby declared that it shall be deemed to include the following classes of work:

(a) Any necessary or customary work in connection with divine worship;

(b) Work for the relief of sickness and suffering, including the sale of drugs, medicines and surgical appliances by retail;

(c) Receiving, transmitting, or delivering telegraph or telephone messages;

(d) Starting or maintaining fires, making repairs to furnaces, and repairs in cases of emergency and doing any other work, when such fires, repairs or work are essential to any industry or industrial process of such a continuous nature that it cannot be stopped with serious injury to such industry or its product or to the plant or property used in such process;

(e) Starting or maintaining fires, and ventilating, pumping out, and inspecting mines, when any such work is essential to the protection of property, life or health.

(f) Any work without the doing of which on the Lord's day, electric current, light, heat, cold air, water or gas cannot be continuously supplied for lawful purposes;

(g) The conveying of travellers, and work incidental thereto;

(h) The continuance to their destination of trains and vessels in transit when the Lord's Day begins, and work incidental thereto;

(i) Loading and unloading merchandise at intermediate points on or from passenger boats or passenger trains;

(j) Keeping railway tracks clear of snow or ice, making repairs in cases of emergency, or doing any other work of a like incidental character necessary to keep the lines and tracks open;

(k) Work before six o'clock in the forenoon and after eight o'clock in the afternoon of yard crews in handling cars in railway yards;

(l) Loading, unloading and operating any ocean-going vessel which otherwise would be unduly delayed after her scheduled time of sailing, or any vessel which otherwise would be in imminent danger of being stopped by the closing of navigation; or loading or unloading before seven o'clock in the morning or after eight o'clock in the afternoon any grain, coal or ore carrying vessel after the fifteenth of September;

(m) The caring of milk, cheese, and live animals, and the unloading of and caring for perishable products and live animals arriving at any point on the Lord's Day;

(n) The operation of any toll or drawbridge, or of any ferry or boat authorized by competent deemed to be travellers within the meaning of this Act.

7. It shall not be lawful for any person to advertise in any manner whatsoever any performance or other thing prohibited by this Act.

(2) It shall not be lawful for any person to advertise in Canada in any manner whatsoever any performance or other thing which if given or done in Canada would be a violation of this Act.

8. It shall not be lawful for any person on the Lord's Day to shoot with or use any gun, rifle or other similar engine, either for gain or in such a manner or in such places as to disturb other persons in attendance at public worship or in the observance of that day.

9. It shall not be lawful for any person to bring into Canada for sale or distribution, or to sell or distribute within Canada, on the Lord's Day, any foreign newspaper or publication classified as a newspaper.

10. Every person who violates any of the provisions of this Act shall for each offence be liable, on summary conviction, to a fine not less than one dollar and not exceeding forty dollars, together with the cost of prosecution.

11. Every employer who authorizes or directs anything to be done in violation of any provision of this Act, shall for each offence be liable, on summary conviction, to a fine not exceeding one hundred dollars and not less than twenty dollars in addition to any other penalty prescribed by law for the same offence.

12. Every corporation which authorizes directs, or permits its employees to carry on any part of the business of such corporation in violation of any of the provisions of this Act, shall be liable, on summary conviction before two justices of the peace, for the first offence to a penalty not exceeding two hundred and fifty dollars and not less than fifty dollars, and for each subsequent offence to a penalty not exceeding five hundred dollars and not less than one hundred dollars in addition to any other penalty prescribed by law for the same offence.

13. Nothing herein shall prevent the operation on the Lord's Day for passenger traffic of any railway subject to the legislative authority of any province unless such railway is prohibited by provincial authority from so operating.

Nothing herein shall prevent the operation on the Lord's Day for passenger traffic by any railway company incorporated by or subject to the legislative authority of the Parliament of Canada of its railway where such operation is not otherwise prohibited.

14. Nothing herein shall be construed to repeal or in any way affect any provisions of any Act or law, relating in any way to the observance of the Lord's Day in force in any province of Canada when this Act comes into force; and where any person violates any of the provisions of this Act, and such offence is also a violation of any other Act or law, the offender may be proceeded against either under the provisions of this Act or under the provisions of any other Act or law, applicable to the offence charged.

15. No action or prosecution for a violation of this Act shall be commenced without the leave of the Attorney General for the province in which the offence is alleged to have been committed nor after the expiration of sixty days from the time of the commission of the alleged offence.

16. This Act shall come into force on the first day of March, one thousand nine hundred and seven.

Football Match A Tie

Penticton and Summerland teams meet for first time on Saturday

The Penticton - Summerland football match which took place last Saturday afternoon, resulted in a tie, with three goals scored by each side.

The game, which was billed for 3:00 p.m., did not actually begin until somewhat later, the Maud Moore bearing the Summerland players and a contingent of their friends being a little late in arriving. The day, as regards weather conditions, could not have been more suitable, but the grounds, although well chosen and laid off, were rather rough.

Most of the business places in town closed for the latter part of the afternoon in order to give all an opportunity to be present, and the Penticton people turned out to a good number in consequence. The game was well contested and both sides are to be complimented on putting up an exceedingly clean and straightforward game. The contest was watched with intense interest by the spectators favorable to each party, and, although the Summerland people were numerically unequal to those of Penticton, numbers proved no criterion as to the amount of enthusiasm shown. Whenever the Summerland boys scored, or made a particularly good pass, the ladies especially from that place did not fail to vociferously express their admiration.

A DECADE
IN REVIEW

1910 ~ 1919

Rush Construction on Kettle Valley

Contracts Call for Grading of First Thirty Miles by Next March

SURVEY GANGS BEGIN WORK NEXT WEEK

SEPTEMBER 3, 1910 — Survey parties will be on hand and the work of locating a line out of Penticton to connect with Merritt on one hand and Midway on the other will be commenced early next week according to an announcement made to the Herald by Mr. J.J. Warren, president of the Kettle Valley Railroad yesterday.

"Mr. McCullough, our engineer, is now packing over the trail with surveying outfits from Merritt and should be in Penticton by Sunday, Monday, or Tuesday at the latest," said Mr. Warren.

As soon as Mr. McCullough arrives upon the scene, the survey work will be prosecuted vigorously.

"We have surveys into Penticton from both the south-east and north-west," observed the president of the Kettle Valley, "But we have never linked them together, and this work will now have to be done."

Will Keep to Base of Hill

SEPTEMBER 3, 1910 — The work of locating a line from Trout Creek into Penticton, should, Mr. Warren intimated, be comparatively easy, but several trial surveys will probably have to be made on the Benchlands on the east side of the lake.

"We wish to avoid as much grading as possible," continued Mr. Warren, "And hope to get a good survey for a line that will sweep into Penticton at the base of the hills behind the benchlands."

May Build Wharf This Fall

SEPTEMBER 3, 1910 — "If we can get the necessary heavy timbers and crib work into Penticton this fall we will commence work on the building of our wharf," said Mr. Warren.

This wharf will be constructed at considerable expense and still be built to meet the demands of heavy traffic.

Regarding the construction of yards and roundhouses in Penticton, Mr. Warren stated that these would be built to take care of locomotives and cars as soon as construction work was far enough advanced.

The Kettle Valley has exercised its option on the lakeshore property which will be deeded over by the council, and, as soon as a proper transfer is made, the vendors will each receive their share of the $24,329, the price for which the property was sold.

MERRITT SEPT. 8. — By the end of September there will be engaged at least 1000 men in the construction of the Kettle Valley railroad at this end. Five camps, four of which are working on construction, are now strung along between Railway Pass and Merritt and with the commencement of work by the steam shovels there will be two or three additional camps. The final locating of the line has retarded work to a large extend, but the engineers say that this end will be fully completed in the course of a week or so.

Grading for the first thirty miles will have to be finished by March 1, and barring an unusually severe winter, the conditions of the contracts will be met. It will then require an additional two or three months to complete the tracklaying so that the first thirty miles should be in operation by the middle of the summer. The work of rushing construction on the rest of the line will be proceeded with at once as it is the plan of the company to have the entire line completed within two years.

Surveyors Will Work Down Grade

Kettle Valley Men Will Probably Tackle Eastern Mountain Range Before Winter

A FEW NEW DEVELOPMENTS
President Warren Was in Town During Week and Will Pay Visit to Midway

If you do not see the surveyors of the Kettle Valley railroad in your orchards or in the streets of the town during the next few weeks, do not imagine that Penticton has been sidetracked after all or that the railroad is not making every preparation to place this town on the map of its system.

It is very probable that the survey parties will begin their work on the mountain range east of Penticton so that the most difficult part of the grade into town will be completed by winter. This will give the railroad all the winter for surveying in the valley.

Mr. J.J. Warren, president of the Kettle Valley railroad who has been in town the greater part of the week, stated that there had been few developments since his last visit.

"Survey work will be prosecuted vigorously in the Penticton district from now on," said Mr. Warren. "I do not expect that we shall be able to start upon the actual construction of the road until late next spring. There is a great deal of work to be done around Penticton and I am going to see to it that the preliminary work of surveying is satisfactorily completed. Every endeavor will be made to push along the work."

Steel is Being Laid on Kettle Valley

Track-Laying Machines Working at Both Ends - Twenty Miles by January 31.

Work Delayed By Weather But Fair Progress Has Been Made

Twenty miles of steel on the Kettle Valley railway line will, it is expected, be in position by the end of January. Track-laying is going along simultaneously at both ends of the route from Midway and Merritt.

Work commenced on the Midway end last week and good progress has been made. A big track-laying machine is being operated with a large force of men and under favorable conditions ten miles of steel, to Rock Creek, will be completed before the end of the month. The machine will lay a mile of steel a day, but the severe weather of the past week has prevented such fast progress being made.

At the Merritt end of the Kettle Valley line ten miles of steel highway are being rushed to completion. In the meantime construction work and grading goes on apace, and another ten miles of track will be laid at either end in the early summer.

Several location surveys are now being completed in the neighborhood of Penticton, and as soon as the weather moderates active construction work will be commenced in the town.

Difficulty in securing heavy timbers at this season of the year has retarded the construction of the big wharf which will be built by the railway company but work on this will probably be commenced very early in the spring.

Hundreds of people turned out May 30th, 1915 to greet the first passenger train as it rolled into the Lakeshore Station in Penticton.

Stocks photo Hudson Collection Courtesy of Penticton Museum

Okanagan Fruit Sold Like Hot Cakes

One Thousand Boxes of Peaches Disappeared in Ninety Minutes Among Winnipeg Crowd - Prairie Dwellers Want More

Great Success Crown Initial Shipment of "All Fancy" Fruit from the Southern Okanagan

O, thou Okanagan. Thou land rich in orchards laden with thrice blessed fruit. What can compare with thy luscious peaches, O fruitful valley of far-away British Columbia? When shall the children of the prairies cease sounding thy praise?

This is the psalm of joy that scores of Winnipeggers sang, chanted, hummed and whistled as they pushed through the heavy swing entrance doors of the T. Eaton Company's big store on Portage Avenue and with what

appeared to be boxes of treasure trove under their arms hurried homeward in order to get their precious freight under cover and removed from all chance of pillage from other less fortunate mortals.

Peaches and cream! And real fresh peaches too. What a luxury for the plainsman.

Too late! How the dire significance of these words, the most tragic in our language must have come home to those who, after driving in a distance of twenty miles or more from the country, found they had arrived just one minute after the last box of Fancy Elbertas had been sold.

Someone got a brilliant idea, however, and rushed off to the nearest telephone office and about five minutes later conversations such as these were general.

Important Resolutions Passed by Central Farmers' Institute

The convention of the B.C. Central Farmers' Institute was held in Victoria last week, with W. E. Scott, Deputy Minister of Agriculture, in the chair. The Chairman said the Department intended to continue the reorganization which Capt. Tatlow had started, and now classified the different departments for stock, poultry and horticulture.

A British Columbia Poultryman's Association was to be organized. With the various departments, the Department would be better able to assist the agriculturists of the province. He told of the need of development, instancing the fact that last year the importations of sheep, poultry, horses, etc., to British Columbia

was $10,000.00. These should be raised in British Columbia. He then went on to tell of his trip to England to exhibit British Columbia fruit, and told of the many successes which have been recorded in this regard.

In his report Superintendent Hodson said six new organizations had been formed, and there was now a membership of 4,000, as compared with 3,250 in the previous year. Twenty-five women's institutions had been organized.

Maxwell Smith announced a movement for the holding of the first annual apple show next November at Vancouver. The sum of $25,000 was required, and he suggested that this be voted on by

the Provincial and Dominion Governments and the City in which the show was to be held. There would be many exhibits, which would prove a great advertisement for the province.

A number of important resolutions were passed during the three day session of the Institute. These dealt with matters of considerable importance to the farmers of the province, and interesting discussion arose, the dominant note of which was the anxiety displayed to bring in new settlers and to encourage them as much as possible in their initial efforts.

Among the resolutions was one recommending the establishment of a national apple show,

with its first meeting place in British Columbia, preferably in Vancouver. This was endorsed by James Cook, of East Kootenay. As an advertisement alone such a show would prove a great factor. It was a matter of considerable interest to British Columbia, as the apples of this province were winning medals wherever they competed.

NOVEMBER 24, 1910

Mexicans Revolt

Mexico has been in a disturbed condition following the anti-American riots of a few days ago, which seem to have been made the excuse for a revolt against the Diaz government. The trouble is occurring at various places in the republic, the most serious outbreak as yet being that at Puebla, on Friday, in which it is reported one hundred persons, including the chief of police, were killed. It was precipitated by the attempt of policemen to break up an anti-administration meeting and the battle was opened by a woman who shot and killed the chief. A general combat ensued during which bombs were used and many were killed. The troops were called out and attacked a house in which the rebels were fortified. Heavy firing on both sides caused the loss of many lives, among the killed being Mrs. Jose Cerdan, who killed the chief of police. Several women were found among the dead and wounded, and 11,100 rifles and a large quantity of ammunition were discovered. With the fall of the rebel stronghold order has been restored in Puebla.

JULY 30, 1914

Panama Canal Opens

The Panama Canal will be opened on August 15 for general navigation to ships requiring not more than 30 feet of water. It is intended to provide 50 feet of water later on, but extensive dredging of slides will be required. No ceremonies will mark the occasion, as the official opening of the Canal will take place in March, 1915, when an international fleet of warships will pass through the waterway and up the Pacific Coast.

Noble And Peasant Paid Homage

At Death Bed Of Leo Tolstoi - Church Sought Reconciliation Before End Came

Count Leo Tolstoi, the great Russian author and reformer died peacefully at Astpava on the morning of Nov. 21. His wife and daughter were present when the end came.

Throughout the crisis a crowd waited outside, pressed up around the low hut.

There were distant relatives of the author and many church men, among these was the Abbot Varsofenius, who did not lose hope until the end, of seeing Tolstoi and extending to him the olive branch on behalf of the church from which he was excommunicated by the holy synod in 1901 for his writings on religion and Christian teachings.

All the people alike stood spellbound. The whole population of Astopava was there. Then a voice from the hut quietly announced "Leo Nicholaevich is dead." There was a moment of silence. Then every head was bared, and there were sounds of sobbing everywhere.

Later in the day all the peasants in the district flocked there.

No one was excluded from the death chamber, through which there was a constant stream of visitors including many school children. The chamber was decorated with pine branches.

The body has been embalmed and transferred to Yasnazi Poliana, where Tolstoi played as a child. Friends of the dead author have started a movement for the acquisition of the house where he died as a national memorial.

Grand Duke Nicholas Michaelovich has sent a message to Countess Tolstoi, saying, "My whole soul is with you and your family at this moment," and numerous other telegrams of sympathy have come from friends and individuals.

Count Lyof Nikolaevich Tolstoi was born on August 28, 1828.

At the age of 23 he entered the army and served in the Caucasses and at the defence of Sebastapool.

During the campaign he wrote a series of vivid sketches which ranked him as a man of literary genius. Tolstoi wrote a great deal on national and political reform subjects, but of late years devoted himself to religious teachings. He made "Return not Evil" his golden text, and insisted that the literal interpretation of the Sermon on the Mount was the only rule of the Christian life.

NEWS OF THE DOMINION: 1910

OCTOBER 1, 1910 — A fresh Great Seal has to be made on the accession of every sovereign to the throne, and the delicate work of cutting it on silver, from the drawings of the artist commissioned to make the design, is done at the mint. A document to which the Seal if fixed is the instrument by which the will of the sovereign in regard to all the more important matters of state is declared. The Great Seal is, therefore, affixed to royal proclamations dissolving or summoning parliament, to treaties with foreign powers, to patents of nobility and to the credentials of ambassadors.

FEBRUARY 10, 1910 — That the Canadian Pacific Railway is looking forward to a very busy summer in 1910 in the matter of railway construction, is indicated by a statement made by general manager Bary, of Vancouver. He stated that the large sum of $30,000,000 would be expended in Western Canada this year. This total would include betterments and improvements and great interest is manifested to learn in what parts of the country the corporation will be at work.

FEBRUARY 10, 1910 — The American invasion of the Canadian North-West still continues. Last week, 820 settlers, each of whom possessed from $2,000 to $5,000, crossed the Boundary line.

1910~1919

THE VERNON NEWS

THE LEADING JOURNAL OF THE FAMOUS OKANAGAN DISTRICT

le Number 1067. VERNON, B.C., NOVEMBER 2, 1911.

Vernon's New Provincial Government Building

AUGUST 1911

Word was received this week from the coast that the contract had been let by the Provincial Government for the construction of the new court house in Vernon, a cut of which appears above. The lowest tender was that of Burns & Co., a Nelson firm of contractors, whose figure was $174,000, and they accordingly were awarded the contract. It is stated that excavation work will be started at once.

The building will be admirably situated on a site purchased by the government a couple of years ago at the corner of Barnard and Mara Avenues. The building will be 150x75 feet in size, two stories high, with a basement the full size of the building. It will contain ample accommodation for court rooms, government offices, fire warden, school inspector, horticultural officers and other departments connected with provincial affairs. It will be constructed of the fine red granite from the quarries below Okanagan Landing, and will be the largest, handsomest and most costly government building in the Interior.

OFF FOR OTTAWA.

Premier McBride Will Press British Columbia's Claims at the Capital.

Victoria, Oct. 30.—Premier McBride and Attorney-General Bowser have arranged to leave on Wednesday for Ottawa, where they will be joined by Hon. Mr. Ross, Provincial

position in visiting the national capital just at present and to anticipate any possible criticism that the adopted course might be regarded as precipitate, pointing out the urgency to British Columbia—in these days of her rapid growth and satisfactory development—of early action in this vital matter, especially as the provincial parliament is to assemble early in January and he both hopes

in the nation's thought, especially qualified to unostentatiously promote a larger sympathy and fuller understanding in the imperial family.

"The people of British Columbia in all its parts are already eagerly looking forward to the visit which in the usual course of events His Royal Highness will pay us during the next few months. The Duke of Connaught when he comes to the

the American Land and Irrigation Exposition at Madison Square Gardens, from the 3rd until the 14th inst. The British Columbia exhibit comprises about sixty varieties of extra choice potatoes, a ton and a half in total weight, and is entered in competition for the Stilwell Trophy and $1,000 prize. Should this be won, the advantage to British Columbia in the promotion of agri-

A WARM WELCOME.

Hon. Martin Burrell Gets an Enthusiastic Reception in His Home Town.

Nelson, B. C., Oct. 28.—All the business places of Grand Forks were closed yesterday afternoon and the people of the city and Boundary District, 2000 strong, gave Hon. Martin Burrell, Minister of Agriculture, a

Vernon's New Provincial Government Building

Word was received this week from the coast that the contract had been let by the Provincial Government for the construction of the new court house in Vernon, a cut of which appears above. The lowest tender was that of Burns & Co., a Nelson

firm of contractors, whose figure was $174,000, and they accordingly were awarded the contract. It is stated that excavation work will be started at once.

The building will be admirably situated on a site purchased by the government a couple of years ago

at the corner of Barnard and Mara Avenues. The building will be 150x75 feet in size, two stories high, with a basement the full size of the building. It will contain ample accommodation for court rooms, government offices, fire warden, school inspector, horticul-

tural officers and other departments connected with provincial affairs. It will be constructed of the fine red granite from the quarries below Okanagan Landing, and will be the largest, handsomest and most costly government building in the Interior.

London society under new King

Queen Mary May Not Be Entirely Popular With Smarter Element of Society.

As the end of the year of mourning for King Edward approaches the interest of the British people in the new court grows keener, says a London correspondent of the New York Sun and Toronto Mall and Empire.

The personalities of King George and Queen Mary are not as yet very well known to the great majority of their subjects, but daily the sum of their knowledge increases. Gradually but surely an idea, a mental portrait of them, their characters and personalities is forming in the minds of the people.

It is already safe to say that when that mental picture is complete it will be entirely to the satisfaction of its makers. At the very beginning of his reign certain stories that had long been current to the discredit of King George were wisely tackled and killed. Now a new idea of the man is rapidly forming itself.

Much as they loved King Edward, the English people recognize that a man of a very different type may be equally worthy of their affection. Edward VII loved society for its own sake; it is no secret that George V does not. Like his father, he is a keen sportsman and a hard worker, but possesses less of that superfluous energy which made the late King throw himself with the same zest into the social as into the more serious side of life.

Queen Mary is essentially a mother. It will perhaps be impossible for her to be as much in the public eye from a merely social point as was Queen Alexandra, who came to the throne when the more absorbing side of her domestic duties may be said to have

been at an end. But it was as the devoted mother while Princess of Wales that Alexandra gained that deep hold on the affections of the English people which she has never lost.

As Queen and mother, Mary will probably follow in her footsteps. With the smarter element of society she may not be entirely popular, but that element is not important.

When Queen Victoria died there is no doubt that the court and society as a whole needed a fillip. An idea has been gradually gaining around that in the last year or two society had forced the pace a little, and that had King Edward lived his unerring instinct would have told him this.

His successor has come to the throne at a moment when a brilliant court is less of a necessity than it was ten years ago. The required social impetus has been given, and it is not likely that its effects will quite wear off. A restraining influence, it is felt, will not now come amiss. It must and will be exercised with tact and discretion, for society today can be led, but not driven.

King Edward at the earliest moment possible abolished the somewhat antiquated methods of the Victorian court. The old-day drawing rooms gave place to evening courts. The waiting outside the palace gates, with ladies in court dress shivering in their carriages, was done away with.

Instead of waiting for weary hours before passing the presence, people went to a brilliant evening party, and instead of going empty away, they sat down to a splendid supper. This change was representative of many more. It is unlikely that the procedure of court entertaining will undergo much change in the new reign. But it is probable that the next few years will see more of stateliness and less of brilliance about the court than in the reign of King Edward.

The late King and Queen Alexandra moved about a great deal in society, dining and attending balls at the greater houses during the London season, and constantly visiting about among their personal friends in the country. It is likely that the present King and Queen will go less into general society, pay fewer country-house visits, except for specific purposes, and themselves entertain much less in the country than did their predecessors. For one thing, they possess no adequate country-house of their own, except the far-distant Balmoral, and entertaining at Windsor necessarily partakes more of state than did the cheerful house parties at Sandringham, where King Edward always loved to be.

(CP PHOTO) 1999 (National Archives of Canada/Bassano)

King George V family (George V, King, Edward VIII, 1894-1972, George VI, 1895-1952)

Titanic Sinks!

TERRIBLE DISASTER TO ATLANTIC LINER

Titanic White Star Leviathan, on Her Maiden Voyage, Strikes Large Iceberg and Sinks

ESTIMATED 1,500 TO 2,000 PERISH

Women and Children Saved in Boats - Picked up by Cunarder Carpathia - Harrowing Scenes

The most appalling catastrophe that has ever occurred at sea, befell the new White Star liner Titanic, at 10:25 on Sunday night, when she crashed into a monstrous iceberg at a point believed to be about 500 miles from Halifax. The passengers are supposed to have numbered at least 1,500, while a crew of 800 brought up the total souls on board to 2,300. Of these, only 868 are known to have been saved by the Allan liner Carpathia, which went to the rescue immediately on receiving a wireless message from the doomed Leviathan.

Rumours were rife on the lake towns on Monday and Tuesday, but beyond the fact the Titanic had struck a berg and staved her bows in, nothing definite was known until the Okanagan arrived with the Union Jack at half mast, on Tuesday evening. It was then ascertained that the Titanic had fought her first, and last, fight with the sea and that she had gone down, carrying with her at least two-thirds of her passengers and crew.

The first news of the collision was received at Cape Race at 10:25 o'clock Sunday night, when the Titanic wireless operator called 'C. Q. D.,' the Cunard liner Carpathia picked up the call, and is believed to have been the first vessel to reach the disabled steamer's side.

The Titanic is the largest steamer ever built. She is 882 feet long, and has 46,328 tons displacement. She was launched last May, and this was her maiden trip.

Among her passengers were Colonel and Mrs. John Jacob Astor, Alfred G. Vanderbilt, Major Archibald Butt, military aide to President Taft; F.D. Millet, the artist; Mr. and Mrs. Isador Straus, Judge Widner, of Philadelphia; President Hayes, of the Grand Trunk Railway; J. B. Bruce Ismay, manager and director of the White Star Line; W..T. Stead, and others.

The death bed of the $10,000,000 steamer Titanic, and in all probability of the many who were drowned when she sank, is two miles below the surface of the sea. The calculation was made by an official of the government marine department, who finds the depth in the marine chart at a point about 500 miles from Halifax, and about 70 miles south of the Grand Banks, where it is believed the Titanic went down.

NEW YORK, APRIL 16 —

Messages received shortly after 10 o'clock this morning, by the Marconi Company, from stations at Cape Race and Sable Island, indicates that there are none of the Titanic's passengers on either the Parisian or Virginian.

HALIFAX, N.S., APRIL 16 —

The Allan Line steamer Parisian, reports via Sable Island, that she has no passengers from the Titanic on board. The Parisian has just come into touch with the Sable Island wireless station.

The Parisian steamed through much heavy field ice, looking for passengers from the Titanic. No life rafts or bodies were sighted among the floating wreckage. The Parisian reports that the weather was cold, and that even if any persons had been on the wreckage, they would, in all probability, have perished from exposure before they could have been rescued.

NEW YORK, April 16. -

What is believed to be one of the last messages sent from the Titanic, before she struck the iceberg, was received at the Hydrographic office in Washington, on April 14, the day preceding the night on which the accident occurred, according to advices received here tonight. The message, as given, reads: "April 14, German steamer Amerika reported by radio telegraph, passing two large icebergs in latitude 41.27, longitude 50.08. Titanic." This message indicates that the Titanic had knowledge of ice in her vicinity, as her position, when she struck, was latitude 41.46, longitude 50.14.

ST. JOHN'S, Nfld., April 17 -

When the Titanic struck the iceberg, which sent her to the bottom, she was going eighteen knots an hour. The impact was so terrific that the decks were broken through, her sides crumpled, and the bulkheads forming the watertight compartments, upon which such reliance was placed, were crushed in from the bow to nearly amidships.

This version of the wreck is credited to the British steamer Bruce, en route to Sidney, N.S. She is supposed to have picked up the story by wireless, from other ships near the Titanic. The great liner is declared to have struck with such speed and momentum as to rear half out of the water, tearing her bottom off on the jagged, submerged ice, from the bow clear to amidships. The compartments flooded at once, and she began to settle by the head.

NEW YORK, April 17. -

The Camperdown wireless station at Halifax, today sent the Associated Press the following dispatch: "We are now in communication with the Carpathia, and in position to announce, unofficially, that the Titanic struck an enormous iceberg and sank. Over two thousand lost, seven hundred survivors, mostly women, on Carpathia; harrowing details."

Band Played While Titanic Sank

Ship Was Ripped Open Below The Water Line -
Passengers Only Felt Slight Shock
INSUFFICIENT LIFEBOATS ABOARD
Brave Women Refused to Leave Their Husbands -
Thrilling Story by Passenger

Nearly two weeks have passed since the Titanic, the greatest marine achievement in the history of the world, sank in mid-ocean. Much of her story is still untold, and many a day will pass before the world will fully comprehend the significance of the disaster.

The number of dead possibly will never be positively known, inasmuch as the complete passenger list went down with the vessel. The number of survivors is fixed at 705 by the report of Captain Rostron of the Carpathia. The White Star Line officials believe the death list totalled approximately 1,635. The narratives gathered piecemeal from the liner's survivors pay a tribute, without precedent, to the bravery of the men and women of these modern days, a bravery of impulse, unstudied, unassuming alike in steerage passengers, stoker and millionaire.

The following story was compiled by Carlos M. L. Hurd of the New York Morning World, from stories narrated by survivors of the Carpathia. Facts which I have established by inquiries on the Carpathia as positively as they could be established are:

That the Titanic's officers knew several hours before the crash, of the possible nearness of the iceberg.

That the Titanic's speed, nearly 23 knots an hour, was not slackened.

That the number of lifeboats of the Titanic was insufficient to accommodate more than one-third of the passengers, to say nothing of the crew. Most members of the crew say that there were sixteen lifeboats and two collapsibles; none say there were more than 20 boats in all. The 700 who escaped filled most of the sixteen lifeboats and the one collapsible that got away, to the limit of their capacity.

Had the ship struck the iceberg head-on, with whatever speed and with whatever resulting shock, the bulkhead system of watertight compartments probably would have saved the vessel. As one man expressed it, it was the impossible that happened when, with a shock unbelievably mild, the ship's side was torn for a length which made the bulkhead system ineffective. The Titanic was 1799 miles from Queenstown and 1191 miles from New York, speeding for a maiden voyage record. The night was starlit, the sea glassy. Lights were out in most of the staterooms, and only two or three congenial groups remained in the public rooms.

In the crow's nest, or lookout, and on the bridge, officers and members of the crew were at their places waiting relief at midnight from their two hours' watch.

At 11:45 came the sudden sound of two guns, a warning of immediate danger. The crash against the iceberg, which had been sighted at only a quarter of a mile, came almost simultaneously with the click of the levers operated by those on the bridge which stopped the engines.

Captain Smith was on the bridge a moment later giving orders for the summoning on deck of all aboard and for the putting on of life preservers and the lowering of the life boats.

The first boats lowered contained more men passengers than the latter ones, as the men were on deck first and not enough women were there to fill them. When a moment later the rush of frightened women and crying children to the deck began, enforcement of the women first rule became rigid. Officers loading some of the boats drew revolvers but in most cases the men, both passengers and crew, behaved in a way that called for no such restraint.

Revolver shots heard by many persons shortly before the end of the Titanic caused many rumours. One was that Captain Smith shot himself; another was that First Officer Murdock had ended his life. Smith, Murdock and Sixth Officer Moody are known to have been lost.

Members of the crew discredit all reports of suicide and say Captain Smith remained on the bridge until just before the ship sank. It is also related that when a cook, later, sought to pull him aboard a life boat he exclaimed: "Let me go!" and jerked away went down.

The Penticton Herald

PENTICTON, B.C., SATURDAY, APR

VOL. 2. No. 43.

TERRIBLE DISASTER TO ATLANTIC LINER

Titanic White Star Leviathan, on Her Maiden Voyage, Strikes Large Iceberg and Sinks

ESTIMATED 1500 TO 2000 PERISH.

Women and Children Saved in Boats—Picked Up By Cunarder Carpathia—Harrowing Scenes

The most appalling catastrophe that has ever occurred at sea, befel the new White Star liner Titanic, at 10:25 on Sunday night, when she crashed into a monstrous iceberg at a point believed to be about 500 miles from Halifax. The passengers are supposed to have numbered at least

sighted among the floating wreckage.

The Parisian reports that the weather was cold, and that even if any persons had been on the wreckage, they would, in all probability, have perished from exposure before they could have been rescued.

NEW YORK, April 16.—What is believed to be one of the last messages sent from the Titanic, before she struck the iceberg, was received at the Hydrographic office in Washington, on April 14, the day preceding the night on which the accident occurred, according to advices received here tonight. The message, as given, reads:

"April 14, German steamer Amerika reported by radio telegraph, passing two large icebergs in latitude 41.27, longitude

BYLAWS TO BE PASSED B WILL REQUIRE $128

ELECTRIC EXTENSIONS WILL SWEL

To Build Municipal Hall—Improvement of Light and Water For the Whole Mu Industries to Be Encouraged— From Taxation Reque

An extraordinary meeting of the Town Council, for the purpose of entering into the estimates for the present year, and to consider bylaws to be present-

requeste to ask fo was not tail all to Per

Photo courtesy of the Penticton Museum

Photo courtesy of the Kelowna Museum

The Sicamous was not alone on the waters of Okanagan Lake. By 1914 numerous vessels of all shapes, sizes and propulsion systems (sternwheeler and screw) handled capably the daily chores of moving passengers and freight along the shores of the 86 mile long lake.

At top left the Aberdeen was the first to ply the waters in 1893.

Middle left shows the next ship to appear on the scene, the Okanagan in 1902. She remained in service until 1932.

At bottom the luxurious dining room of the Sicamous, the Grand Dame of the CPR sternwheeler fleet. This magnificent room was 65 feet long and could seat 70 people.

Photo courtesy of the Penticton Museum

SS Sicamous - Queen of the fleet

Some Particulars of the Fine Addition to the C. P. R. Fleet on the Okanagan

("Vernon News")

The "Sicamous" easily Queen of the fleet of Okanagan Lake vessels, is larger and more luxurious than any of the C.P.R. fleet of inland ships, save the "Bonnington" on the Arrow Lakes. The hull is an exact duplicate of the hull of the "Nasookin" now on the Kootenay, being 200 feet in length, 40 feet wide, and 8 feet deep. The height of the "Sicamous" is 53 feet from the level of the main deck to the top of the pilot house. The length over all is 228 feet, and she draws an average of five feet of water.

The hull is of steel construction throughout, and is divided into 20 water-tight compartments. The engines, of the tandem compound jet condensing type, generate from 1,200 to 1,300 horse power, and will drive the new boat at a rate of 19 miles an hour. The entire steamer is electric lighted and steam heated.

The "Sicamous" is rated at 1500 tons gross capacity, and will carry 900 tons net tonnage, besides capacity for 400 passengers, and will carry a crew of 32 or 33.

Construction work was begun on the new boat in September of last year, and she will have cost, when entirely completed, about $180,000. $14,000 of which will have been spent for furnishings.

The dining room, 65 feet long, will seat 70 persons. There are 40 passenger state-rooms, four of which are double suites, and one suite with a private-bath. In addition to the usual state-rooms for the crew, there are special rooms for the mail clerk and express messenger, a cold storage room for meats and poultry, a pastry room, shower bath for the crew, and other conveniences not found on the ordinary inland boat.

The furnishings and fittings of the steamer have been done in Australian mahogany and in teak wood from Burmah, a combination which gives an effect of unusual richness.

The large observation and smoking room back of the upper tier of state-rooms is practically walled with plate glass, and will afford a splendid point of vantage from which to view the scenery of the Okanagan. Writing desks and reading lamps will be put on the balcony above the dining room. The most modern fire fighting devices will be provided, as well as safety devices designed to protect passengers and crew, and six large life boats will be carried.

The SS Sicamous took her maiden voyage on May 14, 1914. Here she is docked at Kelowna in the summer of that year.

Photo Courtesy of Penticton Museum.

LATEST NEWS BY WIRE

Unrepentant Assassin Of Imperial Pair Glories in Deed

BUDAPEST, HUNGARY, JULY 1. — The "Ujasaj" newspaper publishes an alleged confession by Favrio Prinzip, the assassin of Archduke Ferdinand and his wife, according to which he obtained the pistol with which the deed was done from a revolutionary group in Belgrade. He gives not the slightest evidence of remorse, stating: "I have no regret for what I have done, but, on the other hand, am well satisfied because I have accomplished what I had desired to do for a long time."

Servian Churches Destroyed In Bosnian Riots

SERAJEVO, BOSNIA, JULY 1. — Rioting has occurred at Arevo Cubello, where Servian churches have been stormed and destroyed. Martial law has been declared in Bosnia and Herzegovina.

Royal bodies interred

The bodies of the murdered Archduke Francis Ferdinand of Austria and his consort, the Duchess of Hohenberg, were interred on Saturday with simple ceremony in the family vaults in the castle of Artstetten.

No Danger Of Rupture Between Austria and Hungary as a Result of Assassination of Archduke and Duchess

VIENNA, JULY 8. — The fears of a rupture between Austrian and Hungary as the result of the assassination of Archduke Francis Ferdinand and his wife now appear to be groundless. Servia will be asked to clear out the nest of conspirators sheltering in that country. Count Tisza, the Premier, has denied in parliament that there is any danger of a revolution in Bosnia.

Local Soldiers leave the Okanagan to go to war in September of 1914. The SS Sicamous transported thousands of men to Okanagan Landing for their journey to the battlefields in Europe.

Photo Courtesy of Penticton Museum.

Great Britain Declares War

Great Britain Steps Into the Fray, and a Titanic Struggle is Now in Progress - Italy is the Only Great European Power Not Involved in the Conflict - Great Britain, France and Russia Are Ranged Against Germany and Austria-Servia, the Cause of the War, Becomes of Secondary Importance - Fighting on Land and Sea.

Special to the Courier.
Received at 9:15 p.m. August 4.

LONDON, AUG. 4. — Britain has declared war on Germany, and Germany declared war on Britain tonight.

The long-threatened great European conflict has come at last. Two weeks ago, there was no sign that the great powers of the Old World were so soon to be hurled into deadly conflict with each other, and the climax has come so suddenly that many people are still asking in a dazed manner, "What is it all about?"

The rankling wounds left by the Franco-Prussian War of 1870 have been regarded for years past as the probable cause of the next great European war, but the titanic struggle now begun has had its origin in the deep-rooted hate and jealousy not between the Latin and the Germanic races but between the German and the Slav. Since the assassination of the Archduke Franz Ferdinand, heir to the Austrian throne, and his consort in June in Serajevo, the Bosnian capital, the German population of the dual monarchy has been simmering with wrath and the Austrian government resolved to visit signal punishment upon the Servian people, whom it blamed for encouraging, sheltering and protecting the Serb authors of the plot against the lives of the murdered pair. Probably to permit of time for the necessary military preparations, the intentions of Austria were kept entirely secret, and the ultimatum served upon the Servian government on July 23rd, demanding the suppression of the Pan-Servian movement and the punishment of those concerned in the assassination, came upon Europe as a thun-

derbolt from the clear sky. A conciliatory reply was made by Servia, but Austria, like the wolf in "Little Red Riding Hood," had made up her mind not to be conciliated, and on July 28th she formally declared war on the little Balkan state, and immediately followed the declaration by bombarding Belgrade.

Russia, generally looked upon by the minor Slav peoples as their protector, at once began mobilization of her troops, and it was then that Germany took a hand and demanded an explanation of Russia's intentions, and that she cease mobilization. Failing to receive a satisfactory reply, Germany began mobilization of her army through an order signed by the Emperor at 5:15 p.m. on August 1st. and at 7:30 the same evening the German ambassador at St. Petersburg delivered a declaration of war to the Russian government and immediately thereafter left St. Petersburg. Not content with her ultimatum to Russia on July 31st, Germany had also addressed a demand to France, on the same day, desiring to know what would happen if Russia refused to cease mobilization. The diplomatic reply to this peremptory request has not been published, but that it could not convey much satisfaction to the Germans is evident by the fact that shortly after receipt of the

German answer to it, about 4 p.m. on Aug. 1st, a general mobilization order was issued to the French army. No formal declaration of war was made prior to the commencement of hostilities, which seem to have begun along the French border the following day, although the strict censorship exercised by the powers involved has made all the reports received of fighting vague, indefinite and unreliable. It would appear that Germany and France are each seeking to throw upon the other the onus of beginning the war, but Germany is clearly the aggressor, as she has violated the neutrality of Belgium and the independent Duchy of Luxemburg by entering the territory of these states with her troops, hence the direct reasons for Great Britain being drawn into the conflict as one of the powers guaranteeing the inviolability of Belgium.

Following an appeal from the King of the Belgians, the British Government took action as stated in the following telegram:

Special to the Courier.

LONDON, AUG. 4. — The Government gives Germany until midnight to declare her intentions in regard to the neutrality of Belgium.

Details of the negotiations are not yet available, but Germany's assurances were evidently quite unsatisfactory to Great Britain, and the result was that mutual declarations of war were exchanged on Tuesday evening, as stated in the telegram to the "Courier" printed at the top of this page.

More Bright-Faced Volunteers Go To Fight For Empire

Penticton recruits for third overseas contingent are now at Victoria

Church parade Sunday morning Social Saturday evening - Addresses at Hotel Incola

Packed tightly the entire length of the spacious porch in front of the Incola Hotel, flowing down the side steps into the driveway , and spreading fan like out upon the street, it seemed as if the entire population had assembled Sunday night to do honor to the departing soldiers. The band, imbued with its usual high sense of duty, was out in full force and contributed a generous programme of spirited music. Masses in front of the Aquatic Club building and surrounded by torch bearers. "The Best and Biggest Band" lifted the spirit of the crowd to a high pitch of enthusiasm and filled with martial ardor the hearts of the soldier boys.

The reeve was the first speaker and he addressed his audience from the elevated entrance to the Incola. His worship, in his quiet but sincere and impressive way, bade the soldiers farewell on behalf of the townspeople. He touched a vibrant chord in the hearts of many when he said that Penticton with the pick of her youth and manhood had answered readily and nobly to the Empire's call, to the Empire's gain and our eternal glory.

The reeve was wildly applauded and when some man on the outskirts of the crowd, with a voice that would have shamed Stentor Heights, climbed on the gate and proposed three rousing cheers, he

met with a response that must have satisfied him.

Lieut. Dufresne was next called. This popular officer's delayed appearance on the firing line was more in the nature of a strategic advance than a vigorous assault. In other words, as the Lieutenant explained, when his heavy vocal artillery got in action, when the "order of the day" was speech-making it was always difficult for him to get his ammunition unlimbered. However that may be, he made some pretty good hits when he did get the range. Lieut. Dufresne called the Roll of Honor, to which the members of the Overseas force clearly and promptly responded with pride in their tone and the light of high resolve in their sparkling eyes.

There would have been a total eclipse of the Moon if the drill sargeant had had his way, the local luminary was brought from behind a crowd of his admirers and elevated to the military firmament. It was a full moon, too. Full of humor, characteristic bluntness and unexpected eloquence. He complimented the boys upon the efficiency they had achieved in so short a time, giving the credit generously to the motive that had prompted them and to the understanding and intelligence they had shown during the few days of training. That the victims of his productive drilling tactics held no grudge against the sergeant was very evident by the manner in which they show appreciation of his happy speech.

Were Up In The Air!

What?
Why German Airships, Of Course!

There has been considerable excitement during the last two days in connection with a persistent rumor to the effect that two airships were seen on Tuesday evening manoeuvering above Okanagan Lake in the vicinity of Gellatley's Landing.

Word of this unexpected visit was first received over the long distance telephone from Mr. Gellatley, who stated that two air craft appeared about 6 o'clock in the evening, and flew back and forth in an apparent effort to locate their exact position as they used their searchlights continuously.

After scouting for some time at a high altitude they descended to within a few hundred feet of the surface of the lake, when apparently having located their position they shot skyward and

disappeared in a northwesterly direction towards Kamloops. Corroborative reports come from Oyama and Vernon, where glimpses of the flying machines were also had.

Mr. Gellatley, who was the first to observe the weird visitors, telephoned the startling news to Kamloops, where a careful watch was instituted without any results, so far as has been learned.

Much speculation is being indulged in as to the purpose or object of the aerial visit, the opinion being freely expressed that if they were craft of the enemy, they must have started some secret point across the boundary and headed for a point where operations might have the effect of creating a feeling of insecurity in the western part of this country.

We should worry.

Review of 1916 by General A.W. Currie

Canadians Win Every Time, But Hun Morale Unbroken, Says Head of First Division

"We expect fully that next year will see some hard and fierce fighting," said Major-General A.W. Currie, of the 1st Canadian Division, writing in December, 1916, from Canadian headquarters in France. The letter in part says: "The old division is still going strong, though the original members are getting very, very few; of all the officers and the infantry and the brigade and divisional staffs who came over to France in the beginning, there are only three of us who have never been away from the division for any reason, other than ordinary leave. Of course we still have a number of officers who have come back after being sick and wounded."

General Currie was among the first to offer himself for active service, and left Canada in command of the 50th Regiment, Victoria, with the first Canadian Contingent, and has been in France on active service since. He has been decorated by President Poincare with the Legion of Honor with the title of Cross Commander. He left Canada as colonel and received his promotion on the field.

Drafts Do Well

The letter continues: "The health of the troops is simply splendid. Everyone is cheerful and optimistic. The new drafts are very good physically and are willing and anxious to learn the game quickly and get into it at once. I feel certain the splendid reputation already enjoyed will be maintained. The corps did extremely well on the Somme, and the old division just a little more than its share. We had the unique distinction of going in three times. It was a great compliment. As long as there is a man left, the old division still has a fight in it. Our men do not whimper and do not quit.

"We fully expect that next year will see some hard and fierce fighting, for the old Boche is by no means licked. It always annoys me to read in our papers that the German morale is very low, that the German soldier is so sick of fighting that he surrenders at the first opportunity. Such stuff is all balderdash. You'd think we had nothing to do but go over and they would hold up their hands. All rot, any that we have been opposite have always been ready for a fight

though we've licked them every time we have come to grips. We've licked this year, we've shown him that we could take his strongest works, and anything and everything we've taken from him this year still remains ours. We have inflicted more casualties than we have received, and whenever you do that in this war you win, for it is a war of attrition. We have given him a taste this year of what he may expect next year, and as soon as the weather gets right we're going at him again and knock the very devil out of him.

Shuns Peace Talk

"About his peace proposals, I think everyone is agreed that he is like the poker player who, having all the chips in his stack, thinks it a good thing to break off the game. You've met those fellows, haven't you, and you've usually agreed they were pikers. Well, the old Boche is worse. He knows he has more now than he'll ever have again, and of course he wants peace, but he won't get it, and he knows he won't. It is a long, long time since we left Canada; we are all longing for the time to come when we'll get home again."

Russians Triumph Over The Germans

Have now the advantage of strength and position say experts - War news

PETROGRAD — Russia finally has established a superiority as a fighting power over Germany, high military observers here say, and the turning point of the war on the Russian side has now been reached. The bottom has fallen out

of the German campaign, these experts say, and all that the Germans are now seeking to accomplish is to cover the failure of the strategic plan or possibly the absence of any adequate plan by frantic rushes at frightful cost in every direction.

Czar Nicholas riding in front of his troops drawn up for review in Petrograd before leaving for the front.

WAR DIARY

British Losses Now Show Big Decreases

LONDON, MAY 9. — In the House of Commons, today, Andrew Bonar Law, the chancellor, referring to the west front, said that the rapidity of our attack had forestalled the enemy, who had to fight in the open with heavy losses because they had no time to prepare trenches. Since April 1, British forces had taken 20,000 prisoners, 257 guns and 227 trench mortars. While in the first four days of the somme drive we had advanced three and one half miles on a six mile front, we had now advanced from two to five miles on a 20-mile front, where there were twice as many German divisions against us as there had been on the Somme when half of them had to be withdrawn. In spite of all this, our casualties in the present offensive were from 50 to 75 per cent, less than they had been on the Somme. Our successes were largely due to our distinct artillery superiority, in connection with which the Chancellor paid warm tribute to the flying corps.

Pte. Fred Crouch Dies Of Wounds

NOVEMBER 4, 1917 — Just at the time when the end of the war is apparently in sight, Lance Corporal Fred Crouch, a well known and very popular Penticton man, has fallen in battle. Word of his death was received by his wife on Saturday.

Corporal Crouch enlisted in Penticton in the 172nd three years ago. He was overseas for two years. He was first wounded on April 10, 1917, in the shoulder and foot during a bloody encounter at Vimy Ridge. He was mentioned in battalion orders for highly efficient and courageous work in a raid on enemy trenches in Hill 70.

His death took place on October 1 from gunshot wounds in the left leg and hand.

Corporal Crouch had lived in Penticton for six or seven years prior to enlisting and had a wide circle of friends here. He is survived by his wife, there being no family.

Advance at Vimy told by officer

Well-known Penticton man relates dramatic story of battle of Arras

This letter is one of the most interesting and descriptive ones that has been received since the beginning of the war, and it will be read with great interest by the people of Penticton, who have so much reason to be proud of the boys they have given to the great cause:

My Dear Guernsey, – This is Easter Sunday evening, and the eve of battle – a battle for which we have been preparing for many months. No operation has been more carefully prepared, thoroughly thought out, or more assiduously trained for than this one. It may prove historic; it will add lustre and glory to the records of the Canadian corps in France. The bombardment of the Huns' trenches which is going on now and which has been going on for days, is more intense than anything which has gone before – not excluding the battle of the Somme.

At the moment of writing our trenches are crowded with men all eager to go over the top, all waiting calmly but determinedly for the passing of a few short hours which will bring them to close grips with the foe. Never were troops in better spirits nor better prepared for the ordeal of tomorrow. They are splendid and one is proud to be in it with them.

I am writing this in our battle headquarters, forty feet below ground, just a few hours before the show. What the next few hours will bring forth has no fear for us; we know we shall win, although the cost may be heavy. Everyone is in good spirits, but not excited. It is perhaps a curious condition of mind which precedes a great battle like the one which will be fought in a few hours. There is no undue or unnatural excitement – just an elation of spirits like the effects of a glass of good "bubbling."

Everything has been so thoroughly prepared and thought out that we have nothing to make us anxious.

April 12 – Since I wrote the above lines the great battle of Arras has been fought and you know the result. It has realized our highest hopes and crowned the efforts of months with the completest success.

The show started at 5:30 a.m., just as day was breaking. The bombardment had been going on with considerable intensity for some days without cessation, but half an hour before zero hour there was a lull. Then punctually to the minute our guns burst out simultaneously into a terrific roar accompanied by the rat-tat of hundreds of machine guns. I was 500 yards from the German lines at the time,

and in front of all our guns, so that the full fury of the bombardment was passing over my head. It was the most appalling pandemonium that the mind of man can imagine. The Hun lines were hit from end to end with a sheet of flame from the bursting shells and soon S.O.S. signal rockets added to the spectacular effect as the Huns in frenzied haste sought to warn their batteries of their danger. For three minutes this tornado of steel rested on the front trench of the enemy's lines, then it lifted farther onwards, and as it did so our infantry sprang from the assembly trenches and swept over the first objective. The barrage moved slowly on and our troops keeping close under it did what was expected of them. The stronger positions were treated with a more lingering regard by the barrage of shells until they were pulverized beyond recognition, and were then dealt with by our magnificent infantry. The final objective was taken and consolidation started two hours from the commencement of the show and Vimy Ridge was ours.

- Thos. H. Wilson

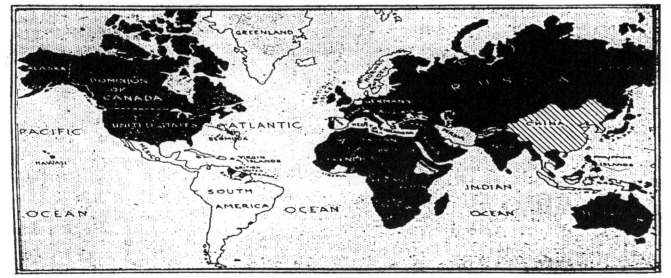

Two-Thirds of the World at War

The resources of the United States and the Entente Allies compared with the Teutonic Allies				
Country—	Population	Wheat production in bushels	Pig iron production—tons	National wealth
United States	103,000,000	1,000,000,000	33,600,000	$230,000,111,111
Entente Allies	779,000,000	2,170,000,000	27,500,000	305,000,010237
Teutonic Allies	147,500,000	415,000,000	16,000,000	133,750,000,000

Will Have Revolution Before Conscription

French Canadians Promise Opposition to Bill for Compulsory Service

MONTREAL — "Down with conscription" was the sentiment which prevailed at a gathering in Park Lafontaine tonight, at which it was estimated that between 15,000 and 20,000 people attended. The crowd was largely comprised of men and boys whose ages ran from 15 to 30. Marcil, the proprietor of the local French language daily, "La Liberte," said that he had received a letter from Sir Wilfrid Laurier in which the Liberal chieftain said he would oppose the prolongation of parliament and conscription. "I want to register this statement," said Marcil, "that before we have conscription we will have revolution." M. Briton, who presided over the meeting, said that "it is the duty of all men to protest against this damn conscription." Speaking further, he said, "Let us show the government that the French Canadians are not sheep." He considered that "Canada had done her whole duty when she sent 400,000 of our fellow citizens to Europe." The meeting was orderly.

Keep up the Food Supply and Help Make Victory Sure

"I AM assured that my people will respond to every call necessary to the success of our cause—with the same indomitable ardour and devotion that have filled me with pride and gratitude since the war began."
HIS MAJESTY KING GEORGE

OUR soldiers must be fed; the people at home must be fed. And—in spite of Germany's murderous campaign to cut off the Allies' Food supply, by sinking every ship on the High Seas—an ample and unfailing flow of food to England and France must be maintained.

This is National Service—
Not to the Farmer only—
But to YOU—to everybody—
This appeal is directed

WE must unite as a Nation to SERVE —to SAVE and to PRODUCE. Men, women and children; the young, the middle aged and the old—all can help in the Nation's Army of Production.

EVERY pound of FOOD raised, helps reduce the cost of living and adds to the Food Supply for Overseas.

PLANT a garden—small or large. Utilize your own back yard. Cultivate the vacant lots. Make them all yield food.

WOMEN of towns can find no better or more important outlet for their energies than in cultivating a vegetable garden.

For information on any subject relating to the Farm and Garden, write:
INFORMATION BUREAU
Department of Agriculture
OTTAWA

Be patriotic in act as well as in thought.

Use every means available--
Overlook nothing.

Dominion Department of Agriculture
OTTAWA, CANADA.
HON. MARTIN BURRELL, Minister.

Spent A Bad Year In Hands Of Germans

Chris Kay, returned soldier, was brutally treated while wounded and a prisoner

Chris Kay was severely wounded at Messines in June of 1916, when the Germans blew up a dug-out in which he was located with some companions, he had both of his legs broken, one of them in two places, in addition to some other minor injuries. The three companions with him in the dugout were instantly killed. He succeeded in crawling into the open, where he lay for five days before he was discovered by the Germans, who were consolidating their position. In fact he was first discovered by some Canadian prisoners who were in the hands of the Germans.

When found, Mr. Kay was in very bad shape, his wounds terribly inflamed and his condition pitiable. The only attention given to him when he was first found was to tie bandages around his injuries without any dressing or even a first aid description. At a German base hospital somewhere in Belgium, which he reached some hours later, his broken bones were set and his other injuries attended to with considerable care. Indeed, he relates that while he was in hospital in Belgium he received very good care. Later, however, he was taken to a hospital in Germany, and here the

treatment was much different.

The convalescing soldier said that while a prisoner of the Huns he never knew what it was to have enough to eat, and that he is sure he would have starved if it had not been for the parcels that came quite regularly from the thoughtful friends at home. When he would get a parcel, which although always opened by the authorities before it was given to him, was seldom interfered with, he never stopped till he had consumed everything in it, that was edible. He received many parcels during the ten months that he was in the hospital,

and they were all that made his life endurable. Mostly the regular fare served to prisoners in Germany at that time was bread made from sawdust and potatoes, soup from horse chestnuts and coffee from burnt acorns. Now and then a special treat would be macaroni and dried fish bones. Kay weighed 162 pounds when he was taken a prisoner, but only 83 pounds when he was sent to Switzerland to be exchanged.

Mr. Kay, who is still somewhat weak, returned last week to Victoria, where he is receiving treatment at a military hospital.

1910~1919

Kelowna soldier dies a gallant death

Capt. C.K.L. Pyman, D.S.O. pushed attack home before hit by sniper's bullet

A letter received by Mr. W.G. Benson from Mr. F. Pyman, brother to the late Mr. C.K.L. Pyman, of Kelowna, gives some particulars of that gallant soldier's death upon the battlefield on the 10th August, meagre details of which reached here about the 20th of the same month.

The letter states that Colin Pyman "was in command of the 5th Canadian Infantry Battalion in the attack on the 9th August and had set a splendid example by his dash and energy in pushing the attack home, moving about from one part of the field to the other under constant fire, quite regardless of his personal safety. About 5 o'clock when approaching the Vrely-Rouvroy Road (west of Chaulnes) he was hit in the groin by a sniper's bullet. The advance had been so quick and so far that they had outstripped the field ambulance, and it appears that he lay in an exposed position in excellent spirits, but in great pain for some time, until the stretcher bearers came up and carried him away. At this time he was conscious. He reached the doctors too late for an operation to have any chance of saving his life and died on the 10th. Since his death he has been awarded the D.S.O. for a particularly gallant raid which he organized and carried out near Arras on July 26."

Four More Soldiers Come Back To Kelowna

Just in time for the Good Friday and Easter holiday, four more Kelowna men returned from Europe last Thursday afternoon and were accorded a warm if somewhat quiet welcome. These men consisted of Ptes. A. Gibb, Pte. Smith, F.O. Bussill and Plant. All of them have done good service for the Empire and deserve every form of welcome that can be given to them.

How to make our soldiers happy

A doctor writes: "If you go to any of the military hospitals where they bring the wounded, the first thing that strikes your attention is the packet of cigarettes by the side of the bed. The nurses know it is useless to hope for a man's speedy recovery until he has the taste of tobacco on his lips."

The best and surest way to make our troops, wounded or unwounded, happy; the best way to make them think that Canada is not unmindful of their great courage and fortitude, is to send them enough tobacco.

In the trenches, or in the hospital, a packet of tobacco is the most acceptable gift in the world.

Do not delay, send a contribution today to: Canada's Tobacco Fund (Organized by the Over-Seas Club).

The Kelowna Courier will receive your contribution and send it on without delay to Canada's Tobacco Fund, which has been organized by the Over-Seas Club.

Don't Let Tommy's Pipe Go Out.

1910~1919

"In Flanders Fields" touched thousands

Evoked Wide-Spread Response and Death of Author Brought Sadness and Sorrow

"In Flanders Fields," by Lieut.-Col. John McCrae of Guelph, Ont., has touched thousands in Canada and the Untied States as probably no other lines on the war have done. The publication of his poem has evoked a widespread response, some of which is also in verse.

When the war broke out Dr. McCrae was a distinguished physician on the staff of McGill University, Montreal. He at once entered active service on the staff of Brig.-Gen., Morrison, and up to and through the second battle of Ypres served with his brigade in the double capacity of staff and medical officer. Later he was appointed to the medical side of Canadian Hospital No. 3, McGill unit, Boulogne, France, at which post he continued till his death a short time ago of pneumonia. He was a son of Lieut.-Col. McCrae, of Guelph, was 45 years of age and unmarried.

In Flanders Fields

In Flanders fields the poppies blow
Between the crosses, row on row.
That mark our place, and in the sky
The larks, still bravely singing, fly,
Scarce heard amid the guns below.

We are the dead; short days ago
We lived, felt dawn, saw sunset glow,
Loved and were loved, and now we lie
In Flanders fields.

Take up our quarrel with the foe!
To you from failing hands we throw
The torch; be yours to hold it high!
If ye break faith with us who died
We shall not sleep, though poppies grow,
In Flanders fields.

Terms of Thirty Day Armistice

Allies to occupy all Germany west of the Rhine
HUNS TO PAY FOR ALL DESTROYED SHIPPING
Brest-Litovsk treaty cancelled

LONDON, NOV. 11—

The armistice terms include the cessation of hostilities for a period of thirty days. They also include the evacuation of all occupied territory, including Alsace and Lorraine, also the evacuation of the left bank of the Rhine and the surrender of a vast amount of guns and equipment, also the surrender of all rolling stock in occupied lands. It further includes reparation for damage done, the repatriation of all allied prisoners and exiled peoples, the restoration of allied shipping destroyed, the uncon-

ditional surrender of the German army in East Africa, the surrender of all advantages gained under the treaties of Bucharest and Brest Litovsk, the evacuation of the Black Sea ports, the surrender of 160 submarines and larger craft, the concentration of aircraft at stipulated points, also the surrender of two thousand airplanes, two thousand five hundred big guns, thirty thousand big guns, thirty thousand machine guns, the restoration of all allied and American merchant vessels. The Germans are to reveal the whereabouts of all mines, they are to delay all acting fuses on all evacuated territory, they are to pay for the keep and cost of occupation of troops in the Rhineland

country west of the Rhine. The immediate repatriation of all prisoners of war and the removal of German troops from evacuated territory is to begin at once.

Further terms include the restitution of all gold taken by Germany or yielded to her by Belgium, Russia and Roumania, transfer of this to be made immediately to the allies and held in trust by them. In addition to the surrender of 160 submarines, all others must be disbanded, the crews paid off at once and the submarines must then be placed under allied supervision. Six battle-cruisers, ten battleships, eight light cruisers, including two mine layers and fifty destroyers of the most modern type shall be interned in neutral ports with only caretakers left aboard, all other warships shall be concentrated in a German naval base to be designated, the

crews of these boats shall be paid off and the vessels completely disarmed. Notification is to be given to neutrals that the freedom of navigation shall be given to all allied vessels without exception. All naval and mercantile prisoners of war held in Germany are to be repatriated at once. All vessels of the German auxiliary fleet are to be disarmed. Mine fields in territorial waters are to be swept by the allies at positions indicated by Germany. Freedom of access both to and from the Baltic is to be granted to the allies, and to ensure this and other terms the allies are to be enabled to occupy all German forts, batteries, defence works, etc., from Cattegat to the Baltic. Blockade conditions so far as the allies are concerned are to be unchanged and any German merchant ships found at sea will be liable to capture. All German aircraft is to be assembled and demobilized at specified German bases. In abandoning the Belgian coast and ports Germany must abandon all ships, tugs, lighters, etc., all stores and apparatus of all kinds. The Black Sea ports are to be evacuated and all Russian war vessels are to go back to the allies. All neutral vessels are to be seized and returned. All Germans must leave Russia at once.

LONDON, NOV. 11 —
Hostilities ceased at 11 o'clock this morning.

Crowd Burns Kaiser In Effigy; Peace Celebration

Rousing welcome given news of ending of great world war

BIG BONFIRE MADE ON NEARBY HILLS

Street parade with plenty of noise told of local enthusiasm

The greatest war in the history of the world is over; the fighting is ended, and "Dyer Tag", which the blatant Germans have toasted, pledged and bragged about for many a long year has come at last, but its coming finds the Hun in humbled and sullen mien which his conquerors rejoice and give thanks that civilization is once more triumphant and that the world has really be made safe for democracy.

Monday morning the joyful news that an armistice had been signed, with Germany practically surrendering unconditionally in the field, was wired into The Herald office. An "extra" was hurriedly run off and within an hour these were being eagerly snatched up and read by the people of Penticton. A false alarm last weekend had stampeded the populace and threw them into hysterics and a premature celebration

was the result.

This time, however, system was injected into the preparations and by ten o'clock Reeve F. M. Smith had issued a proclamation calling on the merchants to close their places of business at noon Monday.

The half holiday was utilized in the organization of a big bonfire and parade to be held at night, and all afternoon autos were kept busy trucking boxes, dry goods cases, logs, shrubbery, and inflammables of every description to the site selected for the bonfire on the north side of Guernsey's pond.

The streets presented an animated appearance and crowds seemed to spring up from nowhere. Everybody carried one or more Union Jacks and stocks of flags and fireworks in the stores were quickly depleted. The crowd was apparently restive and eager for the start of the "big noise," but gradually thinned out toward the supper hour.

The scene on Main Street about 7 p.m. augured well for a night of hilarity and Penticton never looked so gay one many facetiously remarking that "This town gets more like New York every day." However, Fire Chief Ellis, marshal of the parade, started the fun when he undertook to line up his forces. The honor position at the head of the line was given to the returned soldiers, dressed in uniform, immediately followed by the veterans who had seen service in other wars, particularly the Boer war and the Riel rebellion. Next in order came the honorably rejected men, those who had volunteered their services to their country but were turned down on account of physical unfitness. Then the marshal asked the general public to fall in behind, these to be followed by the long line of automobiles which were strung along both sides of the street, staring with bright bulging eyes at the unusual proceedings in a generally sedate and demure young city.

Revolution in Russia; Czar Abdicates

People in revolt run and slay in streets of Russia's capital.

Shots Fired

During the early stages of the Russian revolution Petrograd students and soldiers fired across the Molka canal at the police who sided with the supporters of the old regime.

Most Unusual Photograph of Russian Revolution

The scene is the Novski Prospect. The large building in the background is the public library and it was from the roof of this building that the machine guns mowed down the people on the street.

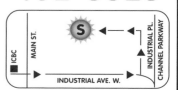

1910~1919

Munition ship explodes in Halifax Harbour

STREETS OF THE CITY THICK WITH DEAD — HOSPITALS FILLED TO OVERFLOWING

CP PHOTO) 1998 (National Archives of Canada)

This picture was taken almost opposite the scene of the explosion and shows how it completely destroyed industries and homes were leveled to the ground.

SIXTY PER CENT OF THE CITY'S AREA DESTROYED BY FIRE

Worst Disaster in the History of Canada

RELIEF RUSHED FROM ALL QUARTERS TO THE STRICKEN CITY.

HALIFAX, DEC. 8 —

Four thousand persons were killed in the burning and destruction of the buildings resulting from the explosion on a munitions ship in the harbor on Thursday, according to estimates tonight by officials. This estimate, higher than any other heretofore, was made after a survey of the devastated district of Richmond, where acres of debris probably will not be cleared for a month.

Right in the heart of this area, fires starting on Thursday blazed tonight like bonfires, and the crowds moving along the rough snow paths caught something that made the atmosphere here well-nigh unbearable. It was the odor of burning flesh.

The flames leave little trace, and this fact may give substance to the new official estimate of 4,000. There was no accurate census of the population of the Richmond district.

Relief Organized

The total lives lost as a consequence of the explosion on the French munitions ship Mont Blanc on Thursday may never be known, but for the moment the number is of secondary importance. The outstanding fact that has been faced by the local authorities is that twenty thousand persons are destitute, and of that number perhaps one out of every seven is suffering from injuries, which in many cases are bound to prove fatal.

Tonight the work of organizing the various relief units into a workable whole, with a general direction that will avoid duplication of effort and tend to greatest efficiency, was well under way.

Federal, provincial and Red Cross aid, supplemented by volunteer units from other cities and the United States, were being utilized to the best advantage. The Massachusetts relief train, which had been stalled most of the night in snowdrifts near the Nova Scotian border, arrived today, bringing the first contingent of physicians, nurses and supplies. It was the first of several trains en route from the American side.

Cause of Disaster.

Inquiries in every quarter confirmed reports as to the cause of the explosion of the French munitions steamer. Many suspicions have been expressed, but the most thorough investigation, it is asserted shows no evidence of an enemy plot.

According to the officially accepted version, the French ship was coming into the harbor through a channel not more than a third of a mile wide when she was rammed by the Norwegian relief ship Imo, outward bound, due to a mistake in signals. When the crash came tanks of benzine on the deck of the Mont Blanc were broken and it is supposed the liquid ran down into the engine room.

The government pilot, officers and men, realizing what would happen, escaped in the small boats to Dartmouth and ran. They were still running when they were knocked down by the force of the explosion.

Experts declare that had the same amount of explosive been let loose on land every living thing within a radius of ten miles would have been killed.

Worst in History.

MONTREAL, DEC. 8.— The staff correspondent of the Star at Halifax wires:

"It is probable that there has never been an explosion of such force, even in the war zone. To begin with, the vessel contained 2800 tons of the highest explosive known, three times as powerful as fulminate. A powder expert has since reckoned that had the cargo had a solid foundation under it there would not have been so much as a live cat or rat left. Debris from shells, steel plates and shrapnel have been found within a five-mile radius within an area of ten square miles.

"Something about the scope of the explosion has already been reported. At Orangedale, Cape Breton, 150 miles distant on an air line, and at Sydney, 200 miles away, the shock was that of a severe earthquake.

The explosion raised a tidal wave in the harbor that was forty feet high.

Federal Aid

OTTAWA, DEC. 7.— Federal aid will be granted by the government to the sufferers from the holocaust in Halifax as soon as things become more settled and the extent of the need can be sized up.

Meanwhile by rushing supplies to the cities, sending special trains with doctors and nurses, and having the military help in policing the city, the Dominion authorities are rendering every possible aid in the greatest of Canadian disasters.

A Shock Upon Deadened Nerves

The Halifax disaster, with four thousand dead and the business section of the city laid in ruins, as a result of the explosion of the munitions cargo on a vessel, comes as a tremendous shock to the people, as indeed to the whole world.

But the ruin of the Atlantic seaport is by no means of the tremendous import to us it would have been had the devastation come four years ago. A nation which has gone through more than three years of the greatest war of the world, and which is facing at least a year or two more of terrible conflict, is not so readily stirred. The explosion at Halifax, if it had occurred four years ago, would have stirred us for months. Now the impress will fade in weeks.

Thus does Nature dull the sensibilities to meet the onslaughts of misfortune.

Britain Will Adopt Woman Suffrage

House of Commons Favors It By Majority of 279

LONDON —

After an interesting debate today, the House of Commons, by a majority of 279, expressed its approval of legislation on the lines of the speakers' conference recommendations for franchise reforms. The small minority against such a measure represented not the actual opponents of reform, but rather members who were desirous of postponing legislation of such contentious matter until after the war. A great feature of the debate was the frank acceptance, by Ex-premier Asquith and Bonar Law, of the woman's right to vote as the result of her war sacrifices and services, and Premier Lloyd George's whole-hearted acceptance of the recommendations of the conference with the exception of proportional representation. Premier Lloyd George was even willing to go further and make the qualifying period three instead of six months. A small party in the Commons, during the course of the debate, expressed their continued opposition to woman suffrage, but their numbers were too small to carry weight. The Nationalists announced that they would support Mr. Asquith's motion. As a result of the debate, the government, as Mr. Bonar Law announced, will proceed with legislation to give effect to the recommendation, except proporence. The bill will embody all recommendations, except proportional representation and woman suffrage, these will be omitted, first, because the government is still undecided on the question; and, secondly, because it is held that parliament must first of all express the acceptance of the principle of woman suffrage.

Presbyterian women's temperance union meets in Penticton c.1917.

Photo Courtesy of Penticton Museum.

Butterfly Nurses to Go
Decolletee Ladies to Be Replaced in France

The lady nurse must go! That is the decree which has gone forth in France, and it has caused no small sensation.

Volunteer nurses in hospital where military sick and wounded are cared for are to be replaced by professional paid nurses. The volunteer infirmiere who came forward at the beginning of the war, when there was a great shortage of trained women, was pressed into service after a short superficial training. She has done nobly, toiling day and night and spending her money freely on the wounded besides paying her own personal expenses. She asserts that the new regulations are inspired by political motives, as it was

feared that the poilus were becoming too much attached to their aristocratic nurses and were in danger of forgetting the maxims of equality and liberty in their exaggerated respect for titled attendants.

Doctors frankly prefer the professional nurse, who can be ordered about in a way her volunteer sister would resent. They say that the unpaid assistant has her own ideas of discipline. The lady nurse, too, is apt to err in matters of taste. I saw one step out of a luxurious car the other day much overdressed. A lady friend said, "Look at those stilts; one cannot call them heels. How can she run backwards and forwards in the

wards all day in those?"

As the butterfly nurse got out of the car she raised her snow-white uniform and displayed yards of billowing petticoats in batiste and embroidered white silk. "A nice get-up for a days work," remarked my pessimistic friend. "How the paid nurses must love her"

The doctors of the Paris hospitals have sometimes been obliged to suggest that volunteers should go home, discard their diamonds and dress more discreetly.

Public sentiment supports the doctors in their efforts to replace voluntary workers, being convinced that they are acting in the true interests of the sick and wounded.

NOVEMBER 15, 1917

High Power Line To Cross S. Okanagan

Similkameen to be Served with Hydraulic Developed Electric Energy

It appears to be probable that the southern end of the Okanagan Valley will, in the not far distant future, have electric power generated from hydraulic energy. An extension westward of the high power line of the West Kootenay Power Company is to be made from the Boundary district across the Okanagan Valley and into the Similkameen, as far westward as Princeton. These lines already extend west and supply "juice" to the mining and smelting industries of West Kootenay and Boundary, as well as for domestic use at Rossland, Trail, Grand Forks, Phoenix and other towns. The proposed extension into the Similkameen is primarily to supply power to Copper Mountain, near Princeton, where the Canada Copper Company has planned to spend $2,500,000 within the next two or three years in development work. It is also intended to tap Camp McKinney, where construction camps have already been opened to initiate the power installation work.

It is understood that the new line with laterals and sub-stations will cost between $2,000,000 and $2,500,000. The project has been under consideration for some months but work has now been definitely started. Mr. J.J. Warren, the president of the Kettle Valley Railway, and managing director of the Trail Consolidated, is also managing director of the Power Company. The power line will cross the Okanagan Valley at Fairview, and it is thought possible that a lateral will run up the Valley to Penticton and Summerland, at the former place it would no doubt be used in the K.V.R. workshops and yard.

Absolute Prohibition After April 1

Stringent restrictions on the liquor traffic were passed on Saturday by the Cabinet Council at Ottawa under the War Measures Act.

After December 24, no more intoxicating liquors can be imported into Canada; and after April 1, 1918, no liquor can be transported into any province where the sale of same is illegal. These restrictions are to remain in force until twelve months after the declaration of peace.

After April 1 there will, therefore, be bone dry prohibition in every province in the Dominion with the exception of Quebec. The total stocks of liquor in bond in Canada amount to sixteen million gallons.

Drinking Habit Expensive

The drink habit is an expensive one in every way. The following is a bill which a drinking man had to pay through ill treating his wife when drunk:
Doctor's bill for mending my wife's ribs, etc. $35.
Extra things for nursing $12.
To the landlord for smashing door and banisters $7.
Nurse's wages, two weeks $35.
For broken crockery $2.
Loss of week's work $18.
Fine with costs $20.
Cost of the liquor which caused the trouble 20cts.
Total $129.20

Spanish Influenza Rages in Canada

Thousands of cases reported with many deaths

Those who are most susceptible to it

"Fruit-a-tives" - The wonderful fruit medicine - gives the power to resist this disease.

The epidemic of Spanish Influenza which played such havoc in Europe, has reached this continent. Thousands of cases of the strange malady have appeared and many deaths are already reported; Surgeon-General Blue of the United States Public Health Service having stated that Spanish Influenza will probably spread all over the country in six weeks".

Practically every ship which touches our shores from abroad, brings those infected with the disease.

Surgeon-General Blue urges that "the individual take all the precautions he can against contracting the disease by care and personal hygiene". Plenty of exercise should be taken; the diet should be regulated, etc.

Spanish Influenza affects most severely elderly persons and others whose powers of resistance are weakened by illness, work or worry, especially those who are "run-down" or "not feeling up to the mark."

The really great danger from the disease is not so much in the disease itself, as that it often develops into pneumonia.

What everyone needs now is a general tonic like "Fruit-a-tives". This wonderful fruit medicine is not a germ-killer. It is a body-builder; a strength-maker; a blood-purifier; a power in protecting against the ravages of disease.

"Fruit-a-tives" regulates the kidneys and bowels, causing these organs to eliminate waste regularly and naturally as nature intended. "Fruit-a-tives" keeps the skin active, and purifies and enriches the blood. "Fruit-a-tives" tones up and strengthens the organs of digestion, insuring food being properly digested and assimilated.

Everyone can take ordinary precautions, avoid crowded places, and use "Fruit-a-tives" regularly to insure sound digestion, to keep the bowels and kidneys regular and the whole system in the best possible condition. Then we are safe from disease.

"Fruit-a-tives" is sold by dealers everywhere at 50¢ a box, 6 for $2.50, trial size 25¢ or sent postpaid on receipt of price by Fruit-a-tives Limited, Ottawa, Ont.

OFFICIAL WARNING TO GUARD 'FLU'

Be careful of discharges from nose or throat.

Use handkerchief or other piece of cloth and destroy after use by burning.

Avoid contact with crowds.

Keep out of poorly ventilated places.

Do not come into contact with persons suffering from colds or other sickness.

Do not neglect colds, however simple.

Go to bed immediately if temperature rises, or other symptoms of the disease appear.

Prevention of disease may be assisted by use of antiseptic sprays for nose and throat of such antiseptics as Listerine or Borol, and by inhalation of oil of eucalyptus.

Keep dry and warm, be careful, but don't worry.

R.B. White, M.D., Medical Health Officer

Flu is now almost a thing of the past

Churches open Sunday morning – city schools may open on Wednesday.

Thanks to the prompt and strict regulations imposed upon Kelowna and district by municipal officials, by the Medical Health Officer and by the medical fraternity in general, Kelowna can boast of an early breakdown of the invasion of the Spanish "flu" germ. If progress continues to be made at the same rate as during the week gone, and no new cases appear, Dr. Knox announces that schools will be able to re-open in a few days and the district will be able to declare the epidemic a thing of the past.

The churches are opening again on Sunday morning, one service only being allowed during the day, as although the upper hand has been gained the greatest precaution is still needed. Consequently, there will be no Sunday School as yet, nor will public meetings be allowed until the danger is still further removed. The majority of the rural schools opened last Monday. Rutland was the only exception, because the "flu" got an early start in that district, but the Rutland school will re-open on Monday next. There has not been a case in the whole Ellison district, and consequently that school has not been closed. The city schools, both the public school and the high school, will probably open on Wednesday morning next, though this is not yet definite. The flag at the school will be hoisted two days before opening, so that if they open on Wednesday the flag will be flying on Monday, otherwise a short postponement will be made according to circumstances. Handbills will probably be distributed announcing the opening.

Dr. Knox and the special committee hope to close the city's emergency hospital on Saturday next. Only four new cases have appeared this week, leaving about 50 cases still under medical treatment throughout the district. The Japanese hospital still contains four patients, but the Chinese hospital is closed, although there have been nine deaths amongst the Chinamen. Altogether there have been about 200 cases in the district, resulting in 10 deaths, being the nine Chinamen and one Hindu.

Something about the 'Spanish Flu'

Influenza, which is now sweeping over Canada from one end to the other, is a very old disease. it was known in ancient times, and as early as 1510 it overran the whole civilized world. For centuries it has periodically swept over various parts of the world. The last great world epidemic was in 1889-1890, when it was generally known by the French name of lagrippe. The disease has always travelled from east to west.

Symptoms

The symptoms are similar to those of a heavy cold; more or less severe headache, cold in the head and throat, fits of sneezing, flushed face, chills, aches and pains in the back and limbs, pains in the eye-balls and behind the eyes, general physical depression, and temperature rising to between 101 and 104 degrees.

How to Prevent it

As it is such an old disease, doctors have naturally learned a great deal about its prevention and treatment. The first principle of prevention is to keep away from those inflicted, and the second, to build up the germ-resisting parts of the body by eating nourishing foods, dressing comfortably, getting lots of sleep, and by living in the open air and in bright, well ventilated rooms as much as possible. The mouth, throat and nose should be systematically and frequently disinfected by antiseptic inhalations, sprays and washes. Such preparations as chloretone and listerine are well adapted for this purpose.

In fighting previous epidemics doctors found quinine a useful preventive. One grain of sulphate of quinine mixed with (but not dissolved in) a wine glassful of cold water, makes an excellent antiseptic gargle. The anti-microbic properties of quinine are well known and its use as described above at once relieves the symptoms of sore throat, which result

from the strain of the fight between the white blood corpuscles and the invading germs in the tonsils – the body's first line of defence. Quinine is also given internally with success as a preventive. In one of the more recent outbreaks in Europe an experiment as tried in which the men of one squadron of a regiment of cavalry were each given 7 1/2 grains of quinine in half an ounce of whiskey daily for 22 days, whilst those of the other squadron were given none. The latter squadron had from 22 to 44 cases each of influenza, whilst the squadron treated with quinine developed only four cases. Inhalations of oil of eucalyptus, thymol, oil of mountain pine and the like are also valuable as preventives.

How to Treat it

When a person is struck by influenza, only one course lies open. That is to take to bed with the least possible delay, and call a doctor. Rest, warmth and quiet are three sovereign remedies of the primary disease, and the best preventives of its more deadly complications, of which pneumonia is the most frequent. While there is no specific for influenza yet, there are many drugs which play a useful part in relieving it, such as quinine, aspirin and various tonics, anti-neuralgic, antiseptic and heart medicines, to be prescribed the the physician in charge.

What to Eat

The dietetic rules which apply to any fever apply equally to influenza. Liquid foods at first, solids a little later on in a gradually ascending scale from lightly boiled fresh eggs to chicken, roast joints, etc. Water, cold or hot, may be sipped, or "egg" water may be given. This excellent dish is prepared by blending with a pint of cold water, the whipped whites of from two to four eggs, flavored with salt or cinnamon. Then the

animal broths may be given. There are many cases in which even the lightest foods are spurned with loathing, and common sense must be used in adapting diet to the particular cases in hand.

Precautions Against Influenza

1– The sick should be separated from the healthy. This is especially important in the case of first attacks in the household.

2– Discharges from the nose and mouth should not be allowed to get dry on a pocket handkerchief or inside the house, office or factory. They should at once be collected in paper or clean rags and burned. if this cannot be done, they should be dropped into a vessel containing water.

3– Infected articles and rooms should be cleansed and disinfected. Use disinfectants everywhere. Wash the hands frequently.

4– Those attacked should not, on any account, mingle with other people for at least a period of ten days from the commencement of the attack. In severe cases they should remain away from work

for a longer period.

5– Special attention should be given to cleanliness and ventilation. Warm clothing should be worn, the feet should be kept dry and all unnecessary exposure avoided.

The Daily Courier   **Vernon Times**

PENTICTON HERALD

The **Okanagan** SATURDAY   *The* **Okanagan** SUNDAY

The Okanagan Valley Newspaper Group

HER MAJESTY'S APPLES

Have Been At Express Office For Sixteen Days Since His Royal Highness Expressed A Wish That They Be Sent To Buckingham Palace

OCTOBER 18, 1919 — During the visit of His Royal Highness the Prince of Wales to Kelowna just sixteen days ago, he was good enough to graciously accept a present of six boxes of Kelowna apples. When it was suggested that these apples should be sent to friends of his in England he objected, expressing a desire that they should be sent to the Queen, his mother, at Buckingham Palace. So far, so good, but the unfortunate part of this pleasing episode is that with the customary inertness for which Kelowna must surely be becoming famous the six boxes of apples still lie where they were presented to our future sovereign, at the C.P.R. wharf. It is doubtful whether the apples are improving, yet apples for Her Majesty should be the very best that go out of Kelowna. By a somewhat curious error, the apples were first addressed to "H.R.H. the Queen." Fortunately someone noticed the mistake and the shipment was held back for alterations in the address. The correction was made in some fashion, it now reading "H.M. the Queen," but the apples still lie there unshipped.

A strange callousness, when the matter is one concerning a gift from our beloved Prince to his mother our Queen; a callous indifference which is surely a disgrace to Kelowna.

Heir To British Crown Receives Royal Welcome

His Charming Personality Wins Thunderous Applause from Penticton Citizens

Receives Address at Ellis Public School

H.R.H. the Prince of Wales is seen here on the steps of Ellis School in Penticton on October 2, 1918

Photo courtesy of Penticton Museum

Individually and collectively the people of Penticton excelled themselves in the wonderful welcome that greeted H.R.H. the Prince of Wales and heir to the British Crown last Tuesday morning from the time he stepped off the train at South Penticton until he boarded the Sicamous an hour later for the trip up the lake.

There was little formality about the reception of the Prince here beyond the reading of the address and the reply thereto, and this fact lent a better spirit to the occasion and greatly pleased both the prince and the large crowd that gathered to greet him.

Hundreds of citizens, shouting greeting and waving flags, filled he Ellis school grounds when the automobile bearing His Royal Highness pulled up to the curb in front of the school, and although they had come primarily to cheer the institutions he represented, his boyish appearance, charming personality and winning smile captivated all immediately and a thunderous cheering applause rang out for "the Man."

The front entrance to the school was artistically decorated and the coat of arms of the Prince of Wales was cleverly depicted over the door, above which hung a long streamer bearing the words "Welcome to Our Prince"

Reeve F.M. Smith read the address of welcome from the citizens of Penticton, which was beautifully illuminated on parchment and enclosed in the royal colors of purple and gold. The prince's reply is as follows :

" I am very grateful for the cordial way in which you have welcomed me to this beautiful district, and I beg you to convey my thanks to all the citizens of Penticton.

It is a great pleasure to me to have been able to visit Penticton and the Okanagan Valley, of which I have heard so much, and also to have this opportunity of congratulating you on your fine services to the Empire during the war. I appreciate very much your kind reference to my own modest service as a junior officer in the field.

I will gladly convey your warm expression of loyalty to my father, the King, and I wish all the residents of the district a prosperous future."

Hearty Welcome Given to Prince of Wales

Kelowna is charmed with Royal Visitor - Prince meets War Widows and chats with Citizens.

In a country like the Okanagan where the weather is nearly always fine and sunny, it was but natural that something special should be provided for the honored occasion of the visit of His Royal Highness the Prince of Wales. It was therefore necessarily one of the drawbacks of living in such a fine climate that the weather which greeted the Prince was anything but what would have ordered by any loyal citizen. Yet, in spite of this, no one could class the visit as having been anything but a great success and certainly all those who were privileged to participate in it can never look back to the occasion with anything but the greatest enjoyment. But this is the case where-ever the Prince has gone in Canada, and on Tuesday evening the people of Kelowna understood why. With a sincere but simple personality, the Prince charmed Kelowna beyond the expectations of the most loyal citizen, and even the most stolid socialists were seen to effuse over his affable comradeship.

Street and traffic arrangements were well set. Returned soldiers guarded the approach of every street and crossroad, saluting as the Prince passed and forming quite an impressive and military welcome. C.P.R. police were also on hand in the Park, where members of the Fire Brigade were also doing special police duty.

In spite of his entertainment at other points having slightly detained him, the Prince reached Kelowna well on time, and it was only a few minutes after 6:30 that his car, in which he had driven from Vernon, came down Bernard avenue amid the applause of the citizens who were lining that thoroughfare.

Phone Will Link Up Kelowna With Coast

Railway May Take Over Government Telegraph

With the coming of the Canadian Northern Railway it seems probable that changes will take place in the Dominion telegraph and telephone service, which will link up with the telegraph service connected with the new railway.

W.H. Stevens, manager of the Dominion telegraph and telephone service of the interior of British Columbia has returned from Ottawa, where he went a month ago to consult with the public works department concerning the situation as regards the government telegraph and telephone lines under his management. As

to any changes in regard to the telephone and telegraph lines, he said that a complete policy had not been adopted but that since the federal government had taken over the Canadian Northern Railway he expected that all telegraph lines parallel to this road would be discontinued and the business taken care of by the railway company. So far as the telephone lines are concerned these would be continued and extensions made and in all probability Kelowna district would be linked up with the coast by carrying telephone lines on the telegraph poles of the C.N.R. in

the gap between Kamloops and the telephone line at the coasts. This would give the Kamloops, Okanagan and Yale districts direct communication by telephone with Vancouver. Mr. Stevens also stated that only those extensions deemed absolutely necessary by the government would be constructed, yet he expected that certain extensions asked for in this district would be made.

Prohibition Is Favored By Presbyterians

Point Out Many Benefits Which Resulted From Act

Below is given a copy of a resolution passed recently by the Presbytery of Kamloops, which includes Presbyterian churches in the Kelowna district, to be sent to the provincial government, supporting the present Prohibition Act, providing that it is properly put into effect:

Whereas, the B.C. Prohibition Act has been in force since October, 1917.

And whereas, based on personal knowledge and on interviews with men of all classes, in the over seventy places served by the ministers and missionaries of the Presbyterian Church in this Presbytery of Kamloops, we

believe the Act has been of very great general benefit resulting in:

1. A marked improvement in social conditions and especially in the home life of the community;

2. A great decrease of crime, so much so that many of the jails and police stations now have but very few inmates;

3. A pronounced increase of profitable business to merchants and supply men, not a few now paying promptly, who before could scarce receive credit;

4. An increase in efficiency and safety in industrial operations and especially where large groups of men are employed in lumbering and mining camps.

Dr. Knox Warns As To Small Pox Danger

Dr. Knox, the Medical Health Officer for the Kelowna district, states that he has received an advice from the Provincial Board of Health that small pox is occurring at seaports on the Atlantic coast and at some of the southern ports on the Pacific coasts, 27 cases having been reported in Seattle. In view of the possibility of the disease appearing in B.C., the provincial Board of Health earnestly urges and recommends all precautionary measures be taken, especially with regards to children. One of the chief precautionary measures, says Dr. Knox, is vaccination, which should be attended by the family physician. Our province, being on the seaboard and at the end of the transcontinental roads, makes us especially exposed to the danger of the importation of the disease.

Auntie Fanny's
tells a really neat success story

Furniture is about atmosphere. The pieces you choose and the way you put them together create an ambiance in your home.

Ed and Bonnie Huber understand furniture and have a special feel for what works.

The story of the rise of their business is nothing short of phenomenal. In 1984 they opened an 800 square foot store in downtown Vernon.

Today they have stores in Winnipeg, Kelowna, and two franchised stores, one in Regina and Saskatoon. In 1998 they opened a 15,000 sq. ft. factory in Salmon Arm employing 25 people.

At Auntie Fanny's you'll find gorgeous dining room suites, entertainment centres, and beautiful bedroom suites made from pine or oak.

Picture your family dining around an oval solid wood table, exchanging news and laugh-

ter. It's a picture that seems to need several generations. You may be the parent now, but these diningroom suites will still be treasured pieces when your grandchildren become the parents.

You'll find variety pieces in Auntie Fanny's too—anything from solid oak filing cabinets for your office to an oval mirror perfect for your entrance, or a solid oak magazine rack to add a touch of class beside your favourite recliner.

"And really neat stuff" is what you'll discover at Auntie Fanny's. That slogan is not by accident—it's how so many people describe the store after dropping in.

When Ed and Bonnie look back to 1984—not that long ago—and remember how they quit their jobs and branched out to start their own business, with two children still at home, they shake their heads a little. They have five grandchildren and a bouncing business now, but they have no regrets.

"We didn't expect it to take off like this. It comes partly from not being afraid to try new things. To succeed there is a certain amount of risk," says Ed.

They wouldn't trade all the responsibility for the stress of working for someone else again.

Besides, they are having so much fun, and that enthusiasm is contagious.

PINE & OAK FURNITURE

"AND REALLY NEAT STUFF"!
SINCE 1984

Sellers of Quality Oak & Pine Furniture

1794 Baron Rd., Kelowna
Behind Costco
Mon.-Sat., 9:00 to 5:30
868-8444

HUBER'S
HERITAGE FURNITURE INC.

Manufacturers of Quality Oak & Pine Furniture

5851 Auto Road
(Industrial Park)
Salmon Arm
804-4345

From large basic items to small accent pieces, furniture is an essential element in creating atmosphere in your home.

And, Huber's Heritage Furniture can help you establish the timeless ambiance of the Shaker era, when furniture was hand-crafted with care.

Shaker lines are simple and minimalist and hark back to the turn of the century, says Ed Huber Sr., in charge of sales, advertising and promotion for this family-owned business.

Huber's manufactures classic Shaker bedroom pieces for furniture stores coast-to-coast as well as the Northwest Territories and the Yukon.

"It's more than just a look at Huber's Heritage Furniture," says Huber, "it echoes the solid quality of period furniture." Drawer boxes are dovetailed on the front and back and slide easily on European metal glides. Dressers are double-framed to provide extra strength, with thick tops, five eighth-inch solid slides and absolutely no particle board.

Built to serve you and your heirs, finishing for this custom furniture is available in ten different colours of stain.

Put these night stands, dressers, armoires, high-boys or lingerie chests together with a mission Shaker bed, complete with traditional slatted head and foot boards, finished in a soft wheat stain and you have a room set in timeless elegance, says Huber. The Shaker style is just one of the looks customers can create with furniture from Huber's. The company manufactures three styles of bedroom furniture in solid oak or solid pine. Look for jelly cupboards, bookcases, benches, love seats and deacon's benches and solid oak, padded dining chairs.

Restaurants, hotels and motels are impressed with the quality of the manufac-

turing, says Huber, as well as the large selection of fabric choices.

Huber's wife Bonnie is the president of this family-owned business and Ed. Jr. is in charge of the day-to-day operations at the Salmon Arm plant. This 15,000 square foot factory sits on an acre of land and is already too small, in just one year of business.

A 10,000 square foot addition is in the works and the company's staff of 25 employees will grow by five more. "Phenomenal growth and runaway sales are business principles as traditional as our furniture," Huber says. "Build a good product at a reasonable price and people will come and buy it."

A DECADE
IN REVIEW

1920 ~ 1929

The Day of the Automobile

Quebec Telegraph.

The wonderful development of the automobile business in Canada, and the enormous increase in the use of this comparatively modern mode of locomotion and traffic since the days immediately preceding the war, are illustrated by the number of registrations made in the different provinces of the Dominion each year from 1913 to date. In the entire Dominion only 50,498 cars were registered in 1913, of which total Ontario contributed 23,700. The sister province increased this number in 1918 to 109,374, and estimates at least 140,000 for 1919. The total number registered in all Canada in 1918 was 269,727, while the estimated total for 1919 is 352,700. The province of Quebec had only 5,452 automobiles in 1913, but had increased the number last year to 28,338, and the estimated number of registrations for the current year is 40,000. It is noticeable that since 1912 the number of cars in use has approximately doubled every two years.

In the United States the greatest increase in the use of motor cars has been in the agricultural districts. The farmer has found the motor so helpful that it is now as much a necessity as other modern farm implements. In many parts of Canada, the experience is similar, the records of motor vehicle registration showing the largest increase in the use of cars to be in the agricultural districts, while the same fact, within the last few years, has been increasingly true of the province of Quebec.

From...

To...

1920~1929

Now a Complete Truck

HEREAFTER Ford One-Ton Trucks may be bought *complete* with bodies and cabs, ready for the road.

The body as well as the chassis will be planned to give Ford service.

'This will insure the utmost efficiency from the Ford Truck; give the purchaser Ford value in every part of his truck; produce better bodies at lower prices.

Two types of Truck bodies, the Stake and the Express, will be kept in stock, set up, painted (or in the lead) and ready for prompt delivery.

They have oak floors, sills of seasoned hickory and specially designed forgings and castings.

The construction at every point provides for rough usage such as every truck is bound to get. Both bodies have closed cabs to protect the driver.

These cabs have sliding windows and two-way, double ventilating windshields.

Call and learn what it will cost to use these complete trucks in your business. Look them over carefully. See how they outclass other trucks in every detail.

Price (Chassis only) $750 f.o.b. Ford, Ont.

Standard Ford Bodies extra. Get our prices

THE MORRISON-THOMPSON HARDWARE COY.

DEALERS - KELOWNA, B.C.

Acreage In Fruit Trees Totals Twenty Thousand

Penticton Leading In Area of Peaches

Tables showing the results of the orchard survey recently conducted in the Okanagan Horticultural district under the direction of W.T. Hunter, district horticulturist, have now been issued.

For purposes of comparison the district was divided into Northern Okanagan and Southern Okanagan. In the Northern Okanagan are the following sub-districts: 1, C.P.R. Main line except Salmon Arm, but including Kamloops, Walhachin, Spences Bridge, Lytton, Chase and Sorrento; 2, Salmon Arm; 3, Armstrong and Enderby; 4, Vernon and Oyama; 5, Okanagan Center and Duck Lake; 6, Kelowna. In the Southern Okanagan are Westbank, Peachland, Summerland, Naramata, Penticton and Keremeos.

The fact that the district contained twenty thousand acres in fruit trees is a surprise to many persons. It was not known either that the Okanagan contained well over a million apple trees. While main line points are included in the horticultural district, it can be seen from the table that they are by no means an important factor in the totals as compared with the points in the Okanagan valley proper.

Total trees covered by the tables of the varieties shown come to

1,344,379.

The table shows that Kelowna has the largest fruit acreage, with almost five thousand acres, Vernon being a close second, Summerland is third and Penticton fourth.

The same order is preserved in the number of apple trees. Penticton takes second place to Kelowna in the number of pear trees planted, with Vernon third and Summerland fourth. In plums, Vernon is first, Kelowna second, Summerland third and Penticton fourth. Vernon also leads in prunes, with Kelowna second; Penticton displaces Summerland for third position. In total cherries Kelowna leads, with Penticton second, Summerland third and Vernon fourth. In apricots Summerland barely noses Penticton out for first place, Naramata being third and Westbank fourth. In peaches Penticton has a long lead, with Summerland second, Peachland a good third and Naramata fourth.

The table shows twenty-eight of the most popular varieties of apples and divides them up in each district into those five years old, those between five and ten, and those over ten. Seven varieties of pears, seven of plums, six of cherries and five of peaches are similarly shown. Apricots and prunes are not divided into varieties.

Jonathans lead the apples, there being 265,787 trees of this variety, with 159,651 of McIntosh.

Semi-Weekly Herald To Be Another Mark in Penticton's Progress

Important Step to be Taken by Newspaper in May - First Publication in Okanagan to be Issued Twice a Week Since the War - April Held Open for Those Who Wish to Subscribe at Reduced Rate - Advertising Will be Lower.

MARCH 31, 1921—Beginning in May, it is our intention to commence the publication of a semi-weekly paper. The Herald, therefore, instead of reaching its many hundreds of readers as a weekly issued in twelve-page size each Thursday, will greet them as a semi-weekly, published Tuesdays and Fridays.

VIVID PICTURE OF NEW YORK NIGHT LIFE

"While New York Sleeps" Abounds With Spectacular Incidents

JULY 21, 1921 — The press agent who has announced "While New York Sleeps," an eight-reel Fox Special, which is billed for Wednesday, July 27, at the Empress Theatre, as "the most sensational and artistic melodrama, of all time" does not realize how close he has come to the mark. Competent critics who have seen the picture cannot find it in their hearts (or their experience) to disagree with him.

Night life in New York among the several strata of society in that cosmopolitan city is pictured with wondrous fidelity in the three acts or episodes which compose the picture. The play abounds with spectacular incidents and yet the thing that remains in the memory after seeing "While New York Sleeps" is the almost intolerable suspense with which Director Charles J. Brabin has succeeding in endowing his picture. Some magnificent views of the bright spots along The Great White Way have been used in the picture. For instance, there is a dancing number from Florenz Ziegfeld's popular Midnight Frolic girl-and-music show, together with gorgeous cabaret scenes from the Cafe Palais Royal.

Then the action plunges over to the East side, where we see a tragedy in the life of a tempestuous shop girl, her puny, gentle-hearted husband whom she despises, the saintly, paralytic father of the man, and the gangster leader of a band of thieves. In this episode occurs a thrilling revolver battle between the famous New York police boat and a launch full of desperados.

In addition to the remarkable intensity of the three stories and the interest in connection with the spectacular features that the director has introduced into the picture, are the splendid characterizations effected by the small but eminent cast of players who portray the principal parts. Seldom if ever in the history of the screen has any group of players acquitted themselves so admirably.

The cast is composed of Estelle Taylor, one of the most beautiful and capable of the younger actresses of the screen today; Mare McDermott, who has for many years enriched the screen with his ability; Harry Southern, nephew of E. H. Southern. William Locke and Earl Metcalf, a star in his own right.

"While New York Sleeps" is a picture that no devotee of better art on the silver sheet can afford to miss.

Super Heat Cars and Kills Pests

A meeting took place between Messrs. A. Sturrock, assistant superintendent Motor Power; T. Acheson, agricultural representative, both of the Canadian Pacific railway company, and Messrs. Arthur Gibson, Dominion Entomologist, A. F. Barss and R. C. Treherne in the C. P. R. headquarter offices at Winnipeg on June 16th. The matter under discussion related to the subject of treating empty foreign fruit refrigerator cars with steam to offset the introduction of Codling Moth into the fruit raising valleys of British Columbia. Mr Treherne had previously received the sanction of Mr. F. W. Peters, general superintendent, Vancouver, to further the matter in the manner above recorded. Substantial progress was made and the matter is believed to have been started definitely on the road which will spell success or failure to the principle under consideration. The Master Mechanic of the C. P. R. has now taken the matter in hand and the fruit growers of the province may reasonably expect a definite opinion in the near future.

View looking north from Penticton's East Benches c.1920

Phot courtesy of Penticton Museum

1920~1929

Motoring on the Roads of the Southern Interior

Being a Page of The Herald devoted to the Interests of Autoists, Good Roads Enthusiasts, Garages, Motor Agencies and Allied Interests

STUDEBAKER HAS GOOD RUN SOUTH

Average of 24 Miles to Gallon Obtained on Long Run to Wenatchee

The local Studebaker agency sent a light six down to Wenatchee with the party of growers who made the trip this week to look over the fruit lands. The car was sent down for demonstration purposes.

During the trip a distance of 453 miles was covered, using 19 gallons of gasoline for an average of 24 miles to a gallon. The 195 miles from Penticton to Wenatchee were made in between seven and eight hours actual running time, an average speed of twenty-five miles an hour.

The Studebaker ran beautifully the whole time, making the trip down over every kind of road without having to change from high gear. No tire or engine trouble was experienced and the drivers stated that the engine had an exceptional feeling of power. The engine did not get over-heated in spite of the very hot weather and the lack of vibration in the car was very noticeable.

The car was driven by Mr. Roy McNicoll and Mr. Stanley Woodruff, who both declared themselves more than satisfied with the running of the car.

Auto Question Drawer

L. F. F., Penticton — Do two cylinders work together all the time on a twelve cylinder engine?

Answer: On a twin-six cylinder (twelve cylinder engine) there are twelve periods of 14 degrees,

when three pistons are working together and twelve periods of 46 degrees when two pistons are working together. This naturally gives steady power.

J. J. W. Penticton — Can I use a telephone generator taken from an old phone for ignition?

Answer: No; this generator generates high voltage, but practically no amperage or quality of current at all. If you were to run it at high enough speed, say 3000 revolutions per minute, and had a proper transformer or coil to "build up" the current, that is, to reduce the voltage and make a higher amperage, it might be used with a make-shift system of ignition.

SERIES 21 BIG-SIX
Seven-Passenger, 50-horse-power, 126-inch wheelbase
$2786 f. o. b. Walkerville, Ont.

IN times of adjustment when people consider carefully what they get for every dollar they spend, a product of merit, properly priced, receives just consideration. Also the standing and reputation of a manufacturer is given much thought in times like the present. These are the reasons why the great Studebaker factories are taxed to capacity to meet the present demand for Studebaker cars.

"Built-in-Canada"
INTERIOR MOTORS LIMITED
H. A. FINCH, Local Manager
FRONT STREET   PENTICTON, B.C.

NEW PRICES OF STUDEBAKER AUTOMOBILES
f. o. b. Walkerville, Ontario, effective June 1, 1921

Touring Cars and Roadsters		Coupes and Sedans	
LIGHT-SIX 2-PASS. ROADSTER	$1850	LIGHT-SIX COUPE ROADSTER	$2350
LIGHT-SIX TOURING CAR	1865	LIGHT-SIX 5-PASS. SEDAN	2635
SPECIAL-SIX 2-PASS. ROADSTER	2275	SPECIAL-SIX 4-PASS. COUPE	3250
SPECIAL-SIX TOURING CAR	2335	SPECIAL-SIX 5-PASS. SEDAN	3435
SPECIAL-SIX 4-PASS. ROADSTER	2325	BIG-SIX 4-PASS. COUPE	3995
BIG-SIX TOURING CAR	2785	BIG-SIX 7-PASS. SEDAN	4085

ALL STUDEBAKER CARS ARE EQUIPPED WITH CORD TIRES

This is a Studebaker Year

IMPERIAL
Polarine
FRICTION REDUCING
MOTOR OILS

Keeps Motors Smooth Running

Quality maintains economy. You may pay less "per gallon" for other lubricating oils but you get more lubrication "per dollar" when you buy, Imperial Polarine Motor Oils.

USERS of Imperial Polarine Motor Oils enjoy a singular freedom from engine trouble, which is at once a source of profit and pleasure to them.

Every bearing and rubbing surface is cushioned with an unbreakable oil film which relieves friction and minimizes wear. Good compression is also maintained, saving both fuel and oil and increasing power.

Lessened repair bills, lower upkeep costs, better satisfaction and longer service from your car follow the use of Imperial Polarine Motor Oils.

Consult our Chart of Recommendations for the grade of Imperial Polarine best suited to your motor. See Charts at your dealers or write to 56 Church Street for "Automotive Lubrication," a booklet which contains the Chart and other valuable information.

IMPERIAL OIL LIMITED
Branches in all Cities

WE GIVE
IMPERIAL
Polarine
MAKES A GOOD CAR BETTER
CRANK-CASE
SERVICE

FOR A CLEAN EFFICIENT MOTOR

The crank case of your motor should be drained, cleaned and refilled with fresh Imperial Polarine every 1,000 miles or less. Dealers who display this sign give expert crank case cleaning service, using Imperial Flushing Oil, a scientific cleaning agent which removes all dirt, grit and impurities, which are so harmful to your engine. It will pay you well to employ Imperial Polarine Crank-Case Service to-day.

IT'S OUR BUSINESS
To give you the best service, and it is yours to see that you get it—Give us a trial

A-1 AUTO LIVERY AND EXCHANGE
FRONT STREET   PHONE 300

—SEE THESE
Reduced Prices!!!

MASTER SIX SPECIAL	$2,515
MASTER SIX REGULAR	$2,335
LITTLE SIX SPECIAL	$1,935

Stop at our garage—Look them over and listen to the steady purr of the motor—Good stock of parts—reliable Mechanic.

Ewart & Harris - Penticton Garage

Hatfield Motors
Chevrolet Distributors
PENTICTON, B.C.

Lindbergh's Historic Transatlantic Flight

LINDBERGH TO MAKE AIR TOUR OF EUROPE

PARIS, MAY 26. — The Paris edition of the Chicago Tribune says that Lindbergh has virtually decided to make an air tour of Europe. It states that in addition to Brussels and London, he will visit Copenhagen, Berlin, Vienna, Rome and possibly Madrid.

A medal commemorative of Lindbergh's New York-Paris flight will be struck by the French mint before the aviator leaves Europe.

Lindbergh had one-tenth of his gasoline supply left when he landed at Le Bourget Flying Field last Saturday night after flying from New York to Paris.

Wealth means nothing to Lindbergh, and he intends to continue as a plain aviator when he returns to the United States.

"My mind is absolutely made up about that," he said. " I haven't any idea of accepting any offers at all at this time."

Lindbergh Gets Woodrow Wilson Peace Award

NEW YORK, MAR. 1. — The Woodrow Wilson peace award has been conferred by unanimous vote of trustees of the Woodrow Wilson Foundation upon Col. Chas. A. Lindbergh, for his flight across the Atlantic and his other flights in the cause of international friendship.

Flies New York to Paris - Lands Safely With Little Gas To Spare

PARIS MAY 20 — It has been discovered that Capt. Lindbergh had only one-tenth of his gasoline supply left when he landed here from New York on Saturday. This measured about 47 1/2 gallons.

Aviator Charles A. Lindbergh stands beside his plane, The Spirit of St. Louis, in 1927 before his historic solo flight across the Atlantic to Paris.

(AP Photo)

King George to Receive Lindbergh

Transatlantic Aviator is as Generous as he is Modest

LONDON —

King George will receive Captain Charles Lindbergh in audience on Monday, it was announced officially today. The King's reception is expected to be informal, and it is understood that the Prince of Wales will be present and that the youthful aviator will be invited to join with them in a real informal chat about his journey. London is preparing to make Lindbergh's visit a gala occasion.

Perhaps the most gracious act Lindbergh has performed and one which has won for him even greater admiration, has been his gift of 150,000 franc to the fund for the families of French aviators who have lost their lives in promotion of the science of flying. The sum was awarded to Lindbergh by the Aero Club of France, having been donated by Mm. Deutsche de la Meurthe for the purchase of a cup. The hero of the first long transatlantic flight promptly turned the money back, stating that he greatly appreciated the honour extended to him but that it was his desire that the money be paid into a fund for the relief for those who had given their sons and husbands to the science of aviation.

Concert is Broadcasted from 10AY

Remote Control Successfully Employed To Send Out Two Hour Musical Programme

History was made in Kelowna on Monday night, when remote control was employed for the first time to broadcast the complete programme of a two hour concert, held to celebrate inauguration of the up-to-date apparatus lately added to the equipment of the local station, 10AY. Through the kindness of the Empress Theater management, the concert was arranged to commence at 9 o'clock, immediately after the conclusion of the Beery and Hatton feature picture, "Now We're In The Air,".

The microphone was installed in the orchestra space, raised so as to be about three feet above the level of the stage. Rev. A.K. McMinn acted in the capacity of announcer. It was a little difficult, perhaps, for many in the audience to realise that his remarks were not intended primarily for them so much as for the hundreds of unseen listeners scattered over a radius of possibly a thousand miles or more. It might seem that he indulged in a great deal of repetition, but such is necessary in radio work, as many hearers only catch part of the programme, and, unless the name of the station is given from time to time, it is difficult to tell whence to programme emanates. Mr. McMinn used the phrase "Station 10AY, Kelowna, the Orchard City of British Columbia," to localize the broadcasting point, and in his commendably brief prefatory remarks - for longwindedness is not beloved of radio fans - he explained the nature of the occasion as celebrating inauguration of remote control at Station 10AY. He then introduced Mayor Sutherland, who likewise was brief and to the point. In order to insure the best possible reception by his invisible audience, His Worship read his address from manuscript, as follows:

Address by Mayor
"Station 10AY, located at

Kelowna, B.C. is on the air to broadcast its first amateur programme from the Empress Theater over a newly installed remote control system. If this initial programme meets with favor, we trust to be on the air frequently in future.

"10AY is by no means a new station, taking into consideration what a recent thing broadcasting is; it is one of our pioneer stations, being installed by G.H. Dunn, our enterprising City Clerk in 1922. In 1924 he obtained an amateur broadcasting license bearing the number 10AY, and assigned a wave length of 250 meters. It is a 50 watt station, that being the greatest power allotted by the Radio-Telegraph Department to any amateur station.

"Having made brief reference to 10AY, I wish to give those who are listening in at a distance some idea of what we are doing in the Okanagan, which is the best known fruit district in Canada. As the 1927 returns are not yet in complete, I will give you a summary of the fruit shipments for 1926. In that year we produced and shipped 3,614,000 boxes of apples and 900,000 boxes of peaches, apricots, cherries, and other soft fruits, making a total of 4,500,000 boxes, or 6,000 cars. In addition to this, our local canneries took 3,622 tons of fruit. The total acreage on which tree fruits are grown is 20,164 acres. But our activities are not confined to fruit alone. Our vegetable shipments for this year amounted to 521,000 crates and 29,546 tons shipped in sacks, and in addition 10,932 tons were canned in the local canneries.

"In connection with these shipments various subsidiary industries are maintained. For instance it takes 26,000,000 feet of lumber to make the boxes and crates for these shipments.

"With this brief introduction to 10AY and the Okanagan, we will proceed with the programme. I trust you may enjoy it. If you do

please send us a postcard."

The musical portion of the programme followed, each item being announced by Rev. A.K. McMinn, who took advantage of an interlude to inform listeners-in that Kelowna was supposed to be the Garden of Eden. A number of requests were received for special selections, but, owing to the length of the programme, it was possible to grant only one number, an orchestral rendering of "Blue Heaven".

In closing, Rev. Mr. McMinn expressed the deep obligation of the Kelowna Radio Association to the artists who had so kindly given their services and to the management of the Empress Theater for cooperating in the arrangements. With the singing of the National Anthem, Kelowna's first public concert broadcast then came to a close.

Cariboo hwy through Fraser canyon

(Special to the Herald)
VANCOUVER —

The new Cariboo highway through the Fraser Canyon is now open for traffic. Okanogan-Cariboo Trail from Wenatchee, Wash., to Vancouver, B.C. is generally in very good condition but further improvement in some sections is very necessary. Work of widening and improving curvatures is in progress in many places, but extra care in driving must be exercised between Lytton, Cache Creek, Savona and Kamloops. A number of sharp grades and short curves are encountered on these sections. Average running time on trip is also reduced by condition of road from Rosedale to Hope. Preparations for accommodation of large number of tourists, which grandeur of scenery is certain to attract, are being made, particularly in the Fraser Canyon section.

Vancouver Man Talks To Brother in London

VANCOUVER, MAR. 8.— The longest telephone call in the history of the world was put through from Vancouver to London by J.P.D. Malkin to his brother, W.H. Malkin, this morning.

The distance covered was seven thousand miles via land lines to New York and across the Atlantic by radio telephone. The call lasted four minutes and cost $76.00. Reception at both ends was good except for a brief fading.

Princess Mary to Spend Vacation in Egypt

LONDON, MAR. 8 — Princess Mary and her husband, Viscount Lascelles, left today for a vacation trip in Egypt.

Talented Professor Denounces Rejuvenation

VIENNA, MAR. 8 — Professor Tandler, one of the foremost anatomical authorities in Europe, has expressed absolute lack of confidence in rejuvenating operations. Lecturing before an Austrian science society, he said that physiological changes, due to increased age, can not be influenced by an operation.

Amendment to Gasoline Tax Carried

VICTORIA, B.C., MAR. 8. — A slight amendment to the Gasoline Tax Act, which was strongly urged by the Opposition members and also supported by members from the Liberal side, was accepted by Attorney-General Manson in the Legislature on Wednesday. The inspectors, by this amendment, will have their powers of search without warrant restricted to premises other than actual domiciles.

The new Gasoline Act, which creates the vendors officials of the Government for collecting the tax, passed through committee without any other amendment.

1920~1929

ROYAL PRESENTATION WAITING LIST GROWS

Too Many Names Submitted for Scheduled Courts at Buckingham Palace

MAY 26, 1927 — A "waiting list" will be a novel feature in connection with this year's royal court, because of the unusual number of applicants for presentation to the King and Queen at Buckingham Palace. The first court is not scheduled until May 24, but close to 800 too many aspirants for presentation at this and three subsequent courts, it is said, have already sent in their names.

The vacancies will be filled from waiting lists in the event of successful applicants not being able to attend, owing to illness or other cause. The main reason for excess applicants is the growing desire of people from the Overseas Dominions to be presented. With the atmosphere of the courts tending to become less stiff, the formal yearly ranks from which the debutantes are drawn are becoming increasingly representative.

DEHYDRATOR PLANT PROCESSING APPLES

Report Is That Market Has Been Found For All They Can Turn Out

FEBRUARY 23, 1928 — Bulmans Limited, dehydrator plant has been operating this week on apples. A start was made on four cars on Monday and if others can be obtained they will be processed. The apples were secured from Vernon, Kelowna and Coldstream.

It is understood a market has been secured for all the processed apples they can turn out.

STORM SWEEPS SHIPPING FROM THE GREAT LAKES: SIX DEATHS REPORTED

Lakes Superior, Huron, Erie and Michigan Lashed to Fury by Winds

CHICAGO, ILL., OCT. 24.— The worst storm of the year churned eastward over the great Lakes on Wednesday. Ships were tossed up on the rocky shores of Huron and Erie and others drifted uncontrolled on Superior in a gale, sea walls crumbled and homes along the shores of Lake Michigan were ruined by floods as the owners fled in a panic.

Six deaths are reported.

Knox kept huge hoard

Death of Wealthiest Man in the Okanagan Who Lived Without Ordinary Comforts

NEVER MADE WILL

A. B. Knox Came to Okanagan in 1874 and Accumulated Fortune Variously Estimated at From $400,000 to a Million — Chief of Police Cracks Safe and Uncovers Hoard of Negotiable Securities and Cash

That a man could have $200,000 in bonds and in cash in his house and no one know of it or even suspect it, is one of the curious facts about the late A. B. Knox which has been revealed by his death and the search for a will. The cash and negotiable bonds were in the safe in Knox's home on Lake Drive, Vernon, and Chief of Police Clerke, turned cracksman, opened the safe in the presence of three witnesses, extracted the documents and conveyed them for safekeeping to the strong boxes in the Royal Bank. Included among the documents in the safe was an envelope bearing the inscription "Copy of my latest will," inside there was a printed form of a will that had never been filled out. The writing on the envelope was said to be that of the deceased man. That Knox died intestate is the opinion of most men who knew him, and this is corroborated by a statement made by him to Dr. B. F. Boyce, Kelowna, to the effect that he was not going to make any. This is supported by a report which has not been confirmed, that he told Mr. Jackson in Kelowna, some years ago that after he was gone "They could fight for it." The battle has started already in a contest over who will be official administrator of the estate. Estimates of the value of the estate vary from $400,000 to $1,000,000.

The fragmentary story of the life of the late A. B. Knox sounds like a wild stretch of the imagination, his death and burial, was in keeping with his life. He has, for about three years past, spent a very great deal of his time at Gellatly where he had taken over the Gellatly estate, and was engaged in farming it. Though 76 years of age, he worked hard and two years ago it was his proud boast that he did more work on his farm than any hired man on the place. He lived as hard as he worked, scrimping and saving, spending it is believed hours alone in his home in Vernon behind tightly drawn blinds, gloating over his wealth. Locking up the old safe he would go off to Gellatly, being away for weeks at a time, working slavishly to add to his horde.

Not The Only Cache

The securities and money which were removed from his home to the bank was not his only cache. It is said that he had a very large sum on deposit in the Royal Bank here, though on this point particulars cannot be obtained, as bank officials naturally refuse to make any statement.

Knox became ill some time ago and on Monday, April 18th started from Gellatly for Kelowna. On arrival of the boat at Kelowna he staggered by Mr. McGuire, who assisted him to the stairway on the Rowcliffe building and summoned Dr. Royce. He was taken to the hospital and death resulted the following Friday morning at five, due to acute arthritis (rheumatism), and endo carditis (inflammation of the heart). Interment was made at Kelowna.

To run sheep on O'Keefe estate is marked change

For More Than Sixty Years the O'Keefe Estate Has Been Noted For Cattle

The O'Keefe estate is changing over from beef to sheep raising. While this announcement does not sound important it marks a decided change in operations on these large holdings. For more than 60 years the O'Keefe place has been devoted to cattle raising. Price Ellison is authority for the statement that about that many years ago, Messrs. Greenhow, O'Keefe and Tom Woods combined together and sent to Oregon for cattle for their then vast ranges. The owners, all but Tom Wood, have passed on, but the nature of the operations has continued until the present time.

The recent death of Mrs. O'Keefe places control in new hands and the decision to raise sheep is the first changes in a large way.

R. A. Davidson, the sheepman who has been operating here for the past few years, and who has had sheep on Hunter's range the past two summers, is reported to have gone to Calgary to purchase the sheep.

It is said that the O'Keefe estate raises sufficient feed to permit the wintering of large flocks.

It is the winter feeding which appears to hold back the sheep industry in the interior of the Province.

Marketing the tobacco crop is most difficult

Proposals Presented to Members Of Growers' Association At Kelowna

NEW OFFER TO PAY GROWERS WHAT TOBACCO BRINGS ON THE MARKET

About a hundred tobacco growers, members of the British Columbia Tobacco Growers' Association, met a group of men representing the B.C. Tobacco Products Co. Ltd., Vancouver, in Kelowna on Monday evening for a discussion of the marketing of the 1927 tobacco crop.

A good deal of the inside history of company affairs was disclosed. Of $50,000 subscribed and paid in the major portion has been expended leaving insufficient to finance the 1927 crop. After O. Brener secured assurances last Spring that there would be about 400 acres planted to tobacco in the Okanagan in 1927 he went to the Old Country and the United States to get acquainted with conditions and if possible to dispose of the crop. Alleged dissatisfaction with the Ontario crop proved an obstacle and an outlet was not secured for the profitable disposal of the crop under contract. When the crop was not taken up according to the contract H. C. Collett, Kelowna, went to Victoria to interview the Cabinet asking for assistance in financing the movement. This could not be arranged.

A group of men owning stock in the B.C. Tobacco Products Co. submitted tentative proposals.

They offer to advance a small sum per pound on delivery of the tobacco and to forward it East where further processing will be given. Then if an advantageous offer is received they will sell. If they do not receive what they consider a fair offer, they will send it to Mr. Kelley in Great Britain, for him to dispose of.

A contract for a term of years, which does not fix the prices to be paid, is being prepared. This is to be submitted first to the Association and later to the growers for their approval.

Canadian Women Win Fight With Supreme Court

To the right are three of the five prominent Canadian women who appealed to the Privy Council against the decision of the Supreme Court of Canada that women were not eligible to become members of the Canadian Senate of Canada. Left, Hon., Irene Parlby, one of the first women in the British Empire to be come a Cabinet Minister. Right, bottom, Judge Emily Murphy, of Edmonton, and top, Mrs. Louise McKinney, first woman to be elected to the Alberta Legislature.

WHISKEY BOTTLE FULL OF VINEGAR

Doukhobor Who Bought For Police Got Little For His $7.00

OCTOBER 24, 1929 — One of the shocks of a lifetime came to Police Chief Davies the other day when he opened a bottle thought to be full of whiskey and discovered that the contents were only vinegar. The chief, it may be explained, was opening the bottle in his official capacity and the shock therefore was purely of an official character.

The incident occurred in connection with a raid on Thursday night of last week upon the premises of Thomas Hanson, Front Street, who is now charged with keeping liquor for sale. The case was up in court this morning and was adjourned until tomorrow.

A similar charge has been laid against Corey Dow, also of Front Street.

H.H. Boyle is appearing for the prosecution and M.M. Colquhoun for the defence.

A Doukhobor had been employed by the chief as a preliminary to the raid. It is understood that he went into the Hanson place and asked for a bottle. Hanson gave him a bottle in exchange for seven dollars in bills. Shortly afterwards Chief Davies and Constable Allercott entered the premises and demanded an examination of the money, which upon scrutiny was found to correspond in bill numbers with numbers which the chief had marked down in his notebook.

Hanson is said to have told the chief that the bottle did not contain whiskey and it is further alleged that when the chief examined the bottle he found it to be full of vinegar.

Later in the evening the police scoured the premises at the rear of the Hanson place.

The same night they visited the Dow place and found a small quantity of beer, three bottles of Scotch and some gin.

Was Successful In Antarctic Flight

Commander Richard E. Byrd and three companions left Little America, Antarctica, in a tri-motored Fokker aeroplane for the South Pole, 1,600 miles from their base. The flight was successful and the party was back in a little over 24 hours. The layout shows Commander Richard E. Byrd, who is in charge of the expedition and the plane in which the historic trip was made.

School Not To Be Opened

Six Cases of Scarlet Fever Found This Week

Six new cases of scarlet fever were developed in Penticton over the weekend, thought to have resulted before the schools were closed on Wednesday. The first signs of these cases were general on Saturday and Sunday, with others from then to Tuesday.

So far, the parents have co-operated well with the doctors' orders and have kept the children off the streets much better than has been previously known. With no apparent cessation of the disease at the present time, the schools with be closed for another week, or until further notice is given.

One new case among the older students was discovered on Sunday when a Kaleden girl was taken ill. She was attending high school in Penticton but had caught the malady through her associations in Kaleden.

It is not thought necessary to close the high school as the only case there was obtained from an out-of-town source.

Five Billion Dollars Swept Away

NEW YORK —

Five billion dollars in market values were swept away today in the greatest selling wave in the history of the New York Stock Exchange. Then some of the nation's most powerful bankers gave support, which stopped the break.

It was the greatest day in the history of the market, more than 11,000,000 shares having been exchanged frantically by 2 p.m.

Impetus was given buying United States Steel by the fact that directors were to hold a special meeting after the close today. At that time it was expected some action would be taken to acquire Columbia Steel Company of Pittsburg, Cal. Some were against talking of a split up in United States Steel common stock on a two for one basis.

A stronger tone came into the stock market about 1 p.m.

A meeting of big bankers at the offices of J.P. Morgan and Co. gave confidence to some of the traders who had been dumping stocks overboard regardless of price.

About 1 p.m. the tape was running 92 minutes behind. At that time United States Steel was being bid at 204 1/2, up from a low of 195.

Wheat Market Has Collapsed

Prices In Some Cases, Dropped Thirteen Points Today

(Special to the Herald)
WINNIPEG, —

Wheat was literally pounded into the pit here today as traders started one of the heaviest liquidation movement witnessed here in some time, and prices tumbled from 8 1/2c to 13c below yesterday's quotations up to noon.

CHICAGO, OCT. 24. — the grain market was demoralized today under an avalanche of selling orders without a buyer, wheat prices collapsing nearly 12 cents a bushel without a pause in the rush.

Prices Rally On New York Stock Exchange

Stock prices rallied in spectacular fashion at he opening of today's market, which has been delayed two hours to give harassed brokerage employees an opportunity to rest. Scores of issues showed initial gains of $1 to $12 a share, with several large blocks changing hands.

(Later)

NEW YORK — Heavy profit-taking halted a wild stampede to buying in today's stock market after scores of issues had been marked up $5 to $30 a share and gains of $75 and $95 a share had been registered by a couple of high-priced specialities.

Losses from high levels ranged from $2 to $12 in most of the popular shares. Trading was conducted at a furious pace, sales from noon, when the market opened, to 1:30 p.m. totalling 4,472,400 shares.

The opening gains in many cases were even more spectacular than that of the past week.

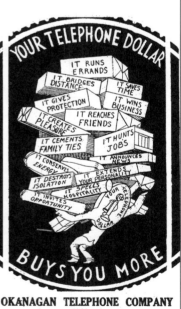

OKANAGAN TELEPHONE COMPANY
Division of
CANADIAN PUBLIC SERVICE CORPORATION, LTD.

RUTHLESS RAID ON NEW YORK STOCKS

Wall Street Brokers Experience Panic and Stock Prices Go Crashing Down

NEW YORK, N.Y., Oct. 24.— Hundreds of millions of dollars in market values were washed away on Wall Street yesterday as bears staged a new ruthless attack on stocks.

Just as the market began to show renewed stability a powerful drive against vulnerable issues sent traders into a panic and holdings were dumped overboard at any price. Several issues were reported down from $30 to $96. The break came in the closing hour with amazing swiftness.

NEW YORK STOCK MARKET HOLIDAY

Exchanges Open Half Day Today and Then Close For Two Days

NEW YORK, N.Y., Oct. 31.— Governors of the stock exchange have voted to delay opening Thursday until noon and to close on Friday and Saturday.

The selling frenzy which has swept the world stock markets during the past week appeared to have passed here Wednesday and prices on all leading stocks rallied briskly, scores of issues jumping up from $5 to $30 a share. C.P.R. stock moved up nearly 20 points.

Montreal and Toronto to Close

MONTREAL, Que., Oct. 31.— Conforming with New York, the Toronto and Montreal stock exchanges will close Friday and Saturday.

Records Broken at New York Clearing House

NEW YORK, Oct.31 — Settlements through the New York Clearing House yesterday totalled 3,500,000,000 a record for all time . It was attributed almost entirely to the abnormal exchange of cheques in settlement of Stock Exchange transactions.

The previous record for one day was 3,034,000,000 on January 2nd last, when the figures were swelled by the month-end and year-end payments, dividends and other settlements.

OGO Believe

AUGUST 9, 1928

Ogopogo seen at Osoyoos

"Ogopogo" Is Also Seen By Swimmers At Osoyoos Lake

OLIVER — Manuel Louie, an old timer, tells of his son and five friends receiving a severe shock while enjoying a swim at the north end of Osoyoos Lake last Saturday afternoon.

Their description of a "large whale" about 100 feet long coming to the surface, making in their direction and then disappearing under water again, makes one inclined to think that the Ogopogo has changed its abode, probably due to severe floods experienced in the district this season.

AUGUST 16, 1928

Ogopogo Now Coming South

Summerland Couple See Lake Monster Through Field Glasses

The Ogopogo is coming.

A report from Summerland this morning said that the famous lake monster is heading in this direction. According to the rate of speed he was travelling, he ought to have arrived some time ago.

Early this morning, when the Pentowna was leaving Naramata, Mr. H. Neill, C.P.R. freight agent at Summerland, noticed a commotion in the lake. He hurriedly obtained his field glasses and with his wife ran to ascertain the cause.

By this time the Pentowna was heading for Penticton. Focussing the glasses on the spot where the disturbance could be seen, Mr. Neill plainly made out the head of the animal or fish. The head was the only part of the creature which was visible, but the water behind was agitated. Mr. Neill states that the head resembled that of a sheep.

Mr. Neill then handed the glasses to his wife, who could see the creature in the water still. To obtain further spectators they ran to the station, but by the time they returned all traces of the Ogopogo were gone.

Saw Splash

He Saw Splash Of Ogopogo Nearly Fifty Years Ago

Editor, Penticton Herald:

Our local paper carried a reprint of an article in The Herald about that thing you have in the lake you call "Ogopogo". I steamboated that lake for nine years without seeing that joker.

However, during the summer of 1960 we were rounding Squally Point on a hot day with the lake as calm as a millpond. Captain Shorts sighted something ahead which looked like a big log floating on the water and he headed our little craft for it, and when he got close it gave one big lunge and disappeared. He yelled out to me, "Harry, that's the devil fish the Indians talk about". However, I saw nothing but rings on the water. I had been busy poking wood into the little boiler.

Our boat was about 40 feet long, driven with a 4-h.p. engine – the first and only steamboat on Okanagan Lake at that time. We seldom made more than one trip a week from the head of the lake (not Okanagan Landing).

Freight was hauled from Sicamous to Enderby by the Enderby Flour Mills boat "Red Star," thence by freight teams to the head of the west arm of the lake on the Indian reserve, and return to Enderby with a load of wheat. The milling company had a large warehouse on the lakefront. We hauled the wheat from the Mission (now Kelowna) to the head of the lake. Wheat, cattle and hogs were all that came out of

POGO
it or not!

937

of Ogopogo

Ogopogo Seen By Local Men

Subterranean Monster Puts In Annual Appearance Here

Penticton's summer visitor, the dim and mysterious denizen of the deeps of Okanagan Lake, has won over another skeptic for the Ogopogo has returned to harry the scientific guesser once more.

On Sunday, Mr W. X. Perkins and Mr. "Mike" Larama, of the Grand Forks Garage Co., were out enjoying the cool breezes of Okanagan Lake, in their launch. While they were about a mile from Squally Point, at 1 o'clock in the afternoon, they suddenly observed something strange, something that seemed to be following the wash of the boat. But there was a stretch of untroubled water between the wash and the "unknown."

Finally, the "something" turned, and Mr. Larama, who had witnessed the Okanagan phenomenon previously, said "That's it!" Mr. Perkins gave the usual description, of a body longer than their boat, round, and dark, or black. The body could be seen clearly, he said.

Then suddenly, as if tired of its pranking, the "Ogopogo" dropped out of sight. The dip was a sudden one, Mr. Perkins said, creating a big disturbance in the water.

Ogopogo Seen

PEACHLAND — After a disappearance for over a year, Ogopogo once again showed himself here when he was observed by a dozen men who were returning from the Osprey Lake fire on Wednesday afternoon, August 30. The truck was driven by Arnold Ferguson and, as they rounded the last turn on the Princeton road, just the distance of the P.N. Dorland orchard from the lake, they saw a commotion in the water and six feet of the creature out of the water.

Although none of the men could describe the appearance of the head of the monster, they all agreed that the size of the body and the commotion in the water behind could belong to nothing else but the Ogopogo. There are now no skeptics in that party. The lake was calm and the truck was stopped on the corner so that all might see, but almost immediately the object of their attention went down and disappeared from sight.

the Okanagan in those days.

The farmers grew wheat all summer and played poker and danced all winter. Everybody had money and wore a smile. It took us two days to steam from the head of the lake to Penticton.

When night came we nosed into some sheltered bay and tied up for the night, built a camp fire on the beach and baked our bannocks. Our ship ran at the right speed for trolling and we were always well supplied with fresh fish.

The country was full of deer. When we wanted venison we ran along the shore line until we could shoot one from the boat. Then we would run ashore, take the hindquarters and leave the rest. It did not cost much to live in the country in those days.

Our landing at Penticton was just inside the mouth of the river, on a sand bar. A pack train worked from there through the south country which was mostly owned or controlled by four men, Tom Ellis of Penticton, Dick Cawston and Frank Richter at Keremeos, and Judge Haynes on the boundary line. The Lord help you if you tried to pre-empt any land among them.

In the fall of '90 Jack Coryell surveyed several quarter sections of land wherever it was any good between Penticton and Squally Point on those benches for Tom Ellis. He bought those patches for one dollar an acre and controlled the rest to keep out squatters as they were beginning to come into the valley. The railway started to build in from Sicamous on May 1, 1890.

Yours respectfully,
H. Colbeck
P.O. Box 744, Revelstoke, B.C.

LAKEVIEW MARKET

SERVING KELOWNA FOR 52 YEARS!

- QUALITY MEATS
- FRESH PRODUCE
- INSTORE BAKERY

Open 9 a.m. - 9 p.m. 6 days a week
Corner of K.L.O. & Pandosy

A DECADE IN REVIEW

1930 ~ 1939

Hundreds Of Men Soon To Be Put At Work In Relief Camps In This District

TRANSIENTS ARE RECEIVING DOLE

Government Issues 40 Cents Each to 178 Unemployed In One Day

JULY 16, 1931 — More than 150 transients have been receiving here the government dole of 40 cents per day for the past week or ten days.

Each morning, between 9 and 11 o'clock, there is a line-up outside the provincial police office, stretching across the driveway and sometimes touching the fence on the property directly opposite.

All manner of men and boys are in this line. There are Scotch, Irish, English, Swedes, Germans, and all other types of foreigners. The average of the dole each day amounts to between 150 and 180. One day this week slips were handed out to 178 unemployed.

Each transient, when he reports to Constable Hatcher, is given a number. He shouts his number as he enters the office, signs the slip, and then leaves. This slip is value for 40 cents worth of groceries, or, if so desired, can be handed to a restaurant for a 40-cent meal.

Transients From Prairies Arrive

JULY 23, 1931 — The provincial government's 40 cent dole to the unemployed is still continuing at the provincial police office, with an average of 180 transients appearing daily. This week there have been an increased number of hoboes from the prairies arriving to receive the dole. These men frankly admit they heard of the B.C. dole while in Calgary or other points and immediately rushed to this province for a hand-out.

It was rumored at the first of the week that the government offices in Kelowna and Vernon were going to make the men do odd jobs, such as cleaning streets and vacant lots for their dole. It is a certainty that 42 transients came down the lake on a barge in one day, and it is thought that this was the reason.

Many humorous sidelights on the transient situation are heard on the street. One man employed two transients at $2 a day and board each. They worked hard the first day, but failed to make an appearance until after 11 o'clock the following day. When asked why they had come so late they replied that they could not get the government dole until nearly ten o'clock, and so could not get to work any sooner.

Relief camps on road construction work are being opened up in many sections of this district and several road projects, held over for some time, are now being launched in order to provide work for the unemployed.

One of these is the crossing of the two Rock Creek canyons on the road to the Boundary country, a short distance east of Bridesville. Long the dread of timid motorists, these crossings are about to be replaced through the construction of a new road a mile and a half long, across the mouth of the canyon and below the point where McKinney Creek and Jolly Creek meet, although still above the location where the combined creek flows into Rock Creek. The diversion is to provide for a canyon bridge 100 feet high and 300 feet long. The situation calling for changed conditions in this road was forced by unemployment in the district and accentuated by the recent fire which damaged the existing log-supported road through the canyons.

It is understood that a relief camp of 100 men will be established in that locality at once in order to have the new canyon road finished this year.

New Yellow Lake Camp

The new Yellow Lake road camp near the Parker ranch, and housing 100 men, will be ready for use in very little more than a week. This camp will be at work on a new road to get away from the Parker hill road, which is narrow, steep and winding.

Full blast on Hope-Princeton

More than 100 men are now working on the eastern end of the Hope-Princeton link and at least four camps will be operated. They have, in fact, already been built, and it is believed that this force of 100, which is an expansion of the 30 men working all summer on the link, will be increased very soon to 250 at least. One camp is at Friday Creek, another at Copper Creek, a third near the junction of the Roche and Pasayten rivers, and a fourth further ahead. The intention is to have the road pushed through the Allison Pass, the summit about 50 miles out from Princeton, by the end of the year, if weather permits.

More On Hope End

Information is that at the western end of the link, covering the 38 miles from Hope to Allison Pass, the camps will be even larger than on this side in order to take care of many Vancouver unemployed.

A relief camp is to be built at Shuswap Hill on the Vernon-Arrow Lakes road, with another at Mars Lake on the Trans-Canada Highway. Two small camps are now working on the Kelowna-Carmi road, which as a pilot road, is practically completed.

A camp is operating at Cascade for the purpose of improving the highway near the Cascade bridge and west towards Grand Forks.

The Osoyoos camp will continue. The new bridge there is nearing completion insofar as the central structure is concerned and the approaches are now being put in hand.

Falls Bridge Under Way

The new bridge at Okanagan Falls is now under way. Material has been ordered and the approaches are being constructed. This bridge would be finished in about six weeks or two months.

Relief camp near Princeton c. 1932

No Depression in Okanagan

Fifteen substantial residences have been built in Penticton since spring. A modern hotel to accommodate tourists and the ever-increasing demand of the travelling public, is now being erected on Main Street.

These are only a few evidences of progress to be seen in the city at the southern end of Okanagan Lake.

At Kelowna and Vernon several business blocks have been, or are being erected, and numerous modern residences are appearing on many residential streets in both these centers.

More buildings have gone up in Vernon this year than were built in three years before.

When Fear rules man's will, nothing can be done; but when man or community casts Fear out, the world becomes his or its oyster.

To lose money is nothing, but to lose hope, to lose nerve and ambition, that is what cripples the individual or the community.

So far as the Okanagan is concerned, this silly depression is ended. It exists more in the minds of people than in actual experience.

Sympathetic effort may yet be necessary to carry through the winter, but isn't it time to end this senseless depression talk?

— ENDERBY COMMONER

Everything Dying On Ranch, Owner Says To Collector

SUMMERLAND —
Municipal collector C.E. Pineo receives some strange letters at times. Generally they have some pointed remarks, but recently one with stoical resignation about it draws a smile and perhaps some sympathy. It reads as follows:

"Mr. Pineo. I got your notice about my dog. I have no dog; it died a unnatural death. It swallowed some flume water. Everything is dying. My cow is slowly passing out because it gives less milk. My hens died of 'hooping coff,' hooping for water. There was none. All I have is dead and I think I will be dead before taxes come to you, and you can have my dead ranch and everything on it, except my wife. I wish you all good and make desert blossom as rose.

"Yours truly,
(Signed) —————"

Men In Concentration Camp At Vernon Refuse To Work And Start For Vancouver

UNEMPLOYED IN B.C. AT 65,000

Highway Work Offers the Only Temporary Solution, Says Bruhn

(Special to the Herald)
VICTORIA, FEB. 25, 1932 — The number of unemployed in the province has risen to 65,000 and highway construction and non-productive public works hold the only temporary solution to the problem, Hon. R.W. Bruhn, minister of public works, told the Legislature Wednesday in a clear-cut defence of the government's policy.

When the fiscal year's program of works is completed, over ten million dollars will have been spent on relief in B.C., he said. The province had received sound value in return for its expenditure. There was only one province which had set up relief camps as cheaply as this one. Of the total cost, $689,200, at least a third would be receivable in salvage.

Hon. R.L. Maitland turned a caustic attack on the leader of the Opposition. The only solution Mr. Pattullo had offered, he said, was a repetition of the South Okanagan settlement scheme on a larger scale. That project, he declared, cost the taxpayers $4,500,000 and only took care of 1,000 men. Based on the figures of the present unemployment, such a plan would cost over $300,000,000.

Men Must Go To Work or Get Out Was The Verdict

VERNON —
"On to Vancouver," shouted about 65 indigents, quartered in the local unemployment concentration camp, when informed by O.P. Roberts, assistant district engineer, that the camp was officially closed at 1:30 o'clock Wednesday afternoon. Another 16 boarded the north-bound 5 o'clock train, of whom nine had not belonged to the camp.

Steadfastly refusing to accept the government's stipulations that in return for 120 hours of labor per month they should receive board, lodgings and an allowance of $7.50, the large crowd spurned the invitation to climb aboard trucks bound for Lumby.

As had been previously announced, the trucks arrived at the concentration camp shortly before 1:30 p.m. Only a mere handful signified their willingness to go to Lumby, where relief work is planned. Ten threw their belongings into the vehicles. About a score, in the course of the next half hour, drifted towards Vernon, the railway tracks and in other directions.

The great majority, however, numbering about 65, lined up in the basement quarters of the premises. They declared that they would not leave until official notice was given them that the camp was closed.

When he arrived Mr. Roberts offered the men a last chance to go to work. He declared that the trucks were ready for them. In reply the men asked if the camp was definitely closed or not.

"Yes," answered Mr. Roberts.

"That's all we wanted to know," shouted several men. In less than ten minutes the camp, home for about 100 men since last November, was practically deserted. Singing and shouting a parade disappeared toward Armstrong. Trucks arrived to remove food supplies.

Before leaving, leaders of the men declared that it is their avowed intention to carry the so-called "parade" right to Vancouver. En route they expect to be joined by a number of the 54 quartered at Mara, and by a large number at Kamloops.

"We won't stop till we air our grievances before the very highest provincial authorities," stated one man.

On Sunday last all men were informed that work was to start. It was explained that in return for 120 hours of work per month, either five hours a day for six days of the week, or six hours a day for five days in the week, that they should receive board and lodgings and a monthly allowance of $7.50.

All men, from "A" to "H," were to move on Sunday. There was a straight refusal. On Monday the men once more refused and the local government officials laid down a decisive ultimatum. The camp was to be closed on Wednesday.

A committee of ten was appointed by the camp inmates to represent them. This committee made representations to the local government officials, protesting against the low wage.

Some of them declared that they would lose membership in certain unions if they worked for such low wages. When the point was stressed that the $7.50 monthly was not a wage, but a "bonus" or "allowance," the men then answered that they would not be sure of receiving the money.

"If we work, we'll be helping to batter down wage levels in this province," declared one of the leaders.

A counter proposal, that married men be paid $4.00 per day for four days a week, and that single men receive $4.00 a day for three days of the week, was advanced.

This was promptly refused at the Court House here, and after communication with Victoria, the authorities repeated their statement that the camp was to be closed on Wednesday.

Sparce comforts are afforded to laboureres in Hope-Princeton relief camps 1930-37   Hatfield Collection courtesy of the Penticton Museum

Victor in the International Fisherman's Races

Here is the Bluenose, successful Canadian defender of the trophy for international races between fishing schooner. She defeated the American challenger, the Gertrude L. Thebaud, of Gloucester, Mass., in the recent races off Halifax, winning twice in succession. Capt. Angus Walters was her skipper.

Parents Urged To Thresh Boys

Oliver Youths Who Damaged Property Hallowe'en Are Before Court

OLIVER —

Magistrate G.F. Guernsey, of Penticton, sitting as Juvenile Court judge here Wednesday, bewailed the fact that the powers that be had abolished the clause in the Juvenile Act which allowed the presiding judge to impose a good sound thrashing as punishment. Magistrate Guernsey uttered these remarks when sitting in judgment on four youths charged with causing wilful damage to the district school on Hallowe'en. He gave them all six months' suspended sentence and admonished their parents to give the boys a sound thrashing. The parents will have to pay the amount of damage caused by the boys to the school, and also the costs of

the court.

Three other youths, also implicated in the Hallowe'en depredations, were made to assist in paying the costs of the damage caused to the school and the court costs.

On Hallowe'en, following a party given by the teachers to the children to keep them out of mischief, the district school building was broken into and the fire hoses turned on. Water was sprayed over the walls and ceilings and the basement was flooded. Damage to ceilings and other fixtures ran to a considerable figure. The high school building was also broken into and valuable books belonging to the principal, Dr. Masterton, were ruined. Ink was spilled over walls and floors, and other damage caused.

Provincial police who prosecuted the youths did not lay a charge of breaking and entering,

for the reason, Constable Laird said in court, that the boys in that case would have to go to a higher court for trial and would likely have their futures ruined. In place of this the charge of wilful damage was laid, which could be dealt with summarily by the magistrate.

All pleaded guilty to the damage charges, some admitting they had put carbide in the ink, and others to tampering with the fire hose. The boys who appeared before Magistrate Guernsey ranged in age from 14 to 17 years. They were given a severe reprimand and, together with their parents having to foot the damage costs to the school, they also will have to report to the provincial police on the first of every month for the next six months.

The damage to the school and the teachers' books, etc., were assessed at $21, and the costs of

the court at $13. One of the fathers of the accused boys was unable to pay his share of the costs, and the other three boys, who voluntarily gave themselves up and confessed their part in the raid on the schools were made to pay this man's share.

New Commercial Radio Station Takes The Air

1930~1939

After Testing This Week, CKOV Begins Regular Schedule On Sunday

Radio Station CKOV, the commercial station operated by Okanagan Broadcasters Limited, with Mr. J. W. B. Browne as announcer, is on the air this week with test programmes. Reception throughout the valley, checked at various points by listeners-in during the day and evening on Tuesday, was found to be excellent, and for the first time since Kelowna has had a broadcasting station Vernon radio fans were able to tune in on Kelowna in the evening. Owing to interference made by so many stations on the air in the evenings, Vernon resi-

dents were never successful in getting 10AY at night. CKOV, with greater power of 100 watts, cannot be drowned out.

Commencing on Sunday, the following schedule will go into effect: Sunday, 11 a.m. to 1.30 p.m.; 6 p.m. until close of evening church service at 9 p.m. Every day, 8 a.m. to 9 a.m.; 11:30 a.m. to 2 p.m.; 4:30 to 7:30 p.m. On Tuesdays, Thursdays and Saturdays, additional programmes will be broadcasted from 9 p.m. to 11 p.m., and on Thursdays and Saturdays, the station will go on the air at midnight for two-hour broadcasts.

The new home of CKOV is located north of Jolley's Service Station. All necessary equipment has been installed by the Canadian Marconi Company.

J.W.B. Browne — "The Voice of CKOV" — during a broadcast c. 1932.

Photo courtesy of Kelowna Museum

Fatal Injuries Inflicted by Motor Car

Mr. A. A. Ballard, Widely Esteemed Citizen, Succumbs As Result Of Street Accident

Succumbing to fatal injuries received when he came in contact with a motor car at the corner of Pendozi Street and Lake Avenue, Mr. Archibald A. Ballard, an esteemed resident of this city for many years, died in Kelowna General Hospital on Sunday, shortly after 11 p.m., six hours following the accident.

According to the evidence of eye witnesses, Mr. Ballard and Mr. W. McEwan were crossing to the east side of Pendozi Street from lake Avenue when a car driven by Robert Knox, son of Dr. W. J. Knox, approached from Pendozi Street north. The driver sounded his horn two or three times and checked the speed of the car, which was not travelling fast, at the same time pulling over to the left to avoid the pedestrians. Mr. McEwan, who had seen the car approaching before he started to cross, halted in the street to allow the car to pass. Mr. Ballard, who apparently did not see the car in time, put up one arm, which shattered the window in the right front door, when he came in contact with it. He was thrown backward, falling on the back of his head and fracturing his skull. Dr. Knox was called immediately and the uncon-

scious man was taken to hospital in the ambulance. The accident occurred at 5:30 p.m.

The verdict of the Coroner's jury, which heard the evidence of eye witnesses at the inquest held by Coroner J.F. Burne in the Court Room, Casorso Block, on Tuesday morning, exonerates Robert Knox. It follows:

"That Archibald Anderson Ballard came to his death as a result of coming in contact with a motor car driven by Robert Knox at the corner of Pendozi Street and Lake Avenue in the city of Kelowna. It would appear from the evidence given that Robert Knox did everything possible to avoid the accident.

"We strongly recommend that the City Engineer look into the matter of lighting and grading this part of the road to avoid further accidents."

Agnes Macphail Pleads Cause of Disarmament

Urges Canadian Club Hearers to Sign Petitions

February Conference will Show Trend of World Feeling

Stressing the fact that by signing the League of Nations petitions for disarmament, people can aid greatly in the success of the February conference, Miss Agnes Macphail, only woman member of the Canadian Parliament, made her first Penticton appearance at a Canadian Club supper last night in the Oddfellows Hall. It was an open meeting and some 100 members, friends and wives attended. Rev. H.P. Barrett, president of the Penticton Canadian Club, was chairman of the meeting. Secretary M.C. Kendall presented the guest speaker with a bouquet of chrysanthemums.

Miss Macphail has greatly enjoyed her B.C. visit. She had never before appreciated the extent of this province, she said. Canada is a great country and there is a sturdy national spirit prevalent, made more so by the work of the Canadian Club. This organization is helping to hold Canada together.

But there are great difficulties in getting this big country together on any one subject. To aid the disarmament problem, Miss Macphail volunteered to tour the provinces for a month, giving the Canadian clubs an idea as to the progress in this matter and what still has to be done.

The disarmament committee of the League of Nations sent petitions to all parts of Canada, Seeking support for the cause. But there was not enough publicity given to this, and the public was not versed on the subject.

Miss Macphail then outlined the problems in gaining world peace. First there is the psychological aspect, the bravery of the service against the institution of war itself. The latter is becoming unpopular, and should be done away with as soon as possible.

Opposed to War

That the world is becoming antagonized to war is borne home when such men as Sir William Robertson, one of the greatest army men in England, and Sir Arthur Currie, denounce it. "We have become frightfully efficient in the art of killing," continued Miss Macphail. In the Great War a mere 33 planes invaded London and did great destruction. Today France alone could muster 2,500 planes at a moment's notice. The destruction by war at the moment would be so complete it would be slaughter, and all-inclusive.

In past years a small scrap between nations in one corner of the world would not attract other nations, but now the world has become so closely knit that all nations must join.

Canada is not a military nation, yet out of every dollar of the budget, 45 cents goes towards wars, past and future. In the United States 65 cents is spent, Great Britain has about the same, while France is slightly higher. The Balkan states spend 90 cents or more. To carry this further would leave the world helpless to meet the ordinary requirements of life.

League Has Grown

Turning again to the League of Nations, Miss Macphail asserted that it is almost unbelievable that the nations met as a League. Since its inception the League has grown in power.

The world must face the facts. It is not paying sufficient wages to buy back the products of the machine. The problem not yet mastered is how to get the produce distributed. Everybody is racing to dump goods on the world markets, but nobody is racing to buy. The economic causes of war are currency, war debts, and trade barriers. Miss Macphail was never excited about the gold standard, she said, and considered Britain should never have joined in 1925. Currency lies at the root of most of the difficulty.

Then coming back to the disarmament problem, Miss Macphail pointed out that, despite the Versailles Treaty and the restrictions placed thirteen years ago, there is 70 per cent more armament today than in 1913. This is the time for a definite decision "for in February we must say whether we meant all that we have said about disarmament or state that we will not disarm."

The League believes the world has been woefully slow in making up its mind as to this question. The disarmament committee met first in 1925 and for four years talked of the budgetary and numerical systems of disarmament. Then there was a compromise resolution brought forward, advocating disarmament by publicity. No one knew what that meant, but it passed with only five dissenting votes. A delegate on that committee told Miss Macphail that, when the resolution passed, a movement and a shudder went over the assembly caused by the members' quivering consciences.

It took Viscount Cecil two weeks to convince the League that this method could not succeed, but finally it was turned down. Next year a really good plan was produced.

The People Control

The government is willed by the people, stressed Miss Macphail, and if the people will only go after disarmament, then they will get it. But if they never stir from their homes, the government will do as it pleases. In Holland, 50 per cent of the adult population voted for disarmament, while in Great Britain and the United States more than a million and a half persons signed the petition. Canada's objective is 500,000, and Miss Macphail pleaded that, if a little country like Holland could give such support, then Canada could muster far more than the sought-for votes.

In conclusion, the speaker stressed the need to send over capable men to the conference in February. In the past, the minister of national defense was sent, but in her opinion he was not the man to go. Precedent counts for much in a government, and it will be only through the will of the people that some other representative will be sent. She named a number of prominent statesmen such as Sir Robert Borden, Rt. Hon. Arthur Meighen, Ernest Lapointe and Herbert James, who would be ably suited for this position. But in all Canada only ten or fifteen men could be found suited for the position, as it is a terribly responsible task. A tremendously high standard must be upheld and it is unlikely that the prime minister will send any of his leading cabinet ministers, for he will need them at home at that time.

In Western Canada there are just as capable men as in the East, Miss Macphail concluded, and it is up to the western people to bring these men forward and bring them to the attention of the government.

Mr. L.B. Boggs moved a hearty vote of thanks to Miss Macphail, and it was seconded by Mr. W.R. Long. Rev. H.P. Barrett was in accord with the League of Nations Society and urged every person gathered in the hall to send a subscription to that body and receive the literature which will give a comprehensive survey of the work being done.

1930~1939

1930~1939

The Empress Theatre on Front Street in Penticton in the 1920's. Notice the poster for Polish actress Pola Negri's American debut movie, "Bella Donna" which was released in 1923.

New Pictures For Empress Reflect Change In Taste Of Patrons Of The Talkie

Wholesome, human type of show is popular.

That there has been a decided change in the taste of the theatre-goer during the past year is the opinion of Manager J. Watt of the Empress Theatre, Penticton.

"Both screen and stage for several years have been reflecting conditions that have drawn upon it a great amount of criticism," stated Mr. Watt, "and by mirroring these conditions it has gone a long way to bringing the realization of such conditions to the consciousness of the nation."

"We have been passing through an age of real sophistication, and naturally the screen has been influenced by that type of material. But we know that the most successful type of talking picture is that which is wholly away from sophistication, and the old type of postwar thought, which found its life in sex and frankness, is dying.

"For some time, mankind has known that such stories are out of step, but citizens have been afraid to admit it. Today they are not. The world wants to believe in Cinderellas and not in gold diggers of Broadway.

Back to Wholesome Type

"There is something sane and sound in the people which makes us hurry back to the wholesome, human type of entertainment before any great damage is done. Humanity is as healthy as its entertainment – drama, literature, art and sports.

"The war caused our most recent era of sophistication because it shattered the ideals of youth. In spite of the fact that adults believe they set the standards for the world, youth has always moulded the thoughts of its elders because grown-ups want to appear in line with youthful ideas."

"But don't you think our youth is still 'flaming' and prides itself on its frankness?" the interviewer asked.

"No, I do not," said Mr. Watt emphatically. "This age of frankness is now passed. Today's generation is the first in many when all young men have been iconoclastic, wanting to tear down the old and reform the world, at some time in their lives.

"I do not mean that wrongdoing cannot be depicted on the screen, but whenever and however it is used, it must be properly presented to show that punishment is the result of all wrong."

Juvenile Pictures Please

"There is a lot of truth to the phrase, 'When you reach the heart of a child, you reach the heart of a nation.' And for that reason Paramount for its 20th Birthday Jubilee Year has paid a great deal of attention to pictures which will appeal to everybody from eight to eighty years of age."

"Another trend is the leaning toward the return of music to the screen. There will be a sprinkling of operettas with a reasonable number of musical comedies. For years motion picture audiences had been trained to realism. The stage had a dramatic licence which was impossible in pictures. Audiences could not get used to music coming from nowhere on the screen. A more skilful technique will make them popular again."

"Paramount has also developed a perfected recording of sound on the film which is another big step in advance and which makes Paramount pictures stand out in tonal excellence."

New Personalities Arise

"Personalities come first with the public in most cases in judging entertainment. With this fact in mind, Paramount is building the largest star list in the history of Paramount. If you will look over the list of stars in most companies you will find that they were 75 per cent made stars in Paramount pictures. New personalities and youth are the demand of the theatre today, seasoned by a few established favorites."

"First, perhaps, should be mentioned Maurice Chevalier in the adaptation of Oscar Straus' famous operetta of Viennese life, titled for the pictures as 'The Smiling Lieutenant'. Claudette Colbert, Mariam Hopkins and Charles Ruggles are the featured players."

"Everyone has been waiting for the playing dates of 'An American Tragedy,' Theodore Drelser's much-talked-of novel, which has been called 'The Great American Novel.' Those who have seen the picture version of 'An American Tragedy' pronounce it to be the most powerful picture to reach the screen in all its history. Phillips Holmes rises to great heights in this picture and Sylvia Sydney and Wynn Gibson give remarkable portrayals which stamp them as rising young stars.

"Then we have such important productions coming soon as: 'Sporting Blood' with Clark Gable and Madge Evans; 'Hell's Angels' with Ben Lyon, James Hall and Jean Harlow; 'Whoopee' with Eddie Cantor; 'Raffles' with Ronald Colman.

"You see I am enthusiastic about the new season," Mr. Watt concluded. "And I have every reason to be. I have seen some of the new pictures, been in on their selection and booking, and know the wonderful entertainment fare I will be able to offer to Penticton this year.

ARE LINKING UP MOVIE HOUSES

Representatives of Independent Theatres Are Forming Co-operative

NOVEMBER 14, 1929 — That within two years silent movies will be things of the past was the prediction made here last week my Messrs. W. A. Barnes and Charles Stephenson, who have been touring the interior of the province linking up independent movie houses into an association. Mr. Barnes, former manager of the Orpheum at Vancouver, is now secretary-buyer in B.C. for the Exhibitors Co-operative of Canada. Mr. Stephenson is connected with the Tiffany Stahl Productions of Hollywood. He was at one time manager of the Dominion in Vancouver.

They have been visiting the Kootenay and in this district also spent some time in Grand Forks, Summerland and Princeton. where independent houses are located.

The tremendous investment being made in talkie equipment meant the relegation of silent pictures to the discard, said the visitors. This created a serious situation for the small independent houses not linked up with such circuits as the Famous Players, which now operates a large string of theatres in Canada and the States, including the Berry houses in this district.

The independent theatres mush shortly install talking equipment and under existing condition must pay three times as much for talkie films as for the silent type. This would mean ruination for most of them unless they got together andbought films as an entity, thus cutting down costs, said the visitors.

Fight Pictures Here Saturday

Tunney-Dempsey Fill Will Also Be Screened Monday

OCTOBER 6, 1927 — The Tunney-Dempsey fight pictures are to be screened at the Empress on Saturday and Monday night. Announcement made from the theatre this week of the prompt arrival here of movies of this famous ring encounter was greeted with great interest by the fight fans of the district and the Empress is certain to attract big crowds for Saturday and Monday.

Regular feature programmes will also be screened. Harold Lloyd will be here Saturday in "Never Weaken" and Art Young in "Alaskan Adventures," these two pictures are also being show on Friday.

1930~1939

No Word Yet of Lindbergh Baby

Family is hopeful, however that youngster will be returned

(Special to the Herald)

HOPEWELL, N.J., MARCH 3 — There is a well-defined expectation that the Lindbergh baby might be returned today. Although police are silent on the subject, there are thought to be secret negotiations between the Lindberghs and the kidnappers for its return. The deadline around the Lindberghs' home from which newspapermen were turned back late yesterday was extended even to police today and the house is completely isolated for four miles. Lindbergh has appointed two agents to deal with the kidnappers, and one of them, Arthur Springer, secretary of the late Dwight Morrow, Lindbergh's father-in-law, has drawn $50,000 from the flyer's account.

(Special to the Herald)

HOPEWELL, N.J., MARCH 3 — There is still no word of Charles Lindbergh Jr., the baby held by kidnappers for $50,000 ransom. It was stolen from its crib Tuesday night.

All night the Lindbergh home blazed with lights. For five miles it could be seen, standing against the black skyline, a beacon inviting the baby's kidnappers to bring him back home, but the coming of a dull dawn found the little crib empty.

Friend of Hauptmann Questioned

Anita Lutzenberg, attractive woman friend of Bruno R. Hauptmann, photographed after she had been questioned by District Attorney Samuel Foley as to her knowledge of Hauptmann, the man indicted for extortion in connection with this possession of Lindbergh ransom money.

There was a hint of hope. First there was a postcard, mailed in Newark yesterday and received by Col. Charles A. Lindbergh later in the day, stating the baby was safe and for him to await further instructions. Second, there was the intimation from the household itself that the child might possibly be restored to its parents today.

There was no explanation of the expression of belief that the 20-month-old baby would be returned today. Perhaps it was predicted upon negotiations with the kidnappers, although the police deny this.

Rumors arose all through the night and all through the hours of this morning that the child had been seen at distant or near places, that suspicious cars had been sighted, that suspects had been caught; but all of these, when each was pursued to its foundations by a corps of police, aviators and volunteer searchers, was proved untrue.

On the appeal of Mrs. Lindbergh, the daily diet of her baby was broadcast by radio last night and an appeal was issued on her behalf that the kidnappers should take care of the child, which was suffering from a cold when taken.

CHICAGO, MARCH 3 — "It's the most outrageous thing I ever heard of," said Al Capone from his prison cell when he heard of the kidnapping of Baby Lindbergh. He suggested that he be allowed out of jail to assist in the search. He said he had friends all over the country who would help him to run down the kidnappers.

Al Capone offered a reward of ten thousand dollars for the capture of the kidnappers.

Pat Crowe, kidnapper of the Oudahy baby 30 years ago, who is now lecturing on good citizenship, offered to go to New Jersey to help the search.

Photographers perched in every vantage point follow aviator Charles A. Lindbergh, center without hat, as he leaves the courthouse in Flemington, N.J., in this Jan. 10, 1935, photo. The trial of Bruno Richard Hauptmann, charged with the kidnapping and murder of Lindbergh's infant child, drew one of the largest press corps in history and was the first time newsreel cameras were allowed in a courtroom.

(AP Photo)

Dumping Apples

Southern Okanagan growers are getting their first bitter taste of apple dumping. To what extent they will have to pursue this method of getting rid of the surplus fruit is not yet clear. Apparently dumping may be extensive this year and will cost something. Definite hauling charges will possibly have to be marked up against the fruit going from the packing houses. The costs of delivering to the packing sheds have already been incurred and charged to the grower, but this additional expense seems something from which there appears at present no way out.

There are apples now going out to owners of livestock. At Summerland they get these apples for their animals by paying the hauling charges and returning the boxes to the packing houses. The sheep herders there are using about 100 boxes a day, and several dairies and stockmen are using as many more of sizes which could not be marketed except by way of the bulk deal. These are of low grades of off varieties.

Where shippers have slightly oversold, under their allowance with the cartel, it is understood they are buying for dumping purposes from some shippers at other points in the valley who have a surplus stock. Some of the shippers with branch houses at different points will probably dump all at one place, it is understood, but from the unpacked stock they still have in warehouses. Good varieties which are holding up are not as yet being sacrificed, for it is hoped some market may appear to reduce the quantity which it now appears will go into the discard.

If the apples could be held in sound condition they might pay as fertilizer if plowed in. Certain it is, they must be covered to prevent any which have codling worms from producing the moth, also odor of decaying vegetation.

Some market might be created for sweet cider if small plants were available. Two glasses for a nickel or a quart to take home in one's own container at a nickel might use up a quantity. While it would be only a small outlet, it might be expected to expand. Some of the unemployed might create quite a market with some profit to themselves. The fruit would cost nothing this year. Whatever is to be done with the surplus must be planned in the next few weeks.

Across the line, to prevent some of the dumping and lessen spray costs for the next crop, growers in many orchards are cutting out every second row of trees, and these rows are not fillers. The situation has not come to that pass here, but the problem of dealing with the next season's crop is surely worth considering now.

If the market is not in sight by harvest time next fall, it would be much better to warn growers at picking time what part of the crop cannot be taken to market. Profiting by this year's experience may mean that some of the crop in 1933 would be better shaken from the trees and plowed under. That would be cheaper than may be the case this year of having to haul the fruit to the packing house and again paying to have it hauled away, dumped and covered.

The sensible solution of the problem of the surplus is to devise such unified action as will mean that the extra fruit is not picked. The cost stops right there. The modified amount sold would bring prices sufficiently better to provide for some payment to owners of unpicked fruit.

Nearly Million Boxes Of Apples Still In Storage In Okanagan

| | APPLES | | | |
| | Common Storage | | Cold Storage | |
	Packed	Loose	Packed	Loose
Salmon Arm	2195	39818		
Armstrong	625	3575		
Vernon	21353	42969	129314	14057
Oyama	2160	25273		
Winfield	256	10724		
Okanagan Centre	500	17700		
Kelowna	52929	71634	89519	50360
Westbank	254	16094		
Peachland		13800		
Summerland	16221	88993		
Naramata	1225	25204		
Penticton	9960	69565	57135	53846
Kaleden		1000	57360	10438
Oliver		28552		
Keremeos		12250		
Total	**107678**	**467151**	**333328**	**128701**
Creston	1500	20000		
Kootenay	47950			
Grand Forks	2000	1064		
Total	**51450**	**21064**		

Okanagan Total—
Apples, common (packed boxes) 419112
Apples, cold (packed boxes) 419128
Onions, common (tons) 4658
Onions, cold (tons) 1187
Potatoes, common (tons) 9200
Kootenay Total—
Apples, common (packed boxes) 65492
Onions (tons) 86
Potatoes (tons) 4350

NOTE—Totals are given in packed boxes. One loose box taken as equal to 2-3 packed box. Figures as at December 31, 1932.

1930-1939

Important Gold Strike Claimed At Grand Forks; Find Is Close To City

GRAND FORKS, B.C. — What bears all the earmarks of being the most important gold strike made in this district in many years came to light a day or two ago when news was received of several assays of ore that had been sent to the Hecia Mining Co.

Four assays vary from one ounce to four ounces of gold to the ton and were taken from the surface of the mountain a few hundred yards directly east of the old Granby office. It is a hungry looking quartz and those visiting the property say there is a veritable mountain of it.

Will Puritch and John McLeod are the two operators, but very little work has been done. They have been backed in their effort by H.O. Patton.

News of the strike had the whole city agog Wednesday as the quartz showing on the face of the hill stands out like a sore thumb and has been gaping at businessmen for years, being less than a mile from the main business corner.

A riot in mineral claim staking got under way in the afternoon.

Grand Forks new hydro plant will no doubt be a boon to any development activities that take place.

BEFORE YOU BUY ANY CAR DRIVE A FORD V-8

Know the thrill of V-8 performance — the getaway in traffic, the power on hills, the speed on the open road. Know the comfort of a roomy body and easy riding on all 4 wheels. Get behind the wheel today. Remember the Ford V-8 is the only car under $4,000 that gives you a V-8 engine.

ASK FOR DETAILS ABOUT OUR LOW DOWN-PAYMENT AND EASY TERMS

E. A. BEGERT - Ford Garage - Penticton, B.C.

WORLD'S FIRST "TEST-TUBE" TWINS

Reposing peacefully in their mother's arms (just like any other twins), Victoria and Marilyn Lauricella are quite unaware of the storm of commotion they have caused in the world of science. They are the world's first "test-tube" twins. The mother, Mrs. Lillian Lauricella, of Lawrence, L.I., had been childless for eight years. The twins were brought into the world by Dr. Frances Seymour, who at different time has officiated in connection with the birth of thirteen such "test-tube" babies. She was loath to reveal details of the experience except to say that it was accomplished by artificial means and without a major operation.

Codling Moth Found For First Time in B.C. In Peachland Cherries

JULY 19 — Codling moths have been reported by The Herald to be intoxicants and really to appreciate home brew of a lower type, but they always stuck to their apple trees in this province, up to a short time ago.

But this year, for the first time in the history of the province, the codling moth has been discovered in cherries. It is believed that this was merely an eccentricity of the worm in suddenly changing its favor to the stone fruits, and it is not feared that this will become general.

The discovery was made at Peachland.

Four Paralysis Cases At Kelowna

Three More Young People Stricken in Northern Area

SEPTEMBER 27 — Three new cases of infantile paralysis have been reported this week from Kelowna, making the total number of cases to four in that city. All three new cases were in contact with the initial one, it was reported by Dr. G.C. Paine, who was in communication with Kelowna authorities this morning.

Only the school in the South Kelowna district has been closed. Public meetings have not been shut down for adults, but children under 18 years are barred from all gatherings there.

There have been no cases reported in the South Okanagan district.

Surfacing of Main Highway From Osoyoos to Kamloops Adopted By Trade Boards

SEPTEMBER 27 — Completion of Hope-Princeton Link to Coast Also Favored

Almost the entire discussion at the first monthly dinner meeting of the Board of Trade fall session, held at the Incola Hotel on Wednesday evening, centered around the deplorable condition of B.C. Interior roads and the results of the convention of Associated Boards of Trade of the Fraser Valley and the Okanagan, held at Harrison Hot Springs Hotel on Saturday last.

Mr. H.B. Morley and Mr. W.J. Allerton, Penticton delegates to Harrison Hot Springs, reported at length to the board meeting, which was fairly well attended. The Harrison meeting was practically entirely devoted to road questions, and the possibilities of greater revenues from good roads throughout the Interior.

Bargain Excursions to Europe

THIRD CLASS ROUND TRIP AS LOW AS $110
TOURIST CLASS ROUND TRIP AS LOW AS $139
Allowing 15 days in Europe

The chance of a life-time to spend Christmas and the New Year in the Old Land.

Apply to any Steamship or Railway Agent for details, or to

CUNARD WHITE STAR LIMITED
ANCHOR-DONALDSON

CANADIAN PACIFIC STEAMSHIPS

"After a busy day there's nothing like a glass of delicious beer, such as B.C. Bud, to quiet the nerves."

"I find a little beer improves my digestion and induces sound sleep naturally and healthfully."

DRINK B.C. BUD!

Pure and wholesome malt beverages like B.C. Bud sparkling lager are carefully and scientifically brewed from only the choicest malt, hops, and yeast. Their use promotes temperance and they are healthful and satisfying.

COAST BREWERIES LTD.
VANCOUVER, B.C.

Also Brewers and Bottlers of
OLD MILWAUKEE LAGER   SILVER SPRING LAGER
ENGLISH BITTER BEER   BURTON Type ALE
XXXX INVALID STOUT

These British Columbia malt beverages are obtainable at all Government Liquor Stores.   New Low Prices.

This advertisement is not published or displayed by the Liquor Control Board or by the Government of British Columbia.

Desperate State Of Germany Seen As World Threat

Canadian Club Thrilled by Capt. Scott Lecture On Europe

The Weary Dove ———————— by A. B. Chapin

"It must be thoroughly understood that the lost lands will never be won back by soulful appeals to the good God, nor by pious trust in the League of Nations, but only by the force of arms." This statement by Adolf Hitler of Germany summed up one of the keys to the European situation as outlined to the Canadian Club on Tuesday night by Capt. H.G. Scott.

With every supper place at the large horseshoe table filled, and a number of members coming to the lecture afterwards, the world traveller, on this his second visit to Penticton, held the absorbed attention of the audience while he outlined the many facets of the German and German-Austrian position in the puzzle that is Europe today.

Hitler made this statement to his parliament within recent months with regard to the lost colonies and provinces Germany sacrificed as the price of her defeat in the World War.

Only fifteen years since the close of the last great conflict, Europe is again on the verge of another, the speaker stated. Germany, who was, prior to the last conflict, a world power, stands today a crippled nation, having lost one-seventh of her territory in Europe, one-twelfth of her population, all her colonies, and also her huge world trade, which was entirely gone at the end of the war.

As most of his hearers might know, Capt. Scott said, Adolph Hitler was not a German, but a Austrian by birth. He had neither birth nor breeding. What then was the secret of his rise, and his power? Simply that he expresses the German bitterness at defeat, and an overwhelming desire to win back the old place in world affairs.

Platform Style Known Here

To the German people, Hitler was something of a novelty as a leader. Most of the German leaders were stolid and unemotional, especially while on the platform, but Hitler was emotion personified. His speeches did not contain a great deal of real matter, having only one or two basic ideas. Roughly, these were that Germany has been badly treated, and that Germany must seek her old place in the world.

Although to the Canadian mind the whole thing might appear ridiculous, to a German the Nazi salute was a serious thing. This had now reached the stage where two persons on the street passing might raise their right hand and shout "Heil Hitler" — also, the exclamation was used in letters. It was just as if, in B.C., two strange persons, passing on the street, were to shout to each other, while holding aloft their right hand, "God save Pattullo". (Laughter.) Unfortunately, the Germans have no sense of humor, and cannot see how absurd this form of "idol worship" is.

1930~1939

Hindenburg Is Dead; Hitler Assumes His Office of President

AUGUST 2, NEUBECK, GERMANY — President Paul Von Hindenburg died at 9 o'clock this morning.

Shortly after word came from Von Hindenburg's country estate that the 86-year-old hero had died, announcement was made at Berlin that Chancellor Hitler has assumed the presidency. The cabinet went into session immediately an receipt of his death.

In a nation-wide broadcast, Paul Joseph Goebels, propaganda minister, announced that the office of Reich president will be united with that of chancellor, giving Hitler unlimited powers.

Italian official circles in Rome received news of Hindenburg's death calmly. They adopted the attitude that no outside criticism was called for.

Sincere grief and considerable apprehension over he political future of Germany was caused in British Government circles.

"The New Germany Of Hitler" Upheld In Rigorous Manner Before Kelowna Rotary Club

OCTOBER 4, KELOWNA — "The New Germany of Hitler" was the title of an address delivered to the Kelowna Rotary Club last week by J.R. Brendel, a German national who has been a great admirer of Hitlerism and who has kept in touch with current German conditions by the study of periodicals and through his many relatives still residing in Germany.

The Hitler movement, the speaker stated, considered from the point of view of its astonishingly rapid growth up to its crowning moment when its leader, Adolf Hitler, took over the reigns of government, is without a doubt one of the most characteristic and impressive events. A radical change has occurred in the inner political situation of a great country set in the heart of Europe. It is a sudden change of such truly revolutionary character that it certainly is bound to awaken lively interest in the rest of the world.

The Capone Touch

The series of political assassinations, conducted under the eye of Herr Hitler, and carried out by summary court-martial under the presidency of Herr Himmler (a most promising Fouquier-Tinville of the third Reich) establishes the extent of the gulf which separates Germany today with other western nations. Nobody particularly laments the dead Nazi leaders, but what is most ominous is the method of their passing. That the ethics of the gangster should

replace the forms of law which, as the safeguards of justice, are regarded as sacrosanct in every modern and civilized State, augurs ill for the re-establishment of international relations on a footing of good faith and good will. The sharp deterioration of Germany thus marked by internal disorder and by the recent declaration of a moratorium on its medium and long-term debts and on the service of the Dawes and Young loans, is a more positive menace to the

peace of Europe than any amount of sabre-rattling. "The cauldron," says an observer lately returned from Munich, a B.C. man, by the way, who has been living in Germany these last five years, "the cauldron is beginning to boil"; which means that the time is fast approaching when the failure of the national-Socialist regime will be marked by adventures in the foreign field. British Columbia, happily, is far removed from the pangs and fears of Europe, but no part

of the Empire, however distant from the storm-center, can afford to remain indifferent to events so big with future consequences to all the world. Curiously enough there is a link with B.C. in the late "clean up," for one of the victims, Herr Werner von Alvensleben, is a scion of that Alvo von Alvensleben who, in the palmy days before the war, was a notable figure in real estate circles in Vancouver enjoying the patronage of the All-Highest in his city lots.

King George Succumbs To Heart Weakness After Only Four Brief Days Of Illness

Bronchial Catarrh Contracted As Result Of Chill When Riding Impairs Action Of Heart And Causes Death Of Beloved Monarch

PRINCE OF WALES SUCCEEDS TO THRONE AS EDWARD VIII

Death Comes Peacefully To 70-Year-Old Sovereign

Nine days ago King George, despite wintry weather with snow on the ground and a keen wind, was riding along the roads around Sandringham, his Norfolk estate, returning with his accustomed courtesy and kindliness the greetings of the country folk, to many of whom he was a more important figure as the local squire than as the ruler of a great Empire. On Friday a small item in the dailies stated that he was confined to his room with a cold, but that court officials said it was not serious. By Saturday it was blazoned across the top of front pages that the King was showing indications of cardiac weakness, which, in the guarded language of his physicians' bulletins, "must be regarded

with some disquiet." His condition remained much the same on Sunday, while the first bulletins issued on Monday conveyed the reassuring news that he had passed a more restful night. Further bulletins gave encouragement by explanation that the appointment of a Council of State to deal with matters usually handled by the King was due rather to the likelihood of his illness being prolonged than its severity. As the day wore on, however, bulletins received by wire and posted at the Courier office told of a failure to regain strength, then at two o'clock, or 10 pm Greenwich time, came the fateful message: " The King's life is moving peacefully towards its close." The end came peacefully five minutes before midnight and the sad news was flashed immediately around the world, being received in Kelowna within a few minutes.

His Majesty was unconscious for the last hour or two of his life and he passed way as in sleep. At his beside were his devoted wife, his daughter, the Princess Royal, Countess of Harewood, and his sons, the Prince of Wales, Duke of York and Duke of Kent. The Duke of Gloucester, who was ill at Buckingham Palace, was the only member of the family unable to be present.

As the end came the Queen, who had preserved her superb self-control to the last and sat by the bedside stroking her husband's hand, burst into tears and the Prince of Wales gathered her into his arms and consoled her.

There is not interregnum in the

British monarchial system and the Prince of Wales immediately succeeded to the throne as King Edward VIII. He flew from Sandringham to London next morning to meet the Privy Council and to be proclaimed as King. The House of Lords and House of Commons met to take the oath of allegiance to the monarch and proclamation of the accession of Edward VIII, to the throne was carried out yesterday with all the traditional pageantry in the courtyard of St. James Palace at Charing Cross, at Temple Bar and at the Royal Exchange.

The body of King George was removed to the little parish church of Sandringham on Tuesday, where it lay in state until today, guarded by workers on the royal estate. His removal to London today is told in dispatches received this morning.

PENTICTON, B.C., THURSDAY, JANUARY 23, 1936

Beloved Empire Ruler Dies

The King Is Dead   **Long Live the King**

His Majesty King George V. died at Sandringham at 11:55 p.m. (Greenwich time) Monday. The end was not unexpected. The Empire probably never before felt such a sense of personal loss in the death of a monarch. King George's voice had entered the homes of millions through radio during the past two or three years.

The same agency of radio brought to Empire households the proclamation of a new King Wednesday morning when the Prince of Wales was received at the boundaries of London as King Edward the Eighth.

Nearly Two Thousand Gather To Pay Homage To His Late Majesty

Scout Hall Jammed to Overflowing - Extra Audience At School Auditorium - Simple Service Marks Penticton's Tribute To Late Monarch Who Had Been Buried In Old Country But Few Hours Before

Never before in the history of Penticton has so large a gathering attended a single function, held indoors, as completely filled the Scout Hall, and partially filled the Senator Shatford Auditorium on Tuesday afternoon. Such was the fitting tribute paid by local citizenry in honoring a dead King, and a splendid gentleman.

Simple, yet sincere, as the man the service was honoring, was the Memorial Service for the late King George Fifth, who the same day had been laid at rest with his fathers in the Motherland over the sea. Although there was such little time for preparation, the service did not lack dignity for that reason. Rather, the service was the more

impressive because all extraneous details, all unnecessary ceremony was omitted. Those who arranged the service did it splendidly, people remarked on every hand, as the huge gathering poured out of the two halls and wended a quiet way homeward.

A public address system had been fitted up, so that those in the Senator Shatford Auditorium found themselves an integral part of the main service held in the larger Scouts Hall. It would be impossible to accurately estimate the number which thronged the latter building, but it is thought it approached 1500, with about 200 or more on the lower floor of the Auditorium and the stage filled with singers.

Rebels threaten Madrid

A Fascist revolution is sweeping across Spain and threatens to oust the Social Government. Apparently having seized control of all Spanish Morocco and the ports on the Mediterranean, Fascist Monarchist forces are threatening to bomb Madrid. British warships have been rushed to the scenes of rioting along the Mediterranean Sea to protect British nationals. Led by Jose Antonia Primo de Rivera (above) the revolt has spread to all centers indicated in the above map by black dots. Below is a typical scene of disturbance in Madrid as loyal troops attempt to quell a riot.

Loaded Pistol Presented at King Edward

LONDON, JULY 16, 1936 — A man presented a loaded revolver at King Edward as he rode on horseback at the head of the parade to present colours to the Brigade of Guards at Hyde Park today.

Scotland Yard has issued the following official statement:

"A man pushed his way to the front of the crowd near the Wellington Arch on Constitution Hill. Exactly what happened has not yet been ascertained, but a revolver fell in the roadway between the King and the troops. The man was promptly arrested. The revolver was found to be loaded with five cartridges."

LONDON, JULY 16. — Sir John Simon, Home Secretary, informed the House of Commons today of the incident in grave tones, stating: "The whole House will be profoundly thankful that the risk to which His Majesty was exposed was so promptly averted."

The London papers state that the man pointed a pistol at the King and that a woman dressed in grey immediately knocked it from his hand. The Duke of York, riding behind the King, saw the whole affair.

FEBRUARY 20, 1936

New Dominion cabinet

This is the first picture to be taken of the Cabinet of the Right Hon. W.L. Mackenzie King, new Prime Minister of Canada. Seated: (left to right), Hon. Fernand Rinfret, Secretary of State; Hon. J.C. Elliott, Postmaster General; Hon. P.J.A. Cardin, Minister of Public Works; Hon. T.A. Crerar, Minister of Interior, Mines and Immigration (to be merged in Department of Natural Resources); Rt. Hon. W.L. Mackenzie King, Prime Minister and Secretary of State for External Affairs; Hon. Ernest Lapointe, Minister of Justice; Hon. Charles Dunning, Minister of Finance; Hon. W.D. Euler, Minister of Trade and Commerce; Hon. Ian Mackenzie, Minister of National Defence.
Standing: (left to right), Hon. C.D. Howe, Minister of Railways and Canals and Marine (to be merged into Department of Transportation); Hon. J.E. Michaud, Minister of Fisheries; Hon. C.G. Power, Minister of Pensions and National Health; Hon. J.L. Iisley, Minister of National Revenue; Hon. N. McL. Rogers, Minister of Labor; Hon. J.G. Gardiner, Minister of Agriculture. (Hon. R. Dandurand, Minister without portfolio and Government Leader in the Senate was absent when this photo was taken.) Those Ministers seated in front row were members of the previous Liberal Administration.

New Playhouse Has Everything

No Effort Spared To Provide Perfect Entertainment In New Amusement Center For Entire District — Finest Equipment Aids Presentations

The Capitol Theater, of Penticton, the most modern theater in any community of the same size in North America, opens its doors under the management of J.H. Black and begins a new era in the amusement life of the municipality.

In this, the latest edition to the Famous Player string of picture houses, no expense has been spared to provide the people of Penticton and district, and their visiting friends, with the finest that modern ingenuity and science can devise. In two sections, seating and lighting, there will be innovations for the entire North American

Continent. In every other department, modernistic decorations and up-to-date equipment will play their part in providing Penticton with a show house to which it may point with pride.

Constructed of re-inforced concrete, the new Capitol Theater raises its imposing facade on Main Street, adjoining the Three Gables Hotel, and, with its dazzling white exterior illuminated by a flashing Neon sign, adds greatly to the appearance of downtown Penticton.

Modernity has been kept as the guiding feature in the construction, and decoration, and the entire building, inside

and out, has been designed with this motif in view. No chance has been lost to take advantage of science's latest discoveries to create an impression that will be a lasting one to all who visit the theater.

New lighting, the latest in projection and seating equipment, sound absorbing wall board, twenty degree angle floor, luxurious furnishings, these are just a few of the features that go to make up the Capitol. To those interested in its construction, it means the culmination of months of effort.

As a result of the careful planning it will be possible for a

member of the audience, no matter in what portion of the building he or she may be seated, to get a clear, undistorted reception of sound, and to have a clear view of the stage.

When the first scenes of "Private Number", starring Loretta Young and Robert Taylor flash onto the new screen, they will do so after having passed through the most up-to-date equipment money can buy and the voices of the stars will be heard through the finest sound reproduction facilities that have ever been installed in any theater.

Soft, luxurious carpets and drapes will add their own note of elegance to the surroundings and will create an atmosphere that will be more that welcome to Penticton amusement seekers.

The lighting fixtures, embodying a radically new idea in illumination, will be the object of wonder and curiosity. Their exact construction is a matter of patented secret, but their appearance and the addition they make to the general effect leaves nothing to be desired.

The new home of the first class theater entertainment in Penticton would well grace any city in the world and does credit to the organization and individuals who have made it possible.

Crowds queue up on the 300 block of Main Street, Penticton for tickets for a Capitol Theatre movie c.1936.

Photo courtesy of the Penticton Museum

Huge Crowd At Premiere

First Audience Fills New Theatre – Addresses by Reeve Morley and G.A.B. Macdonald

A capacity house greeted the premiere perform-ance of the new Capitol Theatre in Penticton on Monday night. Prior to the opening of the doors the patrons of Penticton's new motion picture house stretched along the side-walk for a considerable dis-tance, while parking space for autos was at a premium.

Reeve H.B. Morley was called to the stage by Manager Harry Black after the audience had been seated. In his remarks Penticton's first citizen said he considered the Famous Players had shown great faith in the future of Penticton in erecting this theatre. They had been a far-sighted organization for many years, showing shrewd judgment in locating their hous-es. Evidently they considered Penticton had a great future, for otherwise they would not have erected this splendid new build-ing at such great cost. Some per-sons might have criticized the company for spending this amount of money. But certainly they knew what they were doing, and their confidence in Penticton must be based upon a concrete analysis of the commu-nity, the district, and its future.

"Addition to Penticton"

Following the address by Reeve Morley, G.A.G. Macdonald, president of the Penticton Board of Trade was called upon. "This will be a great addition to Penticton," said Mr. Macdonald, "and one of which we can justly feel proud. It must mean that the tourist trade will have a great place in the future of Penticton, the Board president indicated, for the Famous Players

Company to invest so much money in the new addition to the life of the community."

It would be a pleasure to attend this theatre, said Mr. Macdonald, where the air was clean, and where it would never be either too warm or too cold. Continuing his remarks, Mr. Macdonald referred to a pam-phlet issued by the Famous Players announcing the new theatre in which they called the Okanagan the "Garden of Eden of Canada." Well, it could be noticed that we had, likewise with the original garden, some difficulty over the apple. This sally was greeted with laughter, as were further witty remarks from the President of the Board.

Fine Reproduction

Then, finally, the lights were dimmed, and the sound came on. There were some gasps, and considerable amazement at the accuracy of this and the clarity of tone.

When the first house had poured out of the building, these comprising it found another long line, patiently awaiting entry to the second showing of the films. For there was not only one good house on Monday night, but two. As many of those comprising these audiences came from out of town, it is pos-sible the new theatre will draw considerably from the outlying areas, thus providing citizens in the smaller communities with first class entertainment.

Try This On Roller Skates

A tap-dance on roller skates, with a gay song accompaniment! That is the novelty presented in this number by Ginger Rogers and Fred Astaire, here caught in action by the camera, in the screen musical hit, "Shall We Dance," for which George and Ira Gershwin wrote the music and lyrics. Produced for RKO Radio by Pandro S. Berman, this is the sixth in Fred and Ginger's long line of smash screen successes in which their dancing and singing are outstanding features. Showing at the Capitol Theatre Friday and Saturday.

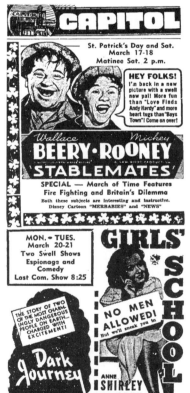
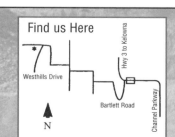
1930~1939

Sports World

Olympic Athletes Sail For Berlin

Managers of Canada's Olympic fortunes, P. J. Mulqueen, of Toronto, chairman of the Canadian Olympic Committee, Abbie Coo, of Winnipeg, manager of the track and field team and W. Fry, of Dunnville, Ontario, president of the Amateur Athletic Union of Canada, photographed on board the Duchess of Bedford as the Canadian contingent sailed from Montreal. Below are three charming members of the Canadian Olympic squad enjoying the sun on the deck. They are Roxy Adkins, Toronto; Hilda Cameron, Toronto; and Betty Taylor, of Hamilton.

Jesse Owens shown in action in a 200-meter preliminary heat at the 1936 Summer Olympics in Berlin. Owens was viewed as something of an oddity by the German crowds. Not only was he a brilliant sprinter, but he was the best long jumper in the world, as well. And, oh yes, there was one more thing.

GEORGE VI IS NAMED SUCCESSOR

THE VERNON NEWS
THE LEADING JOURNAL OF THE FAMOUS OKANAGAN VALLEY

VOL. XLV, No. 31.—Whole Number 2377.   VERNON, B. C., THURSDAY, DECEMBER 10, 1936 $2.50 Payable in Advance

THE WEATHER

	Max.	Min.
Dec. 2	39	29
Dec. 3	32	24
Dec. 4	33	20
Dec. 5	16	12
Dec. 6	19	13
Dec. 7	25	14
Dec. 8	27	14

Snow, 15.9 inches

1930~1939

Edward VIII Abdicates Throne

Announcement of Abdication Made In House Of Commons Is King's Irrevocable Decision

Days of Suspense End In Dramatic Scene In The British Parliament

"The King has abdicated."

These words that may echo and re-echo down through the centuries as the most momentous in the history of the greatest Empire the world has ever known were uttered by the speaker, before the crowded House of Commons in London this afternoon, Thursday.

As the climax came after days and nights of nerve-racking suspense, constituting the gravest national crisis since the Great War, British subjects throughout the world realized that the worst had happened and that King Edward VIII, once the idol of the world, has chosen the love of Mrs. Wallis Simpson to the British throne.

In his place is George VI, by the Grace of God, of Great Britain, of Ireland, and of the Dominions beyond the Seas, King, Emperor of India, Defender of the Faith. With him reigns his consort, Queen Elizabeth, whom he married April 26, 1923.

Abdication will be followed by a meeting of the Accession Council to which representatives of the Dominions will be invited. The new King will then take the Oath of Accession which will be followed by legislation in Great Britain and all the Dominions to confirm the accession of the new King to bar any issue of Edward VIII and Mrs. Simpson from the throne, and relieve him of any disabilities under the Royal Marriages Act, which would otherwise forbid him marrying without the consent of the sovereign.

It is from this direction that the first trouble in this fast-moving drama may come. The present Irish Free State government may follow its avowed intention of refusing to pass any legislation of this kind, not as any personal reflection on the King but upon a policy of non-loyalty to the British Crown.

It is thought that Great Britain's legislation may contain financial provisions recognizing King Edward's 25 years of service to the nation.

It became evident on Tuesday that Mr. Baldwin had received Edward's decision and that he had withheld it for a threefold reason. First, to allow the King the opportunity of an eleventh hour change of heart; second, to give time for communication with the Dominions; and third, to prepare the masses for the blow that was to come.

From the skein of King Edward's romance has been woven a momentous future for a fair-haired little girl. Princess Elizabeth, 10 years old and known as the Little Sweetheart of the Nation. She becomes the heir presumptive. Only the birth of a son to the new King and Queen can come between her and the British throne. Immensely popular, she is a typical British child and vigorous training for Queenship will be her lot from now on.

It is believed the date of the coronation will not be altered.

This is the first time in British history that the sovereign has voluntarily abdicated. The last King to abdicate was James II.

King's Statement Read In House

This afternoon Prime Minister Stanley Baldwin appeared at the Bar of the British House of Commons and handed to the Speaker a statement from His Majesty King Edward.

In part, it was as follows:

"After long and anxious consideration I have decided to renounce the throne to which I succeeded upon the death of my father and I am now communicating this my final and irrevocable decision.

"Realizing the gravity of the step I can only hope that I will have the understanding of the people in the decision I have taken. I will not enter now into a discussion of my private feelings but beg them to remember that the burden constantly on the shoulders of a sovereign can only be borne in circumstances different from those in which I now find myself.

"I conceive I am not overlooking the duty placed in the forefront of public interest when I declare that I am conscious I can no longer discharge the task efficiently and satisfactorily to myself. I have therefore executed the following instrument:

" 'I, Edward VIII, King of Great Britain and Ireland and the Dominions beyond the Seas, Defender of the Faith, Emperor of India, do hereby declare my irrevocable determination to renounce the throne for myself and my descendants forever and desire that effect be given to this decision immediately.

" 'To this I have set my hand this tenth day of December. My execution of this declaration has been witnessed by my three brothers, the Duke of York, the Duke of Gloucester and the Duke of Kent.' "

"I deeply appreciate the spirit which actuated appeals to me before I took this decision," the King's statement continued. "I have pondered over them but my mind is made up. Moreover, further delay cannot but be injurious to the people I have tried to serve both as prince and king. Their future happiness and prosperity is the constant wish of my heart. I take my leave of them in the hope that this course is the best for the stability of the throne and Empire and for the happiness of the people.

"I am deeply sensible of the consideration which has been shown to me both before and after accession to the throne, and I hope that the same consideration will be shown to my successor.

"I am most anxious that there be no delay in giving effect to this instrument so that my lawful successor, my brother, the Duke of York, should ascend the throne."

King George VI,(left to right) Princess Elizabeth, Queen Elizabeth (Queen Mother), Princess Margaret taken in 1937, the year after King George ascended to the throne.

World's First Surviving Quintuplets

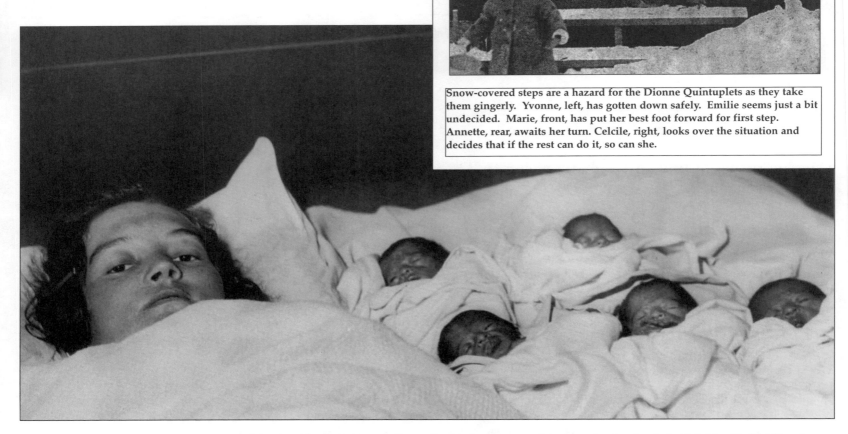

Snow-covered steps are a hazard for the Dionne Quintuplets as they take them gingerly. Yvonne, left, has gotten down safely. Emilie seems just a bit undecided. Marie, front, has put her best foot forward for first step. Annette, rear, awaits her turn. Celcile, right, looks over the situation and decides that if the rest can do it, so can she.

Elzire Dionne, at home in Corbeil, Ontario, with her five identical girls - Cecile, Emilie, Marie, Yvonne and Annette, shortly after their birth May 28, 1934. Born two months premature and weighing less than 2 pounds each, they are the first known surviving quintuplets.

APRIL 2, 1936

Father Appeals To King

Mr. A. Dionne, father of the famous quintuplets, has written a personal letter to King Edward VII, requesting that his five pretty little daughters be given to his care rather than let them remain under the control of the government. When the girls were just infants, the Premier of Ontario issued a court order to remove them from their parents care. The Ontario Government has since put them on display for as many as 6,000 people a day at "Quintland", where people can watch them play behind a one-way screen.

No Word Yet On Earhart

SAN FRANCISCO, Cal — No trace has yet been found of the round-the-world flyer, Amelia Earhart, and her co-pilot, Fred Noonan. The search Wednesday turned to the Phoenix Islands, 300 miles south of Howland Island, after 100,000 square miles in the vicinity of the latter had been carefully searched by the coast-guard cutter, "Itasca," and by a mine sweeper.

The U.S. navy Wednesday night officially denied the truth of a report that the U.S.S. "Colorado" had contacted Miss Earhart.

George Putnam, new York publisher, waiting here for news of his wife, said that if she were to die she preferred to "go out" this way.

Lost in the south Pacific with her navigator Capt. Fred Noona, Miss Earhart has now been given up for lost. The search cost the United States Navy $4,000.00.

Health Board To Enforce Measles Regulations Here

Prosecution For Delinquents – Elementary School Opening Postponed For Week –

APRIL 1, 1937 —

The Penticton board of health has decided to issue definite orders barring all children of 12 years and under from public gatherings, forbidding children 15 and under to leave or enter houses where there are known cases of measles, and retarding the opening of the elementary schools for an additional week.

Police have been instructed to enforce the orders, a special patrol will be appointed to keep watch on homes with known measles cases, and prosecutions will be instituted against anyone found breaking the regulations.

This was the outcome of a special session of the council on Tuesday morning, when the measles question came up for considerable discussion, as did the action of the newly-appointed medical health officer, Dr. J.C. Parmley, in issuing restrictions on children 12 years and under on Thursday, March 25, without the knowledge or consent of the council.

When the advertisement appeared, a section had been added, forbidding the attendance of children under 12 years of age at public gatherings. This was a complete surprise to the council, said individual members on Tuesday morning.

No effort had been made to enforce the regulation and Manager Harry Black, of the Capitol Theatre, appeared at the Tuesday morning meeting and asked that some definite policy be followed. He reported that he had lost considerable sums over the weekend through the confusion that the advertisement had caused.

B.C. Bracewell, municipal clerk, took strong exception to the procedure that had been followed by the medical health officer. He explained that in certain church programs in which he had been interested, children under 12 years of age had been eliminated from the Easter services. Then children of the same age were observed to be attending the services and the theatre.

Cases in the municipality are on the increase. One hundred and eighty pupils were away from the elementary schools on Wednesday and 225 on Thursday. On Saturday 30 measles cards were put up by Mr. Drake as sanitary officer, bringing the total to 80, and another 20 cases were reported over the weekend. There are now over 100 known cases.

Question of enforcement of regulations was discussed and it was agreed unanimously that, if the regulations were put into effect, prosecutions would be made in the cases of delinquents.

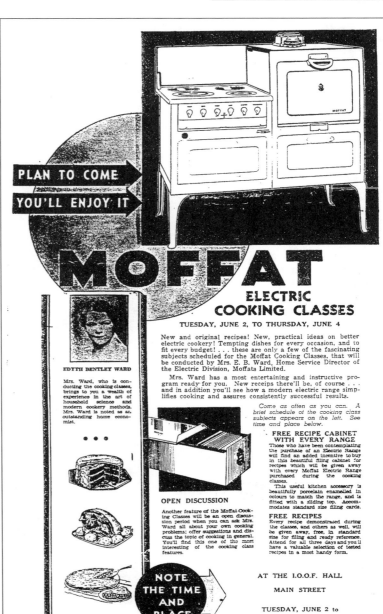

PLAN TO COME
YOU'LL ENJOY IT

MOFFAT

ELECTRIC COOKING CLASSES

TUESDAY, JUNE 2, TO THURSDAY, JUNE 4

New and original recipes! New, practical ideas on better electric cookery! Tempting dishes for every occasion, and to fit every budget! . . . these are only a few of the fascinating subjects scheduled for the Moffat Cooking Classes, that will be conducted by Mrs. E. B. Ward, Home Service Director of the Electric Division, Moffats Limited.

Mrs. Ward has a most entertaining and instructive program ready for you. New receips there'll be, of course . . . and in addition you'll see how a modern electric range simplifies cooking and assures consistently successful results.

Come as often as you can. A brief schedule of the cooking class subjects appears on the left. See time and place below.

FREE RECIPE CABINET WITH EVERY RANGE
Those who have been contemplating the purchase of an Electric Range will find an added incentive to buy in this beautiful filing cabinet for recipes which will be given away with every Moffat Electric Range purchased during the cooking classes.

This useful kitchen accessory is beautifully porcelain enamelled in colours to match the range, and is fitted with a sliding top. Accommodates standard size filing cards.

FREE RECIPES
Every recipe demonstrated during the classes, and others as well, will be given away, free, in standard size for filing and ready reference. Attend for all three days and you'll have a valuable selection of tested recipes in a most handy form.

EDYTH BENTLEY WARD

Mrs. Ward, who is conducting the cooking Classes, brings to you a wealth of experience in the art of household science and modern cookery methods. Mrs. Ward is noted as an outstanding home economist.

OPEN DISCUSSION

Another feature of the Moffat Cooking Classes will be an open discussion period when you can ask Mrs. Ward all about your own cooking problems; offer suggestions and discuss the topic of cooking in general. You'll find this one of the most interesting of the cooking class features.

NOTE THE TIME AND PLACE

AT THE I.O.O.F. HALL

MAIN STREET

TUESDAY, JUNE 2 to

THURSDAY, JUNE 4

Daily from 9:15 a.m. to 11:30 a.m.

L. A. HOWSON

PHONE 259   PENTICTON, B.C.   MAIN STREET

POLICE WILL RECRUIT MEN

AUGUST 31, 1939 — According to an order received from the Commissioner, B.C. police will act as recruiting officers in each district. This is following the practice carried out in 1914-18, when the officers performed a similar duty. The wire reads:

"The district O.C. of Military District No. 11 advises that recruits are required for the following permanent units: Royal Canadian Artillery, Royal Canadian Engineers, Royal Canadian Ordinance Corps. You might see that this information is give proper publicity in your area, and that if recruits present themselves to your office, decide upon their suitability, and if it is felt they fulfill requirements, arrange for local representatives of the Royal Army Medical Corps to make necessary physical examination. When this is done, and the men have passed, advise this office, when we will communicate with the officers commanding the units concerned with regard to transportation. It may be that local boys desiring to enter the police would care to consider the foregoing. – Commissioner."

B.C. Dragoons Send Troops To Aid In Canada Guard Work

AUGUST 31, 1939 — "C" Squadron Men, From Summerland, Penticton, Sent to Northern Parts of Province As Canada Moves To Protect Vital Points From Attack Or Sabotage.

Note Exchange Between England, Germany Halts-Situation Becomes Grave

Evacuation Of London Proceeds As All Europe Tenses Itself For Catastrophe —Vatican Issues Appeal For Peace As Hitler Claims British, Polish Mobilization Has Aggravated Situation

Warclouds which had lifted during the past few days have grown ominously darker within the last few hours, as Europe becomes an armed camp, ready for any eventuality.

Claiming that Britain's mobilization of her fleet and partial mobilization in Poland had increased tension in the crisis, Hitler, late Thursday, halted diplomatic exchanges with Britain.

It was made plain, however, that negotiations had not been completely broken off.

Meanwhile, with practically complete mobilization in force, Britain prepared to evacuate millions of her people from congested areas.

A warning from the Vatican that the present situation could not be endured longer than until Sunday was addressed to five nations,

incorporated in a peace appeal.

Before Hitler broke off diplomatic exchange with Britain he had been preparing an answer to the latest British note which, it is understood, merely asked him for further elucidation of some of his former points. Foreign Minister Von Ribentrop had already communicated orally to British Ambassador Sir Neville Henderson what the reply would be.

Speed Mobilization

In the meantime, Britain sped her mobilization and precautions. The royal navy was ordered fully mobilized and all regular army and supplement reserves were called up.

Evacuation of three million children, women, invalids and aged persons from congested metropolitan areas in London, Glasgow,

Birmingham and other large cities started early today (Friday), states a report received by The Herald by special wire, just a few moments before going to press.

Each child carried a gas mask and rations. Country homes were ordered to receive and keep them on payment by the government of $2.30 per child per week.

Exchange Closed

Owing to transportation tie-up, the London Stock Exchange is closed and will remain closed until the evacuation has been completed.

In Poland, additional mobilization increased the army to more than two million men. Communiqués charged that German patrols had crossed the border at several points.

For a time, all telegraph and telephone communications between the continent and London, between London and America and between the continent and America was cut off. When it was resumed, British censorship of transatlantic news and commercial wires was started.

Stop Press

BERLIN — Germany has submitted a 16-point offer to Poland for settlement of their dispute, it was announced early today (Friday).

Point one demands the immediate return of Danzig to Germany, and point two said from Marienwerder to Grudziasz Kulm and Bydgoszc, is to be subject to a plebiscite to determine whom it belongs.

Later developments indicate Hitler's 16 points were submitted to Poland before Britain sent her latest reply to the Fuehrer's note. The demands were insistent that Poland send an envoy to Berlin to discuss the terms of settlement. They declared he must reach Berlin by August 30, now past. Poland, it is understood, agreed to meet Germany on neutral ground but not in Berlin. Hitler's 16 points have been communicated to Britain and France.

PARIS — After an urgent 21-hour meeting, the French cabinet unanimously re-affirmed its promises to support Poland if attacked.

LONDON — Food rationing has been ordered by the government.

All Walks of Life In Kelowna Affected By War Declaration

War Welcomed As Relief From Uncertainty — Men Leave For Home Guard Duty — Business Affected When Orders For Large Pieces Of Merchandise Are Cancelled — News Followed Closely — No Civil Disturbances Reported —

Sugar, Flour Hoarding Evident

Effects of the declaration of war by Great Britain and the uncertainty of the situation late last week before Prime Minister Chamberlain's historic broadcast early Sunday morning, have reacted in may ways in the Okanagan Valley although far from the scene of the actual crisis. So close is the world brought together by means of fast transportation, wireless and other modern sciences that the war in which Hitler has engulfed Europe and Britain has been felt keenly here in many respects.

On Sunday a general feeling of relief was evident. The long strain of uncertainty was ended and the knowledge that we were at war was considered better than the uncertainty and the unexpressed fear that we might not fulfill our pledges to Poland.

The declaration of war by Britain was received quietly and with satisfaction. There were no outward demonstration, no cheers, no parades. On Saturday there had been some fear that Britain might disregard her Polish pledges and let Hitler do his will with that country.

This was changed on Sunday and a quiet confidence that right was on our side and that British arms would eventually triumph.

Business Affected

Uniforms appeared suddenly on the street and have now been accepted as commonplace. Station scenes recalling '14 were enacted as friends and relatives bid what was hoped was only a temporary farewell to militiamen who were leaving for home guard duty.

Business was affected with truck, automobile and refrigerator orders being temporarily cancelled. This reaction has been caused by many people temporarily adopting a wait and see policy. Many local residents receive money from Britain and fear that this regular income might be curtailed or stopped altogether. In the meantime, they decided to preserve their resources.

Germans Taken Into Custody

Two Men From Osoyoos, Ten From Vernon, Reported Picked Up

The Royal Canadian Mounted Police commenced action at Osoyoos on Tuesday, September 5, when they took Rudolph Hentschel and Heinrich Schalge into custody. The two remained at the provincial police office overnight and were taken to Vancouver on Wednesday morning. They will be interned at Vancouver for the time being. Certain actions taken by these men for some time past has led to their arrest. They have both been active in German organizations, Hentschel being leader of the "Strength Through Joy" league, while Schalge was leader of the Canadian Society for German Culture (the Bund). The arrests were made in the late afternoon of Tuesday, based on the records of the two men over the past several months. Ten men, it is understood, were picked up in Vernon and transported to the Coast.

OLIVER — Rumor has been running rampant during the past few days that the German population at Osoyoos has made a run on the Canadian Bank of Commerce at Oliver due to the international situation. Although there is some truth in this inasmuch as there were numerous pay cheques cashed on Saturday and also advances to growers from various packing houses, the "run" was certainly not due entirely to matters relative to international affairs. Ready cash at the bank has been depleted before, due to a similar situation, that is, a large payroll and amounts paid to growers. Authoritative reports indicate that more money was deposited by Germans resident at Osoyoos and Oliver than was withdrawn.

1930~1939

Claim Hitler Will March

"Peril Of War Imminent" Says Chamberlain - Think Nazis To Strike At Once

"Britain faces the imminent peril of war." Prime Minister Chamberlain told the House of Commons in London this morning, just before he was given full war powers over all activities of the nation.

"Britain will not back down from her pledge to Poland under any circumstances," Foreign Minister Lord Halifax told the world in a message broadcast over shortwave radio at noon.

It is the considered opinion of the most competent military observers in the world that Hitler is ready to march on Poland at any moment.

Poland Mobilizes

Poland officially began mobilization this morning, after she had thrown a division of troops around the free city of Danzig, presumably to meet with any force, any move by Germany to occupy the city.

"If Britain is called upon to fight, it will not be fighting for Poland, but to preserve the safety of all the peoples of the world," said Chamberlain.

Ratification of the Russo-Nazi anti-aggression pact today is felt to have removed Russia as a likely combatant if war comes. If Russia does not field their armies, the armies of the opposing side would be fairly evenly matched, and observers have ventured the opinion that the British Empire would be fighting for its very life.

Hitler's demand for a free hand in Europe and his statement to Neville Henderson, British Ambassador to Berlin, that any country which interfered would be to blame for the ensuing war, have raised a storm of indignation in the Old Country.

English Troops in France

British War Forces Land On Continent - Rhineland Industrial Centers Hit

Belgian News Sources Report Rioting In Cologne and Other German Towns As Food Shortage Makes Itself Felt Throughout Reich - Rumor Mussolini To Propose Peace Move

Early Thursday morning dispatches from Europe were highlighted by the announcement from Paris that British troops had landed in France and were assisting the French in their drive on the Seigfried line… Swiss sources report extensive French and British air raids on the Rhineland with thousands of bombs being dropped on industrial centers… Neutral observers express the belief that Hitler will make peace overtures through Mussolini as soon as Poland is subjugated… Berlin announces that the Bremen has reached a friendly port and will remain there… The German consul on the Pacific U.S. Coast and Hitler's former company commander during the World War, resigned from his exclusive club Wednesday when 161 members signed a petition stating that if he did not do so, they would…

A Norwegian vessel reports sighting a German sub off Key West, Florida… Flour and other staple foods have risen sharply in price in the United States and shortages are reported in some centers… Belgian reports state that there is much industrial unrest in adjacent German cities with rioting reported in Cologne and other centers. Workers are complaining of the poor food… Krakow is reported as captured but the Poles are said to be standing firm outside Warsaw and neutral observers express the belief that the Poles are prepared to fight a major engagement along these lines… Swiss reports state that a German cruiser was sunk during a British air raid on the mouth of the Kiel canal… German bombs fell in Lithuania… Col. J. C. Ralston of Montreal, has been appointed minister of finance succeeding Hon. C. Dunning who is in ill-health. Ralston was formerly minister of defence in a former King administration…. The first B.C. war casualty was a pilot of the R.A.F. whose home was at Qualicum Beach. His parents were advised by the British war office on Wednesday that he had died on active service… Although Berlin denies there is any fighting on the western front, the first casualties reached Paris Wednesday night… Swiss reports state that French troops have entered the outskirts of the German city of Saarbrucken… The Swiss also state that over 300 French planes were engaged in one raid on the Saar mining area… Polish reports claim that 30 Polish planes successfully bombed Berlin Wednesday and returned without casualties… British sources report the same incident… Mahatma Ghandi has sent a peace plea to Hitler and a pledge of loyalty to Britain… The French are reported as having taken the first line of pillboxes of the Seigfried line and are advancing steadily into German territory… Poles are still holding a munitions dump in Danzig harbor. It was against them that the first shots of the war were fired.

Drive into the Millenium...

Great deals on new Volkswagens at least 'til the end of the century.

(Not as much of a selling point as it used to be)

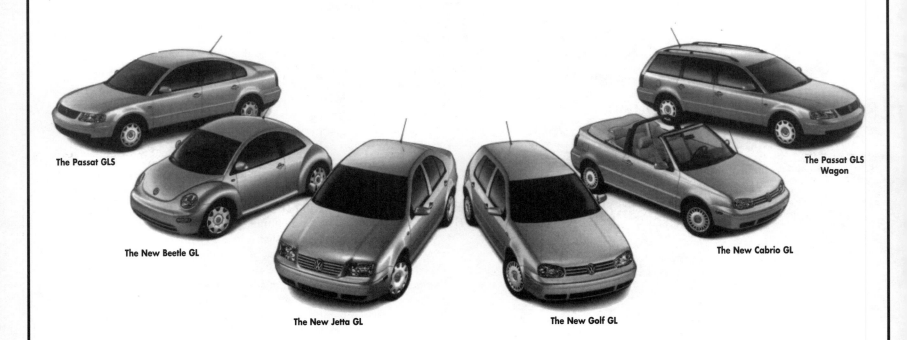

The Passat GLS

The New Beetle GL

The New Jetta GL

The New Golf GL

The New Cabrio GL

The Passat GLS Wagon

Mervyn Motors is holding a Millennium celebration with the whole family of cars, you're bound to find something that fits. So, come down for a test drive, lease or purchase.

Mervyn Motors proudly serving the Okanagan Valley since 1950 offering quality products, value and service.

Drivers wanted.®

A DECADE
IN REVIEW

1940 ~ 1949

WANTED!
MEN TO FIGHT FOR FREEDOM!

Get into the battle against Hitlerism—Enlist Now!

This is Canada's fight—and YOU are Canada. Everything for which you have worked and planned—your life, your home—are threatened by the fiendish attacks of the Huns and though we toil in the factories to produce weapons with which to crush them, these weapons are useless without MEN.

The Canadian Active Army requires men for Artillery, Engineers, Signals, Armoured Cars, Tanks, Infantry, Transport and Supply, Medical, Ordnance and other branches of the Service. The Army is prepared to teach many trades, and to train you to efficiently handle Canada's weapons of war.

Go to your nearest District Recruiting Office. Find out about these Units; how they work, what they do. See just where *you'll* fit in. See where any particular skill you possess can best be utilized. Then join up for *ACTION*.

Apply to nearest DISTRICT RECRUITING OFFICE
or any local Armory.

You are wanted NOW!
for ACTIVE SERVICE

RATES OF PAY IN THE RANKS

$1.30 per Day with Board, Lodging, Clothing, Medical and Dental care provided. EXTRA: (1) Rates varying from 25¢ to 75¢ per day for skilled tradesmen while employed. (2) Dependent Allowances in Cash: $35 to wife, $12 each per month for 2 children — only 3 dependents per soldier.

DEPARTMENT OF NATIONAL DEFENCE
CANADA

War Long and Costly

Hon. J. L. Ralston, Minister Of Finance, Recently Before The Canadian Club Of Toronto, Gave A Convincing Exposition Of The Subject: "Government And Business In Wartime"

It was an exceptionally able address and a straight statement from a member of the Cabinet whose energy and ability have been expropriated by the government for the management of war finances.

Colonel Ralston explained the operations of the various control boards set up in a way to leave no doubt of the wisdom and necessity of the steps taken, and even dealt with taxation in a manner calculated to make the public almost like the imports levied for war purposes. There was an indisputable weight of sincerity behind his interpretations.

Above all, his speech presented the economic and financial side of the war effort in a clear light. Why was there, apparently, so little to show for the vast sums of money involved, compared with the last war? The effort then was represented almost by manpower. A division in the present war costs twice as much, largely due to the amount of mechanized equipment. Instead of two light cruisers and fifteen hundred men in the naval

service, we now have six thousand officers and men, six destroyers and a flotilla leader, five naval mine-sweepers and thirty auxiliary craft.

Forty million dollars are being spent on this branch in the first year, compared with less than four million in 1914. There was no Canadian Airforce in the Great War; this time there are more than eight thousand officers and men in the defence of both coasts, equipped with flying boats, bomber reconnaissance machines, fast single-seater fighters. An estimate of Canada's share of cost in the first full year of the air training scheme is one hundred million dollars.

Up to September First the army will have cost $197,000,000; the navy, about $40,000,000; the air force about $88,000,000 and the air training scheme about $50,000,000.

From a money point of view we cannot fail to realize that we are at war. During the first full fiscal year, ending March 31st, 1941, Colonel Ralston estimates, the cost will be $500,000,000. It is a stu-

pendous sum for a country like Canada, virtually doubling the peacetime expenditures of the Federal Government. Nor can funds be borrowed, from Britain or the United States, as in the last war.

This vast money undertaking in itself invites sober thought, but the Canadian people are not seeking a way of escape. Their honor and the integrity of their country are at stake. In thinking it over they must also give heed to Col. Ralston's warning that there is a long war ahead. "I think," he said, "we should strangle on sight those twin offspring of wishful thinking which get in our way and hinder our effort. One of these is the idea that the enemy is likely to collapse and that therefore the task will be easy; the other is that an early peace will be negotiated and the war will be short. I am convinced that no more dangerous fallacies and no more subtle menaces to aggressive war effort could be imagined."

It is not a "phony" war, and Canada's part in it is not "phony".

Recruiting In This District Exceeds Expectations As Men Answer Empire Call

Estimate Valley Has Sent Total Of 500 Men Since Start Of War — Many Leaving Jobs To Aid Struggle

Swelling the total of men that have already left the Okanagan, recruiting in Penticton has been carried on at record-breaking rate in the local Armoury. It is estimat-

ed that more than 500 men have left this valley since the commencement of hostilities.

Men from all parts of the district and also some from Coast points have been pouring into the big Nanaimo Avenue building for the past few days. Large contingents left on Monday, Tuesday and Wednesday nights. Crowds of people flocked to the C.P.R. station on each night to join in the send-off

given the troops.

Three local bands participated in the farewell at the depot. The Penticton Band was on hand each night, playing a number of patriotic selections and marches. The Canadian Legion Pipe Band played on Tuesday night, and the Sea Cadets Band on Wednesday. Every recruit leaving Penticton was given cigarettes by the Penticton branch of the Canadian Legion.

1940~1949

Inside Germany

Seven Lean Years Have Left the Country's Cupboards Almost as Bare as Mother Hubbard's. Already a Long Way on Road to Inflation.

By Wilson Woodside

The Nazis are amusing themselves these days broadcasting to the world that Canada is having an election on whether to stay in the war, that South Africa is on the verge of leaving the Empire, that India is seething with discontent, and England itself overrun with Irish revolutionary bombers. The Empire, in fact, is on the verge of breaking up-just as it was at the beginning of the last war.

Supposing we in our turn take a look inside Germany - but on the condition that if I find some serious difficulties there you won't immediately jump to the conclusion that she is on her last legs. She isn't. She can still put up a

terrific scrap, just as she could by the Spring of '18. But symptoms of her final collapse are also just as evident as they were by early 1916, or certainly mid-1917.

We have examined in other articles of this series Germany's supplies of iron, oil and other vital raw materials of war. There is another war material - Dr. Schacht once said that it was the most important of all - which we didn't mention. That is money. Germany's monetary situation is badly deteriorated.

Before the last war a German mark was equal to an English shilling, or almost twenty-five cents. Even up to the last few months of the war its value hadn't been shaken. Germany still held half a billion dollars worth of gold in her Treasury and still had credit with the neutrals. After the Armistice the mark began to slip and in 1923 the German Government, to defeat the Reparations and the French occupation of the Ruhr, pulled the pins out entirely. By the fall of that year you could buy four billion marks with an American dollar.

Hitler's Germany is, however, a long, long way on the road to inflation. There has been no accounting given of the national finances since the Nazis came to power seven years ago. Not until the opening day of the war was there any admission of the colossal sums poured into armaments; aeroplanes, cannon, uniforms, tanks, trucks, all the great factories for the

making of these and the wages of the million of workers engaged, the great Western fortifications and the wonderful new roman roads. Ninety billion marks, Hitler boasted, have gone into this greatest spree in history. This is almost as much as the cost of the last war to Germany, or over half of the U.S. national debt, big enough to cause that rich country to worry.

Financially, Germany has fought her war already. The Nazis have used up all her gold reserve, as well as the gold which they were quick to get their hands on in Austria and Czechoslovakia. They have plundered the Jews. They have called in all the foreign stocks and bank accounts of German citizens. They have cleaned out all available funds in the banks, the savings banks and the insurance companies. They have quietly robbed the old age pension fund of eight billion marks. They have cleaned out the unemployment insurance fund and continue to take a heavy deduction from the pay envelopes of the workers, although unemployment has long ago ceased to exist.

The German population, as well as the German finances, have fought a considerable war already. They have experienced all the restriction, censorship, nervous tension, spy-hunting, food and clothing shortages, and forced saving which we associate with wartime. For years farmers have been unable to sell their own eggs or hogs where they wanted and

city folk have been on butter, fat and cream rations.

That doesn't mean that the Germans are starving, however. Many millions are still getting more to eat than they did during the Depression of 1931-32-33, and all are faring much better than in 1918. But they are hungering. And the worst time of the year is yet to come, before gardens grow again and the harvest fills the granaries.

To make it worse, they are cold as well. On the one hand the roaring armament industries, the busy railroads and the artificial processes for making gasoline are hogging the coal, and tired and underfed miners can't be pushed any harder. On the other hand wool is one of the scarcest of all materials in Germany. The country's cupboards, which were filled to bursting in 1914, have been emptied in the seven lean years of Hitlerism until they are as bare as Mother Hubbard's.

Does this mean that the German people are on the verge of revolt? Certainly they are not happy. There is plenty of grumbling. But it is a long way from grumbling to revolt in Germany.

Their spirit may not be as confident or united as in 1914, but it would be unsafe to reckon that it is worse than in 1918. And there may be some who remember that Germany put up an effort even then that came uncomfortably close to winning the war. Until she has been defeated in the field, she will remain a dangerous enemy.

War Picture Coming Here

Minister of National Defence Applauds "The Lion Has Wings"

Timely as today's headlines and more exciting than any adventure, "The Lion Has Wings" is the first full-length documentary picture of the war. To see it the King and Queen braved a London blackout.

Complete in every detail, this picture, which plays at the Capitol in Penticton January 4, 5 and 6, has won enthusiastic comments from reviewers everywhere.

Hon. Norman McL. Rogers, minister of national defence, has made the following approved statement in connection with it:

"With Canada's war efforts so deeply concerned with the strengthening of the Allied air forces, this film, "The Lion Has Wings," is a record for all

Canadians to see, of what the mastery of the air means to the Allied cause.

"One of Canada's most spectacular contributions to the common cause will be the Empire training scheme by which, for aerodromes across the country, pilots from the Dominions will be trained for overseas service. Here, in "The Lion Has Wings," is dramatically recorded the story of what it means in organization, skill and human courage. Indeed, the film gives to civilians an interesting insight into the intricate new military art of aerial warfare.

"I have been much impressed by the film, and not least by the reconstruction of the raid on the pocket battleships at Kiel, which is one of the highlights of the picture. This motion picture is performing a valuable national service in bringing us, while the news is still fresh in our memory, a record of the efficiency and daring with which this Allied war effort was planned and executed."

Opening Of Local Airport To Be The "Biggest Day Penticton Ever Had"

Gyros Plan For Visit Of Officials, Planes - Arrange Navel Auction

The wholehearted support of the Penticton municipal authorities was assured by the local Gyro Club in its sponsorship of the opening of the Penticton airport. At a regular dinner meeting on Tuesday evening in the Incola Hotel, the entire council and J.R. Wiglesworth, municipal clerk, were present to listen to the various reports brought in to the assembly and to take part in a general discussion on the subject.

Wilson Hunt, the president, welcomed Reeve R.J. McDougall, Councillors Johnson, Sutherland, Cousins and Tough, and also Mr. Wiglesworth. He then outlined the whole plan. This will consist of two distinct features. The opening of the airport, and a monster queen contest, embracing the entire district. Prizes of $1,000 in war savings stamps have been tentatively suggested for winning "queens."

Mr. Hunt explained that, due to the war, the usual July 1 celebration staged by the club would be cancelled for this year. A celebration of this sort at this time would be in poor taste, he decreed.

The opening of the new airport will not only be a splendid patriotic means of obtaining funds for war purposes, but would also be an excellent method of publicizing Penticton for the tourist traffic throughout a very wide area.

Every effort will be made to bring in military planes and, if possible, a bomber. Formation flyers will be sought from the U.S.A., as it is very doubtful if our own machines will be available in numbers at the time of the opening.

A large influx of visitors will be expected and a civic banquet arranged for prominent guests in the evening. All boards of trade in the district will be asked to cooperate and also other service clubs. The Gyro leader emphasized the size of the undertaking, pointing out that it will probably be one of the largest events ever staged in Penticton. Pointing out the keen interest shown by other districts in similar ventures, he stated that in Lethbridge, at the opening of the airport there, the sponsors, the local Gyro Club, were absolutely swamped by the cast assembly.

First On New Airport

The Department of Transport Lockheed twelve seen above, landed at the local airport on Friday morning, using the new local airfield for the first time. Observers report that the machine made a highly successful landing, and an equally good take-off later. In the latter case, the machine purposely tested what had been considered to be the softest part of the runway. The plane was in charge of J. Hunter, of Lethbridge, Assistant Airways Inspector for the government, Pilot Clarke being his co-pilot. In addition to testing and inspecting the field, the men also tested the range station under landing conditions.

The six-mile drive to the airfield took hours to cover, thousands upon thousands of automobiles were in Lethbridge, and all plans laid by the sponsors were practically overridden by the very size of the crowds.

All committees will be appointed before the next meeting and very careful preparation given to every detail.

Cliff Greyell reported on his recent trip to Vancouver. He had, he stated, interviewed many officers in connection with the opening. The plan was enthusiastically received by all. W. Templeton, manager of the Vancouver airport, stated that planes for passenger flights would probably be available. It was possible, too, that a Trans Canada plane may be up for the show. Carter Guest, who is in charge of civil flying in B.C., was also enthusiastic in his praise for the project.

"Torch Day" Plans Are Impressive

Dedicatory Service To Be Held In King's Park

Determined to go "all out" in the forthcoming Victory Loan drive, starting the effort to raise this district's $479,000 quota, Penticton will stage one of the biggest "days" in its history on Saturday. Although rapidly organized, the local "Torch Day" program will be an impressive one.

It will commence with a parade at 11 o'clock in the morning, which will be one of the largest, in point of the number of persons marching, ever to be held in this community. Following the parade, which will proceed from the north end of Main Street to King's Park, by way of Main Street and Eckhardt Avenue, there will be the impressive "torch ceremony" in the latter location.

At the same time, a plane will fly overhead, and shower "bombs" of leaflets on the community.

Designed to focus national attention on the Victory Loan-drive, the torch ceremony plan consists of forwarding a bomber plane, bearing a sculptured five-foot metal "torch," which is inscribed "Part of the Tools - Canada's Victory Loan, 1941," from Victoria, B.C., across Canada and eventually to London, where it will be presented to the Rt. Hon. Winston Churchill, in the name of the people of Canada.

The "torch" will serve as a challenge to the Canadian people to hold on high the torch which has shown the path of freedom and the democratic way of life down through the centuries.

BLACKOUTS

Blackout Dos and Don'ts

DECEMBER 11, 1941 — The signal is the continuous scream of the fire siren for two minutes. At night this is accompanied by the turning out of the street lights.

Responsibility for the protection of property rests with the householders. A shovel, pail of sand and a hose should be placed in readiness.

The city will place piles of sand at convenient points throughout the city. Householders are expected to fill their pails from these piles.

During alarms the telephone is to be used as little as possible.

All qualified nurses are asked to volunteer for service in first aid posts.

All owners of light delivery trucks are requested to volunteer the service of the trucks.

All householders are asked to prepare for a complete blackout. All openings such as windows should be covered with heavy paper, blankets or other material. No light should be showing.

Electric signs, window lights and night lights in stores must be put out at the sounding of an alarm.

Central A.R.P. headquarters has been established at police office.

Central first aid post has been established at the junior elementary school.

The city has been divided into seven districts under district wardens. The location of the district headquarters and first aid posts in your district should be familiar to you.

In case of an alarm, keep off the streets.

Do not touch any fallen wires.

A.R.P. men will wear white armbands.

Learn how to fight incendiary bombs, as explained in this issue.

Motorists should get home as soon as possible. If travel is necessary, headlights must be blinded save for a vertical strip three inches long and one-quarter inch wide. Tall lights must be covered save for a small disc in the centre.

Penticton Boy Wins Honors In Air Force

R.A. Barton Awarded Bar To High R.A.F. Decoration

Squadron Leader Robert Alexander Barton, son of R.A. Barton, well known Penticton surveyor and engineer, has been awarded the bar to his Distinguish Flying Cross, it was announced last week.

The Penticton airman, who had destroyed four enemy aircraft over the United Kingdom when he won the Distinguished Flying Cross a year ago, has accounted for four during his service at Malta, and his personal total now stands at 11.

The citations paid tribute to the courage and leadership of the local man as follows: "This officer destroyed seven hostile aircraft during his period of service in the United Kingdom. Since his arrival at Malta, he has led his squadron on all interceptions and fighter patrols, during which he has destroyed four hostile aircraft, including one at night."

"Squadron Leader Barton," the despatch continues, "has throughout shown a high standard of courage, leadership and initiative, and has contributed materially to the results obtained by the fighter effort on the island."

A note accompanying the official announcement of his award said, "Barton's outstanding leadership has contributed materially to the many successes obtained by his squadron," and added that "his skill was particularly displayed on one occasion when his squadron destroyed 20 enemy aircraft."

Weekly War Diary

Air Aid To Italy

From material gathered by British United Press, foreign correspondents, and transmitted to the Penticton Herald by the Vancouver Bureau of the British United Press.

THURSDAY, JANUARY 2

Italy, for the first time today, officially admitted that Germany is diverting part of the Nazi air force to aid the bogged-down Fascist military machine in Albania and North Africa. General Francesco Pricollo, Italian undersecretary for air, announced that German air squadrons will fight for Italy in the Mediterranean basin.

Vichy dispatchers described Franco-German negotiations as at a standstill and reported evidence of Nazi displeasure at the attitude of the French. Dispatches from Vichy said the Germans are preoccupied with preparations for a great attack on Britain. On the war fronts, action was limited. London reported a raid of exceptional severity had been made upon Bremen.

WEDNESDAY, JANUARY 1

German and British war planes were grounded, the British said, because of bad weather, but the Germans claimed it was because of an unofficial truce for New Year's.

In Albania, Greek troops continued to score on all fronts against the Italians. In Catro, the Middle East command of the Royal Air Force said that, beginning on Monday night, the R.A.F. bombers had subjected Italy to widespread attacks. Survivors rescued from lone Emaran Island, south of the equator, where they were marooned by German prison ships, said at least two, probably more, German sea raiders are loose in the South Pacific.

Canada At War

The Japanese on Sunday dropped a bomb on Hawaii and the dropping of that first bomb moved **CANADA CLOSER TO THE CONFLICT** and brought British Columbia from a quiet backwater of the war right into the front line. On Sunday night Canada formally declared war on Japan and thus became the first British nation to do so, hours before similar action was taken by Britain herself or the United States. The action was taken at ten o'clock on Sunday night and took effect on Sunday. Leaders of all Opposition parties in the House of Commons were consulted before the acton was taken. Canadian armed forces were immediately ordered to engage the enemy wherever he may be found.

The first Canadian force to see action against the Japanese was the **CANADIAN CONTINGENT AT HONG KONG** which landed at the British outpost two months ago. During the past two days the base has been attacked by Japanese land and air forces and while there has been no definite word of the part Canadians played in the defense of the base, it is more than probable that they were in the thick of the actions which saw the attackers repulsed on several occasions. On Wednesday it was admitted that the outer defenses had been pierced at one point.

War in the Pacific brought **WAR CONDITIONS** to the British Columbia coast and all air, naval and army units were made ready for instant action. Air patrols have been scanning the seas for enemy shipping and submarines, but especially for Japanese air craft carriers which were reported to be a few miles off the coast. As yet no report of these has been received. The army was instantly on the alert and it was expected that British Columbia reserve units would immediately be mobilized for active duty in the defense of Canada. However, so far as is known, none of the B.C. reserve army units has been called, and certainly not the local unit, B.C. Dragoons.

An **AIR RAID ALARM** at San Francisco early Monday night spread northwards along the whole Pacific coast and B.C. authorities announced that an attack was "imminent". Vancouver, Victoria, and all costal points were blacked out more or less effectively and all radio stations were off the air. The black out in coastal points will continue indefinitely and the radio station "blackout" which applies to stations in B.C., Alberta and Saskatchewan, will continue indefinitely during the hours of darkness. Cities through the Interior brushed up on their blackout preparations and placed everything in readiness in case an attack should come.

Smoke billows from the USS Arizona after a Japanese attack on Pearl Harbor. The attack triggered the U.S. entry into World War II.

VALLEY FLIER REPORTED KILLED

Body of Pilot Officer Bell, of Okanagan Mission, Found in Sea

KELOWNA — One Kelowna home was saddened this Christmas with the news that their beloved son has been killed while fighting for his country over the Kiel Canal. Pilot Officer Brian Stallard Bell, younger son of Mr. and Mrs. J.W. Bell, of Okanagan Mission, has been reported killed after his family had waited months for word of their son.

On the night of July 31, Pilot Officer Bell was in command of a British bomber raiding the Kiel Canal. The engine of his plane was shot away and he and his crew of three men were forced to bail out on the North Sea off the Yorkshire coast.

In November, the American Embassy in Holland notified the Air Ministry in London that the body of Pilot Officer Bell had been recovered from the North Sea and had been buried in the cemetery at Petten, North Holland, on September 12.

The young aviator was the younger son of Mr. and Mrs. J.W. Bell of Okanagan Mission. He was born and educated in Kelowna and joined the Royal Air Force in March, 1938. He was 22 years old at the time of his death.

Citizens Urged To Prepare For Blackout

"The one fact which must be impressed upon the general public is that the protection of his property during the air raid depends entirely upon himself," Chief Warden R. Whillis told a meeting of A.R.P. wardens and department chiefs on Tuesday night, when final organization steps were effected. "The individual must make all preparations to fight any fire that breaks out in his premises and he must take all necessary steps to see that his premises are blacked out. If he cannot control the fire some assistance may be possible from headquarters but this is not at all certain."

1940~1949

Airline Manager Hopeful Of Facilities Here When War Over

"You may rest assured that when equipment becomes available after the war, Penticton will undoubtedly become one of the areas served."

Such is the comment made by G.W.G. McConnachie, general manager for western lines, Canadian Pacific Air Lines, in a recent letter to H.B. Morley, secretary of the Penticton Board of Trade.

The letter was in response to a communication from the board, which sought inclusion of a Penticton stop in the Vancouver-Prince George service, and which drew further attention to Penticton's desire for such air service as can generally be made available.

Mr. McConnachie, who visited here on April 9 and inspected the airport, said that it was most difficult to make extensions at the present time. He pointed out that the Penticton airport is 150 miles off the run to Prince George. The 1939 service from Oliver, however, had amply demonstrated the value and necessity of interior linkage by air, and he therefore gave assurance that when equipment becomes available, Penticton will not be overlooked.

"I think this is a reassuring statement from this official," observed F.G. Pye, vice-president of the board, who presided at the executive meeting on Monday evening, at which Mr. McConnachie's letter was read.

HOUSING

HOUSING

Vets' $360,000 Housing Scheme Commences Here

Construction of First 20 Homes Begins At Cricket Grounds - 100 To Be Built In Seven Or Eight Months - Work Being Rushed As Fast As Possible

OCTOBER 4, 1945 — Amid the whirr of saws, the clatter of hammers, and the clean, pungent odor of freshly cut lumber, the biggest single housing project ever undertaken in Penticton this week got into active construction at the old cricket grounds where 20 houses, the first of 100 Wartime Housing rental homes to be built here for war veterans and their dependents, are being constructed.

The total cost of the 100 homes will be $360,000.

The 18-inch excavations for the basementless homes have been completed for 13 houses and while the Herald reporter was present yesterday afternoon No. 17 was laid out on the ground ready for the excavating crew.

Okanagan Constructions, composed of Kenyon-Killick and J. Dairymple, are determined to keep the work going at as fast a pace as possible.

Says Ottawa Buys 700 Acres For Vets On Cawston Bench

"Actual Development At Earliest Opportune Moment," States Murchinson Letter To Similkameen M.L.A.

JUNE 28, 1945 — Of wife interest to the whole southern Okanagan area is the news that Ottawa has definitely purchased 700 acres of the Cawston bench lands from the provincial government.

This information is contained in a letter recently received here by Bernard Webber, Similkameen M.L.A., from Gordon Murchison, Ottawa, director of soldier settlement and veterans land act, department of veterans affairs. This letter is dated May 31.

The letter states further:

"Advantage was taken of the time during the purchase negotiations to have irrigation surveys made by the Prairie Farm Rehabilitation Administrations. Their reports are now in our hands and we will be in a position to proceed with the actual development at the earliest opportune moment consistent with the best estimate we can make of the probable requests by returned men for establishment on this project, and the availability of labor and material."

Air Hero's Funeral Today

Buried At Dartford Kent, Father's Birthplace

Flying Officer Gregor S. Moore, of Penticton, who earned a hero's death in the war torn skies of England, was laid to rest today, Thursday, in the typically English cemetery at Dartford, Kent, the birthplace of his father, the late A. E. Moore.

Last Thursday FO Moore, son of Mrs. T. C. Robertson, Rigsby street, Penticton, sacrificed his life so that student pilots under his tutelage, could live to fly and fight again.

This 20-year-old Penticton airman, a flying instructor, was out on dawn exercises with a flight of training planes when a Nazi fighter bomber zoomed into sight and raked Moore's plane with machine gun fire.

The German, thinking the unarmed trainers an easy bag, started to turn to deliver a second attack, when Moore crashed his own training plane into the Nazi aircraft, which fell a flaming wreck into the streets of a little village below.

"We all owe a debt to Moore," said the chief flying instructor at

GREGOR S. MOORE

his station. "The Nazi aircraft would have been a wolf in a pack of sheep if it had not been for Gregor's action."

Mrs. Robertson received word late

Saved Student Pilots From Certain Death

last week of her son's death, but no details were given as to how he paid the supreme sacrifice.

When informed of these details she said quietly:

"That is just the kind of thing he would do."

Last October following his graduation from No. 3 S. F. T. S., Calgary, FO Moore was home on leave, after which he went on active service.

He was born and educated in Penticton and one year prior to his enlistment in the air force worked with the C.P.R. here.

A brother, Warren A. Moore, is now serving overseas with the Princess Patricia's Canadian Light Infantry, while a step brother, Bombardier James Robertson, is on the Royal Canadian Artillery in England, and a step sister, LAW M. Robertson, is in the R.C.A.F., women's division, in Canada.

Present for the last rites of this young Penticton airman were his step-brother, and two uncles and three aunts living in Dartford.

Kelowna Area Suffers Casualties As Allies Advance In Italy

Past Week Has Seen Several Local Men Wounded Or Missing - None Have Been Reported Killed In Action - Most Wounds Apparently Suffered During Breaking Of Hitler Line - Letters Have Been Received From Men Wounded Less Than Two Weeks Ago

As a natural sequence of the recent heavy fighting in Italy, in the thick of which a number of Kelowna men have been, casualties from this district are being reported in increasing numbers. During the past week there have been some half-dozen, but for the most part, the official telegrams have indicated the wounds have not been of a serious nature.

Word has been received that Trooper Alfred Johns is suffering from severe multiple burns of the third degree sustained in action on May 25th. He is the son of Mr. and Mrs. H. Johns, of Okanagan Mission. He is a gunner in one of

the tanks of the 9th Armored. A further telegram on Tuesday stated that he is "seriously ill but improving."

Mr. and Mrs. Olaf Peter Olson, Five Bridges, R.R. 3, Kelowna, have had word that their son, Acting Corporal Olaf Olson, has been slightly wounded. The date and nature of the wounds were unknown. He, too, was a 9th Armored man.

Still another member of the same regiment who is reported to be slightly wounded is Lieut. H.N. (Red) Williams, son of Mr. and Mrs. A. Williams, Strathcona Avenue.

Mrs. H.N. Williams is a member of the teaching staff of the Kelowna schools.

Andrew J. Cook, of Winfield, has received word that his son, Sergt. W. Cook, was wounded in Italy on May 25th.

On Friday, L.D. Browne-Clayton, of Okanagan Mission, received word that his son, Lieut. R.D. Browne-Clayton, had been reported missiing following action in Italy on May 23. Lieut. Browne-Clayton was a member of the Princess Pats. The action on May 23, apparently, was that in which the Hitler Line in Italy was cracked.

(CP PHOTO) National Archives of Canada-Gilbert Alexander Milne)

Personnel of the 9th Canadian Infantry Brigade landing from LCI(L) 125 of the 3rd Canadian (264th RN) Flotilla on 'Nan White' Beach on D-Day.

JUNE 22, 1944

Penticton's First Invasion Losses

Tpr. Donald Hilliard Killed On "D" Day

The first Penticton boy to pay the supreme sacrifice for King and Country in the invasion of the Normandy beaches, so far reported to the Herald, is Trooper Donald Brock Hilliard, 21, who was killed in action on "D" Day, June 6, 1944, according to information reaching his father here, W. Brock Hilliard, of the Herald staff.

Tpr. Hilliard was a member of the tank corps and was probably in the first wave of Canadian troops to storm the beaches.

Prior to his enlistment he was a member of the Betts' Electric staff here. In November 1942, he enlisted in the Canadian Active Army in Penticton and arrived in England May, 1943, and was attached to the Fort Garry Horse, now an armored formation.

Tpr. Hilliard was born at Huilcar, near Armstrong, in January, 1923, and lived there until 1941 when he took up the electrical trade in Vernon. He came here in September, 1941, in the employ of Bett's Electric.

His older brother, Tpr. Douglas Hilliard, enlisted at the same time and went overseas in June, 1943. He is now in a reconnaissance unit attached to the Third Canadian Division which is also fighting in France.

This young Penticton soldier leaves, in addition to his father and brother, three sisters: Mrs. William Parker and Mrs. Robert Coldicott, of Armstrong: and Mrs. Charles Hardwood, West Broadway, of Vancouver.

Cpl. H. Murfitt Dies Three Days After Landings

The second Penticton soldier to die in the invasion of France was probably Cpl. Herbert Arthur Murfitt, 37, nephew of William Murfitt, of Penticton, who was killed in action June 9, just three days after "D" Day, June 6, 1944.

According to information reaching his uncle here Cpl. Murfitt was serving as an instructor up to a short time before his death.

Cpl. Murfitt, who had lived at his uncle's home here at one time, had worked at the Summerland Box factory before his enlistment in the Seaforth Highlanders in the fall of 1939 at the outbreak of war. He went overseas with the first division. However he did not go to Italy with his regiment but remained in England on instructional duties.

His father, Charles William Murfitt, resides in Bakersfield, California, where the family went from England. Cpl. Murfitt came to Penticton about 14 years ago and was well known both here and in Summerland. He was an ardent hunter and fisherman. He was single.

Surviving are his father, one brother, Arthur Murfitt, of London, England; four uncles, William Henry Murfitt, of Penticton; Fred, Sidney, and Harry Murfitt, of London, England; and two aunts, Mrs. Edith Batterham, and Mrs. Chrissie Uphill, both in the Old Country.

EDITORIAL

D Day

JUNE 8, 1944 — Four years and two days after we had been driven out of Europe and the tattered remnants of our army had regained British soil, we went back to Europe. Four years ago the British Commonwealth stood alone against the seemingly invincible might of Germany and her allies; this week we returned to Europe with the most powerful nations in the world marching shoulder to shoulder into Europe with us. Four years ago the Royal Navy had three old Gladiators to provide it with fighter protection on Monday morning the invasion fleet was protected by eleven thousand planes. Four years ago we had two tanks armed with two-inch guns to repel any invading German army; today literally thousands of the most heavily armored tanks are rolling from ship to French beach. Four years ago we had three field guns to repel any German attack on the British Coast; today our armies are the best equipped in the world, provided with the finest equipment science can devise and man can make.

On Monday morning, June 6th, we commenced what history will probably record as the beginning of the final stage of the war against Germany. The preparations have been long and, we may rest assured, thorough. For fifteen months now the German industrial army has been subjected to a great attack from the air; an attack that has been gaining in crescendo with every passing month; an attack that has wiped out cities and drastically curtailed the production of supplies and equipment for the German army; an attack which played no small part in the success of the Russian armies. But if German production has been blasted, more recently the communication and transportation systems of Germany and northern France have endured a pounding equally severe. We have sea supremacy and air superiority which is rapidly changing, apparently, to air supremacy. Added to these factors there is the vitally important one of morale. Our men have waited four long years for the word which was given on Sunday night and their morale is unquestionable.

This does not mean that there will be an easy victory. The German is too great a soldier for us to have any hope of that. We may have a beachhead, but he will do everything in his power - and his power must be recognized as still considerable - to throw us out. There will be bloody battles and many cruel casualties. These are the price free peoples must pay to retain their freedom; this history has proved many times.

But there is one thing of which we can be sure. The Allied Supreme Command did not send our armies across the Channel without the sure conviction that everything has been done that could be done, that the time is ripe, and that Victory for our arms is as certain as any battle can be considered certain. The fact that we have made the crossing leads one to believe that Allied Headquarters knows that conditions behind the German lines are such as to cause Hitler's generals great concern; that the German people are approaching the crumbling stage, supplies are short, production curtailed and transportation inadequate. In short, that Europe is like an egg; once the hard shell is broken the remainder will run out.

Our men are now in France, marking the beginning of the end, and of the end there can be no doubt. It is a time of action and excitement for the men in the services.

For the people at home it is a time for anxiety and concern. Though the Great Adventure is in full stride in France, we at home can only sit and wait - and hope - and pray - and have abiding faith.

Tribute To First Invasion Dead Here

A fitting tribute in verse to Penticton's first two invasion casualties, Tpr. Donald B. Hilliard, Fort Garry Horse, and Cpl. H. A. Murfitt, Seaforth Highlanders, was received here this week from Dr. Robert Mathison, pioneer Kelowna dentist and former printer.

Dr. Mathison is a close personal friend of Tpr. Hilliard's father, W. Brock Hilliard, of the Herald staff, and sent the latter the verses reproduced below in tribute to his fighting son, who was killed in action on "D" day.

They apply equally well to Cpl. Murfitt, who is the nephew of William Murfitt, veteran member of the municipal staff here.

Cpl. Murfitt was well known both here and in Summerland, where he worked at the box factory. He died on "D plus 3," three days after the first wave of Allied troops hit the Normandy beaches.

WHEN I GO DOWN

I want to go when the fight fares fast,
When the cannons roar with the loudest blast;
I want to go when the bayonets flash,
I want to go when the sabres crash.

I want to go when the pulse runs strong,
When the head is high and the breath is long;
I want to go when the eye is bright,
When the heart is young and full of fight.

I want to go when the summer sun
Shines full in the face of deeds well done;
I want to go ere life grows tame,
I want to go while I play the game.

CPL. H. A. MURFITT

TPR. DONALD B. HILLIARD

THE PENTICTON HERALD, THURSDAY, APRIL 26, 1945

Page Seventeen

P.O.W.

PRISONER OF WAR PARCELS

You Can Help To Bring Them Back Alive

BY SUPPORTING THE P. O. W. DRIVE ON — **SAT. APRIL 28**

★

$1.00 SUBSCRIPTION

TICKETS WILL BE SOLD BY THE CADETS OF THE THREE SERVICES. THE PURPOSE OF THIS DRIVE IS TO RAISE $50,000 TO SEND PARCELS THROUGH THE RED CROSS TO PRISONERS OF WAR.

100 Percent Of The Proceeds Of This Drive Goes Direct To The Canadian Red Cross.

Each Parcel Contains:

1 lb. tin Creamery Butter, ¼ lb. pkg. Tea, 1 lb. tin Orange Marmalade, ½ lb. tin Salmon, 12 oz. tin Corned Beef, 16½ oz. tin Kam (Pork), ½ lb. Sugar, 1 small pkg. Salt, 7 oz. pkg. Raisins, 5 oz. pkg. Chocolate, 1 pkg. Biscuits, 1 lb. tin Klim, 6 oz. pkg. Prunes, 1 bar Toilet Soap, ¼ lb. Canadian Cheese.

THIS DRIVE IS IN THE FORM OF A PRIZE DRAW

1st PRIZE . . . . $2500 VICTORY BOND
2nd PRIZE . . . . $600 IN WAR SAVINGS STAMPS

And 26 other HIGH PRIORITY PRIZES, INCLUDING an ELECTRIC WASHING MACHINE, SIX PAIRS NYLON STOCKINGS, ETC.

ALL PRIZES DONATED BY B.C. BUSINESS FIRMS.

This Message is Sponsored by the Following Public Spirited Penticton Businessmen and Merchants

MODE SHOP LTD.
PACIFIC PIPE & FLUME LTD.
PENTICTON NURSERIES—G. Robinson, Skaha Lake
McKEEN'S DRUG STORE
STAR CLEANERS
PERCY BENT LTD.—Ford Dealers
F. R. STEWART CO.
MODERNE BEAUTY SALON
PAUL'S HARDWARE
WEBSTER'S LADIES' WEAR

HENDRY'S CAKE SHOP
DUCO BILL'S AUTO METAL SHOP Bill Hodgson, Prop.
GRAND FORKS GARAGE LTD.
GRANT KING CO. LTD.
GEDDY'S BOOT SHOP
PYE & HILLYARD
NEVE-NEWTON PHARMACY
O. L. JONES FURNITURE (Penticton) LTD.
PENTICTON FLOWER SHOP— W. Powers, Penticton

INTERIOR CONTRACTING CO. LTD.
BASHAM & FINCH
CLARKE'S BUILDING SUPPLIES
PENTICTON DRAY & EXPRESS
PENTICTON TRADING ASSOCIATION
HUNT MOTORS
EARLEY'S SHOE STORE
R. J. LONG LTD.
INCOLA HOTEL
COOPER & GIBBARD
PENTICTON POULTRY ASSOCIATION

THREE GABLES HOTEL
OVERWAITEA LTD.
BENNETT HARDWARE
ESSON'S BAKERY
WILKIN'S MACHINE SHOP & FOUNDRY Ltd.
McLENNAN, McFEELY & PRIOR (Penticton) LTD., "MC & MC"
PENTICTON TIRE HOSPITAL & GARAGE
PENTICTON RETREADING & VULCANIZING
WHITE'S GARAGE
UNIQUE FISH AND CHIPS

Penticton Offers Thanks On VE-Day

Citizens Mark End Of War In Europe Quietly

A deep and sincere undertone of thanksgiving marked Penticton's VE-Day celebrations.

This feeling will find further expression this Sunday when Penticton churches, like those all over Canada and the Empire, will hold special services.

Legion members will parade to St. Savior's Church on that occasion after "falling in" at the Legion hall at 10:45 a.m.

As far as Penticton was concerned Monday, the day before the official VE-Day, was the most boisterous. This pattern, if radio broadcasts were any indication, was followed all over the Allied world. Once the surrender of Germany was apparent, the common people gave vent to their joy and would not wait for the official pronouncement by Great Britain, the United States, and Russia.

The first official celebration was that staged by the elementary school students who marched to the Gyro Park Monday morning at 11:30 o'clock under the supervision of their teachers. School closed Monday noon and did not re-assemble until yesterday,

Wednesday.

Stores here closed at noon hour Monday and opened yesterday. Monday night the Gyro sponsored VE-Day eve dance was held, which proved to be the gayest of celebrations here. Far into the night some of the more exuberant car owners drove through the town sounding their horns. But these exhibitions were not very numerous and didn't occur often enough to interrupt the sleep of the less wakeful citizens.

The government liquor store was well patronized Monday morning when long line ups formed as it became apparent that Germany had "thrown in the towel".

There was a "run" on flags of all kinds Monday morning as homes and cars suddenly became decked with the flag of the United Nations.

There was little to give the police concern here during Monday and Tuesday. One or two fights did occur but these were not serious and the participants soon cooled off after a few hours in the lockup.

The Municipal council met Monday night as usual and transacted routine business. However, the occasion was noted in the minute book at the suggestion of Municipal clerk J.R.Wiglesworth.

The well organized VE-Day program, presented by the community under R.N. Atkinson, provided an opportunity for residents to give thanks and to hear music, oratory, and songs appropriated to the occasion.

The siren at the firehall did not usher in VE-Day here because, according to Fire Chief H.M. Foreman, the code word from A.R.P. officials did not come through. "We had strict orders not to sound the siren until the code word was received. It didn't come through."

Naramata and Kaleden joined with Penticton in observing VE-Day.

Every Community In South Okanagan Celebrates Victory

Every community in the South Okanagan marked VE-Day with special celebrations, dances and parades. Some of these were planned far in advance, others were impromptu affairs organized when the good news was flashed around the world that the Nazi Germany had surrendered unconditionally.

A deep feeling of thankfulness characterized all of the srevices for the end of the war in Europe. But there was the realization that a careful and determined foe must still be dealt with in the Pacific.

THEY ARE NOT FORGOTTEN

MAY 10, 1945 — V-E Day was a sad day in many homes in the Central Okanagan. That statement should not be surprising if one stops to reflect upon the score of homes in this small community which have sustained casualties as a result of the war.

To the people of these homes - the mothers, fathers, wives, sons, daughters, brothers and sisters - VE-Day could be nought but painful. Of course they were happy the war in Europe was over; of course they were glad that the servicemen and women would soon be returning to their homes; but deep within their hearts there was a dull ache for VE-Day meant that the loved ones of others would be returning while in their homes the vacant chair would remain unoccupied.

This week the people of Kelowna did not forget these homes. True, there was not any outward demonstrations, but the memory and the sympathy were there, sincere and living. A long procession of casualty reports have marched through the pages of The Courier during the past five years, the most distressing type of news which this or any other paper has to handle. Many of the wounded, missing or killed men and women were known to us personally or they lived in the next block, the next street, the next farm. In a small closely knit and compact community such as the Kelowna area, the suffering of one affects the whole and, so, casualties are

Home They Come

The return of Canadian warriors from long years of service overseas is in full swing. Two big troopships laden with thousands of servicemen docked at Halifax. As the Samaria and Scythia eased into their Halifax docks, the great throng of soldiers, airmen, nurses and war brides with their children lined the ships deck rails cheering and singing as an expression of their delight at being in Canada again. Military and port authorities supervised the landing with all possible speed and special trains left Halifax on the final leg of the westward trip on an average of one every hour.

1940~1949

(AP Photo)

The world's first atomic explosion is shown in this photo on July 16, 1945, on what is now known as the White Sands Missile Range about 50 miles northwest of Alamogordo, N.M. Debate has raged over the morality of U.S. bombs dropped on Japan less than a month later. Declassified documents have added to what is known of Japan's own efforts to build an atomic bomb late in World War II.

(AP Photo/Nippon Eiga Shinsha Ltd.)

Gas Rationing Lifted

AUGUST 16, 1945 — Minister
of Munitions and Supply, Hon C.D.
Howe, announced in an official
statement on Wednesday morning,
that all restriction on gasoline and
fuel oil have been removed.

A man walks through the rubble
near the remains of the Hiroshima
Chamber of Commerce and Industry
building, (now the Atomic-Bombing
Dome), in this image made from
newly-recovered footage of the
western Japanese city shot just
weeks after the Aug. 6, 1945 atomic
bombing by the United States.

1940~1949

Russia at War With Japan

Generalissimo J. Stalin

"Russia has de-
clared war on Jap-
an."

In this cryptic,
terse statement
President Truman
announced the lat-
·est development in
the war with Japan
to the world.

The date set is to-
day, August 9, but
allowing for dispar-
ity in the time, the
declaration took ef-
fect at about 4 p.m.
Wednesday after-
noon, Pacific day-
light time. Fighting
on a 300 mile front
in Manchuria has
already commenced.

The graphic an-
nouncement, which
inevitably came out
of the Potsdam Conference, was made immediately after
the atomic bomb had struck the military city of Hiroshima. Last. night still another of the terrible, destructive atomic bombs struck Nagasaki.

Hiroshima has a population of 318,000.

City Crowds Go Wild With Joy
As News Sweeps The Nation

Throngs Laugh, Sing, Dance, Weep With Joy

AUGUST 16, 1945 —
Never has such a public
demonstration of joy, happiness and relief been experienced in
Vernon as that seen here late
Tuesday afternoon, through the
evening, and on into the night, as
the news of Japan's unconditional
surrender swept the city like a tidal
wave.

Citizens, members of the Chinese
community, holidaymakers and
troops went wild with unrestrained
joy. Within half an hour of Prime
Minister Attlee's announcement
over the air, decorated cars filled
with laughing, cheering and some
weeping men, women, children,

began an impromtu parade.
Crowds thronged the downtown
area during the early evening,
where a military band played
songs at the Bank of Montreal corner. All traffic was suspended on
Barnard Avenue. The throngs
paraded up and down, sang,
cheered, and otherwise gave vent
to feelings which had sometimes
been stretched taut during the
nearly six years of war.

More than 2,000 people jammed
into the Civic Arena for the free
juke box dance. The entire floor
space, the largest in the Interior,
was practically one solid mass of
people. Crowds were also in the
bleachers surrounding the dancers.
The music continued until 2 a.m.
when the multitudes slowly dispersed.

Today, the United Nations, partners in freedom, have triumphed!

Valor, determination, unity, inspired leadership, and above all courage have been given unselfishly to retain the freedom that is our heritage.

★ ★ ★

We, the undersigned, offer our heartfelt thanks to all our fighting men who, by their courage, devotion and sacrifices, have once again made us all proud to be called Canadians.

MODE SHOP LTD.
PACIFIC PIPE & FLUME LTD.
PENTICTON NURSERIES—G. Robinson,
    Skaha Lake
McKEEN'S DRUG STORE
STAR CLEANERS
PERCY BENT LTD.—Ford Dealers
F. R. STEWART CO.
MODERNE BEAUTY SALON
PAUL'S HARDWARE
DeLUXE CLEANERS
HARRY'S MARKET

HENDRY'S CAKE SHOP
DUCO BILL'S AUTO METAL SHOP
    Bill Hodgson, Prop.
GRAND FORKS GARAGE LTD.
GRANT KING CO. LTD.
GEDDY'S BOOT SHOP
PYE & HILLYARD
NEVE-NEWTON PHARMACY
O. L. JONES FURNITURE (Penticton) LTD.
PENTICTON FLOWER SHOP—
    W. Powers, Penticton

INTERIOR CONTRACTING CO. LTD.
BASHAM & FINCH
CLARKE'S BUILDING SUPPLIES
PENTICTON DRAY & EXPRESS
PENTICTON TRADING ASSOCIATION
HUNT MOTORS
EARLEY'S SHOE STORE
R. J. LONG LTD.
INCOLA HOTEL
COOPER & GIBBARD
PENTICTON POULTRY ASSOCIATION

THREE GABLES HOTEL
OVERWAITEA LTD.
BENNETT HARDWARE
ESSON'S BAKERY
WILKIN'S MACHINE SHOP & FOUNDRY Ltd.
McLENNAN, McFEELY & PRIOR (Penticton)
    LTD., "MC & MC"
PENTICTON TIRE HOSPITAL & GARAGE
PENTICTON RETREADING & VULCANIZING
WHITE'S GARAGE
UNIQUE FISH AND CHIPS

V-J Celebration

Crowd Jammed Bernard Avenue

V-J Day in Kelowna was marked by an enthusiastic but comparatively orderly celebration in which several thousand persons gave full vent to their feeling of relief that the war was completely over and their enthusiasm that the Japanese had been brought to their knees in a humble plea for peace. On Wednesday morning a survey of the results of Tuesday night's celebration showed that only one car had been stolen, one window smashed and one nose broken and several score of flags stolen. Police authorities and civic officials generally agreed that the celebration was surprisingly peaceful.

A car belonging to W. B. Hughes-Games was stolen from in front of the home of A. McKim, 111 Bernard. A car crashed the front of O. L. Jones Furniture Store, breaking one of the large windows. A brief fisticuffs occurred in the Royal Anne. Those, as far as the police were aware, were the sum total of V-J Day disturbances. On Tuesday night the business district was well decorated with flags : three remained out on Wednesday morning. Six disappeared from in front of The Courier office and other business premises were likewise stripped.

Nevertheless, the crowd was an orderly one and incidents were surprisingly few. Spirits ran high but they found incidents were surprisingly few. Spirits ran high but they found release in pranks and fun rather than in destruction.

All Kelowna gathered on Bernard Avenue in the evening and were joined by most of the people of the entire rural area. At one time it is estimated that a thousand couples were dancing on the street in front of the Royal Anne while many more thousands watched.

The actual official news reached here with Prime Minister Clement Attlee's broadcast at four in the afternoon. A minute after four the

fire hall siren started and was quickly joined by all whistles in the city and the horns of automobiles. The church bells joined the clamor and tin pans and whistles were used by youngsters to excellent advantage.

Except for the housewife who had refused to heed the adequate warning and scurried at the last moment to obtain provisions for the two-day holiday, business to all intents and purpose ceased at four o'clock and people poured into Bernard Avenue, which was quickly jammed with impromptu parades of cars, bicycles and pedestrians. Trucks and cars with youngsters and grown-ups hanging from all available footholds toured the streets.

Stores were raided for toilet paper and this was used to excellent advantage as streamers. Some confetti miraculously appeared and some colored crepe streamers. The result was that Bernard quickly took on all the aspects of a first rate celebration.

Flags, too, quickly appeared in front of practically every business house and the city workmen quickly strung the city flags to the intersection.

Youngsters on bicycles dragged long strings of cans behind them.

The sidewalks and the street itself were jammed with people carrying broad smiles. Jim Browne, of CKOV, was on the street making a street-scene broadcast. The broadest grins of all were carried by members of the Chinese community who celebrated the end of the decade-long war between their country and Japan. At six-thirty a parade formed under the direction of the Junior Board of Trade and the Canadian Legion and headed down a packed Bernard Avenue.

Led by B Squadron of the 9th Armored (R) with its vehicles and anti-tank guns, it was composed of veterans of this and other wars, the Chinese community, the Pacific Coast Rangers, representatives of the three armed

services, both men and women, members of the Women's Auxiliary of the Canadian Legion, the Canadian Red Cross Corps, the Sea Cadets, the Scouts and Brownies and the Girl Guides. Trailing it were a score of cars.

Three bands participated in the parade, the Canadian Legion Pipe Band, the Bethel Baptist Boys Band and the Sea Cadet Bugle Band.

Actually it was a pretty fair parade for an impromptu affair in a small town. Oddly enough the only foreign flag present was that of China, proudly carried by members of the Chinese community.

The announcement Sunday night that the Japanese had accepted Allied peace terms caused premature peace celebrations in the city.

The fire department siren started wailing shortly before 6:45 p.m., and the local telephone exchange was flooded with telephone calls by local residents. However, even after the peace terms were officially denied at 7 p.m., the previous announcement had enough spark to set off celebrations.

Scores of people gathered in the streets, and while no parades were formed, many motorists drove through the streets blowing their automobiles horns.

SURRENDER

Carnival Of Joy On Main Street as Japs Surrender To Allies

AUGUST 16, 1945 — "Hurray, Old Man Mars is dead!"

This shout, by a smiling teen-aged youngster last Tuesday night, as the flames shot up around the seven-foot effigy of the mythical Greek God of War, carried with it a fervent hope as well as the wishful-thinking statements of fact. In the joyous hearts of the estimated 3,000 Penticton residents who watched the brutal features of the God of War vanish in the smoke and flames, there was probably the same prayer, inaudible, but there all the same:

"Let us hope that never again shall the scourge of war be visited on mankind."

Thus the burning of the effigy of the War God was symbolic of the hopes of all mankind and an act most appropriate to the occasion of the end of the greatest war in human history.

But on Tuesday afternoon and evening there was little of solemnity and contemplation.

People were too thankful for anything except an outburst of joy. This spirit, if radio reports were any indication, was duplicated in just about every town and hamlet in the Allied world.

Reports of Japan's surrender had been flying back and forth for almost 48 hours and everyone was keyed to fever pitch. When the news did come late Tuesday afternoon this feeling welled up and bubbled over in a carnival of joy.

FRUIT INDUSTRY

Biggest Apple Campaign In History To Boost Sales As Coast Program Starts

JAUNUARY 25 — Sixty-Six Thousand Apples To Be Distributed Free To Vancouver School Children - Ten Cars Already Have Left Valley To Meet Increased Trade - Big Program Arranged

Today, Coast apple centers are commencing their annual B.C. Apple Week and numerous organizations are combining to make this 1940 effort one of the biggest publicity campaigns ever organized to boost the sale of B.C. apples. Vancouver, North Vancouver, New Westminster and Victoria are combining in the promotion of apple sales from today, Thursday, January 25, to Saturday, February 3. Sixty thousand apples are being distributed to school children in Greater Vancouver while the Apple Ambassadors, who made such a hit in their jaunt around the prairie centers in November, are being welcomed at the Coast centers.

Ten cars of apples left the Okanagan last week.

Herald's New Home

Photo by photo credit

Situated at the corner of Nanaimo and Winnipeg streets, the new premises of The Penticton Herald are now completed. Modern in every detail, the new building forms an attractive addition to Penticton's business district. The building extends ninety feet on Nanaimo and eighty feet on Winnipeg. The printing equipment is contained in the portion of the building under the word "printing", extending to the rear of the structure. The editorial offices are in that section under "Publishing", while the general offices are directly behind the entrance.

Big Convention Under Way

Control Of Export Deal Likely To Be Most Important Question Coming Up At Grower Gathering

Growers from all points of the Interior of British Columbia are gathered in Penticton today for the annual deliberations of the British Columbia Fruit Growers' Association., and the growers are looking forward to big developments for the benefit of the fruit industry. Although up to the time of going to press most of the important functions of this session, the furtherance of the selling agency, as initiated this year, is definitely in the minds of the growers and will occupy the spotlight at this conference.

One of the most important points to be considered at this conference will be the next steps to be instituted by B.C. Tree Fruits Ltd. The taking over of the export deal will be discussed at length, reliable sources reveal,

and it is probable that this will be the main topic for Thursday afternoon.

The governors of Tree Fruits are said to have discussed this angle thoroughly and are ready to bring in recommendation. It is fairly certain that these recommendations will include that of taking over the export deal this coming season and providing one more step nearer to the final objective of the complete central setting deal.

– Welcome –

B. C. F. G. A. Convention

We, the Merchants and Professional Men of Penticton, Welcome Most Cordially the Official Delegates and Visitors to the British Columbia Fruit Growers' Convention.

We trust that your efforts at this gathering will meet with every success in bettering the great industry of the Okanagan.

Your Success is Our Success . .

Our Combined Good Wishes Are With You.

Fruit Juice Company Is Formed Here

Okanagan Fruit Juices Ltd., Incorporated

A new business was born in Kelowna last week when Okanagan Fruit Juices, Ltd., was incorporated under the Companies Act.

The new organization is composed of a group of local business men with D.K. Gordon as chairman of the board of directors and O. St. P.

Aitkens as managing director of the company.

Officials of the company were reticent about the new organization, maintaining that the present is a little premature but the notice of incorporation gives the company a wide variety of activities. It states that the objects of the company are to extract, can, pack, process, dehydrate evaporate, preserve, or in any other way to obtain, treat, or deal with the juices of fruits and vegetables of all kinds, and all products

which may be made from or which are derived from any such juices, and to purchase, produce, raise, can, pack, preserve, process, dehydrate, evaporate, cure, pickle, or in any way treat or deal with all kinds of fruits, vegetables, nuts, cereals and dairy products.

The authorized capital of the company is fifty thousand dollars, divided into twenty-five thousand management shares of one dollar each and twenty-five thousand Class B shares.

Gold Prospect At Tulameen

Eight miles from Tulameen, about two miles up Bear Creek from the Tulameen River, lies Grasshopper Mountain, and on the slopes of this mountain are buried the hopes and fortunes of three brothers of Tulameen.

Sometime in 1937 the three brothers, Daniel, Thomas and Patrick Rabbitt, all residents of the Tulameen area, were returning home from a trip up the side of Grasshopper Mountain when they came across some "float" or loose quartz which appeared to have gold content. Assays reported favorable on the ore, and the attention of mining men was drawn to the location of the claim. The brothers were heartened with the results, and staked out a number of adjacent claims, which came to be known as the B.C. Gold Group.

In 1938, the Pioneer Gold Mines Limited took out an option on the property, but for some reason the option was allowed to lapse. The brothers found themselves burdened with what appeared in the eyes of experienced mining men to be a property of little value. However, they were not to be detracted from making an effort to prove the worth of their property. The vein was known to extend up the side of the mountain, so they commenced the tedious task of surface mining with simple tools. They shipped a speculative truckload to the smelter at Trail last year, and were vindicated of their faith in the property by the rich return obtained from the load. Other loads quickly followed, and even better returns were obtained on each trip.

In December of last year a syndicate of mining men financed the mine and a 65-horsepower diesel, and air compressor and drills were shipped to the property from the Coast and development work commenced in earnest under the direction of Mort Richmond, mining engineer. A drift is being driven into the mountain, and a small crew is constantly employed with the project.

First Fighter Designed Here

March 16, 1939 — Canada can not only build airplanes of all kinds, but can design them, and the one pictured above is being demonstrated before the Dominion government officials at Ottawa. It is the Gregor, the first singe-seater all metal fighter, with a speed of 300 miles an hour and the exceptionally low landing speed of 57 miles an hour. It was designed by Michael Gregor, chief designer of the Canadian Car and Foundry Co., at Fort William, and was assembled at St. Hubert airport preparatory to flying to the Capitol.

The Okanagan Builds Up

Interesting figures on building in the Okanagan are revealed in this week's issue of The Herald. They show that, during the decade just brought to a close, during what was considered to be a period of world-wide depression, construction valued at over three million dollars was carried out in the three major towns of the Okanagan - Penticton, Kelowna and Vernon.

Kelowna is in the lead with $1,320,582, Vernon was second with $1,217,754, while Penticton was third with $1,127,303.

It is interesting to note that over the ten-year period, the race was strikingly close, less than two hundred thousand dollars separating Kelowna and Penticton, with Vernon mid-way between the two.

The growth represented in these figures provides real proof that the Okanagan Valley is one of the favored spots of the Dominion of Canada.

Many centers throughout the country, on checking up at the end of the ten-year period just past, can find little or no progress of any kind. In many cases there are distinct signs of back-sliding.

But the three major towns of Okanagan have all shown real progress and can look back with justifiable satisfaction of the "thirties." Individual business returns have not been as satisfactory, perhaps, as we would like to have seen them. But, sound businesses have been able to get by and to make progress.

Nor is this building progress confined to the major Okanagan towns alone. More spectacular, perhaps, are the strides which have been made by some of the smaller centers, particularly in the extreme southern portion of the valley.

We refer to Oliver and Osoyoos, where such changes have taken place that persons who had not seen either of these communities since the twenties would have real difficulty in recognizing them.

Summerland, too, has gone ahead, with Peachland and Westbank residents adding to the attractiveness of their communities with new homes and places of business.

The Herald has been accused, on occasion, of having boosted local building figures, and of giving the impression that there was more prosperity here than really was the case.

The fact that Penticton is at the bottom of the list would not indicate that there has been any undue "boosting."

However, each of the three major towns has set up a record of which to be proud and has established a high mark at which to shoot in the decade which is now opening up before us.

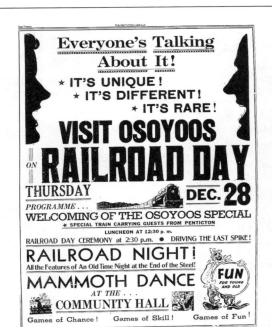

Herald Plant Destroyed By Fire

Early Morning Blaze Does $45,000 Damage

Interior of Mechanical Division Of Local Newspaper Structure Is prey To Fierce Flames And A Tremendous Heat - Building Substantially Saved

In a fire that illuminated the whole downtown section of the city area shortly before 3 o'clock on Saturday morning, the Penticton Herald's mechanical department was wiped out, that part, of the attractive year-old building was completely gutted, and the administration offices suffered water and smoke damage.

Flames that fed on inflammable vapors from inks, oils, and other materials in the plant of the newspaper, which were ignited after the fire had been under way for a period, made a sweeping torch that swept through the building, demolishing much more than woodwork. The heat was so

intense that it melted metals completely. The fine precision machinery and a large assembly of general printing equipment, are claimed as a total loss. Coupled with damage to the building the destruction is tentatively placed at about $45,000.

The flames spread around the entire interior of the mechanical building, but the structure as a whole is substantially intact. The blaze got through the roof at only one point and there did not do great damage.

The interior on Saturday morning, after dawn broke, offered a sorry spectacle to a multitude of townspeople who flocked through the premises.

Charred and blackened over every inch, drenched with hose water, it was a very different scene from the splendid printing and publishing establishment erected in the late autumn of 1939 by R.J. McDougall, and regarded by all experts as a model plant, fitting for

the operations of the newspaper which for two years in succession was judged the best weekly community publication in the entire Dominion.

Exactly how the fire started could not quickly be determined, according to Fire Chief Jack Ellis. Various theories were all examined carefully, but were not easily confirmed.

The opinion that seems to have the most weight with those who have studied the situation is that the fire started under the cement floor of the furnace casting room. Heat from the furnace fire or the ashpan which sits on the floor in some way affected the wooden foundation beneath the cement. This apparently ignited at some time Friday afternoon, according to this theory, as this would have been after the melting of ingots. The blaze spread up a partition, and the whole conflagration eventually resulted.

Application Made For Radio Transmitter

Application has been made by Okanagan Broadcasters to erect a transmitting station here, to be known as CKOK, with 250 watts of power and a broadcast frequency of 1450 kilocycles.

This was the information given by J.W.B. Browne, manager of CKOV Kelowna, when speaking to the Penticton Rotary Club at the regular weekly luncheon meeting in the Incola hotel Monday.

Mr. Browne stated that the licence and equipment for the undertaking had been secured and all that is now needed is government approval of the transmitter site.

However, he warned that studio facilities will not be available here in the immediate future as such equipment is now unobtainable. He stated that the transmitter is being installed here to overcome the "difficulties" now faced by listeners in Penticton who tune in to CKOV. The transmitter will be fed by direct line from Kelowna. Mr. Browne did

say that it might be possible to have some local hookups, even with the transmitter.

He stressed that as the southern area grew in population he hoped to expand facilities here into a full fledged station.

Mr. Browne also reviewed the progress made in the field of radio and pointed to the fact that the Okanagan station has grown from "a man and a boy" 13 years ago, to a point where it now employs a staff of 17, and has a yearly payroll of $30,000.

He stated that CKOV had originated school broadcasting in Canada under the direction of Cyril Mossop, former Kelowna music teacher, and well known throughout the valley, and Kenneth Caple, of Summerland, now director of school broadcasting in B.C.

Mr. Browne recalled that the first of these broadcasts was given in November, 1936, under the direction of the Okanagan Valley

Teachers' Association.

Farm broadcasting was also a feature of the Okanagan station's programs many years ago and they "have to set the pattern" for similar programs which are now broadcast nationally and regionally, Mr. Browne stated.

The three great developments of radio in the future will be television, frequency modulation, and radio facsimile transmission, the speaker asserted.

The last named has to do with the broadcasting of the printed word or pictures and it would not be beyond the realm of possibility to have newspaper contents transmitted in this manner.

The development of radio and its allied science of electronics has, under the stimulus of war, been amazing.

The applications of these new discoveries and techniques to peacetime living will have a far-reaching effect, it was predicted.

TRANS-CANADA TO BE COMPLETED

APRIL 10, 1941 — For long years motorists have dreamed of travelling by an all-Canadian highway from Canada's Atlantic shores to where the Pacific beats on its western coast. They realized that to complete the road would take time; that many engineering problems would have to be solved, and that a huge financial outlay would be required. Few thought that the trans-continental trip would be possible by airplane before the road was completed. During those years waiting the airplane has passed through the experimental stage to reach its present state of perfection. The automobile has also improved. It is faster, more comfortable to ride in, and is not subject to those fire and mechanical ailments which afflicted automobiles of an earlier vintage, but it has not developed wings. Airways require no filling and grading, no miles of pavement between landing fields.

The motor road must have all these and more. Until the road is completed, or wings permit the car to fly, motorists will have to wait, and that period of waiting is drawing to a close.

As a bridge is built across a wide river, extending from either shore to meet in the centre, so the Trans-Canada highway has developed. There now remains to be built either the 150-mile stretch between Hearst and Geraldton in Northern Ontario, or the longer one along the north shore of Lake Superior between Sault St. Marie and Schreiber. This northern gap will in all probability be completed during 1941. Breaking its war-time policy of making no capital expenditures on roads, the Ontario government is proposing to spend $6,000,000 on completing the highway. It is estimated that an expenditure of $27,000,000 will be required to complete the southern route.

Almost thirty years ago an author dreamed as he wrote of this highway and of Canada as a tourist country, "Where one automobile has travelled, a hundred will be ready to follow, and a thousand eager to travel a four thousand mile highway through a panorama, unique, varied rugged and consistently sublime. The house beautiful will be set in order. There will be the perfected road running from sea to sea. There will be good hotels; wholesome little inns will be as plentiful as scenery. Invitations will go out to all the world to tour the Dominion." The waiting has been long but motorists will perhaps this fall, or next year, travel America's longest highway.

1940-1949

Alaska Highway Opens Nov. '42

Difficulties Of Alaska Road Construction Are Outlined

Trade Board Hears N.P. Steacy

Something of the tremendous difficulties involved in the construction of the Alaska highway were outlined to members of the Penticton Board of Trade at their regular monthly dinner meeting on Wednesday night of last week at the Incola hotel by N.P. Steacy, western manager for the Borden Milk Company, who spent considerable time in the north country when the "road" was under construction.

"The road was built for military reasons," explained Mr. Stacey, "to ensure that supplies, troops, and ammunition could reach Alaska in the event of a Japanese attack."

One month after Pearl Harbor, United States and Canadian authorities had agreed on the need for the road.

"Canada was very generous," the speaker added. "She gave the United States the right of way through B.C., the Northwest Territories, and the Yukon."

The United States Engineer Corps, which actually had charge of the work, were faced with the task of pushing the road 1,667 miles through a country, wild, desolate and totally unexplored.

"There was nothing to go on," Mr. Stacey pointed out, "and every politician and chiseler had his own ideas on where the route should go."

However, officers of the U.S. Engineer Corps made a preliminary survey of the route from the air and orders were then given for the actual commencement of work.

On March 22, 1942, the first 4,000 men of the U.S. army arrived in the sleepy little town of Dawson Creek, from which center the road starts. At that time the thermometer was down to 22 below zero and there was very little accommodation for the men.

However, more troops and civilian workers poured into the town until a force of 15,000 road builders had been assembled.

The immediate task was to establish working bases every 500 miles along the road and this had to be done before the spring breakup and thaw.

At first a terrible "bottleneck" occurred in the Northern Alberta Railway which was not equipped to handle the huge volume of supplies sent over it. However, this was soon corrected and the assault on the road was commenced.

With a total of 50,000 men and 10,000 pieces of road making equipment the great task was started. From the northern end crews worked south with supplies sent in by boats from Seattle, Vancouver, and Portland.

About three-quarters of the equipment was taken over the various rivers, many of them as large and as swift as the Fraser River, to establish bases when a "chinook" blew up and threatened a thaw.

"However, the Gods were on the side of the Allies," Mr. Stacey said. "It froze again and the rivers were solid sheets of ice. Thus the equipment was transported to the various bases in time."

In the actual construction of the road the huge bulldozers led the attack. Their massive iron sheathed snouts ripped through virgin forests, cutting down trees, uprooting hillocks, and gouging out of the right of way.

Behind the bulldozers came the scrapers, used for leveling the road, which in turn were followed by the ditchers, which dug ditches on each side of the route.

Soft spots were ballasted with gravel and rock, and rolled until they became firm.

North of Fort Nelson the engineers encountered their toughest enemy - muskeg. This has still to be licked.

At first the overburden was stripped off and the road foundations carried down to the glacial ice. It was thought that the road bed and gravel would provide enough insulation to keep the ice from melting but this proved to be wrong. The ice did melt and water "boiled" up through to the road bed making huge soft spots in which trucks and equipment became bogged.

Later it was found that building the road right over the top of the muskeg was the most satisfactory procedure. However, this problem still remains to be solved adequately.

The first 85 miles of the highway is 36 feet wide as to the travelled portion, but after that it narrows to 24 feet. However, the right of way is cleared 100 feet wide along the entire route. When the road is completed Mr. Stacey estimated that the grades would run between five and eight percent. He admitted that they are considerably more than this in some places at the present time. At one spot there is a 27 percent incline.

Beyond Fort Nelson are five ranges of mountains over which the route was taken, the peak being Soldiers' Summit, 3,500 feet above sea level.

Something of the engineering problem involved can be gathered from the fact that there are 36 large bridges and 100 smaller structures along the route. The large bridges are about the size of the First Narrows suspension span in Vancouver. The material for all these bridges had to be transported over the road through a desolate wilderness.

Along the road are hospitals, gas stations, repair depots, and other facilities to keep the road and its fleets of trucks operating.

The men who built the road, many of whom came from the warm southern states, faced incredible hardships in the construction of the route. Weather and insects seemed to be the greatest problems.

In November 1942 the Battle of the Alaska road was won and trucks loaded with supplies rolled over the route for United States bases in Alaska.

Activity On Alaska Road Route Plans

Penticton Council Endorses Suggestion From Kamloops Chamber of Commerce

Penticton council, at Tuesday morning's meeting, went on record as endorsing a suggestion from the Kamloops Junior Chamber of Commerce, which asked for unremitting activity in obtaining the Okanagan routing for the Alaska highway, when and if it is built.

The council decided to instruct its representatives to the Alaska highway meetings to act with that end in view.

A letter from the Kamloops body reviewed the entire situation and reiterated the reasons favoring the Okanagan route.

The letter reads as follows:

The proposed Alaska highway has recently received a good deal of publicity, and at present is engaging the attention of both the Canadian and United States governments. Our organization has become interested in this project and would like to place before you certain facts for your consideration.

Two Proposed Routes

There are two proposed routes through southern British Columbia:

1. From Seattle, Vancouver and through the Fraser Canyon, joining the present Cariboo road north of Ashcroft.

2. The Interior route entering B.C. via Osoyoos, thence north through the Okanagan Valley, Kamloops, along the North Thompson River highway to the Cariboo road, and Prince George.

In favor of the latter route, public opinion is strong, both in the United States and Canada, as it is felt by both civil and military authorities that it possesses very definite advantages over any alternative routes. We would, therefore, urge your strong support of this route.

In assessing the worth of the road in post-war years Mr. Stacey was of the opinion that it will not constitute a tourist attraction until the wild country through which it runs has been settled to a greater extent than is now the case.

Under present conditions a run of 5,000 miles over the road and back would be needed for a tourist trip. This would take too long for the average holidayer's vacation.

However, he did paint a glowing picture of the richness and beauty of the country through which the road passes.

Beyond Fort Nelson is a "hunter's paradise," the speaker stated, with scenery unparalleled for beauty anywhere.

The mineral wealth of region, including coal, oil, and other deposits constitutes an unlocked storehouse of wealth.

Along the road is a chain of airports and these will of course be an immense benefit to civilian flying when the war is over.

After hostilities the Canadian government will take over the road, and in this regard Mr. Stacey underlined the importance of a connecting link south into B.C. in order to provide a freight route from the Peace River block, which would thus be saved a long costly haul east.

Prince Rupert and Vancouver would both benefit by an Alaska highway road connection, it was stated.

The speaker admitted that the north country is a "hard land" with temperatures dipping down to 60 and 70 below in the winter. However, in the warmer spots temperate vegetables and flowers can be grown in the summer, during which time the sun never sets. Conversely in the winter it is night for 24 hours a day.

"Believe me no engineering feat was ever so successfully carried out in the face of such difficulties," Mr. Stacey summed up.

Churchill's Defeat
A World Of Loss

Much of the unofficial American world, unable immediately to view the defeat of the Churchill government from the standpoint of British domestic policy, is dismayed by the British election results. During the grave years, in which the fate of nations has hung on wise and aggressive leadership, the Churchill Government has been Winston Churchill, half American, who typified, nevertheless, unbeatable John Bull, and through whose inspirations the British people earned undying admiration in an unparalleled test of courage. Wherein had he failed the people who, at the first opportunity, rejected his guidance, his job still incomplete?

Prime Minister Churchill was not the sole possession of the United Kingdom in these critical days, and there will be a searching for the answer to this question wherever Ministries are challenged on their record. No British leader has wielded so great influence abroad. A spirited summons to his own folk was a clarion call to democracy everywhere. He, it was, who marshaled the free nations, later plotted the course of victory with President Roosevelt, following which was constituted the original Big Three, in whose hands rested the fate of mankind. Confidence in him was international, but at home it is withdrawn.

His successor cannot substitute the fire and zeal, the catching phrase and winning personality that made Churchill acclaimed in the United States. The foreign policy of the new United States. The foreign policy of the new Government may be all that is desired, but the atmosphere for diffusing it will be different. The British people were greatly heartened by President Roosevelt's re-election for a fourth term because of the assurance in continuity of policy which deeply concerned them, and were gratified by President Truman's promise to carry on. They cannot complain if the American people look for active confirmation from Prime Minster Attlee before giving him their full confidence noting, as they must, that the only remaining member of the original Big Three, toward whom Mr. Attlee's party leans sympathetically, had not eliminated from the American Republic all doubts as his foreign policies.

It is an old saying that the public is a hard taskmaker. When heroes are being singled out for awards it would have seemed equitable to have given the master hero of civilization in this war the mark of confidence he earned and sought. He will remain the genius of the day, despite determination by his own people that he may not speak for them longer. The United Kingdom has lost the world of leadership to satisfy a domestic ideology.

In England there is a church with fossils in its stone walls. Some other churches have them elsewhere.

Diamond Jubilee Of Historic Railway Event

One of the most important dates in the Dominion's early history was the completion of the C.P.R. at Craigellachie, B.C., in 1885. The diamond jubilee of this historic event, which actually sealed the pact of Canadian Confederation, was re-enacted on Dominion Day at Revelstoke, B.C., 28 miles east of Craigellachie, by Kinsmen who held an exciting three-day show to buy milk for Britain and support their local civic centre. Inset shows Miss Joan Barnes, carnival queen, being congratulated by C.A. Cotterell, assistant general manager, C.P.R., Vancouver, with Superintendent A.R. Everts, of Revelstoke, making the introductions.

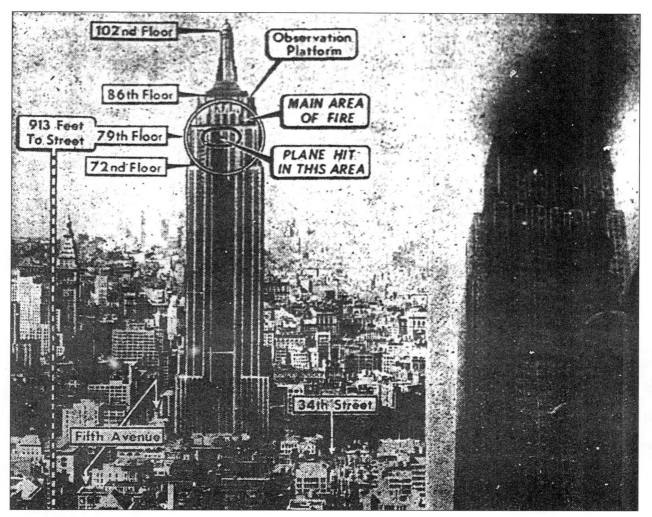

Key areas involved in the recent bomber crash into the 79th floor of the Empire State Building, the world's tallest, are shown in this view looking south from the north side of the structure. This picture was made prior to the accident, with a death toll of 13. On the right smoke billows from the building immediately after the crash from fires started on the upper floors of the building.

Japanese Issue Is Debated As Associated Boards Meet

Want Ottawa To See "Repat" Japs Sent To Homeland

The explosive Japanese issue was debated at some length at the quarterly meeting of the Associated Boards of Trade of the Southern Interior held last Friday night in Kaleden.

After much discussion it was finally decided to ask the government to see that all those Japanese who some time ago agreed in writing to repatriation to their homeland carry out that undertaking. It was pointed out that the majority to them are now trying to renege on this undertaking.

The Japanese question, which touched off a wide discussion, was introduced by T.B. Young, of Summerland, immediate past president of the associated boards, who stated that there are a number of resolutions which had been shelved in the past for action when times were more favorable. Among these, he said,

was the one dealing with the Japanese.

George Fraser, of Osoyoos, asserted that such a resolution had already been passed by the associated board.

John Hope, of Oliver, stated that the White Canada Association is now circulating a petition calling for Jap expulsion and he suggested support in this regard. Mr. Hope said that the petition is now in Oliver.

"Send it up to Penticton and we'll sign it," stated E.J. Babcock.

Dr. George Cope, of Oliver, then stated that Japs in the Slocan Valley are now seeking to renege on their agreement to go back to their own country. This written undertaking had been given by them at a time when it appeared that Japan had some chance of winning the war, he said. They had agreed to this step voluntarily, without compulsion. They should be made to honor their word, he added.

Dr. Cope asserted Eastern inter-

ests are anxious to get the Japs back in British Columbia. The speaker stated that the Winnipeg Free Press had been advocating such a course.

W.H. Laird was not satisfied with merely seeing that those who had signed for repatriation keep their word, he was emphatically in favor of sending all Japs back to Japan. "Shoot 'em all back," he stated. "Thank God there are no Japs in the south end," Mr. Laird favored the deportation of Chinese because they like the Japanese constitute an economic menace in his

opinion.

Mr. Young submitted the suggestion that the Japanese should be dealt with by Canadian and Allied servicemen and others.

"One Of Healthiest Places In Canada," Report Of Unit Director Indicates

But Penticton Must Have Sewerage System To Stay In Category

According to the annual report of the Okanagan Valley Health Unit, the Okanagan district continues to be one of the healthiest places in Canada.

In his annual report to the Union Board of the Okanagan Valley Health Unit recently, D.P. Avison, M.D., D.P.H., stated that in 1945 there had not been one case of typhoid fever, polio, diphtheria, or smallpox in the entire district. The district covered by Dr. Avison and his staff includes a population of approximately 30,120, with 22 school districts, and 5,020 school children. It stretches 76 miles north and south in the valley.

There was an epidemic of measles with 564 cases reported throughout the year. This epidemic was interesting, the report stated, in that it showed how a large body of water like the Okanagan lake can hold the spread of disease for sometime. Commencing at the northeast side of the lake in January, it first affected large numbers there and petered out by the end of June, only to cross the lake at the opening of school in the fall and spread down the west side to the south.

There were 59 cases of tubercu-

losis reported throughout the area in 1945. Most of these were reported by doctors in connection with their work or by the Travelling Chest clinic but, of 6,755 X-ray pictures taken by the Mobile X-ray Unit which worked in this district for 29 days, there was not one case of the disease reported. The reason for this, the report stated, was that people who suspect they might have the disease stay away from the mobile unit for fear the disease may actually exist and be discovered.

Venereal diseases, Dr. Avison reported, showed a marked increase toward the end of 1945. Although the percentage of afooted persons is much lower than in many other parts of Canada, the authorities are apprehensive because of many obviously unreported cases.

A thorough system of immunization and physical examinations of school children has been in operation throughout the Okanagan district. Children, including infants, pre-school and school children, were immunized to prevent smallpox, diphtheria, whooping cough and scarlet fever.

The Southern Okanagan Dairymen's Association was organized by Mr. Black in the early part of the year, and this brought many of the district milk producers together. It has resulted in the employing of better methods, bet-

ter sanitation and better all-around dairy conditions.

Mr. Black reports that the standard of restaurants throughout this district has improved 100 percent. Restaurant owners have come together under the district sanitary inspector's guidance and this has resulted in a great many improvements such as supervision of the cleanliness of employees, sanitary dish washing methods and many other changes essential to good health.

Many complaints were received by Mr. Black during the year. Most outstanding of these were complaints of overflowing septic tanks and of badly kept outside toilets.

The matter of water supplies has become a major problem for the district sanitary inspector. Frequent tests have been made, and show pollution in all unchlorinated supplies.

Mr. Black's report on sewage disposal pointed out that the present situation is an ever increasing menace to Penticton, that the situation has reached its peak and that an epidemic is imminent when the ground is completely thawed. "Thirty percent of my time," reported Mr. Black, "was used in 1945 for the supervision of proper disposal pits and the inspecting of unhealthy septic tanks and toilets. There is only one thing left to do, and that is to have a sewerage system for Penticton."

Kelowna May Organize Hockey Association

KELOWNA –

Hockey plans for this year began to take shape last week as a large gathering of 50 supporters of Canada's national sport decided to form a new Kelowna Hockey Association, responsible for icing organized teams in proposed, but not yet defined, Valley leagues. Two things appeared definite and one important decision is expected in a week's time.

By an overwhelming vote, the meeting decided to form an association with a live-wire executive, and the meeting unanimously endorsed a resolution to have at least minor teams playing this year. An all-important factor – where ice

can be obtained for practises – is under investigation by a large committee which will report back at another meeting next Tuesday.

Bill Moebes was elected president of the association and F.L. (Doc) Fitzpatrick "gave in" and agreed to act as vice-president. Eric Loken was chosen as secretary-treasurer. The following were put on the executive: E.R. Oatman, Bill Sands, Damon Verity, E.R. (Pinky) Raymer, Charlie Dore, former secretary-treasurer, Jack Schell and Horace Simpson.

Enthusiasm over getting into the Okanagan Valley Intermediate League was just as high, particularly among the many players who

have recently come to the district from the Prairies. Most of them hold they are eligible for intermediate ranks, but too old for junior. Discussion on setting up teams was adjourned until the ice situation could be looked into.

Moebes made the suggestion that a rink for practices be created in the Black Mountain area, where ice can "be had three to four months of every year." He said the place he had in mind was seven miles from the city and easily accessible.

He reported that the pond was already frozen over and that he thought it would be ready for use in about two weeks time.

M.L.A. Owner Is Progressive Merchant

W.A.C. Bennett Has Great Faith in Okanagan

Although he is a British Columbian by adoption only, W. A. C. Bennett, M.L.A. has proved that he is an exceedingly thorough one. This is true not only of his business life in the province, but also in his public activities.

The South Okanagan member has evidenced his faith in the future of British Columbia in a concrete way, by erecting the present new store building in Penticton. He has stated, both publicly and privately, that he is convinced this province is on the verge of a new era of expansion which may well surprise even the most optimistic.

He has stated that the province is now definitely in the industrial field in a new way, that the war has crystallized this into a definite phase of growth. In giving this opinion, he also indicates that the industrial era, far from being confined to the lower mainland region, will spread throughout the province. De-centralization of industry will be more completely possible here, through the ready access to raw materials and power sources.

At the same time Mr. Bennett has a highly sympathetic attitude to the needs of the fruit growers, and realizes the growing importance of this industry in the overall picture of the province. In his legislative activity he has made it apparent that he understands the urgent needs of the main industry of his constituency fully.

A similar idea has been fol-lowed in the institution of both the present new, and all other Bennett Hardware stores, each of which makes it a point to feature the requirements of the fruit-growers. With the opening of the new premises, a more expanded line of these implements will be carried.

Born in New Brunswick, Mr. Bennett enlisted in the last war air-force in 1918. Feeling the call of the west, immediately after demobilization he moved to Alberta, where he owned and operated hardware stores in Westlock, and Clyde.

As to so many others, Canada's Pacific province called; and in 1930 he sold out his business on the prairies, and moved to the Okanagan, where, in the same year he bought out the pioneer Leckie Hardware business at Kelowna.

From this he first expanded in 1931, to Vernon. This at a time when many firms were seriously considering retrenchment, rather than growth. His past, and present faith in the Okanagan has more than proved itself, however.

In 1941 he instituted the branch in Penticton, the same year in which he first became member of the B.C. legislature for the Southern Okanagan, being re-elected in 1945 as a coalition member.

Mr. Bennett is a member of the Kelowna Gyro Club, and the Kelowna Canadian Club, and is immediate past-president of the Kelowna Red Cross Society, a post he held for some time. Both he and Mrs. Bennett take a keen interest and an active part in community affairs at Kelowna, where they make their home.

New Bennett Hardware Store Opens

Building Reflects Modern Trend In Design, Utility
Structure Completed On Schedule Despite Many Difficulties

As modern as tomorrow and designed for it. This is the keynote of the new Bennett Hardware store, which opens its doors tomorrow, Friday, September 6.

Completed in record time, considering the handicaps through material shortages and kindred problems, the building is a credit to Main street, and may well indicate a new era in building here, such as was developed a decade ago, by the erection of the Capitol Theatre and post office buildings.

New "Okanagan" Tugboat To Be Handed Over

C.P.R. Boat Cost $200,000 — Generates 800 Horsepower

Today, Thursday, the new C.P.R. tugboat "Okanagan" will be formally handed over to the railway company by its builders, the West Coast Shipbuilders Ltd. Of Vancouver.

In addition to being the second boat on Okanagan Lake to bear the name, the new craft is the first diesel tug owned by the Canadian Pacific on this water.

It is also the most powerful tug boat built in British Columbia to date, not only for inland, but for coastal waters as well.

Cost of the new craft is approximately $200,000.

It can develop 800 h.p., and is entirely of steel construction.

It is 110 feet long, 24 feet wide, twelve and a half feet deep (hull), and has a ten and a half foot draft (at the stern).

It is driven by an eight cylinder, 15 by 20 inch 800 brake h.p. diesel, built by the Washington Iron Works, Seattle, and driving through an eight foot propeller.

Its pumps are all electrically driven. They were made in Vancouver.

The towing winch and anchor windlass were also made by Vancouver firms.

All bedding, fixtures, upholstery, etc., are of B.C. origin, so that with the exception of the steel for the hull, the main engine, and the electric motors, everything in this vessel has been "made in B.C."

The boat has accommodation for a captain, four officers, and a cook, all accommodate in single berth cabins, and twelve crew members, all accommodate in double berth cabins.

The company that has completed the build-ing of this tugboat was organized in 1941 to build cargo ships to replace losses through submarine action. Between May 1942 and January 1945 it has turned out fifty 10,000 ton cargo vessels. Subsequently it has completed three workshop depot ships for the Royal Navy, and converted a large passenger-cargo vessel into an entertainment ship for the Royal Navy, outfitted with theatre, swimming pool cafeterias, and also a complete brewery.

Since the end of the war, they have complet-ed two large 10,000 ton cargo and passenger ships for trade between Vancouver, the South Sea Islands, and Australia.

They are now converting two corvettes into stream-lined passenger vessels for the Union Steamships Ltd. for service between Vancouver and Alaska, and have built a large number of tugs and barges for service on the Mackenzie River and Great Bear Lake.

"FARM" HOCKEY TEAMS FOR VALLEY TOWNS?

Visitor To Kelowna Says Arena May Be Built In Penticton

FEBRUARY 6, 1947 — Today's issue of the Kelowna Courier is carrying a story of a suggested hockey league for the Okanagan, comprising "farm" teams from some of the New York major groups.

It is reported that Bobby Watson, who stated to the Courier that he had been a scout for the New York "Americans," is enthusi-astic about using the Okanagan communities for this purpose. He stated in a Kelowna interview, that the New York hockey interests might be willing to invest a con-siderable sum in this, the expendi-ture to include the building of an arena in Penticton.

Mr. Watson is also reported as saying that the close proximity and easy travelling in the Okanagan would make an "ideal set up" for such a program. He alleged that this is one of the few remaining areas where virgin hockey talent might be developed.

In an interview with a represen-tative of the Kelowna Courier, Mr. Watson said that the suggested arena would be in operation for next season.

Immediately word of the pro-posal reached Penticton, the Herald set in motion all necessary steps to contact Mr. Watson. But at press time today, he had not regis-tered at either of the local hotels, nor had he contacted members of the Penticton Living Memorial Committee, who had been told of the Kelowna release.

Vernon Airport Receives Licence At Long Last

VERNON, — Vernon airport has its license. It was something of an anti-climax at the Council meet-ing last week when City Clerk J. W. Wright read the announcement from the Department of Transport. There was a definite silence, then a routine motion that the letter be received and filed.

Only a few weeks ago the Council had been told to "fix the airport, or blow it up." Last week, mayor David Howrie said, "It's the thin edge of the wedge for air activity centered in Vernon."

There was more jubilation when the licence was turned over to L. and M. Air Service officials at the airport.

"We are going to frame it and hang it on the wall for everyone to see," remarked Manville Pepper, pilot for the concern.

The company will be ready to give sight-seeing trips during the week-end and within a week will have an eight-passenger twin-motored Anson ready for charter flights to the Coast or elsewhere.

"We hope to get some students trained and to sell a few planes to them," added R.H. Laidman.

Kelowna-Westbank Ferry Schedule

EFFECTIVE
April 1st, 1946

LEAVE KELOWNA	LEAVE WESTBANK
12.30 a.m.	12.05 a.m.
1.30	1.00
2.30	2.00
3.30	3.00
4.30	4.00
5.30	5.00
6.15	5.50
7.00	6.35
7.45	7.20
8.30	8.05
9.15	8.50
10.00	9.35
10.45	10.20
11.30	11.05
12.45 p.m.	11.50
1.30	1.05 p.m.
2.15	1.50
3.00	2.35
3.45	3.20
4.30	4.05
5.15	4.50
6.00	5.35
6.45	6.20
7.30	7.05
8.15	7.50
9.30	8.35
10.15	9.50
11.00	10.35
11.45	11.20

TUESDAYS—No 7.00 a.m. trip from Kelowna.
TUESDAYS—No 11.05 a.m. trip from Westbank.

H. W. STEVENS, Assistant District Engineer, DEPT. OF PUBLIC WORKS.

Biggest Enrolment In School's History

Total of 1,760 Students To Flock Back To School Next Tuesday

Penticton Junior-Senior High School will open its doors next Tuesday, September 2, to admit the greatest enrolment in its history.

An estimated 760 students will then be assigned to their grade.

Of these, 34 will make up the senior matriculation class, started for the first time last year. "With 34 in grade 13, we will have reached our maximum capacity," stated H.D. Pritchard, high school principal, in discussing school opening plans with the Herald.

With school population growing steadily without a corresponding increase in accommodation, "classroom accommodation is at a premium with us," Mr. Pritchard said. "Every available corner is filled with desks, in fact, you might say we have made use of every room except the boiler-room."

As a result of this serious overcrowding, organization of the school has been extremely difficult.

"We shall welcome nine new faces on the teaching staff this year," Mr. Pritchard stated. "Following next Tuesday's general staff meeting, I expect things will take shape for the year rapidly."

He added that until such time as additional accommodation is made available, the school will never be free of the problems resulting from serious congestion.

As reported in last week's Herald, the summer recess has

been spent in making necessary changes to classrooms to provide additional desk space.

A corps of carpenters has been kept busy all summer, providing, among other things, lockers for students in the senior high.

"While we may be crowded, we anticipate a brilliant year of school activity," Mr. Pritchard concluded.

Send Your Youngsters . . .

BACK TO SCHOOL

in New Fall Outfits...
From The CHILDREN'S SHOPPE

Wonderful values on everything your boys and girls need for back-to-school! Smart, warm, sturdy clothes . . . good quality garments that we were fortunate enough to get just in time for this week-end.

School Dresses

Our selection of dresses is amazing! Good quality rayons and woollens for girls from 2 to 16 years. See our jumper-type dresses . . . they're darling!

Jumper Skirts

Lovely fall-weight materials in many colors & sizes.

Sweaters

English wool sweaters and "Sloppy Joes" for teen-agers. Look hand-knitted.

From Birth to Sweet Sixteen

RAYON BLOUSES Sizes 14 to 16 SPECIAL 1.98

BOYS Blazers
Blue Blazers with white trim for smart young men.

Boys' Sweater Jackets

Featuring the two-tone sweater-type jackets (with full zipper) that ten-and-twelve-year-olds go for. Corduroy fronts and backs, woollen sleeves.

BOYS' DRESS SHIRTS

Hard to believe? Yes! But we have them. Well-tailored dress shirts for boys whose mothers want their "gentleman Jim" to be neat and smart.

The Childrens' Shoppe
Penticton's Clothing Centre for Boys and Girls   Main St.

1940~1949

More Indian Picture Writings Discovered By Works Official

Interest Expressed In Link With Past

Another set of the ancient Indian picture writings, for which this district has long been famous, has come to light. The find was made by K.G.L. Mackenzie of the Department of Public Works, while he was on reconnaissance.

The pictures were found by Mr. Mackenzie on the south bank of the Similkameen about a mile above its confluence with the Ashnola river. They are done in red ochre at the base of a steep cliff, just above the floor of the valley.

The drawings are said to be well preserved. They represent various animals and men, and what may be a war party. The central figure somewhat resembles figures sometimes seen on the coast totem poles and is thought to be symbolic. It may represent an ancient Indian god, but of course this is not at all certain.

Rev. John Goodfellow, of St. Paul's United Church in Princeton made a special trip down to the Ashnola to view the new find. Mr Goodfellow, who has long been recognized as a leading authority on the valley and its Indian lore, believes the pictures of great importance and to his knowledge, a new find. He states that there are now at least 28 separate pictures in the area, and many more in the Okanagan.

Many local people are becoming more interested in these pictures, one of the few ties which we have with the past.

1940~1949

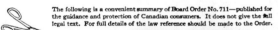

"Heather Bell" Cruises Okanagan on Maiden Voyage

A leisurely cruise up and down Okanagan Lake last week marked the "maiden voyage" of "Heather Bell" one of the valley's largest and most luxuriously-fitted launches.

Built largely by its owner G.H. Hollingworth , of Vernon, the 35-foot, nine-inch craft was launched on March 9. A double-deck cruiser, it is powered by a 115-horse-power Chrysler Crown engine.

With sleeping accommodations for four passengers, the boat is equipped with oil burning stove, electric lighting throughout, and an attractive "galley." All controls are readily accessible to the "skipper" in his pilots seat.

Guests on the "maiden voyage" included Mrs. Dixon. A. Moser, and Mrs. Henning.

New Air Service Links Penticton With Coast, East

Without fanfare or formal ceremony, the long-awaited air service linking Penticton and the Interior with the coast and Calgary was inaugurated on Monday morning when a big Douglas DC 3 dropped to the airport at 10:45 a.m. one and one-quarter hours after its take-off from Vancouver on the first regularly-scheduled flight to the Interior.

A number of company officials and local businessmen were on hand to welcome the plane when it taxied to a stop.

The arrival marked the commencement of a service linking Penticton with Vancouver by air, and will, on September 22, place the community on a "run" from Vancouver to Calgary, with stops in Castelgar and Cranbrook.

Although the arrival of the big 28-passenger plane went unmarked, the occasion has been hailed by local businessmen and civic leaders.

Before You Go ... Let Us

Vacationize Your Car

There's no need to spoil your vacation with unnecessary car troubles that can be cured for beforehand. Let our experienced mechanics "vacationize" your car — put it in the best running condition . . . for smooth, untroubled driving. We'll be open before the month's end — so plan to have Beckwall & Mounk Motors "vacationize" your car.

1940~1949

"Racism" A Vital Problem Of The Day

"Man's Inhumanity To Man" Chiefly To Blame, Anthropologist Tells Club

That problems of race enter into every phase of the lives of fifteen million American Negroes, was the assertion of Dr. H.B. Hawthorn, B.A., M.Sc., professor of social anthropology at the University of British Columbia, in an address to the Penticton Canadian Club on Friday evening.

But the visiting speaker made it plain that, in his view, race problems spring more from "man's inhumanity to man" than from inherent characteristics in different racial groups, for the only group recognized as a race is that with a stabilized heredity.

Three groups of scientists are interested in the human race, the zoologist, the anatomist and the psychologist.

"From the zoologist's point of view, we do not have a human race."

Unlike cattle, where there can be definite strains reflecting clearly defined lines of color, shading, and physical characteristics, the human race must make allowances for very wide variations.

"Our heredity is very much more complex, and I should say it would take 50,000 years to produce a stabilized human strain," and this despite Hitler's claims to a "magic" Nordic race.

As a background to his talk, which covered a complex and highly technical subject, Dr. Hawthorn, a native of New Zealand, explained how he had first become interested in the question through close association with the Maori children of his native island.

"Practically every child in New Zealand goes to school with Maori children," he stated, in pointing out that these natives play a large part in the life of New Zealand, to the extent that of two political parties in the parliament, the four Maori members hold the balance of power.

From this introduction, he made his first point, that our ideas about race are not inherited, and do not form part of our instinctive equipment.

Thus, where race discrimination exists, it has been acquired through the years. Where it does not exist, it has been proven that races can live amicably side by side.

Local Child Polio Victim

"No Need For alarm" - School Opening As Planned

A definite case of polio was diagnosed here in Penticton last week.

The case affects a five-year-old girl. It is described by Dr. A.N. Beattie, director of the Okanagan Valley Health Unit, as a mild case, with a small amount of paralysis in one leg. He states that prospects are good for ultimate recovery.

A strict three-weeks quarantine, in accordance with provincial regulations, has been imposed on the household involved.

There have been no other recent cases in this vicinity, Dr. Beattie emphasizes. Rumors of further outbreaks are without foundation.

There was a case here in May, and more recently two cases in Beaverdell, which is outside this health unit.

Elsewhere in the unit, a case was diagnosed at Benvoulin, just outside Kelowna, in July.

So far as is known, there have been no occurrences of the disease in the North Okanagan Health Unit.

"Control in your own home," is Dr. Beattie's advice so far, as preventive measures are concerned. "this is more important than any public measure."

He said that prevention, "comes down to a matter of cleanliness, and, above everything else - fly control."

Dr. Beattie urges everyone to pay the strictest attention to garbage. Hands should be scrupulously clean, particularly before eating, and this is a point to be emphasized upon children. All fruit should be washed before it is eaten - and kept away from flies.

"We emphasize that control in the home is the fundamental requisite," Dr. Beattie told the Herald. "But the public can be reassured that we are watching the whole situation very carefully, and public measures will be taken if they are really necessary."

The question of any delay in school opening, next Tuesday, has not yet been approached, "because that step will necessarily depend on the conditions then prevailing."

"While the Health Unit is exercising every care in studying the situation," he stated, "it is also fair to add that, under present circumstances, there is no need for undue public alarm in Penticton. There are few seasons in which there are not some reported cases, here as elsewhere."

The unit, he added, "is remarkably free from all other disease at this time."

He admitted that a close eye was being kept on the undulant fever situation in Penticton.

"But we know this disease is going to crop up, we are expecting it - as we do anywhere where raw milk continues in sale."

Two Cases Of Polio At Summerland Close School

Authorities State Every Precaution Being Taken

Incidence of two cases of polio in Summerland has delayed school opening there for an indefinite period, and threatened the continuance of Penticton's new school term, it was revealed this week.

Decision to close the Summerland schools came when a Summerland woman, mother of three, was stricken with the scourge last week. Tests of spinal fluids confirmed the case early this week. While there are no new cases in Penticton, it is understood that the health unit would not hesitate to close the schools here should there be any further signs of the disease.

On Wednesday a 13-year-old Summerland youngster was stricken with the disease and steps were taken to prevent any major outbreak. The case was hospitalized in Penticton.

Several organizations cancelled meetings and the schools will remain closed until all danger is passed.

In Penticton, a major step in preventing any outbreak here was taken when a citizen, Wally Mutch, appeared before council Tuesday night and offered to spray the Main street lanes at the rear of business houses and restaurants with DDT.

Council accepted the offer and provided the DDT, of which 50 pounds were used. On Wednesday morning, Mr. Mutch began his task using a Bee-Kill sprayer supplied by Gerald Duffus Ltd.

All main lanes were given a good dousing and afterwards the vicinity of the school and school grounds was sprayed.

Dr. A.N. Beattie, director of the Okanagan Valley Health Unit, could not be reached this morning for any comment on the possibility of closing Penticton's schools as a preventive measure.

Harry Black, inspector for the health unit, stated that every precaution will be taken here to keep files down and to maintain Penticton's present polio-free condition.

"Final Answer" to Polio Scourge

VANCOUVER, (BUP) - British Columbia health officers began issuing instructions to parents for a mass Salk anti-polio vaccination program today after proclaiming the vaccine to be "the final answer" in the fight against the scourge.

Hopes that every child in B.C. will get free inoculations were expressed by Dr. George Elliott, Deputy Provincial Health Officer. He said free immunization is part of the "normal program of preventive medicine" in British Columbia.

Meanwhile, it was disclosed that the vaccine will be available commercially in Vancouver sometime this week. Two Eastern Canadian firms, the Parke, Davis Co., and the Eli Lilly Co., were licensed by the federal government to distribute the vaccine and a spokesman said the vaccine will go on sale here later this week. Retail price of the vaccine is expected to be $5 for three shots.

A mass inoculation program of 49,308 British Columbia children between the ages of five and seven will get under way on Monday.

Arrangements for the inoculations, which will be given at various schools and health units, were announced in detail today by government health officers.

Expects Vaccine Will Soon Be Available

Dr. W.H. White, president of the Penticton Medical Association, said today that Salk polio vaccine in certain quantities would likely soon be available here.

He said that once authorization for distribution is obtained the "go-ahead" would be given and some of the vaccine would undoubtedly be available in this area.

Asked his reaction to news that the report issued yesterday proved the success of the vaccine in the fight against polio, Dr. White said, "personally, I feel this is a great step forward and heartily endorse its use."

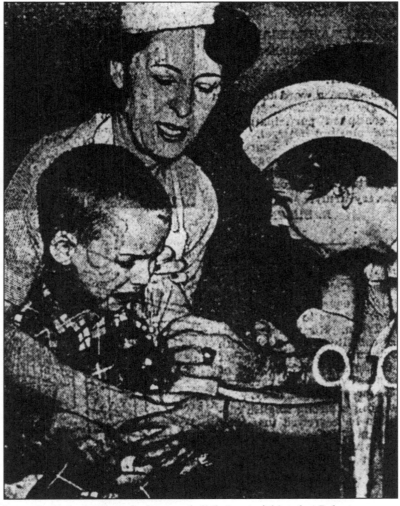

It may be in the interest of science and all that sort of thing, but Robert Henninger, 7, raises a protest in McLean, Va., as he becomes one of first children to be vaccinated in a U.S. test of the new polio vaccine developed by Dr. Jonas Salk. Two nurses and a doctor soothed his hurt feelings with a lollypop. About 1,000,000 children will get shots in the infantile paralysis test, half of them receiving a non-vaccine solution for comparison.

Will Fight Polio With Salk Vaccine

Two thousand children of the South Okanagan, in the five and six years of age group, will this summer receive Salk vaccine in the fight against poliomyelitis. They are part of a group of 48,000 British Columbia youngsters who will receive the vaccine.

This was announced by the Union Board of Health at a meeting of the South Okanagan Health Unit held Wednesday afternoon in the council chamber at City Hall.

START IN APRIL

The plan as outlined calls for the immunization to start on April 17, immediately after the Easter school holiday, with the first injection then, another a week later, and one more four weeks later.

Consent of parents will be sought in each instance, indications being that such agreement is readily forthcoming, when it means relief from the danger of poliomyelitis.

Only sufficient vaccine is available for the age-group specified. The total supply of Connaught Medical Laboratories in Toronto, who have just started manufacturing the material, has been purchased through the dominion and provincial health grants and no vaccine will be available privately this year.

TIDBITS

Health Unit Urges Milk Pasteurization

FEBRUARY 26, 1948 — "Poison cocktails" is how officials of the Okanagan Valley Health Unit describe the use of unpasteurized milk now being served in many Penticton homes, and the organization is bringing to the public's attention the danger of drinking raw milk.

During the week of March 1 to 7, health unit officials will make special efforts to bring this matter to the attention of the public.

"Milk from the healthiest cow can still result in an individual contracting diphtheria, typhoid and paratyphoid fever, scarlet fever, septic sore throat, or dysentery if the milk is handled and contaminated by a germ carrier," it was pointed out. "Unpasteurized cheese, butter, cottage cheese, cream and home-made ice cream can be just as 'lethal' as raw milk."

Pasteurization is the only method whereby milk-borne diseases can be eliminated.

May Develop Snow Mountain For Skiers

FEBRUARY 10, 1948 — Two widely separated sport developments that may, if they prove feasible, mean a great deal to the Okanagan have been under the review by interested groups during the past few days.

One concerns winter sport, the other wider use of the lakes that dot the Okanagan during the summer.

Recently a group of local skiers have been "looking around" for a better locale for their winter sport than is now afforded by the Elk Horn ski bowl. In doing this emphasis has been laid upon the needs of non-competitive enthusiasts.

Some suggestion was made Apex Mountain (Nickel Plate) would be most suited to this, but a well-known local expert, who withheld his name, has declared emphatically for Snow Mountain as the best site.

It is now suggested that this mountain, well known to some local nimrods as a one-time good source for deer hunting, would provide approximately a six-months' ski season, and that it could be easily made readily accessible to Penticton and Summerland.

New By-Law To Mean "Quieter" Local Streets

MARCH 18, 1948 — "Preaching And Praying Aloud" Comes Under Ban

Final reading was given Monday night to a by-law that will be welcomed by a good many ideal residents.

The by-law stipulates that "no person shall preach or pray aloud, or make any oration or haranguer any unnecessary noise or boisterous outcry, or any political or other demonstration on any Penticton street, without permission of the council."

It is aimed specifically at travelling sound trucks, but was not passed until after considerable discussion last week and this.

Postal Delivery To Start On Monday

Eight New Postmen Will Inaugurate Long-South House-To-House Service

"PUBLIC MUST CO-OPERATE" SAYS POSTAL SUPERVISOR; DISTRICT IS DIVIDED INTO SEVEN ROUTES

Postal delivery service starts in Penticton next week.

Culmination of a strenuous campaign by civic officials and the Penticton Board of Trade, the long awaited system will at last get under way, with the new "posties" starting out with their bags of mail after an official send-off on Monday morning. Boundaries have been established, routes tentatively mapped out, and the eight new members of His majesty's postal service appointed.

Supplies and equipment have been installed at the Oddfellows' lower hall, which will serve as the sortation sub-post office until a new addition to the post office building is erected.

G.C. Stewart, postal supervisor at Vancouver, has been in Penticton this week, getting the carrier delivery details fully organized, and instructing the new postmen in their duties.

He told the Herald; "We are doing our part. It is up to the people of Penticton to do theirs."

"This means they must have letter-slots in their doors or approved mail boxes outside, or their mail will have to come back to general delivery.

It is also up to them to notify their correspondents, and especially any publications they receive, of the change in address.

"These are bound to be problems, and some mail will pile up, because we cannot find the right party. But we shall do our utmost. Co-operation will minimize the difficulties."

Ceremonies marking the inauguration of postal delivery in Penticton will be held at 10:00 a.m. Monday in the post office with G.H. Clarke, postal supervisor of Vancouver, in attendance.

Reeve Robert Lyon and members of the council will participate.

Last Flume In Urban Area To Be Dismantled

Irrigation Court Turns Page In History

While there was very little to mark the occasion, a page in local history was turned at the irrigation court of revision held at the municipal hall on Monday.

The Municipal Avenue-Scott Road irrigation line, the last flume passing through the urban area of Penticton, was legally ousted and the users of it formerly served deleted from the irrigation roll, by appeal of the municipality.

Back of this simple act lie months of negotiation before the last of those on the line signed agreements relinquishing their rights.

But all have now signed the new agreement giving them 108,900 cubic feet of domestic water per season at irrigation rates. The municipality supplies special pipe services to each property, and the water may be applied to the whole of the land for general agricultural, horticultural purposes.

The new agreement eliminates the necessity for the maintenance and repair of the flume, bringing ditch riders through town. The users will be able to irrigate when they wish, instead of when the water is running.

Portions of the flumes had already been removed. The municipal council, anxious to curtail expenses in the upkeep, and replacement of the flume, will now remove the remainder.

New Sales Tax Is Feature Of Budget Speech

Three Percent On Sales Announced; Will Provide Aid To Municipalities

VICTORIA —

The imposition of a sales tax was the feature of the Hon. Herbert Anscomb's budget as minister of finance, presented to the legislature at Victoria this week.

Imposition of this three percent sales tax to raise a further $12,000,000 revenue, increasing of timber royalties to pick up another $900,000, increasing financial aid to municipalities by $4,000,000, there-

by bringing the total financial aid to more than $17,000,000 annually, increasing financial aid to rural areas in respect to education by $11,00,000 reduction in the net debt by $10,000,000, insistence that the Dominion government implement its social security proposals now that seven provinces have entered into tax agreements, announcement of a $28,000,000 public works programme of a capital nature in addition to other provisions for high-

ways and bridges, are only a few of the highlights which marked the second budget speech delivered in the legislature on Wednesday afternoon by Mr. Anscomb.

The minister sounded a sharp warning with regard to rising costs of social security, welfare, education, and other public services as well as in connection with the spiral of inflation. These rising costs could only be met by restraint in expenditure and added revenues.

Kelowna's Memorial Arena Complete

The Kelowna and District War Memorial Arena, constructed to perpetuate the memory of those who paid the Supreme Sacrifice in Great War II, will be officially opened Thursday morning immediately following the Remembrance Day Service in The City Park.

Finishing touches are now being put on the $235,000 structure, and this morning officials said plans are now complete for the two evening ice attractions which will be presented Thursday and Friday nights.

The arena, which will hold approximately 2,500 people, is rated as one of the most modern in the interior of the province.

Test pilot Chuck Yeager sits in the cockpit of an unidentified jet aircraft in this photo released by the U. S. Air Force in June 1948. Yeager became the first man to break the sound barrier October 14, 1947, as he piloted an X-1 rocket plane.

(AP Photo/)

New Invention Makes Orchard Pruning Easy

An attempt to ease one of the most annoying orchard tasks has led to a new invention, and the commencement of a small manufacturing business at Trout Creek Point. Announcement of the new venture, the Trout Creek Implement Co., was made this week by J.M. Landry, head of the company.

The task referred to is the gathering

of prunings in the orchard, heretofore laboriously picked up by hand. Now, through use of a machine designed by Mr. Landry, weeks of back-breaking work can be accomplished in the matter of hours.

The instrument, called the "Trout Creek Brush Rake," is extremely simple, will be low in cost, but highly efficient.

1940~1949

Arabs Bomb New Jewish Capital As Both Sides Claim Victories; Jews Admit Being Hard Pressed

MAY 17, 1948, TEL AVIV — The army of new-born Israel claims it is near the capture of the Arab city of Acre to the north, and struck seven miles into enemy Lebanon. Ten lives have been taken at the cost of Arabs by air raids which have been pressed on the new Jewish capital of Tel Aviv for the last three consecutive days. Tel Aviv was bombed this morning. It is believed that only two planes took part in the bombardment, one of them a light or medium bomber. The bomber raid was apparently aimed at the port area.

It was admitted that certain Jewish settlements were being pressed by the Egyptian Army in Negeb (in the southern desert and by Iraq - in the northern Jordan Valley. The Israelite Army, Hagana, said Acre is expected to surrender at any moment.

CAIRO - The Arab higher executive committee said today Egyptian troops have driven within 30 miles of Tel Aviv after an advance of 34 miles into Palestine. The office said the Jewish Agency has authorized the surrender of Jews in the city of Jerusalem.

The condition of surrender provides the Jews to give up their arms. The men will be considered as prisoners of war and the women and children will be handed over to the International Red Cross.

The office, quoting a middle east broadcasting station, said Syrian and Iraqi troops have joined forces in the Samaks area, at the southern tip of the Sea of Galilee. Arab volunteers have captured Lydda Airport inside Israel territory, less than 10 miles from Tel Aviv. They also captured another strip at Qualandiya, a Jewish colony.

ARABS READY TO FIGHT TO LAST MAN

BAGHDAD - Iraq ministers pledged today the Iraq Army, with other Arab armies, would fight to the last man to rescue Palestine, irrespective of the nature and extent of he foreign support for Israel.

ATOMIC WEAPONS TEST SUCCESSFUL

WASHINGTON - The White House today reported tests involving three atomic weapons of improved design had proved successful recently at the Enlowetok Atoil in the Pacific. The tests were called a "mile-stone" in atomic development."

Hedley Homes Dynamited As Raging Flood Waters Tear through Similkameen Valley

Swollen Flood Waters Rise With Appalling Speed - Many Homeless

Homes have been wiped out, land and orchards eroded or washed away, water supply lines have been cut, and highway and roads blocked or severed as the Similkameen valley, during the past ten days, bore its share of the province-wide flood conditions.

While flood water has been the cause, it has not come form the same source. Creeks have contributed a major share of the damage, with the Similkameen river responsible for the remainder.

Hardest hit community of the valley was Hedley, but the gravest threat was to Keremeos, where, but for heroic measures, much of the town, and a vast area of orchards would have been inundated or washed out.

The sudden rise of creeks and river caused alarm prior to Empire Day, but it was felt that unless the long-delayed warm weather came with extreme suddenness, danger would not be too great.

Then, in Hedley, the first real blow came.

On Sunday, May 23, the town water supply was cut off, by the rapidly-rising waters of Twenty Mile creek. By the morning of the holiday, the after service had been restored, but it did not remain so for long.

Further rising of the creek, as upland snows melted, rendered it impossible to reach or repair the washed-out mains. Steps were then taken for water for home and café consumption to be hauled a distance of two miles.

Next, telephone lines were outed, then re-connected as a B.C. Telephone crew was flown in from Princeton, itself commencing to feel the flood, as waters from several sources rose.

Strenuous effort on the part of the West Kootenay Power & Light Co. maintenance crews, working under direction of J.D. McMynn, kept the "juice" lines open. As soon as one set of poles was washed away wires were hooked up from another.

The local medical man, Dr. Badger, took health precautions, ordering all water for drinking to be boiled, and commencing inoculations against typhoid.

All this was prior to Thursday, when disaster struck and a nightmare-battle with Twenty Mile Creek ensued.

The struggle ending only when 20 homes were a total loss, ten more badly damaged, and between fifty and sixty families evacuated.

The rising, rushing stream

undermined a 60-foot gravel embankment, normally above its flow, as waters reached a 50-year all-time high.

This bank, a mixture of free sand and gravel commenced sifting into the stream, entirely altering its course. It was this that caused the gravest threat, the considerable damage.

Freed of the bonds of more than twenty years, the swollen stream leaped over the wire-bound boulder banks and tore into the houses.

Several rows of houses were damaged, and others, near the highway bridge, were in danger of slipping into the stream, and causing a jam near the bridge.

On Friday some of these were dynamited, to prevent their creating a jam at the bridge, and further diverting the water, to endanger Hedley's main business section, some of which was dangerously-close to the rampaging stream.

Penticton Airport Proves Its Worth

On Sunday morning, just when according to a Vancouver newspaper report, it was well under water, Penticton's city airport entered into what proved to be the busiest period in its history.

The boom began at about 2:30 a.m. Sunday when C.P. Airlines began to fly out stranded main line railway passengers who had been brought to Penticton by bus from Kelowna. The passengers had previously been detoured at Kamloops because of floods in the area.

For the emergency period, CPA used a shuttle service of five extra aircraft, three from Vancouver and two from Edmonton, as well as the regularly scheduled flights. And when flying ceased temporarily early on Monday morning, 26 flights had been made and 500 passengers had been removed to the coast.

After a break of a few hours, flying resumed again and this time TCA joined in with their new 42-passenger North Star airliners.

It was the first time that this type of aircraft had appeared on the Penticton airstrip, but, before the day was out, two of them had combined to make seven flights.

The total number of passengers removed in the two day period was slightly under the 1200 mark - an impressive figure - but passengers were not the only cargo.

In addition, the airlines have flown in freight and express goods for the valley towns, including films for the local theatres. And, while official figures are not yet available, it is known that the volume of airmail has jumped tremendously in the past week.

Lake Level Hits Record Reading of 104.6 Feet

Little Hope For Relief In South As Dam Discharges 1,100 Feet per Second Into Okanagan River

As waters recede in various parts of British Columbia, and a special session of the legislature, to meet on July 7, has been called to discuss flood problems, the flood picture of the Okanagan remains acute.

Creeks have subsided, but in some districts are still a potential source of trouble. In others, the dropping waters have lifted the drama, but not the tedium of battling the damage they have left in their wake.

Okanagan lake, now at the all-time high since levels were first recorded in 1909, was at 104.6 on Monday, the last time the level was taken, and has risen since then.

An unofficial record states that in 1894 the lake was at least at 107, and boats plied Bernard avenue in Kelowna. The 1942 peak was 104.12, and the 1928, the last all-time record, 104.50. Recent heavy rains will almost surely raise it still higher.

Discharge into Okanagan river is now 1,100 cubic feet per second, which is agreed by engineers to be the limit that can be poured down into the lap of the Oliver project.

Coupled with the discharge from Ellis and other creeks, particularly McIntyre, the amount passing below the syphon at Oliver is estimated to be at least 1,600 cfs.

This extra discharge has caused several people living in low-lying areas west of Penticton to evacuate homes. Water had worked its way around and into gardens,

basements and on the roads leading to and from their premises.

The sandbag dyke bordering the main highway, west of the control dam is holding, but officials are serving notice to motorists that damage to this dyke will be "severely dealt with."

One unknown motorist ran into it recently damaging some of the bags.

Any give-way at this point could easily flood out scores of people and damage many farms.

People in the Oliver region are prepared for "a long siege." Major Don Hodsdon, Southern Okanagan Lands Project engineer and manager, estimates that it will be three months before the

lake will return to its normal peak height of 102.5. C.F.P. Faulkner, Dominion engineer in charge of lake levels, has expressed a similar opinion.

For this reason it is expected that flood conditions of meadows and other areas near Oliver will continue "for some months."

At Kelowna, the city park has been closed. It is covered by water from one to six inches in depth over most of its area. Only the road to the Aquatic building remains open.

It is anticipated that the heavy rains that fell yesterday and the day before will send Mission creek "on the ram-

page" again. Mill creek there, like Penticton and Ellis, is now behaving itself.

Residents of the lakeshore area at Kelowna are sandbagging homes. Damage to some, through seepage, is already mounting.

Summerland reports that its creeks are in satisfactory shape. There is 14 inches of water going over the spillway at Thirsk dam, but F.J. Nixon, municipal clerk, states that this is a "normal" condition for the time of year. Canyon dam has been partially filled, to keep it in service.

PENTICTON NOW A CITY

Bill 69 Creates City Of Penticton

APRIL — While it may never become known simply as Bill 69, as is the provincial government's famous Bill 39, a government measure bearing the number 69, introduced in the house a week ago by the Hon. R.C. MacDonald, minister of municipal affairs, is of considerably more importance to Penticton.

Bill 69 is the measure whereby Penticton's status is changed from the Corporation of the District of Penticton, to the Corporation of the City of Penticton.

The new city, the bill states, shall continue to be subject to the Municipal Act and "shall be a city municipality continuing to own the assets and rights, and to be subject to the liabilities of the Corporation of the District of Penticton in the same manner as if a change of name only had occurred."

Upon issuance of letters patent, the municipality will cease to exist and a new city will come into being.

The reeve and councillors, the bill adds, "shall be the first mayor and first alderman respectively of the City of Penticton."

The new city's charter will be presented in a ceremony to be held at King's park on the occasion of the visit here May 10 of His Excellency Viscount Alexander, Governor-General of Canada.

Incidentally, Bill 69 is the first measure to follow the introduction of the government's new sales tax, its provisions having been included in Bill 68.

Governor-General Will Present New City's Charter

Ceremonies At Kings Park Will Include Inspection; Freedom Of City To Be Conferred On Viscount Alexander

Details of the civic holiday next Monday to mark the visit to Penticton of the Governor-General of Canada, His Excellency Field Marshal The Viscount Alexander of Tunis, K.G., G.C.G., G.C.M.G., C.S.I., D.S.O., M.C., L.L.D., have been released by Reeve Robert Lyon who worked out the details with Major-General R.F.L. Keller, honorary ADC to the Governor-General.

Highlight of the visit for Penticton will be the presentation by His Excellency of the charter formally incorporating Penticton as a city and conferring on the Governor-General of the Freedom of the City. This will be marked by the presentation of an illuminated scroll and golden key.

Two district men who were honored by His Majesty for war work will receive their awards. E.J. Chambers, prominent Penticton fruit man, will be invested with the insignia and relative warrant of the decoration Order of the British Empire, received in the Dominion Day Honors List of July 1, 1946.

Mr. Chambers received his award for his work as administrator of fresh fruits and vegetables for the Wartime Prices and Trade Board. He was stationed at Ottawa during the war.

Also to be invested will be Arthur Millar, of Oliver. In the 1946 Birthday Honors List he received the O.B.F. for his work on the Joint Board of Inspection for the United Kingdom and Canada, being stationed at Ottawa.

There will be ceremonies to mark the unveiling of a plaque on the new addition to the Canadian Legion building and an inspection of veteran housing.

In the evening, the city council will be hosts at a banquet at the gyro hall at which the toast to the new city will be given by Hon.

R.C. MacDonald, minister of municipal affairs.

The Governor-General's special train will arrive in Penticton late Sunday night from South Slocan and will remain here overnight.

At 9:15 a.m., Their Excellencies will be met at the train by Reeve Robert Lyon and Mrs. Lyon. It is expected that the train will be moved overnight to trackage at the north end of Main street.

At 9:30 a.m., the vice-regal party will proceed to King's Park for the official welcome. His Excellency will reply, after which councillors and their wives and other civic dignitaries will be presented.

Then follows the charter presentation and attendant ceremonies, and the investiture of Mr. Chambers and Mr. Millar.

A review of "C" Squadron, Night Recce Regiment, members of the Canadian Legion, Scouts, Guides, Cadet Corps, and school children will follow.

District men who served in the very famous 8th Army will, at His Excellency's request, parade separately and the architect of Desert Victory will have a special word with them.

New Entertainment For Movie Fans

Interior's First Drive-In Theatre Will Be Completed Here Next May

Accommodation For Over 300 Cars

The Interiors' first "Drive-in" theatre, shortly to be erected on Main street, south of Ellis creek, will provide a novel type of entertainment for Penticton.

The theatre will provide up-to-date movie fare that patrons can enjoy without leaving the comfort of their own cars.

Such a project requires detailed preparations, and the promoters of the scheme have been working on their plans now for nearly four months. Purchase of the site from the city for $5,500 was completed a week or so ago by H.S. Kenyon, Jack Dairymple and R.P. Brown.

A drive-in theatre, such as the structure that will be built here, might be described as a huge carpark, with the autos arranged in rows above each other on sloping ground facing a large screen.

Weather conditions have also been taken into consideration, and windshield visors will be available in the event of rainy evenings.

Unlike the screens used in indoor theatres, the huge drive-in screens sometimes measure over 60 feet by 30 feet, but Penticton's drive-in screen will be somewhat smaller. It is understood that the actual film area will be 30 feet by 45 feet here. The actual screen itself will likely be constructed of masonite.

Big feature of the theatre will be the new-style listening devices, or "speakers." Each car will have such a speaker, attached to posts alongside the car ramps.

With eight or nine months of fair weather in most years, the theatre

would be closed for only a short season each year.

The theatre will be erected on 3 acres of former Indian reservation on Main street, just south of Ellis Creek, and may be completed by May according to present plans.

For the first few months, it will hold about 250 to 300 cars, but about 500 cars will be accommodated easily when the whole project is completed.

Admission charges will compare with ordinary theatres, each adult in the theatre being required to buy a ticket.

In some drive-ins admission is so much per car, regardless of the number of passengers.

Main difference between the proposed theatre and the only other drive-in in B.C., located at Burnaby, will be that this theatre provides speakers for every vehicle.

Now that plans are ready, it is intended to commence building immediately once the cold weather ends.

So far as the films are concerned, it is expected that a general variety of dramas, musicals, wild west, and comedy movies will be represented, with news-reels and cartoons a permanent feature of the drive-in showings.

The concern will spend in the neighborhood of $75,000 on the project, only one third of the money that would be involved for an indoor theatre.

"Don't you think that we're not doing this for profit," smiled Mr. Kenyon. "We hope to make money out of this business, but we're also glad that we'll be doing something tangible for the community."

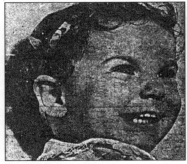

BASHA JITKOFF, 12-month-old dental wonder of Houston, Texas, displays eight of her 16 teeth. It is believed she has the greatest number of teeth for a child of her age which has been reported in the United States.

South Okanagan To Benefit By Huge Highway Program

Important information relating to highway construction in the Similkameen and South Okanagan is contained in the speech made by Hon. E.C. Carson, provincial minister of public works, to the legislature last Friday.

In addition to an indication of the continuance of the "permanent" policy for construction of highways, and making these conform to an integral plan, the address touched upon several Rems of importance to this district. These include:

Hope-Princeton highway - 74 miles to be paved this year; official opening date set as Labor Day, September 5. Cost of road given as $12,000,000.

Completion of Penticton's court house noted, but no further allocations for public buildings in the Okanagan.

Half million dollars voted for reconstruction of the Anarchist Mountain road for this year.

A further $700,000 voted for the Osoyoos-Rock Creek sector to be spent in 1950.

$200,000 voted for reconstruction of the Penticton-Trout Creek road for 1949; and a further $400,000 for the Penticton-Peachland sector, for 1951.

$60,000 (upped form $28,000 voted about two years ago, but not used), voted for Osoyoos Lake bridge; $15,000 for a bridge at Keagon Creek.

$40,000 to be spent on completion of Waterman Hill work from half-way down to the Okanagan River bridge.

Public works garage to be built at Princeton, and on the new highway link.

New equipment for maintenance of the Hope-Princeton.

Hopes that centre-line marking of main highways, in this area, will be commenced this year. Equipment now in the district for this.

While the official opening date for the Hope-Princeton highway has been set for Labor Day, it is unofficially hoped, in some quarters, that the road may be open for traffic a short time before that. Weather conditions will govern this to a considerable extent.

It is expected that paving on sections of the road already completed will be started as soon as the weather is warm enough, leaving only the now-uncompleted portions to be paved later on in the summer. Details of this are expected to be announced from the public works engineer's office in the next few weeks.

Board's Support For Central Trans-Canada Highway Questioned

One of the most interesting reports delivered to the regular meeting of the Penticton board of trade last Thursday was that of F.G. Pye, chairman of the board's highway and transportation committee.

Mr. Pye's report provoked a discussion on the position taken by the committee with respect to the Trans-Canada Highway, a position that has, the report made clear, committed the board to supporting the central route, via the Big Bend, rather than the Southern route, urged by Kootenay centres.

The committee was asked for a more detailed explanation of the action taken with regard to requests from Nelson and Trail for support.

Mr. Pye replied that the committee had felt that it was always the provincial government's intention to continue the southern route, and that by supporting the central route, there would be two main highways serving the interior, "and two routes are better than one."

He reminded the meeting that some 35 or 40 miles would eventually separate Penticton from the route of the southern highway, which would involve a detour for any travellers proceeding through to the coast.

"But if the central route is the main route, and we can secure a first-class highway right through the valley, then by branching off at Sicamous or Revelstoke a traveller might save 20 or 30 miles, pass right through the valley and link up with the Hope-Princeton."

He emphasized that the committee had studied the question and felt quite justified in not supporting the southern route.

Mr. Pye also reported on the joint board meetings at Westbank that resulted in a strong demand for better ferry service between Westbank and Kelowna.

Huge Crowd Sees Opening Of Kelowna Airport

KELOWNA — More than 3,500 cars, carrying approximately 10,000 people, choked roads last week as Kelowna's new civic airport was officially opened by Mayor W.B. Hughes-Games. Opening of the $40,000 field was the culmination of 20 years of hard work by the city and business leaders.

While thousands of people craned necks to watch, the mayor "buzzed" the airport in a plane flown by Andy Anderson, of Okanagan Air Services, before landing to cut a silk ribbon and formally open the field.

Many people, however, failed to see the airshow. Cars were locked bumper to bumper along the nine-mile stretch, and long before the parade started from the Board of Trade office, autos were parked four deep up the main street. The Board of Trade expected possibly 1,000 cars to be parked nearby. But another 2,500 turned up to crowd surrounding fields and park even in ditches. Canadian Pacific Airlines paid tribute to the new field by sending in the first "heavy" plane to land on the 3,000 foot runway.

For Marlon Patterson and Robert Goldie, it was like coming "home" again. Daughter of Mr. And Mrs.

Andy Patterson, Marlon joined C.P.A. one month ago as a stewardess. Pilot was Bob Goldie, son of Mr. And Mrs. James Goldie, Okanagan Mission. The other stewardess was Evelyne Mermod, Victoria, who has been with C.P.A. 18 months.

Mayor Huges-Games praised pioneers who first began working for an airport for this thriving city. Among them were Dave Chapman, D.C. Paterson, former

manager, Bank of Montreal in Kelowna, and Bob Willis, real estate broker. Alderman Jack Horn during the last year or so, has done a great deal of spadework leading to the opening of the airfield.

Herbert Hollick-Kenyon, one of Western Canada's pioneer fliers, now with C.P.A., predicted his firm will establish an interior air route through Kamloops, Vernon and Kelowna to connect with regular flights to Vancouver.

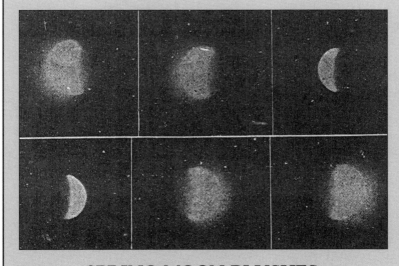

SPRING MOON BLUSHES
APRIL 28, 1949 — Shown above are six stages of the recent lunar eclipse which was visible in Canada. It was claimed to be a "once-in-a-century" totally black eclipse.

Interior To Be Linked By New Fast Air Service
Valley Firm Inaugurates Daily Flights Connecting With C.P.A.

On Monday next, September 26, L&M Air Services will be in regular operation, connecting Penticton, Kelowna, Vernon, and Kamloops by daily flights.

Kelowna will be only twenty minutes from here, by this new passenger and air freight service, now being inaugurated.

The tentative schedule being launched on Monday will knit the four principal interior centres into closer transportation than ever before in their history.

Within about two hours' time,

each place will be serviced on the one-way run.

Start of the flights will mark the climax of a long-desired convenience.

Since the inter-valley schedule will be dove-tailed into the regular C.P.A. runs out of Penticton, usage will be that much more advantageous.

Commencement of service also finalizes a long-cherished ambition of the principal figures operating this new air line.

It was about two and a half

years ago that an application was first made for such a charter. This was received last May. The operating certificate came through last month. Now the "L&M," which incidentally stands for "land and marine," is all set to go.

For their valley schedules the L&M will use a six-passenger Beechcraft twin-engine seaplane.

Berthing will be at the Lakeshore here in Penticton, and those in charge of the company are hoping that this community will speedily install a reasonable landing float.

1940~1949

HIGHWAYS

Premier Pattullo Endorses Early Completion Of Hope-Princeton Highway

JULY 4, 1940 — Declaring he stood for the early completion of the Hope-Princeton highway, Premier T.D. Pattullo thrilled a dinner gathering at the Incola Hotel here on Wednesday night. "I think the great majority of the people want that road completed," said the Premier, adding that he was one of that number himself.

He stated that he had never gone to Ottawa without urging the authorities there that a campaign of road construction be carried out. He said he had urged the government to get people to work on the highways. "I would like to see a program laid out, spending, say, $5,000,000 per year for ten years. You can build and spend economically with a long-term program. We could then get all our trunk roads completed with a program of that kind," he said, adding that he would work for the early completion of the link.

He also referred to the unpaved portions of Interior roads, stating "I do not like washboard, and I know others do not either, but we may have to do a little more oiling, and less construction now, however, until we can catch up. The whole thing today is the war; the big thing is to win it, and the next thing is our internal conduct - to maintain those things we have achieved, our health, education and similar legislative advances. Are we going to lose the benefit of that? Let us endeavor to lose no ground, not to slide back."

U.S. Route To Connect With Hope Highway

MAY 4, 1944 — A road to be built by the state of Washington, from a valuable stand of Timber south of the border, to connect with the Hope-Princeton highway, was greeted by the Penticton Board of Trade executive, at a meeting Monday night, as a welcome development.

"From what we know of the facts, this seems to be a most helpful situation," declared W. Watts, chairman of the board's transportation committee. "Its effect will be to put valuable traffic on the Hope-Princeton, and to ensure improvement of the latter."

Background of the situation was explained by J. Harry Black. The Seattle Light and Power Company is proposing to build a dam at the junction of the Skagit and Cedar rivers. When this is done it will mean flooding of, the timbered area and it is in advance of this that the timber interests are seeking to take out their products. The lumber will move in big trucks, connecting with the Hope-Princeton at about Cedar Flats, and going back to the United States through Hope and Sumas. There is no practical route south of the border.

Final Construction Of Hope-Princeton Highway Commences

Greeted with enthusiasm throughout the Interior is the news that work on the final construction of the Hope-Princeton road has commenced. Reproduced below is the route, showing the unfinished portion now under construction.

Late last week four power shovels and a gang of 50 men swung into action on the west end of the road four miles from Hope. This work is under the direction of the Anderson Construction Company, of Fort William.

Shortly, six trucks with five power shovels will be employed with an eventual 150 workmen.

The contracts for the road aggregate total $2,892,586. For its 83-mile length there will be no costlier project, say engineering experts, who point out that in some places the figure will amount to $100,000 a mile.

The Fort William firm will handle the western section and W.C. Arnett and Company, of Toronto and Vancouver, will work on the eastern portion.

In commenting on the Hope-Princeton road "Construction World," contractors' magazine, states that the construction is going to be a gigantic task. It has gripped the imagination of contractors right across Canada, as witness the many firms outside British Columbia who have looked into the plans and offered bids.

The Anderson company will build section "A," 27 miles from Hope to the Skaist River, for $1,316,477. The Arnett Company will do 56 miles from the Skaist River to Princeton for $1,576,109. In addition, materials, engineering, and contingencies will cost $357,414.

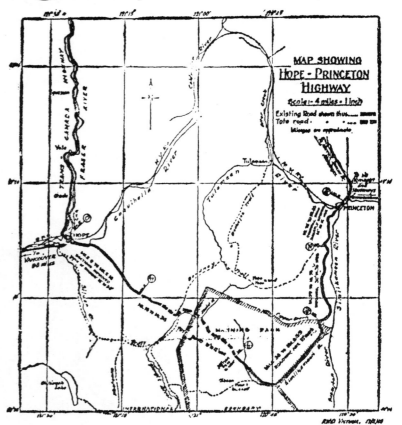

Want Hope Road Paved, Opened By Sept. 1

Two Views Of Associated Board Delegates Merged In Strong Resolution Passed Last Night

Two opposing views on the Hope-Princeton highway project were merged at the quarterly meeting of the Southern Interior Associated Boards of Trade, held in Okanagan Falls last night, Wednesday.

One faction wanted to be assured the road would be surfaced before being opened to traffic. The other wanted the road opened at the earliest possible date, regardless of surfacing.

Finally the two "camps" came together in the following resolution: "That the hard surfacing of the Hope-Princeton highway be commenced at the available opportunity in 1947, and that the road be opened for use, as a fully surfaced highway by September 1, 1948."

This resolution, drafted and moved by P.D. O'Brian, of Penticton, passed almost unanimously. It seemed to meet the views of both groups, and, according to statements made by delegates, is fully possible.

The discussion was opened by P. F. Eraut, president of the Penticton Board of Trade. He mentions a special luncheon meeting with Hon. E.C. Carson, in which this matter was discussed. The minister had advised against pressing for opening until the road is surfaced.

Mr. Eraut said that the government is purchasing a half million dollars worth of the latest road-making machinery, including paving equipment. If this arrives in time, work can be pushed forward considerably.

Thousands Witness Highway Opening

Province-Wide Acclaim For New Short Route To Coast

PREMIER OFFICIATES AT SIMPLE CEREMONY AS HOPE-PRINCETON ROAD OPEN TO TRAFFIC

The history of the interior reached a point of very real climax yesterday.

When Premier Byron Johnson unlocked a gate in Allison Pass, the official opening of the Hope-Princeton link of the Southern Trans-Provincial Highway was cheered by an enthusiastic crowd far outnumbering the advance predictions of the most optimistic supporters of the project.

Thousands of cars and even more thousands of people, jammed on either side of the barriers, testified to the significance of the occasion.

Literally and figuratively a gate was swinging open to the great interior of British Columbia.

The Hon. E.C. Carson, minis-ter of public works, acted as chairman, and a short address was given by the Hon. Herbert Anscomb, minister of finance.

There were greetings from nearby Washington, and from as far away as Ontario.

In attendance were a score of legislative representatives from all parts of the province.

But, by and large, the ceremony was simple. It needed no fanfare. The greatest commentary was in the size of the crowd itself, emphasizing the magnitude of the undertaking, then being declared completed.

Not a cloud marred the sky as Charlie Bonniver, of Princeton, for 54 years a resident of the district, prepared to cross through the gate girst, an old prospector with his pack horse. The beauty of the weather summed up an

Left to right — H.V. Anscombe, Minister of Finance, "Boss" Johnston, Premiere, Robert Carson, Minster of Public Works.

obvious feeling of enthusiasm in the event. Charlie's horse balked. But he himself was "the first across," with the premier opening the way for him - as a gesture to the old-timers who have long dreamed of the day.

It was "the day" for many

another, too many to mention in any detail - the government leaders and their deputies, construction men, and residents of the whole area, young and old.

For the day there were caravans from all over.

Crowds of people attend the long awaited opening.

Thousands of cars jammed the Hope-Princeton Highway in anticipation of the opening ceremony.

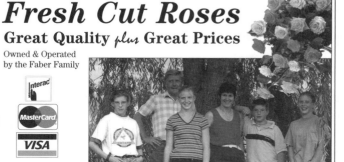

WHO WANTS SICAMOUS?

Kelowna Makes Bid For "Sicamous" — Wants It For Sea Cadets

May 26, 1949, KELOWNA — The Orchard City may be the resting place for the pioneer lake steamer, S.S. Sicamous.

Following months of deliberation, due largely to the controversial point as to who would maintain the ancient stern-wheeler, City Council decided to ask the Canadian Pacific Railway to moor the ancient vessel in Kelowna.

Final decision was not made until Tuesday of last week. The previous evening, representatives of the Kelowna Yacht Club appeared before council and pressed the city to take action.

Majority of aldermen felt the boat could be moored inside the present break-water behind the A.J. Jones Boat Works Ltd. At a special meeting held in the power house, City Council went on record 4-2 in favor of asking the C.P.R. to moor the vessel in Kelowna.

In making application for the boat, it was clearly understood that the Kelowna Yacht Club would be responsible for bringing the pioneer lake steamer here, and that the club would look after the mooring and maintenance of the vessel.

Fresh from an extraordinary general meeting, a six-man delegation from the Kelowna Yacht Club appeared before council, and advised city fathers they were prepared to accept the city's "offer" and assume responsibility of the Sicamous. The vessel has been laying idle at Okanagan Landing for nearly 20 years.

Suggested mooring was beside the breakwater at the foot of Doyle Ave. The steel deck, 215 feet long by 45 feet wide would be used to store boats. Free space, would be provided for all Sea Cadets' activities.

Believing the Sicamous would be a tremendous drawing card for tourists, the Yacht Clubmen said they proposed to charge a small fee to sightseers, which fee would help defray the maintenance costs.

Vernon B. Of T. Wants Sicamous

JULY 28, 1949, VERNON — The Vernon board of trade would like the old S.S. Sicamous to remain at its present mooring at Okanagan Landing. The board feels that Vernon has a prior claim over Penticton, which reports that the steamer has been placed at the disposal of authorities there, who plan to have it permanently moored at the lakeshore for use as a museum.

The Vernon Kinsmen Club made an effort to buy the old sternwheeler some time ago, and when the trade board council met on Friday, members decided to contact the C.P.R. pointing out this fact, and urging the city's prior claim.

Sternwheelers are gradually disappearing. They will soon become unique, and of great interest to visitors, the trade board states. Efforts will be re-instituted to purchase "Sicamous" for Vernon.

Photo courtesy of the Penticton Museum

S.S. Sicamous being berthed Ausust 1951 at the western end of Okanagan beach at Penticton

Last Resting Place "Sicamous" To Penticton

The final resting place of the brave old S.S. "Sicamous," pioneer lake steamer of Interior waterways, is to be on Penticton's lakeshore.

This information, known unofficially for some time, has now been formally confirmed with the signing of an agreement between the city and the Canadian Pacific Railway for the transfer of the historic relic.

The city will pay the railway company a nominal $1 for the purchase of the vessel and pay towing charge from Okanagan Landing where the old steamer is presently moored. The move will likely be made this fall.

Other centres, notably Kelowna, have frequently made spirited efforts to secure the boat, but it was Penticton's assurances that it would not be used in any commercial way that swung the deal in local favor.

According to the agreement, the city will maintain the boat as long as possible, undertake not to use it in any way in competition with the C.P.R. and demolish it when it can longer be kept in good repair.

It is anticipated that the "Sicamous" will be used in connection with plans for the development of the lakeshore as a park area, although final details have not yet been worked out.

Among suggestions that have been advanced is that the Okanagan Historical Society will be invited to participate in the care and use of the steamer. A museum might be the eventual outcome. Then too, it has been suggested that a small playhouse be constructed so that performances by the lake could be given during the tourist season. The new interest in dramatics in Penticton has fathered this thought, which finds much favor in the eyes of Mayor Lyon. The whole situation will be fully canvassed before a decision is reached.

S.S. "Sicamous," the third and last of the Canadian Pacific sternwheelers to ply the waters of Okanagan Lake made its week-day runs from Penticton to Okanagan Landing and return for eighteen years. Launched in 1914, this three-decked, steel-hulled vessel had a gross tonnage of 1,786 tons and was over 200 feet in length.

Luxuriously-furnished saloons, staterooms and dining and smoking saloons made travel on this imposing vessel an affair of leisurely living, and thousands of passengers saw the Okanagan Valley from the decks of this steamer each year.

Consternation was general when in 1931 C.P.R. officials made it clear that the service rendered by the S.S. "Sicamous" since its launching in 1914, was rapidly being superseded by bus and motor travel. It was pointed out towards the last that the daily loss of keeping this steamer on her run amounted to as much as $200.

Inevitable as the change was it brought only regret for the passing of an era - the close of a chapter in the history of the Okanagan Valley.

Sicamous Comes Home

City Royalty Welcomes Famous Stern-Wheeler

Like a tired but proud old lady, the still seaworthy S.S. Sicamous — a vessel steeped in the colorful history of the Okanagan Valley — came home on Monday to her final resting place.

Hundreds of Penticton citizens left their homes and offices to extend to the famous paddle-wheeler the royal welcome she deserved. They lined the beach as the S.S. Sicamous moved slowly into shore, arousing pleasant nostalgia in the hearts of pioneers who saw vivid pictures of the old lake steamer plying the Okanagan Lake, of the Sicamous seemingly joining the revelry of moonlight cruises.

The pathos of the ship's arrival — heightened by a light drizzle of rain — was most evident in the features of a grizzled old-timer who watched the high-riding ship, with its golden bells and checkered red-and-white flag fluttering in the breeze, continue her final voyage.

Said the old-timer, gazing through misty eyes: "I never thought she would come to this."

The S.S. Sicamous is home but not as a derelict and weath-er-beaten hull, its importance as the main transportation link between Okanagan communities forgotten. The old lady will have her face lifted. She will be dressed in a new and gleaming coat of finery and serve as a tourist attraction, a centre for your activities, under the sponsorship of the local Gyro Club.

Her curtain call after an outstanding role in the drama of Okanagan progress marks the end of an era in which the valley has changed from frontier land to Canada's major fruit-producing area. And when a giant CPA airliner droned over her, the S.S. Sicamous seemed to salute the New World with a "you take it from here".

There was also something rather tragic in the motionless stern wheel, the wheel that had pushed the Queen of the Okanagan through thousands of miles of lake water. And it was evident that the Queen would have been happier to make her last trip under her own power, without the assistance of the diminutive but powerful M.S. Okanagan.

"This Is Her Home", Says Skipper

One valley veteran with a special reason for the lump in his throat was Otto Estabrooks, son of the original skipper of the S.S. Sicamous when she began her career in 1914. Mr. Estabrooks, who later served as mate and also skippered the vessel, boarded her at Summerland with press and radio personages.

Now holidaying from his run on the Columbia River with a CPR ship, Mr. Estabrooks is hoping to retire on the same day that the Sicamous is beached. "She was a fine boat and it's a good thing she's here," he said. "For Penticton was really her home port. She was tied up here every night and what wouldn't Kelowna give for another chance of getting her! I'd have bought her myself if I'd had the chance."

RENOVATING COST HIGH

Capt. J. Weeks, Former Skipper Of Lake Steamer, Interviews Council

MAY 18, 1950 — Costs of renovating the S.S. Sicamous, 36-year-old lake paddle steamer, to provide a tourist attraction, would amount to some $25,000 in the opinion of Capt. J. Weeks, who for 13 years skippered the old stern wheeler.

Capt. Weeks appeared before city council last week, and his report on the Sicamous was a body blow to those who hope to see the vessel established as a tourist attraction and feature of the lake front park now being developed by the city.

The 1949 council purchased the steamer from the CPR, for the nominal sum of one dollar.

Capt. Weeks told council, the vessel, built originally to accommodate 310 passengers, had been subject to structural changes that reduced its carrying capacity and that it would not be suitable for a grand stand.

Rails are of light construction, and he warned, this would constitute a danger to children. Paint and decks are in poor condition; the interior, constructed of cedar, is very inflammable and the cost of proper moorings and maintenance would be high, Capt. Weeks said.

Council thanked Capt. Weeks for presenting his views, but took no action towards deciding the fate of the old steamer which is moored at Okanagan Landing.

1940~1949

Penticton Herald

PENTICTON, B.C., THURSDAY, AUGUST 30, 1951

VOL. XLII.—No. 35

Three Sections — 22 Pages

Temperature		
	Max.	Min.
August 23	76.2	45.3
August 24	76.0	42.0
August 25	79.4	46.2
August 26	78.2	55.0
August 27	61.8	53.9
August 28	56.2	45.9
August 29	64.4	50.0

Rain and Sunshine		
	ins.	hrs.
August 23	.01	8.0
August 24		9.7
August 25		5.8
August 26		4.3
August 27	.50	
August 28	.64	
August 29	.04	

Sicamous Comes Home; City Royally Welcomes Famous Stern-Wheeler

Like a tired but proud old lady, the still seaworthy S.S. Sicamous — a vessel steeped in the colorful history of the Okanagan Valley — came home on Monday to her final resting place.

Hundreds of Penticton citizens left their homes and offices to extend to the famous paddle-wheeler the royal welcome she deserved. They lined the beach as the S.S. Sicamous moved slowly into shore, arousing pleasant nostalgia in the hearts of pioneers who saw vivid pictures of the old lake steamer plying the Okanagan Lake, of the Sicamous seemingly joining in the revelry of moonlight cruises.

The pathos of the ship's arrival — heightened by a light drizzle of rain — was most evident in the features of a grizzled old-timer who watched the high-riding ship, with its golden bells and checkered red-and-white flag fluttering in the breeze, conclude her final voyage.

Said the old-timer, gazing through misty eyes: "I never thought she would come to this."

The S.S. Sicamous is home but not as a derelict and weather-beaten hull, its importance as the main transportation link between Okanagan communities forgotten. The old lady will have her face lifted. She will be dressed in a new and gleaming coat of finery and serve as a tourist attraction, a centre for youth activities, under the sponsorship of the local Gyro Club.

Her curtain call after an outstanding role in the drama of Okanagan progress marks the end of an era in which the valley has changed from frontier land to Canada's major fruit-producing area. And when a giant CPA airliner droned over her, the S.S. Sicamous seemed to salute the New World with a "you take it from here".

There was also something rather tragic in the motionless stern wheel, the wheel that had pushed the Queen of the Okanagan through thousands of miles of lake water. And it was evident that the Queen would have been happier to make her last trip under her own power, without the assistance of the diminutive but powerful M.S. Okanagan.

"This Is Her Home", Says Skipper

One valley veteran with a special reason for the lump in his throat was Otto Estabrooks, son of the original skipper of the S.S. Sicamous when she began her career in 1914. Mr. Estabrooks, who later served as mate and also skippered the vessel, boarded her at Summerland with press and radio personages.

Now holidaying from his run on the Columbia River with a CPR ship, Mr. Estabrooks is hoping to retire on the same day that the Sicamous is beached. "She was a fine boat and it's a good thing she's here," he said. "For Penticton was really her home port. She was tied up here every night and what wouldn't Kelowna give for another chance of getting her! I'd have bought her myself if I'd had the chance."

THE OLD AND THE NEW—It was a red letter day for the wheeler, shown below, her flag fluttering in recognition of a career lasting more than two decades of service to the Okanagan Valley when the S.S. Sicamous began, back in July. Hundreds of Penticton citizens lined the lakeshore to give the erstwhile Queen of the Lake the welcome she deserved. Now the "grand old lady" will be beached.

WHEN ROY HUFF and Nita Roylance shown above became engaged recently, they planned a wedding in the spring followed by a honeymoon trip to California . . . but Lady Luck had other ideas. Roy invested 50 cents in a Peach Festival ticket—number 41886—and it was drawn out of the raffle barrel shortly before the festival wind-up last Thursday night. The outcome: Roy and fiancee Nita will travel by a CPA airliner to Hawaii and spend their honeymoon in tropical sunshine under swaying palms. Roy is convinced that he made a wise investment.

Power Switch Averts Blackout

Whatshan-generated power saved Penticton and other points in the south Okanagan from a complete blackout of eleven hours duration on Tuesday of this week.

West Kootenay Power and Light Company transmission lines failed, from as yet undetermined causes, with some suspicion that sabotage may have been the cause of the outage.

OGO
Believe

JUNE 1944

Ogopogo On Parade For Twenty Minutes

MR. AND MRS. R.W. CRAIG, OF NARAMATA, DAUGHTER AND HOUSEKEEPER, CONVINCED

"I've been unbelieving about the Ogopogo before, but not any more. It is really there all right."

These were the words used by R.W. Craig, K.C., after he told a Herald reporter early this week about seeing the Ogopogo disport itself for about 15 minutes in the waters of Okanagan Lake in front of his Naramata home last Sunday at 8:00 p.m.

Mrs. Craig, her daughter, Mrs. R.E. Curran, now visiting at her parents' home from Ottawa, and Miss McIvor, housekeeper, were others who saw the lake denizen that night.

"It was the most extraordinary thing I ever saw," said Mrs. Craig.

Mr. Craig stated that the monster was bout one third of the way across the lake between Naramata and Summerland, at a point just below the orchard of Mrs. G. Hayman. She called to Mrs. Curran was the first to see it from the dining room of the Craig home. She called to others, including Mrs. Craig and Miss McIvor.

They were later joined by Mr. Craig, who at that time was rather skeptical about the whole thing. Not for long was he to remain in that frame of mind.

"You could see it quite plainly with the naked eye," Mr. Craig stated, but added powerful Zeiss field glasses were used to study the Ogopogo at close range.

"At first it looked as though it might have been a log fixed up by some practical joker, but we soon found out that the thing was real all right. It swam around, submerged and reappeared on the surface of the water and moved back and forth and generally fooled around in a space of water about one quarter of a mile square. We watched it from ten to fifteen minutes.

"It looked like a big serpent of some kind. Its body was mostly submerged but you could see the big head quite plainly. Its back was serrated and looked as though it was covered with scales. We saw about 10 to 15 feet of it, but how much of it was under water I couldn't say. The head looked like that of a dragon or a large horse. We could see it quite plainly through the glasses."

JULY 14, 1949

Skaha Lake Rival For Ogopogo Seen

Ogopogo no longer reigns supreme as the monster of all the surveys within the waters of the Okanagan Valley.

A somewhat smaller competitor, according to witnesses, made his initial appearance in the waters of Skaha Lake shortly after 6 a.m. yesterday morning.

The two men who reported seeing the Skaha Lake edition were Al Williams, manager of the Blue and White Cafe, and Tom McClenaghan, meat department manager of Superior Food Stores, who were on an early morning fishing trip.

According to the two men, the monster was about ten feet long, about six inches in diameter, black in color and slimy in appearance. The men were able to obtain a close-up description of the beast as it came very close to their boat. However, they only saw the body as the head and tail were not visible.

The animal propelled itself across the water in the style of Ogopogo, its body appearing as a series of humps, each about a foot long.

"My first impression when I saw it in the distance was that it was a school of fish, but when it got closer up it appeared to be a huge overgrown eel and was the same thickness throughout its body," Mr. Williams told the Herald.

"It appeared to come from the river mouth and moved through the water at quite a speed. It came directly across the lake at our boat which was about 200 yards from shore."

"I could almost have hit it with an oar, it was so close to the boat, but even then we could not see a head or tail. It's appearance made shivers go up and down your spine."

"We were both cold sober and we both couldn't have been wrong."

Those who have looked with pride on Ogopogo's lengthy residence in Okanagan Lake are pointedly muttering that this upstart in Skaha Lake is the work of Steve Stogre, whose Skaha Lake fish derby has been lurking enthusiasts to the other side of town. "It's the work of Steve Stogre," they say, adding that Mr. and Mrs. Stogre have been seen working quietly, at night, in tightly closed quarters on some mysterious object.

It is anticipated that Ogo, who is nothing if not tourist-conscious, will make a determined effort to restore his prestige as the valley's only watery phenomenon.

POGO
it or not!

AUGUST 1950

Ogopogo Goes Berserk - Herald Reporter Too!

EDITORS NOTE – A reporter's life is not an easy one, and Ogopogo, flying saucers and the odd flying ice cream cone popping up repeatedly do not tend to improve conditions. Recently Ogopogo popped up in Skaha Lake and a Herald reporter was sent to investigate. Here's what happened.

Ogopogo was scared stiff. He'd had so much publicity lately things were getting out of hand. His wife was mad too, and besides, she said, the neighbors were talking.

In fact, things had become almost unbearable. Last night his wife had said, "I'm sick to death of this, every time I lift up the paper, I see your ugly face."

Then she proceeded to show him a picture appearing in a recent newspaper. There he was with two of the most beautiful gals he'd ever seen.

"Look" wife pointed, and he read: "Beauty and he Beast – Lovely Betty Ball, former Lady-of-the-Lake and former princess Sharon West captured Ogopogo some time ago, and judging from the look on Ogo's face, he doesn't mind having the rope around his neck. But who would when roped by such charming girls!"

"Well?–" his wife said.

"I swear I wasn't dear–" and that was all Ogo remembered. Next thing he knew he was in deep water.

There wasn't much Ogo could do, so he went home to his mother who lives in Skaha Lake.

Of course, even in Skaha Lake, Ogo had to have his fun.

The next day Mrs. Pogo (his mother) read in the Penticton Herald the following account:

Ogopogo has deserted Okanagan Lake.

Early this week a "monster" was sighted in Skaha Lake by local residents and Vancouver holidayers.

"It was definitely something big and strange" said Evan Lougheed, Vancouver merchant.

Mr. Lougheed's version agreed with that of Mrs. Henry Swift of Beachside Motel, Mrs. A Borsato and Mrs. L.C. Way of Vancouver, all of whom were basking on the beach at the same time.

Said Mrs. Swift: "The lake was calm, there was no wind. All of a sudden waves rolled into shore. There was no motor boat on the lake or anything like wind to disturb the calm surface. A few hundred feet off the river mouth we saw a strange object heading out toward the west shore. We didn't see a head but there were three distinct black humps spaced a few feet apart. We watched it for five or ten minutes then it disappeared."

Several other unidentified sunbathers also watched the mysterious object.

This is the second year of such reports from Skaha Lake. In 1949, two local men claimed they sighted a similar "monster" breaking the surface in approximately the same location.

Mrs. Pogo was mad. She said, "Well–"

"Honest mom, I was only–" and that was as far as he got, as the quick lash of a parental tail sent him back to his spouse in Okanagan Lake.

SEPTEMBER 14, 1957

Ogopogo Seen Anew - Seemed To Be Drunk

Ogopogo, legendary monster inhabitant of Lake Okanagan, is claimed to have been seen by a Penticton-bound bus-load of 22 passengers near Peachland, Friday afternoon.

This time it was suggested that the monster was drunk because he was going around in circles.

The passengers and driver saw a churning swirl going around in a circle on the water accompanied by a white mist about half a mile from shore. The bus was stopped at a view point above the lake to let the passengers have a closer look. Some were reported to have seen the humps of the monster quite clearly but not his head.

Former Pentictonites Mr. and Mrs. Kingsley Morgan now living at Victoria, were among the group of sighters. Mrs. Morgan, who has had some doubts about Ogopogo's existence before, said she was now firmly convinced she had seen him. Mr. Morgan now has confirmation of the belief he has always held that there must be something behind the many reported sightings of the monster.

Bus driver T.A. Bond, of Penticton, didn't want to say definitely that it was Ogopogo that was seen.

"But there was definitely something there churning up the water," he declared. "It looked like the wake of a boat but there was no boat to be seen. Whatever it was I haven't seen anything like it before."

Mr. Bond added with a hearty chuckle, that if it was Ogopogo", he must have drunk some of that Kelowna wine because he was going around in circles."

A DECADE
IN REVIEW
1950 ~ 1959

More Danger From Space Bodies Than Atom Bombs, Chemist Says

Big CBC Show Here May 27 In School Gym

MAY 14, 1950 — Almost hidden behind a mass of arena blueprints, staging details, music memos and production notes, Canadian born theatrical producer Frank Eckersley may be found these days planning the final moments of the Western Canada tour of the famous CBC show "Leicester Square to Old Broadway." This spectacular review of gay 90's will hit interior points, including Kamloops, Vernon, Kelowna and Penticton.

SUMMERLAND —

Dr. A. Harris, a UBC chemist home for short vacation, told Summerland Rotarians at their meeting last Friday that we are in more danger from possible collisions of space bodies with the earth than we are from atomic bombs.

Another year has gone by and no one has dropped an atomic bomb, he stated, adding that now there is the hydrogen bomb to worry about.

One space body did land on earth last year, he said, but as it was in Russia little has been learned about it.

Dr. Harris drew attention to the impact of the chemist on everyday life of the nation and pointed to the development of machinery which has resulted in the virtual banishment of the horse from commerce and agriculture.

This has changed the economy as farmers previously raised horses and grew feed for them. Now they must buy the machinery and the gasoline to run it.

Dr. Harris recalled that several years ago he had predicted the manufacture of several items from coal. At that time he had been laughed at, he said, but the predictions had been correct.

In the same way chemists can relieve many of the shortages now apparent, he believed. As an example, chemists developed a method of augmenting the short supply of nitrogen by taking it from the air.

Increases in population, he believed, will force a change in the economy of the entire world.

As an example, trees won't be used for either fuel or building, he said, and people of the future won't resent chemical foods any more than our forefathers resented white bread.

Nylons will be a thing of the past, he believes, and clothing, such as a shirt, might be turned in and come back in the form of food.

Chemists are now coming out of their laboratories and are taking a greater interest in public life, Dr. Harris believed. They are keeping the public better informed as to the work of chemists as it is the people that must provide the funds for research, he stated.

Plane, Flying Saucer, or Smoke Ring – It Was Seen Here Twice

It's a bird! It's a plane! It's a flying saucer?

Tuesday evening at the CPR depot a "something" was seen in the sky which various people described as resembling a tadpole and an ice cream cone.

About nine o'clock as the train from Nelson was standing at the station someone cried: "Look, it's a flying saucer."

Norman Phipps, a railway employee, said he also saw something which he thought looked like a flying saucer.

"It was shaped like an ice cream cone and coming from the west. It was about three feet long," he said.

But J.A. Young, chief dispatcher for the CPR said he saw the whole thing, "and it wasn't any flying saucer."

"As the passenger train was getting ready to leave, smoke from the engine formed what looked like a perfect smoke ring. As it went up into the air it formed an odd shape, rather like a tadpole, and then disappeared," he said.

While this may explain Tuesday night's occurrence some explanation still has to be found for last Friday's apparition.

Miss Chelan Edwards and Bill Sutherland, a Greyhound bus driver, were fishing in Okanagan Lake across from Naramata about 8:30 in the evening, when they saw something in the sky.

It was about 1000 feet in the air about eight feet in diameter, and gleamed silver in the setting sun, Mr. Sutherland said.

"It was like sun shining on glass, I thought at first it was a plane," Miss Edwards explained, "there was no noise."

According to Mr. Sutherland it hung stationary in the sky for about five minutes and then disappeared in the direction of Naramata.

Other people who saw the same sight at the same time, but in a different place, were Mr. and Mrs. Tommy Bond, Mr. and Mrs. Marvin Bond and George Moore, who were swimming out at Skaha Lake.

Third Ferry Goes Into Operation At Westbank In July

South Okanagan MLA Says Long Range Plans Include Highway And Bridge

KELOWNA —

Long range government plans call for a modern highway on both sides of Okanagan Lake from Penticton to Vernon with a bridge across the centre of the lake between Kelowna and Westbank, W.A.C. Bennett, MLA (South Okanagan) declared at a Coalition meeting held in the Orange Hall here last week.

Mr. Bennett admitted construction of a bridge across the lake is a major undertaking and will have to be studied carefully by capable engineers. As a temporary stopgap, a third ferry will be put into operation early in July in an attempt to solve the traffic problem which is expected to hit a new high this summer.

Touching on the over-all transportation picture in the valley, Mr. Bennett pointed out the Okanagan had developed tremendously during recent years.

"I am an idealist. I believe we must have a long range plan and a short range plan," he declared, referring to the traffic problem across the lake. As a temporary expedient, we are getting a third ferry. But on a broad plan, we must have a highway clear around the lake, and we must also have a bridge across the centre of the lake. But the government can only meet these problems as they arise, and they can only be taken one at a time."

The speaker thought the present 22-minute ferry service is adequate for the time being. He apolgized on behalf of the department of public works and himself as MLA, for the traffic tie-up over the Easter weekend, and admitted that someone in the public works department had erred.

The third ferry, which will be ready July 11, will cost $344,000 and there is a penalty clause of $10,000 if the vessel is not completed by that time, he continued. Mr. Bennett said the new boat would handle 50 per cent more vehicles than the present vessels.

Touching on politics as a whole, the local MLA said he is in favor of a transferable ballot, which would prevent a candidate being elected on a split majority vote.

"Suppose we did have a Liberal and a Conservative candidate running in a three-way fight in the next election? What of it?" he asked. The transferable ballot, which may go into effect before the next provincial election, would prevent a candidate being elected on a split minority vote. The Coalition government would continue, and it will tend to allow more free talk on the floor of the legislature, he said.

Irate Naramata Citizens Call for East Side Highway

150 Attend Emergency Meeting To Protest Report That Naramata Against East Side Road

Over 150 irate citizens, packed into the Naramata Community Hall on Tuesday night, voted unanimously for completion of a highway to Kelowna on the east side of Okanagan lake.

Three delegates were elected to present the case for Naramata to the government at Victoria.

They will make the trip armed with a petition drawn up at the meeting and signed enthusiastically by almost everyone there.

A collection taken up in the hall yielded $35, to be used to help finance the journey.

J.V.H. Wilson, one of the delegates chosen, branded as "preposterous rubbish" the representations of "certain elements in Kelowna" that construction of the highway was not feasible.

The "certain elements" pressing for a bridge, Mr. Wilson believed, would not be satisfied with the bridge alone.

"Do the people realize that the bridge is just a beginning?" he said. "The next thing will be a move for completion of the Peachland-Princeton cut-off."

"This is a nice dream," he said, "to be paid for by the taxpayers of B.C. It's a nice dream but not for the present."

Loud applause greeted Mr. Wilson's remarks that the west side road and the ferry were adequate for local needs.

"It is not local traffic that is causing the bottleneck," he said.

They ignore the thriving communities of Okanagan Mission and Naramata when they say that there would be no contribution to a road on the east side, he stated.

"This is the eleventh hour," Mr. Wilson added, "and we must decide soon for strong action."

The meeting arose out of a radio report which stated that W.H.

Whimster, secretary of the Naramata Board of Trade, had said that the people of Naramata did not want an east side road.

The statement was said to have been made when Mr. Whimster was speaking as a delegate at a meeting last week, in Keremeos, of the Associated Boards of Trade of the Southern Interior.

TRADE BOARDS FAVOR BRIDGE AT WESTBANK

FEBRUARY 23, 1950 — The Associated Boards of Trade of the Southern Interior have endorsed a proposal for construction of a bridge across Okanagan Lake - if it is feasible - as the real solution to the Kelowna-Westbank ferry bottleneck.

Ten member Boards were represented at the quarterly meeting of the association held in Keremeos last Friday evening.

Summerland delegates added that, even with a road on the east side of the lake, the Westbank - Kelowna ferry service would still have to be maintained.

It was also pointed out that the initial cost of a bridge would be higher than that of a road. But it was added that, over a period of years, the necessary maintenance of a road would place its cost higher than that for a bridge.

In voting, the delegates felt that the immediate solution to the bottleneck problem lay in the construction of a bridge with a road on the east side of the lake to follow at some later date.

Okanagan Lake Bridge Would Cost $20,000,000

FEBRUARY 8, 1951 — Thumbnail sketches of his CCP compatriot members of the B.C. Legislature, some pungent remarks on past and present administrations, and a number of tense comments on B.C. roads were contained in the address given to the Penticton CCF club on Friday by Rupert W. Haggen, (CCF) MLA for Grand Forks-Greenwood.

One of the most startling statements made by the MLA concerned Okanagan and Boundary road routes. In making these statements Mr. Haggen spoke not only as a member of the legislature, but also as a surveyor and civil engineer with approximately 50 years of experience in all parts of the province.

Mr. Haggen stated that, according to information he had received, it would cost approximately $20,000,000 to build the proposed Westbank-Kelowna bridge, and that even, then, the engineers on the task, are not yet certain of having sufficiently good foundations.

BCFGA Asks Prompt Action To Enable Growers To Carry On

The BCFGA executive in session at Kelowna yesterday called for immediate government action to enable some growers to carry on pending relief as requested at the June 15 emergency conference.

The executive was informed earlier in the week by the Hon. Harry Bowman, provincial minister of agriculture, that the necessary inspection of orchards, to ascertain extent of damage, could not be made until the latter part of next month.

Meanwhile, a conference will probably be held with the Hon. J.G. Gardiner, Dominion minister of agriculture, he said.

The telegram dispatched by the executive yesterday to Premier Byron I. Johnson and to the Hon. Mr. Bowman, stated that "immediate aid is urgently requested to alleviate distress conditions in the tree fruit industry."

"Conventional loans are unprocurable under present conditions," it continued, "and the BCFGA implores you to take immediate government action to enable some growers to carry on pending relief as requested at the emergency conference June 15."

The telegram received from the provincial minister of agriculture on Tuesday read: "Have discussed the problem in cabinet this morning and pending a discussion with Ottawa and ascertaining the extent of the damage, no definite policy will be decided upon. My officials state the necessary inspection of orchards cannot be made until the latter part of next month but expect to see Mr. Gardiner mean-

time. The provincial government will then, upon receiving the complete report, decide what course is to be pursued and advise you."

The proposed meeting with the Dominion agriculture minister is in accordance with the submissions made by the emergency conference on June 15.

The conference requested the B.C. government to set up the machinery to alleviate the distress conditions in the tree fruit industry at this time and to approach the Dominion government for co-operation.

The matter has been under consideration ever since the conference, according to a letter to the BCFGA from Premier Johnson.

Orchardists Are Winning Battle For Pest Control

Fruit Producers Facing Less Expense And Less Difficulty Than Believed Possible Even Five Years Ago

For the orchardists as a whole, few if any reports presented at the annual convention of the BCFGA hold as much interest as that of the pest control committee.

This year's convention, held at Vernon this week, has not been an exception in this regard. The committee's detailed survey was followed with keen attention. No grower is unaffected.

The committee comprises executive members of the association and Ben Hoy, R.P. Murray, Dr. H.R. McLarty and J. Marshall.

The report in full is being carried because of its interest to so many producers. It was as follows:

Generally speaking British Columbia fruit growers are controlling orchard pests with less difficulty and with less expense than they might have believed possible even five years ago. In the face of the steadily advancing costs of other fruit production operations this is a timely and fortunate development.

In 1950 green apple aphid, two-

spotted mite and Williamette mite were the pests that caused most concern; codling moth and European red mite were in the background. Apple scab was troublesome only in the Kootenay-West Arm districts. Apple powdery mildew was of little importance. Mice caused extensive loss during the winter of 1949-1950; they have not subsided to their ordinary level. Deer have been causing considerable damage in some Kootenay and Salmon Arm orchards.

The behaviour of DDT and other pesticides in the soil is now a subject of long term study. So far, it appears that DDT accumulates mainly in the upper two inches of soil under Okanagan Valley conditions. Very little was found at the 2 to 4 inch level even under sprinkler irrigation in light soil. The point is important because an excessive amount of DDT in the soil is known to be injurious to plant life and it

tends to persist unchanged for several years and so to accumulate. British Columbia orchards do not seem to be in danger from this type of soil poisoning. The investigations have not yet given any indication of the effects of spray chemicals on beneficial soil organisms.

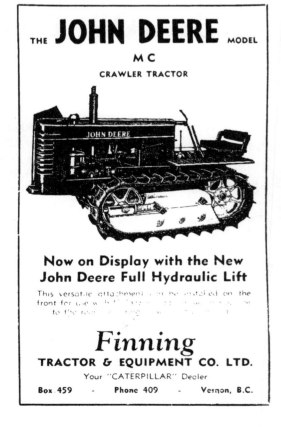

B.C. Presents Mace To Tenth Province

A sterling silver, gold plated mace, British Columbia's token to Newfoundland in commemoration of her entry into Confederation, has been presented to the Newfoundland Legislature in St. Johns, by the Honorable Herbert Anscomb, Minister of Finance and Acting Premier.

Accompanying the presentation, was an illuminated formal address which was delivered by Mr. Anscomb on the floor of the Legislature.

This address will be kept in the Newfoundland Archives and a copy of it in the British Columbia Archives.

While in Newfoundland, Mr. Anscomb was the guest of His Honor the Lieutenant-Governor, Lieutenant-Colonel L.C. Outerbridge, CBE, LLD, DSO.

The mace is made of British Columbia precious metals and designed and fashioned by British Columbia craftsmen of Henry Birks & Co. of Vancouver.

A description of the mace was given during the course of his address by the Honorable Mr. Anscomb as follows:

"In designing the mace, we sought to incorporate not only characteristics of the nation of which you and I are members, but symbols that are representative of our respective Provinces, and above all to embody emblems that denote the allegiance of all countries within the Commonwealth of Nations to one common sovereign."

"At the top of the mace is a replica of the British Crown, complete except for the jewels, which are represented by gold-plated and silver insets."

"This symbol is unique in that it represents one of the most interesting devices in constitutional history for the holding together of a group of independent countries in a cohesive whole known as the Commonwealth of Nations. "

"Each country is free to act as it deems best; yet each country gives allegiance to one Constitutional Monarch, who represents in his person all the cherished rights and liberties of which the British people are so proud, and which they have so jealously guarded throughout the years."

"Below the replica of the British crown is a band of entwined dogwood flowers, British Columbia's floral emblem, and maple leaves, representative of Canada as a whole."

"The dogwood is one of our earliest-flowering trees. Because of its appearance in spring, it denotes youth, or a young growing country. "

"Also, because it sends its roots down deep and is consequently difficult to transplant, it represents the people who have established their roots in British Columbia, so that their succeeding generations may contribute to the building of a great nation as native-born Canadians."

"The maple leaf, with its glorious blending of colors in the fall of the year, is truly indicative of Canada as a new country, merging together people of all races and creeds."

Seventeen Liberals so far elected in Newfoundland election with Pro-Cons electing two, Independent one.

MAY 30, 1949. ST. JOHN'S, NEWFOUNDLAND — The Liberal party has won Newfoundland's first election as a province of Canada. Returns today confirmed the trend of landslide proportions that became apparent in the early counting following the election on Friday.

With 25 of 27 seats heard from, the tally showed 17 Liberals were elected, two Progressive Conservatives and one independent. Liberal leader Joseph Smallwood, who won a thumping majority in Bonavista North, termed the election a "remarkable victory," and told reporters the new province's first legislature would sit on June 24. He said the victory was a magnificent endorsation of confederation and a "complete repudiation of George Drew and Toryism."

(AP PHOTO) 4/1/49

After 400 years as a British colony, Newfoundland became Canada's tenth province in a simple ceremony at St. John's that saw Canadian Secretary of State Colin Gibson present a token certificate to Canadian citizenship to Sir Albert J. Walsh, Newfoundland's first Lieutenant Governor. Newfoundland's provisional Premier, J. R. Smallwood, is shown being interviewed at a reception following the ceremony.

1950-1959

KOREA

Canada's Tribal Destroyer Nootka will be brought out of mothballs for active duty and will join the three other Canadian destroyers, now serving in Korean waters, in 1951. Depth charges set by destroyer is shown above. At full strength, the Nootka, now lying at the naval dockyard in Halifax, numbers 240, including 17 officers.

Wounded Veteran Of Korean War Writes Graphic Account Of Action

JULY 12, 1951. —

While aboard an army hospital ship, carrying him out of Korean combat, the first thoughts of Corporal Wong Suey W. Lee, Kelowna infantryman, were of his parents. He was afraid they would worry after receiving official notice that he was wounded. Despite the severe pain, he dropped a line home. The letter follows:

Dear Folks:

I guess by now you have received the telegram from the war department saying that I was wounded in action in the fighting near Yonchon, North Korea. I imagine there are many things of doubt and obscurity in your minds about what and how it happened.

First I would like to explain to you that I wasn't an interpreter in the army, but instead I was a combat infantryman in a rifle platoon. I denied you the truth because I didn't want you to worry about me while I was in the war. The Red Chinese we are fighting against do not even speak the same language as I do. They do speak Mandarin. All of them are from Northern China.

I have been in the front line combat since January. Since I have been with the 7th Can. Regt. I have fought in many noted battles, Hill 202, Hill 578, Hongechon River area, Hwachon Reservoir, Uijonglur Injin River and now up to Yonchon in North Korea.

There are many things I guess I should have wrote and told you,

but I thought it was best not to until it was all over or until something like this happened.

On June 2, or somewhere around there, our regiment jumped off on the attack from the Injin River. This attack turned out to be the fiercest, heaviest, bitterest, and stiffest fighting I have ever encountered since I have been over here. Every time we carry the war into North Korea, the enemy fights much harder and stiffer. Misery and physical suffering was added due to the heavy rainfall and cold wind at this time of the year. Fighting in these steep, muddy Korean hills is extremely difficult and miserable. The terrain is another battle in itself. I can never put down on paper or in words just how miserable and difficult it is to fight a war in this steep terrain and under adverse weather conditions.

During the first three days of the offensive it rained continuously in a heavy volume. I was so thoroughly soaked, cold and miserable that I didn't sleep for three consecutive nights. Sitting in a muddy fox hole or laying in the mud throughout the night without dry blankets or any cover, didn't help the situation any. It was difficult to keep our weapons from malfunctioning due to the extreme rust.

Last winter it was the weapons freezing up. During the windy season it was the dust that got into the mechanism. The weather is a big problem for our ordnance department and us.

One night I was on outpost about 40 yards from our main com-

pany defense perimeter with six other men from our company. Our mission was to detect the enemy's approach, we would pull back to our main perimeter and alert the whole company. We were set up on the top of a very steep hill and night was rainy, cold and extremely dark and windy. This made the detection of the approaching enemy very difficult.

That night we were also expecting a Red counter-attack, for the hills across from us were still swarming with Communists.

The night went on without anything happening until 4:30 in the morning when we heard a lot of movement in the brush below us. We couldn't see because it was too dark. The noise of movement became heavier and the shooting started. I threw two grenades in that direction and then I decided to pull the seven-men outpost back to the main perimeter rather than take any possible chance of letting the enemy overrun us. On the way back to the main perimeter a deadly fragmentation grenade thrown by the enemy exploded by us and wounded four out of the seven men. I got the worst of it because I was the closest to it. The explosion caught me by surprise and the grenade seemed to come out of nowhere.

Next thing I knew I was lying on the ground in great pain and shock, with blood spurting out of me. The other unhurt men picked me up and helped me back to the C.P. where I got first aid and morphine injection to reduce the pain.

I lay on the wet ground for about two hours wrapped up in a blanket while waiting for the stretcher party to carry me off the hill. I lay there shaking and shivering from fear and shock. This was

the first time I had ever been on the front line unarmed and helpless.

Finally, after a treacherous trip down off the steep and slippery hill, we arrived at the battalion aid station where jeeps were waiting to take us to the regimental collecting station.

Upon arrival, I found out the road which we were to drive over was zeroed in by heavy enemy artillery and mortar fire. I began to pray again. Finally I arrived at the collecting station. From there I started the long process of going from one hospital unit to another and also emergency surgery …

Most of the shrapnel penetrated into my right forearm, some into my right buttock and into the right side of my forehead. Some of the larger pieces of the shrapnel have already been removed by an emergency operation near the front. I am getting the best medical care and in about two months or so I will be good as new again.

The doctors say I will be hospitalized from two to three months. When I get out of the hospital I don't think I will have to go back into combat any more. I will have more than adequate time for rotation and I have now been wounded twice in action. I am quite sure my fighting days are over with now.

Tomorrow I will be leaving by plane for Japan. I will receive further surgery and hospitalization at some hospital in Japan. You will not hear from me for a while again as they will be cutting into my arm to remove the shrapnel. I am having quite a painful time trying to put out this letter. Please do not worry at all about me as everything will turn out alright. Will write when I can.   Love Suey.

N WAR

Canadian Destroyer Hangs Up Enviable Record

On Board the "Sioux"

FEBRUARY 2, 1951. — After six months of service with the United Nations naval forces in Korean waters during which she added plenty of laurels to her masthead, the HMCS Sioux is resting proudly in her berth at Esquimalt.

With the other two Canadian destroyers, Cayuga and Athabaskan, the Sioux took part in the Inchon invasion in mid-September, and figured in bombardments and mine destruction during patrols off Korea's west coast. She also participated in the 8th Army's withdrawal from Chinnampo, port for the North Korean capital of Pyongyanp, in early December.

The Sioux, smallest of the three RCN destroyers that left the British Columbia port on July 5, just 10 days after the outbreak of the Korean War, has acquired her share of individual records and achievements among United Nations

ships.

She rolled up more miles and days at sea than any of the Canadian destroyers, establishing a new fueling-at-sea record for British Commonwealth ships, rescued 29 UN soldiers and sailors, ran a close second to the Cayuga for the distinction of being the UN destroyer with the longest patrol during the Korean war and was close behind the Athabaskan in the "mines destroyed" column.

Probably the individual record of which quiet-spoken Cdr. Paul Taylor and his crew are most proud is the fueling-at-sea mark. It was a sweet triumph over not only British, Australian, and New Zealand warships but also the Cayuga and Athabaskan.

The previous record time had been eight minutes, set by the destroyer HMS Chequers in the Mediterranean when the Duke of Edinburgh was her First Lieutenant. On her first try the

Sioux dropped the time to six minutes. The Cayuga knocked a half minute off that – and then the Sioux registered the present mark of four minutes and 39 seconds, which has withstood the attempts of all British Commonwealth ships to lower it.

During her Korean service the Sioux rescued 28 South Korean soldiers and sailors and one British naval pilot. The 28 ROKs were drifting helplessly in an engine-less tug in heavy seas and with no food or water when the Sioux picked them up in mid-October. The Canadians fixed the tug's engine and supplied the South Koreans with food and equipment before sending them on their way to complete their mission.

Two months later, The Sioux picked up a naval pilot from the British aircraft carrier Theseus when his Sea Fury developed engine trouble on returning from a raid over North Korean territory. The pilot was 15 miles away from his floating air base when he ditched his aircraft. The Sioux rushed to the scene and pulled the pilot from the cold waters off the west coast of Korea, near the 38th parallel.

The Sioux logged more than 41,000 nautical miles on her patrols, topping both the Cayuga and Athabaskan by some 3,000 miles, and averaged 22 days at sea per month.

Another experience which the Sioux men relate with pride was the full-scale typhoon they ran into during a three-day passage to Hong Kong in mid-November. The storm, which the most toughened North Atlantic veteran claimed as the worst he had ever seen, bent guard rails, swept a boat overboard, warped watertight doors and snapped a funnel stay. When the Sioux limped into Hong Kong, she looked as if some giant fist had

swept in a vicious arc along her port side.

In the matter of mine destruction the Sioux showed the way among the RCN destroyers until late in the campaign, when the Athabaskan topped her mark of eight.

The Sioux registered a mark of 44 days at sea on continuous patrol duty. This was better than all other UN destroyers except the Cayuga, which holds the unofficial United Nations destroyer record of 50 consecutive days of patrol without hitting port.

"At least that record is still in the family. And we don't mind it too much," is the way one fiercely bearded Sioux tar expressed his feelings.

Korean women are on the march again, following the victorious Allied advance, driving the Chinese north.

KOREAN YULE DRIVE OPENS IN VANCOUVER

OCTOBER 16, 1952. — Local residents are invited to "open their hearts" to the third annual appeal for funds to send Christmas comforts to B.C. and Canadian boys fighting in Korea. The fund, sponsored by the Women's Auxiliary to the Princess Patricia Canadian Light Infantry, opens on October 20 and donations of any amount are welcome. Contributions may be forwarded to the Korean Christmas Fund, The Women's Auxiliary, P.P.C.L.I., c/o Toronto General Trust Corporation, 590 West Pender St., Vancouver.

The work of the Women's Auxiliary is far-reaching. Besides sending comforts, both at Christmas and each month of the year, the ladies visit patients from Korea in Shaughnessy Hospital at Vancouver; they meet planes, trains and boats and serve refreshments to returning veterans; they also sponsor a Christmas party for children of the men who cannot be home with their loved ones during the festive season.

The objective is $3,000 and donations to this worthy cause are deductible for income tax purposes.

Half Kelowna's Population Down With Flu; Child Dies

KELOWNA —

First death believed due to the current outbreak of flu in the Okanagan occurred in hospital when an eight-month-old boy died from pneumonia. He was Edward Philip Zerr, son of Mr. and Mrs. Daniel P. Zerr.

Medical health officials estimate that at least 50 per cent of Kelowna's 10,000 population is down with the flu. And there is no indication the epidemic has reached its peak. Over 1,000 school children are away from classrooms.

Even physicians, including the medical health officer, Dr. Helen Zeman, have been stricken with the disease.

Scores of public meetings have been cancelled until danger has passed. Sunday school classes were closed while attendance at church services was negligible. Stores and offices are operating with reduced staffs.

While school teaching staffs have been curtailed, school board officials gave no indications classrooms would be closed.

Families in outlying areas have

also been hit. In many cases the entire household is in bed.

Physicians warn people who have flu symptoms to go to bed. If no improvement is shown within 24 to 48 hours, they are advised to call a doctor. This type of flu is not serious, however, and an individual in good health, should recover within three or four days, they state.

Visiting Kelowna General Hospital has been restricted to immediate relatives of patients. Hospital authorities state this is merely a precautionary measure.

The flu epidemic struck the Central Okanagan during the middle of last week, and medical health authorities do not believe the peak will be reached for another two or three days.

The southern part of the Valley was hit first, and the "bug" gradually crept northward. To date, the northern part of the Valley has escaped the epidemic.

Effects Of Cigarette Smoking Analyzed In "Digest" Report

The tidal-wave increase in cigarette smoking in a single generation, stands as one of the most remarkable mass changes of human habit in all history, declares Roger Williams Riis in The Reader's Digest for January. Last year, 400 billion cigarettes were consumed in the United States and 15 billion in Canada. About 800,000 American non-smokers are joining the smoking ranks annually.

The Digest article, one of the series of "Reports of Consumers", appraises the effects, harmful and otherwise, of this "nationwide cloud of cigarette smoke" upon public

health, as shown by medical findings to date.

Two chemicals in cigarette smoke – benzo-pyrne and nicotine – are under grave suspicion, though medical science "has so far not proved a case" against them. Nicotine, in pure form, is so violent a poison that the amount contained in two cigarettes would kill a smoker quickly if injected into the bloodstream. But in smoking, most of the nicotine escapes into the air, and only a slight percentage is absorbed by the mouth and lungs.

Though benzo-pyrene is an irritant rather than a poison, it is a greater threat to heavy smokers than is nicotine, according to many physicians. Throat irritation, the most common charge against smoking, is blamed by doctors on incompletely burned tar products, of which benzo-pyrene is the chief ingredient.

Medical opinion differs on smoke-induced damage to the lungs. Cancer of the lungs has show a marked increase in recent years, and some authorities attribute this higher incidence to a parallel increase in cigarette smoking. Others do not. The American Cancer Society formally

states that no answer can yet be accepted as scientifically valid.

It is generally agreed, however, that cancer of the mouth, tongue and lips is "unduly prevalent among smokers". Researchers in Michigan, Illinois and Pennsylvania have come independently to the conclusion that the majority of victims of cancer of the tongue are excessive users of tobacco.

Cigarettes retard hunger, the author states, by suppressing stomach-wall contractions which produce the hunger sensation. Hence smoking interferes with appetite and thereby with good nutrition. A gain in weight is commonly experienced by persons who have forsworn the smoking habit.

Heartburn and gastritus may be caused by excessive smoking. The article gives no evidence that stomach ulcers are so caused, but states that excess acidity of the stomach, produced by smoking, "provides the kind of climate ulcers like." Ulcer patients who smoke have more relapses than those who do not.

On the effect of tobacco on pregnancy, doctors have concluded that "smoking does not do pregnant women any more harm, or any different harm, than it does anyone

else." Mothers' milk has been found to analyze 1.4 parts nicotine in ten million, among moderate smokers; 4.7 parts among heavy smokers. But no effect on babies has been detected.

The Reader's Digest article reports evidence that smoking impairs athletic prowess and retards the growth and chest development of college-age men. Coaches are almost unanimous that muscular power is lowered and that fatigue begins earlier in smokers.

Heart disease is more prevalent among smokers than non-smokers, and smoking may intensify existing heart disease, Riis states. Smoking speeds the pulse by as much as 28 beats per minute, and raises blood pressure "markedly and quickly". As yet, however, no proof exists that smoking causes heart disease or high blood pressure.

Studying the life span and smoking habits of more than 6,000 white American males, a physician at Johns Hopkins concluded that 66 per cent of non-smokers at the age of 30 will reach 60, but that only 61 per cent of light smokers and a mere 46 per cent of heavy smokers will double their age at 30. Other doctors disagree.

Civil Defence Commission Plans For Preparedness

Communities in the Okanagan Valley must be prepared to shelter and feed an influx of 18,000 men, women and children who, experts predict, would flock into the valley within the space of two days in the event of an atomic attack on the coast metropolitan area.

This information was divulged when members of Penticton's civil defence commission met in the City Hall last Thursday night to formulate their role in billeting and caring for evacuees and – just to be sure – measures of recovery in the event that an A-bomb landed here.

Under the chairmanship of Alderman Wilson Hunt, they made their first steps toward civic preparedness: formation of a central committee which will take over if an atom bomb drops. It consists of Paul G.W. Walker, city engineer; Miss Joan Appleton, public health nurse; Dr. J.J. Gibson; Alderman J.G. Harris and G. Winter, chairman of the Red Cross disaster services committee.

After discussing the myriad of problems which would confront an A-bombed community, they will appoint sub-committees.

Mass Evacuation

The local civil defence commission is working in conjunction with the Vancouver organization headed by Alderman J. Cornett who, in a letter to Alderman Hunt, said that the people of the Okanagan should be prepared to care for 18,000 people in two days.

Dr. Gibson, representing the medical profession, claimed that it would not be required to play an overly active part in commission planning. "Our main concerns would be beds, blood and more personnel," he said. "We would have to utilize space in Oliver and Princeton. The Armory, too, could be used as a hospital.

"Blood is most essential," he stressed, adding that a card-index system should be instituted to give rapid information of blood donors and blood types.

Suggests Blood Bank

Dr. Gibson suggested a blood bank here in Penticton. "It could be accumulated with several weeks," he informed, explaining that blood in Vancouver would be sorely needed there in the event of an emergency and allotments to other centres would be insignificant.

"Suppose our own hospital was blitzed – should we be responsible for decentralization of supplies?" asked Alderman Hunt.

"Yes", answered Dr. Gibson. "I think we should plan to use the Kaleden hall for storage of materials."

Another problem discussed was the extent of the power of the local civil defence commission. Orders from several sources, it was suggested, would confuse the measures for survival, would eliminate co-ordination of emergency efforts.

Work With Police

"How much authority have we over the police?" asked Mr. Winter.

Mayor Rathbun replied that the city of Penticton has jurisdiction over seven members of the RCMP. He offered to write a letter to Attorney-General Wismer for full information on the powers of a civil defence commission.

Alderman Hunt stated that complete authority should be vested in the central committee, that council should discuss the matter with the RCMP.

Mayor Rathbun pointed out the difficulty of a group of leaders trying to lay comprehensive plans. "We can't just sit around a table and plan our activities. All we can do is organize the leadership, then find someone who has the time and ability to head the various sub-committees, to speak to people and determine those who are willing to serve on the commission."

Alderman Hunt will attend a meeting from centres throughout the Okanagan Valley in Kelowna on March 1 which is designed to co-ordinate measures of preparedness throughout the Interior.

1950~1959

Tips On How To Survive "A" Bombing

APRIL 26, 1951 —

Stating that "your chances of surviving an atomic attack are better than you may have thought," an article in the current issue of Health, official magazine of the Health League of Canada, lists "survival secrets" for atomic attacks:

1. Try to get shielded. If you have time get down into a basement or subway. Should you unexpectedly be caught out-of-doors, seek shelter alongside a building, or jump in any handy ditch or gutter.
2. Drop flat on ground or floor. To keep from being tossed about and to lessen the chances of being struck by falling and flying objects, flatten out at the base of a wall, or at the bottom of a bank.
3. Bury your face in your arms. When you drop flat, hide your eyes in the crook of your elbow.
4. Don't rush outside right after a bombing. After an air burst, wait a few minutes then go help fight fires. After other kinds of bursts, wait at least one hour to give lingering radiation some chance to die down.
5. Don't take chances with food or water in open containers. To prevent radioactive poisoning or disease, select your food and water with care. When there is reason to believe they may be contaminated, stick to canned and bottled things if possible.

Official Opening Of CKOK's Studios And Big Power Increase Mark Three Years Of Progress

From two-hundred and fifty watts with office and studio space less than seven hundred square feet. To one thousand watt power and more than two thousand square feet studio space — that briefly sums up the rapid growth of CKOK, an independent Canadian radio station fast becoming recognized as one of this country's most progressive.

And CKOK is one of Canada's youngest stations. Only on the air since September of 1948, with a small staff of seven people and one sponsor, it now has a staff of sixteen. Its studios and equipment are the latest word in modern broadcasting.

TROUBLE! TROUBLE!

Popular production manager Vince Duggan, who has been with the station since its inception, recalls that during the first several days of operation, programs had to originate at the small transmitter at Skaha Lake. Somebody had slipped up, for the studios on Main street were not completed when the station was ready to go on the air. To further plague the limited staff, the ordered records and transcribed shows failed to arrive. It was a matter of programming "by gosh and by gee." But in spite of all that, some of the original programs have survived the trying times: programs such as "Coffee Time," "Saddle Serenade," "Town Meeting In Canada," and one or two others. News service was limited but credit managed to edit six newscasts daily. Today there are fourteen with full coverage of local activities along with national and international happenings.

The new studios on Nanaimo Avenue are acoustically right in every detail. Chief engineer Jim English made exhaustive surveys of leading stations here in Canada and in the U.S. before putting plans before the building contractors. While everything is on a much smaller scale, the exacting science of proper acoustics has been thoroughly adhered to in every instance. And the same applies to all the new equipment. A second survey proved that General Electric appeared to do the best job for most of the leading stations on this continent. As a result, the new CKOK transmitter carries the name-stamp "GE" as does most of the studio equipment. A new 205 foot steel tower at the transmitter will add its part to the intention of CKOK to give full and satisfactory coverage for listeners north of Oyama, south beyond Osoyoos and west to Princeton.

Valley Hockey Clubs Vote Coast Pucksters Out; Will Form New League

KELOWNA —

If you know of any senior hockey teams on the loose and not too far removed from the Lower Mainland, then you likely would be welcomed with open arms by the directors of the Nanaimo Clippers and the Kerrisdale Monarchs.

For last year's league champions from Nanaimo, who went on to the Allan Cup semi-finals, and the Kerries are oddly all that is left of the Mainline-Okanagan Amateur Hockey League.

The two coast teams, since yesterday, are virtually orphans while a new hockey league, embracing four Interior clubs has taken over in place of the MOAHL.

This turn of events was not a surprise. It was started officially last month when the MOAHL's annual meeting began in Penticton. But when Penticton's entry into the league appeared uncertain at that time, the annual meeting was given a hoist until Sunday afternoon.

No sooner had Penticton's entry been accepted than the four upcountry teams (Kamloops, Vernon and Kelowna are the other three) started off a long, haranguing, pleading and sometimes bitter session on their proposal to "withdraw".

This "withdrawal" was finally accomplished in the face of earnest representations from the coast teams and impassioned pleas by league president, Dr. Mel Butler, of Kelowna, and league vice-president, Dr. Ralph Hughes, of Kamloops.

Leave Meetings

In their arguments for the "withdrawal" spokesmen cited geographical and financial reasons and playoff "ball-ups" in previous years.

After the vote was taken with four interior clubs voting for and the coast clubs against, Nanaimo delegate Blair Cook and Kerrisdale representative Fred "Cyclone" Taylor walked out of the meeting.

Team delegates then set up what is known as the Okanagan Senior Amateur Hockey League. Dr. Ralph Hughes, of Kamloops, is the new president, with Art Crowe, of Vernon, vice-president. Dr. Butler was elected honorary president.

FIRST STEP TOWARDS HOCKEY CLUB MADE

FEBRUARY 8, 1951. — Luminaries in the local world of sports gathered in the Three Gables Hotel Tuesday night to formulate plans for a Penticton entry in the Okanagan-Mainline Hockey League.

At the private meeting called by A.E. Tidball, parks commissioner, they formed two three-man committees to investigate the initial problems confronting large-scale sport promotion: costs of operation and methods of financing.

To determine anticipated costs, local pundits will benefit from the experiences of other cities now sponsoring clubs in the Okanagan-Mainline circuit. Lowell Gove, J. Thom and J.B. MacNeil will discuss expenditures with officials of the Kamloops Elks, Kelowna Packers and Vernon Canadians.

Also attending the meeting was George Cady, well-known throughout the interior as a former athlete and sports promoter, who is well aware of the fact that an arena such as the one designed for Penticton must have a hockey club to finance its functions.

It is his contention that the puck-chasers would be "the major drawing power," that receipts from skating only would not provide sufficient revenue to keep the arena out of financial difficulties.

Four-Team Valley Junior Football League In Offing

A four-team Okanagan Valley junior football league may be in operation come early September. Eligible to play would be boys under 21 on September 1, 1950.

Merve Davis, backfield coach of the Penticton Scarlet Marauders, has been contacted through local business men by Norman Howard, of Vancouver, who is going all out to have the loop formed. Howard is connected with the Big 4 Canadian Rugby Football League.

Likely entrants will be Penticton, Kelowna, Vernon and Kamloops, although Vernon has not formed a team as yet.

The four would play off at the end of the season for the Okanagan Valley championship and then play the winner of the four-team Vancouver junior football league for the provincial crown.

Possibilities of a Canadian final are being discussed.

Through their own efforts last fall, a score of local junior football players formed their own association, bought their own equipment, staged practice sessions and arranged their own games. One local business man helped in the purchase of the $900 worth of equipment now owned by the team.

Association executives are Les Wiseman, president; W.X. Perkins, honorary president; Chuck Raitt,

vice-president; Merve Davis, secretary-treasurer; and Maury Moyls, manager.

Further word on the proposed league is expected by Davis in the next few weeks.

Vancouver Blue Bombers are known to desire exhibition matches with the interior teams now organized, Kelowna, Penticton and Kamloops.

The Scarlet Marauders hope to play exhibition games with teams from Washington, this fall. American teams will be contacted at the beginning of the season for this purpose.

Marauders will start practising at the end of August.

Penticton Is Valley's Largest City

Population has nearly doubled in past decade

Penticton's population has jumped from 5,777 to 10,517 in the past ten years.

This was disclosed this week in the latest preliminary census figures released by the Dominion Bureau of Statistics.

The official count establishes Penticton as the fastest growing city in the Okanagan Valley and among the fastest growing cities in B.C. Penticton had a slight lead on Vernon and Kelowna when the 1941 census was taken and was trailing behind Kamloops but, during the past ten years, Penticton has far outdistanced the other valley centres in the population race.

Comparative figures, with 1941 figures in brackets, tell the story:

Penticton 10,517 (5777).
Kelowna 8466 (5118).
Vernon 7778 (5209).
Kamloops 7988, (5959).

This city's population is 24.2 per cent higher than Kelowna's; 35.2 per cent over Vernon and 31.7 per cent above Kamloops.

Not Surprising

Mayor W.A. Rathbun termed the census figures "satisfying but not at all surprising in view of the physical evidences of the city's growth especially during the years since the war."

Some ardent Penticton boosters are frankly disappointed, having estimated the population at anything from 12,000 to 14,000.

The census figures, incontrovertible evidence of Penticton's expansion, are nevertheless only another link in the chain of evidence which includes this year's more than $2,000,000 building program of which tangible proof is available to the eye this week in the new Memorial Arena and Hotel Prince Charles.

1950~1959

Flying Saucer Seen By Osoyoos Couple

AUGUST 9, 1951. OSOYOOS — A flying saucer has been seen by Osoyoos residents.

A well-known local couple, Mr. and Mrs. Cecil G. LePoidevin of the LePoidevin Greenhouses, were relaxing on the lawn at their home across the lake when the object was first sighted by Mrs. LePoidevin.

Almost at the same time Mr. LePoidevin noted it too.

It was a round disc which had the shiny appearance of aluminium or glass. There was no wind and the object glided by noiselessly at a height of about 2000 feet. It is estimated the object was travelling about 500 miles per hour.

The couple saw this mysterious object at 6:40 Friday evening, and its rapid progress quickly took it out of sight, proceeding in a direct north to south path.

Expansion Plans Of Okanagan Telephone Co. Subject Of Talk

A comprehensive discussion of the development plans of the Okanagan Telephone Company was presented by that organization's engineer, George Wormull, when he spoke before the Rotary Club at its Monday luncheon in the Incola Hotel.

Introduced by George Carter, the local manager, Mr. Wormull gave his chief attention to the question of conversion to the dial system, but he also reviewed many other aspects of the utility's activities, and his address, in full, was as follows:

The purpose of this short talk is to acquaint you with the Okanagan Telephone Company's development plans as applied to the whole system and, more especially, to the city of Penticton, reviewing the development to date, the immediate plans and those for the future.

The modernisation of the company's plant and the conversion from manual operation to dial have been in the development stage for the last four years. The initial decision was to introduce automatic switching in order to improve the then existing service and provide a system that could cope with the rapidly increasing demand for telephones.

At that time the system provided service through the principal centres, Penticton, Kelowna and Vernon, and in the south in some rapidly developing communities that were served through small exchange areas such as Summerland and Peachland. In the north end of the valley exchange areas were already established in Armstrong, Enderby, Salmon Arm and Revelstoke. The growth of demand for telephone service throughout the system has been phenomenal since 1945, and telephone companies throughout the continent were likewise flooded with requests for service beyond their ability to accommodate the demand. They then entered into large expansion programs.

The use of the long distance service is a comparatively modern trend in our daily lives, and prior to the last war was only considered as a business convenience or a luxury. The habit of "visiting" over the long distance service was developed during the war when so many were travelling across the country, but for a long while the average person was nervous and consequently not at ease when speaking over long distance. This was partly due to a new custom and also partly due to inferior connections whereby telephone users had difficulty in hearing each other.

Rapid strides were made in the improvement and reliability of long distance connections, especially with regard to the intelligibility of the conversation. These improvements were the prime factor in encouraging the use of long distance calling, and the endeavour of the utility to improve the grade of service resulted in such demand that the operating companies were met by problems that they themselves had not foreseen.

It is the demand for service by the public that leads to development of an industry, and calls to mind the old adage, "necessity is the mother of invention".

Impressive Ceremonies As Memorial Arena Opens Here

"Unless groups and individuals of all ages use the varied recreations and entertainment which can be provided here the purpose of the dedication will fail."

PENTICTON—

This exhortation to use the memorial arena was made by A.E. Tidball, parks board chairman before the arena was thrown open to entertainment which included broom ball, figure skating, pee-wee hockey and a race between representatives of city organizations.

Prior to the dedication service Mr. Coffin spoke briefly on the purpose of the arena.

"It is a memorial to those who gave their lives for King and Country" he said. "It is for the men who answered the call in a time of distress and made the supreme sacrifice."

"It has been built especially for the children and not only for recreation and entertainment."

Following the singing of "God Save the King" the Rev. Mr. Eagles urged that the valor and sacrifice of the men who died must never be forgotten. "It would be fitting if the whole community could gather here for services every year and to have a schoolboy place a wreath in memory of the men who must never be forgotten.

"I ask your promise never to forget," he said.

The Last Post and Reveille rang out through the stilled arena marking the one minute of silence in memory of the warrior dead.

Further tribute was paid as the Pipe Band droned while cadets and veterans stood to attention.

Turning the arena over to the parks board for administration Mayor Rathbun outlined the planning and discussion which had gone on for six years prior to the completion of the memorial.

He praised those who had struggled to have the arena built and who had contributed towards the cost.

Summerland Arena Will Open Saturday

SUMMERLAND — This Saturday evening, February 3, another mile-stone in the sports history of Summerland district will be passed with the official opening of the new Summerland Arena.

Built almost entirely with volunteer labor and spark plugged by George Stoll, president of the Summerland Rink Association, the rink has come into being largely through the persistence of this one man.

Although held up at various stages by official red tape and sometimes lack of enthusiasm on the part of a few, Mr. Stoll bullied, pleaded and cajoled until his enthusiasm ignited the spark which was needed to make a success of the venture.

Since the first of the year gangs of volunteers up to thirty in number have been seen, hammers in hands, fitting the lumber onto the original framework.

Cost of the project to date is $25,000, raised practically entirely by sale of debentures and from a small loan at the bank.

A full-size hockey surface plus three sheets of curling ice are included in the big building, besides kitchen, dressing rooms and auxiliary units.

The roof and part of the ends are covered with aluminum sheeting , which will last a lifetime and adds greatly to the smart outside appearance.

If let by contract, the building would have cost at least $75,000 it has been estimated by many quarters. Hundreds of spectators from all parts of the Okanagan are expected to converge on Summerland this Saturday evening to see for themselves what can be accomplished with the proper co-operative spirit.

Kelowna Council Takes Initiative in Planning Major Sidewalk Program

FEBRUARY 8, 1951 — A total of five miles of sidewalks will be constructed in Kelowna this year under the local improvement by-law, providing city residents in the affected areas approve the scheme.

Concrete steps toward the sidewalk construction program were taken by city council last week. The city has decided to take the initiative , and under the plan taxpayers will have an opportunity to object to the scheme. Notices will now be sent out to the individuals affected and majority of owners, representing at least half of the total assessed value of land, must object within one month, otherwise the city can proceed with the scheme.

W.A.C. Bennett, MLA Goes Over To Social Credit

W.A.C. BENNETT

Constituents Laud Bennett's Rebellion

MARCH 29, 1951, KELOWNA
— British Columbians may see a new political party in the field when they go in the polls in the next B.C. general election.

And the cornerstone for this new party may well have been laid in Kelowna Tuesday night, the hometown of W.A.C. Bennett, MLA (South Okanagan). At one of the largest political rallies ever held in the history of Kelowna, the independent member of the B.C. House, who bolted the ranks of the Coalition Government last week, was obliged to address two meetings when the Empress Theatre was unable to accommodate the record crowd.

Over 700 people jammed the theatre to capacity, and another three to four hundred stood outside when the meeting got underway. After Mr. Bennett announced he would speak a second time, over 300 returned an hour-and-a-half later to hear the fiery MLA give his reasons for crossing the floor of the House and also criticize the government on its policies during the past year.

STAND ENDORSED

Both meetings unanimously endorsed Mr. Bennett's stand in opposing the increase in the B.C. Hospital Insurance premiums, and also commended him for bolting government ranks to sit as an independent.

The Kelowna merchant was careful in announcing future political plans. Only reference to a new political movement came during the question period.

"I am going to do one thing at a time," he replied when someone asked him if he was going to form a new party. "I am not making any announcement. What I decide to do after this meeting will be done after I have taken you in my confidence and have consulted my constituents. I believe in doing one thing at a time."

The well-known MLA for South Okanagan, one of the most vigorous political figures on the provincial scene, has thrown something of a bombshell into the current scene.

He made his statement to the Penticton Herald today and, in so doing, called his new affiliation "a government of the people."

A province-wide convention of this party, relatively new to B.C., will be held next February.

At that time, it is being predicted, Mr. Bennett could be chosen as leader of the whole Social Credit movement in the province and as an aspirant to the premiership in the next B.C. election.

In his statement to the Herald, Mr. Bennett acknowledged that he was joining Social Credit, but on other phases of development, such as his possible leadership, he would make no comment.

The Kelowna businessman, who is the owner of a widespread hardware business throughout the interior, including a branch in Penticton, was selected as a coalitionist at the last polling in South Okanagan. Since then he has crossed the floor of the house.

Twice before, in his political career, he contested the leadership of the Conservative Party in B.C., losing out on both occasions to Herbert Anscomb. His first election to the house in Victoria was as a straight Conservative, and he has been an unsuccessful candidate for the federal field, also a straight Conservative.

His full statement, in announcing his change of party affiliation, was addressed to the electors of his constituency of South Okanagan, and was as follows:

"When I reported to you at meetings in the Empress Theatre, in Kelowna, during the Easter recess of the B.C. legislature, I stated in answer to questions as to whether I would favor a new provincial party, that I was a person who did one thing at a time, and that I would inform the electors of my constituency of South Okanagan immediately a decision was made.

"During the months since that time I have studied the provincial governments of all Canada and the problems and opportunities facing our province of B.C.

"I have come to the belief that a Social Credit government similar to the one operating in our neighboring province of Alberta would be the best for our province and our people - a government based on free enterprise - opposed to monopoly either of the right or left - a government of the people.

"I have therefore decided to join the Social Credit movement."

Bennett Surpasses Mark As Longest-Serving Premier

VICTORIA (CP) — Premier W.A.C. Bennett today becomes the longest-serving premier in British Columbia history, surpassing the 12-year, six-month, 14-day record of Sir Richard McBridge who served from 1903 to 1915.

Tributes are expected from all sides of the legislature when it meets later today and a number of testimonial dinners will follow for the premier who was sworn into office in August, 1952.

Mr. Bennett, who will be 65 in September, will be guest of honor as the first of these here tonight. On Feb. 17 he will be made a freeman of the city of Vancouver at a dinner to be held there.

A former conservative, Mr. Bennett left the Liberal-Conservative coalition in 1951, crossed the floor of the legislature to sit as an independent and then joined the Social Credit party.

He led the party to a minority victory in 1952.

He then won a clear-cut majority the following year and has since easily survived provincial elections in 1956, 1960, and 1963.

The King Is Dead

This Was A Man

His life was gentle, and the elements
So mixed in him that Nature might stand up
And say to all the world, "This was a man!"

Today we mourn the passing of George VI. We mourn him as our Sovereign. We mourn him as a friend and a man.

In looking back over the events of the King's life before his accession to the Throne, we can trace the impress of a strongly marked character. Without Prince Albert's (he was known by that title then) pluck and perseverance, without the capacity for minute and patient study which he carried into every new sphere of activity, and without this keen unswerving sense of duty they would show a very different shape.

On the threshold of manhood he knew the kind of frustration that has disheartened many who became his subjects. He wanted to be the sailor son of a sailor. His training ashore and afloat did not differ from that given to other naval cadets of his generation, and he had the gratification and honor of serving with distinction at the Battle of Jutland. Then, by the accident of illness, he was forced to relinquish the profession which aptitude and hard work had made his own. Undiscouraged, and still determined to serve his country in arms, he turned to the air, and in the new service his enthusiasm and concentration won for him merited promotion.

When the war ended Prince Albert once more refocused his energies, this time upon the problems of peace. He went up to Cambridge and while in residence there as an undergraduate trained himself to undertake the work which for many years was to color his manifold and multiform activities – the promotion of industrial welfare. Everything he did bore the mark of conscientiousness and revealed qualities which were an assurance that he would shrink from no task, however arduous, unexpected, or undesired, that the country might call upon him to perform.

These traits stood him in good stead when, by wholly unforeseen and tragic turn of destiny, he ascended the throne in 1936. His bearing throughout at that time was faultless. He said no word which did not speak movingly of his affection for his brother whom he was succeeding. None doubted that he assumed his splendid but awful burden reluctantly, yet with taut determination.

As the new King emerged into the fuller light of the Throne, there were many who, with a sudden lift of the heart, recognized in his gaiety, his simplicity, his modesty and his conscientiousness the very qualities of his father, George V of happy memory. One remembers vividly his first Christmas broadcast. Not because he has an especially agreeable voice, but the impediment in his speech, which he reduced to an occasional slight pause between words, gave somehow a characteristic and marked impression of a man meeting, and mastering, a difficulty.

King George occupied the Throne for fifteen years and during that time there has been crisis after crisis. No monarch of modern times saw his reign punctuated so regularly with major alarms as he, Europe was in a turmoil when when he ascended the Throne and within three years his country was plunged into war and held the battle line for the free world, desperately and alone, for many long months. The war's aftermath was no less distressing, with industrial crisis following financial crisis continuously while Britain fought her way through the postwar turmoil. It was a nerve-wracking reign for the Monarch, but he was a "crisis king" and remained cool and collected, doing his best to instill confidence in the minds of the people. That was King George's role in the tense years he occupied the Throne. For him they were years of acute uncertainty, but he devoted his time to setting for his people an example of coolness and national service that had an incalculable effect on the nation.

At the time of his accession he said to the Privy Council, "With my wife as helpmate by my side, I take up the heavy task which lies before me." Those words were no mere formality. He performed his heavy task in such a manner that verily, nature may stand up and say to all the world, "This was a man!"

QUEEN VICTORIA   **QUEEN ELIZABETH II**

On Tuesday when Queen Elizabeth the Second ascends to the throne of England amidst imposing ceremony, embodying the traditions of a thousand years, many of the older generation will recall another Queen. She was Queen Victoria whose death in 1901 ended her 60-year rule. Queen Victoria was the last reigning Queen until Queen Elizabeth succeeded to the throne on the death of her father George VI. In the long history of British monarchy there have been only been five ruling Queens, Mary Queen of Scots, the first Elizabeth, Queen Anne, Victoria and the lovely woman, who on Tuesday will be crowned Queen of the realm.

Dowager Queen Dies In Sleep

Coronation Date Unchanged

LONDON —

Dowager Queen Mary, queen through a half century of social and political change, died peacefully in her sleep Tuesday.

A report, entirely unofficial, circulated that her last wish was that the coronation of her granddaughter, Queen Elizabeth II, should go on as scheduled in June.

Mourning Period

There will be a period of mourning befitting a royal figure revered by millions of British subjects, but the great pageant which people are coming thousands of miles to see may not be affected.

The Queen Grandmother, whose life spanned a momentous period of history, will have a state funeral. She will be buried in Windsor Castle beside her husband and the son she outlived, George VI.

The 85-year-old grandmother of the Queen succumbed after a prolonged battle with a gastric ailment. The official announcement of her death was made by Prime Minister Churchill to a hushed House of Commons.

Queen Mary was the widow of King George V, who died in 1936. Her long life spanned the period from the imperial 19th century days of Queen Victoria, through two world wars, to the tense times of the atom bomb and the cold war.

Churchill Weeps

The end came peacefully. Churchill sobbed as he announced in the Commons that the revered widow of one king and mother of two other monarchs had died at 10:20 p.m., 5:20 p.m. EST.

"I have with great regret to make the announcement that Queen Mary has died while sleeping peacefully," Churchill said.

Churchill's own political career began in the same Victorian era which saw Queen Mary's entrance into the Royal Family through her marriage to a son of the then Prince of Wales.

City Joins Empire Wide Celebrations

Pays Homage To Elizabeth II

Penticton forged its link in the chain of Empire wide celebration yesterday when thousands of city residents gathered at Gyro Park to participate in the Coronation Day program.

At 10 a.m. yesterday morning hundreds of flag waving school children, members of Scout and Guide groups, cadets of army, navy and air force, the City Band and the Pipe Band, members of C Squadron of the B.C. Dragoons, and other city organizations assembled outside the schools to start the parade which moved down to Gyro Park for the Coronation program.

Enough Breeze To Stir The Flags

More than 3,000 stood in the park enjoying one of the most pleasant spring days of the year. Bright sunshine and just enough breeze to stir the flags added zest to feeling of celebration that was everywhere.

Down at the park, after the singing of "O Canada", the Rev. A.R. Eagles offered the dedication and also prayers for the Queen and for peace. Before the prayer for peace he said "our country is doing more to bring about peace than any other country in the world," and later he said, "let us dedicate ourselves to follow the example of service set by the Queen."

Mayor W.A. Rathbun then delivered his address which is reported elsewhere in this section.

Solemn intonation of the oath of allegiance followed the Mayor's address as the throne repeated the oath, administered by Judge M.M. Colquhoun, reaffirming loyalty to the Crown and to Canada.

Then, on the spring air, rose the strains of the official Coronation Day hymn "All People That On Earth Do Dwell" as the massed choirs and bands, under the direction of Mrs. Monica Craig Fisher, joined the audience in the hymn of praise.

Musical tribute was paid to the new monarch as the massed choir

sang, "Hail Elizabeth", from "Merrie England." Then followed a selection of the national dances of England, Scotland, Ireland and Wales.

Three Cheers For Her Majesty

"Hundsden's House", an English country dance, was the first of the dances which delighted the audience. This dance was performed by junior high school pupils Patsy Armstrong, Maureen Pritchard, Wendy Grove, Verna Spaurel, Lily Lynch, Patty Parmley, Jeannine Chapman and Elvira Hedin, under the direction of Mrs. Edgar Dewdney.

Next came Ireland's contribution to the program, with a jig danced by Haillie Marie Smith, a pupil of the Mary Pratton School of Dancing. Accompanist was Mrs. W. Swift.

From Scotland came the dance "Sean Trubhas", performed by Joanne Hill, Linda Leslie, Donna Day Washington and Brenda Parker, pupils of the Mary Pratton School of Dancing who were accompanied on the bagpipes by Robbie Laird.

The final dance was Welsh, a number performed by Lorraine Drossos, accompanied on the piano by Mrs. Swift.

Then with the color parties on stage, the voices of the massed choirs and the audience, swelled into the familiar strains of "Land of Hope and Glory", and then, with the color parties holding dipped flags and the audience at attention the bands broke the silence with the opening bars of "God Save the Queen" and over three thousand voices joined in singing.

Then with "Three Cheers for Her Majesty" Penticton's official celebration ended.

1950-1959

(AP PHOTO)

The Archbishop of Canterbury, foreground, reads the Benediction to Britain's Queen Elizabeth during the coronation ceremony.

MARCH 11, 1953

Third Section **Penticton Herald** — Third Section

VOL. XLIII—No. 10   PENTICTON HERALD, WEDNESDAY, MARCH 11, 1953

✚ **PENTICTON'S NEW HOSPITAL** ✚

Penticton's New Hospital Official Opening Today

Another Milestone In City's Onward March

Yardstick of a community's progressiveness and of the public spiritedness of its citizens is to be found in the degree of excellence of its school plant, its fire department and its hospital.

Penticton's school plant is second to none in comparable communities. Its fire department can also stand comparison and today Penticton caught up with the third requisite of a community bent on keeping abreast of the times and keeping pace with its area's growth.

A striking testimonial to the progressiveness of Penticton and district is the city's new $1,500,000 hospital on Carmi Avenue, which was officially opened today.

The gleaming structure, standing on a commanding eminence, is Penticton's finest building. It is generally conceded to be unmatched in the Okanagan Valley and it rates with the province's best.

The structure's clean lines, gleaming glass and architectural concrete and cross design excite the admiration of all who see it,

but apart from its architectural beauty the four-winged building is regarded by hospital planners as outstanding.

Penticton's need for a new hospital was recognized more than a decade ago, but the war prevented any immediate action. Then came the post-war period, when Penticton's population increased beyond all expectations. The old hospital on the hill, out-dated and inadequate, was bursting at the seams. It was imperative, that a new hospital must be provided.

JANUARY 11, 1953

Asbestos Finds May Mean New Industry In O.K. Falls Area

$125,000 For Further Exploration

Extensive asbestos deposits have been uncovered on a large tract of land six miles east of Vaseaux Lake, which lies four miles south of Okanagan Falls.

Extent of the asbestos field is not yet known, but sufficient has been uncovered to justify, in the opinion of the Western Asbestos and Development Ltd., the expenditure of $125,000 over the many thousands of dollars already expended, in further exploration of the field.

If the extended exploration program planned for this year substantiates the findings of last season's probing of the property the company expects to swing into full scale mining.

Philip D. Graham, Vancouver, president of the company, informed the Herald that he expects at least one hundred men will be employed year-round and he said, "In my opinion this new industry will be a very stablizing influence on the economy of the valley."

Okanagan Falls would be the first community to feel the impact of a new industry with an annual

payroll which, it is estimated, will reach a quarter of a million dollars a year. Penticton, as the nearest urban centre, would also benefit directly by the establishment of a mining industry employing at least 100 men, possibly more, on a year-round basis.

"A preliminary budget of $300,000 has been drawn up for the coming year's operations. This expenditure will keep the properties in good standing for three years and should block out sufficient ore to ready both properties for the installation of the necessary machinery for production.

"The main task now is to obtain an

underwriting commitment so that the program may be carried out. The company has a good deal of value at the present time and a great potential for the future. This should interest the public and provide the necessary funds.

Miracle Mile Broken

SPORTS RETORTS

Britain's Roger Bannister flashes to the tape at Oxford, England, May 6, 1954 to become the first man ever to run the mile in less than four minutes. He was timed in 3:59.4 in his unprecedented performance.

(AP Photo)

By John Yeomans

AUGUST 11, 1954 — Far down the list in human drama appeal, but still tops in spectator interest, was the Mile, that race about which there was more ballyhoo and build-up than at the sod-turning ceremony for the construction of the Great Pyramid. It was also one of the few incidents in history where advance rave notices were neither overdone nor let down by the actual event.

Oh, sure, Bannister won and Landy was second, and both ran the "miracle mile" in under the four-minute spike barrier. Pick up any copy of the daily papers and you'll read all about it, complete with personal interviews and off-the-record confidentials.

Not so much has been said, though, about who came third. In case you don't know, it was a Canadian by the name of Richard Ferguson, and he ran the mile in four minutes, four and six-tenths seconds, about as fast as Bannister could do it around a year ago.

What is even more unknown is the fact that Ferguson has only run the mile a few times with any serious intentions. His previous best was something like 4:08, a peasant's time these days.

The first two laps of the race told the story. The mile constitutes four times round the track, and at the half-way mark the fellow from Down Under and the chap from Old Blighty were pulling away from the pack.

Then came Ferguson's moment of glory. That guy hardly lost a yard on the two great leaders for the entire last half of the race. He was about 40 feet behind the pair at the second lap, and ended up more or less the same distance behind at the tape, beating out such well-known chappies as Milligan, of Northern Ireland, and Halberg, of New Zealand.

Just as Rich Ferguson was one of the most underrated runners of the entire games, Canada had perhaps the most underrated team of the meet. True, England was expected to finish second behind the Aussies, and came first handily. But Canada certainly wasn't expected to almost come second, to almost beat the supposedly unbeatable Australians. Perhaps it should be worded this way: Australia was the most overrated team at the games.

While England was regaining past glories by coming first with 514 1/2 points. Canada came a raging third with 339, as compared to Australia's 363 3/4. South Africa surprised the field by placing a solid fourth, with 260 3/4 tallies, the only other country with a really respectable score.

Landy, Bannister Scare Off Other B.E. Games Milers

The much discussed BE Games "Mile of the Century" event, to be staged at Vancouver, August 5 and 7, will not be a particularly crowded affair, when compared to other events. When Landy, Bannister and Co. roar off in the finals of the great race, eight men out of a semi-final total of only 17 will be gunning for the winning laurels.

The situation is quite different in the 220 and 440 yard races, for example, in which the total number of entries is 34 each.

1950~1959

Bowsfield Joins Red Sox Organization

Southpaw Inked Contract Monday, But Mum On Money; Reports July 1

Promising southpaw Ted Bowsfield launched a budding career in pro baseball Monday afternoon as he inked a contract handed him by Boston scout Earl Johnson and within a matter of a week the talented youngster will leave for the United States to flex his muscles

TED BOWSFIELD – BASEBALL BONUS BABY?

Scouts Flock Here; Pro Contract For Ted Maybe

JUNE 2, 1954. — Tonight in Summerland ball park some of the best scouting eyes in big league baseball will be in the stands taking a final look at their number one pitching prospect, southpaw Ted Bowsfield, before making their bid for his budding talents. Five years ago Ted was just another freckled-faced kid playing ball – then with the idea of becoming a good slugger and first sacker. Today, with four years of pitching experience behind him, he seems destined for a career on the mound of big league baseball.

Bill Marshall, Milwaukee Braves; Earl Johnson, Boston Red Sox; Tony Robello, St. Louis Cardinals; and Red Rolfe, of the Cleveland Indians are all here and each, no doubt, have a crisp new contract in their hip pocket, all filled out and ready for Bowsfield's signature.

To qualify for this higher echelon in the big league world, a player must be signed for a total bonus and salary of $6,000 or better. Under the rules of the baseball association, such "bonus babies" are not to be farmed out to a minor league for seasoning for a period of at least two years.

Bowsfield's rapid rise to pitching fame under the coaching of Les Edwards has echoed across the western provinces each season and his talent is well known in the ball parks of the west coast, right down to California. He has set pitching records here that will go a long time unaltered and in 1953 sixteen strikeouts per game was just an average performance.

in the Red Sox organization. Thus the first act is finished. For the past three years big time baseball has had its eyes on the 19-year-old chucker from Penticton and, with Ted's graduation, scouts flocked here to have a final look see and make their bids.

"What price was paid for Bowsfield is not known. In reply to the burning question Frank Bowsfield said only, "Ted is being well paid, but I am not at liberty to disclose the contract amount at present."

On July 1, Ted will report to the San Jose, California club and will likely finish out the season there. San Jose is "C" class ball. Next spring, however, the young Penticton hopeful will go to the Albany, New York club of the eastern league, to which he has been signed. Albany is "A" class ball. The Sox don't have an extensive farm club organization, just six clubs in all.

Ted will be coached by the well known "Red" Marion, whose brother Monty, made a big name for himself with the old St. Louis Browns.

In a press interview following

the signing, agent Earl Johnson remarked "In the not too distant future I think you will see the name of Ted Bowsfield on the roster of the major league. He has an outstanding future ahead of him, requiring only the experience of better ball to put him in the top brackets."

Ted Bowsfield displays the pitching form that made him the centre of attention in the eyes of four big league baseball scouts, now in Penticton, reportedly with contracts ready for his signature.

Morrison photo

Big Ted Pitches While Waiting For The Spring

Spring training for big leaguers may not start till warm spring sunshine brightens the southern states of the U.S., but big Ted Bowsfield doesn't believe in waiting for the sun.

While the rest of us shiver our days around the nearest furnace vent the only homegrown big leaguer from western Canada heaves mean left-handers down a specially constructed pitching tunnel.

Ted, due to be honored next Saturday night with a $10-a-plate testimonial dinner, intends to be ready when Boston Red Sox give the call this spring.

Gliss Winter, master of ceremonies for the dinner, told the

Herald yesterday that ticket sales for the event had been exceptionally good. "There are few tickets left, but only a few."

Top Speakers

Four top personalities in the sports world will be guest speakers.

Hec McDonald, former president and manager of the Penticton baseball club, now a resident of Vancouver; Annis Stukus, sports writer for the Vancouver Sun and former coach of the B.C. Lions; Herb Capozzi, general manager of the Lions, and Cedric Tallis, general manager of the Vancouver Mounties.

Honor Paid Ted Bowsfield Has Been Well Earned

About 12 or 14 years ago, a young fellow named Teddy Bowsfield used to take the mound, tug his cap, look over his shoulder, adjust his glove, and fire sizzling left-handers at boys his own size.

Some recognized Ted as major league potential right away. Others thought he'd fade and lose interest when he reached his teens. And some, we suppose, never noticed the difference between the ability of the Bowsfield boy and their own youngsters.

Ted Bowsfield didn't lose his early promise. He didn't fade when he reached his teens, and before too long he established himself as being definitely superior to the other boys playing minor ball.

Tomorrow night some of the men who watched Ted walk out to the mound when he was hardly big enough to get a ball over the plate are honoring him with a testimonial dinner.

Even the most optimistic among them in those far-off days never dreamed of such a day.

A Penticton boy honored as rookie of the year by an American major league club. A Penticton boy hitting the headlines of all sports pages on the North American continent. A Penticton boy whipping the New York Yankees at their own game.

Ted Bowsfield did it and the city as a whole, whether sports fans or not, should be proud that a youngster from a small interior city could hold his own with the best in his chosen field.

Tomorrow night's dinner has two objectives. It honors Ted Bowsfield, and it raises money to encourage other youngsters to tread the same magic trail to the big-time.

As the first man from B.C. to break-in to the ranks of the major leagues Ted Bowsfield will always be remembered. Along with that memory, whenever his name is mentioned in the future, will be the reminder that he was a Penticton boy. Over the years he will doubtless be joined with others, but no one can take his place at the top of the list.

The honors awarded him tomorrow have been well earned.

Works Minister Gaglardi Visualizes Highway 97 Paved From End To End

A paved highway running all the way from Los Angeles to northern British Columbia within the next few years, was visualized by Public Works Minister P. A. Gaglardi, when he addressed directors of the Okanogan-Cariboo Trail Association Friday night.

Mr. Gaglardi painted an optimistic picture on highway development in B.C. and gave a resume of what the present government has done in highway reconstruction and what it plans to do during the present year. He paid tribute to the late E.C. Carson, former minister of public works, and said that Mr. Carson's highway planning had assisted him immeasurably in carrying out road building projects.

He commended the Okanogan-Cariboo Trail Association for the interest the organization is taking

in tourist development, and lauded American members for working hand-in-hand with Canadian directors in promoting travel over Highway 97.

The works minister then referred to the vast undertaking of reconstructing and hard-surfacing roads in northern B.C. Total of 88 miles will be reconstructed south of Prince George, in addition to 86 miles of paving. Over 100 miles of paving will be done over the entire highway 97, he said. On top of that, 15 bridges will be constructed. In the last three budgets, we have made provision for $120 million to be spent on highways, plus $22 million for buildings for a grand total of $142 million, the speaker continued.

Work on reconstructing the Summerland road will be started in September, he said. Reconstruction

was delayed until after the fruit crop is harvested, at the request of growers in that area.

The works minister said the government had saved 25 percent on every contract made in the last year. "We have done more road work for the dollar than any other administration," he said. Mr. Gaglardi pointed out that due to less rock work, the cost of reconstructing Highway 97 in northern B.C. will not cost as much as in the south.

"Out of 23,000 miles of highway, we now have 3,000 miles of paved road," he continued, pointing out that this is somewhat unique as there are only 1,200,000 people living in B.C. In the last three years, 665 miles of highway have been black-topped.

Alderman Herb Geddes thanked the speaker on behalf of the OCTA.

Death Claims One Of The World's Greatest Physicists, Dr. Einstein

PRINCETON, N.J., (BUP) — Dr. Albert Einstein, one of the greatest physicists of all time, died today at Princeton Hospital at the age of 76.

The frail, little cosmic genius, whose theory of relativity unlocked the door to the atomic age, died quietly at 1:15 a.m.

Dr. P. Guy Dean, Einstein's personal physician, listed the cause of death as "inflammation of the gall bladder."

Einstein entered the hospital secretly last Friday. News of his death was withheld for nearly seven hours. Miss M. Hall, director of nurses at Princeton Hospital, said Einstein's family "held up news of the announcement."

(AP Photo/File)

This is a 1955 file photo of Albert Einstein. In the only study ever conducted of the overall anatomy of Einstein's brain, to be published in this week's issue of The Lancet, a British medical journal, scientists at McMaster University in Ontario, discovered that the part of the brain thought to be related to mathematical reasoning – the inferior parietal region – was 15 percent wider on both sides than normal, making Einstein's brain anatomically distinct.

1950~1959

VEES TAKE WORLD T

Penticton Herald

PENTICTON, B.C., MONDAY, MARCH 7

Provincial Library
Periodicals Dept.
Parliament Bldg.

May 55

5c Copy

VOL. XLIV.—No. 27

City Goes Wild At Great News

By VINCE DUGGAN

Sunday quiet was shattered as Penticton jubilantly and recklessly hailed the Vees for their 5-0 triumph over Russia. Cars piled four deep on Main street as folks abandoned the usual Sunday calm to hail their heroes "the world champs".

An estimated 6,000 persons, led by the RCMP and fire truck, joined a spontaneous parade of 11 miles in length as banners and the Union Jack floated in the breeze and auto horns and factory whistles blew the signal of victory.

Although places of business were closed, people wanted to go somewhere and they went, nowhere. But it didn't matter. Come what may, the local boys had done it again and who was to question the outburst of enthusiasm?

Traffic lights were ignored and while it was a parade it didn't move slowly. Main street looked more like an Indianapolis speedway.

"We did it," said the people, "we beat the Russians" — we, meaning the team and the people because who would question the fact that the two are all and one the same?

As the crowd milled around, centre of attraction being Warwicks' Commodore Cafe, I saw a little boy shake hands with an elderly man. "Gosh, this is great," said the youngster. "Son," replied the old man, "I've lived here a long time and this is it."

★ ★ ★

The parade moved up Main street and then broke off at the home of Mrs. Grant Warwick. "I'm so thrilled and happy," said [...] Grant Warwick's wife, "the fans have been wonderful and this

Vees Crack Russian Hockey

Penticton Vees - New World Hockey Champions

5-0

CANADA
RUSSIA
CZECHOSLO
UNITED ST.
SWEDEN
GERMANY
POLAND
SWITZERLA
FINLAND

KREFEL
kids, the Pe
vincing ma
hockey cha
surprising
"Pravd

Vees Win Title

KREFELD, GERMANY, (BUP) —

Canada's Cinderella kids, the Penticton Vees, did it. And they did it in convincing manner - wresting the title of world amateur hockey champions from the Russians here Sunday with surprising ease.

"Pravda" may write a different story to this one, but one thing is certain, the Russian journal cannot hide the score 5-0, and the Russians are lucky it was not 10-0, a score which would have been a better indication of the superiority of the Vees.

Actually, the Canadians won the world title a week ago Saturday when, in a typical Vee comeback, they defeated the Czechoslovak national team 5-3.

The Czechoslovaks were the team to beat in this tournament, not the Russians.

LIKE CLOCKWORK

It took the Vees about two minutes to size up the Russian style of play and for about that length of time the more than 10,000 fans saw something of the vaunted Russian hockey machine. It worked like clockwork and it also busted up like the works of a clock under a sledge hammer when the Vees cut loose.

A wobbly wrist, hurt again on the boards, kept playing coach Grant Warwick sitting out most of the game but the dynamic Vees mentor master-minded the show, throwing a bewildering combination of lines against the Russians.

Russian ace Bobrov was checked to a

standstill and never did look dangerous. Darling of the pro-Canadian crowd was Ivan McLelland, who chalked up his third shutout of the tournament.

The Vees' star spangled goalie wasn't kept busy as a solid four-man defence, George McAvoy, Jack Taggart, Hal Tarala, and Kev Conway were decidedly hostile to Russian intrusion over their blueline, but when the Russians did get through there was McLelland, degrees cooler than the ice he was standing on with his reflexes lightning fast.

Opportunity knocked for the Russians when the Vees collected a total of six penalties to the Russians' one and for the last minute of the game the Vees played with two men in the sin bin. The Russians did try, but McLelland took what heart they had left out of them with a great stop that drew thunderous applause from the fans.

NO MATCH

The Canadians had been warned many times that the Russians were in superb condition, that they skated like the wind and laid down perfect passes. That, as far as it applied to this game, was also so much wind. The Russians couldn't match the Vees in any of those departments.

Where some of the Canadians got their stamina from, stuffed up with colds, this writer doesn't know, but the Vees, as usual, when the chips were down, came through.

The Vees' second goal, a driving play by

the Jack McIntyre, Bill and Grant Warwick line, seemed to break the Russians' will to fight as the puck, driven out by Bill, catapulted off a Russian defenceman and into the net.

Other than that break, the Canadian goals were clean cut and an answer to the question "have the Canadians lost hockey skill through too much bodily contact in the game?"

The fans, including 2,000 Canadian and RCAF personnel, welcomed the Vees with a roof-lifting roar as they skated onto the ice. They looked like champions, skating easy and confidently. Up in the press gallery, it was the tower of Babel.

Nine nations were broadcasting, three were televising and there were five newsreel cameras.

BIGGEST SHOW

It was Sunday, March 6, the "biggest show on earth". Amenities were observed throughout, apart from Doug Kilburn and Kev Conway showing signs of a desire to punch noses in return for sly digs in the short ribs.

But the man who left his mark on the opposition was Hal Tarala, the Vees' massive defenceman. He was hitting hard and often.

The Russians opened with their first line. The Vees countered with McIntyre, Grant and Bill Warwick. With two Swiss referees on the ice, with other international referees acting goal judges and another as the penalty time keeper, the game was kept well in hand.

Vees' defenceman Jack Taggart weaves his way around a Russian during the final game, won by Canada 5–0.

Reaction From Communist Press

MARCH 7, 1955 , BERLIN (BUP) – East German Communists hoped today the Canadians will benefit from their hockey game yesterday with the Russians and learn to play a clean game.

The East German Press said the Canadians, in winning back the world hockey title yesterday, 5–0, scored a "deserved victory" but said they marred their triumph by "unfair" tactics.

The Communists also attempted to detract from the Canadian victory by referring to The Canadians as professionals. The Communist Party Newspaper Neues Deutschland said the team was composed of "ex-professionals."

OTTAWA CHEERS VEES' VICTORY

MARCH 7, 1955, OTTAWA (BUP) – Governor General Vincent Massey and Prime Minister Louis St. Laurent led the list of national leaders who wired happy congratulatory messages to the new world leaders hockey players from Penticton, in Germany.

1950~1959

"WHERE DO YOU EXPECT TO PLAY YOUR NEXT GAME?"

Final Standings

	G	W	L	T	Pt	GF	GA
CANADA	8	8	0	0	16	166	6
RUSSIA	8	7	1	0	14	39	13
CZECHOSLOVAKIA	8	5	2	1	11	63	22
UNITED STATES	8	4	2	2	10	33	29
SWEDEN	8	4	3	1	9	40	16
GERMANY	8	2	6	0	4	28	43
POLAND	8	2	6	0	4	19	59
SWITZERLAND	8	1	7	0	2	15	59
FINLAND	8	1	7	0	2	16	72

WELCOME WORLD CHAMPS

Penticton Herald

THE PENTICTON HERALD, THURSDAY, MARCH 17, 1955   5c Copy

VOL. XLIV.—No. 31   Five Sections — 40 Pages

THOUSANDS GREET VEES AS TITLE COMES "HOME"

It wasn't Shrove Tuesday and it wasn't St. Patrick's Day, but it was still a Mardi Gras celebration when the victorious Vees arrived home last night.

Despite a delay of three hours in plane schedules, thousands upon thousands of Peach City banners, applauded the "Welcome Home Champs" banners, waved. Peach City Promenaders in their street square dancing, landed the many hands who ably took up the slack and prepared themselves for something that couldn't be denied this community in spite of any delay.

It was almost dusk when the CPA airliner from Calgary slipped into this valley. Hot fans, ranging all the way from young-sters who had to be shouldered and the elderly who had never seen anything like it, lined Main street in anticipation.

There was disappointment when word arrived that the Vees would be late, unavoidably.

Main Street "Tremendous Scene"

They were all there — the bands, the officials, and the people. They milled around Main street, on what is an ordinarily quiet Wednesday afternoon where the Jaycees had painted huge "V" signs in green and white, adding just another touch of festive air together with the tons of crepe paper and balloons that became festoons in the tremendous scene.

The heady, holiday mood that prevailed in the city was painted up forcefully when the CPA plane carrying the Vees on the last leg of their journey home flew overhead. As soon as the plane was sighted approaching Penticton a spontaneous, exultant cheer broke out from the thousands patiently lining the streets ... As if the party telling ing overhead could hear and see them — pennants waving, everybody cheering.

"We did it for you, the people of Penticton", was how coach Grant Warwick described the World Tournament triumph as

Three Dollars Per Hour To Watch

Penticton's spirit was shown by a couple of old-age pensioners, unable to stand for any length of time, but who rented a taxi on Westminster avenue, waiting the team's original time of arrival at 7:45 p.m. at three dollars an hour, and said, "we'll wait".

Very proud was John Bowen Caldoust whose cat gave birth to a single kitten, a white one, reported to have a grey "V" on the forehead. The pussy was immediately christened "Giant". People lined the Main street

he stepped off the plane. It was all the coach could say as he and the rest of the party were swept up in a warm greeting from their families and loved ones.

They didn't foresee the tremendous outburst of enthusiasm awaiting them on Main street. "Welcome Home Champs" was in every window, people stood on roof tops as if trying to put to shame anything that had ever before been attempted here.

They came from Kamloops, convoy of 60 cars, joined by folk from other valley towns all the way down. They came down across the border, visitors from Spokane picked up well wishers at Wenatchee and points north.

There was the Firemen's Band from Vancouver and Miss Laurel Newlen from the same city, also known as "Miss Vancouver". And there were all the newspapers, radiomen and representatives of television who came to this exultant town to cover the big event.

sidewalks but as the parade arrived they closed in, cutting down the thoroughfare to half its size as final congratulations could be heard not only seen.

The big parade fleet, donated by the BC Tree Fruits Ltd., and carrying the world championship cup, brought a tremendous cheer from the crowd. A band followed and youngsters marched in the gathering dusk, picking up a tempo and never missing a step, proud to be part of it all.

Familiar Scene For World Champs

MERO COMES HOME to the the applause of what Grant, himself, termed "the best people in the world." Coach Warwick is shown riding down Main street in the victory parade with Mrs. Warwick and son Grant, Junior. Daughter Gail is in there, too, behind Mrs. Warwick.

ALL THE WAY FROM MOSCOW came this world championship cup. Bearing it proudly to the stage at the Memorial Arena last night were Rickey Sutherland and Bruce Voiden.

MIKE SHABAGA, with happy wife and daughter beside him, waves to the cheering throngs along the parade route.   —Redivo photo

MOSCOW PREDICTS FLIGHTS TO MOON

OCTOBER 5, 1957. London (AP) — A Soviet jet propulsion expert said today the launching of the first earth satellite means flights to the moon will be possible within a few years.

Speaking over Moscow radio, Dr. K.P. Stanyulkovich told Soviet listeners:

"It can now be said with confidence that in a few years flights to the moon with instruments will become as much a reality as the launching of the first artificial satellite."

"In the near future, new artificial satellites will be equipped with special instruments which will make it possible to study the more precise properties of the uppermost layers of the atmosphere and cosmic space."

1950~1959

Claims Red Spies In U.S. Missile Setup

OCTOBER 7, 1957. Toronto (CP) — The Toronto Telegram says Igor Gouzenko has informed President Eisenhower that spies in the United States missile production set-up enabled Russia to launch the first earth satellite.

The paper says Gouzenko, former cipher clerk in the Russian Embassy in Ottawa who exposed a Canadian spy ring in 1946, wrote to the president Sunday.

The Telegram quotes the letter as saying the launching "Indicates the work of well-organized Soviet spy rings in the U.S. missile production system."

The story adds that Gouzenko said in an interview that the size and design of the Russian satellite appears similar to the information originally published on American satellite plans.

Many Operating

"I exposed only one spy ring," Gouzenko is quoted. "Even at that time a further nine were operating in Canada. There are far more now than when I came out."

"I don't believe there is much difference in ability between Russian and American scientists. But the Russians have a first-class espionage system to help them, so they're ahead."

Earth Satellite Launched

Russians inspecting the U.S. earth satellite at the International Geophysical Year Rocket and Satellite conference in Washington said nothing about their own country's plan to be first in outer space.

1st Earth Satellite Shot Into Space

Moon Circles Earth

MOSCOW (AP) —

Russia announced today it has launched the earth's first man-made satellite 560 miles out in space and it now is circling the globe at tremendous speed. The dramatic claim that Russia had beaten the United States in the satellite race came in an announcement saying the artificial moon was launched Friday by mutli-stage rockets. The site of the launching was not given.

NEW YORK — Russia has won a race to step first into space with a baby moon.

It brings her enormous popular prestige, and world-wide congratulations of scientists.

Something fashioned by human hands and minds is whirling around the world as a Columbus of space. That's the tremendous initial impact. A link is broken in the chain binding humans to earth.

Baby moons are the first messengers to tell us what space is like, to answer some mysteries of the void between earth, sun and stars.

Now the question is: Just how elusive is this first messenger, and what will it actually tell us about space?

Three Questions

It can be valuable only if:

1. Scientists or amateurs in Russia or anywhere else can spot it often enough to learn its orbit, to predict where it goes next, and so learn what happens to it.

2. It radios back information about what it learns.

3. It lasts long enough before falling back close to earth and perishes like a shooting star.

Moscow, announcing its triumph only hours after the launching, has not yet reported success in accurate tracking.

This first official picture of the Soviet satellite Sputnik I was issued in Moscow October 9, 1957, showing the four-antennaed satellite resting on a three-legged pedestal. Working in obsessive secrecy, the Soviets propelled the Sputnik satellite into space on Oct. 4, 1957, making it the first man-made object to reach the limits of the earth's gravity. It mattered little that the small, silver orb had little purpose beyond achieving orbit and sending back a monotonous bleep-bleep signal as it circled the globe every 95 minutes during its three-month existence. At the height of the Cold War, Sputnik was one of the Soviet Union's most glorious victories and it touched off near panic in the United States, where political and military leaders forecast grave consequences if America lagged behind.

Satellite Will Cross Province Once A Day

Scientists To Interpret Signals

VANCOUVER, (CP) —

Scientists here today said the Russian launched satellite would cross Canada three times a day and British Columbia once a day.

Dr. A. Crooker, of the physics department of UBC, said it would not be possible to estimate times the satellite would cross British Columbia until the exact orbit was established.

He explained that the satellite followed a set course around the earth, but the earth was rotating 24 degrees while the satellite made each circuit.

So the satellite would cross every country of the world each day.

After lengthy calculations Dr. Crooker concluded that the satel-lite could not be as high as the Russians claimed.

He said an object circling the earth every 95 minutes must be at a height of about 350 miles, not 560 as the Russians claimed.

Dr. R.J. Clark, secretary of the Vancouver Astronomical Society, said United States and Canadian scientists should easily be able to track the path of the satellite and interpret its signals.

"The Russian satellite is apparently much heavier than the one the United States plans to launch and probably is carrying many instruments," he said.

"The satellite should be able to tell us previously unknown atmospheric pressures, in temperatures and electrical conductivity of the upper atmosphere."

"It should not be difficult for Canadian scientists to interpret the signals transmitted from the satellite," he said.

Dr. Clark said the information sent by the satellite would be invaluable to scientists everywhere.

The launching of an earth satellite caught Canadian scientists by surprise.

But amateur radio operators said last night they had picked up signals on the wavelength on which the Russians say the satellite is broadcasting.

Dr. C.S. Beals, Dominion astronomer, said he knew Russia, like the United States, was working on the satellite, from discussions with Russians in connection with International Geophysical Year.

"We were a little surprised to learn they had got it going so soon," he said.

Special Stations to Record Atomic Blast

TORONTO (CP) —

Canadian seismologists are scrambling to set up special stations in Ontario and British Columbia to record next Wednesday's underground atomic explosion in Nevada.

Dr. John H. Hodgson, Canada's head seismologist or earthquake expert, said Friday in an interview stations will be set up at the University of Toronto, the University of Western Ontario, London near Guelph, and somewhere on the pre-Cambrian shield in Northern Ontario.

Another party will set one up on Ripple Rock, the stubborn crag off Vancouver Island which is itself to be blown to bits next year.

The scientists hope that shock waves from the A-bomb explosion next week will give them valuable new facts about the earth's composition.

Shock waves from the bomb, to be touched off 800 feet underground Wednesday, will be measured scientifically around the world. The experts hope the waves will penetrate far down toward the earth's core. The time the waves take to bounce back will tell what they met on the way down.

Dr. Hodgson said the four stations in Ontario and the fifth on Ripple Rock are being set up in a hurry by Dr. Patrick L. Wilmore, geophysicist in the Dominion Observatory's seismological division.

He said the Ripple Rock station is being established because when the rock is blown, United States authorities will listen to the shock waves at a station on the site of the underground A-bomb blast.

This would provide "cross reference" readings on the waves from the two stations.

Dr. Hodgsons said he could not report the size of the charge to be exploded under Ripple Rock in Seymour Narrows, 100 miles north of Vancouver, but it would be one of the two biggest nonnuclear explosions known. The other was the 6,700-ton charge by the Royal Navy which blew up German fortifications on the island of Helgoland in the North Sea in 1947.

New Hydrogen Bomb Exploded By Russia

Big Blast Follows Satellite Success

LONDON (CP) —

The Russians announced today they had successfully exploded a new-type hydrogen bomb. The announcement said a "powerful hydrogen device of new design" was tested at a great altitude Sunday.

The announcement was made over Moscow radio while the world was still looking in stunned amazement for the Soviet manmade moon circling the globe.

The emphasis the Soviet announcement put on the "new design" of the latest hydrogen bomb attracted special attention here. And the speed with which the Russians disclosed the explosion – the next day – was significant. Usually they wait or even keep the tests secret even after they are detected outside the Soviet Union. The last previous reported Soviet nuclear test was Sept. 24.

In the race for nuclear power supremacy, the U.S. Atomic Energy Commission, also announced the firing of the 24th - and last - explosion of the 1957 test series early today at the atomic test site in Nevada.

Code-named Morgan, the shot was detonated from a balloon tethered 500 feet above the Yucca Flat desert test area.

The flash was visible for a few seconds in Las Vegas, 75 miles away. Observers on Angels Peak, 45 miles from the detonation point, said the fireball lasted 12 to 15 seconds.

The mushroom cloud rose rapidly to 20,000 feet. It was tinged with pink after the brilliant yellow of the flash faded.

The A.E.C. said the energy yield was below nominal or less than the equivalent of 20,000 tons of TNT.

MOCK H-BOMB HITS CITY DURING CD EXERCISES

OCTOBER, 1956. — Saturday night Penticton was devastated by a mock H-Bomb and nearly 80 Civil Defence officials from southern B.C. evacuated the city for West Summerland.

The civil defence delegates left the city in a long convoy of cars proceeding at the rate of 40 m.p.h. The procession was orderly and according to schedule.

Leaving Penticton at 7:45 p.m., the convoy proceeded directly to a welfare centre set up by the Summerland Civil Defence committee in the West Summerland High School Auditorium.

At the welfare centre the "victims" were registered, entered inquiries for lost relatives, received first aid treatment, clothing and food.

Registration was done on official blue forms issued by the federal Civil Defence organization. In evaluating the procedure, Sunday morning delegates at the Civil Defence Forum felt that the registration forms were rather complicated.

One delegate suggested that instead of having evacuees fill in forms there would be a registered staff interviewing and completing the data.

After The H-Bomb – What? Common Cold Still Problem

OCTOBER, 1956. — This is the season of the year when people go around saying "They can make an "H" bomb – why can't they find a cure for a cold?" Irritating as this statement is, it's also very true. "They" seem to be as far from finding a simple solution to the problem of colds as they ever were.

In the meantime the ordinary citizen will just have to "sweat it out". Literally that – because a hot bath, a hot drink and a warm bed seem to be still the best cure for colds until something better turns up.

T-B X-Rays

OCTOBER, 1956. — The mobile x-ray unit that periodically appears in towns and cities, gives every Canadian a chance to avoid tuberculosis. These chest x-rays are free and by their aid, the earliest symptoms can be discovered and treatment given usually successfully at this stage.

1950~1959

Television Comes To Okanagan!

In the days, months and years that lie ahead, the management and staff of CHBC-TV will strive to bring the latest and finest in television entertainment.

Many months of negotiations, planning and hard work plus more than a quarter million dollars, have been poured into the creation of this ultra-modern television station. CHBC-TV is unique in several ways and judging from the laudatory comments of visiting television men from major Canadian cities, the station is the envy of many.

One Year Ago

More than a year ago, the owners of radio station CKOV, CKOK and CJIB decided that the people of the Okanagan Valley should have their own local television station. Each station management body investigated the feasibility of erecting a station to serve their own particular city and trading area. This investigation proved that the only solution would be to combine forces as a single television company and serve the whole of the Okanagan Valley from one master station.

The Okanagan Valley Television Company Limited was formed, with two directors from each of the three Valley radio stations: Vernon, Charles Pitt and Richard Peters; Kelowna, James H. Browne and Mrs. J.W.B. Browne; Penticton, Roy G. Chapman and Maurice P. Finnerty.

Then application was made to the Canadian Broadcasting Corporation, through the Department of Transport (which regulates all forms of broadcasting in Canada), for a licence to operate a television station in the Okanagan Valley.

Because of the three-station application and the need for television coverage of the Okanagan, the CBC Board of Governors recommended that the licence be granted immediately, and "Operation Okanagan Television" began in earnest.

Appointed Managing Director of CHBC-TV was Roy Chapman, well known throughout Canada as well as the Okanagan Valley as co-owner and Manager of Radio CKOK, Penticton. To Mr. Chapman fell the tremendous task of building a complete television operation.

Problem number one was geographical and pertained to the type and method of transmission best suited to the mountainous area of this valley region. From the RCA Victor Company in Montreal came their finest television engineers. Mountain tops in the vicinity of Kelowna, Vernon and Penticton were investigated for best line-of-sight coverage (because a television broadcast signal, unlike a radio signal, cannot bend and can be transmitted only as far as the horizon). It was finally decided that, to guarantee the clearest signal possible to each of the three major centres and their envisions, a three-transmitter system would have to be employed.

Logical Site

Kelowna was selected as the logical site for the master station, and Blue Grouse Mountain, because of its height, was the site chosen for the master transmitter. Satellite transmitters (smaller versions of the master unit) would be located on mountain tops in the vicinity of both Penticton and Vernon.

This three-transmitter system, with a main transmitter and two satellites, is unique in that it is the only system of its kind in Canada.

The finest and most modern transmitter, studio and control room equipment was then ordered from RCA Victor Company, pioneers in television research.

Next came the problem of studio and office space. Because of the high voltage involved in television broadcasting, the building must be of steel or stone construction.

Studio areas must be free of posts or other supports, to facilitate easy movement of camera, equipment and sets, and the studio ceiling must be at least 15 feet high to accommodate the myriad types of lighting needed for well-lit studio broadcasts.

Floor area of the whole building must be sufficient to allow for a full-size studio, control room, telecine room, darkroom, executive offices and a general office. The ideal location turned out to be the premises at 342 Leon avenue, occupied by the Smith Garage, and used for maintenance work on huge trucks and trailers.

Top-flight craftsmen with local contractor Jim Allan supervising, went ahead with reconstruction work.

Meanwhile, a staff to operate CHBC-TV had to be found. From previous associations, with members of the television and radio industry in Canada, Mr. Chapman hand-picked those individuals who met his qualifications regarding experience, ability and personal characteristics.

As a result of this tremendous behind-the-scenes work, CHBC-TV is on the air!

MAIN TRANSMITTER AT 4,300 FEET

On Blue Grouse mountain, 4,300 feet above sea level, the main transmitter of the Okanagan's own television network sends its signals north and south to Vernon and Penticton. On the metal pins of both neighbouring cities satellite stations pick up the powerful towers's and relay them to the homes of viewers.

SERVING THE OKANAGAN

Bringing the world of entertainment to Okanagan homes the CHBC-TV network is the first of its kind in Canada. A main transmitter in Kelowna, and satellite stations in Penticton and Vernon, promise the finest reception possible of televised scenes for the entire valley area. Rushing work on the Penticton satellite company officials say that within the next few days the full services of the new project will be available to TV set owners in Penticton. First test patterns were sent out from the main transmitter on Sept. 18. Stars of stage and screen, world news and top sporting events will all take their place on CHBC's regular program. Four years in planning the network will constantly strive for high quality performances for Okanagan Valley viewers.

♦ Canada's First Network
♦ Coming to Penticton
♦ With First Class T.V.

TV Bringing Family Back Together Now

Of all the surprising aspects of television, perhaps the most amazing is what it has done to the institution of the family.

Before television appeared on the scene, sociologists were lamenting that the home appeared doomed, that family life had become almost non-existent and that the members of a family hardly saw each other from the beginning of the week to the end.

The function of the home had come to seem something like that of the pits at an automobile race track. Members of the family skidded in individually, were replenished, obtained minor adjustments, then roared off as quickly as possible, followed by shouted words of advice.

Now all that is being changed. Television is reuniting the family, physically at any rate, and luring it back into the home.

A study made by Rutgers University revealed that families with television spent 50 per cent more evenings at home than non-

television families. They average five evenings a week in the home, and three hours and 50 minutes watching television.

New Friends

Chances are that, in addition to the family circle, a number of friends, friends of friends, and just passersby are among living room audiences. A noticeable increase in visitors was reported by 70 per cent of the set-owners. Twenty-six per cent said their television sets had been instrumental in making new friends for them.

Other notable changes in people's daily pattern of living are being made as a result of owning a television set. They listen to radio more during the day-time hours. Their reading habits change, too. Most people read less than before.

In many other ways, television is influencing and altering family life. Mothers report with amazement that their children come right home from school instead of loitering until past supper time. Instead of romping noisily about

the house, they plop right down in the floor in front of the set, where they gaze spellbound at the screen.

Discipline Easy

Discipline is no longer a problem, as mothers threaten to deprive their offspring of their favorite shows.

As far as intra-family conversation is concerned, television has already made notable contributions. Before acquisition of a television set, members of the average family were apt to have little to say to one another, their individual interests being so diverse.

But now it is not uncommon for a housewife to display an unusual grasp of what happened in last night's wrestling matches, when discussing them with her husband at the breakfast table. That subject disposed of, father is quite capable nowadays of turning to his 10-year-old daughter and discussing the latest escapade of a puppet group.

All this takes place only in a home that has a television set.

CARE OF TV SET OUTLINED

SEPTEMBER 28, 1957. — There are two things to remember in taking care of a television set. First, treat it like any other prized piece of furniture, and second, if anything goes wrong, call the TV serviceman.

According to RCA Victor Service Department technicians, it's likely that more TV sets have been damaged by the home handyman's tinkering than for any other reason. It should be a strict household rule that the husband keeps his hand out of the workings of the set and that the children don't use it as a plaything.

Sitter Problem

SEPTEMBER 28, 1957. — Television has caused a mild revolution in the "babysitting" business.

Just ask parents who own sets. There's little trouble in getting a babysitter, they say.

There's little time for tots to get into mischief and cause headaches for the sitter – the youngsters are too busy watching TV horse operas and bedtime stories.

And they no longer demand stories from their sitters, either.

1950~1959

Snarling Mob Fights Police

Negro Pupils Withdrawn

LITTLE ROCK, ARK. (AP) — Little Rock school officials withdrew the eight Negro students who entered Central High School today.

Mayor Woodrow Wilson Mann radioed an announcement at noon CST saying, "Tell the crowd the Negroes have been removed from Central High School."

The radio announcement was sent to police officers at the scene.

Earlier a swirl of snarling men and screaming women tried to break though police lines after the Negro students slipped through a side door at Little Rock Central High School.

A handful of police fought off the crowd of angry whites, clubbing two men and apparently threatening another with a gun. None of the mob got through.

The Negro students walked quietly, and without hurrying, into the school while a diversionary group of Negro adults fought with the assembled whites.

Women Cried

It was a frightening sight.

Women burst into tears and a man, hoisted up on a wooden barricade, roared, "Who's going through?"

"We all are," the crowd shouted. But they didn't.

Students coming out of the high school said three of the Negro boys who entered the school had "blood on their clothing" and fights had broken out inside the school building.

The students told reporters the "Negroes were chased through the halls when classes changed" and were attacked by other students.

The climax of three weeks of integration struggle in Little Rock came just after the buzzer sound-

ed inside the big 2,000-pupil high school at 8:45, signalling the start of classes.

Suddenly, on a street leading toward the school, the crowd spotted four Negro adults, marching in two's down the centre of the street.

A man yelled, "Look, here come the niggers."

They were not the students. One appeared to be a newspaper man. He had a card in his hat and was carrying a camera.

Whites jumped the man with the camera from behind, rode him to the ground, kicking and beating him. They smashed the camera to bits.

BULLETINS

Tip Received On Threat To Queen's Life

SEPTEMBER 25, 1957. London, (CP) — A report circulated in London last night that Scotland Yard has received a tip of a possible threat to the life of the Queen during her visit to Canada and the United States next month.

The information is understood to have been given to security officers by Lady Patricia Fairweather, 41, sister of the Earl of Inchcape. It was based on a conversation she overhead during a recent visit to Barcelona, Spain.

Officials at Scotland Yard refused to confirm or deny the report. Said a Yard spokesman, "We don't discuss security matters."

Hoffa Indicted On Charges Of Perjury

SEPTEMBER 25, 1957. New York (AP) — James R. Hoffa, vice-president of the Teamsters Union, was indicted by a federal grand jury today on five counts of perjury.

The indictment charged that the 44-year-old union leader, a candidate for the presidency of the teamsters to succeed Dave Beck, lied to a grand jury during its probe into alleged wiretapping in teamster union headquarters in Detroit.

James Hoffa

Troops Use Armed Force In Race Fight

Two Hurt In Clash

LITTLE ROCK, ARK., (AP) — Hard-eyed paratroopers, in battle dress and with bayonets at the ready, brought nine Negro students quietly into Central High School today in a new climax to the hate-filled struggle over integration in Little Rock.

One man was clubbed and the other stabbed in the arm by the soldiers in fights that followed.

A few white students from the school left after the Negroes entered but there was no sign of a mass exodus. A school official said 1,250 students were in class today, making 750 absentees. It was 50 more than Tuesday when it was known the Negroes would not appear.

In an arc two blocks wide around the high school, the paratroopers kept breaking up clusters of people, moving them back, herding them onto porches and keeping the area clear.

They moved with swift purposeful actions.

It was in these operations that the two men were injured. C.E. Bake, 46, a railroad employee, tried to grab a paratrooper's rifle, soldiers said. The trooper, quickly reversing it, struck Blake over the eye with the butt. He fell to the

street but did not appear seriously injured.

Paul Downs, of Springfield, Ark., got a bayonet cut in the arm apparently when he was too slow in obeying an order.

Jess Mathews, a principal of the high school, reported "everything is calm inside the school and education is proceeding normally.

Armed Troops Take Over

Moving swiftly, armed paratroopers with bayonets ready escorted nine Negro students into Central High School today at Little Rock, Ark. The paratroopers kept yelling to clusters of spectators. "Back… back on the sidewalk." And they enforced it as they had done with bystanders earlier. The tense scene was not without violence. In two incidents, one man was clubbed and another stabbed in the arm by the soldiers.

Trans-Canada Highway Builders Battle Snow

By Jim Peacock
(Canadian Press Staff Writer)

GLACIER, B.C. —

The threat of avalanche that drove a railway into a mountain nearly 50 years ago is proving the major problem to builders of another transportation route – the Trans-Canada highway.

But the highway builders are beating the snow-slide problem without a tunnel as they swing the roadway back and forth across the narrow Rogers Pass to avoid the worst avalanche slopes.

They have do doubt the difficulty will be beaten, if not by the 1960 deadline for highway completion, then a year or two later.

Built Famous Tunnel

In 1916, the Canadian Pacific Railway abandoned the beauty of the steep-sloped Rogers Pass for the safety and easier grade of the five-mile Connaught Tunnel, driven through Macdonald Mountain from the valley of the Beaver to the Illecillewaet.

The railway sought refuge from the snow slides that between 1883 and 1916 wrought havoc with traffic to and from the west coast and took the lives of 236 workmen.

Today, as workers with hand axes, power saws and bulldozers clear the right-of-way of the Trans-Canada highway through the same pass, experts tramp the high slopes seeking an economic and lasting solution to the avalanche problem.

The federal government faces the major task. It is responsible entirely for the 28 miles of the highway through Glacier National Park, a region about 200 miles west of Calgary, and for 7 1/2 miles through Revelstoke National Park, about 25 miles farther west.

British Columbia is building the highway outside the national parks, with financial help from Ottawa, and is working from the east and west sides of Glacier to complete the remainder of the 90-mile distance between Golden and Revelstoke.

Present Link

These two east-central B.C. points now are linked by the Big End highway, a gravel route open from mid-May to mid-Oct. and taking 192 miles as it skirts the Selkirks to the north, following the Columbia River.

Construction of the all-weather Trans-Canada highway, 48 feet from shoulder to shoulder, is costly in the mountains, where huge timber must be removed and side hills of solid rock cut out. Through Rogers Pass it will cost an average of $350,000 a mile, more than three times the average cost of prairie highway building.

And this figure does not include the avalanche protection, which officials at first feared would cost nearly as much as the rest of the highway. Today the total cost of avalanche protection, including about 4,000 feet of snow-shedding, is estimated at less than $750,000.

THIS IS OUR FIRST ISSUE ON ENTERING DAILY FIELD

SEPTEMBER 9, 1957. — Today is a "red letter" day for the Central Okanagan and particularly for The Courier, for this is our first issue on entering the daily publishing field.

For the next three weeks, we will be hampered considerably, as we are obliged to print on our old press in our former Water Street offices. The maximum number of pages this press can take is eight pages, hence the reason for running the paper in two sections. It also involves trucking the newspaper forms over to the former building, thus a considerable amount of time is lost.

When our new press is erected, we will be able to publish a much larger newspaper. The press is also geared to run off 40,000 papers an hour, compared with 3,000 on our present press.

The Courier's news-gathering facilities will give readers up-to-the-minute world-wide, provincial, interior and local news.

Switching over from a bi-weekly to a daily is no easy task. We will endeavor to publish around the same time, but if your paper has not been received by 7 p.m. please telephone 2802 and one will be delivered.

Education Prevents Disease

SEPTEMBER, 1957. — National Immunization Week will be celebrated in Canada this Fall from September 22 to 28 for the fifteenth consecutive year. This annual event is planned to call to the attention of the people through Canada the importance of immunization against certain diseases. In the past years these have included diphtheria, whooping-cough, tetanus and in parts of Canada tuberculosis.

This year, because of the development of the Salk vaccine, poliomyelitis, or infantile paralysis, will be added to the list. Immunization has already achieved remarkable results. For instance in 1944 there were over three thousand cases of diphtheria in Canada; in 1956 there were only 135 cases. In 1944 there were over 13,000 cases of whooping cough; in 1956 – 8,513. Polio, a disease which even in the absence of vaccine varies in incidence, jumped from 327 cases in 1943 to 8,878 in 1953. However, by the use of the Salk vaccine it is hoped that its incidence may be reduced to the vanishing point.

THOUSANDS CHEER QUEEN ELIZABETH

OTTAWA (CP) —

Queen Elizabeth and Prince Philip arrived here safely today after a 13 1/2 hour flight from London for a four-day visit to the Canadian capital.

As officials sighted the plane, the RCAF band played God Save the Queen.

The plane taxied slowly up a runway half-hidden from the crowd by a low rise of land.

As it rolled slowly along, the Queen's personal standard stood out stiffly in the breeze on the nose. A 21-gun salute thundered across the airport.

Overwhelming emotion swept the scene. Thousands rose to their feet before the aircraft had even entered the final gate leading to the hanger in which the official reception party waited.

By the time the plane had rolled to a halt the entire audience was on its feet, shouts rang out still as the ramp was wheeled up to the aircraft.

There was a pause of a few seconds as the door to the aircraft opened, and a uniformed attendant stood by.

The crowd hushed while waiting for the Queen to appear, then she appeared at the entrance, paused briefly and stepped down the ramp, followed by her husband.

The cheers were deafening. The royal couple stepped into the brilliant sunshine of an autumn afternoon. The temperature was about 55 above.

They've Completed A Bridge Many Said Couldn't Be Built

Not two minutes from this city's main street, they've completed the bridge people said couldn't be built.

The $7,311,000 structure, built for the B.C. Toll Highways and Bridge Authority, shoots out almost a mile across Okanagan Lake from Kelowna on the east side, to Westside.

It is the bridge that people here dreamed of for years but virtually ruled out because of the distance and the cost.

Out on an eight acre site three blocks from where the bridge pushes across the lake, more than 250 workers one year ago were hammering and sawing and planning as they built pontoons and piers.

At the same time tons of fill were being dumped into a thin line, 1,400 feet from the Westside shore and 300 feet from Kelowna to form the causeway of the structure.

During the intervening 12 months, local citizens watched and waited anxiously for the huge pontoons and piers to be completed and placed in position to form a bridge 4,585 feet long, including causeway, pontoons and spans.

The pontoons, 2,100 feet of them, were placed in position early in the year. Two weeks ago the last of three spans was put into position.

Building a bridge is slow work, according to the men who plan the jobs.

"It's all the preparation that takes time," remarked Tom Coul, chief engineer for the Kelowna Bridge Company, when his firm first started assembling materials for the giant concrete pontoons.

The company faced the task of building most of its own equipment and bringing in machinery from Vancouver before it could start to work.

"This isn't an industrial area," Coul remarked, "so we had to bring in things. We even built a concrete plant, waterfront facilities, a pile driver – why we even brought in a tug by rail."

Kelowna Bridge Company crews started arriving here in the fall of 1956. First they began setting up their base camp and then they dredged the lake.

It was in the dredging that the workers met a problem they hadn't counted on – ice.

"We knew the lake froze over," Mr. Coul said, "but it was bad enough to make us stop dredging. it put us back a week in our schedule.

On the waterfront site, workmen scooped out tons of earth to an 18-foot depth to build the graving docks where the pontoons were built.

They left a huge bank of earth at the end of the docks facing the lake before constructing huge timber doors.

When the pontoons were ready, the lake's water was allowed to fill the docks so that the pontoons could be floated out to be placed in position at the bridge site.

Each dock was kept dry through a system of pumps. The lake was prevented from seeping through by sheets of steel driven into the ground by a pile driver.

Ten of the 12 pontoons are 200 feet long, 15 feet deep and 50 feet wide. The other two are 50 feet long.

They are made of reinforced concrete and make up the longest section of the bridge.

"They are built like egg crates," the company's office engineer Bob Prior explained. "They are divided into 56 cells, 14 along the 50-feet side.

Mr. Prior said each group of four cells is connected by openings in the walls to the others but that if the outside wall of one section is damaged, "the rest of the pontoon won't sink."

A total of 146 bolts were used to connect each pontoon to the next. They are separated by thick rubber on each corner.

The pontoons are attached by a huge hinge at the Westbank side to a small transition span, 175 feet long, which has a clearance of 15 feet.

The hinge allows the span to roll slightly with the rest of the bridge.

At the Kelowna side, two 188-foot spans are separated by a 260-foot lift span which has a clearance of 55 feet to allow larger vessels to pass up the lake.

July 19, 1958, will be written into the history books as one of the greatest days for the Okanagan.

Pertinent Bridge Facts

Do you know that:

The entire bridge project is over 2 1/4 miles long? That this includes:

One mile approach road, connecting the existing highway on the west side of the lake with the bridge site.

The rock fill embankment runs 1,400 feet from the west shore.

The west transition span between the rock fill and the pontoon section is 175 feet.

The pontoon section is 2,100 feet (12 reinforced concrete pontoons).

The east transition span between the pontoons and the west main pier is 175 feet.

The lift span is 175 feet.

The east approach span from the east main pier to the rock fill embankment is 175 feet.

The rock fill to the east shore runs a total of 300 feet.

The approach road through the City Park is 1,400 feet long.

Aerial view looking south of the floating bridge nearing completion March 24, 1958.

Royal Opening Of Lake Span

H.R.H Princess Margaret is shown the official dedication plaque for Kelowna's new state of the art floating bridge.

Photo courtesy Kelowna Museum

Big Crowd Breaks Security Barrier

KELOWNA —

Princess Margaret was almost mobbed by an estimated 6,000 persons of the 25,000 attending official opening ceremonies for the $7 1/2 million Okanagan Lake Bridge today.

Her Royal Highness had just officiated with the words: "I have great pleasure in officially declaring open this magnificent new Okanagan Lake bridge" and, departing from the procedure planned, decided to walk with Premier W.A.C. Bennett to unveil the two plaques on opposite sides of the structure, instead of riding in her limousine convertible.

Those in the forefront of the crowd swarmed through RCMP ranks onto the bridge crowding behind the Princess. After unveiling the plaques, one recording the official opening by Princess Margaret and the other listing those responsible for the bridge construction, Her Royal Highness stepped into her car and was driven across the structure and back to conclude the ceremonies.

As a memento of the occasion Princess Margaret received a section of the cable used to anchor the pontoons on the bridge, with an inscribed plaque attached.

Presentation of the bridge to Premier W.A.C. Bennett, chairman of the B.C. Toll Highways and Bridges Authority, was made by Harry C. Anderson, vice-president and general manager of General Construction Ltd., on behalf of his company, Dominion Bridge Ltd., Pacific Bridge Ltd., and the other contractors involved in building the structure.

Among the 400 dignitaries present were the governor of the State of Washington, Hon. Davie Fulton, minister of justice; Mayor C.E. Oliver and his city council from Penticton; and civic government members from communities throughout the valley.

No other bridge in British Columbia will have started its life "so proudly" as the Lake Okanagan bridge, Highways Minister Gaglardi said today.

Mr. Gaglardi said people of the province and especially of the Okanagan district are "very proud and happy that you (Princess Margaret) have consented to honor us today by officiating at the opening of this new crossing."

"We have numerous bridges in the province, some longer, some higher, but none that will have begun its life so proudly."

Premier Bennett said it was "a rare occasion indeed when all the circumstances of a particular action combine as happily as they do at this moment."

"Your gracious consent to officiate at the opening of this new Okanagan Lake bridge lends this ceremony a deep and abiding significance."

"That we should also have the great honor and privilege of your presence not only perpetuates the historic link between our people and the Crown of Empire and Commonwealth, but serves as a most auspicious entry into the century that lies ahead."

H.R.H Princess Margaret cuts the ribbon to officially open the new Okanagan Lake floating bridge.

Photo courtesy Kelowna Museum

Lake Bridge Will Solve Big Problem

Okanagan Lake Bridge will solve one of the British Columbia Government's most vexing highway problems. Highway 97 north of Penticton runs along the west side of Okanagan Lake. It now crosses the lake at Kelowna and runs northward on the east side.

The crossing has hitherto been by ferry and this point has always been a bad bottleneck in travel along the main north-south highway through British Columbia. Despite the continuous operation of three government-owned ferries, traffic has continued to be subjected to long delays. Normal local traffic has been augmented by an increasing volume of through traffic between Alaska and U.S. points, as Highway 97 provides the shortest route.

The construction of the bridge not only links the two sections of highway, it eliminates for many years the necessity of building 40 miles of first class highway southward from Kelowna on the east side of the lake, and another 40 miles north on the west side. Both these highways would be costly because they would pass through rocky and uninhabited country.

The bridge was the logical solution.

Mighty Blast Shatters Ripple Rock

Mild Shock Wave Hits Island Areas

1950~1959

By Al Markle and H.L. Jones
Canadian Press Staff Writers

CAMPBELL RIVER, B.C. — A mighty charge of high explosive – man's greatest non-atomic blast – was set off today in the heart of Ripple Rock.

The tremendous explosion, designed to decapitate the west coast's worst underwater shipping menace, shook the blast area of Vancouver Island. This community of some 3,000, eight miles to the south, felt only a mild shock.

Houses suffered for a split moment but there was no other recognized effect here.

In a great swirling mass, a giant water-spray blossomed from the Rock sharp at the scheduled hour of firing – 9:31 a.m. PST.

The water, rock and debris shot thousands of feet into the air, and a great smoke cloud fanned out, forming a picture-like curtain.

From observation bunkers, where the press and distinguished visitors watched, it appeared the firing was a success.

But it will be some hours before a definite report can be made.

"It looked a success," an engineer on the project said.

A survey ship prepared to move in to make tests.

Seconds after the count-down, watchers saw a giant spray of water shoot skyward and a pall of heavy grey smoke, tinged with brown from nitrous oxide – a product of the explosion of the nitramex 2H – blanket Seymour Narrows, 150 miles northwest of Vancouver.

A tidal wave 12 to 15 feet high roared to the shoreline.

The shock wave took six seconds to reach cameras in an observation bunker 7,000 feet from the rock.

Just In Time

The big blow was set off just in time. Minutes later the area was deluged by rain, which could have caused delay.

It was this heavy rain-laden overcast standing between Campbell River and the narrows seven miles north at the time of the blast, that apparently helped lessen the shock on this area.

People who had cut their power and gas lines, removed pictures from the walls and left their doors and windows open needn't have bothered.

The ground shake was so slight that many people gathered in groups outside their homes tensely awaiting the big blow didn't know that it had gone off.

Unaware Of Blast

Minutes after many were still standing outside, unaware that it was all over.

Mr. and Mrs. Paddy O'Halloran whose home is on a bluff overlooking the village and harbor, said "we didn't even know it had gone off."

Hope Abandoned For 95 Men Sealed In Mine

79 Saved From Shattered Colliery

By Ian Donaldson and Harry Calner
Canadian Press Staff Writers

SPRINGHILL, N.S. —

Ninety-five men are feared to have died in the shattered depths of North America's deepest coal mine.

With hope virtually abandoned for men trapped almost three miles inside the Cumberland No. 2 Colliery, rescue workers were engaged in the grim task of bringing out the bodies.

By mid-afternoon six bodies had been brought out and more were expected.

A sudden upheaval Thursday night shook loose tons of rock and released deadly gas, trapping 174 men deep in the Dominion Steel and Coal Corporation colliery.

By 3 p.m. today 79 men had been rescued. Thirteen injured were taken to hospital.

Harold Gordon, chief of colliery operations for Dosco, brought up from the depths the grim news that there was no hope for most of those still below and only the faintest chance that others were alive.

He said the only reason hope

was not abandoned for at least some of the men was that rescue workers had not yet been able to locate them.

Mr. Gordon, who spoke to reporters on his return from almost nine hours underground directing desperate efforts to save the missing men, said there was no hope for those on the two lowest levels, at 13,400 and 13,800 feet. Earlier reports had indicated some 55 men were at these two levels.

Between 60 and 70 men worked frantically to reach the entombed men through piles of fallen coal and stone. Gas set free by the bump endangered the rescue workers.

Mr. Gordon, who prepared to go back

into the mine after the press conference, said the two lowest levels are completely shattered. The bump ripped up the floors and jammed machinery and conveyors against the roof.

Third Ordeal

For the 7,000 people of Springhill, Nova Scotia's hard-luck coal town 73 miles northwest of Halifax, it was the third agonizing ordeal in less than two years.

Just a week short of two years ago, 39 died when more than 100 men were trapped by an explosion in nearby No. 4 mine. The day after Christmas last year fire destroyed a large part of the town's business district.

FIRST LADY OF BALLET TO LIVE IN PENTICTON

By Marjorie Vanderburgh

NOVEMBER 13, 1958. — Frank Morriss of the Winnipeg Free Press once wrote that when Gweneth Lloyd, director, and Betty Farrally, her most brilliant pupil, set up their ballet shop in Winnipeg, they should have had their heads examined.

That they knew what they were doing has been well proven now, some 20 years since they first came to Canada. Gweneth Lloyd, First Lady of Canadian Ballet, has worked unceasingly to establish ballet in Canada on the firm foundation of the Royal Academy of Dance in London from which she came.

Miss Lloyd established the Canadian School of Ballet at once on arrival and in the same year, she, and Mrs. Farrally, organized a ballet club out of which the Winnipeg Ballet has grown.

The Canadian School of Ballet has branches in Winnipeg and Toronto and now the third and latest branch has opened in the Okanagan Valley with headquarters, at present, in Penticton.

She drove out from Toronto last week and is living with Mrs. Farrally at Kaleden. They have been associated with ballet for 25 years.

Mrs. Farrally came last year to the Okanagan and has been tackling and overcoming all sorts of problems so that already classes of the Canadian Ballet School are going great guns in Vernon, Westbank, Summerland and Penticton and are in the formative stages in Oliver-Osoyoos.

'Life Is Grim For Beatniks'

By Bob Thomas

NOVEMBER 10, 1958.
HOLLYWOOD (AP) —

"Let's go watch the beatniks," my friend said.

It sounded like a good idea. After all, this was a phase of my own beat, the entertainment field. Coffee houses are springing up like mush-

rooms on Hollywood and Sunset Boulevards and other byways of the beat generation. So we went.

The joint was nestled among the agents' offices and steam baths on the Sunset Strip. It was dark, narrow and loud with the efforts of a three-piece combo of questionable jazz talent. The small tables were

tightly packed with young people. They glowered over their coffee cups.

"Why don't beatniks laugh?" I asked.

"Because life is grim, life is earnest," my friend said. "They can find nothing to laugh about in this age of anxiety when the bomb may

fall any moment."

"But we grew up in a depression in time to face a war," I said. "and we managed to laugh. As a matter of fact, when the grape was flowing up at the glen, we laughed it up quite some."

"The beatniks drink coffee," I was told.

Rebels Take Control Throughout Cuba

Dictator Batista's Regime Falls

By Larry Allen

HAVANA (AP) —

Supporters of rebel leader Fidel Castro took over Cuba today from the disintegrated regime of fallen dictator Fulgencio Batista.

Castro celebrated his triumph after 25 months of rebellion with speeches in Santiago, the eastern-most Oriente province and birth-place of his battle against Batista.

As the Santiago celebration continued into the morning, Castro was expected to appear before the roaring thousands and proclaim Manuel Urrutia as provisional president of Cuba. The celebrations were being broadcast.

Effective Strike

There was little doubt this island republic would accept Urrutia, a former judge about 56 years old who long has been Castro's choice to succeed Batista. Castro called a general strike across Cuba until Urrutia was installed, and the strike appeared to be 100-per-cent effective.

Until Urrutia takes over in Havana, however, Castro's announcements from Santiago provided the only framework of government.

Castro, a lawyer who has been a rebel for more than a third of his 32 years, outlined in 1955 the plat-

Cuban revolutionary leader Fidel Castro speaks to supporters Jan. 8, 1959 at the Batista military base "Columbia," now known as Ciudad Libertad. On Jan. 1, 1959, dictator President Fulgencio Batista fled the country and Castro's rebels took control.

(AP Photo)

form he would follow.

It included nationalization of U.S.-financed and operated utilities, splitting up American owned sugar estates among the peasants, confiscation of all properties acquired through corrupt government and breaking the hold of some big business men on Cuba's economy.

No Communist

The bearded guerrilla warrior has denied Batista's charges that he is a Communist or is Communist influenced. Castro says his goal is to end corruption and establish democracy.

Castro and Urrutia were expected to make a triumphal entry into

Havana soon.

In Ottawa, the external affairs department said the Canadian consulate in Havana has received a report that a Canadian is being held by Cuban rebels. He was identified as Adam Bessarabia, a native of Foxford, Sask.

The capital quieted down Thursday night after celebrating, looting and retaliation against supporters of Batista. Three policemen and 10 looters were reported killed.

Batista gave up the presidency and fled to the Dominican Republic early Thursday. His family and scores of his official departed hastily went with him or in planes and boats for the United States.

Cuban Workers To Stage Huge Rally

HAVANA (AP) —

Workers took the day off in Havana today to stage a massive rally in support of the executions by Cuba's revolutionary government.

Fidel Castro called for 500,000 persons to throng the park in front of the Presidential Palace this afternoon. The revolutionary leader said this would be Cuba's answer to foreign criticism of swift retribution for those convicted by military courts of crimes

against the people during Fulgencio Batista's dictatorship.

The first of a series of public trials in Havana was announced to begin at 12:00 p.m. MST Thursday in the city's 15,000-seat sports palace.

A total of 216 men are known to have died before firing squads after military trials. Thirty-nine were reported under sentence of death in Oriente province and 15 in the western province of Pinar de Rio.

Directed To U.S.

Castro said the rally in Havana would support justice and "demand that the United States return the war criminals." No formal requests for extradition of Batista followers who fled to the United States have been reported so far in Washington.

Castro claims 93 per cent of all Cubans favor continued trials and executions as a means of purifying the country and restoring order quickly.

FIERCE FIGHTING RAGES IN CUBA

By Larry Allen

DECEMBER 30, 1958. Havana (AP) — Street-fighting raged in Santa Clara Monday night as rebels trying to cut Cuba in two waged their first big open battle against President Fulgencio Batista's forces.

The government used bombers, tanks, armored cars and artillery to support troops fighting from house to house against the out-numbered infantrymen of rebel leader Fidel Castro. Government sources claimed rebels were being dislodged from key positions.

The rebels said their forces were in position to attack Santiago itself after taking 14 towns in Oriente. The port city, Cuba's second largest, is defended by 10,000 to 12,000 troops. Castro is believed trying to make it his capital and proclaim a provisional government headed by Dr. Manuel Urrutia, who as a judge once freed the rebel leader.

Canadian Acted As Castro's Agent

JANUARY, 1959. Montreal (CP) — A.R.L. (Andy) McNaughton, 42-year-old Montreal consulting engineer, today let it be known he served as an international agent for Fidel Castro, leader of the successful revolt in Cuba.

A son of Gen. A.G.L. McNaughton, famed Canadian soldier, scientist and statesman, Mr. McNaughton said he travelled throughout North and South America under the code name "Esquimal" to provide Castro with information and arms.

"My role was not that of a soldier of fortune. I received no pay for what I did. It cost me thousands of dollars in expenses as well as many thousands which I contributed directly to the (rebel) cause."

As a reward, he said, he was named an honorary citizen of Cuba. He was able to help Castro after falsely leading the Batista regime to believe he was working for the deposed president.

"To help Castro I had to know what Batista's government was doing. As his (Batista's) purchasing agent in Canada, I could find out what materials he was getting in Canada. If he was successful it was my job to arrange for their hi-jacking."

Long-Range Airliners Added To Three CPA Routes

VANCOUVER —

Introduction of Bristol Britannia jet-prop airlines on three major international routes linking Canada with Europe, the Orient, and Hawaii, highlighted 1958 for Canadian Pacific Airlines Ltd.

The remarkable flight characteristics expressed in these long-range airliners have enabled the Canadian carrier to offer superior service on all three routes.

For example, the Britannias have put Canada into the lead on the airways linking the Orient and North America, just ten years after CPA commenced its North Pacific service. Now, the airline offers the fastest non-stop service between Japan and Canada.

So far these 100-passenger, 400-mile-an-hour jet-props have broken all existing records for commercial airlines on all CPA routes where they are in service. On the return inaugural flight from Tokyo to Vancouver, for example, the Britannia covered the 4,752 miles non-stop in 11 hours and 44 minutes.

To set the stage for the introduction of jet-prop service, CPA last spring took delivery of six model 314 Britannias, and commenced to implement its plan to become one of the first air carriers in the world to operate the jet-props on all its international routes.

Royal Itinerary For Canadian Tour

OTTAWA (CP) —

Queen Elizabeth and Prince Philip this summer will see Canada from the rugged shores of Newfoundland to balmy Vancouver Island and the uranium and gold-mining communities of the northland, it was shown in an "outline" itinerary of their visit issued today by the government.

The royal couple will arrive by air at Torbay airport, St. John's, Nfld., on Thursday, June 18, to open a 15,000 mile six-week visit to this country. They will tour every province and the northern territories before leaving Halifax for home by air Saturday, Aug. 1.

The itinerary left unclear the arrangements and actual site for the official opening of the St. Lawrence Seaway, main purpose of the visit. The opening will take place June 26 and 27 at Montreal or Cornwall, Ont., or both.

Announcement Later

A special announcement covering the seaway portion of the tour is to be issued as soon as details are completed. Today's itinerary, which lists 78 Canadian centres and one American stop, Chicago – gave no times or details of the programs at the various towns and cities the royal couple will visit. These also are to be announced

(CP Photo)

Queen Elizabeth II will officially open the St. Lawrence Seaway on June 26, 1959 as part of her six week Royal Tour of Canada.

later.

The Queen and Prince will cruise the St. Lawrence River and Great Lakes in the royal yacht Britannia and depend heavily on air, train and car for transportation to other areas.

They will travel north at least as far as Whitehorse in the Yukon. It is possible they may go even far-ther north, to Dawson City of gold - rush fame. The Queen will be the first sovereign to visit the northland.

The itinerary sets aside July 12 and 13, a Sunday and a Monday, for a rest period in British Columbia. The locale is not specified, but the itinerary indicates it will be in the Kamloops area.

1950–1959

Russian Scientists Working On Manned Flight into Space

RUSSIA'S 'LUNIK' ROCKETS WILL MISS MOON TARGET

Will Become Sun Satellite

JANUARY 3, 1959. MOSCOW (CP) — Russia's new rocket will pass within 5,000 miles of the moon early Sunday and become a new "planet" of the solar system, the Soviet news agency Tass said today.

At 1 p.m. Moscow time (3 a.m. MST), Tass said the moon rocket launched Friday had reached a height of 209,000 kilometres (130,000 miles). This is well over half way to the moon, which is about 250,000 miles from the earth.

The Tass statement said measurements taken on the rocket's course confirm it will pass "close to the moon and will become a new planet of the sun."

The Soviet government predicted the rocket will reach the vicinity of the moon about 7 a.m. Sunday, Moscow time (t p.m. MST) today.

Not Too Close

It will pass between 3,750 and 5,000 miles from the moon, Moscow Radio said.

At the time when U.S. scientists thought an American moon shoot would pass the moon and head toward the sun, they said the rocket probably would be burned up in the sun.

The Soviet announcement indicated otherwise. The Kremlin expects its rocket to survive the fierce heat around the centre of the solar system. How, the Russians didn't say.

And there was no indication of how long Soviet scientists expected the rocket to survive as a planet.

MOSCOW (AP) —

The Russians say the chief unsolved problem in sending men cruising among the planets is how to bring them down again.

Soviet scientists expressed this view Tuesday as they reported cosmic rocket Mechta still speeding toward an orbit around the sun. One physicist, Prof. Vladimir Dobronrarov, commented:

"A perfectly realistic foundation for the development of inter-planetary travel already exists and in the near future man can set foot on other planets."

Set Temperature

During the 62 hours and 370,960 miles Mechta was radioing information back to earth, Dobronrarov said, its internal temperature and pressure remained within set bounds. The temperature had been reported earlier at 50 to 60 degrees.

This means Russia soon will know how to create proper climatic conditions for men inside rockets, Dobronrarov claimed.

But the reentry problem – getting man back through the earths atmosphere – remains, vice-president Alexander Topchiev of the Soviet Academy of Sciences told the press conference on Mechta's achievements.

"I can assure you we will not stop at this," Topchiev said.

No man has yet flown in a rocket, physicist Anatoly Blagonravov said. "How soon he does fly will depend on how soon we have assurances he will be able to return safely."

In 10 years, the American Astronautical society was told in Washington, there could be a space station orbiting hundreds of miles above the earth. The report was made to the society by scientists of Lockheed Aircraft, who said the various sections of the station could be rocketed into space to be gathered and assembled by manned craft. This illustration shows the manned craft, lower left, guiding a piece of a cylinder into position where, joined to others, it would be the living quarters for the space community.

U.S. Scientists Develop New Rocket Engine

CHINA LAKE, CALIF. (AP) —

A new rocket engine that should make space ships about as easy to drive as automobiles:

A safe way of packaging dangerous fuels – so missiles can be delivered to troops in the field ready to fire without long countdowns.

A prediction that this combination of engine and fuels will enable man to land gently on the moon – and take off again.

All these were disclosed Sunday by scientists of the U.S. naval ordinance test station here, where rocket propulsion studies have been under way for 14 years.

Douglas D. Ordahl, head of the missile propulsion division here, told a press conference "We hope to make a test vehicle within the next six months."

The new engine can be controlled remotely by radio, or by a simple hand lever," Ordahl said. "It is capable of repeated starting and stopping, accelerating or decelerating from zero to full throttle, and changing course by varying the direction of rocket thrust."

When completely assembled, the space station would be powered by a nuclear assembly and could travel to any desired spot above the earth. Inhabitants would be well shielded from harmful rays and would have their own atmosphere sealed into the cylinders joined together in the shape of a wheel and distant from the atomic jet exhausts that propel the craft.

Canada's Forces to Get Nuclear Weapons

OTTAWA (CP) —

Prime Minister Diefenbaker today made clear that Canada's armed forces will be armed with nuclear weapons but that the atomic warheads will remain in the custody of United States forces.

The prime minister informed the Commons that the government now is examining with the U.S. government questions connected with acquisition of nuclear warheads for the Bomarc anti-aircraft missile "and other defensive weapons for use by the Canadian forces in Canada and the storage of warheads in Canada."

"Problems connected with the arming of the Canadian brigade in Europe with short-range nuclear weapons for NATO's defence tasks are also being studied," he said.

"We are confident that we shall be able to reach formal agreement with the U.S. on appropriate means to serve the common objective."

It would be "some time," however, before these weapons became available for use by Canadian forces.

Mr. Diefenbaker said the full potential of the Bomarc and the army's surface-to-surface Lacrosse missile is achieved only by arming them with nuclear warheads.

The government believed in the importance of limiting the spread of nuclear weapons at the independent disposal of national governments.

Full Study Of Defence Policy Urged

OTTAWA (CP) —

Opposition Leader Pearson today called for a "complete and comprehensive" parliamentary examination of Canadian defence policy.

He spoke in the Commons immediately after Prime Minister Diefenbaker announced the government's decision to terminate the Arrow jet interceptor program and equip Canada's armed forces with nuclear weapons.

Mr. Pearson said the prime minister had stated that Defence Minister Pearkes and the chiefs of staff now were engaged in further studies of various alternatives for improvement of Canada's defences.

This pointed up the desirability and necessity of a complete and comprehensive examination of the whole concept of Canadian defence policy by a committee of the Commons.

"Where are we going from now on in this vital matter?" Mr. Pearson asked.

"In recent months it has come to be realized that the bomber threat against which the CF-105 (Arrow) was intended to provide defence has diminished, and alternative means of meeting the threat have been developed much earlier than was expected.

Refers to ICBM Threat

Mr. Diefenbaker said the Arrow could be fully operational in the RCAF only after mid-1962 by which time "the threat from the Intercontinental Ballistic Missile will undoubtedly be greatly enhanced, in numbers, size and accuracy and the ICBM threat may be supplemented by submarine-launched missiles."

"By the middle 1960's the missile seems likely to be the major threat and the long-range bomber relegated to supplementing the major attack by these missiles."

"Canadian requirements for civilian aircraft are very small by comparison with this huge defence operation and frankness demands that I advise that at present there is no other work that the government can assign immediately to the companies that have been working on the Arrow and its engine.

The prime minister also said the U.S. government "after full and sympathetic consideration of proposals that the U.S. air force use the arrow has decided it would not be economical.

"Already the U.S. air force has decided not to continue with the further development and production of U.S. aircraft having the same general performance as the Arrow. The development of interceptor aircraft that now is proceeding in the United States and abroad is on different types."

Mr. Diefenbaker said Canada has taken no decision to acquire other aircraft to replace the CF-100, now in use, "which is still an effective weapon in the defence of North America against the present bomber threat."

1950-1959

Women's Page

Order To Shorten Skirts Causes Revolt Among Airline Employees

Not Fashionable

By M. McIntyre Hood
Special to The Penticton Herald
LONDON —

An order issued by British European Airways to its 700 hostesses, receptionists and ticket clerks that they cut from two to three inches from the length of the skirts of their uniforms has started a revolt at the London Airport. The opposition to the new order is outspoken and verbose.

The trouble over skirt lengths and raising of the hemline started when Lady Douglas, wife of the chairman of the BEA, Lord Douglas of Kirtleside, suggested to her husband that the skirts worn by these girls should be shortened. A former model, she thought the present long skirt was quite out of fashion and was not becoming. Like a model husband, Lord Douglas agreed with his wife. The BEA personnel staff was consulted and they agreed with their chairman. So out went the order, in effect, "get busy with the scissors and cut from two or three inches off the calf-length skirts."

But many of the grey-uniformed girls have chorused "Never".

Said one girl, "I would not shorten my skirt for the Queen – let alone Lady Douglas."

Not Consulted

Much of the opposition stems from the fact that many of the girls feel they should have been consulted before the order was made. One receptionist said: "Let's be honest. It is ridiculous to assume we all have Monroe figures and nice legs. We are all shapes and sizes. A short skirt would look ridiculous on some of us. We have not all sylph-like figures like Lady Douglas."

Investigation, however, shows that 70 per cent of the girls are in favor of the change, with 30 per cent in opposition.

By observation, it can be said that the uniformed girl employees of the other major air lines using the London airport have been wearing the short skirts, two or three inches below the knee, for some time, with no complaints.

Every Woman Can Have Electric Kitchen

Whether an apartment dweller or a Newfoundland cottager, every woman has her dream-kitchen. Now it can be a reality – with built-in livability, where dishes all but do themselves, waste foods dispose of themselves and the whole family finds fun in everyday push-button kitchen activities. And the marvel of it is that each new appliance added to the dream finds its right place in a built-in plan.

Such a plan may have its beginning in something as simple as a new fluorescent fixture. Bigger things can come later, taking full advantage of today's straight line, squared corner styling, plus a dramatic use of color.

Because of this practical straight-line design in some new electrical appliances, the built-in trend which started with ranges and ovens, now extends to other appliances. With no curved tops, sides or back, the straight-lined appliances can be placed either flush against a wall tightly in a corner, or in line with other appliances or cabinets.

Many appliances, including the dishwasher, can be installed either waist-high at counter level, placed beneath a work surface, or even mounted atop each other. Many designs make possible freer appliance placement to open up floor space. Wall-hung refrigerator freezers color-matched to kitchen cabinets, make cold storage space seem almost non-existent to the eye.

No matter what type of home it is, or where it is, the new trend in modern kitchen and kitchen electric appliances means dreams do come true, whether in whole or in part at a time, when you plan to live better electrically.

Financially Troubled Farmers 'Need Help'

Uneconomic Land Cited By Walls

By Jim Hume
(Herald Editor)

VERNON —

Charles E.S. Walls, manager of the B.C. Federation of Agriculture, told the 70th annual convention of the BCFGA here this morning that they must never cease to try and help the man who sank his life savings into high-priced property and then because of changing economic conditions, discovered he could not make a living.

Speaking to a crowded auditorium, Mr. Walls said, "there are two types of small farmers working uneconomic land. There is the urban worker with a longing for the outdoor life. We can help him as much as we can in advising him on how to grow his crop and market it. But the other class is more important to us. This is the man who sank his life savings into high-priced property at a time when that property could maintain him and his family in a decent way of life.

Outside Employment

"Changing economic conditions have forced this man to find employment off the farm. When he seeks this outside employment his farm suffers even more. These are the men we must never forget. They cannot, must not, be dismissed, just because their land is no longer economic. They must be helped."

Mr. Walls appealed for a greater understanding between all branches of agriculture. "All phases of agriculture are faced with the same problems. Fruit growers are not alone. Ever spiralling costs of marketing, great changes in economic conditions, are making it increasingly difficult for the farmer."

Praising the BCFGA for lifting its voice until it got a royal commission into the fruit industry, Mr. Walls said all branches of agriculture were not so fortunate or so well organized.

"You would not have been granted this commission had your voice not been strong, and your organization sound. Others lack your organization and your voice but they are watching with avid interest the way you meet your problems. The eyes of everyone engaged in agriculture are focussed on you at this present time."

Mr. Walls stated that one of the greatest features of the MacPhee report and one of the greatest benefits achieved so far, lay in the press publicity given to the report at the coast. "As a result of that publicity, there is already greater understanding among farmers who before did not understand your problems."

Puck World Wonders Whether Rocket Richard Can Come Back

By Marven Moss
Canadian Press Staff Writer

Can a 37-year-old athlete, bone-weary from 17 seasons of National Hockey League competition, make still another comeback after suffering a crippling injury?

Shrouded by the question is dark-browed, grizzled Maurice (Rocket) Richard, Montreal Canadiens rightwinger and hockey's greatest all-time scoring star.

The Rocket suffered a fractured left ankle when the high riding Habs fought to a 1-1 saw off with the resurgent Black Hawks in Chicago last Sunday night.

Out For A Month

Resting in his north-end Montreal home, his leg in a cast, he won't be permitted to don skates again for at least four weeks.

And then?

"I want to see what happens when they take the cast off," he told reporters. "I will not decide whether to continue in the game until I'm able to skate again."

Although in the twilight of his brilliant career, at the time of his injury, the Rocket was still one of the most feared forwards in the league.

He was named the top Canadian athlete of 1958 in a poll by The Canadian Press and he also received a "Big Brother" award as the Canadian providing the greatest inspiration to youth.

Frank Selke, Sr., vice-president and general manager of the Canadiens, states simply: "Maurice will come back. This may be a blessing in disguise. He needed a rest. Now he'll have one and help us win the Stanley Cup."

Selke and the fans can also point to Maurice's record of durability.

A broken ankle in his first NHL season almost nipped his career in the bud. That came 16 games after he first joined the club, but he bounced back the next year to pot 32 goals.

And last year an almost-severed achilles tendon knocked him from action for three months after he had pushed off to one of his highest-scoring starts in years.

Again he returned with all his natural flair for the dramatic, firing two goals in his first game back from the sidelines. Then he went on to accumulate 15 tallies for a 28-game season and lead the playoff snipers with 11 goals.

606 Goals In Career

Before he fell near the boards in Chicago Sunday night – and felt something snap in his ankle – he bagged 17 goals in the current season, running his NHL total to 606 including playoffs.

RAGING BLIZZARD HITS NEW MEXICO

DECEMBER 30, 1958. DUMAS, TEX. (AP) — A raging blizzard Monday buried New Mexico's largest city under its heaviest snowfall, stranded thousands of motorists and claimed four lives. And more snow hit the southwest today.

Winds up to 60 miles an hour whipped the snow into drifts of up to six feet, blocking highways across eastern New Mexico, the Panhandle of Texas and part of western Oklahoma.

Four hundred motorists – most of them Iowans bound for Pasadena, Calif., and the New Year's Day Rose Bowl football game between Iowa and California – were stranded at Tucumcari in eastern New Mexico when snow blocked all roads in the area.

IGY Projects To Be Continued At Observatory

JANUARY 2, 1959. VICTORIA (CP) — While the International Geophysical Year officially has ended, some IGY projects will continue at the Dominion Astrophysical Observatory in nearby Saanich.

Dr. R.M. Petrie, director, said four projects carried out by his staff for IGY are being done on behalf of the National Research Council and the Dominion Observatory, Ottawa.

"Some are to be carried on as continuing ventures," he said.

Costly equipment has been installed and results are useful even though study is no longer on an international scale, he said. It is up to Ottawa to say when projects are to be halted.

A study of the ionosphere, a region of electrically - charged gases 50 to 250 miles above the earth, is expected to end shortly.

Another project, measurement of the products of fission in the atmosphere, will be prolonged at least three months. Both are for the National Research Council.

Dr. Petrie said the operation of a magnetic observatory in a small prefabricated aluminium and plywood dome below the office building will be continued for some time.

All records from these studies, as well as the auroral camera, are sent to Ottawa for processing.

Mystery of Anastasia Continues to Deepen

MAX FACTOR MAKES FEARLESS PREDICTION

By Bob Thomas
MARCH 5, 1959.

HOLLYWOOD (AP) — Fifty years from now, a woman of 50 will be just as alluring as a girl of 20.

That is the fearless prediction of Max Factor, head of the cosmetics concern that is celebrating its first half-century. To signal the event, he reviewed the past and the future of makeup - a word the Factor family helped popularize.

"When my father started the company in 1909, women scarcely used cosmetics at all," he commented.

"The movie stars helped us spread the use of makeup. As the stars became popular, the public copied their dress and grooming.

What about 50 years hence?

"People will be living longer. When we started in business, the life expectance was 40 years or so. Now it is in the 70s and it will go higher."

"I firmly believe that in the future women of 50 years or more will look as appealing as girls of 20. We are keeping in touch with scientific experiments in Europe on youth-giving cosmetics.

"Skin creams are being prepared with the aid of antibiotics as a means toward preserving a youthful skin."

Factor also foresees the extensive use of cosmetics by men 50 years from now, and for the same reason. To keep young. Among his predictions: A pill which will forestall the greying of hair.

Lawyers Arrive In Montreal

MONTREAL (CP) —

Did the Communists kill the grand duchess Anastasia with other members of the Russian royal family in the 1918 massacre at Ekaterinburg or did she survive to become Mrs. Anna Anderson of Bad Liebenzell, West Germany?

And if Mrs. Anderson is not Anastasia, then who is she?

The mystery has split Europe's royal families and intrigued historians since the 1920s. Even Hollywood got into the act by coming through with a motion picture called Anastasia in which Ingrid Bergman was the heroine.

The Hamburg civic court is the latest tribunal to attempt to decide whether Mrs. Anderson is truly Anastasia, as she claims.

Gather Evidence

Two West German lawyers, both representing Mrs. Anderson, came to North America this month to gather evidence from former dukes and princesses and others related to the imperial house of Russia. West German consular officials in the United States and Canada are helping them.

The two, Dr. Kurt Vermehren and Paul Leverkuehn, first went to Cassville, N.J., where they talked to Glen Botkin, 58, the son of the late czar's personal physician and a playmate of Anastasia.

They questioned persons in New York City March 16-18 and were to open the Canadian phase of their investigation today in Montreal with the former Duke and Duchess Dimitri of Leuchtenberg as voluntary witnesses.

The former duke and duchess have been living quietly for many years in the Laurentian resort centre of Ste. Agathe, Que., north of Montreal.

The lawyers are expected to move to Toronto next week to question Mrs. Nicola Koulikovsky of Cooksville, Ont., the former grand duchess Alexandrovna of Russia who has said she is convinced Anastasia is dead.

On arrival in Montreal from New York City Thursday, Dr. Vermehren said in a brief interview:

"We are here to interview people, what more can we say. There are those who say Anna Anderson is an impostor and there are those who swear that she is Anastasia. They will never change their minds."

Mrs. Anderson petitioned the Hamburg court to recognize her claim to the German fortune left to Anastasia, and to Anastasia's three sisters who died in the Ekaterinburg massacre.

The House of Heese in West Germany is contesting Mrs. Anderson's claim to be the youngest daughter of the late Czar Nicolas I. The Heese family has undertaken to prove the woman was a Polish farm laborer.

The late czarina, Anastasia's mother, belonged to the House of Hesse and the Hesse family was declared heir to the Czar's German estate in 1933.

Mrs. Anderson unsuccessfully appealed the 1933 court decision. The Second World War interfered with a second appeal, but on Jan. 29, 1957, a Berlin court discounted her claim to be Anastasia.

Anthropologists and geneticists have said Mrs. Anderson showed little physical resemblance to the Grand Duchess Anastasia who would be 57 years of age if she were still alive.

One witness at the 1957 Berlin court hearing which went against Mrs. Anderson testified that he personally had seen 11 royal corpses, including that of Anastasia who was 17 at the time.

Queen Invited To Visit Penticton Area

Naramata Home To Be Available

By Vic Misutka
(Herald City Editor)

Her Majesty Queen Elizabeth and Prince Philip have been invited to visit the Penticton and area when they tour Canada this summer.

In issuing the invitation, Penticton Board of Trade has pointed out that some 60,000 people in the South Okanagan and Kootenays would have a better opportunity of seeing the royal couple if Penticton is put on their itinerary.

At the same time, Her Majesty and Prince Philip would be able to relax amid some of the finest scenery in British Columbia, a board of trade spokesman said today.

At the request of the board, Mr. and Mrs. Carol Aikins have agreed to make their stately Okanagan lakeshore residence near Naramata available for the royal visitors' convenience.

Arrangements for the royal visit in British Columbia are being coordinated by a special committee headed by Lieut.-Governor Frank Ross. The board's invitation has been referred to Mr. Ross.

Lieut. Gen. Graham expressed warm appreciation for Mr. and Mrs. Aikins' hospitality and the board of trade's interest.

The Aikins' residence where the queen and her consort would stay while in this area, is about three quarters of a mile south of Naramata, set in a scenic and relaxing atmosphere. The spacious and attractive two-storey home of stone construction is on a gentle slope to the lake, and is surrounded by a wide expanse of lawn, trees and shrubs.

Overlooking Okanagan Lake, the home has its own beach along a small bay just to the south and affords a clear view of Penticton, the West Bench and Naramata.

Diefenbaker Opens First Nuclear Reactor

By Peter Sypnowich
Canadian Press Staff Writer

HAMILTON (CP) —

Prime Minister Diefenbaker opened the British Commonwealth's first university nuclear reactor Friday with a plea for agreement on ending nuclear bomb tests.

He told students and dignitaries at McMaster University he has hopes, despite the unprecedented political problems, that negotiations resuming at Geneva Monday may bring a test ban.

"If we bring about steps toward disarmament then we can see a day ahead when the disarmaments race will end and the world will realize the unlimited benefits of nuclear energy."

Would Remove Fear

Disarmament, said the prime minister, will not only end suspicion and fear but it will remove the secrecy surrounding nuclear advancements.

"I believe we must negotiate, that there is no hope for us if we fail to realize the alternative to negotiation is destruction."

McMaster's new reactor, Mr. Diefenbaker said, is a practical example of Canada's determination to put the arts of peace before the science of war.

The $2,000,000 reactor was built in 18 months through grants from the federal government, the Ontario Hydro-Electric Power Commission and private industry. Canada has four other reactors at Chalk River, Ont.

Dr. H.G. Thode, McMaster's vice-president and director of research, said that although the reactor would be used to test materials and gather data for development of commercial reactors, its primary purpose would be for teaching and research.

The reactor building is circular and windowless, 72 feet high and 82 feet in diameter. The reactor itself is of the "swimming pool" type with a potential of 1,000 kilowatts. Uranium 235 is burned in a constant chain reaction 25 feet below the surface of a pool containing 100,000 gallons of circulating water. Radioactive material is handled by a 12-ton crane operated from a catwalk.

Cigarettes, Fallout Add To Cancer Hazard

Increase Shown In U.K

ATLANTIC CITY (AP) —

Cigarettes and nuclear bomb fallout may together present an intensified lung-cancer hazard, a team of St. Louis scientists said today.

Doctors V. Suntzeff, E.V. Cowdry and A. Croninger, all of the Washington University Medical School, said experiments with mice suggest the following:

That the combination of cigarette tar and fallout radiation can produce tissue damage over and above what might be expected from the sum of two agents together.

That is, they told the annual meeting of the American Association for Cancer Research, the experiments indicate a 'synergistic effect" – a phenomenon in which each of two materials enhances the action of the other.

In a preliminary report of their research, they said their conclusions to date are based on tests in which skin cancers were produced in mice by a combination of cigarette tar and radiation from strontium-90. The latter is potentially the most dangerous product in nuclear bomb fallout.

However, in the present controversy over whether there is a link between cigarette smoking and lung cancer there are scientists who argue that there is no present evidence of any such link. They contend, for one thing, that conclusions about lung cancer in man cannot be drawn from skin cancers in mice.

1950~1959

Priest Discovers 16-Year Prisoner

APRIL 10, 1959. BOSTON (AP) — A widow and her daughter were at separate hospitals today after a priest and police discovered them in a rubbish-strewn, foodless apartment.

The emaciated 33-year-old daughter had been held prisoner in her own home, police said, for 16 years.

Police Lieut. Chester A. Henchey said the situation was discovered by Rev. Kenneth Murphy, a Catholic priest, who operates Rescue Inc., a non-sectarian service for potential suicides.

Father Murphy and policemen went to the home of Mrs. Catherine Stearns, 59, Friday night after neighbors said she had threatened suicide. After taking Mrs. Stearns in hand, police searched for half an hour before they found her daughter, Mary, 33, under a pile of debris and blankets.

Henchey said the daughter was in such a wild state she had to be tied. She was calmed and taken to hospital.

A doctor said the daughter's thighs were "no thicker than a man's wrist." She weighed between 40 and 60 pounds.

Father Murphy said the apartment was "full of debris and in a condition that smelled and looked as if it were a town dump instead of a home."

A DECADE
IN REVIEW

1960 ~ 1969

Cuba Invasion Starts With All-Out Attack

Castro Claims Mercenaries From U.S. Are Involved

By the Associated Press

Invaders seeking to overthrow Fidel Castro landed in Cuba today by sea and air.

The Cuban premier, acknowledging the attack, said it was launched by mercenaries organized by the United States. He declared his troops are advancing against the invaders and are certain of victory. He called on Cubans to maintain order and discipline.

Castro told his people by radio that the invaders landed at several points in southern Las Villas province.

Cuban exile sources in the United States said forces also had gone ashore in extreme eastern and western Cuba and on a beach southeast of Havana.

The exiles declared "the battle to liberate our homeland" had been joined.

Fidel Castro

Castro's regime charged before the United Nations that the invaders were armed and financed by the United States.

Raul Roa, Cuban foreign minister, told the UN the invaders came from Guatemala.

Secretary of State Dean Rusk declared the American people sympathize with those fighting against dictatorship but the United States will not intervene. Rusk said his reports indicated

there was no large-scale invasion.

The Soviet government newspaper Izvestia echoed Roa's charge of the use of Americans in the action. Izvestia declared the Communist world stands behind Castro, but it made no mention of Premier Khrushchev's pledge last summer, later toned down, to support Cuba with rockets if necessary.

A Dutch airliner could not land at Havana. The pilot was told all Cuban airports were closed.

Telephone and telegraph communications with Cuba were cut off early today, shortly after a Cuban army officer confirmed one landing on the south coast.

The Cuban government radio was heard summoning all militia units to report at once to their stations.

Rebel sources in the United States said some military units had joined the invaders, possibly from the naval station, where defections from Castro's ranks have been reported in recent weeks.

Bombs Blast Cuban Cities

By Harold K. Milks

HAVANA (AP) —

Raider planes made low-level bomb and rocket attacks at dawn today on airports in Havana and Santiago and on Cuban air force headquarters at San Antonio de Los Banos.

The government radio, warning

the attacks may be the "prelude to an invasion," said Cuba's delegation to the United Nations in New York has been instructed to lodge a protest blaming the United States for "direct responsibility."

Premier Fidel Castro's foreign ministry summoned all foreign ambassadors for a mid-morning

meeting to receive a declaration from the government.

The government immediately ordered all soldiers and militiamen to their posts.

Several of the marauder aircraft were hit by anti-aircraft fire, the radio broadcast said, and one was seen fleeing in flames.

Cuba Invasion May Lead To Total War – Russians

U.S. Warned By Khrushchev Reds Will Stand By Castro

(CP from AP-Reuters)

MOSCOW —

Soviet Premier Khrushchev today pledged all necessary support to the Cuban government and warned

of the possibility of the fighting there developing into a world "conflagration."

Khrushchev said in a message to President Kennedy that Russia would give Cuba all the help it needed to repel the invasion by anti-Castro forces. He asked Kennedy to end the "aggression against the Cuban republic."

Khrushchev's note, delivered to the American charge d'affaires, came as groups of students marched on the American Embassy to demonstrate against "aggression" in Cuba.

A howling mob of about 500 students, shouting "Hands off Cuba," stoned the embassy, hurling rocks through the windows.

Defeat Of Cuban Rebels 'Enormous Blow' To Kennedy

Castro Sees Final Destruction Of Anti-Government Forces

HAVANA (REUTERS) —
Fidel Castro was reported to be directing mopping-up operations against anti-government forces today as the first detailed reports were disclosed here of the defeat of the invading rebels.

The Cuban national radio network said the premier is "engaged in supervising the final destruction of the criminals" who attempted to overthrow his regime.

It also painted a picture of heavy losses suffered by the invading force and of their rout by government troops.

The radio said that 10 aircraft were shot down – "mostly flown by American pilots" – and that three Sherman tanks were destroyed and five captured. Large quantities of American-made arms also were seized, the radio said in an official account of the fighting.

LONDON (REUTERS) —

Russia today described the defeat of anti-Castro forces in Cuba as "an enormous blow" to President Kennedy's prestige but warned that "the defeated adventurers are spoiling for revenge."

The official Communist party newspaper Pravda reported in a story from New York that American "political adventurers are angry and wringing their hands in despair" over the failure of the "dirty Cuban operation."

"Weeping and gnashing of teeth can be heard today over the U.S. radio and in the monopolist press," the article said.

"The interventionist gangs have suffered a crushing defeat. The Cuban escapade has brought Washington nothing but shame …"

The newspaper said that political commentators were declaring that "the anti-Cuban escapade has struck an enormous blow at the prestige of the U.S.A. as well as the personal standing of President Kennedy."

"The powerful wave of protest which has engulfed the whole world and the explosion of popular wrath in Latin America have seriously disturbed U.S. leaders," Pravda declared.

Russians Confirm Man Orbited Around Earth

CP FROM AP-Reuters

MOSCOW —

Russia fired a man into orbit around the earth today and brought him back unharmed after 108 minutes in space.

Maj. Yuri Alekseyevich Gagarin made a little more than one complete orbit of the globe in a five-ton spaceship and then was brought down to a safe landing at a pre-arranged spot in the Soviet Union.

"I feel well," he said as he emerged from the spaceship after landing. "I have no injuries or bruises."

Gagarin, a 27 year old father of two young children, one of them born just a month ago, told the official Soviet news agency Tass that everything went as planned both during the flight and on the landing.

He asked Tass to report this "to the party and government and personally to Nakita Khrushchev."

The Soviet premier, holidaying at a Black Sea resort, immediately sent a telegram to Gagarin saying: "I warmly congratulate you, I embrace you."

The astronaut was put into an orbit that took him around the earth in 89.1 minutes. He reported by radio during the flight that he was "feeling well" and "withstanding the state of weightlessness well."

Russia followed up Gagarin's safe return to earth with a statement proclaiming her lead in the space race and appealing for world peace and disarmament.

The appeal, issued by the Communist party's central committee, the Presidium of the Supreme Soviet (parliament) and the Soviet government, declared that Russia's space achievements "are not being put to the service of war but are designed for the peace and security of all people."

A statement from the Soviet government and the Communist

Yuri Gagarin, left, Soviet cosmonaut, became the first person to achieve orbital spaceflight when, on April 12, 1961, he circled the earth once in Vostok 1. John Glenn, right, was the first American and the third person to be put into orbital spaceflight when, on Feb. 20, 1962, he circled the earth three times in Friendship 7.

party said the satellite space ship Vostok (East), with Gagarin aboard, rose into outer space at 9:07 a.m. Moscow time "and having rounded the globe, safely returned to the sacred soil of our homeland, the land of the Soviets."

Vostok landed at 10:55 a.m. Moscow time, 108 minutes after the launching, the Russians said. Neither the point of the takeoff nor the location of the landing was announced.

1960–1969

$1,000,000 BLAZE DESTROYS FOUR K.G.E. PACKINGHOUSES

The Daily Courier

Smoke Pall Covers City, Hundreds Watch Flames

Vol. 57 — Price 5 Cents — Kelowna, British Columbia, Tuesday, March 14, 1961 — Ten Pages — No. 188

Smoke Pall Covers City, Hundred Watch Flames

Fire ripped through three warehouses owned by Kelowna Growers' Exchange here today, causing an estimated $1,000,000 damage and sending a dense pall of smoke hundreds of feet into the air over downtown Kelowna.

Two other buildings were threatened.

No injuries were reported at presstime.

R.P. Walrod, general manger of B.C. Tree Fruits Ltd., predicted at the scene of the blaze that the damage may seriously affect packing house operations for fruit growers throughout the Valley.

The blaze was discovered at 6:25 a.m. when employees of the S.M. Simpson Ltd. sawmills noticed smoke pouring from the KGE warehouse.

In minutes, the entire Kelowna volunteer Fire Brigade was on the spot as calls for assistance went out to neighbouring areas.

Vernon, 30 miles away, sent equipment and men, as did nearby Rutland and Westbank. Organizations were thanked by KFD Chief C.A. Pettman.

R.P. (Tiny) Walrod, general manager of B.C. Tree Fruits, said at the scene of the blaze, "Tree Fruits, although not directly involved, is concerned with the

loss of storage space and the possible effect the fire may have on insurance rates that might have to be paid by the industry."

"The loss is important to the industry, if we have a heavy crop year. Up to now we've had plenty of storage space, but this fire could leave us short."

"We can ill afford to lose this space."

As he spoke, mere feet from the raging inferno, the south wall of the three-story number five building thundered to the ground, drowning out his words. A huge crowd of spectators recoiled from the searing heat.

It was considered fortunate

there was no wind and a light rain fell intermittently. Had there been a wind from any direction than the west, other packing houses would have been seriously threatened and probably lost.

The Laurel is just across a railway siding to the east and B.C. Fruit Shippers is just beyond that across Ellis.

It became evident to the fire brigade early that the Laurel would be in considerable danger. Not only was the air movement from the lake shifting the column of smoke and embers to the direction of the Laurel but the intense heat of the burning building was a constant threat to the building.

Kelowna Boy Enjoys Limelight

Kelowna's Wayne Hicks (8) joins Chicago Black Hawks teammates in admiring the Stanley Cup, won only seconds before the photo was taken Sunday night in Detroit. Hicks, 24, is the son of Mr. and Mrs. Marlow Hicks of Kelowna and twin brother to Warren Hicks of the Kelowna-Penticton Combines team. The hustling young forward was brought up by Chicago from Buffalo Bisons for the Stanley Cup finals.

Berlin Phone Links Cut By E. Germans

Iron Curtain Slams Shut On Fleeing Refugee Hordes

BOY, PAGE HOUDINI!

Communist East Germany severed telephone connections with the West today and closed the Brandenburg Gate, the chief crossing point between East and West Berlin, as the divided city seethed under the Communist clampdown on the flow of East German refugees to the West.

West Berliners clambered for sharp counter-action against the blockade of East German travel, imposed at the sector border by heavily-armed East German troops and police.

Barbed wire barricades, tanks and soldiers with machine-guns

cut off the great refugee flow from East Germany. And none of the 80,000 East Germans with jobs in West Berlin showed up for work. Henceforth, they must have passes to get past the barricades.

The closing of the Brandenburg Gate, one of 13 crossings left open when the Communists barricaded the sector border Sunday, was described as temporary. Karl Maron, East German interior minister, blamed "continued provocations" at the gate, which was the scene of riotous demonstrations by West Berliners

Sunday night.

A dozen street crossings remained open, however, to such West Berliners and foreigners as wished to enter East Berlin, among them about 15,000 persons who regularly work there.

A spokesman for the Bonn postal ministry said the East German government gave no explanation for severing phone connections, but West Germany believed this was another arbitrary measure to keep the 17,000,000 East German people from openly expressing their views, particularly on the Berlin developments. The Brandenburg

Gate closed, as big crowds built up there.

The crowds began assembling late this morning after some 5,000 West Berlin workers staged a march to the West Berlin city hall in protest against the Communist closure of the border.

West Berlin's Mayor Willy Brandt told the demonstrators "we have resolved to be calm" and appealed to Communist policemen not to "be made use of" in shooting fellow Germans.

Communists Seal Off Berlin Escape Hatch

Soviet Premier Nikita Khrushchev, who regards West Berlin a bone in the Communist throat, acted this week to alleviate the pain.

Moving swiftly Sunday night, troops and armed police of the Communist East German satellite sealed off West Berlin from the eastern sector with barbed wire, tanks and armored cars.

For West Berliners, long a focal point in the East-West struggle, it was the start of a week of dangerously heightened tension.

For East Germans, it marked the closing of the escape route to the West - a path some 3,000,000 of their disillusioned countrymen have taken.

Angry clashes and demonstrations broke out almost immedi-

ately on both sides of the barricade. At one point Sunday night East Berlin police threw tear gas bombs across the border into a crowd of West Berliners.

At a huge West Berlin protest rally Wednesday night Mayor Willy Brandt called on the West

to retaliate with "more than words." Demonstrators carried signs asking "are we being betrayed by the West?"

At home, meanwhile, the Western powers were reviewing their own fighting strength in view of the worsening crisis.

In Washington, steps to strengthen all three services were announced during the week.

In Paris, President de Gaulle on Thursday ordered French ground and air force reinforcements in both France and Germany. Britain simultaneously ordered limited reinforcement of its tactical air units in West Germany and announced recall of an armored unit from Kuwait to start formation of a new strategic reserve division.

On Wednesday the Prime Minister met with his cabinet for three hours and said afterward that, while Canada already is filling its NATO commitments, it will consider increasing its contribution if the need arises.

Defecting East German soldier Hans Conrad Schumann leaps over a barbed wire barricade at the Bernauer Street sector into West Berlin on August 15, 1961. Schumann made his break for freedom to join his family which had fled earlier to West Berlin.

(AP Photo/Contipress, Peter Leibing)

Eichmann 'Emotionless' As He Confessed Crimes

By Relman Morin

JERUSALEM (AP) —

Adolf Eichmann was cool and matter of fact – with one notable exception – during the long sessions when he told his story to his Israeli captors and a tape recorder, an informed source said today.

"He showed a little feeling when he said he expects to get the death sentence," the Israeli informants reported.

"I know I may face a sentence of death," said Eichmann in a recorded statement that was played back Wednesday for the three-judge court trying him on charges of mass murder of Europe's Jews.

Seventy-seven tapes were made of the long hours of interrogation that followed Eichmann's capture in Argentina last year.

The prosecution Wednesday

began playing back excerpts at the trial, bringing into the record the former SS officer's own version of the Nazis' "final solution of the Jewish problem" – meaning total annihilation of Europe's Jewry – and the part he played in it.

The trial was in recess today while Israel celebrated its independence day.

When the hearing resumes Friday, Attorney-General Gideon

Hausner is expected to play tape recordings of Eichmann's account of events in Hungary in 1944. Hausner told the court earlier Eichmann was a key figure in the killing of 437,402 of the 800,000 Jews living in Hungary at the time.

Eichmann pictured himself in recordings played Wednesday as a subordinate who recoiled from his work but had to obey commands from his superiors.

1960-1969

Death A Tragic Climax To Marilyn's Sad Life

HOLLYWOOD (AP) — Marilyn Monroe's body lay unclaimed in the county morgue today – the tragic climax of a lifetime of personal sorrow that even wealth and fame couldn't ease.

She was found dead early Sunday in the cluttered bedroom of her $75,000 Brentwood home, an empty bottle of sleeping pills near her body.

Schoolboys could recite her famous measurements, (37-23-37) and her photos, nude and otherwise, had appeared in practically every periodical in the world.

But on her coroner's call sheet, tagged to Crypt 33 in the morgue, were these unrevealing statistics: Weight 117 pounds, height 65 1/2 inches, hair blonde and eyes blue.

Address Unknown

Next of kin – Gladys Baker, mother. Address unknown.

Only Joe DiMaggio, second of her three husbands, showed any relative interest in her death.

Her mother, a patient in mental institutions for most of her life, was last confined to a home in nearby La Crescenta.

Marilyn, who had shifted for herself since early childhood, was known to have made a will outlining plans for her own burial.

A business associate said that it had not been found yet and funeral arrangements were pending until its discovery expected later today.

DiMaggio took the first plane leaving San Francisco for Los Angeles after hearing of her death on the radio. He was in seclusion in a Santa Monica hotel.

Though Marilyn divorced him in 1955, the two had remained good friends.

Playwright Arthur Miller, since remarried, declined to make a statement on the death of his former wife.

Got Divorce

Miller became Miss Monroe's third husband in 1956. They were divorced last year.

Asked in Roxbury, Conn., if he had any comment to make, he answered: "I don't, really."

Meanwhile, a special coroner's so-called suicide team prepared a series of tests to officially determine whether the 36-year-old actress accidentally or intentionally took the overdose of pills that investigators believe killed her.

Coroner Theodore J. Curphey said psychiatric tests would play an important part in the verdict.

"Our investigation so far shows that she she did not die a natural death, and we can make a presumptive opinion that death was due to an overdose of a drug."

He said it might be 48 hours before the verdict can be announced.

Thus in death the screen's sex goddess left behind the same mysterious personality contrast.

Mobbed By Fans

As Marilyn Monroe, movie star, she was under a public microscope – exciting, wanted and mobbed by fans.

Her more than 20 movies since her first big break in The Asphalt June in 1950 had grossed $200,000,000.

At the banks that finance movies, her name on a contract meant unlimited credit for a producer.

Only her last two movies, Let's Make Love and The Misfits, had been disappointing at the box office – a fact which distressed her.

She seemed happy as Marilyn Monroe, the star, with the spotlights beaming brightly.

But when the lights went off in her lonely bedroom, the dreams of Marilyn Monroe, the sex symbol, became the nightmares of Norma Jean Baker, lost waif in a lost world.

Few movie scripts will ever match the drama of the Marilyn Monroe story, the beautiful girl that she evinced in life, who had everything – but personal happiness.

Childhood Tragic

Every movie fan knew the details of her childhood – as tragic as her death.

The unwanted, the unloved waif, boarded at county expense in a variety of foster homes … a little girl who washed dishes and scrubbed floors … her girlish body violated by a roomer in a foster home … her illegitimacy by a

(AP Photo)

Marilyn Monroe

father she never saw … a mother she seldom saw outside of mental homes.

And all the while dreaming of becoming a movie star – and, when she did, her insecure childhood failed to cushion her against the shocking insecurity of the Hollywood jungle.

Marilyn died proving that peace of mind cannot be bought – even on an income of $1,000,000 a picture.

In 1961, she lost two babies while married to Miller. Then came a frustrated love affair with married Yves Montand, the breakup of her marriage to Miller because of it, and the untimely death of Clark Gable, her co-star in The Misfits.

Marilyn's Last Headlines Outshine Even Big H-Test

LONDON (CP) — The front pages of the world's newspapers today paid tribute to the magic memory of Marilyn Monroe, the star whose sex appeal coupled with little-girl charm captivated millions.

The story of the blonde beauty's sudden death in Hollywood was splashed across the headlines in every continent and inside the pages were filled with words of sorrow and admiration from her shocked co-workers.

In Europe her death over-shadowed the news of the resumption of Soviet nuclear testing and European Common Market negotiations.

In the London Daily Mail the headline read "Marilyn's Agony" and in the London Daily Herald "The Unhappy Goddess."

The mass circulation Paris-Jour called her "a woman who was too beautiful to die" and the conservative Le Parisien "a cinematographic symbol of triumphant femininity."

Even TASS, the official Soviet news agency, devoted 100 words to her death and the Rome Communist newspaper IsUnita gave it a four-column headline.

Donald Zec, London Daily Mirror writer, reported a conversation with Miss Monroe in which she once told him "I'll settle for this" as an epitaph, "Here lies Marilyn Monroe – 38, 23", 36."

"The lovely, dazzling tormented creature had sold herself short. The glowing flame has died – and the world that cherished it has

lost a little of its warmth."

Italian actresses Sophia Loren and Gina Lollobrigida, two of her few rivals in the realm of sexual glamor, were shocked by the news of Marilyn's death.

Miss Loren, in bed with laryngitis, burst into tears.

"She was a real star," Miss Loren said. "Now all we can do is pray for her."

Miss Lollobrigida said:

"I am naturally very, very, sorry. I knew her. She was a nice girl. I am greatly surprised."

The Daily Courier

No. 71 SERVING THE OKANAGAN — CANADA'S FRUIT BOWL
Kelowna, British Columbia, Wednesday, October 24, 1962

HIGH AND LOW

12 Pages Not more than 7¢ per copy

Tense World Waits Showdown of Titans

LET'S FORGET ABOUT LAW SAYS MACKENZIE ON CUBA

VANCOUVER (CP) — Dr. Norman Mackenzie, former president of the University of British Columbia and an international law expert says law isn't going to affect the Cuban situation.

"Forget about the law—let's look at the facts," he said in an interview.

"From the point of view of the US this is not a question of right or wrong. This is a practical situation and a damn dangerous one."

Dr. Mackenzie said international law wasn't important or effective during the Second World War.

"It is foolish to point to it if it's on your side and it's embarrassing if it isn't, but it doesn't decide the issue.

"If you want to settle matters by international law, then you don't build missile bases."

US Fleet Heads Toward Cuba-Bound Soviet Ships

An anxious world waited today as the United States and Russia approached an armed showdown on the high seas at midmorning today, as Soviet cargo ships moved toward Cuba and American naval power converged on them.

Strung out along the approaches to Cuba were an estimated 25 Russian ships. Some of them quite possibly were carrying offensive weapons to the Cuban Communist ally, a movement which President Kennedy says must be stopped.

CUBAN BRIEFS

Leave Cut

ISTANBUL (AP)

Cruiser Sails

Two Big Powers Swap Insults In UN D...

US Seeks Quick Action To Cut Out Cuba's Sting

Stunning JFK Victory Hailed Across Europe

WASHINGTON (AP) —

The United States pushed today for fast diplomatic action to nail down Soviet Premier Khrushchev's agreement to pull Soviet missile bases out of Cuba. Washington policy makers held hope that a breakthrough has been scored in the U.S.-Soviet confrontation that bordered on potential nuclear conflict.

Khrushchev's pledge was hailed in Western capitals as a stunning victory for the United States.

The price Khrushchev asked was a guarantee, which Kennedy gave, that the United States would not invade Cuba.

U.S. diplomats concentrated on working out arrangements for United Nations inspection of the withdrawal from Cuba of the missiles and bombers which Khrushchev announced Sunday he will ship back to Russia.

Acting UN Secretary-General U Thant arranged to fly to Cuba today. The U.S. hope is that he can take with him a workable inspection plan to present to Premier Fidel Castro.

The state department

announced that while the "quarantine" against offensive weapons shipments to Cuba continues, it expects no interceptions by the U.S. blockaders.

Washington authorities said they did not know at the moment whether the building of Soviet missile sites in Cuba - reportedly proceeding at a rapid pace Saturday - had stopped.

Khrushchev agreed to pull out the missile bases in a letter to Kennedy. The Soviet leader said "the interests of peace" guided his decision.

Kennedy issued a statement calling Krushchev's decision" an important and constructive contribution to peace." Kennedy said Khrushchev had made possible "a step back from danger."

'Swap Sites In Turkey' Proposal By Soviet

OCTOBER 10, 1962 WASHINGTON (AP) — The White House declared today Russia must stop work on its missile sites in Cuba, render offensive weapons in Cuba inoperable and cease shipping arms to the Castro government before the United States can consider any proposal to settle the crisis in this hemisphere.

The White House thus replied to Soviet Premier Khrushchev's offer earlier today to withdraw from Cuba weapons the U.S. considers offensive if the United States would pull rockets out of Turkey.

Work on missile sites is proceeding "at a rapid pace" in Cuba, the White House said.

"The first imperative must be to deal with this immediate threat under which no sensible negotiation can proceed," the statement said.

As for Khrushchev's call for removal of missiles from Turkey, the White House said the Western allies have long "taken the lead in seeking properly inspected arms limitation on both sides."

It added:

"These efforts can continue as soon as the present Soviet-created threat is ended."

Khrushchev's proposal was reported contained in messages sent to President Kennedy and U Thant, acting secretary-general of the United Nations. It proposed that Thant act as an agent in carrying out the necessary negotiations.

Kennedy thus did not reject Khrushchev's proposal out of hand but did establish firm conditions for any negotiations between Washington and Moscow. In effect he challenged Khrushchev to demonstrate good faith by dismantling missile bases in Cuba before the United States and Russian consider any plan to settle the hazardous dispute.

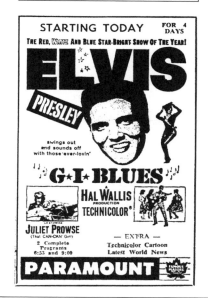

YMCA-YWCA of Kelowna/Westbank

Building Strong Kids, Strong Families, and Strong Communities

1960~1969

JFK Assa

Sniper Fires Barrage Into Texas Cavalcade

DALLAS, TEX. (AP) —
President John F. Kennedy, 35th president of the United States, was shot to death Friday by a hidden assassin armed with a high-powered rifle. Kennedy, 46, lived about 30 minutes after a sniper cut him down as his limousine left downtown Dallas. Reporters said the shot that hit him was fired about 10:30 a.m. P.S.T. A hospital announcement said he died at approximately 11 a.m. of a bullet wound in the head.

Lyndon B. Johnson was sworn in as the 36th President of the U.S. at 11:39 P.S.T.

A hospital announcement said he died at approximately 1 p.m. of a bullet wound in the head.

Automatically, the mantle of the presidency fell to Vice-President Lyndon B. Johnson, a native Texan who had been riding two cars behind Kennedy.

Kennedy died at Parkland Hospital, where his bullet-pierced body had been taken in a frantic but futile effort to save his life.

Lying wounded at the same hospital was Governor John Connally of Texas, who was cut down by the same fusillade that ended the life of the youngest man ever elected

to the presidency.

Connally and his wife had been riding with the President and Mrs. Kennedy.

Jacqueline Kennedy cradled her dying husband's blood-smeared head in her arms as the presidential limousine raced to the hospital.

"Oh no," she kept crying.

Connally slumped in his seat beside the president.

Police ordered an unprecedented dragnet of the city, hunting for the assassin.

They believe the fatal shots were fired by a white man about 30, slender of build, weighing about 165 pounds and standing five feet, 10 inches.

The murder weapon was reported to have been a .30-.30 rifle.

Secret service agents riding with the president and in a second convertible following close behind, immediately drew pistols and automatic weapons.

But they were unable to get a shot at the gunman.

Dallas motorcycle officers, ranged around the cavalcade, took off across a field in the direction from which the murderer apparently had fired.

The motorcade, which had just passed through downtown crowds

President John F. Kennedy is seen riding in the motorcade approximately one minute before he was shot in Dallas, Texas on Nov. 22, 1963. In the car riding with Kennedy are Mrs. Jacqueline Kennedy and Gov. and Mrs. John Connally of Texas.

standing 10 to 12 deep along each curb, broke apart in pandemonium as secret service agents rushed Kennedy and Connally to the hospital.

Ironically, Kennedy was shot to death at a spot where there were few spectators – after driving within handshaking distance of many thousands.

It was the first death of a president in office since Franklin D. Roosevelt died of a cerebral hemor-

rhage at Warm Springs, Ga., in April, 1945.

Kennedy and his wife had just passed the halfway point in a three-day speaking Texas tour.

The president already had prepared a luncheon address for a Dallas audience before he died. In his prepared text, he assailed his ultra-conservative critics.

Dallas is considered a centre of conservative philosophy and finance.

Mrs. Kennedy Cries In Horror

Though Mrs. Kennedy cried "oh, no" in horror and despair after her husband was shot, she did not collapse or give way to hysteria.

When she entered the hospital, her clothing was covered with blood from her husband's wounds.

Lieut. Erich Kaminski of the secret service bureau said, "The assassin's weapon appears to have been a high-powered army or Japanese rifle of about .25-calibre. The rifle had a scope on it."

The entire building where the sniper was located was evacuated. People were working in the building at the time of the shooting.

Dallas Inspector J.H. Sawyer said:

"Police found the remains of fried chicken and supper on the fifth floor. Apparently the person had been there quite awhile."

After the fatal shots were fired at Kennedy,

the stricken president's secret service driver raced away from the scene at top speed – heading for the nearest hospital and trying to get the presidential party out of range of further gunfire.

Kennedy, Connally and their wives had been riding together in the president's dark-blue bubbletop convertible. The transparent plastic roof of the vehicle had been removed for the motorcade.

The horror of the assassination was mirrored in an eyewitness account by Senator Ralph Yarborough (Dem. Tex.), who had been riding three cars behind Kennedy.

"I could see a secret service man in the president's car leaning on the car with his hands in anger, anguish and despair. I knew then something tragic had happened."

Yarborough had counted three rifle shots as

the presidential limousine left downtown Dallas through a triple underpass. The shots were fired from above – possibly from one of the bridges or from a nearby building.

One witness, television reporter Mal Cough, said he saw a gun emerge from an upper storey of a warehouse commanding an unobstructed view of the presidential car.

Kennedy was the first president to be assassinated since William McKinley was shot in 1901.

Shorty before Kennedy's death became known, he was administered the last rites of the Roman Catholic Church. He had been the first Roman Catholic president in American history.

Even as two clergymen hovered over the fallen president in the hospital emergency room, doctors and nurses administered blood transfusions.

ssinated

STOP THE PRESS

Man Denies Link To Assassination

FORT WORTH, TEX. (AP) – Soon after President Kennedy was assassinated, a white man in his mid-20's was arrested in the River side section of Fort Worth in the shooting of a Dallas policeman. The man, who has black curly hair and who wore a red shirt, denied that he was connected with the assassination of the president.

Connally "Good"

DALLAS, TEX. (AP) – Governor John Connally of Texas underwent an operation for gun-shot wound in the chest today, a spokesman said. Connally's condition was said to be serious. But the spokesman said that while the governor "was not out of the woods, his doctors said his vital signs were good."

House Closes

OTTAWA (CP) – The House of Commons adjourned at 2:50 p.m. EST today until Monday as a mark of respect following the death of President Kennedy.

1960–1969

(AP Photo/Dallas Times-Herald, Bob Jackson)

Lee Harvey Oswald, accused assassin of President John F. Kennedy, winces in this November 24, 1963 file photo, as Dallas night club owner Jack Ruby, foreground, shoots at him from point blank range in a corridor of Dallas police headquarters. Plainclothesman at left is J.A. Leavelle. Shortly before President Kennedy was assassinated, the Soviet Embassy in Washington received a letter from Lee Harvey Oswald, a letter the Soviets privately believed was forged to make it look as if Oswald was working for them. The FBI kept systematic track of private bank transactions flowing between the Soviet Union and the United States during the Cold War, enabling officials to stumble upon an attempt by Lee Harvey Oswald's mother to send him $25 after he defected, according to newly declassified files.

The Daily Courier

SERVING THE OKANAGAN — CANADA'S FRUIT BOWL

Kelowna, British Columbia, Friday, November 22, 1963

TRAFFIC TALLY

10 Pages

7c per copy

TODAY'S QUOTE

JFK ASSASSINATED

Sniper Fires Barrage Into Texas Cavalcade

DALLAS, Tex. (AP) — President John F. Kennedy, 36th president of the United States, was shot to death Friday by a hidden assassin armed with a high-powered rifle. Kennedy, 46, lived about 30 minutes after a sniper cut him down as his limousine hit downtown Dallas. Reporters said the shot that hit him was fired about 10:30 a.m. P.N.T. A hospital announcement said he died at approximately 11 a.m. of a bullet wound in the head.

Lyndon Johnson was sworn in as the 37th President of the United States...

Storm In House On DC-9 Issue

OTTAWA (CP)—Prime Minister Pearson announced in the House today Trans-Canada Air Lines will buy six Douglas DC-9 jet aircraft...

Mrs. Kennedy Cries In Horror But Doesn't Become Hysterical

MRS. KENNEDY cradling head

LYNDON JOHNSON ... new chief

Speaker Calls For Order As Sequel To Shouting Match By Leaders

Beatles Arrive In B.C.

Beatles batting zero in their attempt to elude fans

VANCOUVER (CP) —

The game of Beatles, Beatles, who's got the Beatles picks up here today where it left off Friday night in Seattle, 150 miles to the south.

In today's contest, it's a fresh multitude of teenagers versus a harried quartet of singers from Liverpool, who so far have been batting zero in their attempt to elude screaming fans.

The game has been played all over the world by teenagers in cities where the famous beat group has appeared.

The latest round began Wednesday in San Francisco, swung over to Las Vegas Thursday and into Seattle Friday. For the teenagers the Seattle contest was the most successful in the current North American tour of the Beatles.

There the shaggy-haired group performed for 29 minutes. The noise of the squealing teenagers drowned out their music and they were lovingly pelted with jelly beans and peanuts.

When it was over between 15 and 20 of them charged toward the Beatles. Police managed to get the group into their dressing room, but getting them out was another problem.

Finally, after 59 minutes in captivity, police backed an ambulance into a dark recess near the exit and spirited the group away.

Vancouver teenagers face the challenge of penetrating a cloak of secrecy that surrounds the arrival and movements of the Beatles today.

Officials at the Vancouver

((CP Photo)

The Beatles, from left to right, Paul McCartney, Ringo Starr, George Harrison and John Lennon speak to reporters at a news conference prior to their 1964 concert at Maple Leaf Gardens.

International Airport, where the group and their party of 40 are scheduled to arrive by chartered plane sometime after noon today, are saying nothing.

RCMP at the airport, city police, officials of the Hotel Georgia where the Beatles will stay, are also non-committal.

Pacific National Exhibition offi-

cials say the Beatles performance at Empire Stadium will be the biggest of the group's career. A sell-out crowd of 27,000 is expected to watch the show.

National Tragedy Averted As Beatlemania Struck

VANCOUVER (CP) —

A city police inspector said today a "national tragedy" was averted by the work of a 100-man police force Saturday night at the performance here of the Beatles.

Insp. F.C. Errington said the estimated 17,000 youngsters watching the singers compared with no other crowd he had ever seen.

During the hysteria of the 29-minute performance itself, Insp. Errington was quoted as saying:

"These people have lost all ability to think."

He told The Sun in an interview today:

"Every policeman there was happy they didn't have to pack away seriously injured children."

"One hundred policemen were there. That's all that stood

between the way it wound up and a national tragedy."

Police strained against steel fences to hold back thousands of teenagers surging toward the platform held by the four performers in their sheepdog haircuts.

They threw children aside to seize a child tramped underfoot, and carried scores of others to the Empire Stadium concourse for

first-aid treatment. There were no serious injuries or broken bones, but many youngsters lay exhausted on cold concrete, their emotions spent from screaming.

The Beatles management said the Vancouver police employed the most effective crowd - control measures of the quartet's tour so far.

It was their first outdoor appearance.

1960-1969

Thousands Cheer As Maple Leaf Hoisted On Parliament Hill

OTTAWA (CP) —

To the cheers of thousands, Canada's new maple leaf flag was officially hoisted today on Parliament Hill.

The red and white emblem became the country's national flag at noon after the Red Ensign had been ceremoniously lowered and sent to the archives. Nearly 10,000 people covered the snow-covered lawns on Parliament Hill to cheer the new flag up the mast.

The ceremony was held a few minutes after Governor-General Vanier issued an appeal for unity under the new banner.

"I appeal to all Canadians to set aside pettiness, selfishness and intolerance where they may exist, and to cultivate a spirit of brotherhood and mutual confidence."

"I hope and pray that Canadians will in this way give an example of fraternal co-existence and that our flag will symbolize to each of us and to the world the unity of purpose and high resolve to which destiny beckons us."

Raised On Peace Tower

As the new flag went up, the Red Ensign was also being replaced on all federal buildings in Ottawa. Because the governor-general's standard was on the Peace Tower pole – it is flown whenever he is on Parliament Hill – it was several minutes before the new design was raised there.

When the new flag was raised on the Peace Tower another cheer went up.

Before the ceremonies began, an unidentified man stood with Red Ensign draped in black. He left before the new flag was raised.

The entire ceremony lasted one hour.

RCMP Constable Joseph Secours raises Canada's new Maple Leaf flag on the flagpole at the base of Peace Tower on Parliament Hill in Ottawa February 15, 1965. Also gathered at the foot of the flagpole are representatives of the three Armed Services.

(CP Photo)

1960-1969

New Flag Flutters Over City

History was being made across Canada today and Kelowna played its part in a tiny scene enacted on the lawn at city hall, at 8:30 a.m.

In a stirring ceremony before 250 people the Red Ensign was slowly lowered and the Maple Leaf raised to take its place.

Scouts, Cubs, Guides, Sea Rangers and Legionnaires saluted the descent of the "old" and the ascent of the "new". The Kelowna secondary school band, in their scarlet tunics, played "O Canada" and "God Save the Queen."

For those who have lived half their life span or more under the Red Ensign, and for those who fought under it, the day Canada achieved her national flag has sad overtones. The day fittingly belongs to Canada's youth, who will live, fight for, and help make history for, their new flag.

Mayor R.F. Parkinson spoke to the gathering before the flag was unfurled.

"This day, Feb. 15, 1965, will be recorded in history as the date Canada, after almost 100 years, unfurled its own Canadian flag."

"As we gather today to honor this momentous occasion, we urge all bickering and indecision be forever relegated to the past."

"I urge we, as Canadians march proudly forward rededicating ourselves to a more glorious and united Canada, displaying tolerance, understanding and a national pride under our flag.

"The revered and beloved Red Ensign, now being lowered, will have a place of honor in our museum to mark this important day in Canadian history."

"The honor of raising our Canadian flag, has fittingly been delegated to a young Kelowna Canadian, who exemplifies the youth, vigor and foresight, so necessary to make our country great."

With Sea Rangers, Guides, Cubs and members of Royal Canadian Legion, Branch 26, saluting, the new flag took its place atop city hall.

Alderman Thomas Angus turned over the Red Ensign to C.R. Walrod, curator of the Okanagan Museum and Archives Association, to be permanently on display in the Kelowna Museum building.

Others among the crowd at the ceremony were aldermen, firemen, clergy and the Sisters of Charity from the Catholic school.

NAT KING COLE'S VOICE STILLED

1960-1969

FEBRUARY 15, 1965. SANTA MONICA, CALIF. (AP) — Singer Nat (King) Cole, who underwent surgery for removal of a cancerous lung tumor Jan. 25, died today. He was 45.

Cole, whose rich voice and bright piano style had made him one of the most popular musicians, went to hospital Dec. 8 for treatment of what was thought to be a respiratory ailment.

At first it was believed he was recovering well but a spokesman at St. John's Hospital said his condition took a sharp turn for worse last week.

Became Worse

The first hint of Cole's illness came when he cut short an engagement at the Sands Hotel in Las Vegas, complaining of a respiratory ailment. The gravity of his illness became more apparent when he was unable to appear in the first popular music concert at Los Angeles' new music centre Dec. 11 and was replaced by Frank Sinatra.

Cole leaves his wife, Maria; daughters Carol, 19; Natalie, 14; and twins Casey and Timolin, 3; and an adopted son, Nat Kelly 5.

Cole, who played his first professional dates with a 14-piece orchestra that earned a total of $1.50 a night, never really meant to be a singer at all. He started out as a pianist.

His recordings of Mona Lisa, Ballerina, Nature Boy, Unforgettable, Too Young and Christmas Song ultimately raised his average annual income to $500,000.

He came to Long Beach, Calif. in 1937. He was 18 and decided to stay in California. He dropped the S from his last name and began playing piano in cheap night clubs for $5 a night or less.

It was in such a club that a drunk one night placed a paper crown on the young pianist's head and said: "Look, King Cole!" The nickname stuck to Nat (King) Cole.

One night at Los Angeles' Swanee Inn, another drunk came up to the piano and commanded: "Sing Sweet Lorraine!"

"We don't sing," Nat said gently.

"Sing!" the man bellowed.

The manager ran up, sized up the situation and told Cole:

"Sing. This guy's a big spender. Sometimes three bucks a night."

Cole sang Sweet Lorraine. He sang from then on.

Russia, North Korea Denounce Use Of "Other Troops" To Expand War

TOKYO (REUTERS) —

A joint Russian - North Korean statement today denounced the United States for "expanding the aggressive war in Viet Nam by dragging in" troops from South Korea and Nationalist China.

The statement, issued here by the (Nok 4) Korean central news agency, was signed by Russian Premier Kosygin and North Korean Prime Minister Il Sung Kim.

The statement claimed the U.S. had heightened the war in Indochina by calling in troops from Nationalist China and South Korea.

Some 2,000 South Korean non-combatant troops are in South Viet Nam.

The two prime ministers also pledged their support to Indonesia in its struggle against the U.S. - British neo-colonialist plan in Southeast Asia," the statement said.

Sworn To Crush It

The Malaysian federation, which links the former British colonies of Malaya, Singapore, Sarawak and Sabah (North Borneo), is locked in an undeclared war with Indonesia.

Indonesian President Sukarno sees the federation as an extension of colonialism in Asia and has sworn to crush it.

The statement said Malaysia was being used as a tool for defeating the national liberation movement in that area of Southeast Asia and menacing independent Indonesia.

It further condemned the United States for turning South Korea into a military base and colony, hampering the peaceful unification of that country.

The statement accused the U.S. of attempting to form a military alliance comprised of Nationalist China, South Viet Nam and the Philippines.

It also demanded complete disarmament and the complete and final destruction of nuclear weapons.

And the two nations declared their support to Asian, African and Latin American peoples in the just struggles of all forms, including armed struggle, against imperialism and colonialism and for national liberation democracy and social progress.

Scattered Fighting Breaks Lull In South Vietnam

SAIGON (AP) –

Fighting has resumed on scattered fronts in South Viet Nam after a comparative lull.

Military sources reported 27 enemy actions during the last 24 hours, most of them in the northern part of the country.

Three U.S. helicopter crew members were reported wounded in clashes Sunday. One was hit in the back by metal fragments while searching for 50 Vietnamese who disappeared Saturday after a Viet Cong attack in Binh Dinh province.

In Quang Ngai province, 330 miles northeast of Saigon, the Viet Cong killed 16 government troops, wounded 30 and captured five. The Communists poured mortar shells into a government outpost in Quang Tin province, killing seven defenders and wounding 12.

Near Da Nang, 80 miles south of the northern border, two anti-government demonstrations broke out today, possibly inspired by the Communist Viet Cong. Troops fired into one of the demonstrations.

(A Reuters news agency dispatch reported about 40 persons were killed by the troops.)

Reports said that about 2,000 demonstrators demanded an end to air and artillery attacks on populated areas and attempted to storm the office of the district chief at Thang Binh south of Da Nang.

In Saigon, Vietnamese leaders appeared ready to announce the formation of a new civilian government with Dr. Phan Huy Quat, 55, as its head.

He served last year as foreign minister to Lt. Gen. Nguyen Khanh, South Viet Nam's strong man.

(AP Photo/Eddie Adams)

South Vietnamese National Police Chief Brig Gen. Nguyen Ngoc Loan executes a Viet Cong prisoner with a single pistol shot in the head in Saigon Feb. 1, 1968.

Grave Danger Seen Of Canada Breakup

B-B Royal Commission Warns English-French Gulf "Deep"

OTTAWA (CP) —

Canada is in grave danger of breaking up unless major changes take place in public institutions and attitudes, the royal commission on bilingualism and biculturalism says in its preliminary report issued today.

In the 85,000-word report, tabled in the Commons by Prime Minister Pearson, the commission said it has found a deep gulf between English-speaking and French-speaking Canadians, deeper than most people realize.

The report stressed three basic conclusions:

1. There is a large, dynamic and distinct French-speaking society within Canada, "strongly dissatisfied" with present conditions.

2. Wide-ranging negotiations must be initiated between the federal and provincial governments to work out a truly equal partnership between the English and French-speaking societies.

3. All Canadians must overcome the myths, prejudices and ignorance separating them and put the development of a great nation above all other considerations.

The 10-member commission said Canada's continued existence is in peril because the French-Canadians of Quebec no longer accept the status of an ethnic minority and want to be recognized officially as "practically an autonomous society."

'Critical Period'

"All that we have seen and heard has led us to the conviction that Canada is in the most critical period of its history since Confederation," the unanimous report concluded.

"We believe that there is a crisis, in the sense that Canada has come to a time when decisions must be taken and developments must occur leading either to its breakup, or to a new set of conditions for its future existence."

FRENCH-SPEAKING CITIZENS URGED NOT TO LOOK SO LARGELY INWARDS

French-Canadians were asked to respond positively to any significant developments leading to such a partnership.

"It would be necessary for French-speaking Quebecers to restrain their present tendency to concentrate so intensely on their own affairs and to look so largely inward."

Must Face Problems

"Problems affecting all Canada are their problems too."

"They would need to beware of the kind of thinking that puts 'la nation' above all other considerations and values ... They would have to avoid blaming English-speaking Canadians for shortcomings which are their own."

In a summing-up chapter entitled The Crisis, the commission said "An important element in French-speaking Quebec is already tempted to go it alone."

"... We must reiterate that we have found overwhelming evidence of serious danger to the continued existence of Canada."

Quebec's "Quiet Revolution" Noted As Not Being Of Anti-British Nature

Quebec's "quiet revolution" was not motivated by anti-English feeling. Rather it was fed by a widespread desire by French-Canadians to assume more control over their political, economic and cultural destinies.

At the same time, most English-speaking Canadians were indifferent to or unaware of the crisis centering on Quebec.

"All 10 of us are convinced that in the present situation there is a grave danger for the future of Canada and of all Canadians."

"There are those who feel that the problems will lessen and go away with time."

"This is possible, but in our view, it is more probable that unless there are major changes the situation will worsen with time, and that it could worsen much more quickly than many think."

"There are hopeful signs; there are great possibilities for Canada. But we are convinced at the present time that the perils must be faced."

The commission said it will recommend concrete "adjustments and accommodations" in its final report, which is not expected until 1967.

The bulk of the preliminary report summarizes and analyzes views submitted to the commission in the first 18 months of the massive inquiry, which has cost about $1,250,000 to date.

Particular attention is given to off-the-cuff remarks made by "average Canadians" at 23 experimental public forums held across the country last year.

The report dropped hints that the commission favors new constitutional guarantees for "cultural equality" between the two main language groups.

Addressing itself to English-speaking Canadians, the commission said:

"They have to face the fact that, if Canada is to continue to exist, there must be a true partnership, and that the partnership must be worked out as between equals."

Prime Minister Lester B. Pearson tabled an 85, 000 page royal commission on bilingualism and biculturalism in the House Of Commons.

1960~1969

ARTILLERY ROARS ON BORDER

Jordanian and Israeli artillery duelled along the border of divided Jerusalem. Damascus said the Syrian army had gone into action on its front with Israel.

Both sides claimed sweeping victories in the air battles, the biggest of which broke out over the Sinai desert.

Cairo radio claimed 70 Israeli planes had been shot down. An Israeli Arab-language broadcast claimed Israel had destroyed 150 Egyptian planes.

"We are on the threshold of the final battle and we hope that God will grant us victory," King Hussein of Jordan said in a broadcast.

Gen. Moshe Dayan, Israel's victorious commander in the Sinai war with Egypt in 1956, declared to his army:

"Soldiers of Israel, we are not setting out for conquest. Our only aim is to frustrate the attempt of the Arab armies to conquer our country."

Israeli Column Cuts Off Egyptian Force In Gaza

Weeks of Crisis End In Warfare

TEL AVIV (AP) —

Israeli headquarters announced tonight capture of Khanyunis on the southern tip of the Gaza Strip.

An Israeli column, by the account here, smashed into the area which was the scene of a battle in the 1956 Sinai campaign against Egypt.

Occupation of the sector appeared to have cut off any Egyptian forces in the northern tip, including the town of Gaza, unless they could break to Israeli territory.

Heavy fighting raged and air battles and bombing raids were reported by both sides. Forces of Egypt, Jordan and Syria were involved on the Arab side.

Kuwait, meanwhile, proclaimed a "defensive war," against Israel and the Algerian press service said troops of the well-trained Algerian army will leave Algeria tonight for the Middle East.

In Rabat, King Hassan II instructed units of the Morrocan armed forces to be sent to the Middle East, officials said.

The fighting began after a series of minor clashes over the last few months across the Syrian-Israeli border, followed by Egypt's command May 17 for the United Nations to withdraw the UN Emergency Force that had separated Israel and Egypt on the Sinai frontier and at the Gaza Strip.

The fighting first erupted on the Sinai desert front between Egyptian and Israeli troops and tanks, then spread to the Syrian and Jordanian fronts. Both sides accused the other of starting the war after weeks of crisis.

Egypt said Cairo and other Egyptian targets were bombed. Damascus radio reported that Syrian air force planes bombed the oil refinery in Haifa and left it in flames. The broadcast said airfields in northern Israel were heavily damaged. Amman radio said Jordanian planes also took part.

The hardest ground fighting appeared to be centred in the Sinai desert front involving Egyptian and Israeli troops.

Israel Firm: 'No Retreat'

JERUSALEM (REUTERS) —

Israeli Premier Levi Eshkol said today Israel would not agree to revert to the pre-war situation in the region, and called on the Arabs to make peace with Israel.

He told the Knesset (Parliament):

"A new situation has been created that could lead to direct negotiations with the Arab countries."

Eshkol described the period between Israel's establishment and last week's war as one in which the Arab states merely prepared for an onslaught to destroy Israel.

"The United Nations," he said, "ignored this Arab approach."

"Let me tell the nationals of the world: Have no illusions, Israel will not agree to revert to the situation which existed until a week ago."

Cheering crowds in the Israeli port of Elath Sunday night greeted the first Israeli freighter to enter the Gulf of Aqaba since Egypt's proclaimed blockade of the gulf led to the Middle East fighting.

The Jewish nation has assured reopening of the gulf by capturing Sharm el Sheikh, from which Egyptian guns overlooked the gulf entrance at the Strait of Tiran.

An Israeli army spokesman said the war against the Arabs wounded 2,563. Jordan has not announced any casualty figures.

Estimates of the number of prisoners taken by Israel mostly Egyptian, range from 13,000 to 15,000. They still are being counted.

The United Nations Security Council adopted today a resolution demanding that Israel and Syria avoid any forward movement of troops and withdraw any units that have crossed cease fire lines established Saturday.

Syria said Israel moved armored units forward Sunday. Israel said its tank movements were entirely behind the cease fire lines. UN truce observers confirmed movement of tanks in the area.

Israeli troops now occupy Egypt's Sinai Peninsula, the biblical cities in Jordan west of the Jordan River and a 25-mile Syrian front which extends 15 miles into Syrian territory.

Foreign Minister Abba Eban told a public meeting Sunday night that Israel would not return to the armistice lines of 1949. For the first time, he said, Israel's Galilee settlements are out of danger from Syrian guns on high ground overlooking them.

(AP Photo)

King Hussein of Jordan, forground, walks through frontline trenches during his visit to the Jordan-Israeli frontier May 29, 1967, accompanied by high ranking officers.

Eastern Premiers Greet The Queen At Expo Site

MONTREAL (CP) – The premiers of Canada's two senior provinces, Daniel Johnson of Quebec and John Robarts of Ontario, today welcomed the Queen to their provinces' Expo pavilions.

Each offered their hospitality in the common tongue of his province – French and English – Canada's two official languages.

The tour by the umbrella-carrying Queen and rain-coated Prince Philip to the Quebec and Ontario pavilions came in mid-morning after they arrived for the world fair visit at 9:39 a.m aboard the royal yacht Britannia.

Thickly-overcast weather and rain greeted the royal couple. Their visit to Expo was under conditions of heavy security following demonstrations by separatists when the royal couple visited Quebec City in November, 1964.

The Queen drove in a black closed car to Notre Dame section of Expo past the high, glass-walled Soviet pavilion, one of the fair's most impressive.

See British Display

Her tour took her to the British pavilion with its mini-skirted hostesses, to the Western pavilion with its 100-ton logging truck about which Prince Philip asked questions, and on to Quebec's boxlike pavilion and Ontario's, one of the fair's best with architecture described as like a great spider fighting under a piece of cloth.

The Queen travelled from the British to Western pavilions in a trailer train called la Balade that travels the fairground pavements. Glass was installed on the side of the Balade seat the Queen shared with Pierre Dupuy, Expo commissioner-general.

In the Quebec pavilion, which many call highly-intellectual because of its sounds and sight, the Queen was greeted by Premier Johnson. He escorted her about, explaining in French points of interest, including a color movie on a huge screen that blasts out its message about developing Quebec industry.

A luxuriously-bound book about the island of Orleans in the St. Lawrence River near Quebec City was presented as a memento to the Queen as well as a quaintly-shaped object that seemed to puzzle her until she was told it was a paper-cutter.

Photo by photo credit

Crowds walk in front of the inverted pyramid shaped structure "Katimavik" at the Canadian Pavilion at Expo '67.

'Appreciate Heritage'

MONTREAL (CP) — Prime Minister Pearson today singled out the British monarchy as an institution of Canada's heritage that has given the country cohesiveness through continuity.

In welcoming the Queen and Prince Philip to Expo 67 at a mid-day luncheon he urged Canadians to appreciate "what the heritage of our past means to our future, in the depths of our roots and the stability that comes from institutions that have proven their enduring value."

He said the monarchy symbolizes the political and parliamentary freedoms Canadians have inherited and broadened through the ages "which gives to our political life the cohesiveness that comes from continuity."

1960–1969

Violence Flares In U.S. After Dr. King's Slaying

Murder, Arson And Rioting Rampant

By The Canadian Press

Violence burst out in cities across the U.S. in the wake of the assassination of Dr. Martin Luther King Jr. as bands of Negroes smashed windows, looted stores, threw firebombs and attacked police with guns, stones and bottles.

A white man was stabbed to death in the midst of violence in Washington and a Negro died of stab wounds in New York, although it was not known if the latter death was related to the violence.

A white youth died in a fire at Tallahassee, Fla., which police said was started by a firebomb.

Scores were injured, including about 50 in Washington, and several score in New York.

Two Negro students of Mississippi Valley State College at Itta Bena, Miss., were wounded by pellets from shotguns fired by highway patrolmen trying to halt 300 student marchers. Police said shots had been fired from the crowd.

Snipers used guns and bows and arrows against police on the campus of Florida A. and M. University at Tallahassee, but no policemen were hurt.

Tallahassee Mayor Eugene Berkowitz and another city official were treated for minor cuts after rocks shattered the windows of their car.

In Detroit, two policemen were shot and wounded as they patrolled a Negro section, but that city escaped the street violence that erupted elsewhere.

In Memphis, where King died, police shot and critically wounded a man they said had been caught behind a store with a rifle.

More than 90 persons were arrested in Memphis and a like number in New York, and scores in other cities in the midst of the violence.

King, 39, died in a Memphis hospital Thursday night less than an hour after he was shot in the neck by a white gunman while standing on the balcony of his motel here.

The body of Dr. Martin Luther King Jr., was put on public view in Memphis today before it was to be taken to the airport for the journey back to Atlanta. Negroes filed past for a last look at the man who made non-violence and the song, We Shall Not Be Moved, the two major factors in the American civil rights movement. The body was in a bronze coffin and King wore a black suit, similar to the one he had on when he was cut down Thursday.

Angry crowds burned and looted stores in a Negro neighborhood just two miles north of the White House in Washington. Some 50 persons were injured and 167 arrested.

Police in Jackson Miss., fired

Dr. Martin Luther King Jr. displays his 1964 Nobel Peace Prize medal in Oslo, Norway, December 10, 1964. The 35-year-old Dr. King was honored for promoting the principle of non-violence in the U.S. civil rights movement.

(AP Photo/File)

tear gas at groups of Negroes on the Jackson State College campus. A white-owned supermarket in a Negro section was firebombed despite a Negro leader's pleas for non-violence.

Disturbances were reported in Nashville, Newark, Boston and a number of smaller cities and towns.

Stand Your Ground, Asks LBJ

WASHINGTON (AP) — President Johnson called on all Americans today to "stand their ground to deny violence its victory" in the wake of the slaying of Negro civil rights leader Dr. Martin Luther King Jr.

His statement was issued after a hastily summoned meeting at the White House of civil rights leaders and various government officials.

He expressed again his sorrow at the death of the Negro apostle of non-violence, assassinated by a rifleman Thursday night in Memphis, Tenn.

Johnson meanwhile kept in abeyance his plans to fly to Honolulu later in the day for Vietnam policy talks.

The president's statement said, "The dream of Martin Luther King has not died with him."

"Men who are white, men who are black, must and will join together now as never in the past to let all the forces of division know that America shall not be ruled by the bullet but by the ballot of free and just men."

Johnson said that when he heard Thursday night "the terrible news of Dr. King's death my heart went out to his people — especially to the young

Americans who, I know, must wonder if they are to be denied a fullness of life because of the color of their skin."

He said he had called to the White House the leaders of the Negro community for consultation, and went on to say:

"No words of ours — no words of mine — can fill the void of the eloquent voice that has been stilled."

White Man Was Killer

MEMPHIS, TENN. (AP) — A single white man following an apparently well-planned procedure, was the assassin Thursday of Dr. Martin Luther King Jr., Police Director Frank Holloman said today.

Holloman said the investigation showed the assassin checked into a main street flop-house at mid-afternoon, shot King from a second-floor window of the building three hours later and then disappeared in the resulting confusion.

The murder weapon apparently was a new .30-.06 Remington pump rifle with telescopic sights, Holloman said. The assassin also carried a new set of binoculars and a new suitcase.

A .30-.06 Remington pump rifle was one of 15 weapons stolen a night earlier from a Memphis sporting goods store, but Holloman refused to say immediately that the stolen gun was the death weapon.

"As far as we know and from the evidence at this time, there was only one man in the physical area of the slaying," Holloman said.

He said one of the 30 to 40 officers on duty in the vicinity of the motel saw the bullet strike King and all immediately converged on the scene.

The fatal shot was fired from the window of a common bathroom in the flop-house, Holloman said. King's room was 205 feet away, through the trees, across a street but in "clear" view of the window.

Holloman said the assassin was a white male, between 26 and 32 years of age, standing six feet tall and weighing 165-175 pounds. Police radios said he had dark to sandy hair, medium build, a ruddy complexion and was wearing a black suit and white shirt.

After the shooting, Holloman said, the assassin left the building through the front door – on the opposite side from the motel where King lay mortally wounded – discarded his weapon and suitcase two doorways away, and fled.

Fingerprint Quest Reveals Clue In Dr. King's Death

WASHINGTON (AP) — The FBI has pinpointed an ex-convict, high school dropout and U.S. Army reject as Eric Starvo Galt, target of a massive manhunt in the slaying of Dr. Martin Luther King Jr.

The FBI said Friday a "systematic and exhaustive search" through its fingerprint files revealed Galt and James Earl Ray – drifter, loner, avid dancer and prison escapee – as the same man.

In its first positive identification of the man sought by the FBI since the April 4 assassination of King in

Memphis, Tenn., the bureau further pictured Ray as a 40-year-old white man in trouble with the law since his youth – and one who "should be considered armed and extremely dangerous."

There were no indications the FBI was any closer to catching Ray than it was Wednesday when it put the name Galt on a fugitive warrant charging him "and an individual whom he alleged to be his brother" with conspiring to deprive King of his civil rights to travel from state to state.

Ray fled the Missouri Penitentiary – where he was serving the seventh year of a 20-year sentence for a 1959 market holdup and auto theft in St. Louis – on April 23, 1967.

Prison officials, who said a 1966 escape try by Ray was thwarted when he was discovered in a ventilator shaft, indicated he succeeded the next year by hiding in a truck carrying bread from the penitentiary baker to its farms.

RAY DENIES KILLING KING

JUNE 27, 1968, LONDON (AP) – James Earl Ray, fighting extradition to the United States to stand trial for the murder of Dr. Martin Luther King Jr., said today he did not kill the Negro civil rights leader.

The man – who is charged here under the alias of Raymon George Sneyd, the name on his Canadian passport – took the witness stand in a surprise move and testified:

"I have never met Dr. King. I have never had any kind of grudge against him."

The Kelowna Daily Courier

Serving The Four Seasons Playground

Kelowna, British Columbia, Friday, April 5, 1968

Vol. 64   No. 208   16 Pages

POLICE VIEW
White Man Was Killer

Violence Flares In U.S. After Dr. King's Slaying

Murder, Arson And Rioting Rampant In Many Cities

By THE CANADIAN PRESS

Violence burst out in cities across the U.S. in the wake of the assassination of Dr. Martin Luther King Jr. as bands of Negroes smashed windows, looted stores, threw firebombs and attacked police with guns, stones and bottles.

A white man was stabbed to death in the midst of violence in Washington and a Negro died of stab wounds in New York, although it was not known if the latter death was related to the violence.

A white youth died in a fire at Tallahassee, Fla., which police said was started by a firebomb. Scores were injured, including about 50 in Washington, and several score in New York.

Two Negro students of Mississippi Valley State College at Itta Bena, Miss., were wounded by pellets from shotguns fired by highway patrolmen trying to

THE BODY of Dr. Martin Luther King Jr., above, was on public view in Mem...

MEMPHIS, TENN. (AP) — A single white man, following an apparently well-planned procedure, was the assassin Thursday of Dr. Martin Luther King Jr., Police Director Frank Holloman said today.

Holloman said the investigation showed the assassin checked into a main street flop-house at mid-afternoon, shot King from a second-floor window of the building three hours later and then disappeared in the resulting confusion.

The murder weapon apparently was a new .30-.06 Remington pump rifle with telescopic sights, Holloman said. The assassin also carried a new set of binoculars and a new suitcase.

A .30-.06 Remington pump rifle was one of 15 weapons stolen a night earlier from a Memphis sporting goods store, but Holloman refused to say immediately that the stolen gun was the death weapon.

"As far as we know and from the evidence at this time, there was only one man in the physical cal area of the slaying," Holloman said.

He said one of the 30 to 40 officers on duty in the vicinity of the motel saw the bullet strike King and all immediately converged on the scene.

The fatal shot was fired from the window of a common bathroom in the flop-house, Holloman said. King's room was 205 feet away, through the trees and across a street but in "clear" view of the window.

Holloman said the assassin was a white male, between 26 and 32 years of age, standing six feet tall and weighing 165-175 pounds. Police radios said he had dark to sandy hair, medium build, a ruddy complexion and was wearing a black suit and white shirt.

After the shooting, Holloman said, the assassin left the building through the front door—on the opposite side from the motel where King lay mortally wounded—discarded his weapon and suitcase two doorways away, and fled.

(See also Pages 2 and 12)

Loggers Gather

Trudeau Hard To Beat

HOW CAN YOU STOP TRUDEAU?

OTTAWA (CP) — Can anybody stop Pierre Elliott Trudeau?

That question was on everybody's lips today as 8,000 Liberals and observers launched the party's mammoth three-day convention leading to the selection Saturday of a new leader and prime minister.

Justice Minister Trudeau's bandwagon roared from high gear into super-high Wednesday when Finance Minister Mitchell Sharp pulled out of the leadership race and jumped aboard bringing three other cabinet ministers with him.

A few hours later Premier Joey Smallwood announced that Newfoundland's 84 voting delegates have decided almost unanimously – and with his blessing – to back Mr. Trudeau.

"Trudeau" and "Pierre" badges began popping up everywhere.

Delegates, party officials, guests and observers poured into the city all day in a growing flood that is expected to see 10,000 in the new Civic Centre for Saturday's climactic vote.

There are 2,476 eligible voting delegates, most of whom were on hand by Wednesday night to crowd convention eve parties thrown by the major candidates and tour the 20 hotel hospitality suites that went into operation early in the afternoon.

Well On Way To Victory As Opponents Drop Out

OTTAWA (CP) —

Justice Minister Pierre Trudeau today charged into an apparently insurmountable lead after the first ballot at the Liberal leadership convention.

A Trudeau bandwagon for victory on the second ballot seemed in the making.

Three candidates – External Affairs Minister Paul Martin, Health Minister MacEachen and Eric Kierans, former Quebec health minister – threw in the towel immediately.

With the second ballot ready to begin, five candidates were left in: Mr. Trudeau, Transport Minister Paul Hellyer, former trade minister Winters, Consumer Affairs Minister John Turner and Agriculture Minister J.J. Greene.

Mr. MacEachen went over and shook hands with Mr. Trudeau after he announced his withdrawal.

Mr. Trudeau got 752 votes on the first ballot to 330 for runnerup Mr. Hellyer.

Mr. Martin tied for fourth place with Mr. Turner on the first ballot. He took his crushing humiliation unblinkingly like the old pro he is.

After the result of the first ballot was announced, Mr. Martin put his arm around his wife, Nell, and they had a whispered conversation.

Mr. Martin said he would throw his support to the next prime minister but did not officially indicate his choice.

Later, he went over and shook

hands with Mr. Trudeau and Trudeau supporters went wild.

Desperately, Mr. Hellyer's forces tried to rally Mr. Winters, Mr. Turner and Mr. Greene to their support.

The task looked impossible.

The Hellyer group also tried to obtain the support of the candidates who had folded.

Mr. Hellyer himself went to Mr. Martin's box seat while the first ballot was in progress. It appeared that Mr. Hellyer was seeking a pledge and equally obvious that Mr. Martin was not giving it.

Mr. Winters, in third place with 293 votes, also visited Mr. Martin.

Mr. Martin told reporters: "I learned long ago how important it is to be generous in victory, as well as generous in defeat. That is my mood and composure now."

Mr. Martin sucked on a cigar stub as candidates still in the running struggled through the crowd to talk to him.

Mr. Winters tried to shake hands with Mr. Kierans but was headed off in the rush as Mr. Hellyer got there first.

Mr. Winters said his strength would show on the second ballot.

"I'm a late starter," he said.

Mr. Hellyer went to Mr. Greene's seat but the agriculture minister was on the floor talking with delegates.

"We're still in," a Greene aide said.

Mr. MacEachen was reported to have withdrawn because he feared his support would plunge on the second ballot.

Mr. Kierans freed his delegates to vote for their own choice.

"Okay, honey?" Mr. Kierans said to his wife, Teresa, as he wrote out his official withdrawal. The jaunty Mr. Greene told reporters he is the only candidate in a position to stop Mr. Trudeau.

"I'm the only one with no enemies in any camp," he added.

It was Trudeau by a nose in the fourth at the Liberal leadership convention at Ottawa, Saturday. Justice Minister Pierre Elliott Trudeau, 46, got 1203 votes - a few more than the required majority - on the fourth ballot. Here he cheers on his supporters just before the fourth and final ballot.

(CP PHOTO) 1968 (stf-Chuck Mitchell)

TRUDEAU PONDERS ELECTION MAYBE 'SOMETIME IN JUNE'

Prime Minister Sworn In And Shuffles His Cabinet

OTTAWA (CP) — Prime Minister Trudeau said today he is examining the possibility of dissolving Parliament for a June election.

He said he scheduled the official swearing-in of his cabinet for today—two days before

Pearson formally handed in his resignation.

Mr. Trudeau took the oath of office in the French language. Mr. Pearson left Government House before his successor was sworn in. He was accompanied

Ben Wicks

Trudeaumania Catches On
Canada Accepts Challenge By New Liberal Leader

By Carman Cumming
Canadian Press Staff Writer

Pierre Elliott Trudeau challenged Canadians to "take a risk with the future" and the voters accepted Tuesday, handing his Liberal government a solid majority in the national election.

The 48-year-old bachelor took something of a gamble himself in calling the election three days after he became prime minister April 20.

But it paid off as the Liberals gained strength in Ontario and the West, just about held their own in Quebec and emerged with 154 seats in the 264-seat Commons.

The final standings:

	1968	1965
Lib	154	131
PC	71	97
NDP	23	21
Cred	15	9
SC	0	5
Ind	1	1
Totals	**264**	**265**

Like the winning Liberals, the New Democrats and Creditistes gained.

Robert Stanfield's Conservatives showed strength only in the Atlantic provinces and slumped to 71 seats from 97 after the 1965 election.

Attack Riddles PCs

It was a black day for the Conservatives as their front-bench line was riddled by the Trudeau attack.

But it was black for New Democrats also as their leader, T.C. Douglas, took a personal defeat in a close and bitter fight with Liberal Ray Perrault in Burnaby-Seymour.

Voting turnout was a record, an estimated 8,295,200. But the percentage of eligibles voting was about the same as in 1965, about 75 per cent.

The election was the sixth since

(CP PHOTO/Chuck Mitchell)

Prime Minister Pierre Trudeau does a dance after his campaign bus broke down in Montreal June 6, 1968.

1957 and the first to produce a majority government since John Diefenbaker led the Conservatives to a landslide win in 1958.

For Mr. Trudeau, lawyer, writer, professor and non-conformist world traveller, it was the climax of a spectacular rise since his entry to politics in 1965.

After only 12 weeks as Liberal leader, he gained the Commons majority that Lester B. Pearson sought unsuccessfully to build in 1958, 1962, 1963 and 1965.

Prime Minister Sworn In

APRIL 20, 1968, OTTAWA (CP) – Prime Minister Trudeau said today he is examining the possibility of dissolving Parliament for a June election.

He said he scheduled the official swearing-in of his cabinet for today – two days before it was intended to give him this option.

It also gave him time to talk to his cabinet about an agenda for legislation if he does decide to meet Parliament as scheduled Tuesday.

But when a reporter asked whether this was a "caretaker cabinet", Mr. Trudeau replied "yes" and added that there would be further changes whether or not an election is called.

He said the date most often mentioned for an election – June 17 – had "no special appeal" and it could be called for other days in June.

The cabinet would meet this afternoon and possibly tonight and tomorrow to "examine all hypotheses."

1960–1969

Kennedy S

Tragedy Strikes In L.A. After Political Triumph

LOS ANGELES (AP) —

Senator Robert F. Kennedy was shot in the head today after a California primary election triumph and police later identified a Sirhan Sirhan as the gunman. The New York senator was in "extremely critical" condition.

A man grabbed by bystanders at the shooting scene in a hotel, who had refused to identify himself or discuss the shooting, was identified 10 1/2 hours later as the brother of a man who lives in nearby Pasadena.

Sirhan was identified as being a Jordanian born in Jerusalem.

Mayor Sam Yorty and Police Chief Tom Reddin told a news conference that Sirhan, 23, was traced through the .22-calibre pistol used to wound Kennedy and five other persons less seriously, and identification was made through a brother, Adel Sirhan, of Pasadena.

Even after the identification, Yorty said, the prisoner refused to identify himself.

As the two city officials made their announcement Kennedy lay in a hospital fighting for life. A doctor said he fears "the outcome may be extremely tragic," adding that a bullet evidently caused serious damage to the cerebellum, the part of the brain at the back of the head.

The New York senator was shot just after jubilantly proclaiming victory in California's Democratic presidential primary election.

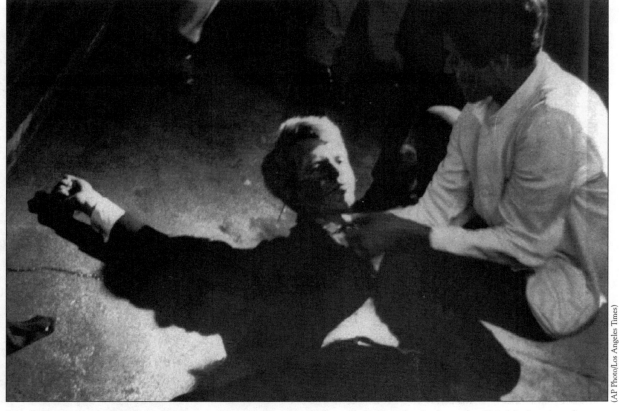

(AP Photo/Los Angeles Times)

Sen. Robert F. Kennedy lies on the floor, waiting for the arrival of medical aid at the Ambassador Hotel in Los Angeles moments after he was shot on June 5, 1968.

His brother, President John F. Kennedy, was shot to death by a hidden rifleman about 4 1/2 years ago in Dallas.

Vital signs – pulse and breathing – are in good order, Frank Mankiewicz, his press secretary, told reporters, but the next 24 to 36 hours will be critical. He said there "may have been some impairment of the blood supply to the centre of the brain" – which controls pulse, blood pressure and tracking of the eye – but "not the thinking process."

The 42-year-old New York senator came from behind in California's crucial primary to accrue a winning lead over Minnesota Senator Eugene J. McCarthy around midnight PDT Tuesday night (3 a.m. EDT today). Kennedy had proclaimed his win to about 2,000 supporters at an Ambassador Hotel rally and was taking a shortcut through the kitchen to a meeting with reporters when shots rang out.

With stunning rapidity at 12:15 a.m., a man emptied the chamber of an eight-shot .22-calibre pistol.

Kennedy fell, hit apparently three times. Five others near him were wounded, none as badly as the presidential candidate.

Kennedy lay for a time on his back in the kitchen, eyes open, the crowd milling around him.

Some observers say they heard him say, as he was lifted into a police ambulance: "Oh, no. No. Don't."

Negro Tackle Grabs Gunman

Roosevelt Grier, giant Negro tackle for the professional Los Angeles Rams football club, quickly grabbed the gunman, wrestled the gun from him and held him for police.

Kennedy was taken first to Central Receiving Hospital where a doctor said he was "practically dead" upon arrival.

Physicians there administered closed cardiac massage, oxygen and adrenaline. "At first he was pulseless," said a doctor who treated him, "then his pulse came back and we began to hear a heart beat and he began to breathe – a little erratically."

The doctor, Victor Baz, said Ethel Kennedy, who accompanied her husband in the ambulance, was frightened – "She didn't believe he was alive because she couldn't see that he was respond-ing. I put the stethoscope to her ears so she could listen and she was tremendously relieved."

Kennedy then was taken to Good Samaritan Hospital. There a team of six surgeons began brain surgery at 3:12 a.m. that lasted about three hours 40 minutes.

Doctors said one bullet struck near the right ear and entered the brain. Another hit in the shoul-der. A third apparently grazed his forehead.

Kennedy's press aide said after the surgery that no further effort is planned for removal of the remaining bullet fragment in the skull. "Some fragments of the bullet went to the brain stem," he said.

Kennedy was moved, unconscious to the hospital's intensive care unit.

1960–1969

hot Down

World Recoils In Shock

FROM AP - REUTERS

Waves of shock, dismay and sorrow went round the world today at news of the shooting of Senator Robert Kennedy.

Members of the Kennedy family in Europe were on the telephone to the United States.

An aide to Sargent Shriver the new U.S. ambassador to France

and the senator's brother-in-law, said Shriver was trying to reach members of the family in Los Angeles.

News of the shooting caused "acute sorrow" at the Vatican, the chief press official there said.

Tass, the official Soviet news agency, reported the shooting briefly and without comment.

Prime Minister Trudeau of

Canada said he was "shocked and horrified" at the shooting.

All Canadians were shocked, he said.

The prime minister said all hope the world some day will be free of violence and that reason will prevail.

Mr. Trudeau made the statement outside his hotel here just before leaving for Montreal to

attend the funeral of Andre Laurendau, co-chairman of the royal commission on bilingualism and biculturalism.

The prime minister made his statement in a low voice and looked deeply troubled.

An aide to the prime minister said it would be fair to assume that more care would be taken in protecting Mr. Trudeau.

Yet Another Blow Endured By Family Of Joe Kennedy

WASHINGTON (AP) —

Once more a Kennedy has been struck by violence.

Once more, a child of Joseph P. and Rose Fitzgerald Kennedy lies in a hospital room – the latest victim of misfortune in a family that had everything going for it – wealth, power and unmatched achievement.

John, the Kennedy who became president, was assassinated. Joe Jr., the oldest, died in the explosion of his bomber on a dangerous mission during the Second World War. He was 29. Kathleen, the third of nine children and a wartime widow, was killed in a plane crash in 1948.

Edward M. (Ted) Kennedy, a senator like brothers John and Robert, lay immobilized for a year after suffering a back injury in a

plane crash. Rosemary, the second oldest Kennedy, has spent much of her life in an institution for the mentally retarded.

Now Robert, at 42, celebrating a major victory in his drive for the U.S. presidency, lay critically wounded from bullets fired at close range in a Los Angeles hotel.

A few years ago, while the family gathered around Edward's bedside, Robert had enough humor left to remark:

"I guess the only reason we've survived is that there are too many of us. There are more of us than there is trouble."

Joseph, the 80-year-old patriarch who was ambassador to England, had been paralysed for years from a stroke.

The son of John and Jacqueline

Kennedy, Patrick Bouvier Kennedy, died of lung disease when two days old. A daughter had been stillborn to them earli-

er and both are buried beside their father in Arlington National Cemetery.

Kennedy Clan Under Curse?

In a very unusual public statement Mr. Kennedy calls rumors false

By Rev. K. Neill Foster

The political career of Senator Edward Kennedy has been placed in jeopardy as a result of the criminal charges laid against him following an accident in which an attractive secretary, Mary Jo Kopechne, was killed. Though Senator Kennedy finally reported the incident eight hours after it happened, serious shadows had been cast upon the Democrats'

leading 1972 presidential prospect.

In a very unusual public statement Mr. Kennedy declared that none of the rumors circulating about immoral or drunken behavior on his part had any truth in them. As he described what it was like to begin to drown before he could clamber out of his submerged car, he publicly wondered if the Kennedy clan itself might be under some awful curse.

Since the assassinations of the Kennedy brothers John and Robert, there are those who have come to believe in such a curse. However, it is not our place here to confirm (or deny) that Joe Kennedy's whiskey millions, gathered from the ashes of broken homes and ruined lives, and reaping a harvest of compounded tragedy in the careers of his sons. But we do not hesitate to say that the Kennedys are under a curse.

All men are. It is the curse of sin and "when it is finished it bringeth forth death."

The reason men die at all is that they are sinners. And for this mortal malady there is no human remedy, only divine forgiveness and eternal life through Christ.

Teddy Kennedy will die as his brothers have done. We hope not in the same way. We hope not soon. But he will die as will we all. Such is this terrible curse.

Apollo Hurtles Out On Voyage Of Ages

Spacecraft 'Perfect' For Flight To Moon

CAPE KENNEDY, FLA. (AP) — With the men and their ship working perfectly, Apollo 11 astronauts hurtled through space today on a voyage of the ages, the first attempt to land men on the moon.

Commander Neil A. Armstrong, 38; Edwin E. Aldrin Jr., 39; and Michael Collins, 38, continued a performance that had been flaw- less since launch. They delicately separated their command module from a spent booster and then linked with the moon lander, still housed in the booster.

The trio started their historic journey on a Saturn V rocket that thundered from Cape Kennedy on schedule at 9:32 a.m. EDT and shot them into an orbit 118 miles high.

Two and one-half hours later, the Saturn third stage fired again to hurl Apollo 11 out of earth's orbit and start it fleeting toward the moon.

Half an hour after their manoeu- vre, the astronauts separated their command ship, pivoted around 180 degrees and gingerly poked its harpoon-like docking mechanism into a connecting device in the nose of the moon landing ship, or lunar module, cradled atop the third stage.

The two ships, locked nose to nose, streaked toward their distant target.

(CP Photo)

Apollo 11 astronaut Edwin "Buzz" Aldrin Jr. walks on the moon on July 20, 1969. Astronaut Neil Armstrong is reflected in his helmet.

'Beautiful, Smooth' Giant Leap For Mankind

HOUSTON (AP) — Here is the conversation between Mission Control here and Tranquillity Base, beginning as astronaut Neil Armstrong left the landing craft Eagle to precede astronaut Edwin Aldrin onto the surface of the moon:

The hatch opened, Aldrin talked Armstrong through his manoeuvres with a television camera and backpack through the Eagle's exit:

Armstrong: How am I doing?

Aldrin: You're doing fine.

Aldrin: All right now, you want this bag?

Armstrong: Yeah. Got it. Okay, Houston, I'm on the porch.

MC: Roger, Neil.

Apollo 11 astronaut Neil Armstrong steps down from the lunar module ladder and becomes the first man to set foot on the moon on July 20, 1969. A huge shadow of the LM is cast on the Moon's surface. This photo was made from 16mm movie film made with a Mauer Camera at 6 and 12 frames per second.

Aldrin: Okay, stand by Neil.

MC: Columbia. Columbia, this is Houston. One minute 30 sec- onds to LOS, all systems, go, over.

Armstrong: Need a little slack?

Armstrong: I need more slack, Buzz?

Aldrin: No, hold it just a minute.

Armstrong: Okay.

Aldrin: Okay, everything's nice and straight in here.

Armstrong: Okay, can you pull the door open a little more? … I'm gonna pull it now … Houston. The MESA came down, all right.

MC: This is Houston, Roger, we copy and we're standing by for your TV.

Armstrong: Houston, this is Neil. Radio check?

MC: Neil, this is Houston, loud and clear. Break, break. Buzz this is Houston, radio check and veri- fy TV circuit breaker's in.

MC: Neil, this is Houston. Loud and clear. Break. Break. Buzz, this is Houston. Radio check, and verify TV circuit breaker in.

Aldrin: Roger, TV circuit breaker's in. And read you loud and clear.

MC: Roger. (Pause) And we're getting a picture on the TV!

Aldrin: You got a good picture, huh?

MC: There's a great deal of contrast in it; and currently it's upside-down on our monitor, but we can make out a fair amount of detail.

Aldrin: Okay. Will you verify the position - the opening - I ought to have on the camera?

MC: Stand by. (Long Pause)

MC: Okay. Neil, we can see you coming down the ladder now. (Pause)

Armstrong: Okay. I just checked getting back up to that first step, Buzz. It's…The strut isn't collapsed too far, but it's adequate to get back up.

MC: Roger. We copy.

Armstrong: Takes a pretty good little jump (Pause)

MC: Buzz, this is Houston. F/2

Armstrong: Okay, I'm at the...

MC: ...1/160th second for shadow photography on the sequence camera.

Aldrin: Okay.

Armstrong: I'm at the foot of the ladder. The LM footpads are only depressed in the surface about 1 or 2 inches, although the surface appears to be very, very fine grained, as you get close to it. It's almost like a powder. Ground mass is very fine. (Pause)

Armstrong: I'm going to step off the LM now. (Long Pause)

Armstrong: That's one small step for (a) man; one giant leap for mankind. (Long Pause)

Armstrong: (Garbled) the sur- face is fine and powdery. I can kick it up loosely with my toe. It does adhere in fine layers, like powdered charcoal, to the sole and sides of my boots. I only go in a small fraction of an inch, maybe an eighth of an inch, but I can see the footprints of my boots and the treads in the fine, sandy particles.

MC: Neil, this is Houston. We're copying. (Long Pause)

Armstrong: There seems to be no difficulty in moving around as we suspected. It's even per- haps easier than the simulations of one-sixth g that we performed in the various simulations on the ground. It's absolutely no trouble to walk around. (Pause) Okay. The descent engine did not leave a crater of any size. It has about 1 foot clearance on the ground. We're essentially on a very level place here. I can see some evi- dence of rays emanating from the descent engine, but a very insignificant amount.

Astronauts Neil Armstrong, left, Michael Collins, center, and Edwin A. Aldrin, are pictured in this 1969 Apollo II crew portrait.

(AP Photo/NASA, ho)

1960~1969

Names In Historic Niche

The touchdown ended a flight of eight days three hours and 18 minutes during which Apollo 11 travelled more than 750,000 miles.

Armstrong and Aldrin etched their names beside history's great explorers on Sunday when they flew the fragile craft named Eagle to man's first landing on the moon.

Hours later, Armstrong, then Aldrin, strode the lunar surface, leaving their footprints in the powdery terrain.

Monday, in another gripping moment in this drama of the ages, Armstrong and Aldrin blasted Eagle off the moon and rejoined Collins orbiting overhead in the command ship, Columbia.

Manhunt On For Suspect In Bizarre Killings Of 5

LOS ANGELES (AP) —
Police pressed a manhunt today for a suspect in the bizarre killings of actress Sharon Tate and four others five miles from where a couple was found slain later in a similar style.

"There is a similarity, but whether it's the same suspect or a copy-cat we just don't know," said Police Sgt. Bryce Houchin.

At the scene of the second slayings, Inspector K.J. McCauley said: "I don't see any connection between this murder and the oth-

ers. They're too widely removed. I just don't see any connection."

The man and woman were stabbed many times in their Hollywood home, Houchin said, the man' s head wrapped in a sheet, the woman's in a night-gown. In the slayings at Miss Tate's home Saturday, one victim's head was covered with a cloth.

The latest victims were identi-fied as Leo A. LaBianca, 44, report-ed to be the owner of a small local supermarket chain, and his wife Rosemary, 38.

Police said their bodies were discovered in night clothes Sunday night by Mrs. LaBianca's son by a previous marriage, Frank Struthers, 14.

Houchin said the two were "stabbed numerous times and their throats were slit."

McCauley said the word "death" was written in an undis-closed substance on the living room wall. Other officers earlier said the words "death to pigs" were scrawled in blood on a refrig-erator door.

At Miss Tate's posh Bel Air home, the word "pig" was written in blood on the front door.

Earlier, police said they were seeking a man whose name "came up in conversation" with a 19 year old caretaker arrested in a guest cottage behind Miss Tate's $200,000 home when the bodies were found.

William Garretson was booked on suspicion of murder, but Detective Lieut. Robert Helder said physical evidence to link him to the crime had not been found.

Murder-Conspiracy Charges Laid Against Clan Leader

LOS ANGELES (AP) —
Charles M. Manson was jailed here Tuesday night on mur-der-conspiracy charges in the deaths of actress Sharon Tate and six others.

The 35 year old leader of a com-munal clan he calls "the family" was brought here after a 300-mile automobile trip from Independence where he had been held on charges of arson and receiving stolen property.

Three women indicted with him Monday by the Los Angeles County Grand Jury were ordered to Superior Court today for

arraignment. They are Susan Denise Atkins, 21: Linda Kasabian, 20: and Leslie Sankstone, 19. Manson will be arraigned Thursday.

Charles Manson - known as both "God" and "Satan" to his fol-lowers - was arrested October 10 with 25 of his devoted followers in a police raid on their secluded Death Valley commune.

Police alleged that Manson and his band made their living by stealing cars. The raid led to other arrests which in turn set police on a trail to the killers of Miss Tate and her four friends, together with

Charles Manson is escorted to and from Los Angeles Court December 11, 1969 for arraignment on conspiracy charges in connection with the slayings of actress Sharon Tate and seven others.

(AP Photo/File)

the stabbing deaths of a millionaire supermarket owner Leo LaBianca and his wife the following night.

Police have claimed that some of Manson's followers set out on a path of violence and murder - a

pseudo-religious program of "lib-eration through death." Some vic-tims were killed to free them from their wealth in accordance with the group's occult beliefs, police said.

Manson Case Death Penalty 'Likely To Be Carried Out

LOS ANGELES (AP) —
A judge has formally sentenced Charles Manson and three women followers to die in the gas chamber for the Sharon Tate mur-ders, and the chief defense counsel says the sentences are likely to be carried out.

Paul Fitzgerald, who argued Monday for reduction of the penalty on grounds that jurors

were swayed by the current mora-torium on executions, said it is invalid to assume that legalities will save the four from death.

There has not been an execution in the United States since 1967. State courts are waiting for a rul-ing from the U.S. Supreme Court on whether the death penalty is constitutional.

Superior Court Judge Charles

Older turned down motions for a new trial, a motion to question jurors about their verdicts, and another to reduce the sentence to life imprisonment. He then pro-nounced sentence and stated his own feeling about the case pub-licly for the first time.

"All that remains are the bare stark facts of seven senseless mur-ders - seven people whose lives

were snuffed out by total strangers for motives that remain known only to them....Not only is the death penalty appropriate but it is almost compelled by this case."

Manson, 36, and three women members of his nomadic hippie-style clan - Patricia Krenwinkel, 23, Leslie Van Houton, 21 and Susan Atkins, 22 - were condemned to death March 29.

Rock Fest Fazes Folk - 200,000 Out Of Hand

WHITE LAKE, N.Y. (AP) —

More than 200,000 young followers of pop music have descended here in rag tag fashion for a three-day rock festival, partially paralyzing this town and jamming area roads.

With increasing numbers of cars being abandoned on the highways leading to this Catskill Mountains resort area, the festival producers today called on "all vehicles to turn back home."

"Everything is quite out of hand," said a state trooper who described the area as "super-saturated." He said troopers at some posts had to be relieved by helicopter because traffic made the roads impassable.

Despite the road jams, intermittent thunderstorms and a shortage of food, most of the young people remained peaceful, taking the inconveniences with good humor and helping each other out.

The town has a population of 3,000 and is about 100 miles northwest of New York City. Normally it is a summer haven for the middle-aged and middle class.

What brought everybody here is something the producers call the Woodstock Music and Art Fair, an Aquarian Exposition. It is set up on a 600-acre farm with the stage at the foot of an alfalfa field that forms a natural amphitheatre.

By early Friday afternoon the crowds had pushed the ticket situation out of control.

"Anybody can get in," said one observer, "tickets don't matter."

State police said 50-60 persons had been arrested on charges of possessing such drugs as LSD, barbiturates and amphetamines.

Elsewhere around the state, troopers reported another 100 youths arrested on drug charges as they made stepped-up spot checks of cars headed for the festival. One car had a half-filled suitcase of marijuana and peyote, police said.

The opening concert Friday night was of folk orientation. Richie Havens opened the bill.

Today's acts included the Who, Jefferson Airplane and Janis Joplin.

For Sunday the billing included The Band, Jimi Hendrix and Crosby, Stills and Nash.

(AP PHOTO)

A young woman revels in the atmosphere of music and togetherness at the three day Woodstock Music Festival located at Max Yasgur's farm in upstate New York.

1960~1969

Photo courtesy of Allan Simpson of ROVER WORKS B.C. Ltd in Summerland

Kaleden 1911

Several families followed James Ritchie to Kaleden. Seaman Hatfield was second in command. He served as the Postmaster, Notary Public, Secretary of the Town and Timekeeper to James' development.

By now there were nearly 100 people who called Kaleden home. The lots were surveyed, 2000 fruit trees were planted, and a modern irrigation system was built. A 17" wooden pipe ran from Marron Lake, a 2 hour uphill horse ride. Water was then piped throughout the townsite, irrigating all the orchards and finally travelling downhill to the luxurious Kaleden Hotel, where, by turning a huge turbine, it generated electric light and water to the building. This unique system supplied all 26 guest rooms with a romantically lit private bath.

This was the first Okanagan hotel to boast such luxuries.

A DECADE
IN REVIEW

1970 ~ 1979

Nixon Has New Problem After Four Students Slain

WASHINGTON (REUTERS) — The slaying of four students in an anti-war clash at Kent State University in Ohio and the threat of more campus upheaval brought new troubles to the White House today as President Nixon sought to muffle rising criticism by meeting congressmen angry over his expansion of the Vietnam war.

The four students – two girls and two young men – were shot and killed Monday by National Guard troops.

Nixon, under mounting pressure over his decision to send U.S. troops into Cambodia, immediately issued a statement expressing his sadness. "This should remind us all once again that when dissent turns to violence it invites tragedy," he said.

But the National Student Association went ahead with plans for a nationwide university strike starting today. Other campus groups already have started boycotting classes.

Arms Talks Hurt?

And the Senate foreign relations committee, in a highly critical report issued on the eve of its visit to the White House at 5 p.m. EDT today, blasted the administration for waging a "constitutionally unauthorized, presidential war in Indochina."

International criticism of the U.S. was capped Monday by Soviet Premier Alexei Kosygin's Moscow news conference in which he denounced Nixon and warned the American incursion in Cambodia would make arms limitation talks now under way in Vienna more difficult.

Despite the clamor, there was no sign that Nixon was about to change course. The White House, in fact, claimed that favorable reaction to the U.S. incursions into Cambodia still is pouring in.

Four Killed

KENT, Ohio (AP) — Four persons were killed and at least 11 wounded by gunfire as Ohio national guardsmen broke up an unauthorized rally on the campus of Kent State University today.

SHOOTING STARTED 'BY ACCIDENT'

MAY 6, 1970. WASHINGTON (REUTERS) — Senator Stephen Young (Dem.) Ohio said today the fatal shooting of four students at Kent State University Monday was touched off when an Ohio national guardsman accidentally fired his rifle after being struck by a tear-gas canister.

Other national guardsmen opened fire on students, he added.

"There was no sniper," the senator said after receiving reports on the incident from two staff members in Kent, Ohio.

Young said that during the confrontation a student apparently hurled back at the advancing guardsmen a canister still partly filled with tear gas, which had been lobbed at the students by the troops.

He said the canister struck a guardsman on the shoulder or upper arm "and his gun fired accidentally."

Other guardsmen "then fired instantly," Young said.

He said that, based on reports from two of his aides who went to the scene, he is convinced the order was given to troops to open fire.

They were "just trigger-happy national guardsmen."

Students Howl Protests In Many U.S. Campuses

The Indo-China War

REUTERS (AP) —

An attempt to paralyse traffic into Washington and student strikes on American college campuses coast-to-coast were planned today as protest against the move into Cambodia by U.S. troops and the death of four students shot by National Guard troops at Kent State University in Ohio.

At Washington, hundreds of Georgetown, American and George Washington university students today planned to disrupt morning rush hour traffic into the capital by throwing human chain barricades across key streets.

A coalition of anti-war groups has called for giant demonstrations in front of the White House Saturday, and New York University students planned a march to Washington today to back a bill to cut off funds for operations in Cambodia.

Student strikes have spread to more than 170 campuses and there are plans to extend them to more, with faculty and administrative backing in many cases.

The presidents of 34 colleges, have appealed to President Nixon to consider the dangers of "an unprecedented alienation of America's youth," and the deans of 15 medical schools sent a telegram to the president urging a quick end to fighting in Indochina.

Some universities shut down altogether, others held rallies, prayer meetings or vigils. There were clashes with police on some campuses Tuesday. On others, there were indications of support for the move into Cambodia.

National Guard troops patrolled at the University of Wisconsin in Madison after, police said, more than 35 persons were arrested in two days of window smashing and firebomb vandalism.

Mary Ann Vecchio gestures and screams as she kneels by the body of a student lying face down on the campus of Kent State University, Kent, Ohio, on May 4, 1970. National Guardsmen had fired into a crowd of demonstrators, killing four.

Baby Bomb Hangs Over World

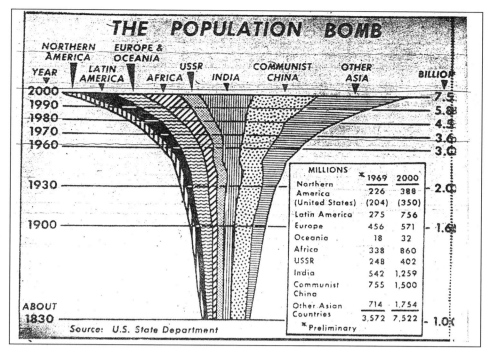

THE POPULATION BOMB

MILLIONS	*1969	2000
Northern America	226	388
(United States)	(204)	(350)
Latin America	275	756
Europe	456	571
Oceania	18	32
Africa	338	860
USSR	248	402
India	542	1,259
Communist China	755	1,500
Other Asian Countries	714	1,754
	3,572	7,522

*Preliminary

Source: U.S. State Department

Here is the U.S. state department view of what is happening to the world population. The threat of over-population hangs over the earth potentially as dangerous a threat of a hydrogen bomb war. If the rate of population continues to grow, pessimists see disaster overtaking the human race, and optimists forecast that family planning will become mandatory throughout the world, with severe penalties for those parents who disregard the laws.

George Shatters World Record

Compiles 5,092 Points

George Athans Jr., of Kelowna, shattered his own world tricks record, but Americans captured the remaining five events Sunday at the International Masters water ski championships, the first held in Canada.

The championships, at the Kelso conservation area, 25 miles west of Toronto, involved 19 American and 16 Canadian master-rated skiers.

Athans, the Canadian champion for the past three years, became the first man to pass the 5,000-point mark in the trick event. He compiled 5,092 points, exceeding his old mark of 4,809.

The 17-year-old son of Dr. and Mrs. George Athans, Okanagan Mission, has been a member of the Canadian National Water Ski team since 1966 when age 14.

Holder of all Canadian men's records, Athans is also the co-holder of the world slalom record, which he set at the World Water Ski Championships in Copenhagen, Denmark, last year.

The Kelowna native, son of Olympic diving champion, Dr.

George Athans Jr.

George Athans, a member of the B.C. Sports Hall of Fame, is rated number two in all the world, behind United States' Mike Sayderhud.

He made a literal leap into world contention when he smashed the existing national jumping record in Winnipeg, Aug. 16.

The Canadian ace bettered his own men's jumping record of 152 feet with a tremendous 157-foot leap, just five feet short of the world mark.

Athans, capping his finest competitive season ever, won the finals in jumping, tricks and slalom for an easy over-all championship and top berth on Canada's national team.

Last weekend, Athans defeated Sayderhud for the first time at the fourth American water ski championships held at Volcanic Tequesquitengo, Mexico.

JANIS JOPLIN FOUND DEAD

OCTOBER 5, 1970. HOLLYWOOD (AP) — Janis Joplin, a Texas runaway who hit the top as a rock music singer selling millions of records, was found dead Sunday night.

Police said her body, with fresh hypodermic needle marks on the left arm, was found in her Hollywood hotel apartment. An autopsy was ordered to determine the cause of death.

"There were no drugs in the room, only tequila, vodka and wine," a police spokesman said.

An ambulance attendant said Miss Joplin, 27, was wearing a nightgown and her death "didn't look like foul play."

"It looked like she had just fallen over," he said.

Miss Joplin was the second rock music star to die in less than a month. Guitarist Jimi Hendrix, who also was 27, was found dead in an apartment in London Sept. 18. A pathologist said he had suffocated from vomiting while unconscious.

Miss Joplin, who lived in the San Francisco suburb of Larkspur, had been here since Aug. 24 to perform for Columbia Records.

1970~1979

Things were taking shape. The town now has its own Real Estate office, Livery, Butcher Shop, and the largest General Store in the Valley.

David D. Lapsley is the proprietor.

Seaman Hatfield operates the Southern Okanagan Transportation Co., a network of paddle wheelers & launches, an automobile stage and the ever reliable horse team and wagon.

Kaleden was now a bustling town.

The impending Great War would change that.

Kaleden 1912

The HISTORIC **1912** Restaurant and Country Inn
fine dining... fond memories

On the shores of Lake Skaha in beautiful Kaleden
250•497•6868

Canada 'Goes To War' On Quebec Terrorists

Emergency Act Invoked: Police Arrest Hundreds

OTTAWA (CP) —

Canada 'went to war' today on members of the Front De Liberation Du Quebec, by invoking the War Measures Act – a move employed only twice since the First World War – and shortly after, police swooped in Quebec and Montreal to arrest hundreds of suspects.

The decision was announced by Prime Minister Trudeau in the House of Commons.

The regulations as of 4 a.m. today make it a crime punishable by five years in jail even to assist a member of the FLQ.

Mr. Trudeau made his announcement to a packed and quiet Commons as the defence department was saying that troops from Alberta and New Brunswick moved into Quebec to reinforce soldiers already deployed in Montreal.

The proclamation of emergency powers came 11 days after the Oct. 5 kidnapping of British trade envoy James Richard Cross and six days after the subsequent seizure Oct. 10 of Quebec Labor Minister Pierre Laporte.

Both men were grabbed from their homes in Montreal and the FLQ issued a string of demands – including release of so-called "political prisoners" – for their safe return.

The kidnappings set off the biggest manhunt – so far unsuccessful – in Canadian history.

Shortly after the powers were declared a spate of arrests under them were reported in Quebec.

More troops also were poured into Quebec and Ottawa in an all-out attempt to turn up the terrorists.

Mr. Trudeau said the regulations, which make it unlawful even to advocate the principles of the FLQ or any successor to it, are effective at least until April 30, 1971.

Labor Leader, FLQ's Lawyer Taken To Cells

MONTREAL (CP) —

Police pounced on hundreds of known Quebec separatists, sympathizers and others today in raids across the province, hours after the federal War Measures Act was invoked.

Among those taken into custody were lawyer Robert Lemieux, who has negotiated on behalf of the terrorist kidnappers of two political figures, and labor leader Michel Chartrand.

A Quebec Provincial Police spokesman reported a total of 238 arrests – 140 in Montreal, 52 in Quebec City, 20 in Rimouski, 15 in Hull and 11 in Chicoutimi – and said others are being sought on warrants.

Police searches resulted in the seizure of "firearms of all kinds," the spokesman said, and huge quantities of literature, posters, books and political pamphlets.

Police Instructed

The Quebec government had set a 3 a.m. deadline for a reply from the terrorists to its "final" ransom offer – that five convicted terrorists be released on parole in exchange for the freedom of the two kidnapped hostages.

The order banning tracts instructs police to detain and bring to the nearest police station "anyone in possession of posters, stickers or pamphlets of a political nature."

In conjunction with the federal war measures action, the Quebec government invoked the Police Act which gives the director of provincial police, Maurice St. Pierre, command of 14,000 police and army personnel.

Hundreds of "special assistants" were used to bolster the anti-terrorist squad in the early morning raids.

ARMED MEN KIDNAP TRADE COMMISSIONER

His Wife Receives Call At Their Montreal Home

OCTOBER 5, 1970. Montreal (CP) — Four men, two armed with sub-machine guns and another with a revolver; kidnapped James Richard Cross, British trade commissioner, after entering his house at 8:15 a.m. today.

The British government office here said that the wife of the trade commissioner later received a telephone call from the kidnappers. Chief Detective Inspector Roland Jodoin quoted a witness as hearing one of the four abductors say: "We're the FLQ."

The Front de Liberation du Quebec, an underground terrorist organization in Quebec, has been linked to dynamite bombings during the 1960s and to demands for the political independence of the province from Canada.

Swap Studied In Kidnapping

OCTOBER 10, 1970. Montreal (CP) — Quebec and federal government officials today were studying the latest demands by the terrorist kidnappers of James (Jasper) Cross that "political prisoners" must be released by 6 p.m. today or the British diplomat will be executed.

In Ottawa, Prime Minister Trudeau and External Affairs Minister Mitchell Sharp were standing by and staying "in touch" with Quebec Justice Minister Jerome Choquette.

The kidnappers Friday night made public two communiques and a note in Mr. Cross' handwriting to show their prisoner was still alive.

The communiques renewed a demand for the release of prisoners in jail on charges connected with terrorism in Quebec province and a demand that police investigation of the kidnapping be curtailed.

'Carte Blanche' Handed Lawyer By Kidnappers

OCTOBER 14, 1970. Montreal (CP) — The terrorist Front de Liberation du Quebec, holding two kidnap hostages, has given its contact man, Montreal lawyer Robert Lemieux, "carte blanche" or full freedom in holding a tough line in talks with Quebec government officials.

In communique No. 9, found today under the entrance carpet of a north-central apartment building by a radio station, the FLQ says it is putting its support behind Mr. Lemieux in efforts to win all its ransom conditions.

Hopes for an early release of British envoy James (Jasper) Cross and Quebec Labor Minister Pierre Laporte, each held by a separate cell of the FLQ, were in doubt today.

Face-to-face talks between Mr. Lemieux and a provincial government spokesman reached a standoff Tuesday night and Mr. Lemieux refused to resume discussions at 10 a.m. today unless the government altered its positions.

1970~1979

Letter Wants Demands Met

Laporte Found Dead

Cross Is Still Alive

Two Men Named As Kidnappers In Both Cases

MONTREAL (CP) —

A government offer to give terrorist kidnappers of British diplomat James Cross safe passage to Cuba stands today, despite the murder Saturday of a second kidnap victim, Quebec Labor Minister Pierre Laporte.

A letter from Mr. Cross Sunday said he was still alive and asked authorities to arrange for his release by meeting the main ransom demand of the Front de Liberation du Quebec – passage to Cuba or Algeria for 23 "political prisoners."

Mr. Cross, 49, was kidnapped at his Montreal home two weeks ago today.

Mr. Laporte, also 49, was killed at 6:18 p.m. EDT Saturday, a week almost to the minute after his abduction from his St. Lambert home on the south shore of the St. Lawrence across from Montreal.

An autopsy report was to be issued later today on whether he died from a bullet or from strangulation.

Negotiations between the government and a contact for the kidnappers collapsed Thursday night and the government Friday invoked the War Measures Act, outlawed the FLQ and gave police power to arrest without warrant FLQ members or adherents.

By early today 319 persons were being detained in the investigation, 183 in Montreal, the others in Quebec City, Sherbrooke, Hull and five other Quebec centres.

Police Sunday issued warrants for the arrest of Marc Carbonneau, 37, a taxi driver, and Paul Rose, 27, a teacher, charging them with kidnapping in both cases. Both are Canadians whose mother tongue is French.

Early today police acted on a tip that Rose might be found in a house in St. Hubert, a town south of Montreal where Mr. Laporte's body was found early Sunday.

The house was empty when police arrived, but they believe the Quebec minister was held captive there until he was killed.

Detective-Sergeant Albert Lisacek said there were blood stains on the floor, the house was messy and there were "chicken bones all over the place." Kidnappers might have avoided detection by using a hole knocked in a wall to an adjoining garage to enter the house.

Trudeau Blasts Terrorists To Applause From All Sides

OTTAWA (CP) —

To echoing applause from all sides of the Commons, Prime Minister Trudeau said today Quebec terrorists are trying to destroy the nation but "they will not succeed."

He made the statement at the opening of a grieving Commons session that paid tribute to the assassinated Pierre Laporte.

Mr. Trudeau said the brutal and cowardly slaying of the Quebec labor minister shows the "moral wasteland" occupied by the Front de Liberation du Quebec.

The FLQ was trying to turn Canadian against Canadian and to inspire fear and hatred and thereby destroy the country.

But Canadians had known freedom and practised tolerance too long to allow themselves to be dominated by criminals.

Looking drawn and tired after an anguished weekend, Mr. Trudeau said Mr. Laporte had devoted his life to the betterment of the people of Quebec.

All Canada grieved for Mrs. Laporte and her children.

THOUSANDS PAY RESPECT TO MURDERED MINISTER

OCTOBER 19, 1970. Montreal (CP) — Long lines of citizens Sunday began filing past the coffin of Quebec's murdered labor minister, Pierre Laporte, lying in state in courthouse next to Montreal's city hall.

The bells of Notre Dame Church, where funeral services will be held at 4 p.m. Tuesday, toiled out across the area.

Those who came to pay their last respects buttoned coats tight around themselves while waiting outside in 40-degree temperatures.

Mr. Laporte, 49, was kidnapped from his suburban St. Lambert home Oct. 10 by the separatist-terrorist Front de Liberation du Quebec and was killed Saturday. His body was found in the trunk of a car.

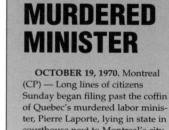

Pierre Laporte

The Kelowna Daily Courier

Serving The Four Seasons Playground

Kelowna, British Columbia, Monday, October 19, 1970

14 Pages   10¢ per copy

No. 66

LAPORTE FOUND DEAD

OSS IS STILL ALIVE

Two Men Named As Kidnappers In Both Cases

CAUGHT IN RAIDS

Olympics Suspended After Terrorist Raid

MUNICH (CP) – Arab commandos seized the Israeli Olympic team quarters today, killed one or two men, held others hostage and brought the 20th Summer Olympic Games to an unprecedented halt. West German police said they were prepared to go in shooting.

Israeli wrestling coach Moshe Weinberg was shot dead when the terrorists, armed with sub-machine guns, climbed the Olympic Village fence in the dark before dawn and burst into the Israelis' apartment.

The Bavarian interior ministry first announced that a second man also had been killed but his body could not be recovered.

A spokesman of the organizing committee said later in the day:

"All we can confirm now is that one man has been killed and his body recovered. If there is a second body in the house we won't know it for sure until police are able to enter it."

Everybody agreed that one hostage was known to be at least seriously wounded.

Olympic officials, in announcing a suspension of the Games for at least a day or perhaps longer, allowed completion of several competitions that already had started when the commandos attacked.

At the end of Monday's program 124 of the 195 events of the program had been completed.

The terrorists burst into the Israelis' apartment in pre-dawn darkness.

Some Israelis escaped but between nine and 13 members of the athletic team – the figure varied in conflicting official reports were held hostage.

The Arabs – five men with charcoal-blackened faces – announced that the rest of the Israelis would be shot if 200 Arab terrorists held in Israel were not released by noon.

Ready For Showdown

The terrorists had twice extended the original deadline of noon – 7 a.m. EDT.

As each deadline approached, West German police, armed with sub-machine guns and wearing bullet-proof vests and armored face protectors, got ready for a showdown.

West German Chancellor Willy Brandt flew into Munich to take command.

Competition started in at least seven sports today but it was an off-day in the big track and field program.

But as the fateful hour approached they were stopped. A joint statement by Avery Brundage of the United States, president of the International Olympic Committee, and Willi Daume, West German chairman of the organizing committee, said there would be no more games for the rest of the day.

The Egyptian basketball team forfeited a game because of the events of the day and sources said the entire Egyptian Olympic team were heading home.

Mark Spitz, the American wonder swimmer who won a record seven gold medals, flew home. Spitz, a Jew, was moved by officials out of the village to a Munich hotel as a safety precaution, but later decided to go right out of it.

By mid-afternoon two tanks were stationed outside the house in the village where the Israelis were held captive. More than 100 police ringed the building. At least one police car filled with guns was driven through the village gates.

Service On Wednesday

Officials announced a memorial service for the dead Israelis would be held in Olympic Stadium Wednesday morning. It was believed the Games would not be resumed until after that, and much appeared to depend on the outcome of the siege.

1970~1979

(AP Photo)

A member of the Arab Commando group which seized members of the Israeli Olympic Team at their quarters at the Munich Olympic Village September 5, 1972 appears with a hood over his face on the balcony of the village building where the commandos held several members of the Israeli team hostage.

Olympic Games Resume After Darkest Day

MUNICH (CUP) –

The Olympic Games were resumed today after a 24-hour halt caused by an Arab commando attack which took the lives of 11 Israeli athletes and officials.

Avery Brundage, president of the International Olympic Committee, announced plans for the resumption as the 20th Olympiad mourned its dead after nine Israeli hostages and a West German policeman were killed in a shootout with Arab terrorists.

The death toll stood at 17, including five Arabs killed in a shootout at an air base outside Munich and two members of the Olympic team killed when the Arab guerrillas invaded the Olympic Village early Tuesday. The terrorists had sought the release of 200 of their own kind from Israeli jails.

Schedule Pushed Back

The fate of the Games, which began Aug. 26, had hung in the balance until the announcement by Brundage, 83-year-old president of IOC.

That pushes each day's schedule back 24 hours and the closing ceremony will be held Monday instead of Sunday.

An official of the Israeli team said the 18 surviving members will leave for home Thursday morning.

"The Games must go on," Brundage said during the memorial service for the dead Israelis.

Brundage was to have met after the service with the full membership of the IOC, but an informed source said the committee was canvassed before and during the ceremony and agreed the Games should continue.

"We cannot allow a handful of terrorists to destroy this nucleus of international cooperation and good will that we have in the Olympic movement." Brundage said. "The games must go on."

Premier Golda Meir of Israel thanked the West German government for trying to free nine Israeli hostages who died at the airport. She endorsed the German decision to use force.

Olympics End On One Last Sour Note

MUNICH (CP) —

The 1972 Olympic Games, bloodstained by murder and rocked by political strife, ended on another bizarre note.

As the Olympic flame was extinguished and the Olympic flag came down before a capacity 80,000 at Olympic Stadium Monday two West German fighter planes patrolled the sky overhead.

They had been sent aloft after Olympic officials received an anonymous telephone call that a stolen airplane would be used to bomb the closing ceremonies.

Radar screens showed an airplane headed in the direction of the stadium, but it developed the plane was a DC-8 charter plane of Finnair, the Finnish airline, which had strayed off its course.

Police said later that no plane had been stolen. They termed the anonymous caller "a madman intent on causing further disturbance."

The fighter planes patrolled over the stadium for two hours, but nothing happened and final ceremonies continued without interruption.

ISRAELI JETS STRIKE AT GUERRILLA BASES

By The Associated Press

SEPTEMBER 8, 1972. — Israeli air force planes were reported to have struck at 10 Arab guerrilla bases deep inside Syria and Lebanon today, a few hours after Israel promised retaliation for the Munich massacre.

The Israeli jets bombed and strafed guerrilla bases and headquarters, striking within four miles of the Syrian capital of Damascus and far into the north of Lebanon above the port of Tripoli, the Israeli military command announced.

The raids were the deepest air strikes by Israel inside Syria since the 1967 Mideast war, and the deepest ever into Lebanon.

All the Israeli planes returned safely to base, a command spokesman said.

Sources in Beirut reported the Israeli planes bombed and strafed two villages on the Lebanese-Syrian border, Deir Al Achaya and Yanta.

There was no immediate confirmation from the Lebanese government.

The Syrian government had put its armed forces on maximum alert and cancelled all leaves, fearing an Israeli attack.

Israeli forces made an eighthour raid into southern Lebanon Thursday, but no major fighting or casualties were reported. The Palestinian guerrillas in Beirut charged Israel with an "unprecedented build up along the Lebanese borders and they expect retaliation for the Arab attack on Israel's Olympic Team.

Kaleden 1932

It is moving day for the Kaleden Packing house. A new, very modern plant with electricity provided by West Kootenay Power has been built on the waterfront just down Main Street from the hotel.

The Kettle Valley Railway has just completed the much awaited Osoyoos subdivision which would become Canada's last major Railway project.

It will provide iced box cars that will transport Okanagan fruit to the world.

Muir Stewert's old packing house will become the community hall, and as for the hotel, Penticton's Mayor Charlie Oliver will soon dismantle its interior after attempts to make it a sanitarium fall through.

SERIES OF THE CENTURY!

First Game Humiliation Erased By 'Team Canada'

Learned Something And Adjusted

SEPTEMBER 5, 1972 . Toronto (CP) – Team Canada played the waiting game Monday night and reaped the fruits of a costly lesson.

"We found out a lot by losing Saturday night," said coach Harry Sinden after the Canadians handed Russia a 4-1 setback at Maple Leaf Gardens to avenge a 7-3 loss at Montreal.

The Canadians, left in the wake of the well-conditioned Soviet players in Game One, made their own breaks Monday and kept the visiting speedsters in check.

Phil Esposito, Yvan Cournoyer, Peter Mahovlich and Frank Mahovlich scored for Team Canada. Alexandre Yakushev broke Team Canada goaltender Tony Esposito's shutout early in the third period.

The Canadians came through with three third-period goals, the first by Cournoyer while the Soviets were a man short and the second by Peter Mahovlich while the Canadians had a man in the penalty box.

McNeill Says Team Canada Faces Bigger Ref Trouble

SEPTEMBER 19, 1972.
Kentvile, N.S. (CP) – Team Canada is going to "run into real trouble in Russia" if the refereeing experienced in Sweden continues, Al MacNeill, coach of Montreal Canadiens in 1970-71, predicted Monday.

"They were having trouble with the refereeing in Sweden, but they are going to have it just as bad in Russia," MacNeill told a service club.

MacNeill, who led the Canadiens to the National Hockey League's Stanley Cup, is here with the Canadiens and his Nova Scotia Voyageurs of the American Hockey League at a training camp.

Although Canada was getting "quite a lesson" in the current Canada-Russia series, "the situation has not gone so far that we cannot correct it," he said.

Up to three years ago, he said, a Russian team could have been "handled" by any NHL club. But physical conditioning was a telling factor in the current series.

Asked whether a team such as Boston Bruins could have made a better showing, MacNeill said he couldn't agree.

"I'd rather have 20 all-star players anytime to play this game, once you had time to work with them."

"But the trouble with Team Canada was that they picked 35 players. That's fine when you are winning. As long as you have players doing the job for you on the ice, the others are not to be playing too much. Once you start losing things get a little tight and players on the bench think they should be in there."

Winner Take All Thursday

Henderson Slams In Stunner To Put 'Team Canada' Even

By Bruce Levett
Canadian Press Sports Editor

MOSCOW (CP) —

Paul Henderson, bouncing off a Russian defenceman in the dying moments of the game, has turned the Canada-Russia hockey series into a sudden-death affair.

His goal, which came with dramatic suddenness, gave Team Canada a 4-3 victory Tuesday night to tie the series at three games each with one tied. The final will be played Thursday night.

Coach Harry Sinden said later: "It forced an eighth game, which might just well be the most exciting game of hockey every played."

And coach Vsevolod Bobrov rapped one of his own players:

"Our defence played well, but (Gennady) Tsygankov cost us the winning goal."

Phil Esposito scored two for Canada with Rod Gilbert and Henderson getting the others. Alexander Yakushev scored two for Russia, Vladimir Petrov getting the other.

The teams were tied 2-2 at the end of the first period and there was no scoring in a somewhat slow second period.

Esposito opened the scoring when Ron Ellis and Brad Park dug the puck out of the corner to the left of goalie Vladislav Tretiak and fed the big Boston Bruins centre right in front of the goal.

Defenceman Bill White was off on a penalty signalled as hooking but announced as interference, when Vladimir Shadrin fed a lead pass to Yakushev at the blue line and Park fell while turning, allowing the Russian to go right in on Tony Esposito and put the puck between his pads.

Defenceman Bill White was off on a penalty signalled as hooking but announced as interference, when Vladimir Vikulov had the puck deflected onto his stick off Park's skate and fed Petrov who went in alone on Esposito, drew him and flipped the puck high into the open corner.

Just over a minute later and with

Canada's Paul Henderson moves down the ice during a game in Vancouver, Sept. 6, 1972 in the hockey series between Canada and the former Soviet Union.

CP PHOTO) 1997 (lls-stf)

less than three minutes to play in the period, Jean-Paul Parise and Serge Savard set up Esposito's second goal to tie the score.

Savard, playing with a cracked bone in one ankle, dug the puck out of the corner and fed Parise at the blueline. Parise passed weakly ahead to Esposito – standing between him and Tretiak directly in front of the net – and Esposito fired through a maze of legs.

The third period was little more than two minutes old when Dennis Hull and Jean Ratelle worked the puck out of the corner, sending it sliding behind the net to Gilbert. Gilbert swung the puck in front of Tretiak as the Russians were caught in the corner, and tucked a backhand behind the goalie.

About 90 seconds later, Gary Bergman was called for holding on Yakushev and, with 11 seconds left in his penalty, Yakushev scored the Russians' second power-play goal of the night.

The third period was fast but, when asked by a Russian newspaper man why it was so rough, Sinden replied:

"It wasn't rough by our standards."

Referees Uve Dalberg of Sweden and Rudy Batja of Czechoslovakia had their hands full preventing a full-scale fight, however, when Boris Mikhailov, who had tangled

with two other Canadians previously, kicked Bergman behind the Canadian net and the teams paired off with gloves off, Mikhailov and Bergman drew roughing majors.

The Henderson goal came off a scrambly play and the Russians became disorganized. With 1:21 left in the game, Ellis felled Tretiak with a shot that appeared to hit the Russian goalie in the face. Tretiak shook off the injury and continued in the net.

Sinden said the refereeing of Dalberg and Batja was better than had been experienced in Sunday's game, won 3-2 by Canada.

"But we're still having difficulties understanding the interpretations of the rules in international hockey," he said.

Bobrov agrees that "the referees did not make certain errors during the games."

"It was a hard game to officiate," he said.

It was announced that Dalberg and Batja would officiate the final game Thursday. In the normal rotation, Josef Komapalla and Franz Baader of West Germany would have worked.

Sinden said agreement had been reached between the two teams so that the West Germans whom he had called "incompetent" after the Sunday game would not appear again.

CANADA WINS

MOSCOW (CP) —

Before the game was five minutes old, more than 3,000 emotional Canadian hockey fans were chanting "Let's go home, let's go home," to their team.

Later, with only 34 seconds left on the clock in the Ice Palace, they were cheering in wild disbelief as Canada scored the goal which gave them a 6-5 win and victory in the hard-fought eight-game series – four games to three with one tied.

Thursday night, they saw hard, fast hockey that rivalled Stanley Cup play in intensity.

Phil Esposito scored twice with the other goals coming from Yvan Cournoyer, Brad Park, Bill White and Paul Henderson, who got the winner. It was the third game – winning goal of the series for Henderson.

The Russian goals were scored by Alexander Yakushev with two, and Vladimir Lutchenko, Vladimir Shadrin and Valeri Vasiliev.

The first period ended in a 2-2 tie and the second with Russia ahead 5-3.

Esposito said of the winning goal:

"I was behind the net and I saw Henderson flying in. I fired on the net and the rebound went out to Paul and he put it away."

Said Henderson:

"This is the happiest moment of my career."

But the game that began with the Canadian players presenting western hats to the Russian players, and Hockey Canada presenting a five-foot thunderbird totem pole to the Soviet Ice Hockey Federation, went on only after diplomatic intervention.

And before it was over, winger Jean-Paul Parise had been thrown out of the game for going after referee Josef Kompalla and stick-swinging Canadian players had to pull team director Alan Eagleson away from a group of Russian police.

Parise was ejected for disputing

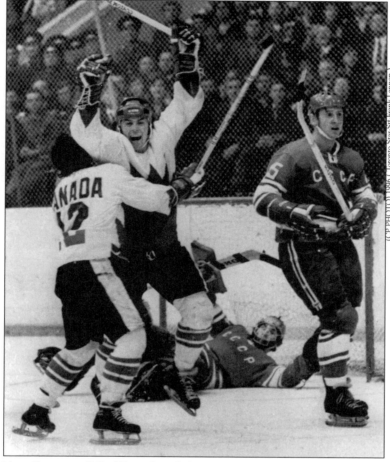

Yvon Cournoyer (12) of Team Canada hugging Paul Henderson after scoring the winning goal in the Canada U.S.S.R. hockey series in Sept. 28, 1972.

(CP PHOTO) 1996 (Toronto Star-Stf-Frank Lennon)

an interference call early in the first period. He protested and Kompalla added a 10-minute misconduct. Players restrained him from attacking the referee, who then threw him out of the game.

At this point, the Canadian bench threw a stool, then a metal chair, on to the ice. Then, when Kompalla skated near, someone in the bench area threw a towel at him.

It was at this point that the fans, unhappy at a pre-game compromise on the naming of officials to work the game, began their slow chant of "Let's go home."

The Eagleson incident erupted when the goal light behind Russian goalie Vladislav Tretiak failed to come on when Cournoyer poked in the tying goal midway through the third period.

Many in the crowd, including the

volatile Eagleson, thought the goal was being disallowed. Actually, the light had failed – it didn't work on Henderson's game-winning goal, either.

Eagleson said he was enroute to the timekeeper's bench to discuss the situation when "about 18" Russian police intercepted him. The players on the ice – led by Pete Mahovlich went over the boards to try to rescue their leader.

Coaches Harry Sinden and John Ferguson ran across the ice and pulled Eagleson away from the melee and escorted him across the ice to the players' bench.

That the game would go on at all was not decided until about six hours before the first puck was dropped.

Earlier in the series, Canada had protested that the West German referees – Franz Baader and Kompalla

were "incompetent" and demanded they not work again in the series.

Then it was announced that Swedish referee Uve Dalberg and Czech Rudy Batsa would work the final game following an agreement with the Russian squad.

After the Canadians tied the series with a 4-3 victory Tuesday, however, the Russians announced they would insist on the two West Germans working the final game.

The Canadians threatened to pull out and a stalemate occurred which brought the interception of Ambassador Ford, Senator Arthur Laing, minister of veteran's affairs, and Ed Ritchie, under secretary of state for external affairs.

After meetings on the diplomatic level, the problem was thrown back to the hockey authorities and it was decided that each team would name one of the two referees.

The Russians named Kompalla and the Canadians Dahlberg. The Russians then reported that Dahlberg was ill with flu and the Canadians' second choice, Batja worked the game with Kompalla.

Park, playing his best game of the series, gave Canada a tie coming out of the first period.

Shadrin took 21 seconds of the second to take back the lead but White tied it up 10 minutes later. Yakushev made it 4-3 for Russia just about a minute after that when Vasihev stretched the lead to 5-3 with Pat Stapleton off for cross-checking with less than five minutes left in the second.

Esposito got one back with less than three minutes gone in the third and moments later Rod Gilbert and Yevgeni Mishakov went off for five minutes for fighting.

Russia played two men short for a brief period when Vasiliev got two minutes for tripping Bobby Clarke, but the Soviets killed the penalties.

That was it, until about the 18-minute mark when Cournoyer scored to tie it up and set off the Eagleson ruckus.

Kaleden 1975

The Reverend Russell combined the Greek word 'Kalos' with 'Garden of Eden' and in doing so named a beautiful hamlet on the shores of Lac du Chien. That was nearly seventy years ago. Much has happened since then. Several pioneer families continue to call Kaleden home. The Swales family operated the Esso for nearly half a decade.

It won't be long before the dock, railway and packing house are gone.

Lapsley's store has housed the K.V.R. crew, been a warehouse and cold storage, a welding shop and is about to become an elegant restaurant.

Fine Dining and Fond Memories.

In the year 2000 we will celebrate our Silver Anniversary.

The HISTORIC
1912
Restaurant
and Country Inn
fine dining... fond memories

On the shores of Lake Skaha in beautiful Kaleden
250•497•6868

'Nam Peace At Hand Kissinger Declares

NIXON ADDS NEW FORCE TO VIETNAM

APRIL 5, 1972 — Washington (AP) – President Nixon is sending additional B-52 bombers to help offset Hanoi's invasion of South Vietnam, but it remains uncertain if the administration has decided on a resumption of widespread air attacks in the North.

About 20 new Stratofortresses sources indicate will augment the 80-plus B-52s already operating over Indochina and will be used to bomb concentrations and other targets in South Vietnam, along the demilitarized zone and in Laos and Cambodia.

Apart from letting the situation ride as it is with U.S. air power limited to the DM2 and the South, Nixon appears to have only one realistic option and that is new and extensive bombing of North Vietnam.

The 7,000 U.S. combat troops are too few to make much of a difference if the North Vietnamese attack continues in force.

Earlier this week, after the size of the North Vietnamese onslaught became evident, the United States ordered two more aircraft carriers to join with two already off the Vietnamese Coast.

WASHINGTON (AP) —

Presidential advisor Henry Kissinger said today 'peace is at hand' in Vietnam.

Kissinger told reporters in an hour-long briefing that most major provisions of a settlement have been agreed to but that one more negotiating session lasting for more than three or four days is necessary.

In breaking American silence of the status of the peace efforts, Kissinger said the nine points outlined earlier today by North Vietnam are essentially correct.

He also said: "I want to stress that what remains to be done is the smallest part of what has already been accomplished."

The presidential adviser said the remaining details are essentially linguistic and technical but need to be settled before the United States and South Vietnam can sign a pact.

He listed what were six or seven very concrete issues that with any-

thing like the good will that has been shown can easily be cleared up.

He included in his examples the need from the U.S. side to specify that no move will be made to grab additional territory between the time of the cease fire and a political settlement.

He also said there needs to be clarification on the timing of the Vietnamese settlement relative to the settlement of the conflicts in Laos and Cambodia. The Hanoi broadcast earlier today said the U.S. had agreed to sign a cease fire agreement Oct. 21.

On the issue of South Vietnam, the presidential aide said there were both agreements and disagreements by Saigon with the draft agreement.

But South Vietnamese President Nguyen Van Thieu will accept a cease fire, Kissinger said. He added that be believed the bitter expression of opposition from the Saigon

leader earlier this week to a coalition government was addressed to a previous plan not this version.

Kissinger said the Oct. 31 deadline for signing a final agreement was set by the North Vietnamese.

While the United States had indicated it hoped to draft a proposed pact by that date, it never committed itself to such a deadline Kissinger stated.

When asked what would happen if the Oct. 31 deadline passes without a signing, Kissinger indicated his belief that negotiations would continue.

"I can't believe that when this progress has been made an arbitrary deadline will break off the negotiations."

"It is up to the North Vietnamese," Kissinger said, "to set the date of the concluding negotiating session." He did not say where that final session should be held, but Paris has been the site of the previous session.

Hanoi's Version Of Peace Terms

HONG KONG (AP) —

This is North Vietnam's summary of the peace terms it says it and the United States agreed to:

1. The United States will respect the independence, sovereignty, unification and territorial integrity of Vietnam.

2. The United States will stop all bombing of North Vietnam and all mining of North Vietnamese waters twenty-four hours after the peace agreement is signed. A cease fire will take effect in all of South Vietnam. All American and allied troops will be withdrawn within 60 days.

3. After signing steps will be taken for the immediate return of prisoners of war held by

both sides.

4. At cease fire the two present administrations in South Vietnam and the South Vietnamese government and the Viet Cong will negotiate with each other to set up elections for a national coalition government. The two administrations will also negotiate with each other on dispositions and reduction of the troops of each side.

5. Unification of North and South Vietnam will be realized gradually by peaceful means.

6. An international committee on military control and supervision will be formed and an international conference on Vietnam will be called within 30 days of the signing of the peace agreement.

7. The sovereignty and neutrality of Cambodia and Laos will be recognized by all parties in the Vietnam War. The United States will end all military activities in Laos and Cambodia, withdraw all troops and not reintroduce troops or weapons into Laos and Cambodia.

8. Ending of the war will create conditions for establishment of relations between the United States and North Vietnam under which the United States will contribute to reconstruction in North Vietnam and throughout all Indochina.

9. The peace agreement will take effect immediately upon being signed by the U.S. and North Vietnam.

'Not Bound By Agreement' – Saigon Lets Sides Know

SAIGON (AP) —

The official Saigon radio emphasized tonight that South Vietnam would not be bound by an agreement between Washington and Hanoi, but left up in the air whether Saigon would oppose it.

"We in South Vietnam have the right of self-determination," said a commentator on the official radio. "A separate agreement

between North Vietnam and the United States does not concern us in any way."

This was the reaction to a Hanoi announcement that the United States had backed out of an agreement on a cease fire withdrawal of U.S. forces and elections for a coalition government.

While the Saigon commentator did not elaborate, unofficial sources in the presidential palace

said earlier that President Nguyen Van Thieu would not be adverse to a Hanoi-Washington agreement as long as the United States continued its Vietnamization and other military and economic commitments to South Vietnam.

"Hanoi has made a declaration 48 hours after Thieu's speech." Radio Saigon said, "The rude language of the declaration reveals

the deceitful intentions of North Vietnam. They dare call ARVN (Army of the Republic of Vietnam) soldiers, mercenaries of the Americans.

"They threaten to engage in separate arrangements with the Americans. They think the South Vietnamese government is composed of servants of the Americans as they are servants of Russia and China."

Last U.S. Forces Leaving Vietnam

SAIGON (AP) —

The last American forces pulled out of South Vietnam today after more than a decade of military intervention that cost 46,000 lives.

As the last 2,500 GIs flew home or to other bases in Southeast Asia, strong American air and naval forces remained on the perimeters of Indochina to keep up the war in Cambodia and to discourage a resumption of major fighting in South Vietnam and Laos.

The 7th Fleet was reported to have four carriers with 200 strike planes within range of Vietnam,

and the Pentagon said there are 202 B52 bombers at Guam and Thailand and more than 400 air force and marine fighter-bombers in Thailand.

Today's departures left a total of 1,034 uniformed American military men in Vietnam – 825 members of the U.S. delegation to the Joint Military Commission (JMC), 159 marine guards at the U.S. embassy and 50 military attaches at the embassy.

CLARK AIR BASE, PHILIPPINES (AP) —

North Vietnam freed its last 67 U.S. prisoners of war today, and two giant C-141 transports

brought them to Clark Air Base for their first stop on the way home.

The release of the 67 cleared the Communist prisons in Indochina of the 587 Americans Hanoi had reported were captives at the signing of the cease fire agreement two months ago. But the Viet Cong turned up another man who will be freed this weekend.

The first C-141 from Hanoi landed 40 men early tonight in a drizzle that failed to dampen the enthusiasm of a cheering crowd of 600 Americans.

The second C-141 touched down 42 minutes later with the other 27.

Calley Claims U.S. Was War's Main Victim

NEW YORK (AP) —

Former U.S. Army Lieut. William Calley, convicted for his role in the My Lai massacre of 1968, said today he considers the American people "the greatest victims" of the Vietnam war.

Calley, appearing on ABC TV's AM America program, said he also considers himself a casualty of the American military presence in Vietnam, "but that isn't to say I was the only victim of the war."

"There were many victims of the war," he said, adding he "most definitely" would include Americans.

"I think they're the greatest victims, and I think that is where the real problem lies," he said. "I see the American people had a very hard time and I think we're still feeling the shock waves of it."

Calley, 31, was convicted by an

Lt. William Calley Jr., left is escorted by Sgt. Stevens to the post stockade at Fort Benning, Ga., today after he was found guilty of the premeditated murder of Vietnamese civilians.

army court-martial in March 1971, of killing at least 22 unarmed men, women and chil-

dren at My Lai, a small hamlet in South Vietnam.

After the former platoon leader had served one year of a 10-year sentence, a federal judge reversed the conviction last Sept. 25 on the grounds Calley has since been free on bond while the army appeals the reversal.

Calley was not asked on the program about specific events surrounding the My Lai massacre, nor was he queried about the partial release Nov. 23 by the army of its own investigation of the incident. He declined all requests for interviews before or after the program.

Calley's television appearance was in connection with a coming dramatization of his court-martial in a Sunday night ABC program entitled Judgment: The Court-Martial of Lieut. William Calley.

DRAFT-DODGERS GIVEN PARDON

Carter's First Command
WASHINGTON.

JANUARY 21, 1977 (AP) — In his first executive order, President Carter today fulfilled his campaign promise and granted a full and unconditional pardon to all Vietnam draft evaders who were not involved in any violent act.

Many of the draft dodgers are in Canada. A number of them have been anxiously awaiting the Carter move in order to return home without facing any penalties.

Those ineligible for the pardon included military deserters and servicemen given less than honorable discharges. The White House said the president has ordered the Pentagon to study the cases of these men.

Press secretary Jody Powell said there are "no good estimates of the number (of persons) that might be affected" by the pardon but that it is probably "well up to the hundreds of thousands, including people who failed to register for the draft." There are an unknown number of persons whose failure to register has never come to officials attention.

Draft evaders who now are overseas may return home under Carter's action, Powell said.

Those who have become citizens of another country can come home to visit families "without fear of prosecution," but if they wish to regain American citizenship they will have to apply under the same terms and conditions as any other alien, he said.

Right Ended

Carter's pardon included an order that the government "forever give up its right to prosecute" any of the draft evaders covered, Powell said. the Carter administration was taking "an abundance of caution" in doing this, so that no future attorney-general could reinstate prosecution and so that the draft evaders need have no fear of future jeopardy.

Draft evaders who joined a re-entry clemency program set up by President Ford's administration are automatically pardoned, too, under the terms of this proclamation and they would no longer be required to continue service jobs, Powell said.

1970-1979

OKANAGAN NEWS

Expansion Of Winery Apace With Demands

APRIL 29, 1972. — Increased demand for top quality Okanagan wines has necessitated a $250,000 expansion program to Casabello Wines in Penticton.

"This will increase the estimated value of the firm to about $1 million," said firm general manager T. Evans Lougheed.

He said the extension program is tentatively scheduled to start this year.

Casabello Wines, founded by Mr. Lougheed and Jim Dawson of Cawston, has grown to a firm composed of 40 shareholders.

"The majority of shares are owned by Penticton residents," said Mr. Lougheed.

During the initial stages of the company, five people were involved. At present, it has 21 on its payroll: two in the testing laboratories, six in wine production, six in the bottling department, four in the office and four in sales.

Must Become Realistic About Sex Education

There's No Baby Under Those Cabbage Leaves

By Sonni Bone

JULY 22, 1972. — It would seem only cabbageheads could believe babies come from cabbage patches.

Yet, many such fallacies about childbirth still exist. That is why Mrs. Ann Mason, senior public health nurse who heads Penticton Family Planning Centre, often begins her sex education program for students by lifting up a cabbage and saying: "See no baby!"

"I am for the wanted child," says Mrs. Mason. "I see the tragedy of so many who are not wanted. That is why I feel people should have all information available on family planning methods and devices, and then make their own decisions."

Most Ambitious Moon Shot Coming With Last Apollo

CAPE KENNEDY, FLA. (AP) — Now comes the last Apollo, the end of an unparalleled era of exploration in which man opened the gateway to the limitless frontier of space.

Apollo 17 next month will carry three more American astronauts to the vicinity of the moon, and two of them will walk the surface. When they come back, it may be 25 years or more before man treads again the dusty lunar soil.

Navy Capt. Eugene A. Cernan, who will command the final Apollo, says the flight is "not the end of space exploration, but the beginning of man's coming together and maybe accepting the challenge to gain knowledge far beyond the moon."

"That's the message we hope to get across on this last mission."

Apollo 17 will be the most ambitious of the moon-landing journeys.

The start will be spectacular. The United States for the first time will launch a manned spaceship at night, with liftoff set for 9:53 p.m. EST Dec. 6. The launch time for the Saturn V booster rocket was dictated by the relative positions of earth and moon and by location of the landing site.

Cernan's crew members are navy Cmdr. Ronald E. Evans and Dr. Harrison H. (Jack) Schmitt, a geologist – the first scientist-astronaut selected for a space flight.

Fill In Gaps

Schmitt and Cernan hope to learn about the early evolution of the moon and of its more recent history, filling in missing chapters on how the moon, and perhaps the earth and solar system, evolved.

Evans in orbit and Cernan and Schmitt on the surface will operate a new generation of sophisticated instruments as they seek secrets of this alien world.

Said Cernan, who will be making his third space flight and the second to the vicinity of the moon:

"We'll be the last men to visit the moon for perhaps a decade or a quarter century."

"Some people talk about it as if it's the end of space. That's not true – Skylab and the shuttle lie ahead."

"But it is the last flight presently planned to fly into what you might call deep space. But to me Apollo 17 is just the conclusion of the beginning …

Now that we've learned to crawl, Apollo 17 says … let's set our sights deeper into space.

Cernan and Schmitt are to land their lunar ship in a narrow valley at a site named Taurus-Littrow in the northeast quadrant of the moon on the rim of the Sea of Serenity.

Won't Be Easy

"It's going to be no piece of cake landing here, but we'll make it," says Cernan.

"We hope here to find some of the youngest and also some of the oldest material on the moon," Schmitt said.

"We may get all the way back to the beginning of the moon 4.6 billion years ago."

The youngest rocks collected so far "are on the order of three to 3.2 billion years," with the oldest "at least" 4.1 billion years old.

"So we have a portion of the history of the moon, you might even say of the history of the solar system, that ranges between three and four billion years."

"Two chapters are essentially missing – the first and the last. At Taurus-Littrow, Gene and I hope to fill in those missing chapters."

The geologist-astronaut said the oldest rock found on earth, in western Greenland, was 3.7 billion years old.

Crash Survivors Ate Dead

From AP-Reuter
SANTIAGO, CHILE (CP) — Despair and anger followed the disclosure that some of the 16 survivors of an Andean air crash fed on their dead companions to stay alive.

Official sources on Tuesday disclosed the cannibalism among the young Uruguayan men during their 69-day ordeal on an icy mountain ledge.

A dozen of the survivors staying at a local hotel "were very depressed and went to their rooms immediately" when everyone told their stories, a hotel employee said.

One newspaper used the headline "Cannibalism Justified" with a subtitle asking "What would you have done?"

The 16 were among 45 persons aboard a Uruguayan air force plane that crashed in the Andes Oct. 13. All of the passengers were either players on a Montevideo rugby team or fans.

The survivors spoke freely with reporters earlier about everything except their food supply. They said 18 were killed in the crash or died of injuries, 8 more died in an avalanche Oct. 29 and the last three died in November and early December of injuries or undernourishment.

Most relatives and friends of the survivors refused to discuss the cannibalism but Domitila de Paez said the reports "soil the grandest miracle of history." She is the mother of Carlos Paez, 20, one of the survivors.

Another survivor who has returned to Montevideo, Daniel Franandez Strauch said: "I prefer not to speak of it, it is a sad incident."

Cesar Charlone, the Uruguayan charge d'affaires in Santiago, said the survivors had made a "solemn pact" to say nothing until they had all returned to Uruguay. There, he said, they planned to make a joint statement.

1970~1979

Death Of Pearson Mourned By Nation

OTTAWA (CP) —

Lester Bowles Pearson, the quiet, likable diplomat who won the Noble Peace Prize and became prime minister died Wednesday night, the victim of cancer.

The 75-year-old former Liberal party leader, prime minister from 1963 to 1968, died at 8:40 p.m. PST, just three days after he cut short a Florida vacation to return Christmas Eve. His condition deteriorated rapidly and throughout Wednesday he was in a coma caused by cancer of the liver.

He was operated on two years ago for a tumor that cost him his right eye, he had returned to hospital about a month ago for renewed treatments.

But the gravity of his condition was not know until he was flown home on a government aircraft with his wife, Maryon.

Mr. Pearson whose personal popularity tended to transcend all political considerations will be buried at Wakefield, Que, an area he grew to love while at the prime ministerial summer home at nearby Harrington Lake following a state funeral at Christ Church Anglican cathedral here.

The date will be announced later.

His death closed an era, spanned the launching of the country's own foreign service in the 1920s increasingly independent of traditional British ties, and Mr. Pearson's decision to provide Canada's own distinctive maple leaf flag achieved in time for the country's 100th birthday in 1967.

He forecast, well before it became a fact of Canadian life, that relations with the United States would become increasingly complex, never again to be taken for granted.

Lester B. Pearson

Harry Truman Dies Tuesday

INDEPENDENCE, MO. (AP) —

For the final time, Harry Truman today travels the half mile from his home to the presidential library that bears his name.

And the country he led from war into the chill of an uneasy peace will have a day of morning Thursday to commemorate the man whose dearest wish was to be known as "The people's president."

Richard M. Nixon, the 37th president of the United States and Lyndon B. Johnson, the 36th, were to be at the library today to bid farewell to the 33rd.

But mostly the honor paying last respects is reserved for close family and friends and the ordinary people with whom Truman so strongly identified in his 88 years.

There will be little of the pageantry of other state funerals for the former president who died Tuesday. In keeping with Mrs.

Truman's wishes, once-elaborate plans were scrapped for rites with simple dignity.

A memorial service is to be held in Washington's National Cathedral within a week after Congress reconvenes Jan. 3 for the dignitaries who could not be accommodated here.

President Nixon ordered all but essential government agencies closed Thursday and flags to half staff for 30 days.

Mrs. Truman, daughter Margaret and her family, and close friends were to be at a private service in the Carson funeral parlor this morning.

The 87-year-old Mrs. Truman, dubbed "The Boss" by her husband, was in seclusion Tuesday after word of the former president's death reached her by telephone. But a family friend, Randall Jessee, said she was calm and composed.

TODAY'S NEWS TODAY
IN THE OKANAGAN'S YEAR-ROUND CONVENTION CITY

The Herald is the only daily newspaper printed on the same day it is circulated in Penticton. For home delivery phone Penticton, 492-4002; Summerland, 494-4319.

VOL. LXVI. — No. 205

Penticton Herald

Penticton, British Columbia, Thursday, August 31, 1972

15c Per Copy
65c Per Week Home Delivered

12 Pages

WEATHER FORECAST

PENTICTON HIGH LOW

B.C. SHIFTS TO NDP

Victoria (CP) – The New Democratic Party turned British Columbia politics upside down Wednesday night in an upset provincial election victory that trampled W.A.C. Bennett's Social Credit party into minuscule opposition.

Premier-elect Dave Barrett, 41, led the New Democrats out of nowhere in an unparalleled rampage through the Social Credit ranks as 11 cabinet ministers went down to defeat.

Standings following B.C.'s 30th general election (with one seat still in doubt) and following the Aug. 27, 1969 election.

	1972	1969
NDP	28	12
SC	20	28
L	5	5
PC	2	0
Total	55	55

At dissolution of the 55-member legislature July 24 the standings were Social Credit 36, NDP 12, Liberals 5 and Progressive Conservatives 2.

Barrett, Bennett Rest Before Switching Jobs

VICTORIA (CP) — British Columbia's victor and vanquished Premier-elect Dave Barrett of the New Democratic Party and Social Credit Premier W.A.C. Bennett dropped from public view Thursday but are to switch jobs early next week.

Mr. Barrett, whose party swept to power Wednesday by winning 28 seats in the 55-seat legislature, was off on a Labor Day weekend fishing trip with his wife Shirley and their three children. His press secretary said he would hold a news conference early next week to outline his plans and announce his cabinet.

The defeated premier who held office 20 years through seven elections, stayed at home in Kelowna, only leaving his house for a drive alone through the streets of the Okanagan community where he settled more than 30 years ago.

His aides said he would stay there during the long weekend then return to Victoria for a meeting with his cabinet.

Eleven of his ministers suffered personal defeat in the NDP sweep.

He is expected then to submit his resignation as premier to Lieutenant-Governor John Nicholson, who would in turn call on Mr. Barrett to form the government.

Social Credit's representation in the B.C. legislature was cut to 10 from 36 while the NDP jumped to 28 from 12. The Liberals remained at five seats while the PCs stayed at two.

Choking Tears Back W.A.C. Steps Down

VANCOUVER (CP) —

On the eve of today's Social Credit leadership vote to choose his successor, W.A.C. Bennett, former British Columbia premier, choked back tears as he told delegates he could take hecklers, brickbats and criticism "but this praise I've never been able to stand."

"I'm glad my critics didn't find my weakness until I was about to retire," said Mr. Bennett, who headed the Social Credit government for 20 years.

In an emotional half-hour speech Friday night, the former premier told delegates that after he handed over the party leadership today to one of the six candidates "I will be a private in the ranks" and his first priority would be to increase the party membership.

He didn't endorse any of the candidates, who include his son Bill, 41, but said: "I'm more optimistic for our party, for our province, for our nation than ever in my life before."

He said his party, which suffered a crushing defeat at the hands of the New Democratic Party in the August, 1972, provincial election, was on the march again in B.C. "The public wants us back, but we've got to deserve to be back."

Five are members

Five of the 10 Social Credit members in the 55-seat legislature are contesting the leadership. The other candidate is Burnaby accountant James Mason.

W.A.C. Bennett

Photo courtesy of Kelowna Museum

voting delegates at the convention Friday.

All six candidates, in their opening statements Friday, presented a united front, attacking the NDP rather than each other. All stressed the need to rebuild the party, to bring in fresh blood and to offer to the voters a strong "free-enterprise" alternative to the NDP.

The other contenders are Langley MLA Bob McClelland, 40; Chilliwack MLA Harvey Schroeder, 40; Columbia River MLA James Chabot, 46; and North Peace River MLA Ed Smith, 47.

W.A.C. Bennett left the Liberal-Conservative coalition government in 1951 to sit as an independent in the legislature. In 1952 he joined Social Credit and was elected leader the same year by the Social Credit caucus.

He said it wasn't a miracle that Social Credit was defeated in 1972. It was a miracle that the party won seven straight elections.

Mr. Bennett said socialism had swept Manitoba, Saskatchewan and now it was in B.C.

"West of us is the Pacific, the widest ocean in the world. They can't swim, so they've got to fight.

"This is where the battle is going to take place."

Bill Bennett, who won his father's Okanagan South riding in a September by-election, appeared headed to take over the party leadership as well from his 73-year-old father.

He drew uproarious applause after a brief speech to the 1,194

1970~1979

Nixon Leaves Without Immunity

WASHINGTON (AP) —

Richard Nixon leaves the presidency without immunity from prosecution, leaving him vulnerable to a host of criminal charges that range across the breadth of scandal that emerged in the two years since the Watergate break-in.

The lead role in bringing an indictment against Nixon after he leaves office would fall to special Watergate prosecutor Leon Jaworski, who said Thursday night there has been no deal sparing Nixon from prosecution in exchange for his resignation.

Congress might pass a resolution urging that no charges be brought against Nixon. Such a resolution is not binding by law; it only expresses the feelings of members of Congress.

Nixon's resignation may have squelched what little support there was for such a resolution.

The chief sponsor, Senator Edward Brooke (Rep. Mass.) said Thursday night he would withdraw the resolution unless Nixon makes a "full confession" of his involvement in Watergate and related scandals. After Nixon made his speech, Brooke said that Nixon acknowledged "errors of judgment but did not state what the errors in judgment are."

By resigning, Nixon apparently saved himself from impeachment by the House of Representatives and trial in the Senate. Congress has the authority to proceed with impeachment even though Nixon no longer holds office, but House leaders said Thursday night there is no need to carry it through.

"The House may have to take

Richard Nixon says goodbye to members of his staff outside the White House as he boards a helicopter for Andrews Air Force Base after resigning the Presidency Aug. 9, 1974.

(AP Photo)

some action, but the president having resigned, the proceedings will have to come to an end," speaker Carol Albert said.

Nevertheless, Albert and judiciary committee members were moving toward a House vote on the committee report detailing the allegations against Nixon.

Gerald Ford, upon becoming president, is the only other person who could block the trial of his predecessor. He would have the authority to grant Nixon a full pardon for all crimes in advance, even in the absence of formal

charges and conviction.

Ford, however, gave no hint of his intentions.

Nixon's resignation strips him of the shield of office that once apparently blocked his indictment on charges of conspiracy and obstruction of justice.

The Watergate grand jury named Nixon as an unindicted co-conspirator when it indicted his former White House and campaign aides for conspiring to cover up the Watergate scandal and obstruct the original investigation.

Ford Takes Office As Nixon Resigns

Gerald Ford ...38th U.S. president

WASHINGTON (AP) — Gerald Ford became the 38th president of the United States today and told Americans "our long national nightmare is over."

"Our Constitution works," Ford said as he assumed the office of the resigned Richard Nixon. "Our great republic is a government of laws and not of men."

At 9:03 a.m. PDT, Ford pronounced the oath of office Nixon was accused of violating in the Watergate scandals.

He was president already; Nixon's resignation was delivered at 8:35 a.m. PDT, and with it, the powers of office passed automatically to Ford.

Ford said he will ask to appear before a joint session of Congress on Monday night to discuss "my views on the priority business of the nation."

"As we bind up the wounds to Watergate, let us restore the golden rule to our political process," Ford said.

Ford said his first speech as president will be no political oration.

"I assume the presidency under extraordinary circumstances never before experienced by America," Ford said. "This is an hour of history that troubles our minds and hurts our hearts..."

Never before had a president resigned; never before had an appointed vice-president succeeded to the country's highest office.

Nixon's Adieu Tearful Scene

2,027 Days End

WASHINGTON (CP) — Spinning out the last act of a shattered presidency, Richard Nixon bid a tearful, choking adieu to the men and women of his administration today before flying off to his San Clemente home in California.

At times his voice cracked as he made his last White House speech, urging those who remained behind to do their best and assuring them that only when a man has hit the deepest valley can he realize "how magnificent it is to be on the highest mountain."

Tears streaming down his face, he said "now we look to the future."

He quoted a passage from a book he said he read during his last night in the White House – a story about a young lawyer from New York whose daughter died.

"It was written by Theodore Roosevelt in his 20s," Nixon said. "He thought the light had gone from his life forever, but he went on."

"This house has a great heart and the heart comes from those who serve," Nixon told his associates, gathered in the East Room of the White House.

Family With Him

With the president, as he received more than five minutes of applause, were Mrs. Nixon, his daughters Julie and Tricia and their husbands.

The chieftains of his shattered administration were there, too: State Secretary Henry Kissinger, Defence Secretary James Schlesinger, his Watergate lawyer James St. Clair.

Nixon and his wife walked on a red carpet from the White House to a waiting helicopter and began

"THAT'S FUNNY — IT WASN'T THIS LONG BEFORE WATERGATE"

their journey to the California home that is the western White House no more.

One last time, as he stepped into the helicopter, the resigning president waved the two-handed V for victory sign he had flashed so many times before from hundreds of political platforms.

Four Found Guilty By Watergate Jury

WASHINGTON (AP) — A United States court jury has concluded another chapter in the Watergate story by convicting three of Richard Nixon's most powerful aides of conspiring to obstruct the investigation of the break-in at Democratic national committee headquarters in the Watergate building here.

Found guilty of conspiracy, obstruction of justice and perjury were former attorney-general John Mitchell and ex-White House aides H.R. Haldeman and John Ehrlichman.

Also convicted of conspiracy was former assistant attorney general Robert Maridan.

The jury acquitted Kenneth Parkinson, a Washington lawyer who represented the Nixon re-election committee, of conspiracy and obstruction of justice.

The four men convicted were expected to seek reversal of the decision in the U.S. Court of Appeals.

Turner Oil Plan Remains In Dark

OTTAWA (CP) —

Finance Minister John Turner called Thursday for major domestic oil price increases but left the Commons baffled on how the government plans to raise the prices.

Higher prices are needed to ensure development of new oil sources and to pay for the high-cost secondary recovery methods needed to pump more oil from conventional wells, he said. But he gave no indication of specific steps planned to change the domestic pricing system.

Domestic oil is frozen by agree-

ment with oil-producing companies at about $4 a barrel, less than one-third the going rate on international markets, and the government is committed to maintaining the freeze until the end of the winter heating season.

The freeze took effect in September.

At the same time, the government imposed a crude oil export tax to ensure that Canadian oil was sold on the export market at going international rates.

The tax, effective since Oct. 1, was pegged initially at 40 cents a barrel, raised Dec. 1 to $1.90, to

John Turner

$2.20 Jan. 1 and is scheduled to hit $6.40 a barrel Feb. 1.

Mr. Turner spoke as the House began debate on a bill to formally approve the levy.

Oil Crisis Warning Sparks Fleet Watch

WASHINGTON (AP) — A powerful navy carrier fleet sailed toward the Indian Ocean today as rumbling persisted over State Secretary Henry Kissinger's interpreted warning of possible U.S. military action in an oil emergency.

The six-ship study mission, led by the 85,000-ton nuclear-powered aircraft carrier Enterprise, was expected to enter the Indian Ocean

within a few days after a voyage from Subic Bay in the Philippines.

Sources said the carrier, the nuclear propelled cruiser Long Beach, two destroyers, a supply ship and an oiler were bound for the Indian Ocean.

Pentagon spokesman William Beecher said Tuesday the group is on an operational mission, but denied reports it is bound for waters off South Vietnam, where

government troops have been reeling under Communist attack.

The White House affirmed the Pentagon statement. At the same time, President Ford was described as watching developments in South Vietnam closely.

Congress has banned any U.S. bombing or other military action in Indochina. Any such move would require prior congressional approval, officials said.

Zurich Gold Trading Soars To Record High

ZURICH (AP) —

The price of gold soared to an all-time high of $147 an ounce today on the Zurich market in the wake of mounting indications that central banks in Western Europe may soon increase the official price.

Opening prices on the Zurich bullion market, the world's biggest, were $145 bid and $147 offered, up from $142 - $144 Friday.

The previous record price in Zurich was $143 Jan. 25.

The bullish weekend trend was touched off by reports from Johannesburg, the mining centre for the West's gold, that a consortium of West European countries, including France, Italy and perhaps West Germany, might begin buying at a price related to the free market price.

The trend picked up because of an interview published today in

which French Finance Minister Valery Giscard d'Estaing said he expected an increase in the official price of gold this year.

The dual price system for gold, with an official price set by government central banks and a free market price for trading by private persons and firms, was terminated last November but governments have continued to buy at the official price at that time, $42.22 an ounce.

ACCORD WORKED OUT ON PIPELINE LANDS

JANUARY 9, 1974. JUNEAU, ALASKA (AP) — Alaska and the United States government have worked out an agreement in their dispute about land control along the trans-Alaska pipeline corridor that will allow the project to get under way soon, state officials say.

Charles Herbert, commissioner of natural resources, said Tuesday the agreement deals primarily with surveillance of construction work and it opens the way for issuance of a project permit by the interior department, possibly by next week.

The permit would allow oil companies to move vast quantities of machinery and material into place for a spring construction start.

Title to parcels of land along the 789-mile corridor has been in question since the project was conceived four years ago, and it remains so even under the new agreement.

The agreement merely calls for issuance of necessary right-of-way permits by both state and federal agencies.

'What Now?' U.S. Asked

Energy Independence Plan Eyed By Canada

JANUARY 31, 1974. WASHINGTON (CP) — Energy Minister Donald Macdonald said today he is keenly interested in determining whether the United States really plans to do without Canadian energy in its long-range striving for self-sufficiency.

Macdonald told a reporter as he opened talks with U.S. energy chief William Simon that he watched President Nixon's State of the Union speech on television Wednesday and noted Nixon's reiteration of Operation Independence.

"One thing we want to clarify this morning is the extent to which the administration sees Canada as one of the foreign suppliers from which it wants to become independent," Macdonald said.

If the U.S. wants to end its reliance on Canadian supplies by 1980, along with those of other foreign suppliers, "we want to know that now," Macdonald said.

Nations Pool Brains To Fight Oil Crisis

FEBRUARY 11, 1974. WASHINGTON (CP) — The 13-country conference of major oil consumers today called for an early meeting with the oil-producing countries to help resolve the world energy crisis.

This agreed approach by the United States, Canada, Japan and the nine-country European Common Market raised hopes that the two-day conference would end Tuesday on a constructive note.

Canada's 1973 inflation was worst in 22 years

OTTAWA (NP) — Higher fuel costs were a major factor in pushing up living costs in December to round out 1973 inflation as the worst in 22 years, Statistics Canada reported today.

The only bright note in last month's six-tenths of one per cent rise in consumer prices was that grocery price rises halted after a sharp year-long climb that food costs more up 17 per

of imported crude oil. These contributed to increases of eight-tenths of one per cent each in housing and transportation costs.

"Fuel oil prices rose, on average, seven per cent as a result of increases in eastern Ontario, Quebec and the Atlantic provinces and rates for domestic gas increased in some centres," Statistics Canada said.

"An advance of 1.4 per cent in

up 19 per cent over the year.

OIL PRICE VARIES

Prices of oil products west of the Ottawa Valley where Canadian crude oil is used by refineries have been frozen by a voluntary agreement between the federal government and petroleum companies. But eastern prices have risen as Arab nations more than doubled the costs of imported oil.

Although supermarket prices were unchanged in December,

156.4 on its 1961 base of 100. The index was 155.5 in November.

The figures mean it took $156.40 per week last month to pay for typical family living costs including food, housing, transportation, clothing, health and personal care, recreation and education, tobacco and alcohol. That was 90 cents a week more than the month before, $13.10 more than a year earlier and $56.40 per week more than a dozen years ago

dry, dry cleaning and shoe repair.

In addition to higher heating oil costs, the housing increase included rises of 1.6 per cent for appliances and six-tenths of one per cent for furniture. Over-all housing costs were up 7.2 per cent for the year.

TRAIN FARES UP

Higher transportation costs, besides gasoline and motor oil increases, were due to train and

last month, and was 2.4 per cent above a year ago

Health and personal care costs rose two-tenths of one per cent in December because of scattered increases for medicines, toiletries and men's haircuts. This category was up 6.1 per cent for the year.

Although grocery prices on average were unchanged last month, there were increases for some items, the report said.

"Higher price levels in the

and fish fell six-tenths of one per cent as poultry and pork prices went down, on average, 4.2 per cent and 1.5 per cent respectively, thus outweighing an advance of seven-tenths of one per cent in the beef index," Statistics Canada said.

EGGS UP

Egg prices rose 1.2 per cent in December and were 40 per cent higher than a year earlier

Processed fruits and vege-

clined fractionally in the latest month, the cereal and bakery products index rose six-tenths of one per cent because of continued price increases for macaroni, breakfast cereal, cookies and cake," Statistics Canada said.

Margarine prices rose almost three per cent in December, contributing largely to the year's 18 per cent increase for fats and oils. Dairy products rose two-tenths of one per cent in

Prices On Rise At Record Pace

OTTAWA (CP) —

Another sharp rise in grocery prices led a one per cent rise in living costs in February, escalating the inflation rate to an increasingly faster pace than last year's 22-year record, Statistics Canada reported today.

Groceries climbed 2.6 per cent last month, and included sharply higher prices for beef, potatoes and sugar products, it said. All other major price categories – housing, clothing, transportation, health-personal care and recreation-reading – averaged five-tenths of one per cent higher, the report said.

The latest increase pushed living costs 9.6 per cent higher than a year earlier, approaching the 10 per cent inflation rate that many eco-

nomic analysts have predicted for 1974. Living costs rose 9.1 per cent in all of 1973.

The February increases brought the government's consumer price index up to 159.2 from 157.6 for January.

The figure means it cost $159.20 per week last month to pay for typical family living costs. That was $1.60 more than the month before, $13.90 more than a year earlier and $59.20 more than the 1961 period on which the index is based.

Put another way, the value of the 1961 dollar has declined to 63 cents in the 13-year period and six cents of the decline has been in the past year alone.

February's one per cent rise in over-all living costs followed an

increase of eight-tenths of one per cent in January, and if that rate of rise continues for the balance of 1974 it would total 10.8 per cent by the end of the year.

February's grocery price rise was more than double January's increase and brought food prices up 17.2 per cent more than a year earlier.

The only declines noted in the report were 1.9 per cent for pork and 4.8 per cent for eggs.

Over the year, beef prices were up 34 per cent, poultry 25 per cent, eggs 26 per cent and sugar almost 60 per cent, the report said.

Alcoholic beverages rose 2.5 per cent in February and were four per cent higher for the year.

Housing costs rose six-tenths of

one per cent in February because of increases for new houses, mortgage interest, home repairs, rents, electricity rate in some areas and furniture prices. Housing was seven per cent higher than a year earlier.

Clothing prices increased five-tenths of one per cent in February and were up 8.3 per cent for the year. Last month's increases were due to higher prices for synthetic fabrics, cotton and wool, Statistics Canada said.

Transportation costs rose two-tenths of one per cent in February, including rises of 3.4 per cent for auto insurance and 1.3 per cent for motor oil. Gasoline declined slightly and a drop in train fares reduced public transportation costs six-tenths of one per cent.

Fans 'Go Ape' Over Gordie

In WHA All-Star

EDMONTON (CP) —

Gordie Howe told everybody the third annual World Hockey Association all-star game would be the last of his distinguished career – then he went out to enjoy it.

Scoring a goal and an assist to spark the West to a 6-4 victory, the first western triumph after two defeats, Howe won a standing ovation from a capacity crowd of 15,326 at the Edmonton Coliseum and accepted his team-mates' tributes after it was over.

"It's hard to say how much Gordie means to hockey," said centre Andre Lacroix, who earned three assists in a brilliant display of puck-handling. "He's the star of every game, just because he's still in it at 46 and because he's the greatest that ever lived."

Howe's goal, one of four in a second period blitz that gave the west an insurmountable 6-2 margin, came on a half-speed backhander that trickled over the line.

"I was trying to pass into the goalmouth," said Howe. "I knew it was in when Andy Brown (Eastern

goaltender) called me a lucky bleep."

The goal gave Howe a bit of an extra kick because he played with Andy's father, forward Adam Brown, early in his pro career.

Howe made it clear his last all-star game was something special. He took his stick home.

'One For The Road'

"Sure, it was fun," he said. "It's nice to wind up with one for the road, but the real highlight was to have the kid score one."

Mark Howe took a flip pass

Gordie Howe
...still wowing 'em

from his father to open scoring in the first period. Forward Mark and defenceman Marty, team-mates with Houston Aeros, gave their father the incentive to come back after a one-year layoff at the age of 44.

SWINE FLU VACCINE

Vaccine Slated For B.C. Oct. 15 Barring Delays

To Combat Swine Flu

SEPTEMBER 21, 1976. VANCOUVER (CP) — Swine flu vaccine will be available in British Columbia after Oct. 15 provided there are no further hitches in manufacture and testing, provincial epidemiologist Dr. A.A. Larsen said Monday.

The first shipment of vaccine is due Oct. 9 and the entire million doses earmarked for B.C. should be in hand by early December, he said, in an interview after a meeting in Vancouver of the provincial health officers subcommittee on communicable diseases.

No Evidence Swine Flu Shots Touched Off Deaths Of Aged

But Eight States Halt Program

OCTOBER 13, 1976. — Medical investigators pressed the hunt today for information about elderly persons in the U.S. who died recently after getting swine flu shots.

Eight states suspended the inoculation program temporarily following three deaths in the Pittsburgh area on Tuesday.

Federal and state health officials stressed that there was no link between the vaccinations and the deaths – 10 in all. They said all the victims were elderly and most had a history of heart trouble.

1970~1979

SEPTEMBER 21, 1976

CP Applies To Abandon Carmi Line

CP Rail announced today it has applied for permission to abandon the 131-mile Kettle Valley line between Penticton and Midway. This will receive opposition from some groups and individuals in Penticton.

CP Rail made known its intention to abandon the line in a press release from Vancouver, noting it has applied to the Canadian Transport commission for authority to drop the line in what is known as the Carmi subdivision on the grounds it is uneconomic.

The release said CP Rail's losses on the line between 1972 and 1974 totalled some $1.5 million. "Traffic has declined drastically since 1970, from 350 carloads, to 32 carloads in 1974," the release states.

The subdivision has been in only partial operation for many years. No trains have operated between Penticton and Beaverdell since June, 1973.

Oliver Psychic's Clue Was 'Incredibly Close'

The description by an Oliver psychic of where Abby Drover might be found was incredibly close to the underground cell where she was discovered Monday night after 181 days of imprisonment, Port Moody police said.

The 60-year-old Oliver resident wrote to Port Moody police on April 5, enclosing numerous maps and drawings.

Const. Wayne Smith, who headed the investigation, said he searched the area described at the time, but found nothing.

"It was just three blocks away from where Abby was found," he said.

Police would not release the name of the psychic. A spokesman for the Oliver RCMP detachment said the man moved from Oliver to Ontario in mid-August, apparently permanently.

Comes Close

"If there were any such thing as psychic phenomena this comes about as close as you can get," said Const. Smith.

The 13-year-old girl was found weak but alive after 181 days in a cell under a neighbor's garage.

She disappeared March 10 while on her way to school. Abby, who turned 13 while captive, was held in a six-foot square room, believed to have been built in the 1960's as a nuclear bomb shelter.

Donald Alexander Hay, 43, of Port Moody, has been charged with kidnapping, rape, gross indecency and unlawfully taking away a female person against her will with intent to have illicit sexual relations with her.

Entrance to the cell where the girl was held was by a shaft under a workbench. The shaft was covered by a sheet of plywood with paint cans piled on top of the plywood to make the area look like a paint storage locker.

The psychic maintained that Abby would be found under the floor at the back of an old garage and the drawings sent to police showed the exact spot was covered by a piece of wood under a workbench.

Although the directions were slightly incorrect, Const. Smith said they contained startling similarities to the location where the girl was found.

During Abby's confinement, members of the 21-member Port Moody police force enlisted the aid of Interpol, psychics-dowsers, sex offenders and hundreds of other persons who thought they might help.

The cell was equipped with a bed, cold water sink, radio and chemical toilet, and there were two light chains fastened to the wall at the head of the bed and another fastened to the wall near the sink.

The girl weighed 88 pounds, down from her usual 95 to 100 pounds when she was rescued.

She was occasionally brought some books and cold food from cans, but was never given a hot meal.

She told her mother that she had only a couple of chocolate bars and water during one six-week period when the Hays were apparently away on holiday.

The family was reported to have visited the Okanagan, California and Oregon during that period.

Police found the youngster by a strange stroke of luck. They received a call from Hay's wife saying that she though her husband had barricaded himself in the garage to commit suicide.

Police forced their way into the garage but found no one.

They left, but were called back when Mrs. Hay said she thought her husband was dead.

The officers found Hay climbing up the secret shaft from the cell when they re-entered the garage. They looked down the shaft and heard Abby crying. She climbed up the ladder unassisted.

Although most of the leads turned in about Abby's whereabouts during the 181 days were fruitless, Const. Smith said he had to pursue all of them, including information from psychics.

He said police don't have to believe in such tips, but there is always the possibility that a murderer could pose as a psychic and lead police to the victim.

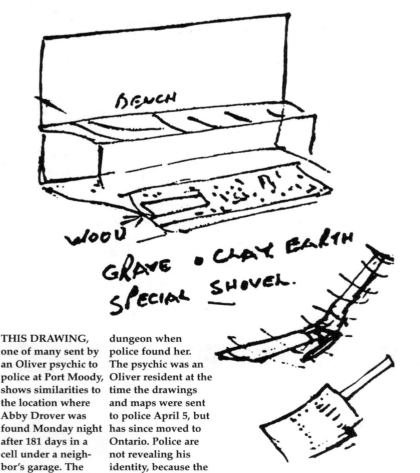

THIS DRAWING, one of many sent by an Oliver psychic to police at Port Moody, shows similarities to the location where Abby Drover was found Monday night after 181 days in a cell under a neighbor's garage. The child emerged weak but alive from the dungeon when police found her. The psychic was an Oliver resident at the time the drawings and maps were sent to police April 5, but has since moved to Ontario. Police are not revealing his identity, because the information was given in confidence.

Chairman Mao Tse-tung Dead

Mao Tse-tung

PEKING (CP) —

Mao Tse-tung, father of the People's Republic of China, died at 12:10 p.m. EDT, Wednesday, the Radio Peking and the official Chinese news agency Hsinhua reported today.

The people of the capital had apparently been prepared for the announcement. Only 30 minutes after the radio solemnly reported that Mao had passed away "because of the worsening of his illness" black armbands appeared on people in the streets.

Grave funeral music followed the announcement and crowds immediately began to gather in Tien Annmen Square in the heart of the capital.

FEBRUARY 21, 1976

"Space Suit" To Free David From Bubble

HOUSTON (AP) —

David, the boy in the germ-free plastic bubble who has never been touched by ungloved human hands, celebrates his fifth birthday today waiting for his most important gift – a "space suit" that will allow him to explore the world outside.

David was born without natural body defences against disease. He suffers from severe combine immune deficiency (SCIDS), an inherited disorder that strikes about one in every 10,000 males. Doctors said the simplest of germs could kill him.

David was placed in the germ-free environment seconds after birth, and his last name has been kept secret by his parents and hospital officials.

Normal in other respects, David runs around inside his nine-by-seven-foot bubble and plays with a ball and several plastic toys. Doctors say he displays consider-able curiosity about the world outside.

His space suit should be ready in December. Officials at the Johnson Space Center and Texas Children's Hospital said Monday the legal documents authorizing David's space suit have been signed, ending more than two years of negotiations that began after space officials were asked to study the possibility of adapting space technology and hardware to extend the boy's environment.

The suit, called Mobile Biological Isolation System, consists of a rubberized garment with a soft transparent plastic helmet. It is connected by a 10-foot-long air hose to a transporter-ventilator mounted on a pushcart.

The system provides a sterile environment which will allow David to make excursions of at least four hours outside his bubble.

He now divides his time between the plastic-walled bubble at the hospital and an identical germ-free bubble at home, travelling between the two in a special van.

David's medical care is paid by a federal grant to Baylor College of Medicine's Research Centre at Texas Children's Hospital.

Baylor now describes David as a "healthy, physically active child and the oldest immune deficient patient in medical history to survive without reconstitution of the body's protective systems."

Doctors have said he is well developed physically, mentally and emotionally.

His curiosity about the outside world began more than two years ago on a visit home. After watching his father working around the house, David said:

"You let me get out of this bubble and I'll help you."

Scientists are still trying to find a cure that will allow David to leave his plastic bubble forever.

1970~1979

Demonstrators Flood Parliament Grounds

OTTAWA (CP) –

Demonstrators, totalling perhaps 1,000 gathered before the Parliament buildings today as part of a national day-long protest by organized labor against the anti-inflation program.

The gathering was much smaller than had been forecast by some organizers, and participants grouped in the windy chill of Parliament Hill, thick with RCMP riot squad personnel.

The now usual steel barricades confronted the demonstrators, who carried placards with the names of scores of unions and labor associations.

The relatively small size of the turnout indicated that few members of public service unions took part.

Downtown Parade, Rally Mark Protest In City

Amana Radarange MICROWAVE OVEN

The first microwave oven with a memory. Makes microwave cooking as easy as 1-2-3!

The Amana Touchmatic Radarange Oven with Cookmatic Power Shift is the king of Amana Radarange Ovens with these great features fit for a queen

- **Exclusive Touchmatic Computerized Controls—**
  Remembers what you tell it to do by touching numbers and words on the control panel.
  Remembers...how long to defrost
  Remembers...to wait for food temperature to equalize.
  Remembers...just how long to cook
  Remembers...to shut itself off and call you for dinner with a pleasant beep
  Remembers...to display the time of day when cooking is completed. In lights!
- **Exclusive Cookmatic Power Shift**
  Puts you in full control of everything you cook. Easy to use. Just slide the shift to the appropriate position for the precise speed of cooking you desire. Even keeps dinner warm until you're ready
- Stainless steel interior... large enough for a family size turkey
- See-through window and interior light so you can see what's cooking

DEMONSTRATIONS
(Kelowna Store Only)
Friday, July 15th, and Saturday, July 16th
10 A.M. - 4 P.M. Both Days
See the RR9 in Action!

do it NOW! **$829.00** ea.

By Ron Watmough
Staff Reporter

Labor's national day of protest was orderly in Penticton with about half the 3,000 organized workers off the job.

The mid-morning parade of the South Okanagan-Boundary Labor Council down Martin St. had about 115 marchers, including some who had been carrying placards as pickets at businesses.

The parade, led by a pair of workers carrying the Canadian flag, moved down Main St. at 10 a.m. to Lakeshore Dr. west on Lakeshore to Martin St. and south on Martin to the Royal Canadian Legion. Dick Larson, Canadian Labor Congress representative, addressed the post-parade gathering.

Penticton's total work force, organized and non-organized, according to Canada Manpower is about 12,000. About 43 per cent of the province's labor force is organized but the percentage is lower than that for Penticton.

Construction was generally quiet, although about half the crew was working at the Atco mobile home plant construction site.

There was no work being done on the Kinsman and Company building across from city hall but brick masons were working on the commercial building across from the liquor store on Martin St. The liquor store was closed and was being picketed this morning.

City Hall

Pickets were also out this morning at city hall, which rescheduled hours from 1 to 3 p.m. as staff observed the day of protest.

Kelowna's Athans Ends Water-Skiing Career

MONTREAL (CP) —

George Athans says he is looking for new fields to conquer after retiring from the competitive water-skiing career that helped put Canada on the map in the sport.

"The first and most important reason for getting out is that I established goals for myself a long time ago and I've reached them all," Athans, the first skier to win consecutive world titles, said in an interview.

"I don't think I'm retiring from my involvement in the sport, but I am going to retire from active competition."

The 24-year old native of Kelowna, B.C., was Canadian champion for more than a decade. In that time he won two world titles, in 1971 and 1973, as well as the United States Masters crown.

"While the sport allows me to cover my expenses, which are in the neighborhood of $20,000 a year, it's hard for me to ski and study and accomplish the other things I'd like to do with my life."

A series of injuries to his left knee have also restricted his activity. He first injured the knee in a jumping competition in California in early 1975.

With training and rehabilitation, he was able to ski in the Ontario-Quebec Challenge Cup, where he reinjured the knee, keeping him out of the 1975 World Championships in London.

Last June, he tore ligaments in the knee the day before he was to take part in the Canadian superstars competition, a television sports feature.

"Going into Superstars I was more motivated than at any other time in my life," Athans recalled. "I probably wanted to prove to everyone that water-skiing involved more than just dragging behind a boat with a girl hanging on your shoulders on a Sunday afternoon."

Athans is studying manage-ment, marketing and advertising courses at McGill to supplement the degree he earned at Sir George Williams University here.

He once was interested in the promotion of athletes and last year served as manager for his brother Greg, the U.S. freestyle snow-skiing champion.

Athans often is asked if he thinks he chose the wrong sport, and he admits that some considerations might have led him elsewhere.

"From a financial standpoint, water-skiing certainly hasn't supplied the secure base that tennis, hockey or some of the other major sports could."

"But you have to look at a sport in its totality. Water-skiing gave me a great education travelling around the world."

City coffee shops try to hold prices

Despite cost increases

City restaurants and coffee shops will try to hold the line on coffee prices despite jumps in the price of bulk coffee and indications of future increases during 1977.

All restaurant managers contacted by the Herald indicated they plan no immediate price increases for a cup of coffee, while a few said a change would take place in the policy of providing refills to customers.

The manager of the catering department at the Three Gables Hotel, Joseph Nagy, said the hotel has made no move on the matter and will not until "it is absolutely necessary."

Coffee at the Three Gables costs 30 cents a cup with no charge for a refill.

"We think of the free refills as a tradition of service to the customer and will continue to keep their cups full as long as it is economically possible," said Mr. Nagy.

He said that coffee cannot be sold for a loss should the prices climb as high as some people have said they might.

A Vancouver coffee merchant, John Murchie, has predicted that the price of coffee could go as high as $6 a pound by the end of the coming summer. A pound of coffee is selling for slightly under $2.50 a pound in Penticton now.

Last May coffee was selling for about $1.60 a pound and was predicted to reach $3 by the end of 1976. Gloomy predictions have called for two separate 85-cent-a-pound increases by the end of February.

Coffee drinkers urged to join price protest

By the Canadian Press

If some consumer groups, particularly in the United States, have their way the familiar question coffee, tea or milk will contain only the latter two words.

Suggestions that consumers reduce coffee drinking as a protest against rising prices have begun to spread across Canada following a fast-growing consumer protest in the United States.

Coffee prices have been rising steadily due, producer sources say, largely to 1975 frost that hit Brazilian plantations, the world's largest exporters of coffee beans.

Consumer anger against the increasing prices found a spokesman last month in Elinor Guggenheimer, consumer affairs minister for New York City, who began a boycott.

Tuesday, Barbara Shand of the Consumer's Association of Canada urged Canadians to resist high prices and switch to less-expensive beverages.

She said she isn't urging an outright boycott, but said the price for coffee is ridiculous.

1970-1979

Reports conflicting on weed kill results

MILFOIL PROBLEM

Wash. State okays lake use of 2,4-D

JULY 4, 1977 — Permission has now been given by Washington State water-weed control authorities to use the herbicide 2,4-D in the control program for Eurasian water milfoil in the state.

Dick Thayer of Oroville, officer in charge of the weed control program, said the permission came following a meeting last week in the state capital involving five state agencies.

Mr. Thayer attended the meeting and showed a color slide presentation of the milfoil situation in the B.C. side of the Okanagan.

"The visual impact was very dramatic and convincing — that an attempt for control must be made immediately" he said.

Mr. Thayer said eight milfoil-infested areas were spotted last week in Osoyoos Lake, from Haynes Point to the Canada-United States border. Osoyoos Lake is an international lake, part in B.C. and part in Washington.

Mr. Thayer said the infestations are relatively small. He said 2,4-D will be used soon in another area of the lake at Boundary Point. Less than 50 pounds of 2,4-D pellets will be used on that weed patch. He said drift from the site will not likely be more than 10 feet so swimming and recreation in the area will not be affected.

Weed Harvesting

JULY 7, 1977 — The Eurasian milfoil water weeds growing in the west side of Skaha Lake are being removed by mechanical means as part of the four-pronged program of weed eradication in Okanagan waters. The program being conducted by the provincial ministry of the environment also includes biological, hydrological and chemical means of controlling the spreading weed problem. Both the mechanical and chemical means have been used to try to cut back the weed growth which has been estimated to now cover 200 acres in Skaha Lake.

Results of 2,4-D use against weeds mixed

There are conflicting reports on whether the herbicide 2,4-D applied to beds of Eurasian water milfoil in Skaha Lake has actually done the job of killing the weeds.

The water investigations branch, in charge of the 2,4-D program, says the weeds are dead or dying. The Okanagan Environmental Coalition says this is not so.

In a late-morning contact with the water investigations branch in Vernon, the Herald learned that first test sample results from Skaha lake silt milfoil, plant material and freshwater clams were favorable to a 100 per cent weed kill, with no significant levels of 2,4-D residue.

The tests were taken four days after 2,4-D was applied to milfoil in Skaha Lake. Karl Marsden, water investigations' branch official in charge of 2,4-D use, said all sediment tests were non-detectable in 2,4-D except one and that was .12 parts per million. Plant material showed 2,4-D uptake between .55 ppm and 9.6 ppm. Most 2,4-D in such application ends up in the plants and the 9.6 ppm is sufficient for 100 per cent weed kill. The tests on freshwater clams revealed no detectable traces of 2,4-D.

Officials of both groups inspected the site before making their comments on the status of the weed kill. Karl Marsden of the water investigations branch, Vernon, covered the site by boat Sunday. Jay Lewis of the environmental coalition was out in a boat Monday inspecting the site.

The coalition estimates 85 per cent of a patch of weeds about 40 yards in diameter was not affected by the addition of the herbicide which was used on about three acres of the lake.

New Shoots

"The weed is definitely alive and is putting out new shoots," said Mr. Lewis.

It is these shoots which break off the weed and float to other parts of the lake where they take root.

Mr. Lewis said the weed patch in question has a few holes in it where the 2,4-D appears to have killed the weed "but for the most part it is still standing and putting out new stems."

"The weeds are dead or dying and some have already decomposed," said Mr. Marsden.

He said the weeds floating on the surface are buoyed up by a flowering structure at the head of the plants. This had already formed before the 2,4-D was applied. Mr. Marsden said this is why it is best to apply the herbicide early in the year. The weeds then just curl up and sink to the bottom.

Says Satisfied

"I'm satisfied with the weed kill in that area. It looks just like it did in test plots last year," said Mr. Marsden.

He said the sequence of the kill is a curling of the tips of the plants in the first one to two days, more severe curling and drooping in the next few days and then decomposition of the stems, and later the leaves, starting in about two weeks after herbicide application.

"In some areas you can see the sand at the bottom where once only weeds could be seen," he added.

Mr. Lewis said "The government essentially has three options to look at now. It can hit the weeds again with the 2,4-D, forget about them and let them spread, or harvest mechanically".

He said he doubted if the herbicide would be used again this summer because it would involve posting beach areas again in the midst of tourist season. Harvesting would make analysis of the results of the eradication program difficult because there would be a question of which method had the most effect in knocking back the spreading weed.

Voices Concern

Mr. Lewis expressed fears that "the government may be preparing the people for another even larger application of 2,4-D in the future.

"I don't know if the massive campaign that is being mentioned for next year will concentrate on mechanical or chemical means of control, but the problem will still be there and something will be done," he continued.

He said people should remember that the four-pronged program to be used against the weeds has to be able to bring their spread under control before eradication becomes a possibility.

Government says 2,4-D worries premature

The provincial government said Monday that complaints by environmentalists about renewed 2,4-D use in British Columbia lakes are premature.

The South Okanagan Environmental Coalition filed a complaint with federal fisheries minister Romeo Leblanc, saying the province has applied for a permit to use 2,4-D on Eurasian milfoil weed in Cultus Lake, near Chilliwack.

The coalition asked Leblanc to ban use of the herbicide anywhere in the Fraser River estuary.

An environment ministry spokesman, however, has denied that any permit application has been made for Cultus Lake or anywhere else in the Fraser Valley. He said the ministry has not yet applied for 1979 permits to use 2,4-D in the Okanagan.

Milfoil appeared in Cultus Lake about two years ago, in nearby Hatzic Lake this past summer, and is expected to show in the Fraser River itself next summer, but so far 2,4-D has not been used on milfoil in the Fraser Valley.

Government officials have neither confirmed nor denied that it will be used in the Valley. The herbicide has been used for the last two summers in Okanagan lakes.

Milfoil battle lost cause

VICTORIA (CP) —

The provincial government has given up any hope of eliminating the Eurasian milfoil weed from Skaha and Okanagan Lakes, Environment Minister Steve Rogers said Wednesday.

Rogers said the only way to combat the weed is to use chemicals, such as 2,4-D, but those chemicals are no longer effective in the two lakes.

"It would appear chemical treatment is out of the question for Lake Okanagan. We can cut it down with mechanical harvesters and clean the beaches off, but as far as eradicating the milfoil, five or six years ago, or even as little as four years ago perhaps we could have turned the tide on it, but now it's not possible".

Rogers said the government will turn over its harvesters to the municipalities of Kelowna and Penticton and will continue to fund projects to combat the weed on a cost-sharing basis.

He said chemical treatment will continue in Wood and Kalamalka Lakes, and any other lakes in the Okanagan water system where the weed takes root.

Environmentalists have protested the use of 2,4-D saying it causes cancer and birth defects.

Protesters of 2,4-D to face RCMP - Mair

Environment Minister Rafe Mair has served notice to opponents of the use of 2,4-D against Eurasian milfoil in the Okanagan lake system that RCMP will be summoned to deal with any incident of obstruction.

Mr. Mair, speaking to a regional Social Credit convention in Richmond at the weekend, said the government would continue to use the chemical even although its application last summer led to confrontations between government employees and protesters.

Mair said the weeds in several Okanagan lakes are too dense to be chemically treated and could only be harvested but 2,4-D will be used in other affected areas.

He said he did not expect there would be a repeat of last year's incidents.

But if there are, "and people obstruct, then of course we'll have to call the RCMP," he added.

In the Penticton area no chemical treatment is planned this year in Skaha Lake but one application is scheduled for Okanagan marina.

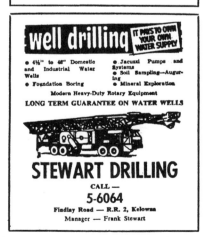

Rock 'N' roll King Elvis dies at age 42

Doctors deny Presley's death was drug-connected

MEMPHIS, TENN. (AP) — Elvis Presley, a one-time truck driver who as a rock 'n' roll singer was idolized by fans and denounced by preachers as the devil's tool, died Tuesday of a heart ailment at age 42.

Dr. George Nichopoulos, long-time physician to the swivel-hipped baritone who was known as the "King of Rock 'n' Roll," said an autopsy revealed a constriction in one of the main arteries to the heart, which restricted blood flow and brought on a heart attack.

"What caused it? Any one of a number of things," he said following Presley's death.

Dr. Nichopoulos said his patient, who carried about 175 pounds on a six-foot frame as a young man but recently had been reported grossly overweight, had been taking a number of appetite depressants, but did not have a drug problem.

Presley's uncle, Vester Presley, chief of security at Elvis' Graceland mansion, said today that the singer's father, Vernon, has decided to open the casket for public viewing between 3 p.m. and 5 p.m.

Jim Stewart, night supervisor at Memphis Funeral Home, said the body would be taken to Graceland and that he understood from the family that the public would be permitted to pay its last respects.

Presley's uncle said Elvis' former wife, Priscilla, whom he divorced in 1973, arrived at the mansion at about 3 a.m. today.

"She is taking it hard," he said. "She is in a total state of shock."

Dr. Jerry Francisco, the Shelby county medical examiner, discounted rumors that Presley, who had been a recluse at his Graceland mansion for 2 years, had suffered from a drug problem.

"There was no indication of drug abuse at all," Dr. Francisco said. "I was aware of the rumors and that is why I mention it."

Delbert (Sonny) West, a Presley bodyguard for 16 years, said in Chicago just hours before Presley died that the singer was heavily addicted to drugs and haunted by fears that drove him into seclusion.

West was interviewed by Sun-Times columnist Bob Greene about the recently released book, Elvis: What Happened?, that West and two other former bodyguards have written about Presley.

"He was on pills all day long, and he would give himself shots in the arm or the leg with those little plastic syringes," West said in the interview. "He would have us give him shots in the rear end. We prayed for this man many times. His drug habit is so severe that I'm convinced he is in danger of losing his life."

Presley, whose recording of Heartbreak Hotel helped to put him on top of the entertainment world 21 years ago, was discovered unconscious at Graceland in suburban Memphis on Tuesday afternoon.

Presley was found dressed in pyjamas and lying face up in the bathroom next to his second floor bedroom.

He was taken to Baptist Hospital in a fire department ambulance while Dr. Nichopoulos and emergency medical technicians worked to revive him.

The doctor said attempts to revive Presley continued because of a slight chance life still existed in his body.

"The reason we continued to resuscitate him was his pupils were constricted," the doctor said at a hospital news conference after an autopsy.

Thousands Mourn Superstar Elvis

MEMPHIS, TENN (AP) — A white cross of flowers from his former wife and his daughter stood by the crypt of Elvis Presley today, as outside the mausoleum hundreds of people paid a final homage.

They came in a steady stream from the time the cemetery gates opened to weep and to kneel and to take pictures of the building where the rock and roll superstar was laid to rest Thursday.

Florists stood behind ropes to give the mourners flowers from the 3,116 displays which lay like a colorful quilt across the lawn of the mausoleum. None of the visitors was allowed inside the building, but they appeared content just to be outside.

Presley's coffin was sealed behind a slab of concrete and marble in a small chamber near the front of the building. Near a window was a three-foot high cross of white carnations, decorated with red roses. A streamer said it was from Lisa Marie and Priscilla.

Lisa Marie, 9, is Presley's only child. Her mother, Priscilla, and Presley were divorced.

Roses cover floor

On the floor of the chamber was the blanket of roses that covered the coffin when it was carried in Thursday.

The mausoleum was kept locked because the family was expected sometime during the day and the crowd was too large.

Some persons waited all night outside the cemetery gates, sleeping on the sidewalks, and when they were admitted, shortly after 8 a.m., some ran the half mile distance to the mausoleum to be the first.

Mourners had waited patiently for hours in the broiling sun Thursday — outside the Presley mansion, along the four-mile funeral route on Elvis Presley Boulevard and in front of the cemetery.

The white funeral that Presley had wanted was carried out: white hearse bore Presley's copper coffin, covered by 500 red rosebuds, and 16 shining white Cadillacs led a procession of about 50 cars from the mansion to the cemetery.

But a commercial atmosphere also crept into the sad occasion. Hawkers sold Elvis T-shirts for $10. Forty-cent picture post cards of Graceland went quickly for $1.50. A small bottle of cola, also $1.50

Floral tributes in front of the mausoleum hid the lawn under a spectacular quilt of color as about 50 members of the Presley family and 150 invited guests arrived for the entombment.

Eight pallbearers carried the coffin inside for five minutes of ceremony.

Vernon Presley, the singer's father, stayed behind for a few private moments with Elvis, watching as workers began to seal the crypt.

1970~1979

Presley records sold out quickly

Sales of Elvis Presley record-ings soared Wednesday as fans of the rock and roll star who died Tuesday, flocked to city record shops to purchase the records they had meant to buy for years.

Four major Penticton record retailers reported they were sold out of Presley recordings

by mid-morning. Large num-bers of people will now have to wait until the shelves are re-stocked in about a weeks time.

Apple Valley Records man-ager Dean Werts said, the 20 to 30 records he had in stock were gone early in the day.

At Kelly's Stereo Mart all Presley recordings had been

sold before noon. The store usually sells about two of his records or tapes a week.

The Bay record department manager Wynn Heaven said, she has had to continue turning people away today after all recordings were sold early Wednesday.

The record department at

Woodward's had sold all of its Presley recordings by 10 a.m. Wednesday. About 25 to 30 of the older recordings of the king of rock and roll were all sold early in the morning.

All stores said there will be no problems ordering any of the entertainer's recordings or movie soundtracks.

1970~1979

'Wired city' a-coming!

Penticton Herald

Published by Thomson B.C. Newspapers Ltd.
186 Nanaimo Avenue West, Penticton, B.C.
G. J. Rowland, Publisher

Even as the debate continues over the pervasive influence of television in our daily lives, we are moving into an age where the one-eyed monster will truly be man's servant.

The spectacular popularity of electronic games that use the television set — like ping pong and hockey — is only a hint of things to come.

Cable television, which is steadily growing in usage and sophistication, may be the wave of the future.

Currently being tested in Tokyo is a cable system that ultimately could provide every household in Japan with a variety of two-way services. The system utilizes the new technology of fiber optics, by which information is transmitted via light beams through hair-thin glass filaments.

With a central computer providing the necessary controls, test subscribers can use special equipment installed in their homes to interact with the system in a number of ways. Some examples:

Request entertainment. By tapping out the proper code on a keyboard, the subscriber activates the computer's video information unit, which switches the designated program into automatic transmission.

Request data. This is transmitted to the subscriber in still-picture form at his option, and includes all types of specialized information, such as news, stock market reports, time, weather and other announcements of interest.

Facsimile. If the subscriber wishes, hard copies of video information can be printed out, including a "home "newspaper.

Computer-assisted instruction. Questions and assignments appear on the screen of the home TV receiver. Students respond on the keyboard and their answers are evaluated by the computer, which regulates the program in accordance with the capability demonstrated by each individual.

Cashless transactions. Store and restaurant bills, rent and utility charges can be paid through the system, with deductions made automatically from the account of the subscriber.

Shopping and reservations. Goods appear on the TV screen, together with prices. The subscriber can order by means of keyboard input, or make theater, restaurant and travel reservations the same way. Again, payment is made automatically from bank accounts.

Burglar and fire alarms. Detectors are installed in each home so that the central computer can sense any abnormality, such as intrusions or excessive heat or smoke. Alarms can be retransmitted to police and fire stations and instructions relayed to the household on emergency measures to be taken while safety units are on the way.

Telemetering and telecontrol. Electricity, gas and water meters are read automatically and charges handled as cashless trans-actions. Telecontrol makes it possible to regulate household electrical appliances and heating and cooling systems from outside the house.

The Japanese project was begun in 1972, but had been stalled because of the cost, bulkiness and other limitations of conventional coaxial cable. Independent investigation into the potential of fiber optics by Arthur D. Little, Inc., an American research organization, was instrumental in persuading Japan's ministry of international trade and industry to adopt the new technology.

According to Little, the Japanese field trial is experimental only in the sense of evaluating the performance of the system and determining modifications necessary to raise it to full-fledged nationwide operation.

Thanks to the computer and fiber optics, the much-talked-about "wired city" or "information society" may be upon us sooner than we think.

Heist could have been the world's biggest!

VANCOUVER (CP) — Several police officers waded knee-deep Tuesday in millions of dollars in cash, jewels and gold, scattered on the floor of a Vancouver vault in the course of what some detectives say could be the world's biggest robbery.

The carefully-executed raid was foiled by a Vancouver Airport baggage handler who became suspicious Monday when he found a suitcase almost too heavy to lift. When a supervisor opened the bag he found a fortune in bullion, cash and jewels.

The RCMP were called in, found eight more stuffed suitcases and arrested three suspects before the raid on the vault had been reported.

Police are still counting the loot, stolen from 2,500 safety deposit boxes in a downtown vault. They estimate the robbery would eclipse the $10 million in jewels, gold bars, cash and securities stolen last year at Nice, France.

"I was knee-deep in valuables," said Jeff Hilton of the police crime laboratory. "It was incredible."

Police also arrested two suspects in Winnipeg who had left Vancouver on a Toronto flight that was forced back to Winnipeg by bad weather. The two were returned to Vancouver Tuesday night.

Police said thieves entered the building containing the vault sometime after closing Friday through a second-floor window near a fire escape.

The thieves opened a ground-floor door to an adjoining lane and moved some equipment to the basement. There they attacked the rear wall of the 40-by-15-foot vault which houses 5,000 deposit boxes.

"They drilled through 24 inches of concrete with diamond core drills and burned through 3 1/2 inches of steel with a thermal lance," said Mr. Hilton.

"The thermal lance causes concrete to flow like lava."

The thieves cut a hole two feet in diameter, levered out the concrete plug in the middle and clambered into the vault. Inside, they broke open about half the boxes, taking only the most valuable items, cash and gold. Before leaving, they hid four empty oxygen and acetylene tanks used for the cutting torch.

The vault had no alarm and the company had not insured the vault's contents.

"They were counting on the thickness of the wall," said one detective.

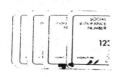
1970~1979

Premiers tackle Quebec proposal

ST. ANDREWS, N.B. (CP) —

As Canada's premiers met on the contentious language issue here today, about 20 English speaking parents representing the Quebec Federation of Home and School Associations demonstrated their opposition to Quebec's Bill 101 outside the hotel.

The premiers met in Premier Richard Hatfield's suite instead of a nearby meeting house, apparently to avoid the placard-carrying middle-aged demonstrators.

Included in the discussions was a compromise proposal on the language issue which would have the 10 premiers affirming French-language rights across Canada with the possibility of referring the issue to an educational council.

There was some concern over whether the compromise would be acceptable to Premier Rene Levesque of Quebec.

The premiers were scheduled to end formal talks shortly after noon and board a ship for a leisurely cruise to nearby Campogello Island.

They were to be met by Lt. Gov. Hedard Robichaud, Senator Edmund Muskie of Maine and Franklin D. Roosevelt Jr. The Roosevelt family's former summer home, now a historic site, is on the island.

The demonstrators from Montreal, the Eastern Townships, Hull and the Laurentian area carried placards condemning the Parti Quebecois language bill.

Audrey Strutt of Hull, a spokesman for the group, said the protesters wanted to get their objections across to the premiers during their language deliberations today.

"The Parti Quebecois party is tending to make political use of a scene in education where the battle has already gone to the French culture in Quebec in that we all — English-speaking Quebecers — agree this is a French province and we must live in it," she said.

An indication of the feeling with which the premiers regard the Quebec proposal surfaced Thursday when Levesque and Premier Allan Blakeney of Saskatchewan exchanged heated words behind closed doors.

Levesque, who challenged Blakeney on his interpretation of the Quebec proposal, later described it as a pretty vigorous exchange.

Blakeney said the proposal is abhorrent to Canadians, but that he was willing to have Levesque explain it further today.

Economic issues and particularly unemployment also were discussed Thursday.

In a communiqué issued shortly before midnight Thursday night, the premiers expressed concern about forecasts of continuing high unemployment for at least the next 18 months. To reduce unemployment, they recommended several short-term measures including:

-Federal personal income tax cuts to improve customer purchasing power.

-Faster housing construction either through tax measures, accelerated government procedures or increased funding.

-Re-introduction of the federal forgivable capital loan fund.

They urged the federal government to announce a termination date for wage and price controls as soon as possible to remove the uncertainty now plaguing the economy.

They were concerned about the period immediately after the removal of controls and supported a monitoring agency for incomes and prices.

'FREEDOM' RECOMMENDED FOR SON OF SAM SUSPECT

AUGUST 19, 1977. NEW YORK (AP) — A pre-trial agency recommended that David Berkowitz, who police say is the Son of Sam killer of six persons, be released without bail because he had a steady job, a permanent residence and no prior criminal record.

The recommendation by the Criminal Justice Agency Inc., a private group funded by the city and the federal government "defies belief," Mayor Abraham Beame said Thursday.

The agency recommended Berkowitz's release on his own recognizance although it knew he was accused of being the .44-calibre killer, Beame said.

The mayor said similar recommendations in less notorious cases "could permit dangerous criminals to walk the streets on little or no bail."

He ordered an immediate investigation of the procedures used by the agency, which interviews every criminal justice defendant who appears before a judge in New York City and makes its recommendations to judges.

Beame said the recommendation was based on information supplied by the 24-year old Berkowitz, a postal worker.

The agency makes only one of two decisions: release without bail or no recommendation. In practice, judges in the city usually order murder defendants held without bail initially.

Meanwhile, The Daily News says psychiatrists examining Berkowitz have serious doubts that he will be found mentally competent to stand trial.

Federal aid announced for grape development

Agriculture Minister Eugene Whelan has announced assistance to the Association of B.C. Grape Growers of Kelowna for a project to introduce German grape varieties and growing techniques in the Okanagan Valley.

Agriculture Canada's New Crop Development Fund will contribute $66,500 over a five-year period to evaluate these varieties, and four others developed at the department's Summerland Research Station for winter hardiness and winemaking quality.

With increasing demand for vinifera varieties, the association is attempting to find varieties with qualities suitable for premium table wines. Because the climate and soil conditions in the Okanagan Valley are similar to those in Germany, the growers feel German vines grown under German techniques may be able to withstand winter climates and produce top quality wine.

Two three-acre plots of land will be leased for the project from two B.C. grape growers. Under the direction of a supervisor, these growers will maintain and complete all work in the plots during the five-year duration of the project.

The federal department's New Crop Development Fund was established to assist in bridging the gap between basic research results and practical application in the field. The fund, with an annual budget of $1 million, is available to groups with workable plans for developing and producing new crops and varieties, or for expanding production areas of established crops.

Mass Suicide Kills Hundreds

GEORGETOWN (AP) — Between 300 and 400 bodies - of men, women and children who were reported to have lined up for doses of poison brewed in a tub - have been found at a Guyanese jungle camp of a California sect, whose members ambushed and killed five U.S. citizens, including Representative Leo Ryan, Guyana's information minister reported today.

The minister, Shirley Field-Ridley, said the whereabouts of the remaining 500 to 700 Americans at the camp is not known, but they apparently fled into the surrounding jungle, in the northwest corner of Guyana, a former British colony in South America.

Well-known U.S. lawyer Mark Lane, who was at the People's Temple camp just before the mass deaths occurred, told The Associated Press here today that suicide was discussed at a community meeting and he was later informed by two sect members: "We are all going to die now."

"They were smiling...," Land said. "They looked genuinely happy."

Death Time Unclear

It was not clear whether the mass deaths occurred at about the same time or some time after the Saturday night ambush of Ryan and his group, which had gone to the camp to investigate reports of alleged large-scale abuse of sect members.

Ryan's party was trying to escort some disenchanted members from the camp when it was attacked at a nearby airstrip.

Adherents of the People's Temple, whose founder Rev. Jim Jones established the agricultural commune last year, were reported to have long planned mass suicide if they felt their sect was threatened.

The hundreds of bodies were found by Guyanese troops who raided the camp Sunday. Miss Field-Ridley said some had gunshot wounds but most showed no signs of violence.

"A witness said that people in the area were having mass suicide," she told a news conference. "He said the poison was being administered to them, that they were lining up for it."

It was not immediately known what kind of poison was used.

She said the military is trying to identify the bodies, some of which were found in homes and some in open areas of the camp, called Jonestown, and that so far Jones himself has not been found among the dead.

Rev. Jim Jones, founder of the People's Temple sect, is interviewed in Jonestown, Guyana, shortly before five members of Congressman Leo J. Ryan's party were slain in 1978.

Jonestown death toll reaches 775

GEORGETOWN (AP) — The U.S. embassy here announced today that at least 775 bodies have been found at the scene of the mass suicide-murder in the Jonestown settlement in Guyana, and the count is still rising.

The count nearly doubled the original figure of about 400 bodies found at the U.S. religious agricultural commune in the northwest Guyanese jungle.

Embassy official Patricia Moser said, that as of 1 p.m. 485 bodies had been removed from Jonestown.

Twenty more have been placed in body bags and a still-continuing count had located 270 more, she said.

She emphasized that the count is still continuing.

The new bodies were found in the Jonestown settlement under previously counted bodies, she said.

"We understand the bodies have been found piled and there were a lot of children," she said. "Many children were found under the bodies of their parents and were not counted originally."

Cultists grimly drank Kool-Aid with cyanide

GEORGETOWN (AP) — U.S. troops flew into Guyana today to begin ferrying out bodies of more than 400 American cultists who drank a lethal brew of Kool-Aid and cyanide in fanatic loyalty to a suicidal leader. But the state of the bodies may force the soldiers to bury them on the spot in the jungle commune where the people died.

The bodies of sect founder Rev. Jim Jones and his wife were among 409 bodies that a police spokesman said Guyanese troops had counted in and around the meeting hall in Jonestown.

Jones and several others had been shot, presumably by their own hand. The others had drunk Kool-Aid into which the camp doctor mixed cyanide.

Jones ordered the mass suicide Saturday after sect members ambushed and killed a U.S. congressman and four other persons who were part of an investigative team that visited Jonestown.

Also found at the camp was $500,000 in cash and some jewelry. Unconfirmed reports also said $500,000 in gold and hundreds of social security cheques had also been found.

Fifteen survivors were reported found, three in the camp and 12 who came out of the jungle. Estimates of the missing ranged from more than 375 to more than 775.

An exact estimate was not possible because reports of the settlement's total population ranged from 800 to 1,200. Most were from California, the headquarters of the sect.

USSR cosmonauts end historic space flight

MOSCOW (AP) —

The longest space flight in history ended today when Soviet cosmonauts Vladimir Kovalenok and Alexander Ivanchenkov parachuted back to earth after spending a record 139 days in space.

The Tass news agency said Kovalenok, the 36-year-old commander, and Ivanchenkov, the flight engineer who celebrated his 38th birthday during the flight, landed near Dzhezkazgan in Soviet Central Asia, 200 kilometres east of the Baikonur space centre.

Both were reported in good condition after a medical checkup.

Their space endurance record totalled 139 days, 14 hours and 48 minutes.

The two men were launched June 16 aboard the Soyuz 29 spacecraft which linked up the next day with the Soyuz 6 space station where they lived during their trip.

They returned aboard the Soyuz 31 spaceship, left docked at their space station by one of two other pairs of cosmonauts who visited briefly and swapped capsules with them.

Break Record

On Sept. 20 the two men broke the previous endurance record of 96 days, set June 17 by two cosmo-

nauts on the previous Soviet flight.

The U.S. record is 84 days, set four years ago by astronauts Gerald Carr, Edward Gibson and William Pogue aboard Skylab 4.

The United States has not made a manned space flight since the 1975 Apollo-Soyuz joint mission with the Soviet Union. No new manned U.S. space flights are planned until the space shuttle goes into operation in 1980.

During the course of their flight, Kovalenok and Ivanchenkov broke another record on Aug. 2, logging enough time to put the Soviet Union ahead of a U.S. record of 937.6 total man days in space.

1,000,000th case rolls off line

By Ron Wade
Courier Staff

Wine drinkers have become accepted in B.C. and more and more people are taking wine with their meals and for social occasions.

As a result wine makers are having bumper sales, and in Kelowna, Calona Wines Ltd., is in the process of doubling its production and sales.

Thursday was a historic day for the 46-year-old firm which saw the millionth case of wine of the year roll down the line.

It was the first million the company has made in a year and by the end of the year, company president Art Davis calculates, the 1978 output will be 1,200,000 cases.

Commemorative bottle

At a ceremony attended by a member of the founding family,

Tom Capozzi, Mayor John Hindle, long-time employees, and growers, who were each presented with a special commemorative bottle of the product, Mr. Davis watched the millionth case roll through a bright banner marking the occasion.

One of those present was Alex Ciancone, the company's first employee back in 1932, and still working for Calona.

"We've come a long way," he said.

"Yes," said Mr. Davis, "and we're going to go a long way further!"

He said the millionth case is tangible evidence of the success of the winery.

"Also, more importantly it is real evidence of remarkable progress in a relatively short time,

★ *The Holiday Treat!*

CALONA WINES

Produced and matured to perfection on the sunny slopes of the Okanagan. B. C. products you'll enjoy and praise and the cost is so much less. Ask for "Calona."

Calona Champagne	26-oz.	$1.90
Calona Sparkling Burgundy	26-oz.	1.75
Calona Italian Vermouth	26-oz.	1.25
Calona French Vermouth	26-oz.	1.25
Calona Clear (White Demi-Sec)	28-oz.	.50
Calona Red (Demi-Sec)	40-oz.	.75
Calona Italian	½ Gal.	1.45
Type (Red Dry)	Gal.	2.85

At Government Liquor Stores

Calona Wines Limited
Kelowna, British Columbia

This advertisement is not published or displayed by the Liquor Control Board or by the Government of British Columbia.

A Calona Wines ad from 1934

of the Okanagan grape-growing industry and the skills of our winemaking and production people," said Mr. Davis.

Before the ceremony, Mr. Davis told the media that the trend is toward wine-drinking. It had been decreed by the B.C. government that wine should be boosted, as a milder drink than the "hard stuff."

1970–1979

Ailments cited in W.A.C. death

KELOWNA (CP) —

W.A.C. Bennett, the former premier who dominated British Columbia politics for 20 years, died in his sleep Friday night. He was 78.

Jon Arnett, press secretary to Bill Bennett, the current B.C. premier and son of W.A.C. Bennett, said Bennett's wife May, daughter Anita Tozer and son R.J. Bennett were at his bedside when he died at 10:30 p.m. at Kelowna General Hospital.

Bennett, who led his Social Credit party to seven consecutive election victories in the 1950s and 1960s, had been in failing health for some time.

Bob Morrison, a brother-in-law of the late premier, said Friday that he wore himself out serving the people of the province and was suffering from a combination of ailments.

He had left politics, his first love, in 1972 after an upset defeat by the New Democratic Party. That loss was avenged three years later when son Bill became B.C.'s premier.

Bennett, a former Conservative whose smile was his trademark, virtually built the Social Credit Party in B.C. single-handedly in the early 1950s. His two decades as premier is unmatched in the province's history.

Before he entered politics, Bennett built up a chain of hardware stores bearing his name in the interior B.C. communities of

W.A.C. Bennett   1900-1979

Kelowna, Kamloops, Vernon and Penticton. After he retired, he went back into the business by minding the Kelowna store.

Bennett's political career was dominated by what he called a "great and holy crusade against socialism."

He took part at first in the disastrous coalition of Liberal and Conservative Parties in the late 1940s and when that government collapsed, was a leading figure in the stunning Social Credit victory of 1952.

In the 1952 election he kept the

old Co-operative Commonwealth Federation (CCF) - the forerunner of the NDP - from forming a minority government by the bare margin of one seat.

Bennett was born Sept. 6, 1900, at Hastings, N.B., to a rural family descended from United Empire Loyalists. Shortly after the First World War, he moved west to Edmonton where he acquired a business education through correspondence courses.

By 1928, Bennett was a partner in two Alberta hardware stores but he sold out two years later to move to B.C.'s Okanagan Valley where he set up his family business.

Bennett became involved with the Conservative Party soon after his arrival in B.C. In 1941, he was returned to the provincial legislature as Conservative member for South Okanagan but he soon fell into disfavour because of his outspoken behaviour.

He tried twice to gain the provincial leadership of the Conservative Party and once tried for election to the House of Commons, losing to a CCF candidate.

Bennett became disillusioned with the coalition government and crossed the floor to sit as an independent for a time before becoming attracted to Social Credit.

After the 1952 campaign, he was chosen leader of the Social Credit government largely because of his legislative experience.

Hundreds mourn at W.A.C. funeral

KELOWNA (CP) —

With tears and tributes, more than 1,000 mourners said goodbye Tuesday to former British Columbia premier W.A.C. Bennett at an emotional service in this Okanagan city which had been his adopted home.

Politicians, friends and family - including his 81 year-old-wife May and his son Bill Bennett, the province's current premier - crowded into the red brick First United Church while several hun-

dred others lined the streets outside under sunny skies.

Bennett died last Friday at the age of 78.

As the Kelowna crowd paid its final respects to the man who shaped the province as premier from 1952 to 1972, memorial services were being held in Victoria and Vancouver.

Among those attending the service in Victoria's Metropolitan United Church, where the former premier and his wife had wor-

shipped while in the capital, were Gov. Gen. Edward Schreyer and Mrs. Schreyer and Lt. Gov. Henry Bell Irving and Mrs. Bell Irving.

In his eulogy, Ray Williston, a cabinet minister under Bennett, said it was not a time for sorrow but a time for rejoicing that divine providence allowed this remarkable man to serve as our leader of government for so many years.

WEPT OPENLY

B.C. Hydro chairman Robert

Bonner, an early ally after Bennett led the Social Credit Party to its first surprising election win in 1952, delivered the eulogy at the Vancouver service attended by about 800 people.

In Kelowna, many couldn't contain their grief and wept openly as the coffin, draped with the sun-emblazoned provincial flag that Bennett introduced, was led from the church by two bagpipers and an honour guard of six RCMP officers from the Kelowna detachment.

1970-1979

Mary Pickford funeral private

HOLLYWOOD (AP) —

A hundred close friends and co-workers of Mary Pickford, the Canadian-born silent screen star, gathered Thursday in the Wee Kirk O' the Heather chapel at Forest Lawn Memorial Park and heard her eulogized as not only America's sweetheart, but truly, sweetheart of the world.

It was the private funeral requested by Miss Pickford, who was once the most famous actress in the world.

Rev. William Hornaday of the United Church of Religious Science told of Miss Pickford's gentle admonition in her will - that there be no weeping, but merely a memorial service with beautiful music.

The star's husband of 40 years,

Charles (Buddy) Rogers, had tears streaming down his face as he was led out into the hazy sunshine by Hornaday.

The eulogy was delivered by John Mantley, producer-writer of the television series Gunsmoke and How the West was Won, and a distant cousin of the Toronto-born star.

"Kings and emperors gave her elaborate gifts, princes vied to be invited to her home," said Mantley. "But most of all, people of the world gave her their love with overflowing."

Miss Pickford died Tuesday at age 86 of a cerebral hemorrhage. She was interred privately in a plot she had purchased at the Glendale Cemetery in 1948. Her mother, Charlotte, her sister, Lottie, and her brother, Jack, are also buried there.

(CP PHOTO)

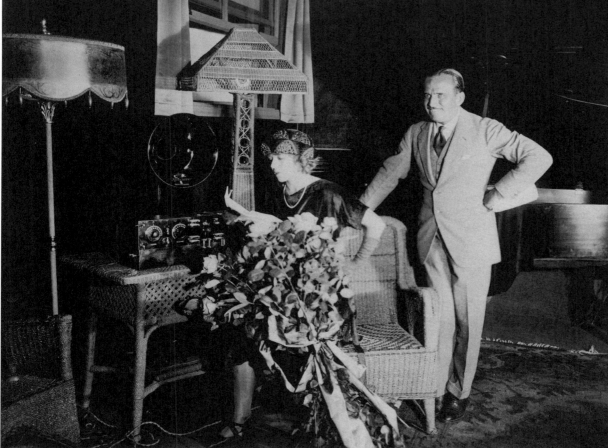

(CP PHOTO)

October 2, 1924 - Douglas Fairbanks and Mary Pickford at CKAC studio (microphone in lampshade).

Political conspiracy link to JFK murder is discounted

WASHINGTON (AP) — A member of the House of Representatives assassinations committee says there is no evidence of a political conspiracy in the murder of John F. Kennedy.

However, Representative Richardson Preyer (Dem. N.C.) said in a statement Monday the U.S. justice department should look into the possibility that individual members of organized crime or anti-Castro Cubans were involved.

"We exculpate all major groups and conclude that changing the institutions of government was not the goal of the possible conspirators." Preyer said.

The committee also concluded that there was no hint of involvement by Secret Service, CIA, FBI or the Cuban or Russian governments.

And although the committee believes that anti-Castro Cuban groups and the national syndicate of organized crime were not involved, this does not preclude that individual members of either group took part.

"This is an area which we believe further investigation is most warranted by the department of justice," said Preyer, chairman of the Kennedy sub-committee of the full assassinations committee.

The committee is asking the justice department to investigate what it calls new evidence that both Kennedy and civil rights leader Martin Luther King were slain as a result of conspiracies.

The department has not responded to the committee's suggestion.

In its report, the committee said scientific evidence shows Kennedy probably was murdered in a crossfire of conspiring gunmen and that circumstantial evidence indicates a likelihood King's murder was also part of a conspiracy.

U.S. Prepared To Guard Mideast Oil

WASHINGTON (AP) — The United States is prepared to use its military force to protect the flow of oil from the Middle East, say two members of President Carter's cabinet.

Defence Secretary Harold Brown said Sunday, the United States would "take any action that's appropriate" to protect the Middle East oil flow, which he said "is clearly part of our vital interest."

In a separate interview, Energy Secretary James Schlesinger, said the administration is considering the "issue of a U.S. military presence" in the Persian Gulf area.

"That would involve military personnel," he said. "Whether it would involve a deployment of troops is another question."

On Friday, Vice-President Walter Mondale said the administration has shut the door on using U.S. troops abroad "except under the most extreme, compelling circumstances."

SAYS OIL VITAL

Brown, questioned on CBS TV's Face the Nation, described the Middle East oil flow as "clearly part of our vital interests."

"In protection of these vital interests, we'll take any action that's appropriate, including the use of military force, but military force is not necessarily appropriate in every instance," he said.

Brown, who recently returned from a Middle East trip, said countries in that area are concerned about possible threats from outside the region and from nearby "more radical states."

Of the Soviet Union, he said, "It's well known that the Soviets are not responsible for all the problems in the area, but they clearly are willing to - in fact, eager - to fish in muddy waters by aiding one country against another."

On a Soviet threat, he said, "The U.S. is prepared to counter such a threat from a major power with whatever means are necessary. Again, let me say, the United States is prepared to defend its vital interests with whatever means are appropriate, including military force where necessary."

VAGUE ON ACTION

Schlesinger, questioned on NBC TV's Meet the Press, declined to specify what action might be taken.

"I think that the point I made is that the United States has a vital interest in the Persian Gulf area, that we have been prepared to discuss the question of a military presence in the area with the states involved and that that would have to be worked out in response to their desires and with some flexibility."

Gas find may be Canada's biggest

CALGARY (CP) —

A natural gas discovery described as possibly the largest in Canada was announced Tuesday by Panarctic Oils Ltd.

Charles Hetherington, Panarctic president, said the find could add at least 10 per cent to Canada's proven gas reserves, estimated at 73 trillion cubic feet.

"This could well be the biggest gas field in the Arctic Islands," Hetherington told a news conference.

He was joined by Bill Hopper, chairman of Petro-Canada, which provides about 80 per cent of Panarctic's financing.

"We're talking in the neighborhood of four to five trillion cubic feet - conceivably double that," said Hopper.

The previous largest discovery in Canada, also made by Panarctic in the Arctic Islands, was at Drake Point where reserves are estimated at 5.5 trillion cubic feet.

The discovery was also announced by Prime Minister Trudeau, who was campaigning Tuesday in Kamloops, B.C. for the May 22 federal election.

SALT II shakeup rejected

WASHINGTON (AP) —

The Senate foreign relations committee today rejected attempts by Senate Republican Leader Howard Baker to add two amendments to the second U.S. Soviet strategic arms limitation treaty that supporters of SALT II said would kill the agreement.

The vote was 9 to 6 against each proposal.

One would have called on the Soviet Union to destroy its 308 large SS-18 intercontinental ballistic missiles. The other provided for the termination of the SALT II treaty on Dec. 31, 1981, unless an agreement has been reached to get rid of all those missiles by 1985.

"Why propose a killer amendment of this kind?" said Senator Frank Church (Dem. Idaho), the committee chairman. "If either of these amendments were to be adopted by the committee we might just as well shut up shop."

By an 8-to-7 vote Tuesday, the panel also rejected a Baker amendment to allow the U.S. to have as many of the large intercontinental missiles as the Soviet Union, a step opposed by the Carter administration as militarily unnecessary.

Athans Pool – A Sound Victory

By Ron Wade
Courier Staff

A second major swimming pool is go for Kelowna.

In what was generally a quiet election Saturday, a complete victory for the $2.5 million Athans Pool referendum was recorded.

All the polls, including Rutland, gave a majority "yes" to the referendum. The final tally was 3,838 for and 1,995 against for a 65 per cent victory.

The Rutland poll tallied the most votes, 1,766 for and 423 opposed. The curling rink poll result was closer at 630 to 558, and the Rec Centre count was 329 to 149.

The Okanagan Mission vote was a clear sign of majority approval with 340 for and 276 opposed.

South Kelowna gave a big percentage nod with 100 for and 66 against, and Raymer poll voters in the South Pandosy area, voted 358 to 315. North Glenmore was almost tied at 189 to 178.

It is a sign that the city is coming together, said Ald. Ben Lee, chairman of the city pool task force committee, when all the votes were counted.

Ald. Lee said his task force had taken plans and a model of the pool to as many functions and groups possible and explained as clearly as they could the benefits

derived from approving the much needed pool without further delay.

"The fact that all the areas outside Rutland gave approval as well indicates to me that at least the city is beginning to realize that it is a city and not just a collection of small communities," he said.

He said the fact of amalgamation has been accepted, at least to a large extent.

Mayor Hammill congratulated the task force for getting out and helping people understand what they are getting.

It was because of lack of this knowledge that the pool referendum failed in 1977, he said.

1970~1979

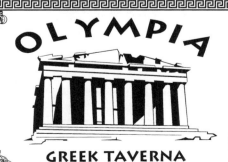

Veteran tough-guy actor, John Wayne, dies of cancer

John Wayne poses for a publicity photo for the 1959 United Artist movie "The Horse Soldiers."

(AP Photo)

LOS ANGELES (AP) —

John Wayne, a Hollywood hero for almost 50 years and 200 movies, built his image as a fearless, determined fighter. That was the way The Duke died - in a courageous fight with cancer.

As the disease began its final assault and as the pain became more severe, Wayne sometimes refused the drugs that might have eased the pain. He wanted, a hospital official said, "to be with his children, his grandchildren; he would tolerate discomfort just to be near his family."

His seven children were at his side when Wayne, known to friends and fans as The Duke, died Monday at the UCLA Medical Centre. His 72nd birthday was celebrated May 26.

"He was – and is – an American institution," said actor Charlton Heston. "It's not surprising that, to the end, Duke gave an example of courage that made him more than an actor and friend."

Hospital administrator Bernard Strohm, announcing the death at a news conference, said Wayne's family plans a private funeral.

Countless fans had been following Wayne's final battle since Jan. 12, when a routine gallbladder operation turned into a 9-hour ordeal as surgeons found cancer in his stomach and removed it.

The next five months brought small successes - release from the hospital, an ovation at the Academy Awards - and gradual deterioration. He was back in surgery May 2. This time the cancer was in his intestines.

Wayne had faced cancer before. The disease claimed part of a lung 15 years ago - but the Duke won. "I licked the Big C," he boasted after that 1964 operation.

Then he went to Mexico and began filming The Sons of Katie Elder, another in the long string of westerns that made Wayne one of the biggest box-office draws in Hollywood history.

Wayne's last public appearance was April 9, when he ambled onstage at the Academy Awards. He was, he told a warmly applauding audience, "mighty pleased that I can amble down here tonight."

Wayne presented the award for best picture, for The Deerhunter, and basked in the lengthy standing ovation, saying it's "just about the only medicine a fellow'd ever need." The face and body were much thinner, worn down by the disease. But the grin was still there. The voice had not changed.

John Wayne never stopped being The Duke, the nickname he picked up from the Airedale dog his family had when he was a child.

He was born Marion Michael Morrison in 1907 in Winterset, Iowa. He moved with his family to California as a boy and played football at the University of Southern California.

After a series of bit parts and odd jobs around the movie sets, Wayne got his first starring role in 1930. He became a star nine years later for his role as a good guy gunman in Stagecoach. He was nominated for an Oscar in 1949 for The Sands of Iwo Jima. He won the award in 1970 for his role as Rooster Cogburn in True Grit.

"A Jumbo In This Business": Hope

Duke "an American institution": Heston

HOLLYWOOD (AP) - "He was - and is - an American institution," Charlton Heston said of John Wayne who died Monday after five decades of film-making.

"It's hard to believe that John Wayne, the most durable of all film actors, is gone," said Heston.

"But it's not surprising that to the end, Duke gave an example of courage that made him more than an actor and friend."

Actor Jack Lemmon said Wayne "was bigger than life but he never abused it. He always gave more than he got."

Comedian Bob Hope said Wayne was "a jumbo in this business. He was a patriot, someone who spoke out for America, who would help you out if you had a worthy cause."

Hope once joined Wayne at the White House to greet returning prisoners of war during the Vietnam war.

More of Wayne's colleagues contributed personal memories to the stream of tributes.

"I put him in pictures 50 years ago, and he was a very fine man, a real good American," said Raoul Walsh, who directed Wayne's first major picture, The Big Trail, in 1930.

"He enjoyed life a lot, working with the crew and the cast and stuff," said Walsh. "He was always on time, paid good attention to his work and everybody loved him."

Actor Lloyd Nolan recalled a rugged John Wayne who lived on his yacht, The Wild Goose, while both were shooting the 1964 film Circus World in the south of Spain.

"It was a great experience," said Nolan, who Wayne once described to the late director John Ford as the perfect man for the role which Wayne ultimately played in Stagecoach. The 1939 movie established Wayne as a major star.

Another star of the western genre, Lorne Greene, said Wayne was "beloved and respected by many millions of people."

"He put up a tremendously courageous fight against his illness that reiterated again the true grit the man had in him," the Ottawa-born actor said.

"He had true character. Not everyone agreed with what he said but they all knew what he did think. They were his honest opinions and he should be respected for them."

Enormous dislikes, immense likes

HOLLYWOOD (AP) —

For all his coolness-under-fire image on the screen, John Wayne was a passionate man in his personal life.

In his western movies, he told his men to hold their fire until the Indians approached the circle of wagons. In interviews, he shot from the hip at almost every topic that was tossed at him.

During a third of a century I found him consistently the most provocative interview subject in Hollywood.

He had enormous dislikes - Communism, the welfare state, rude directors, upstart actors, discourtesy to women.

He also had immense likes - the United States, the movie industry, the University of Southern California, John Ford and Latin women.

Wayne's marriages were to the daughter of a Dominican diplomat, a Mexican film actress and a Peruvian beauty. All three marriages failed.

During his long career in Hollywood, Wayne always stated his own principles, which his critics termed hide-bound.

The 1960s were the toughest time for The Duke. He was appalled by what he saw in the United States - long hair, student demonstrations, the drug scene, the erosion of patriotism, and opposition to the Vietnam war.

Wayne was reviled by activists for his hawkish stand on the war, for his unswerving support of Richard Nixon, for his denunciation of campus unrest.

But the war's end, Nixon's resignation and a return to less-impassioned politics restored John Wayne to his role as American Hero.

Students say hostages will die if Washington interferes

TEHRAN (CP) —

Students holding some 60 Americans hostage in the U.S. embassy here today threatened to kill them if Washington took any action, military or otherwise, to secure their release.

A communiqué from the students read over state radio, said: "The spies who are our hostages are very well taken care of and we declare to America that any military or non-military action will cause the elimination of all the hostages."

The communiqué, addressed to the Iranian Moslem nation, said:

"The spying and plotting centre of the United states will be in our hands until the final conclusion."

The students, who have been holding the hostages for more than 48 hours, are demanding the extradition of the deposed Shah to face trial before a revolutionary court in Iran.

Tehran newspapers today published photographs of male hostages, blindfolded and with their hands tied, being exercised in the embassy grounds.

The students have called on Iranians to track down and detain

U.S. charge d'affaires Bruce Laingen, who was not in the embassy when it was stormed last Sunday.

However, Laingen has been holed up at the Iranian foreign ministry, negotiating with the government of Premier Mehdi Bazargan since Sunday.

(AP Photo)

One of 60 American hostages - his hands bound blindfolded - is displayed to the crowd outside the American embassy in Tehran, Nov. 9, 1979. Some of the militant Iranian students who seized the embassy in the Iranian capital flank the hostage.

Students assault second embassy

TEHRAN (CP) —

More than 100 Iranian students broke into the British embassy compound in central Tehran tonight despite appeals by Moslem leaders not to extend the U.S. embassy takeover to other diplomatic missions in the Iranian capital.

Witnesses said about 120 students were involved at the British embassy, and that 70 embassy staff were in the compound at the time.

There were no reports of violence. Two U.S. consulates in other parts of Iran were taken over today, although at least one of them was unoccupied.

Nightmare is over: 52 fly to Germany

By The Associated Press

A plane carrying the 52 American hostages, freedom bound after 444 days of captivity in Iran, took off today from Tehran's Mehrabad Airport, the official Iranian news agency Pars and a policeman at the airport reported.

The departure was shrouded in confusion, with conflicting reports on the takeoff, and no official announcement from the Iranian or United States governments saying that the harrowing ordeal for the U.S. captives had ended after 14

1/2 months.

(Reuters news agency reported that two Algerian 727 airliners carrying the hostages had departed within minutes of each other.)

The 3,000-mile flight to Algiers would take nine to ten hours, and it was expected the hostages would go on to a U.S. Air Force hospital in Wiesbaden, West Germany.

There were reports from Western sources monitoring the hostage situation in Ankara that flight plans filed by the Algerian aircraft included a refueling stop in Ankara or Damascus, Syria, Rome,

or Athens.

The report on the hostages' departure came in the final hour of President Carter's term of office. He had tried to complete an agreement with Iran on Monday, but as the hours slipped away, Carter was deprived of a chance to greet the hostages before he left office.

Thus, the reported freedom for the Americans - 50 men and two women - coincided with the end of the Carter presidency as power was transferred to Ronald Reagan at inauguration ceremonies in Washington.

1970~1979

Uranium sites disclosure sought

An anti-uranium environmental group is pressing for full public disclosure by a government commission of the locations of 30 Okanagan occurrences of the radioactive metal.

Ann Rounthwaite, counsel for Environmental Alliance Against Uranium Mining in B.C., said in Vancouver her group will challenge the contention of mining consultants D. G. Leighton and Associates that the information remain confidential.

The consultants have supplied the commission with information on the occurrences.

The commission, established by the provincial government to look into uranium mining and exploration in the province, is expected to decide next week if the locations will be made public.

Ms. Rounthwaite said her group will press for disclosure on grounds that there is no legal principle which allows the commission to consider the information privileged and argue that it would be against the spirit of the hearings to deny participants in the hearings access to information.

"We are very strongly opposed to Leighton and Associates' contention that these documents should be kept confidential," she said.

Filed Documents

Dick Culvert, spokesman for Leighton, said the company filed documents on the occurrences several weeks ago and some additional information required by the commission is being prepared now.

The company had asked that the locations of the uranium be kept secret to protect client confidentiality, protect the firm's exploration work in the Okanagan and prevent a panic over health safety.

Culvert said the information is in the hands of the provincial health ministry which should be allowed to talk to residents before the information is released generally.

He said the uranium occurrences are not in populated areas and are not considered radioactive.

One of the sites is near Summerland, where local residents have sent a letter to Energy Minister Jim Hewitt demanding a ban on uranium exploration and mining.

Uranium sites pinpointed

Eight located near Penticton

Location of surface uranium deposits in the Okanagan Valley, including eight sites just outside Penticton, have been pinpointed by the royal commission into uranium mining.

The 46 locations, filed with the commission on Wednesday, include eight from the outskirts of Penticton to 10 kilometres west, 16 within one to five kilometres north and west of Oliver, one within two kilometres southwest of Kaleden, 16 from within the municipal boundaries of Summerland to 15 kilometres to the west and north, one eight kilometres northwest of Trepanier, one near Ellison Lake in North Kelowna, two within four kilometres south of Barnhartvale in Kamloops and one three kilometres north of Lac la Jeune.

Farming near surface deposits in the Okanagan Valley might be hazardous, Dr. David Bates, chairman of the Royal Commission, said Wednesday in Vancouver.

The 46 deposits, are on Crown rangeland, agricultural reserve land and within municipal areas. Many are in areas which supply water for domestic use, cattle, irrigation and recreation.

The deposits are not radioactive but since uranium is a heavy metal associated with lead and thorium, toxicity problems might arise.

"It is possible that using fertilizers on this particular land might have the effect of mobilizing uranium," Dr. Bates said.

The commission intends to find out whether irrigation and fertilization might result in the release of the surface uranium, which is found in soil rather than rock.

Secrecy Urged

The commission made public a report by Vancouver geological consultants detailing the location of the deposits. Existence of the deposits had been disclosed at an earlier hearing but the mining industry argued the locations should be kept secret in the interest of competition.

Socreds Under Gun In Uranium Controversy

A small group of protesters outside a Kelowna hardware store last Friday marked an issue that could be trouble for Premier Bill Bennett's Social Credit government.

The inter-church Committee for World Development Education has vowed to picket the Bennett family store until the provincial government permanently bans uranium mining in British Columbia.

The issue literally sits on the premier's doorstep. Most of B.C.'s known uranium deposits — about 1.2 per cent of the Canadian supply — lie in the Okanagan Valley, which is the heartland of Social Credit's traditional political strength.

With a slim five-seat majority in the legislature, Bennett's pro-development party will look hard at lifting the government's moratorium on uranium mining.

Social Credit answered some opposition with a royal commission in January to consider the impact and hazards of uranium mining. But unlike some commissions, which have diffused controversial issues, this one appears to be unifying opposition to uranium mining.

The inquiry is led by Dr. David Bates, a University of B.C. professor with a background in environmental medicine who commands the respect of all groups involved.

Its mandate is to consider the impact of uranium exploration, mining and milling on the safety of workers and the environment and the adequacy of federal and provincial regulations.

Residents of 10 Interior communities made commissioners well aware of their worries about those dangers by filling schools and halls during public hearings last summer. Major concerns include contamination of the environment and the disposal of mining wastes.

Commissioners pointed to above-normal radioactivity near several Okanagan and Kootenay communities, where exploration could release contaminants into drinking water, and recommended a moratorium on the drilling of adits and shafts.

Uranium moratorium lauded by officials

No matter the motives, Penticton area officials are pleased with the decision Wednesday by the provincial government to place a seven-year moratorium on uranium mining and exploration in the province.

"It was a brave step for this government to take," Ald. Rod Barrett said today, "especially in light of the $300 million contract the government has with Korea to provide uranium to that country.

"I figured the government had a strong commitment to sell uranium to Korea. I think it was certainly a well thought out decision. I don't really think it was strictly a political decision to knock the slats out from under the New Democratic Party."

Barrett says he felt the Rates Inquiry into uranium mining performed a valuable function and helped mold public opinion.

"The inquiry brought out information step by step about the hazard of uranium mining. I'm somewhat unhappy the inquiry has been dissolved. It would have been nice to see the whole inquiry through to the end. I think they should complete the technical aspects of the inquiry, and I think the provincial government should fund completion of the inquiry."

Barrett says the seven-year period should allow other alternate sources of energy to be developed.

"The government will have to spend some bucks on developing alternate sources of energy," Barrett added. "In any event I have heard reports that there wasn't enough uranium in B.C. to make mining of the mineral worthwhile."

Walt Taylor of the South Okanagan Environmental Coalition says the decision will now turn the focus of energy development onto other areas.

"If we work wisely in the next seven years, we will be able to develop an alternate energy source," Taylor said. "Alternate sources have been ignored because of uranium but there are other sources that can provide more and better jobs without the risks.

"A study by a group at the Harvard School of Business concluded that solar energy would be adequate if developed and that uranium energy could be phased out over the next 50 years.

"We are quite pleased with the decision. Now, instead of fighting against uranium powered energy sources, we can look at developing alternate methods."

Taylor said he is worried about the dissolution of the Bates Inquiry in that some important facts could have been brought out. He said he was particularly concerned about the effects of low level radiation.

"I feel we should have a chance to bring out further information from experts on uranium mining."

Taylor claims the decision was politically motivated and could have been made over a year ago.

"However, the decision does take a great deal of anxiety off our shoulders," he added.

Environmentalists throughout B.C. are happy with a moratorium but at the same time they are wondering what motivated the decision.

Premier Bill Bennett, in announcing the moratorium, said that a $2 million royal commission into uranium mining will stop functioning immediately.

Dr. David Bates, who headed the inquiry, was in Australia studying uranium mining when the moratorium was issued and had still to issue his report.

"We have some regrets that all the information wasn't able to get out," John Rogers, a spokesman for the Union of B.C. Indian Chiefs, said Wednesday. "Bennett's decision was based on political issues and not scientific data. He could have made the decision some time ago."

1970~1979

CLARK, CABINET IN POWER

JUNE 4, 1979, OTTAWA (CP) — Joe Clark and a cabinet of 29 Progressive Conservatives were sworn into office Monday as the country's 16th administration since Confederation.

PM resignation official

JUNE 4, 1979, OTTAWA (CP) — Pierre Elliott Trudeau resigned as prime minister of Canada today after 11 years, six weeks and three days in office.

The 59-year-old Liberal visited Gov. Gen. Ed Schreyer for more than an hour in advance of the swearing in of Conservative Joe Clark as the 16th prime minister.

Instead of the long silver bullet-proof limousine that has been his transportation for the last few years, Trudeau arrived and left Government House in beautiful spring weather driving his own Mercedes convertible - an RCMP body guard following a short distance behind.

"I feel free," Trudeau said as he drove away - across the street to 24 Sussex Drive, the prime ministerial home he is losing.

Clark opts to govern despite losses

NOVEMBER 29, 1979 — Prime Minister Clark indicated today he has no intention of calling an election just because his minority government was weakened by two by-election defeats Monday and will encounter more difficulty winning the confidence of Parliament.

"Our policy is to govern; we'll see what the other parties do," Clark told reporters upon entering a meeting of inner cabinet.

"I regret the by-election losses, but there will be other by-elections and there will be other elections."

The biggest upset for the Tories was in the Saskatchewan riding of Prince Albert, held for 26 years by former Progressive Conservative prime minister John Diefenbaker. Stan Hovdebo, of the New Democratic Party, narrowly defeated the Conservative candidate.

In the Newfoundland riding of Burin-St. George's, Liberal candidate Roger Simmons retained the riding for his party. The Conservatives finished third and the NDP placed second.

Trudeau resignation stuns nat'l liberals

OTTAWA (CP) —

Former prime minister Pierre Trudeau stunned his own party today by announcing he is quitting as Liberal leader after almost 12 years so the party can "rebuild itself" and win the next federal election.

The surprise resignation of the 60-year-old Trudeau will likely not be effective until March, his suggested date for a leadership convention.

Trudeau informed Senator Alasdair Graham, Liberal party president, early this morning that he intends to quit.

Liberal MPs and senators, gathered for their weekly caucus meeting, were then informed. Some broke into tears and followed Trudeau to a hastily called news conference.

Trudeau told reporters the Liberal party needs to rebuild itself and the best way to achieve that goal is to have "a change in leadership."

But he promised that "where I am and whatever I do, I will continue to fight for my country" and will participate actively in the Quebec referendum campaign this spring.

Tories face non-confidence vote

Five Socreds Will Abstain

OTTAWA (CP) —

Social Credit Leader Fabien Roy said today his five-member group will abstain from a crucial non-confidence vote in the Commons tonight, conceding it could push the country into an election.

Meanwhile, Prime Minister Clark's office said Clark had cancelled a scheduled speaking engagement in Waterloo, Ont., and was returning to Ottawa in time for the vote tonight.

External Affairs Minister Flora MacDonald is returning ahead of time from a NATO meeting in Brussels.

All Liberal members have been ordered to be in their places for the vote and NDP Leader Ed Broadbent has said that all his 27 party members will vote. The vote is on a non-confidence motion sponsored by the NDP.

Support from the Quebec based group is crucial for the survival of the 6 1/2-month-old Progressive Conservative government, which encountered a barrage of criticism in the Commons the day after the tough, tax-imposing budget address.

Liberal House Leader Allan MacEachen said low-and-middle-income Canadians have replaced inflation as public enemy No. 1 in the eyes of the Tory government.

NDP Leader Ed Broadbent said Prime Minister Clark is guilty of reversing his May 22 election promises and urged Clark to dissolve Parliament and seek a new mandate from voters.

The 136 Tories face a potential combined Liberal-NDP opposition of 140. Should the Social Crediters vote with the opposition or abstain, Canadians could be facing a snap election call and be trudging through the slush and snow to the polls in mid-February.

Clark sets tone for election

OTTAWA (CP) — Prime Minister Clark today announced a general election for Feb. 18 and set the tone by charging that an unnecessary winter campaign had been forced by "two parties playing politics."

Clark paid an early-morning, 50-minute visit to Gov.-Gen. Ed Schreyer to ask for the dissolution of the short-lived 31st Parliament and announced the date a few hours later in the Commons.

He was greeted with a standing ovation by Progressive Conservatives as he stood to make the statement, which was greeted by loud cheers from both sides of the Commons.

The Schreyer visit came 10 hours after the narrow defeat Thursday of Clark's minority Conservative government by a combined Liberal-New Democratic Party vote condemning the government's first budget. The vote was 139-133.

Trudeau's back for second round

OTTAWA (CP) —

Pierre Trudeau announced today he will lead the Liberals in the Feb. 18 election campaign.

Speaking to reporters, Trudeau said that he felt he had a duty to the country and to the party to postpone plans to return to private life and lead the party through the election.

If the Liberals win the election, Trudeau will stay on as prime minister, he said.

"Canadians face serious problems," the 60-year-old Trudeau said, "the party faces an election."

Trudeau agonized over his decision since the minority Progressive Conservative government was defeated Thursday night in the Commons. Liberal campaign plans were placed on hold until he announced his decision.

1970~1979

DECEMBER 18, 1979

Liberals back with majority

The Canadian Press

"Welcome to the 1980s."

Those are the words Pierre Elliott Trudeau used early today as he welcomed his Liberal party back into majority government, ending nine months of minority Progressive Conservative rule under Joe Clark.

The Liberal return to power started in the Atlantic provinces, surged through Quebec and peaked in Ontario, before flagging in Manitoba and dying in the West.

The standings, with figures at dissolution Dec. 14 in brackets:

Liberal 146 (114)
PC 103 (136)
NDP 32 (27)
SC 0 (5)

Voting in one riding - Frontenac in Quebec - was postponed to March 24 because of the death during the campaign of the Social Credit candidate. The Liberals won it in the last election.

Trudeau's words were his way of saying that as far as he is concerned the decade is off to a new start because of the election result.

After the Conservative victory last May 22, Trudeau had announced he was resigning as

Liberal leader and a convention had been set for next month to pick a successor.

Then came the Conservative budget in December, with its roundly booed four-cent-a-litre (18-cent-a-gallon) excise tax on gasoline and other tough measures to battle economic problems.

The budget led to the Conservatives' defeat, and brought a reluctant Trudeau back to the political forefront.

He thanked Canadians for sending him a special Valentine. He also thanked his home riding of Montreal Mount Royal, where he

won easy re-election for the fifth time.

Clark accepted the defeat at the same place in Spruce Grove, Alta., where last May he had welcomed victory.

In all, the Liberals picked up 25 seats from the Conservatives, five from the NDP and five from the Social Credit en route to victory. The NDP also took 10 from the Conservatives, who managed to take one from the Liberals.

The Liberals won 44 per cent of the popular vote to 33 per cent for the Conservatives and about 20 for the NDP.

A DECADE
IN REVIEW

1980 ~ 1989

'It's a miracle Mt. St. Helens survivors alive'

SCIENTISTS STILL WARY

St. Helens' bulge slows

MAY 12, 1980, VANCOUVER, WASH. (AP) — The bulging on the north flank of Mount St. Helens has slowed some, but not enough to cause wary scientists to relax their vigil of the 2,946-metre volcano.

A 1.6 kilometre by 800-metre area on the slope has expanded at a regular rate of about one metre a day for several days, but the bulging slowed over the weekend to about half a metre a day.

Clear skies Sunday allowed the peak to show off with intermittent belches of steam and ash, while scientists were busy trying to guess its next move.

One geologist has gone so far as to predict that the changing gravitational pull of the sun and the moon could trigger a lava eruption on May 21.

VANCOUVER, WASH. (CP) — Small groups of survivors of the Mount St. Helens eruption, including at least two children, have been located huddled in clearings in the devastated landscape.

Military aircraft which made a detailed search of the Toutle River Valley area at the northern foot of the volcano reported finding the survivors late Monday.

"It's impossible to try to say what these people have undergone, what intense heat and horror they have endured," a spokesman for the U.S. Federal Aviation Administration said.

"It's a miracle they are alive."

Police who earlier reported nine people dead revised their total to six and increased the number listed as missing from 21 to 29.

Nine people in relatively safe areas were picked up by helicopters Monday but a rescue attempt to pick up two adults and two children spotted standing in a clearing of the scorched terrain had to be called off as darkness fell.

Five more people were seen waving just north of the river and more were spotted about 32 kilometres away.

Around the survivors, lakes are bubbling beneath torrents of hot mud and a giant cloud of grey ash is drifting as far as the Canadian West.

Late Monday, officials reported waters rising behind a fragile mud dam at the base of the volcano.

Bob Christiansen of the U.S. Geological Survey said a fresh flow of mud, pumice and ash cascaded into the valley of the north fork of the Toutle River on Monday, forming a 60-metre deep barrier at the outlet of Spirit Lake. The material will not be able to hold back rising waters, he said.

The eruption of the mountain Sunday ripped off the top 396 metres of the peak, sending steaming mudflows down in a torrent that laid waste to thousands of acres of pristine forest.

Meanwhile, the daily routine of much of eastern Washington state ground to a standstill Monday as businesses and schools closed, hospitals reported numerous respiratory complaints and fine ash particles disabled hundreds of automobiles.

Hundreds of kilometres of state highways were closed as clouds of ash threatened visibility.

No problems expected from haze

Haze continues to hang over the Okanagan Valley in the aftermath of the Mount St. Helens volcanic eruption in Washington Sunday morning.

Concern has been expressed about health problems, water contamination and crop damage from the fallen ash, but chances of any real trouble now seem slim.

The big blast which blew the top off the mountain was felt throughout the South Okanagan.

It rattled windows, shook houses and sounded — in varying reports — like blasting or thunder.

One Penticton resident said that there was a low rumbling noise to the south and then windows rattled. The vibrations lasted for a couple of seconds, and two other tremors of lesser intensity occurred a few minutes later.

Seismologist Max Wilde of the federal observatory at White Lake south of Penticton, is busy checking the quake data collected over the weekend. His reports are compiled with others gathered in a network of seismographic stations.

The smoke rolled into the valley late Sunday afternoon.

Osoyoos residents saw the smoke first, saying it came boiling up from the south like a storm, and when it arrived, it was no storm — just a hazy look about the air.

The smoke reached Penticton

early in the evening, lending a reddish tint to the sunset.

Monday visibility across the valley was limited, and the smoke hung thick in the air with a flat grey appearance.

The volcanic ash could be seen clearly Monday on automobiles in the Osoyoos areas, but to see the ash in Penticton one had to run a hand across a surface to check for the light grey dust.

Ray Johnson, co-ordinator of the Penticton Search and Rescue, said the volcanic dust

has been monitored by the atmospheric division of the environmental service.

Johnson said he has been advised that volcanic dust being blown into this area poses no danger to local water supplies and no danger to public health.

The minute particles of volcanic ash, which caused hazy fog-like conditions in Penticton and the Southern Okanagan, were blown in from northern

Washington by southern winds. Dale Richier at the Penticton airport weather office said Penticton is not directly in the fallout of the volcanic ash but is experiencing dust because of the wind factor. He said the dust should continue for about two or three days as weather patterns indicate winds will continue to blow from the south.

Just in time for big blast

Premonition led residents to mountain

By RON HOLLAND
Staff Writer

Ever wonder why people climb mountains, raft down raging rivers or swim the English Channel?

Ask Carlos and Nacho Botero why they went to Washington on the weekend to view the eruption of Mt. St. Helens and you would likely receive the same answer.

"Because it was there."

Carlos felt all last week that something was going to happen. Whether it was his sixth sense or a premonition, he doesn't know. He just knew that something was going to happen at the mountain and he wanted to be there.

Three Eruptions

"There were three minor eruptions last Tuesday and then the mountain quieted down," Carlos said. "We left Saturday morning and arrived near the mountain that night. We were staying about 15 miles from the mountain. It looked like Nkwala Mountain from Kaleden. It was that big and imposing.

"We took some pictures Saturday night when we arrived and a few more early Sunday morning before it blew."

The Botero brothers had plans of going up to Spirit Lake early Sunday but decided instead to have breakfast and then try the journey.

"We were just sitting there with one or two other people," Carlos added. "About 8:30 a.m. the whole mountain just blew."

No Warning

"There was no advance warning or anything like that. We were told after we got home that the blast of the eruption was heard in Penticton. But near the mountain there was nothing. We didn't hear a thing. All of a sudden the mountain was blowing up. The only thing we noticed right after the blast was a strong wind of about 60 miles an hour and it got very cold, very suddenly. We had to put on our winter jackets. Another weird experience was the lightning caused by the blast. There was lots of lightning but no thunder.

"It would be interesting to hear why we didn't hear the blast and there was no thunder after the lightning.

Ten Seconds

"It took about 10 seconds for the mushrooming cloud to block out the sun. It was almost impossible to get pictures of the cloud because by the time I could change the filters on my camera it was too far away. All we could get was some pictures of part of the cloud."

Carlos says the sun was blocked out for almost five or six hours.

He says the ash fallout continued for about two hours and that the ash disappeared with the high winds.

"But the resulting smoke and steam kept the sun blocked out until mid-afternoon.

Sulphur Odor

"The enormous cloud of gas and ash rose about 40,000 to 45,000 feet into the air from the top of the mountain. It was just like a nuclear explosion. Then after about two or three hours it became very warm. The temperature rose from about 40 to 90 within a short period of time. There was a distinct sulphur odor in the air. We had no problem breathing and the gasses and so on spewing out of the mountain didn't bother our eyes at all."

Carlos and Nacho said they both had mixed feelings while watching the mountain explode in front of their eyes.

"For awhile we both had a happy feeling," Carlos said. "Happy that we were watching the experience. Then it got kind of scary. It was hard to know what was coming out of the mountain. We didn't know what gases were in the smoke and ash. We didn't know what was in the ash."

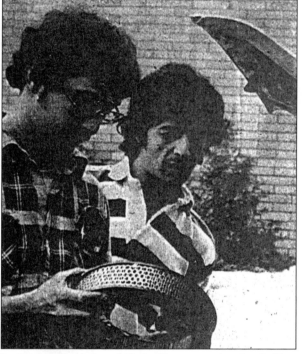

Brothers Carlos, left, and Nacho Botero examine the air filter from their car after returning to Penticton from the scene of Sunday's Mt. St. Helens volcanic eruption.

Mud dam watched

Flood warning follows volcano

VANCOUVER, WASH.
(REUTER) —

A 60-metre wall of water threatening to burst on the devastated area around the Mount St. Helens volcano could force the evacuation of 50,000 people, a prominent U.S. geologist warned today.

The latest danger posed to the scorched and flattened landscape came as a cloud of volcanic ash and smoke left a wide dust trail as far as 2,400 kilometres to the east, bringing small towns to a standstill and damaging crops.

The one-kilometre-wide wall of water, which has built up behind a dam of mud and ash near Spirit Lake, at the northern foot of the volcano, is being closely watched by authorities.

Flood warnings have been issued and a member of the U.S. Geological Survey group, Dwight Crandell, said if the dam collapses millions of gallons of water will be released.

It's Metric Madness

If conversion to metric measurement in the retail grocery sector goes ahead as planned, by Jan. 1, 1981, grocery stores in 21 cities across the nation will display meat and produce prices in dollars per kilo and gram, instead of dollars per pound and ounce. The baffled consumer will once again be scratching his head in an effort to figure out how to get value for his money.

As the Toronto Star points out, although the argument can be made that metrication is valuable in export sales to other nations using the metric system, the benefit of forcing the average consumer to buy his beef steak and bananas in metric measurement has yet to be demonstrated. At best it's a frustrating inconvenience, and since the Metric Commission will be spending millions of dollars on implementation, the tax payer shells out the price of his own annoyance.

Since public antipathy to the system has been clearly demonstrated in three pilot project cities, pressing ahead with retail grocery metrication would also be a fine example of the governmental principle of ignore and conquer.

In Peterborough – considered so typical of public attitudes that it's used widely as a test market for all kinds of products – consumers preferred to drive miles out of their way to shop in stores that offered groceries in pounds and ounces. Some 7,000 people there signed a petition to Parliament telling their legislators emphatically that they did not want, and would not accept, metrication in local grocery stores. Reaction in the other two test centres of Sherbrooke, Quebec, and Kamloops was similar, ranging from confused anger to disgruntled resignation.

Conversion to metric scales is also costly for retailers; that's an additional overhead cost that will inevitably be passed on to customers.

All this discombobulation might be worthwhile if getting to know your neighborhood kilogram had any significant benefit for Canada, or Canadian consumers – benefit that would outweigh the cost, time and effort involved in conversion.

The apparent lack of such benefit ranks metric conversion for fresh meat and produce as low on the scale of usefulness as weather forecasts in Celsius and kilopascals, and metric cookbooks.

It's an idea cabinet should abandon – or at least postpone unless someone comes up with a compelling reason for such an expensive and bothersome business.

Hibernia Oil Find Largest In Canada

TORONTO (CP) —
Confirmation of long-held speculation that the Hibernia oil field off Newfoundland's coast is expected to contain at least 10 billion barrels of crude oil makes it by far the largest find ever reported in Canada.

At that level of reserves, it would be more than six times the size of the previous biggest single field.

Confirmation of the speculation, which has ranged as high as 20 billion barrels, was made yesterday in St. John's, Nfld., by R.H. Carlyle of Calgary, senior vice-president of Gulf Canada Resources Ltd.

He was addressing a two-day seminar on resource management in Newfoundland. Gulf is a partner in the Hibernia test well with Mobile Oil Canada Ltd.

Dinosaur Finds

DRUMHELLER, AL. (CP) —
Teams of eager young detectives are hot on the trail of a mystery among the desolation of a landscape that looks like it belongs in another time or on another planet.

They're working in southern Alberta's badlands on one of the most spectacular dinosaur finds ever recorded.

It's a bed of fossils covering an area the size of two football fields and so rich in remains that one cannot take a step without tripping over them.

About 70 million years ago, during the cretaceous period, most of what is now Alberta was the bottom of a warm, shallow sea and something killed off an entire herd of centrosaurs.

1980-1989

Tune-agers 'wow' audiences while on 7-day tour of B.C.

The Penticton Retirement Centre Tune-agers in the early 1980's.

Photo courtesy of Penticton Tune-agers

By Sonni Bone

The 'Rolling Stones' of the Penticton and District Retirement Centre have just completed their 7th major tour in the 10 years of their existence.

The week long tour of the tune-agers, during which they gave eight performances in five days, was the 'cream' of their performing career, said director Mrs. Helene Scott.

"In my entire life I have never seen a group of people performing who got the kind of heart warming response from an audience that the Tune-agers did.

"Every performance received a standing ovation and the crowds would surge around the stage at the end telling them they had not enjoyed an evening so much in years.

"The rapport that seemed to be established immediately made the Tune-agers give their very best. In the years that I have been coaching them I had never thought they would reach the pinnacle that they did. The question everywhere was 'How the town the size of Penticton could find these kind of performers among their elderly'."

The Tune-agers offered a good repertoire — 35 to 40 group songs and 25 selections for solos and small combos. Each program they did was different using soloists who had friends and relatives in the areas where they performed.

Out of the 52 membership of the Tune-Agers only 37 were able to travel due to illness and other commitments. But the bus was filled with spouses who were a support line during performances.

Record Sales Soar

The first afternoon concert was at Silver Harbor Manor in North Vancouver.

"Our record sales soared. As a matter of fact our total sales of records and donations was almost $2000 over the tour."

Since 1976 the Tune-agers have sold $10,638 worth of records.

1980-1989

Terry Fox ... suffers tendinitis

The People In The News

By Canadian Press

Terry Fox resumed his cross-Canada run today after tendinitis forced him to stop for two days.

Ron Calhoun, national special events chairman for the Canadian Cancer Society, said Fox saw an orthopedic surgeon in Sault Ste. Marie, Ont., after developing pain and swelling in his foot. He developed the problem while running near Marathon, about 220 kilometres east of Thunder Bay.

The 22-year-old university student from Port Coquitlam, B.C., is running across Canada and so far has raised almost $1.6 million for cancer research.

"This has in no way detracted from his determination to run and to finish," Calhoun said. "He is fine and in terrific spirits and he is concerned the story be told accurately."

Terry Fox

Fox Run Draws Con Men

TORONTO (CP) — A Canadian Cancer Society spokesman says people leery of contributing to unofficial fund-raisers inspired by Terry Fox's cross-Canada run should mail contributions to local cancer society offices.

Kay Dabor of Mississauga, Ont., said Monday she has heard of several complaints about door-to-door canvassers soliciting money.

"The cancer society is not doing an official door-to-door canvass in connection with Terry Fox's run but we are aware of many unofficial fund-raisers inspired by

Terry's efforts."

Mrs. Dabor said the society realizes that the fervor inspired by Terry Fox could bring out some "rip-off artists."

Meanwhile, more than 500 people gathered Monday in Sudbury, Ont., to welcome Fox, 22, who is more than half way in his run from St. John's, Nfld., to Vancouver.

Fox said that cancer had caused his right let to be amputated three years ago following lengthy chemotherapy and that he decided to run across the country to bring attention to the efforts of the

cancer society.

Starting his run last spring, Fox has raised pledges of more than $1.2 million so far.

"If you read in the papers that Terry Fox is tired, he's down and he's out, don't you dare believe it," he said. "I'm not going to quit."

Sometime on Sunday he passed the half-way point of his run without knowing it.

"Mentally, today (Monday) was the hardest so far. Because I've been looking for the halfway mark for 3 1/2 months, then I missed it."

HERO'S WELCOME HO-HUM FOR FOX

AUGUST 21, 1980. WHITE RIVER, ONT. (CP) — Terry Fox ran eight kilometres Wednesday in a driving thunderstorm, continuing to amaze those who lined roads to cheer him.

Fox, 22, who lost his right leg to cancer three years ago, resumed his cross-Canada marathon early today in another shower and was south of White River, 320 kilometres north of Sault Ste. Marie.

Fox, running to raise money for cancer research, received his now-customary hero's welcome Wednesday afternoon, dining with White River municipal officials and speaking before about 250 cheering citizens.

White River, which has a population of 1,200, has pledged $3,400 for the Canadian Cancer Society.

TERRY MAKES GUINNESS

By Frank Mackey

JANUARY 8, 1982. LONDON (CP) — Terry Fox, the young cancer victim from Port Coquitlam, B.C., who inspired millions with his attempt to run across Canada in 1980, has made it into the latest edition of the Guinness Book of World Records.

Fox, who died June 28, 1981, just a month short of his 23rd birthday, is credited in the 1983 edition with having raised the greatest amount of money in a charity walk or run.

The full entry, listed in the category of "economic" records, says: "The greatest recorded amount raised by a charity walk or run of $24.7 million Canadian by Terry Fox (1958-81) of Canada who ran from St. John's, Nfld., to Thunder Bay, Ont., with a artificial leg in 143 days from April 12 to Sept. 2, 1980. He covered 5,373 kilometres (3,339 miles)."

Cancer Catches Up To Heroic Runner

But He's Not Given Up

Terry Fox had difficulty getting people to notice when he set out to run across Canada on one good leg and one made from metal and plastic.

But the more he ran, the more they noticed.

And even though cancer has struck him again and cancelled the last half of the coast-to-coast run he started April 12, the 22-year-old from nearby Port Coquitlam, has not given up.

Fox ran from St. John's, Nfld., to Thunder Bay, Ont., but has raised twice as much money for cancer research as he first set as his goal.

Running his daily marathon during the weekend, Fox thought he had a cold.

"We were nearing Thunder Bay. For the past three days I had been feeling a little nauseous, a bit short of breath."

"On Monday I did 18 miles then went to the van for a rest. I had a pain in my neck and chest. I had no idea what it was."

"I ran two more miles and I was feeling pretty sore. I slept for 15 minutes, then I ran another mile."

"It wasn't any better."

He was then 16 kilometres from Thunder Bay General Hospital.

Terry was examined there and on Tuesday, secondary cancer was diagnosed in both lungs.

"The left lung collapsed," he said, "I had to come home."

Gripping his mother's hand and fighting back tears and a persistent cough, he told a news conference Tuesday night in a hospital in this municipality adjacent to Vancouver that he is not disappointed in himself for failing to complete his cross-Canada marathon.

"I'm happy with what I did, I tried my hardest, I did my very best.

"If there's any way I can finish it off next year or the years after, I'll be there. I can't do any more right now. I fainted this afternoon just walking across the road."

It was in the same hospital 3 1/2 years ago that his right leg was amputated above the knee because of cancer. And it was in hospital the night before the operation that he decided on his Marathon of Hope to raise money for cancer research.

It still is his goal.

"I've raised $1.5 million so far," he said, "and I didn't make it to four of the provinces." Cancer society officials said Tuesday the total is closer to $2 million.

Fox said it will take more courage to see him through his second bout with cancer than it took to battle fatigue and the elements on his run.

"All along I've been trying to set an attitude for people who have cancer. I'm not going to quit, I'm going to keep on fighting my best."

"I knew that unless he collapsed he wouldn't stop," said Lynn Bryan, a Canadian Cancer Society spokesman close to Fox's efforts. "There's no way Terry will stay down as long as he's able to move.

"We all knew it could happen but we didn't believe it would. We thought that he was like the eternal flame – he would just go on and on."

Simon Fraser University announced Tuesday the establishment of the Terry Fox gold medal to be awarded annually to an SFU student, along with $1,000 and free tuition for three semesters.

It will be given to the SFU student who demonstrates the personal qualities, as Fox has, of courage against adversity and dedication to society.

BUT HE'S NOT GIVEN UP
Cancer catches up to heroic runner

NEW WESTMINSTER, B.C. (CP) — Terry Fox had difficulty getting people to notice when he set out to run across Canada on one good leg and one made from metal and plastic.

But the more he ran, the more they noticed.

And even though cancer has struck him again and cancelled the last half of the coast-to-coast run he started April 12, the 22-year-old from nearby Port Coquitlam, has not given up.

Fox ran from St. John's, Nfld., to Thunder Bay, Ont., but has raised twice as much money for cancer research as he first set as his goal.

Running his daily marathon during the weekend, Fox thought he had a cold.

"We were nearing Thunder Bay. For the past three days I had been feeling a little nauseous, a bit short of breath."

"On Monday I did 18 miles then went to the van for a rest. I had a pain in my neck and chest. I had no idea what it was."

"I ran two more miles and I was feeling pretty sore. I slept for 15 minutes, then I ran another mile."

"It wasn't any better."

He was then 16 kilometres from Thunder Bay General Hospital.

Terry was examined there and on Tuesday, secondary cancer was diagnosed in both lungs.

"The left lung collapsed," he said. "I had to come home."

Gripping his mother's hand and fighting back tears and a persistent cough, he told a news conference Tuesday night in a hospital in this municipality adjacent to Vancouver that he is not disappointed in himself for failing to complete his cross-Canada marathon.

"I'm happy with what I did, I tried my hardest, I did my very best.

"If there's any way I can finish it off next year or the years after, I'll be there. I can't do any more right now. I fainted this afternoon just walking across the road."

It was in the same hospital 3 1/2 years ago that his right leg was amputated above the knee because of cancer. And it was in hospital the night before the operation that he decided on his Marathon of Hope to raise money for cancer research.

It still is his goal.

"I've raised $1.5 million so far," he said, "and I didn't make it to four of the provinces." Cancer society officials said Tuesday the total is closer to $2 million.

Fox said it will take more courage to see him through his second bout with cancer than it took to battle fatigue and the elements on his run.

VOWS TO FIGHT

"All along I've been trying to set an attitude for people who have cancer. I'm not going to quit, I'm going to keep on fighting my best."

"I knew that unless he collapsed he wouldn't stop," said Lynn Bryan, a Canadian Cancer Society spokesman close to Fox's efforts. "There's no way Terry will stay down as long as he's able to move.

"We all knew it could happen but we didn't believe it would. We thought that he was like the eternal flame — he would just go on and on."

Simon Fraser University, where Fox is a kinesiology major, announced Tuesday the establishment of the Terry Fox gold medal to be awarded annually to an SFU student, along with $1,000 and free tuition for three semesters.

A university spokesman said it will be given to the SFU student who demonstrates the personal qualities, as Fox has, of courage against adversity and dedication to society.

1980–1989

Former Beatle Gunned Down
Suspect charged in Lennon slaying

NEW YORK (CP) —

A 25-year-old Hawaii man who apparently stalked John Lennon for three days was held today on a charge of gunning down the former Beatle, as the music world mourned the death of the legendary songwriter and singer.

The suspect, Mark David Chapman, was taken under heavy guard to the Tombs prison in downtown Manhattan early today to await arraignment.

A police source, who asked not to be identified, said Chapman gave different stories to detectives about the killing. But he said Chapman was "emphatic" that he knew he was shooting the 40-year-old Lennon, who helped make the British rock group into superstars and pop-cult legends in the 1960s.

More than 2,000 people gathered this morning outside the Dakota, the luxury apartment building on Manhattan's Upper West Side where Lennon lived with his wife, Yoko Ono and their five-year-old son, Sean, and where he was shot Monday night after stepping from a limousine.

David Geffen, president of Geffen Records for which Lennon recorded, said Ono, upstairs in one of the couple's apartments, was "very upset" by the crowd after daybreak.

"They're a bunch of crazy people out there... they're drunk and rowdy. It's like a party," Geffen said.

A smaller, more subdued crowd had stood vigil outside the building on 72nd Street across from Central Park late Monday night.

Police said Chapman told them he had a licence for the gun used in the shooting but could only produce a bill of sale for the weapon, a Charter Arms .38-calibre revolver, purchased in Hawaii.

Lennon had autographed a record album for Chapman about 5 p.m. EST when he was accosted by the young man as he left his apartment complex to go to a recording studio.

The police source said that at one point Chapman indicated he was annoyed that Lennon had only scribbled his autograph on the album.

Lennon, who was the co-author with Paul McCartney of such

famous songs as I Want to Hold Your Hand, Yesterday and Let it Be, was returning from the studio when the shooting occurred.

Yelling "I'm shot," Lennon staggered and collapsed face down after the shooting at 10:50 p.m. Police rushed the former Beatle to nearby Roosevelt Hospital in a squad car.

"Tell me it isn't true," sobbed his wife, when doctors pronounced the songwriter dead soon afterwards. Lennon had said in an RKO radio network broadcast only hours before his death that he hoped to die before his wife because he "couldn't carry on" without her.

Even six hours after the shooting, 150 people knelt and recited prayers outside the building.

Hundreds of fans lit candles and ringed the hospital in silent tribute.

McCartney, reported in "deep, deep shock, and saddened" by the killing, was in his Sussex farmhouse in southern England and was refusing to see anyone.

Former Beatle Ringo Starr broke off a vacation to fly to the United States, and George Harrison also was deeply upset and had cancelled a recording session scheduled for today.

Dejected Lennon Fans Take Their Own Lives

Widow Calls For Vigil

NEW YORK (AP) —

Two fans, apparently despondent over the slaying of John Lennon, took their own lives, while Lennon's widow called for a 10-minute silent vigil to honor the memory of the rock star who stepped from five years of seclusion into a hail of bullets.

Meanwhile, the wife of the man accused in the slaying, Mark David Chapman, said she too mourns Lennon, but loves her husband. Guards were checking Chapman's cell every 15 minutes to make sure he doesn't commit suicide.

And lawyers for the Lennon family filed a will estimating the former Beatle's estate to be at least $30 million.

Chapman, who has twice attempted suicide in the past, said his lawyer, was being held for a psychiatric examination.

"I've got a good side and a bad side," The Daily News said he told guards. "The bad side is very small, but sometimes it takes over the good side and I do bad things."

Lennon's death Monday night outside his luxurious Manhattan apartment building continued to bring tributes from music fans.

About 10,000 people huddled in snow and wind Wednesday night for a candlelight vigil in Toronto, 2,000 gathered to mourn in Washington, 10,000 in Baltimore and 1,300 people held hands and sang Lennon's songs on the steps of the New York Capitol in Albany.

Mourns Rock Idol

"To me, his death made a big hole in the world," said Brian Markle, 29, one of the fans who sang in Toronto. "There was no one like John Lennon."

For the third night, a small crowd kept vigil outside the Dakota, where Lennon lived with his wife, Yoko Ono, and their five-year-old son, Sean.

In Brooksville, Fla., a 16-year-old girl who "idolized" Lennon and still was mourning her father's suicide took a fatal overdose of sleeping pills Tuesday, authorities said. Jean Costello said her daughter, Colleen, left a note saying she was depressed over Lennon's death.

In Salt Lake City, Michael Craig, 30, fired a pistol into his mouth Tuesday after becoming despondent at the news of Lennon's death, authorities said.

Lennon's body was released by the city medical examiner on Wednesday and taken to Ferncliff crematorium. There, under heavy security, the body was cremated and the ashes were claimed by his widow.

Ono asked those who wanted to commemorate Lennon's death to observe 10 minutes of silence at 2 p.m. Sunday. A spokesman said "The world will be the place where you are."

LENNON RECORDS SOLD OUT

By Ron Holland
Staff Writer

DECEMBER 10, 1980. — Anyone in Penticton wishing to obtain a record album by the slain John Lennon had better be prepared to wait, because it's going to be some time before they are again available.

Lennon was shot down in a hail of gunfire Monday night outside the New York apartment where he, his wife Yoko Ono and their five-year-old son Sean lived. Lennon was a member of the Beatles, which during the 1960s, developed a music style for an era. Over the years, the Beatles have sold more record albums than any other pop group.

"His records are sold out everywhere, we can't get any," said Vic Mateus, manager of Apple Valley Records. "The run began early Tuesday and the record companies can't keep up with the demand.

"Warehouses in Vancouver, Calgary and Toronto don't even have any. I guess the public has decided his records will be collectors' items. I understand some companies will be pressing new records, but it's going to be two or three weeks before I see any of them."

Mateus said he only had a limited stock of Lennon albums but he was cleaned out in about 20 minutes.

Kevin Harding of Kelly's said some Vancouver retail record stores jumped the price on Lennon's latest album from $7.98 to $10.98 as soon as the news of Lennon's death reached the Vancouver area.

"We only had about 30 of his new albums and they were gone within two hours," Harding said.

Lennon fans gather for tribute

By The Canadian Press

John Lennon wasn't much for dead heroes.

"I don't appreciate worship of dead Sid Vicious or of dead James Dean or of dead John Wayne," Lennon said in a recent interview in Playboy magazine. "It's all garbage to me. I worship the people who survive."

But his words didn't' stop thousands of Canadians, young and old, from gathering Sunday to offer silent prayer and songs as part of a worldwide tribute to the former Beatle who was killed a week ago.

In Ottawa, about 5,000 mourners huddled in the freezing cold and strong winds in front of Parliament Hill's Peace Tower.

Carrying candles and flowers, symbols of Lennon's messages of universal love and peace, they joined in a 10-minte period of silence and sang Lennon's famous refrain, Give Peace A Chance.

A Roman Catholic priest, Father Daryl Kennedy, delivered a brief prayer and then said:

"John Lennon was a man blessed by God but taken from us by man's brutality. His life was a success but not without its moments of glaring failure."

As Beatles music poured out of giant loudspeakers, many young men and women swayed to the music and held up their hands with fingers forming the familiar V-shaped peace sign.

"Lennon Lives Forever," said one banner.

Lennon, 40, was shot dead in New York on Monday night as he and his wife, Yoko Ono, were entering their apartment building.

His body was cremated Wednesday in New York and there was no funeral. Instead, Ono asked everyone to "pray for John's soul" by observing 10 minutes of silence at 2 p.m. Sunday "wherever you are."

In Western Canada it rained most of Sunday, but about 300 people from British Columbia and Washington state attended a Lennon vigil at Peace Arch Park, on the Canada-U.S. border south of Vancouver.

Mourning of Lennon's death is not enough

The sentiment aroused by the slaying of ex-Beatle John Lennon should not obscure the circumstances that led to it and which remain after it.

It is not enough to mourn his death and to dismiss the killing as the work of a lunatic or a misfit. There are two constructive things now that the American public can do.

The first is resolving to come to grips with the symbol and instrument of violence and assassination in America - the handgun. It can be argued of course that stricter gun laws will not prevent the deranged or violent person from committing murder; he will acquire the weapon he needs whether it comes form legal or illegal sources.

But it is incredible that in most parts of the U.S. the people should be able to buy and sell firearms with such ease, and given that situation and the staggering number of weapons in private hands, in good conscience one can only conclude that stricter and more effective gun control laws must be adopted forthwith. A return to saner levels of violence can only come about when the number of arms in private hands is drastically reduced.

The second constructive thing Americans - indeed all of us - can take in the wake of the Lennon shooting is to consider the full range of violence inciting aspects of modern life. Movies which glorify cruelty, television violence, magazines whose editorial lens distorts all events into strife - these daily events poison the social climate.

In life, Lennon built a reputation for fighting with some success for various causes. Could it be that in the current outpouring of grief, his death will bring his greatest success - getting action at last on one of the most pressing causes of all - the control of the sale and possession of handguns?

1980~1989

Flags fly half mast for Terry Fox

DECEMBER 2, 1980, NEW WESTMINSTERS, B.C. (CP) - Tumors in Terry Fox's lungs have shown signs of shrinkage following a course of drug treatments, his doctor said Monday.

Dr. Robert Heffelfinger said Fox has completed chemotherapy treatments and will have a break of several weeks while doctors evaluate his response to treatment.

"There is some evidence of improvement in the size of the lesions which is a great thing, frankly." Heffelfinger said.

He said there probably will be another course of chemotherapy for Fox, the one-legged runner who has raised $2 million for cancer research.

Fox had run more than half way across Canada when the cancer that forced amputation of his right leg was found to have spread to his lungs.

Fox is reported feeling much better than earlier in November when the chemotherapy made him weak.

"It knocked him right out," said family friend Doug Alward. But since then, said Alward, "he's made an amazing recovery."

Fluid diet for Terry

JUNE 24, 1981, NEW WESTMINSTER, B.C. (CP) — Marathon of Hope runner Terry Fox is more restless today but is able to carry on short conversations with his family, the medical director of Royal Columbian Hospital said today.

Dr. Ladislav Antonik said the 22-year-old cancer victim is in critical condition, but he added Fox was in worse shape in February when he underwent surgery to remove a fluid buildup around his heart.

Antonik told a news conference Fox is on a fluid diet by mouth and is receiving morphine for control of pain.

Fox is not being treated with the experimental anti-cancer agent interferon. He had been receiving interferon until June 7 and treatment was scheduled to resume Monday.

Antonik said when doctors saw the condition Fox was in they decided to postpone treatment.

Fox was readmitted to hospital Friday with a chest infection. Antonik said he was coughing and spitting up blood.

Antonik said Fox has lost a considerable amount of weight.

He said he does hope to send him home again, "but right now there certainly is no immediate prospect of that.

"The best you can say is that he's not exactly in a condition where you would expect to send a patient home for home care. It would be difficult to look after him at home."

Antonik said it is debatable whether the interferon treatments have slowed the spread of Fox's cancer "depending on whether you're an optimist or a pessimist."

Antonik said there is no reason to believe the cancer has spread.

By The Canadian Press

Canadians from all social ranks and parts of the country paused Sunday to pay tribute to Terry Fox, the man who helped to bring Canadians closer together by his struggle against cancer.

Provincial and federal politicians were united in praise for the 22-year-old who died early Sunday.

In an unprecedented move, the federal government ordered all its flags to fly at half mast in honor of the young runner whose Marathon of Hope ended last September, an honor generally reserved for distinguished politicians or statesmen.

But apart from the official reaction that poured in Sunday, heartfelt admiration also came from dozens of average citizens polled across the country by The Canadian Press.

"It took the foreign-ness out of cancer," said Debbie Walsh, a 26-year-old student in St. John's, Nfld.

"My aunt is dying of cancer and she wants to continue living her life exactly as she did before. I think it is exposure to people like Fox that will let people let her do it."

Montreal accountant James Gow, 29, said the Marathon of Hope helped bring Canadians together.

"We've been hearing quite a bit about him through the news media," Gow said. "It has brought Canadians a bit closer, perhaps."

In Ottawa, Primer Minister Trudeau said, "Canadians mourn the passing of a young man whose courage and awesome determination inspired this country as no one else has ever done."

Trudeau said Fox's struggle prompted Canadians to give generously.

"The people of this country were eager to respond to the grandeur of his crusade. He told us we could do so by contributing money to

(CP Photo)

cancer research, so that others could be spared from that dreadful disease, or could have greater hope for recovery from it."

As a recognition of Canadians' affection for Fox, the federal government announced plans to lower flags on all federal buildings across the country until the runner's funeral, scheduled for Thursday in his home of Port Coquitlam, B.C. However, flags will be raised Wednesday in line with government regulations for the Dominion Day holiday.

The federal government also announced that a book of condolence was opened in the centre block of Parliament and everyone is welcome to sign the register.

Senator Ray Perrault said other federal government tributes are being planned but he declined to be specific.

Gov.-Gen. Ed Schreyer, on board a submarine in the Atlantic Ocean, also conveyed his sadness at the news of Fox's death, saying the

runner instilled "a sense of pride and hope in all Canadians."

The governor-general sent condolences to the Fox family.

In a message to the Fox family, Opposition Leader Joe Clark said the runner was a symbol of courage to the world.

"He fought for life against overwhelming odds and his courage will stay a beacon for everyone with illness or fears," the Progressive Conservative leader said.

Federal New Democratic Party Leader Ed Broadbent said Fox's life was a triumph over death.

Ontario Premier William Davis said "we can all stand a little taller because there walked among us for a very short time a young man called Terry Fox."

Fox leaves a legacy for Canada to admire and follow, and has shown what determination and courage can do, British Columbia Premier Bill Bennett said in Victoria.

Terry's legacy: an editorial

Few people have left such an impressive imprint on Canada and Canadians as has Terry Fox.

This was the young man who got every one of us caught up in the personal challenge he saw in his incredible cross-Canada marathon to raise money for cancer research. All of us shared the bitter blow when he had to discontinue that valiant effort.

But in no sense could it be said

that he failed to reach his goal. It was taken up more forcefully than he could ever had dreamed of because he gave the people of Canada a cause behind which they could unite.

In death, Terry's spirit lives on. He set an example of courage, endurance, determination and commitment - and of hope - that all of us would like to be able to strive somehow to emulate.

He has reminded us, too, how highly we prize real-life examples of true grit, of selflessness, of modesty and how much we love a genuine hero.

Through the inspiration he provided, we owe it to Terry Fox to continue his mission - not only against cancer but against all the crippling diseases and evils that make a loss such as his such a tragedy.

Local Loverboy hits big time

Empire Stadium in Vancouver will be filled with ecstatic young people, screaming their enthusiasm as Penticton's Mike Reno skips over the stage Aug. 2. When he opens his mouth to sing, teeneyboppers jammed against front stage will wave grasping arms in his direction.

To fans across North America, Mike Reno lives up to his group's name, Loverboy.

Playing to crowds of 10,000 to 50,000, people in up to five different states a week, Loverboy is racing up the charts and pounding its popularity to headliner success.

Yet still, home is best.

"We've played every major city in the U.S. but this is definitely the most beautiful place of all," said Mike Rynoski, home recently for a quick visit with his parents, Mr. and Mrs. Steve Rynoski of Vaseaux Lake. "Everywhere we go, we're always kind of comparing it to home," he said.

Tour Europe

But there isn't much chance to get home with a schedule as heavy as Loverboy's. This coming year, their engagements include a new record, performances in dozens of U.S. cities, and Hawaii at Christmas. From here the five-man rock band will tour Australia, Japan, all of Europe and back

Mike Reno

across Canada.

Vancouver is Loverboy's "home base." It is the home of their management company, and of Doug Johnson, keyboard player, and Matt Frennette, drummer. Both Mike and Matt are formerly of The Great Canadian River Race, local band which hit the charts before it broke up a few years ago. Guitarist Paul Dean is from Windermere, and Scott Smith, bass player, came from Winnipeg.

Loverboy is a full time job, says Mike. "We work pretty well every day. When we're not working we're travelling." In their Silver Eagle touring bus, complete with

stereo and color TV in the living room, a kitchen, bathroom and sleeping for 10, the band and road crew travels to a different city every day. Another truck follows, loaded with equipment. Or, from Miami to New York, San Diego to Seattle, they rent a 10-seater plane.

Loverboy's performances have been described as "minimum fuss with maximum power." This may be true of the road, where, as Mike says, "We're all having a good time... and nobody's got ulcers." "We're all good friends. The camaraderie makes the road easier."

Triple Platinum

The group's record reads like the rushing of a swollen river. Formed only two years ago, they spent the first year getting their act together in an old warehouse in Vancouver. In August, 1980, their first album was cut (a second is currently underway). Over two million of the album "Loverboy" have been sold in the U.S., and it has reached a triple Platinum rating in Canada (300,000).

Loverboy was top winner of the first annual Tribute to West Coast music awards in January. And they were nominated this spring for the coveted Juno awards.

There are four reasons for the group's success, says Mike - a good record company (Columbia), good management company, good

songs, and good musicians. (Loverboy plays only music written by themselves.)

And the group is playing from the heart. "We really mean it, we're not just pretending," says Mike. He has noticed this same depth in other successful groups. Loverboy has appeared with: Kiss, Journey, Bob Seeger, ZZ Top, Heart, Prism, Cheap Trick and Blue Oyster Cult.

High School Band

How did it all start? "It's all they ever wanted to do," says Mike's father, of Mike and his older brother Steven. But they had no music training, nor a musical family. In 1968, aged 13 and 17, the boys organized a band in Penticton called The Blue Webb.

"Mike bought his first drums from a paper route, when he was just a little kid," said Mr. Rynoski. On his 13th birthday, he filled in for a regular drummer in Greenwood. With brother Steve on electric guitar, it was Mike's first professional engagement.

Another band, Synergy, formed by local high school kids, played Friday nights in the Elks Hall. After graduation from Pen-Hi in 1973, Mike played and sang with groups in Calgary and Toronto, until he met Paul Dean, guitarist of Streetheart, and they formed Loverboy.

Gretzky here for Moog roast

Wayne Gretzky, the premiere hockey player in the world, is the latest in sports celebrities who will be attending the Andy Moog Sportsman's Dinner and Roast which will be held at the Peach Bowl Saturday at 6 p.m.

The announcement of Gretzky's appearance at the Andy Moog gala was made by Penticton Knights' public relations officer Sandy Brown this morning. Brown said

that the Edmonton Oilers' star will be arriving in Penticton Saturday morning and will participate in the Penticton Junior 'A' Alumni golf tournament which will be played at the Twin Lakes Golf and Country Club beginning at 9 a.m.

Other personalities include Oilers' general manager and coach Glen Sather, Oilers' Brett Calligan, Buffalo Sabres' captain Danny Gare and Minnesota North Stars' Kevin

Maxwell. Joining these three on the Roast panel will be Andy's father Don, a member of the 1955 World championship Penticton Vees, Rod Phillips, play-by-play announcer of the Oilers, Harvey Roy, Kamloops' Junior Oilers GM, and Andy's minor hockey coach Rick Kozuback, who is now an assistant coach with the reigning B.C. Junior Hockey League champion Penticton Knights.

WAYNE GRETZKY, the Edmonton Oilers' star will be at Penticton's Peach Bowl Saturday night for the Andy Moog Sportsman's Dinner and Roast.

Royal Wedding

Tumultuous Reception Along Procession Route

(AP Photo)

This is a family portrait taken after the wedding between Prince Charles and Princess Diana at Buckingham Palace in London, July 29, 1981.

LONDON (CP) —

A beaming Prince Charles took the beautiful Lady Diana Spencer as his bride and future queen today in a fairy-tale wedding as a hundred church bells peeled, huge choirs sang and thousands cheered.

"O let the nations rejoice and be glad!" erupted the massed choirs when the Archbishop of Canterbury pronounced them wed under the soaring dome of St. Paul's Cathedral.

From Buckingham Palace to St. Paul's and back, the princess, in a cloud of ivory taffeta, and the prince, in brass-buttoned navy commander's uniform, rode in horse-drawn carriages past about 600,000 people who roared their good wishes and waved a sea of Union Jacks.

The joy overflowed when the newlyweds returned to Buckingham Palace, stepped on to the scarlet-draped front balcony and waved to the thundering crowds.

The Queen joined them there, along with three generations of the Royal Family, the five bridesmaids, garlands in their hair, and the two pageboys.

At one point, Charles and Diana kissed, touching off a crescendo of cheers from below. They then retired inside for the wedding breakfast.

Captivates World

Royal kiss touches off a crescendo of cheers

(CP PHOTO)1996(ap-files)

Later, the couple set out for Waterloo rail station and their honeymoon in a horse-drawn landau trailing a dozen silver and blue plastic balloons attached by the prince's younger brothers. A hand-scrawled sign, "Just Married" was tacked on the hack.

The new Princess of Wales, appearing more at ease than during the earlier ceremonies, sparkled in a shiny pink short-sleeved suit trimmed in white with a small corn hat trailing a pink ostrich feather perched on her famous blonde hairdo. The prince, smiling and waving to the crowds left over from morning rituals was relaxed in a light gray lounge suit.

QUEEN DOESN'T GET CURTSY FROM NANCY

LONDON. SEPTEMBER 27, 1981 (AP) — Nancy Reagan reaffirmed U.S. independence with a handshake for the Queen instead of a curtsy but confounded the British press with a nod.

"Mystery of phantom curtsy" read the headline in The Daily Mail. The Daily Express said Mrs. Reagan "made as if to bow then changed her mind."

The U.S. first lady and the Queen met without benefit of press photographers Sunday before Mrs. Reagan joined the Royal Family to watch Prince Charles play polo at Windsor. It was the first meeting of the two women since Mrs. Reagan arrived as the official U.S. representative to the wedding Wednesday of the prince and Lady Diana Spencer.

Mrs. Reagan's press secretary, Sheila Tate, said the president's wife "shook hands with the queen and inclined her head slightly as you would when you meet someone.

"It was definitely not a curtsy."

Whether Mrs. Reagan would bend her knee to the descendant of King George III became an issue in the British press because of the flap in the United States when her friend, Leonore Annenberg, curtsied to Prince Charles on his arrival in Washington earlier this year.

Mrs. Annenberg got in practice when her husband, Walter was U.S. ambassador to Britain. But she now is the U.S. state department's chief of protocol and was welcoming Charles on behalf of President Reagan and the U.S. government.

1980~1989

An Independent

Constitution comes home after 115-year absence

OTTAWA (CP) —

The Constitution "is truly Canadian at last," Queen Elizabeth said today as she declared her "unbounded confidence in the future of this wonderful country."

The absence of Quebec is regrettable, she said, switching to French before thousands of people on Parliament Hill moments after an historic ceremony which gave Canada sole authority over its own constitution 115 years after Confederation.

But it is still "right" to associate the people of Quebec with this celebration because without them, Canada would not be what it is today," she said.

Prime Minister Trudeau also regretted the Parti Quebecois government's decision to reject his cherished new Constitution but said "nothing essential to the originality of Quebec has been sacrificed."

"Moreover, the process of constitutional reform has not come to an end." Trudeau said. "The two orders of government have made a solemn pledge to define more precisely the rights of native peoples.

"At the same time, they must work together to strengthen the charter of rights, including language rights in the various provinces.

"Finally, they must try to work out a better division of powers among governments."

PRAISES ACCORD

The Queen congratulated Trudeau and the nine premiers who signed the Nov. 5 accord leading to patriation on "the wisdom and statesmanship they have shown in reaching agreement on this new Canadian Constitution.

"It has been a long and difficult process of negotiation which I have followed closely for many years."

Quebec was "both the inspira-tion and the principal agent" of "perhaps the most significant step in Canada's history," the decision to take pride in Canada's several languages and cultures rather than deplore the differences, she said.

The Queen praised the new constitutional charter of rights, saying it "guarantees to every person in this country the right to equal opportunity.

"I am glad to see that the equality of women is accorded full respect, that disabled persons are protected against discrimination and that the rights of the aboriginal people are recognized, with full opportunity for further definition."

'SHARE RISKS'

Trudeau declared that "no charter of rights and freedoms, no sharing of powers can take away the need for us to be willing to share the risks and the greatness of the Canadian adventure.

"Without that collective act of

CANADA'S CONST
... from

Trudeau fu

will, our Constitution would be a dead letter and our country would wither away."

Significant moment in Canada's history

By Casy Korstanje
Courier Staff

The constitution respects the federation of Canada and Canadians should mark the occasion with all solemnity and respect it deserves.

Fred King (MP Okanagan-Similkameen) considers the patriation of the constitution a significant moment in Canada's history.

"I hope we can respect this day in Canada's history," said King. The constitution that is coming home represents the combined efforts of the country's first ministers, save one, and respects federation.

When the government first proposed patriation it was presented in a manner that disregarded Canada, said

King. "there was a threat to act arbitrarily," he said.

Input

However the new package represents the province's and the citizens' abilities to demand and gain input into their constitution.

King is delighted the Queen came to Canada.

"She is still the monarch, the queen of Canada and remains that way unless the majority rules otherwise," he said.

King feels the majority-rules concept has been safeguarded within the constitution.

"That's what we (the conservatives) filibustered for and also caused the bell ringing on the energy-bill issue.

(CP PHOTO) 1982

Queen Elizabeth signs Canada's constitutional proclamation in Ottawa on April 17, 1982 as Prime Minister Pierre Trudeau looks on.

Canada at Last

CLAIMED TODAY

e future

his dream

Supreme Court duty to review legislation

The most significant aspect of the new constitution is that it represents a change in the division of political power, says Berry McCullough, chairman of the political science and philosophy department at Okanagan College.

"Some important decision-making power will go to the Supreme Court of Canada. It will have complete responsibility for interpreting the Charter of Rights, property and civil rights."

"Now the Charter will apply right across the board to federal and provincial legislation across Canada."

"That is really what it is all about. It is not a matter of power slipping from the provincial to federal government."

"I wouldn't look for an immediate change to the constitution. The Supreme Court of Canada will move very slowly, very carefully to give teeth to the provisions. Federal or provincial legislation which violates one of the entrenched rights would be unconstitutional."

"Before, the Court was reluctant to do this. It was not inclined to over-rule legislation as long as it was not inconsistent."

"The Charter of Rights is a basic legal document which will be a measuring rod for acceptable legislation."

"There is a definite responsibility for the Supreme Court of Canada to ensure legislation complies. It is now duty bound to review legislation."

1980~1989

Bold but typically cautious Constitution reflects 'mosaic' society that is Canada

By J.P. Squire
Courier Staff

The new Canadian constitution is like Canadian society in that it is a mosaic, says a Kelowna lawyer who has been active in public life.

James Doak, commenting Friday as a Canadian rather than as a solicitor, described the new constitution as "built in Canada for Canadians not of Canadian (legislative) products assembled since 1867."

The new act is a relatively short document with 34 sections focussing on a Charter of Rights, the procedures for amendment and a list of 25 acts beginning with the British North America Act of 1867, he said.

"It is uniquely Canadian - a bold, new picture, but typically cautious. It is the best we could come up with, yet it is a compliment to our first ministers despite their tribulations.

"They set out to provide us with a constitution within the framework of history, the current times and the mosaic of the people and the provinces.

B.C.'s Biggest Mass-Murder Trial Opens With 'Not Guilty' Plea

VANCOUVER (CP) —

Clifford Robert Olson pleaded not guilty to 10 counts of first-degree murder today as the biggest mass-murder trial in the province's history began in B.C. Supreme Court.

Olson, appearing to have lost weight since he was taken into custody five months ago, entered the courtroom under heavy guard. Although his hair was long, he was freshly shaved. He wore a grey suit and carried a looseleaf binder.

The proceedings began with the selection of a jury. Of the 149 potential jurors, 16 asked to be excused for medical of family reasons and five asked to be excused because they were not capable of rendering an impartial verdict.

Moments after the five-woman,
seven-man jury was selected, Mr. Justice Harry McKay announced the jury would be sequestered. Tom Waithe, manager of sheriff services at the downtown law courts building said it was the first time in about 30 years that a jury has been sequestered at the start of a trial.

Olson, a 42-year-old Coquitlam, B.C., construction worker and father of an infant son, was charged last summer following a massive police investigation and discovery of 10 bodies or parts of bodies between November, 1980, and last July.

A series of disappearances of young people in southwestern B.C. during the spring and summer led to a massive police investigation, the arrest of a suspect and the grisly discoveries in isolated areas surrounding Vancouver.

The youngsters were all found within an area 90 kilometres north of Vancouver to the Whistler ski resort and 90 kilometres east to the Fraser Valley community of Agassiz.

Two of the bodies were found buried within a few hundred metres of each other in a bog in Richmond, just south of Vancouver, and about a kilometre from the body of Christine Weller, the first victim. Her body was found in a ditch Christmas Day, 1980, by a man walking his dog.

Five bodies were found in the Fraser Valley. Police did not publicly link the first few disappearances of young children but as the summer of 1981 wore on and the numbers increased, so did public fears.

Clifford Olson

Olson cash deal stirs controversy

VANCOUVER (CP) —

The decision to approve the payment of $100,000 to the family of mass murderer Clifford Robert Olson in exchange for information about his victims was the most difficult the B.C. Attorney General has ever made.

Attorney General Allan Williams said Friday he considered the payment for evidence deal to be revolting when he first learned about it in August last year.

"I went through an extensive analysis of all the factors associated with this case," Williams said in an interview on the Jack Webster television show on BCTV.

"I believe that the decision was then the one that had to be made and I still believe that today."

Williams told Webster he would make no apologies for authorizing the deal Aug. 24, in which $100,000 was paid into an account for Olson's wife, Joan, in exchange for Olson giving police evidence and leading them to his victims' bodies.

Williams also said that if he was faced with the same proposition today, his decision would be unchanged.

Was Correct

"If, in the Olson case, you go back to the 24th of August and advance all those circumstances to today and the information which I was given on the 24th of August was placed before me today, I would make the same decision. In fact, examining what we have uncovered since the decision was made, I'm satisfied it was the correct one."

Meanwhile, Olson's defence lawyer says murderers now will be tempted to kill for cash, because of the police payment for bodies deal.

Robert Shantz said Thursday the RCMP deal to pay $100,000 cash to Olson's family was morally and legally wrong, and in the end, politically dangerous.

"This is the first time I'm aware of in Canadian history when an accused, as opposed to an informant, has been paid money," said Shantz.

"I think it is politically insane and I personally don't approve of it."

Plea changed in Olson case

VANCOUVER (CP) —

The biggest mass murder trial in B.C. history came to an abrupt end today when Clifford Robert Olson pleaded guilty to 11 counts of first-degree murder and was sentenced to concurrent life sentences.

In a surprise move in front of a packed and hushed courtroom, the 42-year-old construction worker reversed his not guilty pleas on the original 10 counts in the deaths of 10 young people. An eleventh count was introduced by the Crown and Olson immediately pleaded guilty.

The bizarre turn came on the third day of what was expected to be a lengthy trial.

After the change of plea, Mr.
Justice Harry McKay called in the seven-man, five-woman jury, which had been sequestered at the start of the trial Monday. He told them that only they could make a finding of innocence or guilt.

They returned after a short deliberation and told Justice McKay they accepted the guilty pleas.

"I don't have the words to describe the enormity of your crime... and the hardships they brought" to the victims' families, McKay said.

No Fit Punishment

He said there was no punishment fit for the crime and recommended Olson never be eligible for parole.

Williams and federal Solicitor General Robert Kaplan said that such a deal would not be repeated.

It was done in the Olson case, Williams said, to ensure that Olson went behind bars where he could not kill any more children.

And it led Thursday to Olson pleading guilty to 11 counts of first-degree murder and being sentenced to a minimum of 25 years.

"He (Olson) advised the authorities that he would provide evidence for four murders
for $30,000 and for another $70,000 he would locate seven more bodies," Williams said.

He arranged for $100,000 to be put in a trust account. Money was paid out, as Olson led police to the bodies of his victims, to Olson's wife Joan, for her and their infant son Stephen.

Mrs. Olson has been paid $90,000 in this fashion. She will not get the remaining $10,000, he said, because Olson volunteered the location of the 11th body without insisting on compensation.

Stanley Cup 'Hat Trick'

VANCOUVER (CP) — Satisfaction for New York Islanders is winning three straight Stanley Cups. For the upstart Vancouver Canucks, the satisfaction comes from just being there.

"The real satisfaction comes from winning it," said Bryan Trottier. "We all wanted the third one so bar that the pressure was tremendous."

"I hope some people don't take us for granted. I hope they don't get tired of us winning. We're certainly not tired of it."

The Islanders became the first American-based team to win three consecutive National Hockey League playoff titles Sunday night when they defeated the game, but outclassed Vancouver Canucks 3-1 to sweep the final in four straight.

Right winger Mike Bossy, named the outstanding performer in the playoffs and winner of the Conn Smythe Trophy, fired two power-play goals in the second period when the Islanders broke open a 1-1 tie.

Bossy scored seven goals in the series to tie the record for a final series set in 1956 by Jean Beliveau of Montreal Canadiens in five

games against Detroit Red Wings.

"We consider ourselves a great team," said Bossy. "We work hard, work together and have fun together."

The Islanders scored eight power-play goals in the series, twice the output of the Vancouver power play, and that was the basic difference in the teams.

"There's only one major difference and that's Mike Bossy because he scores consistently on the power play," said goaltender Richard Brodeur, the shining star of the Canucks in 17 consecutive playoff games." "Until we get that kind of guy, we'll have to do things our way."

The Canuck way in the playoffs was bruising and brutally physical at times. Vancouver played the man with such enthusiasm that the Canucks wore down opposing teams – until they met the Islanders.

"We're pretty happy with what we accomplished in the playoffs," said acting captain Stan Smyl of the Canucks. "We'd have liked to won a game or two in this series."

The Islanders opened the series at home and won the first two games, 6-5 in overtime on Bossy's

goal at 19:58, and 6-4. New York then threw up a wall in front of goaltender Billy Smith in Vancouver and won 3-0 and 3-1.

"We had to play tough, smart hockey in Vancouver to win," said Islander coach Al Arbour. "Our game is not to retaliate, but rather to initiate."

"I guess, as a player, I might have got a little more satisfaction from this series. But I'd like to thank my players, every one of them, for the way they performed."

Playing-assistant coach Butch Goring, the most valuable player in the playoffs a year ago, scored the other New York goal, while Smyl was the lone Vancouver marksman.

Brodeur and Smith, both brilliant in the playoffs, finished off in fine style. Brodeur faced 28 New York shots and Smith looked at 24 Vancouver drives. Smith's win was his 15th of the playoffs, a new record.

The Islanders won their last nine playoff games and finished post-season play with a 15-4 record. The Canucks ended at 11-6 after entering the final with the best record.

CANUCKS MOVE TO FINALS

VANCOUVER, MAY 7, 1982 (CP) — In stores, hotels and bars, and even at the ballet, they whooped and hollered and cheered the night away.

Stanley Cup fever? Why not, considering it's been 58 years since a Vancouver team last had a crack at the fabled hockey trophy and another 10 years before that since they got their hands on it.

Nothing will convince Vancouver fans that their destiny isn't at hand after their Canucks came out of obscurity with a stretch drive and defeated Chicago Black Hawks 6-2 Thursday night to win the National Hockey League semi-final in five games.

Choruses of the now-familiar theme song echoed across the city.

"Na-na-na-na, na-na-na-na, Chicago, GOODBYE."

In the television section of The Bay's downtown department store a crowd of 20 clustered around a bank of TV sets watching the game.

Long after the game, a group of fans in Canuck sweaters roamed downtown streets screaming "We won, we won," and waving white towels – continuing a fad that caught on like wildfire after coach Roger Neilson waved one in token of surrender to the officiating in a Chicago game that was one of only two the Canucks lost in 13 playoff matches.

There'll be no immediate welcome-home ceremony for the Vancouver heroes who went on to New York to meet the Islanders in the first two games of the best-of-seven final starting Saturday night.

Hall Of Fame Induction Set

TORONTO (CP) — Former hockey superstar Bobby Orr and skiing legend Herman (Jack-Rabbit) Smith-Johannsen are among five men who will be inducted into Canada's Sports Hall of Fame in August, the Hall of Fame announced Monday.

Also being inducted are: Jack Bionda, former lacrosse great; Claude (Sandy) Saunders, for 30 years the regatta chairman for the Royal Canadian Henley; and Sam Pollock, former general manager of the NHL Montreal Canadiens.

Orr, 34, was the pivotal hockey player of the 1970s in the

National Hockey League. His records and achievements with Boston Bruins led to his being regarded as one of the greatest players of all time.

In 10 seasons with the Bruins, 1966-76, he won rookie-of-the-year honors, was the top NHL defenceman for eight consecutive seasons, won the Hart Trophy twice as the league's most valuable player and led the Bruins to the Stanley Cup in 1970 and 1972.

Injuries to his left knee forced his retirement in 1978.

Bionda of Huntsville, Ont., is the only other inductee in the ath-

lete category.

His career in lacrosse spanned two decades, from 1948 at the minor level to 1968 for Portland of the West Coast Senior A league. Bionda led his team to five national Mann Cup championships in seven attempts. He holds several scoring records and was voted the most valuable player in the Mann Cup playoffs in 1959 and 1962.

Smith-Johannsen, elected as a builder, is renowned for having developed skiing as a sport in the Laurentians, the Eastern Townships and Ontario.

The resident of Piedmont, Que., who will be 107 later this year, coached the Canadian skiers at the 1932 Olympics, after which he was consulted on the designs of the trails later transformed into the runs used for the 1980 Winter Olympics at Lake Placid, N.Y.

He created the Canadian Ski Marathon in 1967 and was awarded the Order of Canada in 1972.

Saunders, 70, of Hamilton has been involved in rowing for the last 50 years during which he competed for Canada in the 1936 and 1948 Olympics.

1980-1989

Grisly find turns into mass murder probe

KAMLOOPS, B.C. (CP) — Kamloops pathologists were unable to positively identify the charred remains of six people found in the back seat of a burned-out car Monday and have sent the bones and tissue to Vancouver for further tests.

The remains are believed to be those of the Johnsons of Kelowna and the Bentleys of Port Coquitlam, who disappeared in mid-August while on a camping trip north of this interior city.

Police investigators said Tuesday the car and the remains have been sent to the province's main crime lab in Vancouver.

While pathologists try to determine the victims' identities, and what killed them, police are searching for a camper van belonging to the Bentleys. They say they are treating the case as a mass homicide.

Discovery of the skeletal remains ended the massive ground and air search for Bob Johnson, 44, his wife Jackie, 41, their daughters Janet, 13 and Karen, 11, and Mrs. Johnson's parents, George and Edith Bentley, both in their 60s.

When word of the discovery spread Monday, some children who attended school with Janet and Karen left early because they were so upset, said Andrew Craig, principal of Westbank elementary school.

Craig compared the tragedy with the murders of 11 youngsters by Clifford Robert Olson. He said criminals of that nature cannot be rehabilitated and should be eliminated.

RCMP Staff Sgt. Mike Eastham of Kamloops said it appears the Johnson's 1979 American car was pushed off a wilderness road in the edge of Wells Gray Provincial Park north of here and then set on fire.

"It would appear that they were dead before the car was set on fire — but that's subject to confirmation."

Police have issued a continent-wide alert for the Bentley's 1981 Ford pickup truck which carried a Vanguard camper with an aluminum boat on top with a licence plate reading 48 36 FY.

The absence of any trace of the truck makes police further suspect foul play, said RCMP Insp. Vic Edwards.

Coroner Ian McKichan and pathologist Dr. D. J. McNaughton from Royal Inland Hospital in Kamloops were flown to the site Monday morning where they conducted a four-hour investigation.

Fire Intense

"If someone had happened along and looked into the car, they probably wouldn't have identified them as human remains," said McNaughton.

The fire was so intense that it melted the car's rooftop carrier and fused beer bottles that had been in the carrier.

The car had been driven a little more than 1.5 kilometres along a dirt road in the wilderness park. At a relatively level spot at the top of a hill, the car plunged about 40 metres into brush overgrowing an old forest fire burn.

It was a spot that had been searched before, but the bulk was well camouflaged by the brush. it was seen by a man picking berries about a week ago.

The man, whom police have not identified, first dismissed the wreck as merely a burned-out, abandoned vehicle, but later reported it to police.

The Johnsons and the Bentleys had planned to meet Aug. 7 for a holiday in Wells Gray Park.

Police believe six were shot

KAMLOOPS, B.C. (CP) — A Kamloops pathologist who examined the charred remains of six persons found Monday in Wells Gray provincial park says bullet fragments were found in one of the skulls.

Dr. Darryl McNaughton said today the condition of the bodies, believed to be those of the Johnson family of Kelowna and the Bentleys of Port Coquitlam, indicated they had been shot and then burned.

The human remains were found in the back seat of the burned-out Plymouth Caravelle belonging to the Johnsons.

A spokesman at Royal Inland Hospital said the skull is that of a child or a woman. He said there were three large holes in the skull, apparently caused by a bullet. "It's quite obvious from looking at the x-rays that the person was shot," he said.

A preliminary autopsy was performed on the remains in this interior city, but doctors were unable to make positive identification.

The discovery of the Johnsons car followed a tip from an unidentified Vancouver-area man who saw the wreckage while picking berries with a friend on Aug. 22. \

The sighting was just six days after the search for the families had been prompted by Johnson's failure to return to work in Kelowna.

RCMP assisted in search by exposure from media

VANCOUVER (CP) — Media exposure is assisting RCMP in their search for two men wanted for questioning in connection with the deaths of six people in Wells Gray provincial park in central B.C., Kamloops RCMP said Sunday.

On Friday, police issued composite sketches of two men who were spotted in a restaurant in North Battleford, Sask., last week. The men were believed to be driving a camper that matches the description of the George Bentley vehicle.

One of the men is described as about 29 years old, 5 feet, 9 inches tall, 150 pounds, with shoulder-length blonde hair and a shaggy moustache. The other is 6 feet tall, 220 pounds, with black shaggy hair growing below his shoulders and a black beard and moustache.

Johnson — Bentley case

SIX MURDER CHARGES LAID

by Brian Driscoll
Courier Staff

A 24-year-old man appeared today in provincial court in Kamloops to face six counts of second-degree murder in connection with the Johnson-Bentley killings. David William Shearing, a former resident of the Clearwater area, was arrested Saturday and charged Sunday with murder in the deaths of George and Edith Bentley, their daughter Jackie Johnson, her husband

Robert, and their two children, Janet and Karen, all of Westbank. Shearing was remanded in custody to Friday.

The charred bodies of the six victims were found in the Johnson's burned-out car near Clearwater in September, 1982.

According to reports, the suspect is six feet, three inches tall, and weighs 250 pounds. He has medium-length brown hair and wears a drooping mustache.

The police are declining to

release further details of the arrest, saying they do no want to prejudice a fair trail.

The Courier has learned the RCMP do not believe a second person was involved in the murders. However, police will not confirm whether they suspect a second person was involved.

Following discovery of the bodies, a massive investigation was launched by RCMP, who drove a replica of the Bentley's camper truck across the country.

But in mid-October, the burned hulk of the camper truck was found in the bush near Clearwater, two kilometers from the burned-out car.

Following discovery of the truck, RCMP went door-to-door in Clearwater, asking residents if they noticed anyone behaving strangely around the time of the killings.

RCMP are not saying if the renewed investigation in Clearwater contributed to the arrest of the suspect.

Johnson-Bentley suspect admits guilt

KAMLOOPS, B.C. (CP) — David William Shearing, charged in the gruesome slayings of six members of the Johnson and Bentley families, pleaded guilty in B.C. Supreme Court today to six counts of second-degree murder.

The 25-year-old laborer and handyman, wearing a dark sports jacket and beige pants, trembled and spoke softly as he entered pleas.

The hushed courtroom was crowded with about 100 spectators, including reporters, Shearing's relatives from nearby Clearwater and relatives of the victims.

The surprise development came at the start of the trial of Shearing, who was not arrested until more than a year after the slayings in Wells Gray Provincial Park near

the quiet rural community of Clearwater.

Following the pleas, the crown counsel Robert Hunter began laying out the evidence in preparation for sentencing.

Shearing, tall and broad-shouldered with reddish-brown hair, was arrested in November 1983 in Dawson Creek after having gone to the Tumbler Ridge coal fields to look for work.

Hunter indicated a break came in the case when a Clearwater resident told police Shearing talked to him about re-registering a 1981 Ford camper-truck. Shearing said it may have been hot and he wanted to know how to fix a bullet-hole in the door.

Reading from Shearing's statement to RCMP signed Nov. 19, Hunter said Shearing indicated he first saw the Bentley's camper

truck when he was coming home from work one-evening. He went to the site later that night and looked around before fleeing through the bushes back to his home when it appeared someone noticed him.

The next evening, Shearing returned to the area. He came through the bush around the corner of the truck and started shooting.

Hunter said Shearing told police he shot the four adults sitting around the campfire. He then went to the tent where the two girls were and shot them.

He took clothes out to the back of Johnson's car and put the bodies of the four adults in the back. He took tools out of the trunk and put the bodies of the two girls in there.

He then moved the car and the Bentley's truck. He burned the car

Murder suspect David William Shearing leaves courthouse.

the next day and burned the truck a few days later.

The truck wasn't found until late October 1983. Prior to that police used information obtained in extensive interviews with residents of Clearwater, which borders the rugged, wilderness park, and started a nationwide search for two French-speaking men.

'Brutal' slayer given 25 years

KAMLOOPS, B.C. (CP) — Mr. Justice Harry McKay called David William Shearing a cold-blooded murderer and sentenced him British Columbia Supreme Court today to six concurrent life sentences with no eligibility for parole for 25 years.

McKay also prohibited Shearing, who pleaded guilty Monday to six counts of second-degree murder in the slaughter of six members of the

Johnson and Bentley families 20 months ago, from possessing a firearm for five years after any parole is granted.

He also recommended the parole board prohibit him from ever possessing a firearm.

McKay said Shearing, who celebrated his 25th birthday six days ago, had committed "a senseless, brutal, cold-blooded slaughter of six innocent people."

"He devastated three generations of a single family. The Bentleys were enjoying their retirement, the Johnson's were in the prime of their life, raising a family and the Johnson girls had their whole lives ahead of them."

McKay said the killings were a tragedy and a waste.

"And for what" The only motive was that he possibly coveted some of their possessions."

The judge said the letters filled with the court supporting Shearing painted a picture of him as a pleasant, shy and sensitive man. McKay said he had to consider that side of Shearing's personality but there is another side.

"Obviously there is another side to David Shearing that his family and friends are unaware of which makes in my mind a very dangerous man."

Oscar-winning Bergman dies

LONDON (AP) —

Academy Award-winning actress Ingrid Bergman, whose roles ranged from Humphrey Bogart's lover in Casablanca to the tough-minded prime minister of Israel in A Woman Called Golda, has died after a long battle with cancer.

Bergman died in London on Sunday, her 67th birthday, her daughter, Pia Lindstrom, said in New York today.

The Swedish actress, who soared to fame as Humphrey Bogart's co-star in the movie Casablanca in 1943, had been suffering from cancer since 1974.

Bergman, who lived in London's Knightsbridge district, spent her last day with former husband Lars Schmidt, last of her three husbands, and he was with her when she died.

The last role played by the three-time Academy Award winner was a portrayal of Israeli Prime Minister Golda Meir in a film shown on U.S. television this year.

In April, the actress answered rumors that she was fighting for her life by appearing in London and telling reporters: "I am not as young as I used to be. But my health is fine. I am not dying."

She had a mastectomy in 1974 after cancer was detected, and her other breast was removed in a second mastectomy in 1979 after a recurrence of the disease.

Looking back on her career, her three marriages, three divorces and her fight with cancer, Bergman wrote in her 1980 autobiography: "I have always thought that I will go on acting and acting and acting. You need never give up."

She won three Academy Awards for best actress in Gaslight with Charles Boyer in 1944 and Anastasia in 1956, and for best supporting actress for Murder on the Orient Express in 1974.

She was born in Stockholm on Aug. 29, 1915. Both her parents had died by the time she was 12 and she went to live with an uncle and spoke later of how her lonely childhood led her to acting.

A 5-foot-8 beauty, with deep blue eyes, she quickly became a leading lady in Swedish films before producer David O. Selznick invited her to Hollywood in 1939 to co-star in Intermezzo opposite Leslie Howard.

She summed up her remarkable career in a 1968 interview: "I have enjoyed a very beautiful life. A very interesting life. A very lucky life."

Stunned Monaco mourns Grace
Funeral Saturday

MONTE CARLO (AP) —

The body of Princess Grace lay in state today in a 13th-century palace chapel and her subjects came to pay respects to the Oscar-winning actress who left Hollywood 26 years ago but remained one of its most beloved stars.

The former Grace Kelly died in a Monaco hospital Tuesday at the age of 52 from a cerebral hemorrhage, about 36 hours after her car somersaulted 30 metres down a mountainside, trapping her inside.

Her funeral will take place Saturday at 11 a.m. (5 a.m. EDT) at the Roman Catholic Cathedral of Monaco, the royal palace announced.

Guards with black arm bands stood vigil and flags flew at half mast today atop the royal palace in honor of the princess, who reached stardom in 11 films that include High Noon, Dial M for Murder, Rear Window and Country Girl, for which she won an Academy Award in 1955.

The guards allowed only Monaco residents to enter the castle to sign a condolence book, but several hundred tourists gathered outside to snap pictures.

Only the estimated 30,000 residents of the principality were to be allowed to view the coffin later today, the palace said.

The glittering Monte Carlo casinos closed their doors for two days, flags were lowered to half-mast on the banks lining the Boulevard des Moulins and a championship soccer game was moved from the city as Monaco mourned its story-book princess.

Prince Ranier was at his wife's bedside when she died, along with two of her children — Princess Caroline, 26, and Crown Prince Albert, 24.

'Weirdos' sought in cyanide deaths

CHICAGO (AP) — Police hunting a murderer who killed seven people by placing cyanide in Extra-Strength Tylenol capsules are following up several "very substantial" leads, authorities say.

Illinois Attorney General Tyrone Fahner said at a news conference Sunday night that a special police force has at least two dozen suspects, including "malcontents and weirdos who don't act right or did something extremely out of the ordinary."

"We're trying to understand what kind of person could do these things," said Fahner, the chief of a state-federal force with more than 100 investigators looking into the string of deaths. "It is an act of a random murderer who filled the capsules with cyanide and then placed them in the stores."

One of the "very substantial" leads, Fahner said, was the news that two Kane County sheriff's deputies found Tylenol bottles and capsules strewn in a suburban motel parking lot Tuesday, one day before the deaths began.

The attorney general declined to disclose any other leads.

All of the deaths occurred between Wednesday and Friday in Chicago or its suburbs among people who had taken Extra-Strength Tylenol capsules. Autopsies showed the deaths were caused by cyanide poisoning.

The cyanide-spiked capsules probably were placed in the stores Tuesday, Fahner said, apparently on the front of the shelves to ensure they would sell quickly, he said.

Investigators already have interviewed and cleared many suspects and believe someone acting alone obtained bottles of Extra-Strength Tylenol, filled the capsules with cyanide at home and then "salted" store shelves with the deadly poison, Fahner said.

Canadian bests Everest

KATMANDU (CP) — Laurie Skreslet of Calgary today became the first Canadian to stand atop Mount Everest as he reached the 8,848-metre (29,028 feet) summit - the highest point in the world.

Skreslet, 32, accompanied by Sherpa guides Sungdare, 29, and Lhakpa Dorje, 25, planted the Canadian, Nepalese and official expedition flags on the summit at about 9:30 a.m. local time today (11:50 p.m. EDT Monday). Sungdare now holds the world record for his three ascents of the mountain.

Skies were clear but the temperature was around -40C and windy as the trio chipped their way up the final rock and snow face on the South Col route pioneered by Sir Edmund Hillary in 1953, the first to reach the summit.

"We made it," expedition spokesman Earl Pennington reported by radio.

He said the climbers remained on top of Everest for half an hour before beginning their descent today.

The final 941-metre climb from their highest camp, South Col, took eight hours and 15 minutes, a record time.

The assault crew carried a video pack to send the first live television pictures to the world via a sophisticated satellite transmission setup.

But the transmitter's batteries apparently froze in the extreme cold. It is believed the crew is bringing back video film of the final ascent.

Skreslet, a freelance guide and mountain instructor in the Canadian Rockies, is three weeks short of his 33rd birthday.

He has climbed numerous mountains in Canada, Peru, Argentina and last year conquered Mount Nuptse in Nepal, a sister peak of Everest.

Sungdare was among 13 climbers in a mainly West German team which reached the summit in 1979, and he scaled the top again last year with an American medical research expedition.

Canada's highest mountain is Mount Logan in the Yukon. It is 5,950 metres, or 19,520 feet - almost 10,000 feet lower than Everest.

Skreslet got the nod for the final push because he was judged by expedition leader Bill March to be in the best physical shape of all the team members.

IT HAPPENED IN CANADA

WHO'S MORRIS?

MAXIMILIAN OR JUST PLAIN MAX AN ALLEY CAT THAT COST MR. & MRS. DEREK RHIND of Swartz Bay on Vancouver Island ONE DOLLAR IN 1960, WAS ENTERED IN A CAT SHOW AS A JOKE ... AND TOOK TOP HONORS.

FROM THEN ON HE NEVER LOOKED BACK AND WOUND UP AS REGIONAL NEUTER CHAMPION OF NORTH AMERICA

8-25

©1980

1980–1989

Fruit Imports Hit As Protest Draws 700 Here

By Jim Hodgson
Staff Writer

About 700 angry Okanagan and Similkameen fruit growers brought their tractors and trucks to a rally here Monday to protest federal agriculture policies and high interest rates.

Saying cheap foreign imports are forcing farmers off the land, they called on the government to either increase subsidies to farmers or impose tariffs on imported fruit.

More than 220 tractors and 70 trucks formed a convoy at the Kaleden junction and moved in procession to the Penticton Peach Bowl for the rally. Thirty more tractors came from Summerland.

Speaker after speaker complained producers receive only about five cents per pound of apples while consumers pay about 50 cents.

B.C. Fruit Growers' Association president Richard Bullock of Kelowna said returns to farmers were better in 1950.

"Farmers are forced to leave their farms and get jobs elsewhere," he added. "I'm saying to the consumer of this country to leave the farmers on the land."

Bill Ritchie, the crusty Cawston grower who last week chopped down his fruit trees to protest cheap fruit imports, said growers have little control over their cost of production.

He said many farmers have lost hope because of low returns and loan problems with banks. "It doesn't take much imagination to see farmers are in hot water," he added.

"Farmers are dedicated to keeping food on your tables," he told consumers. "At a time of unstable world markets and instability in general, we should be working to food self-sufficiency."

Ritchie said politicians have paid more attention to consumers who want low food prices than to farmers, thus endangering Canadian agriculture. "Politicians should never fear reprisals from voters for paying more to farmers," he added.

What Farmers Got On Sales

The 2,000 Okanagan fruit growers received about $28 million in 1982 of the $150 million gross sales of their marketing companies, B.C. Tree Fruits Ltd. and Sun Rype Products Ltd.

From the $28 million growers must pay the cost of producing their fruit. They also receive a federal subsidy of about $8 million and a provincial subsidy of $10 million.

The $132 million left over from sales is spent preparing the fruit products for sale.

The two marketing companies and 10 interior packing houses owe about $35 million, for which the growers are indirectly responsible.

The B.C. Fruit Grower's Association says a recent bank survey found large interior growers (10 hectares or more) with debts averaging $175,000 while those with smaller orchards (4 1/2 to 6 1/2 hectares) had debts of up to $225,000.

Farmers say federal and provincial subsidies are inadequate, particularly in the face of cheap foreign imports they say are dumped on the Canadian market.

Also, the farmers complain federal subsidies are slow.

Applications for subsidies of last year's crop were made last November. The announcement of what the subsidies would be was not made until August and payment won't be received until November.

They predict a large increase in the number of farm bankruptcies within the next year.

Farmers Mass Here To Protest Cheap Food Policy

FARMERS' PROTEST RALLY 'A LAST RESORT'

Repercussions Predicted

SEPTEMBER 6, 1983. — While organizers of the farmers' protest rally here Monday were clearly delighted with the larger-than-expected crowd, it was clear farmers aren't really used to taking to the streets to make their concerns known.

"This is a last resort," said Keremeos grower Bruce Harker, one of the organizers of the Fair Agricultural Returns Movement.

He and other farmers are wondering if it wouldn't be cheaper to remove the trees from their land and leave the land fallow. Some, like Bill Ritchie of Cawston, have already chopped down their trees.

Lannuy and Julie Martiniuk… tree, signs tell plight

1980-1989

Five Canadians Among 269 Missing

U.S. Blasts Soviet Downing Of Jetliner

FROM AP-CP —

The United States charged today that a Soviet jet fighter plane shot down a South Korean civilian jumbo jetliner carrying 269 people, including at least five Canadians, after tracking it off the Soviet island of Sakhalin.

But the Kremlin said its fighters tried to help an unidentified plane that intruded over its Far Eastern territory Wednesday and that the plane did not respond to signals and continued toward the Japan Sea.

The Canadian Consulate in New York disclosed that as many as 10 Canadians may have been aboard the Korean Airlines Boeing 747 flight which disappeared about 2:30 p.m. EDT Wednesday.

A search is under way for any survivors in the frigid waters off Sakhalin.

U.S. State Secretary George Shultz told a Washington news conference that the Soviet fighter tracked the jumbo for more than 2 1/2 hours before shooting it down with a missile over the Soviet island of Sakhalin. He called it an "appalling act" that caused "revulsion."

Demands Account

President Reagan ordered Shultz to demand an "immediate and full account" from the Soviet Union. Presidential spokesman Larry Speakes, speaking from the U.S. West Coast where Reagan is on vacation, said: "There are no circumstances that can justify the unprecedented attack on an unarmed civilian aircraft."

The official Soviet news agency Tass said "an unidentified plane" intruded twice over Soviet territory before dawn, first over the Kamchatka Peninsula, then over Sakhalin. "The plane did not have navigation lights, did not respond to queries and did not enter into contact with the dispatcher service," it said.

"Fighters of the anti-aircraft defence, which were sent aloft towards the intrude plane, tried to give it assistance in directing it to the nearest airfield. But the intruder plane did not react to the signals and warnings from the Soviet fighters and continued its flight in the direction of the Sea of Japan."

The Tass report did not directly respond to the assertion by Shultz that the plane was shot down by Soviet jets.

But Shultz said thee is no evidence the Soviets had warned the plane, although he said the Soviet pilot was "close-enough for a visual inspection." He said as many as eight Soviet jets were involved.

First Canadian Soars Into Space

By Juliet O'Neill

CAPE CANAVERAL, FL. (CP) — Marc Garneau, Canada's first astronaut, soared into space aboard the U.S. shuttle Columbia today along with six Americans in a spectacular pre-dawn launch that lit up the Cape.

The launch, just before the crack of dawn, went without a hitch. The shuttle left the Kennedy Space Centre on its powerful engines just 43 milliseconds after the scheduled liftoff time of 7:03 a.m. EDT.

The record seven-member crew including Garneau, 35, a Quebec Cityborn naval commander, and two women will orbit the Earth aboard Challenger every 90 minutes for the next eight days.

As Canadians including Prime Minister Mulroney applauded Garneau, the astronaut's parents, Jean and Andre Garneau, were astonished by the dramatic moment that launch director Bob Sieck called "a spectacular sight,"

The parents gaped in awe as Challenger burst into the dark blue and rose-tinged sky with a thunderous sound that bounced back to Earth from clouds around the launch path.

In Ottawa, the prime minister told reporters it was a thrill to see a Canadian roar into space but he couldn't help but show a little green.

"I felt envious. I think it's a tremendous thing and I can still remember exactly where I was the first time there was a landing on the moon. I can still remember my own vicarious thrill."

Canada's first astronaut, Marc Garneau

During the eight-day flight, the crew of five men and two women will use radar sensors and cameras to study Earth's atmosphere and oceans and search for ancient lost cities.

Canada's astronaut, 35-year-old navy commander Marc Garneau will conduct a series of Canadian-designed experiments.

1980-1989

Claims life was ruined

Haymour suit against gov't reaches court

VANCOUVER, (CP) —

A man who contends the British Columbia government ruined his life by obstructing his efforts to build a tourist attraction on an island in Okanagan Lake is suing the government for fraud, breach of trust, malicious prosecution and wrongful imprisonment.

Eddy Anis Haymour, 51, best known for seizing the Canadian embassy in Lebanon in 1976, argues that if he was legally sane when he gave up on his tourism dream and sold Rattlesnake Island to the government for $40,000, he should not have been committed to Riverview Mental Hospital.

If he was insane, he contends, the government had no right to force a mentally incompetent person to convey the island to it.

Haymour is seeking to recover the island from Victoria and collect damages, including punitive damages.

In outlining the case Monday, Haymour's lawyer, Jack Cram, noted an allegation eventually dropped, that Haymour tried to send explosives through the mail to the premier.

Haymour was kept in custody for nine months before being found not guilty by reason of insanity of possessing brass knuckles. After more than a year of further confinement in a mental institution he was found sane, then went to Beirut and held the staff of the Canadian

Eddy Haymour

embassy hostage for eight hours, trying to negotiate the return of his island.

The case is being heard by county court Judge Michelangelo Provenzano, sitting as a judge of the B.C. Supreme Court in chambers.

Haymour immigrated to Canada from Lebanon in 1955 and established barber shops in Edmonton and Calgary. He moved to Kelowna in 1970 and the following year purchased the island.

He contends he was entitled to build on the island restriction free.

However, Cram said, a complaint was made by a neighbor on the lakefront, Des Loan, then a Peachland alderman, to the area's member of the legislature, then-premier W. A. C. Bennett.

The provincial cabinet passed a new building regulation "enacted for the unlawful purpose of preventing" Haymour from completing the facility, Cram said.

In December, 1971, the province zoned the island agricultural forest, although "it was a rock island with a single tree," he said.

The Health Ministry refused

even to consider a proposed sewage system and the Highways Ministry blocked access to the dock serving the island, Cram said.

In July 1973, Haymour, "having been forced by the concerted efforts of the various departments of the province into dire financial condition and suffering from severe strain and mental stress in his efforts to combat the power of the government, offered to sell the property to the defendant for $146,000." This was refused.

"Between July and December 1973, the defendant caused Haymour to be placed under police surveillance, hiring the services of an informer to gain the confidence of Haymour with the purpose of importuning or entrapping Haymour into the commission of a criminal offence," Cram said.

He was charged in late 1973 with threatening to send a letter bomb to W. A. C. Bennett. Eventually, the Crown stayed 37 charges against Haymour, but proceeded with a charge of possessing a dangerous weapon, described by Cram as a child's set of knuckledusters.

After being held for extensive psychiatric examination, Haymour wanted to plead guilty, but the Crown urged provincial court to enter a plea of not guilty by reason of insanity.

In July 1974 — when he had been in custody for seven months and had just learned his wife was divorcing him, his children were on welfare, his home had burned down with its insurance expired and the island property was being foreclosed on — the government had Haymour sign the deed for the island for $40,000.

Governments to bail out ailing wine industry

An imbalance between the amount of red wine grapes planted and the amount of red wine consumed is about to be corrected, thanks to a joint effort by the federal and provincial government, grape growers, and wineries to save B.C.'s ailing wine industry announced Friday.

The $6.8 million bailout will not only save the industry now, but will have long-term effects, according to Gary Tayler, grape grower and past-president of the Association of B.C. Grape Growers.

Tayler said the amount of red wine grapes planted, about 550 acres or one-sixth of the total plantings, will undergo a significant change. And, he said, that will correct an imbalance in the industry.

Out of balance

Previously growers planted about 60 per cent red wine grapes and 40 per cent white wine grapes, while consumption of white wine was about 70 per cent and red 30 per cent. "… way out of balance," Tayler said.

The two levels of government will each kick in $3.4 million to buy out the industry's surplus of red grapes and 2.7 million litres of red wine, and growers and wineries will contribute $5.1 million by replanting with white grapes.

The wine will be distilled and resold to wineries, meaning the government contribution will wind up being less than the budgeted $6.8 million, although Consumer and Corporate Affairs Minister Jim Hewitt said he didn't know how much money the resale would generate.

Association of B.C. Grape Growers president Dick Stewart said Friday wineries and grape growers must now begin a huge replanting effort replacing one-sixth of B.C. grape plants with other varieties.

There are eight commercial wineries in B.C.: Andres Wines in Port Moody, Jordan-St. Michelle in Surrey, Calona in Kelowna, Casabello in Penticton, Mission Hill in Westbank, Brights in Oliver, Okanagan Vineyards near Osoyoos and Beaupre in the Okanagan.

'Unsinkable' Titanic found on ocean floor

PARIS (AP-CP) —

A Franco-American team says it has found the long-sought wreck of the oceanliner Titanic, which struck and iceberg and sank in the North Atlantic off Newfoundland on its maiden voyage in 1912.

More than 1,500 people died in the sinking of the Titanic, a ship many believed to be unsinkable.

The Titanic was the biggest, the most luxurious and supposedly the safest liner of its time, and its passenger list carried such names as American financier John Jacob Astor, industrialist Benjamin Guggenheim and Isidor Straus of Macy's. All three died.

Since the sinking there have been rumors that the ship went down carrying a fortune in jewels and other valuables. Serious students of the disaster call such reports a myth.

The wreck, which has been the object of numerous searches, was found in 3,000 metres of water about 560 nautical miles off Newfoundland, the French Institute for Research and Exploitation of the Sea said Monday.

Many passengers aboard the ship believed that the Titanic was unsinkable because of a magazine article of the day that lauded the

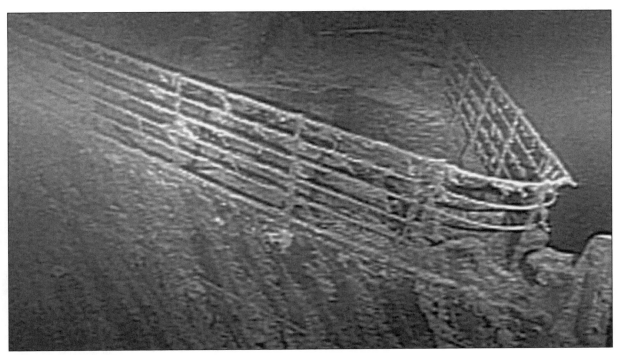

Titanic lays on ocean bottom

safety of its double-steel hull, which was divided into 15 waterproof compartments.

But it hit an iceberg that cut a 100-metre gash across several of the compartments and sank on the night of April 14-15, 1912. A total of 1,513 people died, but about 700 managed to get to lifeboats and were saved.

The French-U.S. team has not suggested bringing up the ship, which apparently broke up on the

ocean bottom, but has proposed making the site a memorial.

A survivor who was seven years old and who lost her father when the Titanic went down said the hulk should not be retrieved.

The wreck was identified by a French-made submarine sonar system and U.S.-made underwater cameras.

A short videotape recorded by the cameras was snatched Monday from the heaving decks of the U.S.

navy research ship Knorr by a helicopter in gale-force winds and flown to St. John's, Nfld., the Toronto Star reported today.

The Star, in an interview with the helicopter's crew, said the men watched fragments of the videotape during their 2 1/2 hour flight back to shore.

It quoted the crew as saying that the fragments showed what scientists on the exploration team believed to be the ship's boiler.

Titanic's salvage: no way

That's what experts say

HALIFAX (CP) —

The dream of raising the Titanic is about as old as the shipwreck itself.

But to Don Kerr, who knows marine salvage inside out, the

idea of raising the world's largest shipwreck from a four-kilometre deep trench off Newfoundland remains the stuff of Hollywood fantasy and pulp fiction.

"Utterly impossible," says the Halifax marine lawyer and head of Atlantic Salvage Ltd., one of Canada's most experienced marine salvage companies.

The Titanic, which sank 73 years ago, was found this week 367 nautical miles from St. John's Nfld., by a French-American research team, 4,000 metres down.

Kerr's belief comes from overseeing more than 140 salvage operations, including the Kurdistan, a British tanker which broke in two off Canada's east

coast in 1979.

He said the record depth for re-floating a large ship is 105 feet (63 metres), set in 1968 by a Dutch firm off Greenland.

The two standard ways of raising a ship by hoisting it on cables or by filling the hulk with compressed air would not work with the Titanic, he said.

ABORTIONS WILL BE PERFORMED AT TORONTO CLINIC

JANUARY 3, 1985. TORONTO (CP) — Dr. Henry Morgentaler says he will personally perform abortions at his Toronto clinic when it reopens Monday – the first time the Montreal doctor will have done so in Ontario.

"I'll be working in Toronto from now on," said Morgentaler.

Morgentaler said he will arrive tonight and will be the only doctor at the clinic next week. Dr. Robert Scott will remain at Morgentaler's Montreal clinic to perform abortions.

Morgentaler set up the Toronto clinic and trained its staff but says he has never performed an abortion inside the building near the legislature. If Morgentaler proceeds with his plans next week he will leave himself open to the possibility of being charged with procuring a miscarriage.

Cola Wars

JULY 5, 1985. Atlanta (AP) — The cola wars are expanding into space with a decision by NASA to allow next week's shuttle flight to carry experimental soft drink cans developed by both Coca-Cola and Pepsi.

Coke officials said the inclusion of Pepsi violates a written agreement allowing Coca-Cola to be the first soft drink in space. But NASA denied that, and Pepsi officials said their experiment was not timed to compete with Coke's.

Charles Redmond, a National Aeronautics and Space Administration spokesman in Washington, said Wednesday the space agency has invited all soft drink manufacturers to develop carbonated beverage containers to be tested aboard shuttle flights.

Smoker Spotted – And Convicted

JULY 11, 1985. Toronto (CP) — A shoe-store owner charged with breaking a no-smoking bylaw after a customer spotted him lighting up in his own store last year was found guilty Wednesday in provincial court.

Jack Herman was given an absolute discharge after the City of Toronto won what is believed to be the first conviction in court after six years of official efforts to crack down on smoking in public places.

Superpowers Agree To Talk

GENEVA (AP) —

U.S. officials fanned out today to brief world leaders on the agreement to resume arms-control talks with the Soviet Union, an agreement the Americans said was nearly

Scuffle Hits Courthouse

Anti-Semitic Charges

TORONTO (CP) —

Four people were arrested Monday outside a downtown courthouse after a scuffle broke out when a man charged with distributing anti-Semitic literature arrived for the start of his trial.

Ernst Zundel, 45, of Toronto is charged with two counts under Section 177 of the Criminal Code, which forbids publication of statements known to be false or likely to cause injury or mischief to the public interest.

Zundel, a German citizen who operates Samisdat Publishers of Toronto, was committed for trial after a week-long preliminary hearing last June. He was charged in connection with publication in 1983 of two articles, one titled Did Six Million Really Die? and the other The West, War and Islam.

derailed by a Soviet walkout.

No date or place has been set for the negotiations, which the two sides – in a joint statement issued late Tuesday – said will be aimed at "preventing an arms race in space" and "the complete elimination of nuclear arms everywhere."

The agreement came after two days of discussions between U.S. State Secretary George Shultz and Soviet Foreign Minister Andrei Gromyko, along with top aides, at the U.S. and Soviet missions in Geneva.

Shultz, before leaving for Washington today, made no comment but gave a "thumbs up" sign. Gromyko, who left for Moscow 45 minutes later, read a brief statement in English in which he spoke of the "immense tasks" that lie ahead for the two superpowers.

Nuclear Plan Disclosed

Defence Minister Denies

OTTAWA (CP) —

Defence Minister Robert Coates said today he knows nothing about a U.S. contingency plan to deploy 32 nuclear depth bombs in Canada in the event of war.

The American plan, outlined in an annual classified memo signed by President Reagan that authorizes U.S. weapons deployments outside the U.S., was made public in Washington Wednesday by a Washington-based defence analyst.

"All I can say is that in view of the fact I know nothing about it, that I've never been consulted on it, I really am not in any position to talk about it," Coates said.

William Arkin, an analyst with the Institute for Policy Studies, a liberal think tank, said in Washington on Wednesday that "Canada really doesn't have much of a choice" about accepting the U.S. weapons. He said the weapons, for use in anti-submarine warfare, would be sent to Canada only in the event of war.

They would be split between Canadian Forces bases at Comox, B.C., and Greenwood, N.S., where long-range Aurora anti-submarine aircraft are based. Anti-submarine warfare is one of Canada's primary obligations as a member of the U.S.-led North Atlantic Treaty Organization.

Coates said he would "ask more details from my officials" about the reported U.S. contingency plans, but he said it was "not something that is of particular interest to me unless there is a submission that comes to the Canadian government."

The External Affairs Department has refused to confirm or deny knowledge of the U.S. plan.

The document from which Arkin quoted U.S. plans is called the Nuclear Weapons Deployment Plan. It is updated annually and specifies what nuclear weapons the United States would deploy in which countries in conditions of peace, military alert or war.

Canada currently has no nuclear weapon on its soil, Coates said. The U.S. plan envisages putting nuclear weapons in Canada only in the event of war.

At any rate, it would be up to Prime Minister Mulroney to make a decision, about whether to accept nuclear weapons on Canadian soil.

Britain Ashamed of Fans' Carnage

LONDON (REUTER) — Britain, accepting the blame for the Brussels soccer riot which killed dozens of fans, offered the equivalent of some $450,000 Canadian today to families of the victims.

Prime Minister Margaret Thatcher announced the gift as an "initial payment" after emergency British cabinet talks on the disaster at Wednesday night's European Cup final between Liverpool and Juventus of Italy.

"These terrible events have brought shame and disgrace on those responsible and their country," she said in a letter to Italian Premier Bettino Craxi.

A Thatcher spokesman said

Britain may make further contributions to a disaster fund for the victims, most of whom were Italians including 10-year-old Andrea Casula.

Thatcher, speaking to reporters after her talks with her ministers, spoke of the "thugs who destroy football" and said she wants them caught, dealt with and banned from grounds.

"It seems from what we saw that citizens of this country were to a considerable measure responsible," she said. "I am deeply concerned."

Soccer chiefs expressed fears that British teams would be barred from European soccer following the riot, in which fans of England's

Liverpool team stormed through the stadium hacking and clubbing Juventus supporters.

"My fear is we will be completely banned," said Football Association chairman Bert Millichip.

European clubs have long threatened a ban on Britain because of the notorious violence of its fans.

South Africa Bomb Hurts Two Police

JOHANNESBURG (CP) — A bomb believed to have been planted in a flower box exploded today at a police station in Cape Town, injuring two policemen and damaging the building, South African authorities said.

It was the 11th bombing in South Africa since a state of emergency was declared June 12, and the first to strike a security force target. Three people have been killed and about 100 injured in the

blasts.

The Bureau for Information described the damage to the police station in a white suburb as minor and said the two officers were only slightly hurt.

The bureau also reported the burned bodies of three black men had been found, raising the official unrest death toll since June 12 to 97. Fourteen other unrest deaths have been reported by authorities in two homelands.

August Opening Seen For Movie

James Forsyth of Penticton, who played the role of Bumper in the movie My American Cousin, said the film is expected to be released in early August. Work on the sound track has caused the delay in release of the film, which was shot in the Penticton area last summer.

"It will probably open simultaneously in Vancouver and Toronto, and in Penticton probably during the opening week."

Sandy Wilson, who wrote the script, would like to see a 50s night at the local drive-in theatre, Forsyth said. "Sandy is still working on it."

Forsyth also worked as a production assistant on My American Cousin, and went on to the University of Victoria last year, majoring in theatre.

LOCAL ACTRESS IN TV SERIES

By Jeane Manning
JULY 23, 1985. — Nicola Cavendish's theatrical career has taken another leap forward. The former Penticton secondary school graduate has a leading role in a forthcoming CBC television series.

Cavendish began rehearsals this week on a ranch near Merritt. The drama, Red Serge Wives, deals with the Royal Canadian Mounted Police and a turn-of-the-century settlement. Cavendish plays one of the daughters of a widower, and is also script consultant.

After Pen-Hi, Cavendish, whose parents are still in Kaleden, graduated from the University of British Columbia in theatre studies and also trained at Old Vic theatre in London. She has recently been acting at the National Theatre in Toronto.

Nicola Cavendish

Tireprints Often Help Crack Crimes

As Important As Fingerprints

JULY 11, 1985. Winnipeg (CP) – An expert says tire impressions left by a vehicle at the scene of a crime can be as important a clue as a set of fingerprints.

Pete McDonald, an Ohio-based specialist in tire design, said tireprints have played a major role as evidence in recent murder trials.

"Much like a fingerprint, a tire can make a very positive identification mark at the scene of the crime," he said in an interview Tuesday.

McDonald now is manager of tire design for Firestone Tire and Rubber Co., but he plans to quit that job next month to focus on tireprint identification, which he began as a hobby seven years ago.

"I hope to instruct more police in the United States and Canada on this very subject, so that at crime scenes, this bit of evidence will not be obscured, but will be recorded so it can be used."

1980~1989

Hometown fete for Fonyo

SALMON ARM B.C. (CP) — About 40 kilometres from Vernon and a weekend of rest and celebration, Journey for Lives runner Steve Fonyo got back on the Trans-Canada Highway today after a warm welcome the night before in "one of my home towns. "

The Fonyo entourage left the tiny community of Grindrod early today and was to run to the outskirts of Vernon, where he now resides, before calling it quits for the weekend.

The one-legged runner, who turns 20 next month, will be toasted Sunday with a parade, reception, banquet and torch light ceremony before running through Vernon Monday on his way to the coast and a finish to his 14 month-long run.

When he completed his run Thursday, the pudgy, curly-haired Fonyo had run 312 kilometres in British Columbia. And 7,311 since leaving St. John's, Nfld. He had 629 kilometres remaining today before he reaches Mile 0 in Victoria. -

A Canadian Cancer Society spokesman said Fonyo received. $6,000 on the road Wednesday and $15,000 that was raised in Salmon Arm, where he was living when he learned, at 12, that he had cancer in his leg.

Donations to the Journey for Lives, which will be used for cancer research, education and patient services, totaled more than $3.52 million in Canada, - excluding government pledges. In British Columbia, the total of money deposited in the bank is almost $220,000. The B.C. government has also pledged $1,000 per kilometre, which will total almost $1 million.

In Salmon Arm Wednesday night, about 700 people roared when Fonyo was described as 'No. 1 in the hearts of Salmon Arm.

Fonyo was escorted to a local park on a fire truck, and then, by golf cart, to a podium at the top of an embankment.

Fonyo had a grinning reunion with two boyhood chums, George Zazzi, 20, and Sandy Reid, 19, who presented him with a greeting card from the town.

Fonyo and friends

Penticton Kiwanis Steve Fonyo Walk-a-Long

May 11th, 1985

"We Build"

Pledge form to be picked up at the walk-a-long office
403 Martin St., Penticton, B.C. (Interior Copy Centre)
Telephone 493-7447
Or
Kiwanis Stand at Cherry Lane Mall
The office and Cherry Lane Stand will be open to May 25th

HOURS: Monday to Friday 3:30 p.m. to 5:00 p.m. Saturday 10 a.m. to 4 p.m.

MAJOR PRIZES FOR TOP PLEDGES RAISED
50% Of Net Proceeds To Steve Fonyo

This message is presented by the Penticton Herald and these community minded businesses:

1980-1989

A modest Fonyo thanks all

VANCOUVER (CP)— Steve Fonyo, masking an inner nervousness behind the beaming smile on his tanned face, delivered the best speech of his Journey for Lives Monday as he was honored by 20,000 people at a B.C. Place stadium celebration televised provincewide.

Reading from a prepared text and displaying a confidence gained in the 14 emotionally draining months he's been in the public spotlight, the one-legged cancer fundraiser shrugged off suggestions he's a hero and paid special tribute to his family, his hackers and a public that has donated nearly $5 million.

"I really want to thank the children who have supported my journey," said the curly-haired, 19 year-old who has drawn children to his side like magnets. "They've emptied their piggy banks and worked hard to raise money.

"Please remember I'm running to help them and to find a cure for cancer."

In shorts, displaying the prosthesis he was once too shy to show, he talked of the anger, bitterness and self-pity he went through when his left leg was amputated at age 12.

He thanked his family, particularly his father, a stern, small-town restaurant owner who has faithfully risen early each morning to drive alongside his son in the escort van. And he apologized for forgetting appointments, for not signing every autograph and for not visiting every Canadian town.

"I have run in cold, I have run on ice, I have run in the rain, I have run in the sunshine. But mostly I've run on hope, the hope that soon there will be a cure for cancer. "

Despite a disappointing turnout in the 60,000-seat stadium - admission and parking were free - it was the biggest celebration of Fonyo's Atlantic-to-Pacific trek.

He will complete the final 13 kilometres of his grueling nearly 8,000-kilometre journey-he has gone through six artificial legs and 17 pairs of running shoes- today and Wednesday on Vancouver Island. He traveled to the Island overnight on a naval destroyer - he is a transportation buff, a lover of fast cars, boats and helicopters - after a private dinner with his family as they celebrated his parents 35th wedding anniversary.

With the television cameras rolling and thousands of people lining the road, the stocky Vernon, B.C., youth ran his 10 kilometres from adjacent Burnaby to the stadium Monday under cloudy skies. It was the first time he moved faster than the walking pace he was forced into last week after developing painful tendinitis in his right leg.

Bubbling like a starstruck kid and calling the reception "fantastic, great," he ran into the stadium to a huge welcome. He then made a symbolic walk across a map of Canada laid out the full length of the football field as his mother, Anna, sat in he stands wiping tears from her eyes.

Then to the continuing applause of the crowd, he did a lap of the stadium before stopping and exchanging emotional hugs with his overjoyed and weeping family.

Steve's journey finally over

$9 million raised for cancer research by Vernon's one-legged runner

VICTORIA (CP) — It was a dream few people thought he could realize, but Steve Fonyo, the one-legged cancer victim with something to prove and a desire to help kids, defied the odds and conquered Canada on Wednesday.

Fourteen months after he dipped his artificial leg into the Atlantic Ocean at St. John's. Nfld., the determined 19-year-old from Vernon, BC skipped down a red carpet on the rocky Beacon Hill Park beach to dunk the prosthesis that takes the place of his left leg into the Pacific.

He had worn out five other artificial legs during his 7,924-kilometre Journey for Lives.

"It's finally over." he said, grinning broadly as he embraced his parents and joined his older sister Suzanne, in emptying the canister they had filled with Atlantic water when the trek began.

With a $1-million federal government contribution announced Wednesday, Fonyo has raised nearly $9 million in private donations and government funding for cancer research, education and patient services.

He had left British Columbia in March 1984 an unknown, chubby teenager who many feared would trample on memories of Terry Fox, the one-legged runner who had tried before him, but fell short when his cancer returned.

But as he passed the point where Fox had been forced to quit near Thunder Bay. Ont., and trudged on through a brutal Prairie winter, he earned admiration.

In the last couple of months, as he struggled with painful tendinitis while adoring crowds lined highways and city streets shouting encouragement clamoring for autographs and pictures, he became something he insisted he was not - a hero.

He brought cancer sufferers to tears and persuaded millions to dig into their pockets.

Thousands jammed Victoria streets in steady rain Wednesday as Fonyo, his short, curly hair and sweatsuit top soaked through, completed the final 10 kilometres of his remarkable journey.

After dipping his leg and laying red and white flowers at the Trans-Canada Highway Mile 0 marker, he moved to an outdoor stage to receive the congratulations of politicians and Canadian Cancer Society officials.

In his only real show of emotion, other than the ear to ear grin he wore at the water's edge, Fonyo stepped to the microphone, raised his hands over his head and shouted " Yahoo!"

"I've been on the road for over a year - 14 months," he said. "Missed a lot of things I like to do and I just want to say that I couldn't have done it without you. I couldn't have done it without the RCMP and my sponsors helping me. I just want to say, thanks, Canada".

Challenger Explodes

Explosion Halts Shuttle Flights

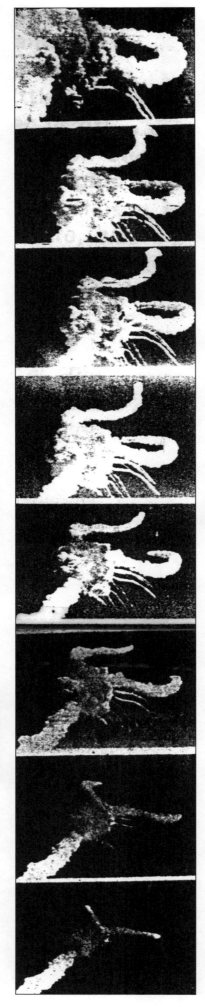

As it happened

The space shuttle orbiter Challenger is shown in this sequence of photographs shortly after it lifted off from Kennedy Space Centre, Tuesday morning, with the bottom frame showing the rocket as it starts to explode. Near the top of the sequence, the downward streams of smoke are believed to be debris from the exploding shuttle.

CAPE CANAVERAL, FLA. (AP) —

Search ships retrieved scattered wreckage from the Challenger mission today as investigators sought clues to Tuesday's tragedy in which seven astronauts were killed.

Meanwhile, an investigation team held its first formal meeting today in what is expected to be a lengthy inquiry into why the $1.2-billion space shuttle, seemingly on a perfect course, suddenly blew apart 74 seconds after liftoff, raining fiery debris into the Atlantic.

The seven deaths were the first in flight after 55 successful U.S. man-in-space slights, including 24 previous shuttle missions. The first "common citizen" chosen for a space trip, New Hampshire schoolteacher Christa McAuliffe, was one of the victims.

Lt. Cmdr. James Simpson, a coast guard spokesman, said "there is debris all over the place," with the largest piece being about three metres long and half a metre wide.

Lieut. Joe Carr of the coast guard, which is coordinating the search, said several small pieces of wreckage drifted ashore in the Cape Canaveral area overnight. He asked residents who find anything that might be a part of the shuttle to turn it in to the coast guard.

The search area is between 50 and 130 nautical miles southeast of Cape Canaveral, the water between 20 and 60 metres deep.

Although the explosion occurred 16 kilometres high and 13 kilometres southeast of the launch pad, the shuttle's momentum of almost 3,200 kilometres an hour propelled the wreckage much father out over water.

Find Pieces

A few pieces 1 1/2 to three metres long were spotted, but most recovered items were thermal tiles. About 30,000 of them covered the shuttle to protect it from re-entry heat, said Col. John Shults, director of Defence Department contingency operations.

The debris will be examined in a hangar at Patrick Air Force Base, Fla.

The investigation could take months, just as it did after the only other U.S. space program tragedy, the launch pad fire that killed three Apollo astronauts 19 years ago this week. The Soviet Union has lost four cosmonauts in flight.

Tuesday's explosion is expected to halt space shuttle flights for months. Jesse Moore, director of NASA's shuttle program, said no shuttle will fly until the cause of the accident is pinpointed and corrections made.

The National Aeronautics and Space Administration had planned a record 15 shuttle flights this year. Challenger was the second. The ship, making its 10th and final flight, had been the workhorse of a four-ship fleet.

Killed along with McAuliffe were commander Francis Scobee, 46; pilot Michael Smith, 40; Judith Resnik, 36; Ronald McNair, 35; Ellison Onizuka, 39; and Gregory Jarvis, 41.

Scobee; Resnik, the second U.S. woman in space; McNair, the second black U.S. astronaut; and Onizuka, a Japanese-America, were making their second shuttle flights. Jarvis, an employee of Hughes Aircraft, was to conduct fluid dynamics tests developed by his company.

There was no immediate explanation for the accident.

Mission Control reported there had been no indication of any problem with the shuttle's three main liquid-powered engines, its twin solid-fuel rocket boosters or any other system. Officials said the shuttle just suddenly blew apart, that radio data ceased at 74 seconds.

The absence of concrete radio information could hamper the investigation, especially if no large parts of the shuttle can be recovered.

Satellites Lost

Lost along with the spacecraft were a $100-million satellite that would have become an important part of NASA's shuttle communications network and a smaller $10-million payload that was to study Halley's comet.

A Canadian-built robot arm was aboard the shuttle, said president Larkin Kerwin of the National Research Council.

The Canadarm, standard equipment on shuttle spacecraft, was to be used to deploy a scientific apparatus that would help investigate Halley's comet.

1980~1989

Canadian Astronauts Shocked, Saddened

OTTAWA (CP) —

The six members of the Canadian astronaut program have expressed shock and sadness today at the destruction Tuesday of the United States space shuttle Challenger and the deaths of its seven-member crew.

Officials of the National Research Council today released the text of a telegram sent to John Young, chief of astronauts at the Johnson Space Centre in Houston. It's the first public comment on the disaster by the Canadian participants.

Canada's only man in space, Marc Garneau, listed his name among the other payload specialists in expressing "sincere sympathy at the loss of the crew of 51-L," the official designation of the ill-starred mission.

The Challenger orbiter lost on Tuesday was the same vehicle Garneau and a NASA crew rode to a successful mission in space in October, 1984.

"We share your sorrow," the two-sentence message concludes.

Along with Garneau and Steve MacLean, the Canadian laser specialist scheduled to ride a March 1987 shuttle mission into space, the Canadian mission candidates are being kept out of the limelight as officials here and in the U.S. ponder the fate of the space program.

The spokesman for NRC, which runs the Canadian astronaut program and pays the participants' salaries, said information was trickling in slowly from the Kennedy Space Centre at Cape Canaveral.

Their Cheers Turned To Tears

CONCORD, N.H. (AP) —

Concord died with Christa McAuliffe.

"Everything just kind of came to a standstill," Karen Nelson said. "People are not moving around like they normally do."

Classes were cancelled. Legislative hearings and court trials were allied off. Flags flew at half mast.

A celebration by McAuliffe's students at Concord High School turned into a wake.

McAuliffe's legion of admirers in this state capital of 30,000 did not want to believe she died.

"I wished the whole day were a dream that it hadn't really happened," Cindy Prescott said. "I think everybody in Concord feels they know her."

Like most people in Concord, Prescott and her three children, huddled on a couch, hollered and screamed in joy when the shuttle Challenger lifted off Tuesday. Moments later their cheers turned to tears.

"Don't cry," Prescott's three-year-old daughter, Mary, pleaded with her mother. "Jesus died and he came back to life. Christa will come back to life."

"I told her that wasn't the same thing," Prescott said. "She was probably with Jesus."

McAuliffe's death touched everyone, from the neighborhood grocer to her students, from her neighbors to the governor.

Edward Shumaker, a friend of McAuliffe's, left a trial in tears, so broken up he couldn't talk.

The Daily Courier
SERVING THE FOUR SEASONS PLAYGROUND

Vol. 74 No. 149 KELOWNA, B.C., WEDNESDAY, JANUARY 29, 1986   40¢ per copy Carriers Delivered $1.70 per week

STUDENTS MOURN LOSS OF CHRISTA
Katharyn Hok, left, and Carina Dolcino, both Concord, N.H. high school students, react during a memorial service for Christa McAuliffe at St. Peter's Church in Concord, Tuesday night.

Loss Devastating For UBC Scientists

VANCOUVER (CP) — The loss of the space shuttle Challenger Tuesday was particularly devastating for University of British Columbia president David Strangway and pathologist Don Brooks.

Brooks lost a friend, research scientist Ronald McNair, 35, when Challenger exploded into a fireball shortly after liftoff. He had trained McNair to conduct an experiment in molecular separation in a weightless environment.

For Strangway, who worked for the Apollo space program for three years in the 1970s and still sits on a committee that advises the U.S. National Aeronautic and Space Administration on planetary projects, the explosion was another reminder of the hazards of exploring new frontiers.

Duchess Is Buried Without HRH Honor

WINDSOR, ENG. (AP) —

The Royal Family buried the Duchess of Windsor today beside the king who gave up the throne to marry her, thus honoring the U.S. divorcee in death after shunning her in life.

Led by the Queen, 175 mourners ranging from royalty to the duchess's faithful butler and chauffeur kneeled in prayer for the woman whose romance with King Edward VIII rocked Britain 50 years ago.

The duchess, who died Thursday in Paris at age 89, was buried beside her husband in a polished oak coffin bearing a single wreath from the Queen. The wreath was made of flowers fresh-ly picked at Windsor Castle.

The plaque on the casket said simply: "Wallis, Duchess of Windsor 1896-1986," without the "HRH" – Her Royal Highness – which the Duke of Windsor had unsuccessfully sought for his wife.

The ceremony in Windsor Castle's St. George Chapel was conducted by the Church of England, which 50 years earlier had been in the forefront of opposition to the king, its temporal head, marrying the twice-divorced Baltimore woman.

The 30-minute service, conducted by the Dean of Windsor, Rev. Michael Mann, included no eulogies and no direct references to the duchess.

Duchess of Windsor

At the service, the Queen was flanked by Prince Philip, Prince Charles and his wife Diana, Princess Anne and Elizabeth the Queen Mother.

Photo by photo credit

Mystery Surrounds Duchess's Jewels

The death of the duchess of Windsor last Thursday in Paris, where she and the duke had lived in virtual exile since his abdication in December 1936, ended one chapter in a love story that captivated the world. She was 89, childless, and with her death Buckingham Palace said the title Duke of Windsor would become extinct.

But the death of the duchess has sparked speculation on who will inherit her jewellery and the rest of her fortune.

The London Daily Telegraph estimated the total estate of the duchess at the equivalent of about $21.7 million Canadian, including property in Europe and North America.

On the duke's orders, the paper said, the jewellery of the duchess, who was divorced before she met the duke, would never be worn by another woman.

News reports speculate her jewellery might go to a Paris museum, or be used to set up a charitable foundation with a few pieces going to some members of the Royal Family – but not the Queen, her children, or Diana, Princess of Wales.

The duke's will was never disclosed and legal experts believe the will of the duchess will not be revealed either.

The death of the duchess also has rekindled the controversy over whether she manipulated a weak man – or was relentlessly pursued by him and tried to stop the romance.

$1 Coins Meet Resistance

MONTREAL (CP) —

A federal government plan to introduce $1 coins has met stiff resistance from a lobby group fighting to keep the $1 bill and from one of the companies that prints the banknote.

Members of the Ottawa-based Committee to Keep the Dollar Bill were in suburban Montreal on Friday to collect signatures for a petition.

The group, whose symbol is a cartoon of a man with his pants around his ankles because of the weight of coins, has collected 47,000 signatures in Ottawa and Toronto.

"We're not against the idea of $1 coins, it has its uses for vending machines and transit companies," said Wayne Boisvenue, an employee with Ottawa-based Canadian Bank Note Co., one of the companies that prints dollar bills in Canada.

"We just think they should keep the $1 bill also."

The $1 coin will be phased in over two years beginning January 1987. After January 1989, the dollar bill will be withdrawn, although it will remain legal tender.

Boisvenue said the new coins will be more difficult for banks, retail outlets and the Royal Canadian Mint to store and will be too hefty to be easily accepted by the Canadian public.

A Supply and Services official, said in an interview the government will save about $700 million over 20 years using coins. Coins last 20 years while $1 bills last about nine months.

It costs five cents to print a $1 bill and 12 cents to mint a $1 coin.

The official said the government didn't "anticipate any job will be lost among the printers who print the $1 bill. The increased demand for the $2 note will offset withdrawing the $1 bill."

Boisvenue said he's heard there are plans to introduce $2 and $5 coins, although the government official said there are no plans yet.

"If we don't stop it here, we don't know where it will end," Boisvenue said.

STRANGE URANIAN MOON PUZZLING SCIENTISTS

JANUARY 27, 1986. Pasadena, Calif. (AP) — Geologists are baffled by the cataclysmic forces that created towering cliffs and ridges, broad valleys and deep canyons on Uranus's major moons, especially Miranda, which has the most complex landscape yet seen in the solar system.

"During the time these moons were being formed, there were severe disturbing forces taking place," said Ellis Miner, deputy project scientist for the exploration of Uranus by the Voyager 2 spacecraft, which took stunning pictures of the planet's five largest moons.

"We're seeing on the faces of these moons, Miranda in particular, the evidence for those strong forces," he said Sunday at Jet Propulsion Laboratory. "However, that still doesn't give us much of a clue as what caused the forces."

During the weekend, information sent to Earth from Voyager's closest approach to Uranus showed 10 arcs, or ring fragments – hints that another 10 rings may encircle the planet in addition to the nine discovered from Earth and a 10th discovered by Voyager.

Today, Voyager was more than 3.2 million kilometres from Uranus, speeding away at more than 53,000 kilometres an hour as it headed toward its 1989 encounter with Neptune, the eighth planet from the sun.

During its closest encounter with Uranus, Voyager came within 81,095 kilometres of the planet, which is 2.96 billion kilometres from Earth.

The existence of large bands of dust among the rings was confirmed for the first time Sunday when Voyager returned a picture of the rings lit in the background by the sun.

The probe also transmitted evidence that a vast, gaseous belt of electrically charged particles, called plasma, is trapped in space by Uranus's magnetic fields, much like the Van Allen radiation belts around Earth.

Scientists were most excited by incredible closeups of the five largest of Uranus's 15 known moons. Voyager discovered the 10 smallest moons, while the five biggest were discovered by Earth telescopes.

Casualty Toll Seen High In Chernobyl Disaster

Second Reactor In Trouble?

MOSCOW (CP) —

An inferno raging at the Soviet Union's devastated Chernobyl atomic power plant spewed more radiation into the atmosphere today amid reports of hundreds of casualties in what could be the world's worst nuclear disaster.

There was still no comprehensive report on the accident from Soviet officials, but the picture appeared to be far worse than that painted by the Kremlin.

In Washington, Reagan administration officials said U.S. intelligence agencies now believe a second Soviet nuclear reactor at the Chernobyl complex north of Kiev either has already experienced, or is experiencing, a meltdown.

The officials, who demanded anonymity, said the first reactor to be destroyed in the disaster apparently began experiencing a "major problem" last Friday.

By Saturday, the problem had evolved into a meltdown of the reactor core. By Sunday, a chemical explosion was touched off that ripped the reactor building apart.

The official stressed that the United States has not been able to verify a second meltdown, but said there are "other indications" beyond just the close proximity of the two reactor buildings to suggest the second reactor is in serious trouble.

Confirms Meltdown

The officials said there is no easy way to verify a second meltdown because "radiation could be venting without (our) seeing it – it wouldn't be visible."

But they dismissed suggestions by some scientists that no meltdown had occurred. They cited in part the presence of radioactive iodine and cesium in the radiation detected by Scandinavian countries.

The United States still has no good estimate of the levels of radiation released nor of the death toll. However, some reports have put the casualty count at several hundred.

There have been suggestions that as many as 2,000 people had been killed. But those reports have been dismissed as wildly exaggerated by Soviet authorities and many officials in the United States.

The Soviet Union has confirmed only two deaths, a claim called "preposterous" by U.S. arms control negotiator Kenneth Adelman in light of the seriousness of the problem.

Although little information is available on what precautions the Soviet Union is taking to protect its people, warnings have been issued in Poland, Sweden and Austria.

Britain and Finland, meanwhile were evacuating their nationals from the Kiev area and the U.S. Embassy issued a warning to its citizens to leave the area.

No specific instructions have been issued by the External Affairs Department for the 18 Canadians – 16 students and two tourists – known to be in the area.

A department spokesman said today that a consular official was being sent to Kiev, the Ukrainian capital 100 kilometres from the Chernobyl complex, to study the situation first hand.

Sweden, more than 1,600 kilometres northwest of the Chernobyl plant, has warned residents on its east coast against drinking contaminated rainwater.

In Poland, parents lined up with their children today at health clinics in Warsaw, Gdansk and other communities in the northeastern part of the country to receive tinctures of iodine.

The iodine saturates the thyroid gland, making it difficult for the body to absorb the radioactive iodine produced by the fallout, which can cause thyroid tumors.

The Polish government also restricted sales of milk from grass-fed cows, urged people to wash fresh fruit and vegetables and said pregnant women and children should stay indoors if possible.

Western diplomatic sources said they understood that radiation levels in the northeast were five to 20 times the normal level Tuesday, but were much lower today.

Radioactive fallout was also reported to have reached Austria today, where some officials advised parents to keep infants indoors.

The fallout is not expected to reach Canada for several days and officials say it should be so widely dispersed by then as to present no health hazard.

Soviet-Type Mishap 'Unlikely' Here

OTTAWA (CP) — Experts said Tuesday that an accident in Canada of the type which struck a nuclear power plant in the Ukraine is a pretty unlikely prospect.

Could such an accident happen in Canada? "It would be considered by any knowledgeable person to be very remote, " says Zig Domaratzki of the Atomic Energy Control Board.

There are some similarities between the Chernobyl plant and Candu reactors, but the designs are radically different.

The biggest difference is called a containment building, a feature of all Canadian and most other western reactors.

The containment building which surrounds each reactor is there to hold any radioactive material released if something goes wrong.

This is a 1986 aerial view of the Chernobyl nuclear plant in Chernobyl, Ukraine showing damage from an explosion and fire on April 26, 1986 that sent large amounts of radioactive material into the atmosphere. Ten years later, the ghosts of history's worst nuclear accident lurk everywhere in the surrounding countryside.

(CP PHOTO)

1980~1989

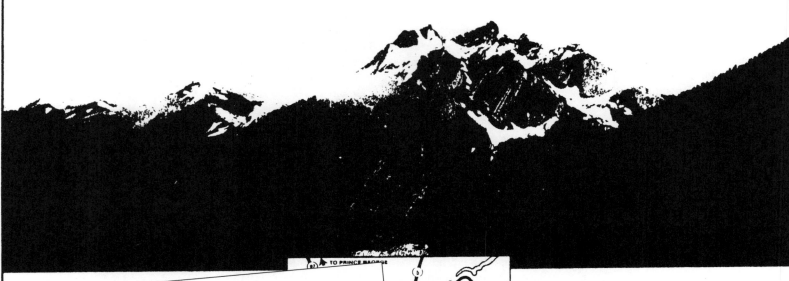

THE COQUIHALLA
...a whole new point of view in British Columbia

OPENING FRIDAY, MAY 16, 1:00pm

Coquihalla officially open

HOPE, B.C. (CP) —
Canada's only toll highway and the province's first toll highway since the 1920s is officially open.

To drive the 115.5-kiolometre Coquihalla Highway, drivers of private cars will have to pay $8, while commercial vehicle operators will have to pay up to $40. The Highways Ministry expects to earn $40 million a year from the tolls.

Premier Bill Bennett and an entourage of dignitaries and reporters began a series of opening celebrations for the $250-million highway with a pancake breakfast here this morning.

Other ceremonies were planned for the 1,240-metre summit about halfway between Hope and Merritt and the Coldwater interchange south of Merritt.

In the afternoon, the premier was to launch the already-announced second stage of the project - at $125-million extension of the four-lane freeway from Merritt to Kamloops that is due

for completion next year.

The finale was a Kamloops reception attended by Bennett and the cabinet. The cost of the day's celebrations is estimated at $50,000.

The highway's four black-topped lanes through the rugged Cascade Mountains cut an hour from the five-hour trip between Vancouver and Kamloops and gives drivers a third route into the B.C. Interior.

It is the first toll highway in British Columbia since the early 1920s when fees were charged for using the Fraser Canyon Highway - now the Trans-Canada.

Today's opening comes more than two decades since former premier W.A.C. Bennett declared highway tolls would never be seen again in the province. The last tolls on tunnels and bridges in the Vancouver area were lifted in 1964, one year after they were removed from the Lions Gate bridge at the entrance to Vancouver harbor.

Engineering feats as spectacular as the scenery

Avalanche zones. Rockslide areas. Delicate ecosystems. Raging rivers. Those are just some of the concerns addressed by the men and women who built the Coquihalla.

As you travel this route, note the stands of timber that have been left to maintain scenic beauty and to offer protection against avalanches. "Avalaunchers" (artillery guns mounted on tracked snow vehicles) are used to release avalanches under controlled conditions, thus reducing any threat of them occurring along the highway. Special bridge footings are placed well above stream beds in areas where flooding is common. Exceptional care was taken to ensure the environment and wildlife of the area were well looked after during and after construction. For instance, sections of three rivers were actually relocated. 10,000 fish were retrieved from the original channels and safely introduced to the rerouted rivers.

Phase II and Phase III to come!

The Coquihalla Highway between Hope and Merritt is just the first phase of a road construction project designed to make travel through the interior easier and quicker.

By Fall 1987, Phase II will be complete, extending the Coquihalla another 75 km (46 mi) to Kamloops. The drive from Hope to Kamloops will then be 80 km (50 mi) shorter than before the Coquihalla was built. The completion of Phase III, will see the Coquihalla Highway reach Peachland in the Okanagan Valley.

"In British Columbia, maintaining and improving our transportation system has always played a key role in the development of our economic potential. Like each of the other routes into the interior, the Coquihalla will help open the door to growth and new investment."

Hon. Bill Bennett, Premier

Hon. Alex V. Fraser, Minister

Canada's junior hockey champions to get big welcome here tonight

The Penticton Knights return home late this afternoon from Dartmouth, Nova Scotia with Canada's most coveted Junior 'A' hockey trophy in hand - the Centennial Cup.

The Centennial Cup champions are scheduled to arrive at the Penticton Airport at 5:45 p.m. A public reception will be held at the Peach Bowl starting at 6 p.m.

The Knights, runners-up in the Centennial Cup championship a year ago, achieved their goal Sunday after defeating the Cole Harbour Colts 7-4 in the final.

The Knights overcame an early first-period deficit to defeat host Cole Harbour Scotia Colts. Tournament most valuable player David Shields, Laine Jeanotte and Cal Brown each scored two goals for the victorious team from British Columbia, last year's runner-up in the national Tier II junior championship for players under 20.

Todd Torrens scored the other Penticton goal, while Kevin Grasse, Glenn Dickey, Gary Thomas and Robbie Mullane replied for the Colts.

The Colts struck early and were ahead 2-0 by 3:10 of the first period, but the Knights came back to lead 3-2 after one and 4-3 after two.

Penticton's slow start came as no surprise to assistant coach Nick Iannone.

"We got progressively stronger and that's just like other series we've been in," he said. "We started off slowly and by the end, we were strong and ended up winning it."

Iannone said the Penticton squad's ability to avoid taking too many penalties was a key to the championship victory.

"If we play five on five, we're tough to beat, but we (often) take a lot of penalties," said the assistant coach.

"If we had taken a lot in this series, we would have been in trouble."

The Colts went through the round-robin portion of the tournament undefeated, including a 6-5 win over Penticton.

The reception tonight is open to the public, and there will be no admission charge. Refreshments will be available.

Tuesday morning a parade will be held to honor the Centennial Cup champions.

The parade will begin at 11:45 a.m. at the Peach Tree Mall and continue down Main Street to City Hall.

Ex-Knights' star, Brett Hull, newest Flame

Former Penticton Knights' star Brett Hull has signed a multi-year contract with the Calgary Flames of the National Hockey League.

Brett, the son of a hockey legend, played with the Knights during the 1982-83 and 1983-84 B.C. Junior Hockey League seasons.

Brett, whose father Bobby is the NHL's fourth all-time leading scorer, was the second-highest goal-getter in U.S. college ranks last season with University of Minnesota-Duluth.

Calgary's sixth-round pick in

Brett Hull

the 1984 entry draft, Brett said he's jumping to the NHL, before finishing two more years of schooling because his play in Duluth has made him an attractive pro prospect.

Terms of the 21-year-old right winger's contract, other than the fact Calgary has offered to pay for all future college courses and provide $5,000 to the Minnesota-Duluth hockey program, were not revealed.

Brett will join the Flames in St. Louis for their third and fourth games of the NHL best-of-seven semifinal series against the Blues. Each team has one win.

Calgary coach Bob Johnson said there are no guarantees Brett will see any playoff action. But the fact the Flames have lost two regulars - Carey Wilson and Gary Suter - to injuries increases the newcomer's chances.

If, after a week, there is little prospect of him playing, Brett will return to university to write his final exams.

Knights Honored

UPDATE...

The Centennial Cup champions Penticton Knights arrived home late Monday afternoon. After being greeted by fans at the Penticton Airport, the Knights bussed to the peach Bowl where the team was honored with a public reception. Knights owner Larry Lund addressed the crowd. The Centennial Cup banner will hang in the Memorial Arena.

1980~1989

Expo opens with new gate forecast

VANCOUVER (CP) — Despite rain and cool temperatures, thousands of Expo 86 visitors were on hand today for the opening of the 165-day fair.

After Expo chairman Jim Pattison ushered a retired Newfoundland couple onto the grounds, the gates were opened to allow into holding areas those who had lined up overnight and in the early hours of the morning.

An anticipated crush of thousands lined up for the opening did not materialize, but as the morning wore on, a continuous stream of umbrella-toting funseekers made their way into the fair.

Most of the early visitors spread out onto the long, narrow fair site, heading for the amusement rides, a favored pavilion or anything that caught their fancy.

Prince Charles and Diana, Princess of Wales prepared to give the fair a royal christening later in the day at B.C. Place Stadium. The royal couple were to briefly tour the fair on the first of three visits. They will visit the grounds two more times next week before leaving the province Wednesday.

The consensus from fair early birds was favorable.

"So far it's great even though it's raining," said Joyce Zimmerman of Wilnow, Ont. "Lineups are going to be long at these pavilions. I have my daughter with me somewhere, but I've lost her already."

The $1.6-billion fair is expected to produce a deficit of over $300 million, to be covered by government lottery revenue.

Fifty-four international participants, seven provinces, three U.S. states and dozens of corporations prepared to tantalize the Expo throngs with their cultural attainments and commercial wares.

In contrast to the unfortunate performances of some previous world expositions, Expo is complete for opening day, though workers were still dabbing paint here and there on Thursday while others swept the site or spruced up pavilion exhibits.

Expo 86 is the largest-ever world's fair with a specialized theme – transportation and communication – unlike Canada's last world's fair, Expo 67 in Montreal, which had the universal theme of Man and His World.

While early world's fairs featured the latest inventions, today's Expos are little more than large, expensive trade shows.

At Expo 86, most participants are touting past and present technologies of transportation and communication. Many deliver thinly disguised advertising for their countries or companies.

The conservative Social Credit government has consistently promoted Expo as a way to spur investment and tourism in B.C.

Although Expo was a success even before it opened its gates – if enthusiastic reaction from international media representatives at a press preview Thursday is any indication – the road to the fair was filled with potholes.

Visitors to Expo 86 in Vancouver, B.C. are dwarfed by the Expo Centre, an exhibit which contains a theatre and various displays. While some regions of the province complained about the lack of spinoff benefits, Expo did generate a mood of optimism and pride that got stronger as one got closer to Vancouver.

(CP PHOTO)

1980~1989

10,000 Welcome Charles, Diana

VICTORIA (CP) —

The Prince and Princess of Wales charmed thousands of British Columbians with their affability and good looks Wednesday.

Charles expressed regret that ill-health prevented Gov. Gen. Jeanne Sauve from greeting him in Victoria – and he added lightly that after the 10-hour flight from London he was "undecided about our own state of health."

But Charles and Diana showed no sign of fatigue at the 45-minute ceremony welcoming them to Canada.

They smiled and waved to the crowd in front of the legislature building, estimated at 10,000. Organizers had prepared for 30,000 to 40,000.

Diana, in a black-dotted blue dress and matching hat, captivated the crowd while letting Charles have the limelight.

"She different; she's even more beautiful than I expected," said Alyson Parker, 11, the flower girl

Diana, Princess of Wales, greets well wishers during the opening of Expo 86.

who presented a bouquet to the princess.

More flowers and compliments were given to Diana as she and Charles stopped repeatedly to chat with bystanders.

"What flavor is the chewing gum?" Charles asked a boy who was masticating blithely in the presence of royalty.

The prince maintained the relaxed tone in his address, winning laughter with a reference to the cool, partly cloudy weather – "certainly the British bit is very much in evidence today."

The cheering was loudest when Charles introduced Diana, making her first visit to British Columbia to see "what a warm-hearted lot you are."

Charles said he and Diana were touched by the invitation to help open Expo 86 in Vancouver on Friday, "and we do very much look forward to seeing the results of all the hard work and planning which I know has gone into this particular exposition."

Expo Greets One Millionth Visitor

Pavilion Death Probed

VANCOUVER (CP) —

Debbie and John Kirkland decided to come to Expo 86 from Portland, Ore., on the spur of the moment.

A surprised Mrs. Kirkland came through the turnstiles Sunday to the sounds of a trumpet and was greeted by Tourism Minister Claude Richmond as the one millionth visitor to the world's fair.

The Kirklands, with their 5 1/2-year-old son, Jamie, in tow, were presented with an Expo 86 duffle bag containing souvenir T-shirts, and a glass vase from Czechoslovakia.

Richmond promised them a VIP tour of the Expo site, followed by dinner at the Czech pavilion.

It was the Kirklands' first visit to the 70-hectare world's fair site .

"What a great welcome," said Mr. Kirkland, a 34-year-old account manager with Pacific Northwest Bell.

Jamie told Richmond what he wanted most to do at Expo was go on the rides.

"This is our lucky day," said Mr. Kirkland.

Meanwhile, an investigation continued into the death of nine-year-old Karen Ford of Nanaimo, B.C., who was killed at the Canada pavilion Friday.

Ford was caught between a stationary wall and one that rotates between two screening areas in one of the pavilion's theatres.

The circular theatre has two screens and rotates 180 degrees so the audience can view both films without leaving their seats.

"The turntable won't be used until further notice," Jim Patterson, a spokesman for Canada pavilion, said Sunday.

However, the theatre reopened Saturday.

Expo chairman Jim Pattison described the incident as tragic. Expo spokesman Gail Flitton said Expo has no jurisdiction over the Canada pavilion, which is a federal government project.

An average of more than 100,000 people have visited Expo daily since it opened May 2. Pattison said last week that Expo had already sold a total of 15 million visits, an average of 91,000 visits every day until the fair ends Oct. 13.

Tests Show Exposure To AIDS May Be Fatal

VANCOUVER (CP) —

Vancouver doctors who attended an international conference on AIDS say new figures indicate all people who test positive for exposure to the virus may eventually go on to develop the fatal disease.

Lindsay Lawson and Alastair McLeod attended a congress on acquired immune deficiency syndrome in Paris. They said information at the conference showed the longer a person has been testing positive for AIDS antibodies

the greater the likelihood he will develop AIDS.

"It was thought it was about five to 10 per cent who (have come in contact with the virus) would eventually get AIDS," Lawson told doctors attending the Canada West Medical Congress.

"But the distressing news is the longer the disease is around, the more people who are positive are converting. We don't know what it will be in the future, but it could be as high as 100 per cent."

Lawson, a respirologist at St. Paul's Hospital in Vancouver, said an estimated 4,000 to 6,000 people in B.C. have been exposed to the AIDS virus. It is estimated that by 1991 about 174,000 people each year in the U.S. will be newly diagnosed with the disease and require hospital care.

Outside of Africa, Canada is the second-most infected country in the world behind the U.S., said McLeod, who is a dermatologist and head of the AIDS care group at St. Paul's.

Record AIDS Deaths

SAN FRANCISCO (AP) —

A record high percentage of San Francisco AIDS victims died of the disease in the first half of 1986, and an unprecedented number of new cases of AIDS were

reported last month, according to the city public health director.

David Werdegar said Tuesday of the 520 new cases reported in San Francisco this year, 67 per cent died from the illness, which

attacks the body's immune system. He said last year's figure for the same period was 58 per cent.

Werdegar said 108 new San Francisco patients were reported in June to have AIDS.

AIDS Carriers Face Quarantine

VANCOUVER (CP) —

AIDS carriers in British Columbia could be quarantined under proposed changes to the provincial Health Act.

The changes, introduced in the legislature Tuesday, would allow a medical health officer to order a person with a communicable disease "to place himself in isolation, modified isolation or quarantine."

Health Minister Peter Dueck said the bill deals with all communicable diseases and does not specifically mention AIDS. However, he said AIDS would be added to the list.

"There are very unique situations that arise with that particular disease," Dueck said. "We have to have the power to protect other people."

Dr. John Blatherwick, Vancouver's medical health officer, welcomed the news.

"We've got a guy now with tuberculosis who won't confine himself to hospital," Blatherwick said in providing an example. "These changes would allow me to order him to stay in hospital."

Bob Tivey, a spokesman for AIDS Vancouver, said the changes will only instill more

fear.

"These sweeping new powers are really frightening," he said.

Tivey, whose group was established to help AIDS victims, said some people with AIDS might be discouraged from seeking treatment.

John Russell, executive director of the B.C. Civil Liberties Association, said his group does not anticipate medical authorities will abuse the new powers.

"But we'll be watching carefully to make sure this broad discretionary authority is used judiciously," Russell added.

Rock Hudson

Heart Operation A Canadian First

Recipient In Stable Condition

OTTAWA (CP) —

Noella Leclair of Ottawa was in critical but stable condition today after receiving a Jarvik-7 artificial heart Thursday night in a bridging operation that was the first of its kind in Canada.

Dr. Wilbert Keon, the doctor who headed the surgical team at the University of Ottawa Heart Institute at Ottawa Civic Hospital, told a news conference today the 41-year-old woman was on a heart-lung machine prior to the operation and was effectively dead.

Doctors hope to find a human heart for Leclair as soon as possible to avoid complications.

The 3 1/2 hour operation ended shortly before 11 a.m. EDT Thursday. Keon said she awoke at 6 a.m. today and was fully responsive. However, she is unable to talk because of a breathing tube in her throat.

Leclair, married with a teenage daughter, seemed to be in perfect health until she started having chest pains April 22, Keon said.

She suffered a heart attack April 25 and further problems in the days that followed. By Thursday, she was unable to sustain blood pressure on her own, and the heart-lung machine was all that kept her alive.

The device implanted in Leclair is a small version of the Jarvik-7 that doctors call the Jarvik-7-70. Keon called it "a masterpiece of engineering."

Keon is one of Canada's leading heart surgeons, and Thursday's operation made it clear that the Heart Institute is at the forefront of clinical work with artificial hearts.

Keon said centres in Montreal, Toronto, London also hope to use artificial hearts for bridging, but none of them has the capacity to do so at the moment.

COURIER ADDS MORE HIGH-TECH IMPROVE-MENTS

1986. — The Daily Courier is now being published with the most up-to-date newspaper computers available.

The Hastech system, made in New Hampshire, has revolutionized the newsroom and classified departments and added new capability to the composing room through the use of video display terminals.

"This installation reflects our commitment to improve the newspaper for our customers and readers," said D.F. Doucette, publisher and general manager. "The Daily Courier is growing with the Central Okanagan."

"Improvements like this show we plan to continue as a leader in the communications field."

A Touching Farewell For Premier Bennett

WHISTLER, B.C. (CP) —

The Social Credit party ended an era Monday night when delegates to the party's leadership convention said a touching thank you to Premier Bill Bennett.

After the voting Wednesday, when 1,300 delegates will choose a new premier and leader from among the field of 12, the provincial Social Credit party will be led by someone other than a Bennett for the first time in more than three decades.

W.A.C. Bennett quit a loose and sagging coalition government to form the populist party under the Social Credit label in 1952. In 1973 the Socreds, who by now had become a coalition of Liberals and Conservatives, chose his son Bill on the first ballot.

Monday night, the party said an official goodbye to Bill in the knowledge that none of his four sons is likely to follow in the footsteps of either their father or grandfather.

Bennett's wife, Audrey, said she hoped none of her sons would enter politics, adding that she did not think it likely they would.

"I could always handle the criticism – but maybe it's because I had more practice handling the criticism – than I could deal with the kindness of friends," the 54-year-old premier told more than 1,500 party supporters in crowded convention centre.

Jimmy Pattison, Bennett's millionaire friend and the chairman of Expo 86, described the last five years in British Columbia as the worst economic times he remembers in his 51 years here. But he said to Bennett: "You've done a first-class job being premier."

Bennett, clearly moved by the praise, took the hand of his mother, May, who was sitting next to him, held it briefly and then stared down at the floor as the applause died.

The Daily Courier

SERVING THE FOUR SEASONS PLAYGROUND

1980-1989

Police, City Meet To Assess The Riot

By Maureen Utley
Courier Staff

People charged in the Regatta weekend riot in downtown Kelowna will begin filtering through the court system today.

Kelowna RCMP Insp. Dave Kilcup said authorities are to meet today with City of Kelowna officials to begin a post-mortem of the early-Sunday morning incident.

Kilcup has neither a damage estimate nor overtime costs for policing. He said the comments he's received regarding police action have been positive.

Kilcup said "the usual crowd of idiots" appeared downtown Sunday night, hoping some action would develop between police and youths, but nothing materialized.

Charges such as assaulting police officers, wilful damage, possession of stolen property and vandalism are emerging.

"Those still in custody are charged with other than being drunk," said Kilcup.

The riot resulted in the arrest of 105 people, 68 from out of town. The inspector said the majority were in their late teens and early 20s.

A spokesman from Kelowna General Hospital said today the emergency department treated about 15 people for minor injuries, mostly cuts. No one was admitted overnight.

"The incident we had last night ... nobody is proud of," said Kilcup Sunday morning. He said around 8:30 p.m. Saturday, reports of flagrant public drinking started coming into the police detachment.

At about 9, "the feeling was, something is going to happen."

At about 1 a.m. Sunday, police decided to close to traffic the foot of Bernard Avenue, the main street, near the landmark Sails sculpture.

"Right, wrong or indifferent, we made it (the decision) and we stand by it," said Kilcup.

"That proved to be difficult ... or a mistake if you like," he said. "It merely seemed to bring a concentration to that area."

"From there it seemed to mushroom," said Kilcup.

The crowd began to throw beer bottles against concrete and at police and their cars.

An estimated 95 police officers were called out. In addition, reinforcements from Penticton and Vernon were called in, as well as the Kelowna Fire Department.

The plan, said Kilcup, was to simply get the crowd moving. But police had to deal with two groups, not just one. There were about three police dogs and handlers at the scene, but Kilcup said they were not used "in the frontline situation" because dogs can become more excited than people."

Tear gas, however, was used.

Kilcup stressed Regatta was not to blame for the riot.

"I don't think there's any connection," he said, but added "It's unfortunate that the Kelowna Regatta attracts that group of people."

He said the number of young people gathering downtown appears to be increasing, and appears to peak at Regatta time.

"It's easier to police those kids when they are in town (compared with bush parties)," said Kilcup.

Kilcup praised his officers, saying they kept control under trying circumstances.

"I am very, very proud of them. It's a scary situation. We can be proud of our policemen," he said, adding the RCMP acted "with what I feel was total restraint last night."

The inspector said when it was all over, he asked his wife: "Have I had a bad dream? Did that actually happen?"

'We'll Come Down Hard' – Mayor

By J.P. Squire
Courier Staff

Mayor Dale Hammill has had it with young people carousing on Bernard Avenue Friday and Saturday nights.

The riot early Sunday morning was "the saddest night I've ever seen in this city," the mayor said today.

Those involved "were just insane, like little animals," he said, and were "mostly punky kids too young to drink" and "probably out for their first unruly time." The alcohol gave them the impetus to break the law, he believes.

"I'm very disappointed that this could happen in Kelowna. I'd like to know how many parents knew where their children were. It was unbelievable, the look on their faces, it was like they had no training at home. Certainly there must be some respect for the law."

He personally favors two years of military training for young people to teach them respect for authority.

"Sunday there was a total disregard for any authority," he said. "It was more than a disgrace the way they treated police. It was a black mark on our community."

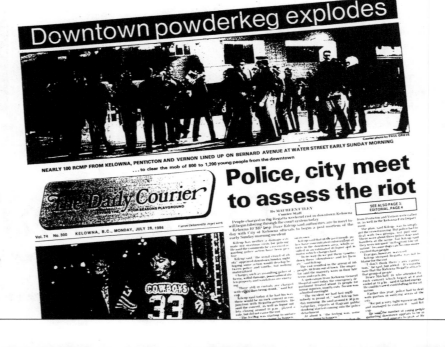

Downtown powderkeg explodes

NEARLY 100 RCMP FROM KELOWNA, PENTICTON AND VERNON LINED UP ON BERNARD AVENUE AT WATER STREET EARLY SUNDAY MORNING
... to clear the mob of 800 to 1,200 young people from the downtown

Police, city meet to assess the riot

Regatta Riot Replay

KELOWNA, B.C. (CP) —
For the second time in as many years, rioting marred the annual Kelowna Regatta early Sunday when more than 1,000 young people smashed windows and threw bottles at police.

Riot-equipped RCMP officers arrested about 190 people after using tear gas to break up the crowd, which, like last year, had gathered downtown for the drinking binge which has come to be associated with the regatta.

In the aftermath, residents worried the riot could spell the end of the 81-year-old event. One alderman said he'll ask city council to lobby the federal government to give police more power to deal with disturbances before they get out of control.

Mayor Jim Stuart read the Riot Act at about 3:30 a.m. Sunday morning, more than two hours after the first indications of trouble. By then most of the crowd had already been dispersed by police.

About 30 people, including four police officers, suffered minor injuries. Damage initially was estimated at about $500,000, most of it broken glass.

Events paralleled almost exactly those of the 1986 regatta riot, in spite of preparation by city officials and police to avoid a repetition.

"We hired street workers and tried to prepare for this with a crackdown on booze sales," said Stuart.

"I felt bad for the police," he said. "They tried hard to keep a lid on it, but couldn't. The police took a lot of abuse."

Sidewalks were filled to overflowing with young people, yelling at friends in vehicles which were crawling along a jam-packed Bernard Avenue.

About 30 uniformed RCMP and a smaller number of plainclothes officers patrolled the street on foot and in cars. They confiscated cans and bottles of beer and ticketed vehicles violating a downtown parking ban put in place for the four day regatta.

The first incident took place about 1 a.m. PDT Sunday, when a few bottles were thrown at police foot patrols from a rooftop.

But the real trouble began when RCMP tried to arrest a young man for disorderly conduct at Kerry Park, near where the 1986 riot began. A crowd converged on the scene and jeered police.

The officers retreated to safety but left more than 1,000 people blocking Bernard Street. The crowd taunted police and threw bottles and cups.

Within a few minutes 40 riot-equipped police arrived and advanced on the crowd, which fled but regrouped several times. A searchlight-equipped helicopter hovered overhead while police hurled tear gas at the crowd, which sometimes sent the canisters back.

Rioters smashed store windows but unlike last summer, didn't steal the contents. A truck-mounted water cannon from the airport guarded a nearby liquor store and drove back a crowd which tried to gather there.

The streets were largely cleared by 4 a.m. except for scattered reports of vandalism. Merchants had arrived to take stock of the damage and begin cleaning up.

"It's getting ridiculous," said Grant Putnam, whose electronics appliance store was hit for the second time in as many years. "The police don't have enough power to stop the vandalism before it happens."

Ald. Tom Treadgold said he'll ask city council to lobby Ottawa to amend the Criminal Code so police can break up crowds before they start trouble.

VENGEANCE NOT GOAL OF SENTENCE IN KELOWNA RIOT CASE SAYS CROWN

JULY 30, 1987. KELOWNA, B.C. (CP) — Angry citizens looking to the courts to mete out vengeance against participants in the riot at the Kelowna Regatta last weekend won't find it, Crown prosecutor Scott Van Alstine said Wednesday.

"Vengeance is not a principle of sentence," said Van Alstine.

Civic leaders have said they will ask Attorney General Brian Smith to instruct judges to hand out stiff sentences to deter a recurrence of the riot which marred the regatta for the second time in two years.

Rehabilitation of the offender, protection of the public and both general and individual deterrence are principals in sentencing in the Canadian legal system, Van Alstine said. Problems arise when individual deterrence requires a light touch but a resident who got the six month jail term was described as one of the main participants in last year's riot. His actions were said to incite others and he showed no remorse.

"That's the balancing act the judge has to go through every time," said Van Alstine.

Van Alstine said that last year prosecutors used a three-page synopsis of the riot to set the scene for the sentencing judge. But sentencing restrictions also apply. Those convicted of summary or less serious offences face a maximum six months in jail, a $2,000 fine and probation for two years.

Sentencing on indictable charges or applying the Riot Act itself provides for a maximum sentence of life in prison. Van Alstine said severe and unusual circumstances are required to apply the act against an individual.

A stand-off between police and out-of-control Kelowna Regatta celebrants resulted in injuries to more than 30 persons, including police officers, and more than 190 arrests.

1980~1989

Kelowna Donates Almost $200,000

By J.P. Squire
Courier Staff

Rick Hansen was presented Thursday with $158,000, more than twice the Kelowna organizing committee's original goal.

And Kelowna's contribution to the Man in Motion World Tour is still growing.

It was only a partial payment since it didn't include the thousands of dollars collected along the route into the city by Kelowna firefighters or the donation of approximately $21,000 from students who met Hansen this morning at KSS.

Thursday's largest donation at $41,000 came from the sale of $10 shares in the Okanagan Lake floating bridge, renamed the Rick Hansen Floating Bridge for this campaign. A total of 5,000 shares are to be sold for a $50,000 donation.

During the city's official welcome in City Park at 4 p.m. Hansen was presented with share number 4,529 and a framed picture of Canada's longest floating bridge.

Okanagan Valley Lions clubs added nearly $19,000 from the raffle of a travel trailer.

"It's nice to be back in Kelowna," Hansen told a City Park crowd. He came to Kelowna for the B.C. Disabled Games in 1981 and 1982, noting this city's history of supporting the disabled.

He urged everyone to join him in the challenge – to remove the barriers that stand in the way of everyone attaining his or her potential.

Hansen Fever Hits Penticton

By Heather Glebe
Family Page Editor

Threatening skies and an hour's delay didn't dampen the enthusiasm of the crowds which turned out to see Rick Hansen on his arrival in Penticton Monday afternoon.

The fever reached a peak when the community's total of $75,000 "and still climbing" was presented to Hansen's fund for spinal cord research.

Strong headwinds had put the Man in Motion behind schedule in his journey south from Kelowna. He arrived in Summerland about an hour later than expected, but was greeted by a large crowd in Memorial Park.

Hansen received a $16,000 cheque from the community, a figure which represents more than $2 per person in Summerland.

Runners from the Penticton Pounders had a hard time keeping up with Hansen as he rolled down the highway to Penticton. While crowds lined Eckhardt Avenue, at King's Park, hundreds of yellow balloons, ribbons and flags danced in the wind.

While the crowd waited until after 4 p.m. for Hansen's arrival, emcee Grant Sherwood listed Hansen's accomplishments as an athlete since 1971. As well as dozens of medals, Hansen competed successfully in 19 international marathons, in most cases breaking world records in wheelchair events.

A roar of cheers and "We want Rick!" greeted Hansen as he entered King's Park.

Mayor Dorothy Whittaker, in officially greeting Hansen, called the Man in Motion tour a "passionate voyage of discovery."

"We understand you have wheeled nearly 40,000 kilometres, equivalent to the circumference of the earth," she said to Hansen. But behind all the excitement is a "simple message" which has touched everyone, she said. "We have each reacted to the depth of your goals. You have given new meaning to the Biblical phrase 'It is more blessed to give than to receive'."

Hansen was then awarded the city's highest honor, the Order of the Peach.

As a finale, Man in Motion committee members, headed by Gordie Gordon were introduced. The total of $75,126 brought a new round of cheers.

1980~1989

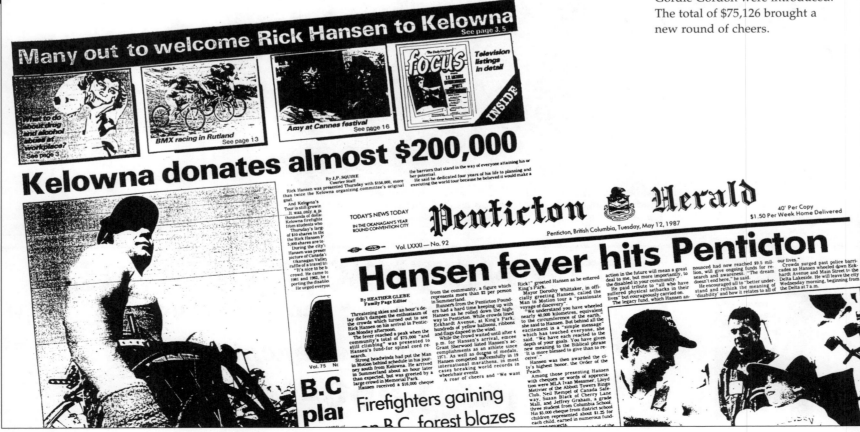

Personal Goal Met

Rick Hansen Rolls Into Vancouver

Overwhelming Welcome

VANCOUVER (CP) —

Rick Hansen, who turned a teenager's determined dream into a personal crusade for the disabled, brought his Man-in-Motion tour home today.

The wheelchair marathoner rolled into Vancouver at 10:39 a.m. PDT, 26 months after leaving the city to circle the globe.

It was an overwhelming welcome. Tens of thousands of people lined suburban streets and connecting highways. They waved yellow balloons, ribbons, streamers and signs.

Some had tears in their eyes. Others were too choked to speak.

"I'm sorry, I'm getting all emotional about this," said a school teacher as she tried to explain how her students have responded to Hansen's message. "It's such an exciting time you know."

A grinning Hansen, wheeling under bright sunny skies with an honor guard of disabled friends, said "there was a raging fire of emotion inside" as he wheeled toward the Oakridge shopping centre – the tour's closing point.

Although he had to wheel only 40 kilometres – about half his daily average – he faced one last obstacle today in the form of a two-kilometre hill in Coquitlam with a demanding 17-per-cent grade.

But wedged into his low-slung chair, his atrophied legs pulled up tight to his chest, he conquered "the steepest hill we've had in North America."

Hansen started the day in suburban Coquitlam, saying he was "floating on Cloud 9."

"I'm just overwhelmed with emotion, with gratitude to not only my crew but to the people who have worked so long and so hard to make this happen," Hansen told reporters gathered in front on his motorhome.

Asked if he considered himself a hero yet, the 29-year-old crusader for the disabled replied: "Not really. I feel like a person who's been fortunate to see his dream come true."

Dressed in a grey T-shirt and blue leggings. Hansen's first stop of the day was in Port Coquitlam – the hometown of one-legged runner, Terry Fox, who died of cancer halfway through a run across Canada.

Hansen told a crowd of several hundred, many waving yellow balloons and ribbons, that Fox "stands as a man who was not afraid to reach for his dreams, a man who knew that failing was not reaching, not trying to be the best you can be with what you have."

As he left the stage, Hansen stopped briefly to shake hands with members of the Fox family.

Fox's mother, Betty, said it was an emotional moment for her. Hansen has raised more than $10 million for spinal cord research and created a new awareness of the abilities of the disabled and their needs.

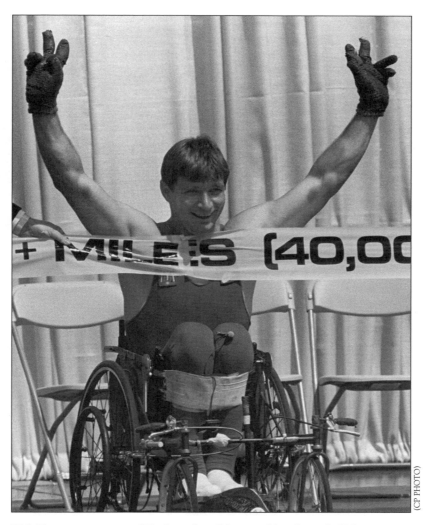

(CP PHOTO)

Rick Hansen prepares to glide through a ribbon marking the end of his two year Man in Motion Tour at a shopping plaza in Vancouver, Friday.

HIGHWAYS CLEARS WAY FOR HANSEN

MAY 5, 1987. Grand Forks, B.C. (CP) — The road home to Vancouver has sometimes been a rocky one for wheelchair athlete Rick Hansen but British Columbia highway crews are literally doing everything they can to pave the way.

In the 581 kilometres between here and Manning Park on Highway 3 there are several stretches of road under construction.

Highways department spokesman Ivan Robertson said Monday, measures will be taken to make sure roads are passable for Hansen who is less than three weeks away from completing a two-year, globe-girdling odyssey to promote spinal cord research and awareness of the handicapped.

"The highways department will do anything to make it easier for Hansen ... all the way to Manning Park if need be."

Robertson says where possible, paving will be done early to provide a single lane of blacktop.

He also says highway crews will grade the shoulders of the highway so Hansen can wheel through construction zones without hitting areas where the road surface has been grouted to help bind the new asphalt.

1980~1989

CANADIAN UNITY

JULY 2, 1987. Ottawa (CP) — Prime Minister Brian Mulroney says the country celebrates Canada Day with a new unity now that Quebec has been brought into the constitutional fold. In his annual Canada Day message, Mulroney referred to the Meech Lake accord as evidence of "the spirit of equality, tolerance and fairness which has enabled us to continue along the path of nation building." Gov. Gen. Jeanne Sauve said: "I do not think Canadians fear change … They believe that the federation must always be open to change."

Second Fastest Mile In History For Runner

Sports In Brief

JULY 8, 1987. Helsinki, Finland (AP) — Said Aouita of Morocco ran the second-fastest mile in history at the World Games IAAF Grand Prix track meet Thursday, winning in three minutes, 46.76 seconds.

Aouita was only 44-hundredths of a second shy of Briton Steve Cram's record of 3:46.32 set almost two years ago.

Markus Hacksteiner of Switzerland was second in 3:55.67.

The pacemaking was excellent as Briton Paul Larkins hit the first 400 in 56.2 seconds. The split time for the 800-metre mark was 1:53.7. Dave Campbell of Victoria, B.C., took over the pacesetting in the second lap after Larkins had dropped out.

I Was Always Kept In The Dark Shultz Tells Iran-Contra Hearings

WASHINGTON (AP) — U.S. State Secretary George Shultz testified Thursday other Reagan administration officials consistently kept him in the dark about key events in the Iran-Contra affair and he was "sick to my stomach" when he learned some details.

In riveting testimony at congressional hearings, Shultz emotionally declared his loyalty to President Ronald Reagan, and said he waged a "battle royal" to make sure Reagan learned all the facts as the affair unravelled last fall.

Shultz said then-CIA director William Casey and then-national security adviser John Poindexter were "on the other side" in the battle and accused them of trying to persuade the president to "bail them out" with inaccurate public statements.

He said Casey even bypassed other high-level officials and secretly talked Reagan into permitting further arms-for-hostages discussions with the Iranians after the controversial earlier dealings became public last fall.

In an appearance that produced one dramatic disclosure after another, Shultz said he didn't know U.S.

This is the cutline style from the style sheet

hostage Benjamin Weir's release from captivity in Lebanon came two days after Israel had sold U.S. made weapons to Iran in September 1985.

He also said he first learned the United States had sold weapons directly to Iran when he read news reports published months after the transaction took place.

Shultz made it clear he and Defence Secretary Caspar Weinberger vigorously told Reagan in December 1985 they opposed any plans to sell arms to Iran.

He described one meeting in the White House where Reagan asked for their opinion.

"So he (Weinberger) gave it to him and so did I," Shultz said.

But the secretary said it wasn't until he told Reagan a year later that Lt. Col. Oliver North's private emissaries were discussing obtaining the release of terrorists imprisoned in Kuwait that "I finally felt that the president deeply under-stands that something is radically wrong here."

Shultz spoke in a sombre voice that belied the astonishing nature of his testimony.

Shultz was heavily criticized last fall for distancing himself from the arms sales when they were made public, and there were calls for his resignation.

He said it was a "very traumatic period" for him, and added: "I frankly felt that I was the one who who was loyal to the president because I was the one who was trying to get him the facts so he could make a decision. But it was a battle royal."

Shultz quarrelled with North's testimony, as well, saying he was unaware of North's secret efforts to funnel arms to the Nicaraguan Contra rebels during a congressional ban on direct or indirect U.S. military aid to the insurgents.

North testified Shultz "knew in sufficiently elegant terms of what I had done."

Wineries Toasting Court Rule

Canadian wineries are toasting an Ontario Supreme Court ruling that says the French are not the only ones who can refer to their bubbly as champagne.

In a decision released Thursday, Mr. Justice W.R. DuPont ruled against an attempt by French champagne houses to stop Ontario companies from calling their product Canadian champagne.

"Canadian champagne is a distinct Canadian product not likely to be confused or even compared with French champagne," DuPont said.

Even people unaccustomed to drinking champagne will realize the difference between the Canadian and French versions. DuPont concluded, noting one way to tell is the price.

The Liquor Control Board of Ontario sells French champagnes at $25 to $30 a bottle, and Dom Perignon sells for about $75.

Bright's President Canadian Champagne, made by Bright and Co. Ltd., goes for $7.95 a bottle.

"The marketing, advertising, labelling and general reputation of Canadian champagne … has satisfied the court that deception and confusion are not likely to occur in Ontario," Dupont said.

David Diston, a Bright vice-president, said he was relieved by the decision.

Bright's sells two thirds of their million bottles of champagne - French or otherwise – sold in Ontario each year, Diston said.

The Herald contacted the local branch of Bright's wines, but they were still celebrating the July 1 holiday today and no one could be reached for comment.

Other area wineries contacted, including Casabello Wines, Sumac Ridge in Summerland and Calona Wines in Kelowna, said they do make a product which could be called champagne.

We Want Vote On Free Trade

OTTAWA (CP) —

Prime Minister Brian Mulroney is mistaken if he thinks Canadian voters will reject John Turner's attempt to use the Senate to force an election on free trade, says a pollster.

Poll after poll has shown that a majority of Canadians want an election before the free-trade deal with the United States takes effect, Michael Adams, president of Environics Research in Toronto, said Friday.

"This is a risk he's taking and a calculated risk and one in public opinion terms makes a lot of sense," Adams said in an interview from Toronto.

Conservative stategists believe Turner handed them an issue on a silver platter when he called on the Liberal majority in the Senate to essentially force an election.

Mulroney was quick to ridicule Turner on Wednesday, suggesting the Liberal leader was using the Senate to hijack the authority of elected members of Parliament.

"I feel like I'm the only Canadian other than John Turner who feels that what he has done makes perfect sense," said Adams.

Surveys have suggested that as many as 70 per cent of Canadians want an election before the trade deal takes effect on Jan. 1.

A January survey taken by another pollster, Angus Reid and Associates of Winnipeg, indicated that 49 per cent of Canadians would support Senate delay of the trade legislation if they thought it was necessary. Thirty-six per cent opposed it.

Adams said the Senate gambit has the added advantage of making Turner look decisive.

"I can't remember the last time John Turner was on the front pages of the nation's newspapers in which he initiated something."

On Wednesday, Turner announced that the Liberal majority in the Senate had agreed to hold up legislation needed to implement the trade deal until Mulroney calls an election.

Under the trade deal, Canada and the United States would begin phasing out a wide range of commercial barriers – from tariffs on imported goods to restrictions on energy exports and foreign investment.

Mulroney could wait until the fall of 1989 to hold a general election. But the agreement would almost certainly die unless Canada has passed its free-trade legislation by Jan. 1, when the deal is scheduled to take effect.

POPE JOHN PAUL PAYS TRIBUTE

JULY 23, 1988. LORENZAGO, ITALY (REUTER) — Pope John Paul, in a rare and intimate conversation with reporters, paid tribute Friday to the "greatness of Nelson Mandela", the black nationalist leader jailed in South Africa. The Roman Catholic pontiff also expressed hope that the Persian Gulf war between Iran and Iraq will end soon. The relaxed and sun-tanned Pope spoke to five Italian reporters and a Reuters news agency correspondent in the garden of a secluded mountaintop house on the last day of his 10-day vacation, in the northern Italian Dolomites near Austria.

Apologizes For Japanese-Canadian Internment

OTTAWA (CP) —

Prime Minister Brian Mulroney formally apologized on behalf of Parliament today for the internment of 22,000 people of Japanese heritage during the Second World War.

As representatives of the Japanese-Canadian community watched and applauded from the public gallery, Mulroney told the Commons the internment was unjustified on moral and legal grounds.

He offered "a solemn undertaking that such violations will never again in this country be countenanced or repeated."

Mulroney said the government has reached a comprehensive agreement with the Japanese-Canadian association to redress their grievances.

Among the details in the $288-million package:

– Official acknowledgement of the injustices.

– Payments of $21,000 to the 12,000 people interned who are still alive.

– $12 million for the Japanese-Canadian community to be administered by the National Association of Japanese Canadians.

– $24 million for a Canadian Race Relations Foundation.

The prime minister acknowledged that "no amount of money can right the wrong."

But "error is an ingredient of humanity," Mulroney said solemnly. "So too is apology and forgiveness. We have all learned from personal experience that, inadequate as apologies are, they are the only way we can cleanse the past, so that we may, as best we can, in good conscience, face the future."

"I am NOT selling out to the Americans!"   "Actually, I'm GIVING Canada away!"

1980~1989

JULY 21, 1988. — Dramatic changes have taken place over the past few months at the Johnson-Bentley Memorial Aquatic Centre in Westbank.

Three months ago, the floor was bare concrete, gravel and reinforcing bars. Now, most of that is gone.

The ceiling, which was once an intricate display of primer-colored steel, is now painted white with blue and yellow suspended acoustic panels.

Blue and white tile are being laid on the floor of the curved L-shaped pool. Floor tile are laid first, then it will take crews another two weeks to do the walls and corners of the pool.

That work can be time consuming. Advanced Building Systems Inc.'s project manager Colin Lee noted it took one worker two days to cut the tile to fit around all the jets in the whirlpool.

The whole facility doesn't look much like what many people might expect to find at a public swimming pool.

The south wall is lined with glass, offering a panoramic view of Okanagan Lake and the hills.

The large whirlpool has room for 40 to 50 people, a wheelchair ramp and shallow playing area for children, all with a great corner view.

Nearby is a steam room (similar to a sauna, but without the dry heat) with windows again offering a view of the lake.

The pool itself has six competition quality 25-metre swimming lanes, with the foot of the L sloping gently into the main pool. A mushroom fountain will help entertain the children playing there.

Adjoining the main pool, but with its own separate heating system, is the circular soaking pool with a canopy to offer "mood lighting."

The pool is substantially finished, other than tile-work, some finishing work in the front visitors' gallery, and the painting of a wall mural.

Lee said water should be in it by the end of July. It will then take two or three weeks to "work out the bugs" and get the YM-YWCA crew accustomed to the complex.

Projects of this size usually take 10 to 12 months to complete, Lee said. Advanced Building Systems had hoped to have it finished by this spring. But delays are inevitable with such a project and the company has taken a slow but sure approach rather than rush the project at the expense of quality, he said.

Johnson Starting To Lose Millions In Sponsorships

TORONTO (CP) —

There were no ticker tape parades when Ben Johnson came home Tuesday, no speeches from adoring fans.

But there were crowds – mostly children chanting, "Ben, Ben, Ben… We believe you." – surrounding his modest suburban Scarborough home.

Canada's fallen hero had nothing to say to the throngs of supporters and media, but one woman seemed to speak for many with a message with some 1,000 signatures indicating a sympathy with what they called "his personal devastation."

High overhead, a plane chartered by a group of local restaurant workers circled with a banner proclaiming: "We believe you, Ben."

The burly sprinter remained secluded after his 14-hour flight from the Olympic Games in Seoul and the biggest drug scandal in sports history. The country and the world was waiting to hear from him.

"I still have my parents," the Boston Globe reported him as saying on the trip home. "My family still loves me."

But it appeared the man once called The World's Fastest Human had lost everything else when he tested positive for the anabolic steroid Stanozolol.

The gold medal he had won will

Ben Johnson

(CP Photo)

be awarded without ceremony to his American rival, Carl Lewis, in an IOC office in Seoul's Olympic Stadium on Saturday.

His title had all but technically been stripped. A world record was expunged from the books and Johnson's name, now forever associated with failure, was struck from the official Olympic history.

Through the 9.83-second record he set last year still stands, firms which a short time ago flocked to his door with big money contracts were scattering like flies.

While Canadian companies said they were content to allow promotional contracts to quietly die, the Kyodo Oil Co. immediately halted Johnson television advertisements

and began taking down his picture from 6,500 gas stations around Japan.

The Italian sportswear company Diadora decided to cancel its five-year, $2.4-million contract with the 26-year-old runner. And a movie company said it would have to rewrite the script for a film about him .

Through it all, Johnson appeared stunned, not comprehending the magnitude of the tragedy as he and his family battled their way through crowds of reporters and cameramen at airports in Seoul, New York and Toronto.

"Why, Ben?" they shouted. "Tell us something, anything."

Johnson, expressionless and dressed in black, said nothing.

During a stopover in New York, he momentarily fought back tears, then managed a slight grin not unlike the one he offered on the victory podium 14,600 kilometres and a world away.

"He wants to be with people who love him now, not the hypocrites who abandoned him," said his sister, Clare Rodney.

Johnson's people have adamantly maintained his innocence since they were first confronted with the test results Monday. They claim he was the victim of a spiked drink.

The IOC rejected the argument and Canadian authorities said they would not appeal.

Tyson Out Of Control

NEW YORK (AP) —

Heavyweight boxing champion Mike Tyson is quoted by the New York Post as saying he suffers from "a manic depression" and realizes he has a problem he has to control.

The article published Thursday was based on an interview Wednesday night just hours after Tyson hurled a radio at a television crew while doing his morning run.

The Post said that after the TV crew incident Tyson had a tearful

talk with his wife, actress Robin Givens, his mother-in-law, Ruth Roper, and psychiatrist Henry McCurtis at which Tyson admitted being out of control at times.

"I was born with this disease," Tyson told the Post. "I can't help it. Maybe that's why I'm successful at what I do. This is the way I was all my life."

Tyson, 22, has had a series of violent incidents in the last year.

In August, he fractured a bone in his right hand in a late night fistfight on a Harlem street with

boxer Mitch Green. Earlier this month Tyson was in hospital for several days after smashing his car into a tree in Catskill, N.Y., where he trains.

Following the car crash, the New York Daily News said sources close to Tyson quoted him as threatening suicide shortly before the wreck. Another source told The Associated Press that Tyson had been depressed because Givens had been staying in New York City instead of his upstate training camp.

Contracted AIDS Virus Through Screened Blood, Court Is Told

OTTAWA (CP) —

A Canadian blood transfusion patient contracted the AIDS virus through a blood sample that was screened by the Red Cross and tested negative, a criminal trial has been told.

It is apparently the first such instance since the Red Cross established universal AIDS screening procedures for donated blood in November, 1985.

Dr. Gail Rock, former medical director of the blood transfusion section of the Red Cross Ottawa Centre branch, said she recently learned of the case from a physician.

Rock was testifying on Tuesday at the trial of a man from nearby Vanier, Ont., charged with knowingly donating AIDS-contaminated blood.

James Thornton, 27, has pleaded not guilty to endangering the lives, safety or health of the public under the Criminal Code offence of nuisance. But he admitted through his lawyer that he donated blood in November 1987 and prior to that, he had tested positive for the antibody, formed from the AIDS virus.

Rock said screening procedures are not 100-per-cent foolproof and do not detect AIDS in all contaminated samples.

She said that by the time a single blood donation that has been screened is broken down into various blood products for use in hospitals, as many as four or five patients could receive the product.

If shipped to the U.S. for extraction of Factor 8, a protein that helps blood clot in a haemophiliac, the infected flood could potentially reach hundreds, even thousands of patients.

In an interview, Rock said the inadvertent transmission of the fatal virus to a Canadian hospital patient occurred within the last three years. But she did not know where the patient lived, or any other details.

Brenda Workers Adjust

The 400 employees who have kept Peachland's Brenda Mines in a profit making position over its 20-year lifespan have often been called upon to adjust to changing conditions.

Before the end of 1990 they will have to make the ultimate adjustment at the permanent closing of the open pit mine that is almost depleted of its copper-molybdenum ore.

Many employees are taking advantage of a labor adjustment program as advance preparation for the imminent shutdown. Jointly sponsored by the federal department of Employment and Immigration, Brenda Mines and the union local, the adjustment program has been operating since the spring, mapping out direction for employees' futures.

The company-union adjustment program is unique in Canada. Whether it fulfills its objective of preparing Brenda's employees for life after the mine will be gauged solely by the numbers who are successful in finding good jobs.

But judging by the attitude of mine workers, the program has already made a positive impact. Employees say they are not worried and seem to have their future plans well in hand.

Negotiations Or War Fate Of South Africa

By Rob Munro
Courier Staff

War in South Africa is inevitable if the government refuses to negotiate, says a spokesman for the African National Congress.

George Lai, who now lives in Vancouver after fleeing South Africa in 1969, spoke to 60 Okanagan College students Wednesday.

"Before we come to a situation of all-out war, we hope to negotiate," Lai said.

The ANC has drafted a Freedom Charter that calls for democratic change giving equal rights to people of all colors in South Africa.

"We have never seen the white people as the enemy, but the system," Lai said. "Violence that is in South Africa stems from the system of apartheid. If they remove apartheid, there will be no violence."

Armed troops in the townships have killed people, Lai said. Non-whites are are now "clamoring for us to retaliate."

But armed resistance is only one solution. Sanctions by foreign countries also put pressure on the government.

Lai suggested Canadians can help by refusing to support companies that do business with South Africa, pressure the Canadian government to live up to its 1985 promise to impose stricter sanctions if the situation did not improve, and to support anti-apartheid organizations like the ANC.

STARS AND FANS HEAR STONES

NOVEMBER 2, 1989.
VANCOUVER (CP) — David Bowie was there. So were Cher and John Travolta. But they were lost in the crowd at B.C. Place Stadium as the Rolling Stones occupied centre stage Wednesday night.

The British rock band entertained a bevy of stars and 53,000 fans with a 25-song show that lasted two hours and 20 minutes.

While critics complained of mushy sound in the domed stadium, the crowd didn't seem to care as the Stones played everything from Satisfaction to Jumpin' Jack Flash.

Other songs included Midnight Rambler, Paint It Black, Sympathy for the Devil, Honky Tonk Woman, Ruby Tuesday, Undercover and a huge industrial-looking stage and spectacular light show but Jagger still managed to win over the crowd with his trademark gestures and dancing.

At $32.50 a ticket, the gross at the gate was $1.7 million, not including the take from Stones merchandise for sale. The band plays another concert here tonight.

Before the show, fans swarmed Beatty Street, flooded Pacific Boulevard, and jammed the stadium but police and security at B.C. Place said the first Vancouver Stones concert in 17 years was a piece of cake.

1980~1989

Canadians Express Outrage

The Canadian Press

As Chinese soldiers completed their bloody ouster of pro-democracy demonstrators from Beijing's Tiananman Square, Canadians coast to coast rallied to express their outrage.

Police in Toronto said 30,000 people marched on the Chinese consulate, while hundreds gathered for protests in almost every major city in the country.

All of the protests were peaceful, but marchers had angry words for the Chinese leaders who ordered the killings of hundreds of student demonstrators in Beijing and the wounding of thousands of others.

Tanks with machine-guns blazing patrolled the Chinese capital Sunday after soldiers cut a bloody path through the city the night before. The orders apparently came from senior Chinese leader Deng Xiaoping.

In Toronto, thousands of protesters jammed downtown streets as they rallied in the colorful Chinatown district and then marched to the consulate several blocks away.

At the consulate, they delivered letters denouncing the violence in their homeland.

While many of the protesters were Chinese Canadians or students on exchange programs, the rallies were also joined by average people appalled by the violence.

The Canadian rallies were part of a worldwide protest, with major demonstrations in Taipei, Paris, London, New York, Los Angeles and Oslo.

The Canadian government also condemned the crackdown, along with Britain, West Germany, the United States, Thailand, Austria, Sweden, Norway, Belgium, and the Netherlands.

External Affairs Minister Joe Clark called on the Chinese to stop "the aggressive and senseless killing."

"We can only express horror and outrage at the senseless violence and the tragic loss of life," Clark said in a statement.

About 600 people gathered outside the Chinese embassy in Ottawa, chanting slogans and burning an effigy of the Chinese leaders.

Similar demonstrations were held in Montreal and Calgary and prayer meetings were organized in Edmonton.

"It is tragic and inexcusable that violence had to be used against those who are demonstrating in a peaceful and non-violent manner for democracy," NDP Leader Ed Broadbent said over the weekend at an NDP convention in Manitoba.

Chinese students at the University of Victoria said they called students in China and informed them of what was taking place in Beijing.

"We called six universities," said Ming Shen, spokesman for the Chinese students and Visiting Scholars at the university. "Students had no idea what was happing in Tiananmen Square."

"Students were astonished when we told them what we'd seen on TV."

Ming said they promised to get the message out to the public.

In St. John's, Nfld., about 300 people demonstrated.

A Chinese man stands in front of a line of tanks heading east on Beijing's Cangan Blvd. in Tiananmen Square June 5, 1989 in front of the Beijing Hotel. The man, calling for an end to the recent violence and bloodshed against pro-democracy demonstrators, was pulled away by bystanders, and the tanks continued on their way.

(AP Photo/Jeff Widener)

1980~1989

Large Rally In Vancouver

VANCOUVER (CP) — More than 500 demonstrators, wearing black armbands, rallied in front of the Chinese consulate here on Sunday to protest the armed suppression of the pro-democracy movement in Beijing.

Chanting "We support democracy," "Shame to the government" and "Down with (Chinese premier) Li Peng" the placard-carrying demonstrators lined both sides of the affluent residential stretch of busy Granville Street where the consulate is located.

"I'm so angry at the atrocities in China," said student Da Peng Chang. "I think June 4 is the blackest day in Chinese history."

Drivers in passing cars honked their horns in support of the protesters, many of them non-Chinese.

The demonstrators said they wanted to see the Chinese consul, but the iron gates remained closed and RCMP officers inside the grounds prevented access. More police watched the loud but peaceful rally from other vantage points.

It wasn't evident whether anyone inside the consulate, sitting at the end of a long, curved driveway, was watching the demonstration.

Xiaobai Yang, a Chinese student studying at Simon Fraser University, said the Chinese government was shameless in its use of force to suppress the pro-democracy movement in Beijing.

"They call it the people's army in China, but they are using the army to kill the people," he said.

"We want the whole world to condemn the brutal massacre by the Chinese government," said Xiaobai, who just received his masters degree in education.

"We want the whole world to know that this fascist government is no longer a government for the people, therefore we have the right to oppose it. We want Canadian public opinion on our side."

The issue does not concern only the Chinese people, said Daniel Overmeyer, head of the Asian studies department at the University of British Columbia.

"It's an issue for the whole world," he said. "The Chinese represent more than one fifth of the world's population. What happens to them happens to all of us."

Panic Selling

HONG KONG (CP) — Panic selling in reaction to the bloody crackdown in China sent stocks in Hong Kong plummeting sharply today, and residents withdrew money from China-run banks in protest against the killings in Beijing.

Officials reported a run on some banks operated by China in Hong Kong.

In London, the British government came under pressure today to re-examine turning over the British colony to Chinese rule in 1997.

The crackdown on the mainland has heightened Hong Kong residents' anxieties over the colony's future.

The stock exchange lost 100 points in the first minute of trading in its morning session, before closing at 2.085.29, down 590.09 points from Friday. All major shares suffered losses.

Real estate specialists said property values could fall between 15 and 20 per cent unless the situation in China stablilizes.

"This is the worst scenario come to pass," said Paul Varty, an executive of a major real estate firm.

"I have had Hong Kong businessmen say to me quite bluntly in the past 24 hours: "Hong Kong has had it," said Bob Broadfoot of the Political and Economic Risk Consultancy.

Some China-run banks said their rate of withdrawal was 30-per-cent higher than usual. Long lines formed outside many of these banks today, and automatic cash machines were drained of money after angry residents heeded the call of a pamphlet to boycott the banks.

The Hong Kong government stepped in, urging depositors against withdrawing their money. The lines dwindled later in the day.

Leading British newspapers said China's military crackdown has intensified doubt that the British colony will be allowed to uphold civil rights and maintain its free-wheeling lifestyle under Chinese rule.

Under the Chinese-British agreement signed in 1984, China has promised to allow capitalism to exist under communism for 50 years in a government run by Hong Kong's 5.7 million people with a high degree of autonomy from Beijing.

British Foreign Secretary Sir Geoffrey Howe said today that work on the agreement to turn over the colony has "been put on ice while all these troubles are taking place."

"But it's much too soon to conclude that we should set all that to one side, because Hong Kong's future is inextricably bound up, geographically and historically, with mainland China," he said in a BBC interview.

The Independent, a London newspaper, said the weekend attacks "have finally destroyed the thread-bare idea that those in power in (Beijing) can be safely entrusted with Hong Kong's future."

1980-1989

A weekend worth of news

Devastation Beyond Imagination

OAKLAND, CALIF. (AP-CP) — Aftershocks rumbled through the battered San Francisco Bay area today as rescue crews searched frantically for motorists under an elevated highway collapsed by an earthquake that jarred Northern California, killing more than 270 people and injuring hundreds more.

"You could hear it crunching down – but you couldn't see anything," said Leroy FitzGerald who works nearby the collapsed highway. "It was just a big white cloud. You could hear people screaming for help."

As dawn spread over the glass-strewn streets of San Francisco, Oakland and other Bay communities, people tried to restore a sense of normalcy, some making their way to work by ferry, by foot or over highways not blocked by damage. The Bay area Rapid Transit system reopened in the morning, as did Oakland Airport and San Francisco International Airport.

The quake Tuesday, 6.9 on the Richter scale, collapsed buildings across nearly 160 kilometres, as well at the San Francisco-Oakland Bay Bridge and at two spans in the Santa Cruz area.

There were no reports of any injuries or deaths among the estimated 100,000 Canadians living in the San Francisco-Bay area, External Affairs spokesman Robert Peck said today in Ottawa.

Severed gas lines sparked fires, including one in San Francisco that destroyed a block of buildings, but all were out or under control today. As many as one million people were left without electricity and other services.

Sixty-thousand baseball fans were evacuated from San Francisco's Candlestick Park before the start of Game Three of the World Series. No major injuries were reported at the stadium, which suffered structural damage.

"The devastation is just horrible and we're just shocked," said Gov. George Deukmejian, who cut short a trade mission to West Germany. Lt. Gov. Leo McCarthy said damage would total "the better part of $1 billion."

In Washington, U.S. President George Bush signed a disaster-relief declaration and said "we will take very step and make every effort" to help. Bush on Tuesday sent Transportation Secretary Samuel Skinner to assess damage.

John Peterson, a state emergency services spokesman, said at least 270 people had died and more than 650 were injured.

At least 253 people were killed when about 1.5 kilometres of the upper level of Interstate 880, the Nimitz Freeway, in Oakland collapsed, said Dave Wilson of the state Office of Emergency Services.

Tractors, bulldozers and dump trucks were called out, and trucks and vans took bodies from the site this morning.

San Francisco Mayor Art Agnos asked the army to help. National Guardsmen were being mobilized, including engineers, military police and medical workers.

Still, Agnos said, "The city is in reasonably good shape. We've survived this so far."

People walked around San Francisco, sat outside dingy hotels or on stoops and curbs, listening to radio reports of the disaster. Without power, there was no television. Restaurants and bars opened with candlelight.

Agnos said five people died in the city after buildings collapsed on cars, and three died in San Francisco's Marina district in a spectacular fire that burned much of the evening before being brought under control.

Up to 20 people were hurt in the fire, officials said.

Police Chief Fred Jordan said the fire appeared to have consumed an entire block, estimated by Agnos to be 12 buildings. The fire apparently was caused by a natural gas leak, Agnos said.

Wilis Jacobs of the earthquake centre said the quake was centred about 12 kilometres northeast of Santa Cruz, or 120 kilometres south of San Francisco, along the San Andreas Fault. That is the major earthquake fault blamed for the 1906 disaster that destroyed much of the city and killed hundreds – 700, according to traditional estimates, and more than 2,500, according to recent studies.

(AP LaserPhoto)

Residents of San Francisco's Marina district wheel some of their belongings along a city street after they were allowed into their homes for a short period Friday, October 21, 1989 to retrieve their possessions.

Tremors Rattling Stricken Bay Area

From AP-CP-AFP-Reuters

SAN FRANCISO (CP) —
Three strong aftershocks from the devastating earthquake rattled Northern California today as relief poured into the bay area from throughout the world.

Workers dug into a 1.5-kilometre long slab of collapsed freeway with fading hopes that anyone might be alive.

An aftershock that measured 5.0 on the Richter scale struck at 3:15 a.m. and was centred about 15 kilometres south of Santa Cruz, said the state Office of Emergency Services.

Two other tremors in the same area measured 4.5 today. The aftershocks caused further damage to buildings in Santa Cruz, near the epicentre of Tuesday's quake, state officials said.

As of midday Wednesday, more than 1,100 aftershocks were recorded. The strongest measured 5.2 on the Richter scale and struck within 40 minutes of Tuesday's quake, according to the United States Geological Survey.

An earthquake of four on the Richter scale can cause moderate damage and a magnitude five quake can cause considerable damage.

Largely because of the collapse of I-880, known as the Nimitz Freeway, the quake was the second deadliest in U.S. history. It killed an estimated 270 people – 250 of them in the rubble of the Nimitz – and crippled transportation, electric power and commerce in the fourth largest U.S. metropolitan area.

At least 21 people died in San Francisco, San Mateo, Santa Clara and Santa Cruz counties. State officials said 1,400 people were injured throughout the Bay area, although hospitals said they treated 2,750 people, many for chest pains.

The cries of the trapped stopped Wednesday and police and firemen said they doubted anyone was still alive. Eight sniffer dogs found only the dead.

Rescue workers peering through the narrow gaps separating the lower and upper roads painted an orange V on rubble wherever they spotted a car. Others wrote DA – meaning victims nearby are dead but inaccessible.

The last known survivor was a seven-year-old boy who had to have a leg amputated before he could be released.

San Francisco Mayor Art Agnos said the quake caused $2 billion worth of destruction in his city alone.

President George Bush quickly declared the San Francisco region a disaster area and directed an initial $273 million in relief efforts.

The earthquake was felt 720 kilometres away. Hundreds of aftershocks followed on Tuesday and Wednesday, including one that measured 5.9 on the Richter scale shortly after the main shock.

Prime Minister Brian Mulroney offered help for the quake victims.

There were no reports of any injuries or deaths among the estimated 100,000 Canadians living in the San Francisco-Bay area.

Quake Was A Warning To Us

As we reported yesterday, it could happen here.

We in the South Okanagan could experience an earthquake as strong as six on the Richter Scale – enough to do serious damage. (The quake that shook San Francisco Tuesday was 6.9.)

While those living in the Lower Mainland are familiar with the eerie feeling of earth tremors and the ever-present possibility of a serious quake, we don't consider it a real possibility here. Since our chances of experiencing such a strong quake are rated as one on a scale of zero to six, we take it for granted that we're safe, that we'll escape any serious damage.

But Dr. Garry Rogers, a research scientist with the Geological Survey of Canada at Pacific Geoscience Centre, says while most of B.C.'s major earthquakes have occurred on the West Coast, the Queen Charlottes and Vancouver Island, "there is a possibility of an earthquake of a magnitude up to six occurring anywhere in the mountainous regions of B.C., including the Okanagan."

Watching Tuesday night's television coverage and hearing the warnings going out to people in the San Francisco area, it became apparent that many of those people – despite living in the most highly prone earthquake zone in North America – weren't prepared for the quake.

We in the South Okanagan can learn a lesson from San Francisco. Individually preparing ourselves for the possibility of a quake here could mean the difference between chaos and order should it ever happen. Page 22 of this year's B.C. Tel directory is a good place to start, with a detailed description of what each of us should do before, during and after a quake.

Berlin Is Again Berlin!

EAST BERLIN (AP) —
East Germany announced today that free passage through the Berlin Wall and the rest of its new open-border policy will remain in effect permanently.

The announcement capped one of the most dramatic shifts in post-Second World War Europe, giving the once penned-up East German people full freedom of travel for the first time since the Berlin Wall was built by the Communists in 1961.

Tens of thousands of East Germans streamed into West Berlin and other parts of West Germany today after a heady night of celebrating the opening of the Berlin Wall and East Germany's other borders Thursday.

They drove cars, took the subway, walked and ran to cross the border in Berlin. Some even abandoned their cars in long lineups and walked over.

Strangers hugged each other like long-lost relatives. East and West Germans danced on the wall. Some took hammers and chisels to the five-metre-high concrete wall, chipping for souvenirs or joining in a symbolic effort to tear it down.

"The Wall is gone! Berlin is again Berlin," proclaimed today's banner headline in the Bild Zeitung, the West Berlin tabloid. People flashed copies of the newspaper, popped champagne corks and waved sparklers.

After thousands of East Berliners had entered the western half of the city, East German radio announced they would be required to get a visa for such trips starting this morning.

But East Berliners who rushed to the wall and to police stations today for visas kept the divided city's border open. They swamped official attempts to control the flow through the eight crossing points.

Police at one station said visa-free travel would probably continue throughout the weekend.

The all-night celebration in downtown West Berlin lasted until about 5 a.m. today. West German television said East Berliners were continuing to cross to the western side this morning. Others, who spent the night celebrating, were returning home.

Also today, a reshuffle of the Communist leadership continued with the firing of one of its new members, appointed just this week. Three non-voting members were also sacked.

East Germany's surprise decision to open the border came at a Central Committee meeting Thursday and followed a series of reforms announced by new Communist leader Egon Krenz.

Plans New Wall

Guenter Schabowski, a member of the ruling Politburo, said the borders were being opened until a law is passed allowing East Germans greater freedom of travel. He did not say when the law would be passed.

The announcement followed months of unrest in East Germany. During that time, thousands left for the West, and hundreds of thousands demonstrated throughout the country for political reform.

East Germans reacted to the news with astonishment and jubilation.

"Is it really true?" asked Mario Schmidt, 18.

(AP Photo)

An unidentified Berliner tries in vain to demolish a segment of the Berlin wall with a sledge hammer early Saturday morning at Bernauer Strasse, where East Germany pulled down segments of the wall for a new passage.

1980–1989

A Weekend Of Reunion In Berlin

EAST BERLIN (CP) —

East Germans headed back to work today after an intoxicating weekend of discovery and reunion in the West, carrying with them new expectations that their government will likely have to address.

One man in blue overalls stepped through an opening bulldozed in the Berlin Wall, stared about for a few minutes and then headed back to the East early today.

"I'm off to work," he said, "I just wanted to take a look."

On both sides of the wall today, the start of a new work week and the reality of having to earn a living brought the city back to something approaching normality.

West Berlin's streets were swept clean of litter left by the flood of visitors, most of whom had returned to the East by Sunday night.

Millions of East Germans exercised their new freedom to travel over the weekend and poured across the Berlin Wall and other border points to take a look at West Germany and visit relatives.

As they walked along streets the older visitors could barely remember and the younger ones had never seen, their euphoria was dampened only by their inability to buy anything with their non-convertible East German currency. The West German government gave each person from the East "welcome money" worth the equivalent of about $60 Cdn.

Lines forming up at banks at dawn today for the money were numbered in dozens rather than the hundreds. Traffic ran normally again on streets that had been log-jammed during the weekend.

Berlin Wall T-Shirt Is The Best Seller

Forget Batman

WEST BERLIN (CP) —

There was virtually no one lined up the Super Kino II today to see the caped crusader's cinematic crimefighting capers or to buy his bat paraphernalia at the nearby kiosks.

No, the biggest selling T-shirt today on the Kurfurstendamm, West Berlin's main shopping drag, was a simple white number showing the odious Berlin Wall with a huge V-shaped cut in the middle.

Through it, East Germans in a wide variety of garb are pouring on foot and by bicycle while airplanes fly overhead.

The T-shirt bears the slogan in huge yellow letters: Der Letzte Macht Das Light Aus!

Freely translated, it reads: The Last One (Out) Turns Off the Light.

Nothing could be more appropriate as thousands of East Germans, freed for the first time in decades by their once-hardline Communist government to visit their western cousins without restraint, poured through the wall to West Berlin from East Berlin for the second straight day.

Sold Out

And nothing could be more popular than the T-shirt.

"I had 200 of these at 9 a.m. this morning," Norbert Gerlach, owner of the Tip-Top Boutique in West Berlin told a reporter this afternoon, laughing. "You just bought the last one."

"I've asked for 1,000 tomorrow but they (the manufacturers) say they can't keep up with the demand."

LOCALS SAY MANY EAST GERMANS WILL RETURN

By Rob Munro
Courier Staff

NOVEMBER 10, 1989. — The flood of East Germans to the west will ease and many will return to their homes, predict Germans living in Kelowna.

Karin Hippler spent five years working in East Germany in the late 1950s before returning home to the west and then moving to the Okanagan in 1967.

"It is going a little bit too fast right now," she said today. "Some of the East Germans are already disappointed and want to go back again."

She said it is wonderful for the people that the border has been opened, but the dramatic change will create "chaos" for both countries.

West Germany doesn't have the housing or the jobs to accommodate the huge influx from the east. The relatively crime-free communist country will now start experiencing some of the drawbacks of the west, she suggested.

"Who can blame the young people if they go across?" said Adolf Illichmann, owner of Illichmann's Sausage and Delicatessen. "They're going to go back. Home is home."

He noted 40 years ago Germans were thrown out of countries like Czechoslovakia and not welcomed in many countries of the world. He is pleased that the attitude in the West has changed dramatically.

"Everything today is happening without a shot," he said. "Let's hope everything turns out peaceful."

Hippler suggests the two countries retain separate governments for the moment, but the border be open. Dramatic changes to the government and standard of living will have to be made to entice citizens back.

Eventually, if the people can compromise, the country might be reunited under one government, she said.

Illichmann said any reunification will be up to the leaders of the United States, Russia, France and Britain.

1980~1989

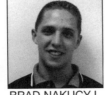

Mass murder worst in Canadian history

Gunman hated 'feminists'

**By Penny MacRae
and Peter Lowrey**

MONTREAL (CP) —

A gunman who said feminists had "always spoiled his life" went on a rampage Wednesday at the University of Montreal, killing 14 women before shooting himself to death with his rifle.

The man, who has only been identified as Marc, carried a three-page diatribe against feminism as he stalked the university's engineering school looking for women to kill, police director Andre Tessier told an early-morning news conference today.

He was quoted by witnesses as ranting" "I want the women" and "You're all a bunch of feminists. I hate feminists."

Police would not give the exact wording of the statement or release a copy to reporters but they displayed the gunman's weapon - a.223-calibre semi-automatic Sturm Ruger rifle with bloody fingerprints on the stock.

Tessier said the statement - which contained a passing reference to Canadian Force Cpl. Denis Lortie, who killed three people May 8, 1984, with a submachine-gun in the Quebec legislature - was dated Wednesday and signed Marc.

The gunman, who was aged between 22 and 25, also wounded 13 other people - nine women and four men - in the bloodiest mass shooting in Canadian history.

The man blamed unidentified women for failures in his life and said he would kill some women in revenge. He said he had not been happy for seven years.

"I can' believe anyone would hate women so much," said Martin Lanciault, a nursing student drinking a morning coffee in the student-centre cafeteria not far from the building. "I can't understand it."

Tessier said the statement indicated the gunman "applied for the armed forces but was refused

(CP PHOTO)

Kate Maclean pays her respects to the 14 women slain at Montreal's Ecole Polytechnique in 1989 during a vigil held at Minto Park's Women's Memorial in Ottawa, Sunday.

because he was antisocial."

Tessier said the gunman, who stood 5-foot-9 and weighed 160 pounds, carried a hunting knife and sheaf, in addition to the rifle, two boxes bullets and a 30-bullet clip.

Two of the wounded were in critical condition while the other 11 were judged out of danger early today.

"I saw death close up and I shook," said Vanthona Ouy, 22,

one of the scores of horrified students who streamed out of the building after the carnage.

"It's our friends who have been killed."

Jacques Dusheneau, a senior investigator for Montreal police, told reporters that between 36 and 37 bullets were fired from the gunman's rifle which had two ammunition clips.

Tessier said the gunman, who wore a navy blue baseball cap

that said Montreal Tracteur (Montreal Tractor), had no criminal record in Montreal and police are trying to determine his identity. The man's fingerprints will be sent to Ottawa today.

He said, within six minutes of the first call they received about the terror caused by the gunman, police arrived at the six-story building, part of the 50,000-student university, the largest in Quebec. He said they thought at first they were facing a hostage-taking incident.

As eyewitness Robert Leclerc put it: "It was just like Rambo. He had at least two ammunition belts across his chest."

Leclerc, 23, an engineering student, said the gunman, who rushed into a packed classroom on the second floor of the university's engineering building, divided the students in the classroom by sex and sent the men into the corridor.

Leclerc said about 15 women remained.

"He told them, ' You're women, you're going to be engineers. You're all a bunch of feminists. I hate feminists!' My friend Nathalie said, 'No, it's not true. We're not feminists.' He fired into the group."

Students who got away were in a state of panic.

The wounded were taken to several hospitals.

Police director Claude St-Laurent said six women were shot dead in the classroom and a seventh was slain in another room on the same floor. The gunman had begun his rampage at about 4:30 p.m., prowling the first floor and killing three women in a cafeteria.

From the second-floor bloodbath, the gunman went to the third floor where he killed four more women in the corridor, climbed to the fourth and fifth where several more people were injured and then returned to the third floor where he took his own life.

Massacre a 'national tragedy'

By Conway Daly

MONTREAL (CP) —

Marc Lepine, a war-movie fan who was "always frustrated by women," was identified Thursday as the gunman who stalked the hallways of the University of Montreal, killing 14 women and then taking his own life.

"Canada is in mourning," declared Prime Minister Brian Mulroney in Parliament Thursday.

Men and women countrywide gathered at remembrance vigils amid calls on the government for tighter gun-controls.

A bouquet of red roses in a plastic bag fluttered in a snow bank near the Ecole Polytechnique at the University of Montreal, the site of the massacre. The flowers and the Quebec and Canadian flags at half-mast marked the deaths in the bloodiest mass shooting in Canadian history.

Mulroney said the massacre was a "national tragedy" as he and his wife, Mila, attended a candle-lit vigil at the university.

Police spokesman Andre Tessier described Lepine, 25, as a reclusive man who was single, unemployed and with a history of failed relationships with women.

Witnesses said Lepine, who had ammunition belts wrapped Rambo-style across his chest, denounced his helpless victims as "a bunch of feminists."

"He was known to watch a lot of war films," said Jacques Duchesneau, a senior police investigator. He said Lepine didn't have any girlfriends and tended to break off relationships at the first sign of any difficulty.

Lepine had taken courses with the aim of entering the same university engineering school where he hunted female students Wednesday evening.

Duchesneau said Lepine was intelligent but had a number of academic setbacks and had been fired from a job in a Montreal-area hospital. The gunman was born Gamil Gharbi and came from a broken home. His father, an Algerian, left his mother when he was seven, and in 1982 Lepine took his mother's last name and the first name Marc.

A three-page suicide letter found on Lepine's body said he was committing a "political act" because feminists have always ruined my life," police said. The letter had a possible hit list of 15 other women, names that may have been taken from a newspaper.

Copies of the letter have been sent to a psychiatrist and a graphologist for analysis.

Funeral mass today for 9 of women shot to death

MONTREAL (CP) —

Paul Cardinal Gregoire led a procession of white-garbed priests past nine coffins today at a funeral mass for women slain last week at the University of Montreal.

"We have difficulty understanding that one must die so young and that lives must be thus broken before they have flowered," Gregoire said in an opening prayer.

"At all ages, death is tragic… This tragedy makes us feel the absurdity and the pain with an even greater intensity."

Louis Courville, head of the Ecole Polytechnique, the engineering school where the women were killed, read a prayer as mourners, who packed the 3,000-seat Notre Dame Basilica, bowed their heads.

Prime Minister Brian Mulroney, Premier Robert Bourassa and Montreal Mayor Jean Dore attended.

The ornate interior of the cathedral and the white coffins were piled high with flowers.

"A wave of insane violence has cut down our friends," one woman read to the mourners.

"Help us not to despair," a young man prayed. "Make it so we remain untied and fraternal and help each other."

Outside, thousands stood silently on the church's stone steps and spilled into the Place d'armes Square across the street to listen to the ceremony on loudspeakers.

"We've all been deeply touched by what's happened," said Alexina Paradis, 78, huddled in her coat against the sunny cold in the square. "The dead are dead but the parents are going to be in pain for years to come."

"I hope it will bring people to rethink the way they live in society because this type of thing is the sign of a very sick society," said Michael Monty, 25.

On Sunday, more than 10,000 people viewed the caskets of eight of the slain women during a memorial service at the university.

Lepine, 25, also wounded 13 other people.

Psychiatrists draw picture of sick killer

By Sheryl Ubelacker
The Canadian Press

A quiet recluse with few or no friends. A man who feels severely inadequate. A man bent on revenge against feminists - who, he probably believed, had usurped his rightful place in society.

This is the psychological portrait drawn by psychiatrists and sociologists of Marc Lepine, whose apparent brooding hatred of women exploded, leaving 14 women dead and 13 other people, including four men, injured at University of Montreal on Wednesday.

The gunman said in a suicide letter that feminists had "spoiled" his life.

"What we're dealing with here is the person we call the "sudden murderer," Dr. Julio Arboleda-Forex, director of psychiatry at Calgary General Hospital, said in an interview Thursday. "He's an individual with very disturbed personality patterns, usually a passive, inadequate type."

Such a killer usually resents the system, "which he feels is not giving him the perks he deserves. He feels alienated and he starts brooding on this idea of revenge."

Elliott Leyton, a professor of anthropology at Memorial University in St. John's, Nfld., agrees the typical sudden mass murderer is an alienated loner with a "disordered" family background.

"He is likely a person without a network or talents to achieve his ambitions, who begins to believe there is a group which he decides or imagines has excluded him from his rightful place in society," said Leyton, author of Hunting Humans, a study of serial and mass murderers.

Because he chose an engineering class, until recently a male enclave, " he may have felt 'There go the feminists. The women are taking over the males' places,'" said Arboleda-Forex.

He said a killing rampage is often triggered by a particular event, perhaps a rejection in a relationship or at work.

OGOPOGO

1980~1989

MAY 9, 1983

We asked about . . .

AL SLATER   MORNA ZWARICH   CAROLE VOGEL   KERRY PURDY   BERT MACKENZIE   IVAN MESSMER

. . . belief in Ogopogo

Does Ogopogo exist? The question has intrigued the people of the Okanagan for centuries.

And now the Okanagan-Similkameen Tourist Association has posted a $1 million reward for anyone who can positively prove - by photographic means or a live monster - that Ogopogo is real.

The Herald asked some Penticton residents and some visitors if they believed in Ogopogo and whether his existence needs to be proven.

"I think there's something out there," said AL SLATER. He has lived in the Okanagan for 40 years "and I've heard a lot of stories about Ogopogo over the years."

And as a tourist promotion, Slater said Ogopogo is great. "the reward will draw a lot of people into the city in the summer," he predicted.

But MORNA ZWARICH doesn't think Ogopogo exists. From Saskatoon, Zwarich has been in the Okanagan for a month working on a Katimavik project in Summerland.

"I bought a stuffed Ogopogo today though." She said she hadn't heard of Ogopogo before coming to the Okanagan.

Her friend CAROLE VOGEL of Summerland believes in Ogopogo. "Yeah, I saw Ogopogo four or five years ago. We were driving down the Summerland hill and there were cars stopped near Rotary beach.

"We stopped and could see a series of humps and waves. He was about 15 feet (five metres) long and very close to shore," she said.

"I know there's something out there. But we have a lot of fun with the idea too," said Vogel.

"I haven't seen it, but I believe in it," said KERRY PURDY of Fruitvale.

She has been hearing about Ogopogo for years, mostly from her grandparents who live here.

"People think you're crazy when you talk about Ogopogo, but he sure helps the tourist promotion here," said Purdy.

"Sure, I see Ogopogo all the time," said BERT MACKENZIE, a frequent visitor to Penticton from Nighthawk, Wash., near Orville.

"He's neat. He has a long neck," she added. "I'm just kidding you. It's a bit like the tooth fairy and Santa Claus."

She added people in her area know about the Ogopogo legends.

"Sure I do," said MAYOR IVAN MESSMER when asked if he believes in Ogopogo. "I haven't had much time to get out and watch, but I intend to get up on Munson's Mountain to take a look."

FEBRUARY 2, 1984

Triathlon society's fears eased

With all the attention it has been receiving lately, maybe Ogopogo will dive to the depths of Okanagan Lake - never to return.

First the Okanagan-Similkameen Tourist Association promised to deliver $1 million for the live capture of the lake monster. Not to be outdone, Greenpeace voiced its concern over the possible killing of Ogopogo by some zealous bounty hunter. Then the Penticton Triathlon Society became concerned about a possible attack by Ogopogo on one of its competitors.

Well, Lyn Van Ert and other members of the society - rest easy. OSTA manager Bob Sheely says there's nothing to fear but fear itself.

In a letter to the society, Sheeley says that as long as the triathletes don't veer off course, they should be safe. Also, they shouldn't go near Squally Point, reputed to be home of the friendly creature.

"We would also recommend," says Sheeley, "that the society should enlist the help of the Penticton Yacht Club to form a protective barrier on the course. We also recommend that triathlete swimmers wear bright red swim caps as, unlike bulls, Ogopogo tends to shy away from bright colors.

"We have also sent a letter to our insurance underwriters to amend the contract to take into account any forays by Ogopogo into the swim course being used by the triathletes."

Sheeley also assured Van Ert that since Ogopogo is indigenous to Okanagan Lake, swimmers would be well advised to use the side stroke "so they can keep an eye out for Ogopogo at all times while under water."

JULY 4, 1985

Misunderstood Monster Children's Book Hero

Okanagan Lake's mythical creature, Ogopogo, becomes a hero in a new children's book available at the Penticton Chamber of Commerce, Okanagan Books, Woodward's book section, Puff n' Stuff and gift outlets in the area.

Ogopogo, The Misunderstood Lake Monster, is the first of what is planned as a series of Ogopogo adventures written by Don Levers of Kelowna. The "misunderstood monster" is descendant of "a fierce, fire-breathing dragon from the middle ages named Percival," and Nessie, Loch Ness monster in Scotland, is his sister.

No Fire

As the book has it, Ogopogo stopped breathing fire when he started living in the lake, and "because he didn't breath fire anymore, he wasn't a ferocious, miserable, mean, crabby old dragon" anymore.

Now, when people make up stories about a dreaded lake monster, Ogopogo's feelings are hurt.

The plot turns on a storm which blows up the lake while men are working on anchor lines that hold the floating bridge. Three busloads of children are on a section of the bridge which floats away in the fictional storm. Enter the hero …

Levers hopes to export Ogopogo. "He is well-known in the Okanagan, but when I talked to the copyright people, they hadn't even heard of Kelowna, let alone Ogopogo."

New Venture

Doing a children's book is a new venture for Levers and the illustrator, Jack Thompson, formerly of Naramata. The venture took "seven months of hard work." The Kelowna museum helped with his research on how the floating bridge is lashed down.

At the time of his interview with the Herald, Levers had not met the authors who have written serious books on Ogopogo sightings.

"This will be a fun series."

Over 600

More than 600 of the broken-bridge adventure books are in valley outlets currently, from Vernon to Penticton. Total printing was 5,000 and they retail at $4.95. Penticton's Chamber of Commerce have the first purchase order, Levers recalls.

He has been giving readings to children in the schools, and has been encouraged by the reaction from his audience.

Believe it or not!

MAY 9, 1986

Ogopogo Fantasy May Become Movie

Everybody has a dream, a fantasy lingering perhaps from childhood. But few of us bring our fantasies to life, like Doug Simmons of Summerland is doing.

Simmons is building on a boyhood fantasy to make another dream come true - a feature movie about Ogopogo. His original screenplay has drawn interest from producers in both Hollywood and Canada, and is currently in the hands of Peter O'Brian (The Grey Fox, One Magic Christmas, My American Cousin).

THIS DRAWING OF OGOPOGO IS A CAREFULLY RESEARCHED COMPOSITE OF SCIENTIFIC THEORY AND DESCRIPTIONS FROM SIGHTINGS: 40 FEET LONG AND A HEAD SIX TIMES BIGGER THAN A HORSE.

The fantasy began with the impressionable mind of a 10-year-old, seeing the image of a statue of a boy riding a dolphin. "It was a beautiful, life-like statue," Simmons recalls, "a lost treasure, lying at the bottom of the sea." He imagined himself the boy, the statue suddenly springing to life with he and his mount plunging through the waves.

Put that together with summers spent on the shores of - and in - Okanagan Lake, and the fantasy takes shape.

The Simmons family stayed with Doug's aunt and uncle, the late John and Clara Pearson, whose house was on the lake in Summerland. It was there the boy heard his first tales of the mysterious Ogopogo. "My aunt was a God-fearing woman whose every word seemed like gospel," he said. "She was an avid believer in Ogopogo, and told me she's seen it on many occasions. She could describe it in explicit detail." She told him that the lake monster was friendly and had never attacked a human being.

As the summers went by, Doug became a regular "fish" in Okanagan Lake, with his snorkel and flippers. "I had a quest," he recalls. "I would find the Ogopogo, befriend it, then ride it" just like the beautiful statue of the boy and the dolphin.

Although he lives on the edge of Okanagan Lake himself now, Simmons has never seen the Ogopogo himself. "Even so, my childhood fantasies are even stronger today than they were then," he says. He has dedicated his story, Ogi, "to keeping this fantasy alive forever and to all the people who want to ride the dolphin."

NOVEMBER 6, 1984

Ogopogo becomes 'unsolved mystery'

It's now official - a crew form Unsolved Mysteries, a weekly television series, will be in Kelowna next week to begin filming a story on Ogopogo.

Director Michael Talazoa and research writer Cindy Bowles telephoned Ogopogo researcher Arlene Gaal Friday to confirm the filming.

The team along with producer Dan Gomenz, will arrive Saturday and will shoot the segment Nov. 13, 14 and 15.

Producer John Cosgrove was in Kelowna two weeks ago and met with Gaal and Ken Chaplin

Cosgrove had an opportunity to view a film Chaplin shot this summer on the lake creature, said to be the best footage so far on Ogopogo. He also saw two other films on Ogopogo.

Gaal has verified that Unsolved Mysteries has shown an interest in using the two latter films in the segment and an agreement has been reached on their use.

Chaplin sent his video down to California and entered into an agreement with Unsolved Mysteries for an exclusive viewing in the Ogopogo story.

Both Art Folden and Larry Thai, who shot the other films, have agreed to recreate the scene of their Ogopogo shoots.

The Folden film was shot in 1968 north of Peachland. The Thai piece was filmed in 1980 as the animal swam from the Okanagan lake floating bridge past Blue Bird Bay Resort off Lakeshore Road.

"It should prove most interesting as every sighting, photo or film footage shot adds another piece to the puzzle and each has its place in the complete story of Ogopogo," said Gaal, who owns the rights to both the Folden and Thai films.

JULY 30, 1987

Ogopogo Surfaces For TV Crew

The legendary Ogopogo monster of Okanagan Lake would appear to be a bit of a ham.

It didn't take him long to make an appearance when an ABC television crew from Los Angeles came beckoning.

The TV crew was shooting an episode Wednesday on the Ogopogo for a new series called Secrets and Mysteries.

On the first day of shooting they reported sighting Ogopogo – with its several humps – in the lake across from Kelowna.

They even claim to have three minutes of the serpent on film.

Cameraman Michael Tabor and producer David Frank were aboard the Okanagan Princess to hunt Ogopogo's haunts.

Also along was the manager of the Kelowna Chamber of Commerce, Gerry Frederick.

"I was there to make sure what they did was done in good taste and they weren't playing any games," said Frederick.

The chamber takes Ogopogo seriously and has put up $10,000 for the live capture of the monster. There is also some $1.2 million worth of goods and services offered by the Okanagan Similkameen Tourist Association.

Frederick said they were about ready to turn around and go back when the monster appeared.

Tabor zoomed in on the object and suddenly yelled "there it is, there it is," said Frederick.

"It was quite visible," said Frederick. "There wasn't a boat in sight. You could see the dark humps and the wake behind it. We got probably three minutes of video footage."

However, thee was no other confirmation of Ogopogo's sighting.

There was also no word on whether the film will be released now or held for the TV series, airing in the fall.

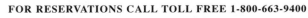

A DECADE
IN REVIEW

1990 ~ 1999

Policeman shot, killed in gun battle

CRISIS

Both sides reinforcing, digging in

JULY 12, 1990, OKA, QUE. (CP) — Three Mohawks sat smoking cigarettes and chatting quietly in the morning sunshine atop their barricade of wrecked police vehicles, the day after a police corporal was killed during an intense gun battle with the natives.

The Mohawk's weapons - two rifles and a submachinegun - lay beside them.

The situation was still tense after Wednesday's disastrous police raid on Indians protesting a planned golf course development onto land they claim as their own.

Down the hill, dozens of flak-jacketed, shotgun-toting police scurried around new sandbagged positions reinforced with concrete blocks.

During the night, police brought in hundreds of officers and manned their barricades in three-hour shifts.

Traffic was blocked on provincial roads and highways through this suburban community just northwest of Montreal as well as around the Mohawk Kahawake reserve south of Montreal where natives blocked a bridge and highways when police moved in on Oka.

Provincial police kept all traffic off the reserve and one officer said, "Nobody goes in. Nobody goes out."

Indians step up protests

JULY 12, 1990, VANCOUVER (CP) — Indian activists plan to step up their protests across the province today and next week with more blockades.

Chief Saul Terry, president of the Union of B.C. Indian Chiefs, said he has directed natives to continue to try to pressure the federal government to resolve its dispute with Mohawk Indians in Oka, Que.

"The government's intransigence and manipulation of policies has become a source of a lot of frustration," he said.

Although representatives of two B.C. tribes met with Premier Bill Vander Zalm on Friday, the talks were inconclusive, and didn't appear to resolve the issues Indians say are responsible for the roadblocks.

The blockades are in the Okanagan Valley — Penticton and Oliver — and in Pemberton and Fraser Lake, in northern British Columbia.

OKA, QUE. (CP) — A provincial police officer was shot and killed as police exchanged hundreds of gunshots with Mohawk Indians on a road barricade today.

Police said Cpl. Marcel Lemay, 31, was killed in the gun battle, which broke out when police swooped in about 5:30 a.m. today to clear the Mohawks from a barricade set up to prevent expansion of a golf course.

Mohawk leaders in the Kahnesetake community said they took a provincial police officer hostage when he was caught behind native lines during the gun battle. There was no confirmation from police.

The slain police officer was shot near the mouth and died about an hour after arriving at nearby St. Eustache hospital, Dr. Denis Archambault said.

The crackle of semi-automatic gunfire and the thud of teargas canisters could be heard from the area as armed provincial police officers, dressed in olive-green fatigues and wearing gas masks, confronted young natives with handkerchiefs tied across their noses and mouths.

As the wind moved the tear gas back across their lines, police quickly retreated and the situation turned into a tense stand-off.

The Indians seized four police cars and two vans and used a commandeered front-end loader to crush and overturn the vehicles to form another barricade. Thick black smoke belched from a pile of burning tires.

Meanwhile, Mohawks from the Kahnawake reserve south of Montreal were blocking rush hour traffic on two main highways into Montreal from the populous South Shore.

The Kahnawake Indians said they were blocking the highways in sympathy with the natives in Oka and no traffic would move until the provincial police left the community.

Oka townspeople started worrying about their safety as police retreated from the Indian community just outside town.

Fights broke out on the street between partisans of Mayor Jean Ouellette who requested police intervention and those who said the confrontation was senseless.

The barricade was set up three months ago to stop the expansion of a golf course on land the Mohawks claim belongs to them.

The dispute between the Mohawks and Oka is over land owned by the town, which is rented to a golf club. The owners of the private course say they want to cut down the white pine forest on the land and expand the course to 18 holes.

In Quebec City, acting public security minister Michel Page said he did not authorize the police action. An aide to Premier Robert Bourassa said the premier was not contacted before police moved in. Earlier this week, John Ciaccia, the minister responsible for native affairs, pleaded with Oka town council to put its plans for a golf course on hold.

Chiefs list resolutions

The following is a list of resolutions issued Friday by the chiefs of Indian bands from across Canada who met in Kahnawake, Que., for three days to discuss the armed standoffs between Mohawks and police in Kahnawake and Oka:

1. Natives have the inherent right to assert their jurisdiction over their traditional lands.

2. The chiefs support the efforts of the Mohawk people to obtain a peaceful, negotiated settlement of all issues in dispute.

3. All military forces and police must withdraw as a gesture of goodwill to enable peaceful negotiations to resume.

4. The prime minister of Canada must actively participate in a peaceful resolution process, and must immediately reconvene Parliament to deal with the dispute.

5. There should be no reprisals, prosecutions or legal proceedings against Mohawks as a result of the dispute.

6. The United Nations should immediately appoint a commission to investigate alleged violations of the rights of the Kahnesatake and Kahnawake Mohawks.

7. Other countries should condemn the government of Canada for its neglect of its native people and impose economic sanctions if the government fails to act promptly on the chiefs' suggestions for a settlement.

8. The chiefs of Canada's First Nations will take the appropriate steps in their respective territories to support the above positions.

Mohawk crisis ends in brawls

OKA, QUE. (CP) —

After 11 weeks of standoff, the Mohawk crisis ended as it began - violently and in mass confusion.

Mohawks left their Kahnesatake encampment Wednesday night, but they didn't surrender to soldiers. In a final protest they tried to snub the army and walk down the road toward Oka.

Initially caught off guard, the military rebounded and wild street brawls ensued as soldiers tried to contain defiant Mohawk Warriors, women and children.

The natives - who had been holed up since Sept. 1 in a treatment centre at Kahnesatake, 30 kilometres west of Montreal - began leaving their compound just before 7 p.m.

The scene became chaotic when some of the group, led by Warrior adviser Loran Thompson and a woman with a child, crossed over the razor wire at the edge of the army perimeter and headed toward Oka.

Soldiers poured into the area and tried to push them back.

Piercing screams of women filled the air. One woman carrying a feather ran up to the razor wire and was bounced back by a soldier who blocked her with his gun. She shouted obscenities at him before being dragged off by another soldier.

Another woman trying to cross the wire and holding a child by a hand, was shoved back. The two fell to the ground and were dragged to their feet by soldiers.

They were pushed again, fell once more, and the woman, still clutching the child's hand,

Canadian soldier Patrick Cloutier and Mohawk warrior Ronald Cross alias "Lasagne" come face to face in a tense standoff at the Kahnesatake reserve in Oka, Quebec, Saturday September 1, 1990. (CP PHOTO)

screamed.

Nearby a man struggling with soldiers yelled: "where the hell is my baby?"

As soldiers tried to gain control, the Mohawks approached a second razor wire barrier. Above the din of screams , two soldiers there quickly but calmly pulled out bayonets and attached them to their rifles.

Blondie, a white teenage francophone from Oka who joined the Warriors early in the standoff, tried to walk around two soldiers on the road, but four other soldiers joined , picking him up and wrestling him to the ground.

While flattening Blondie's face to the ground, one soldier barked: "You're under arrest!"

In the confusion some Mohawks made it down the hill, only to be arrested by provincial police. Pandemonium erupted when three of the Warriors, including Ronald Cross, nicknamed Lasagne, were shoved into police cars.

The Warriors have feared reprisals from the provincial police since Cpl. Marcel Lemay was killed during the July 11 police raid that sparked the crisis.

"You're killers, you're just here to finish the job," shrieked one woman.

Mohawk crisis ends in brawls

OKA, Que (CP) — After 11 weeks of standoff, the Mohawk crisis ended as it began - violently and in mass confusion.

Mohawks left their Kahnesatake encampment Wednesday night, but they didn't surrender to soldiers. In

They were pushed again, fell once more, and the woman, still clutching the child's hand, screamed.

Nearby a man struggling with soldiers yelled: "Where the hell is my baby?"

As soldiers tried to gain control, the Mohawks approached a second razor wire barrier. Above the din two soldiers there quickly but calmly

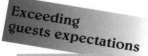

Kuwait Seeks Military Help

KUWAIT (CP) —
Iraqi President Saddam Hussein's powerful army overran the small oil-rich kingdom of Kuwait early today and tank-led troops quickly seized the ruler's palace and other government buildings, Kuwaiti officials said.

Iraq said it had come to the aid of "revolutionary youth in Kuwait" who had toppled the government and set up a new administration. The Kuwaiti ruler fled to neighboring Saudi Arabia.

Meanwhile, in Washington, Kuwait's ambassador appealed today for military assistance from the United States to help oust the Iraqi invaders.

"We have appealed to all our friends around the world, including the United States, to come to our aid and assistance," Sheik Saud Nasir al-Sabah told a news conference.

Asked whether he had asked the United States for military assistance, he said, "Yes sir, we have."

U.S. President George Bush said earlier today the United States was not ruling out any options regarding Iraq's invasion of its oil-rich neighbor and its capturing of the Kuwaiti capital.

Later, Kuwait's new Iraqi-backed rulers said they had sacked the emir and ordered an indefinite curfew, a statement read on Kuwait Radio in the name of the Transitional Free Government of Kuwait said.

A Canadian Embassy spokesman in Kuwait said Canadians in the Persian Gulf state are safe and have been advised to remain off the streets.

"We are advising Canadians to remain in their homes so we can contact them as the situation develops," said charge d'affaires William Bowden in a telephone interview today.

About 400 Canadians are in the country.

There are no immediate plans to evacuate Canadians, Bowden said.

Bowden said "The situation around the embassy is quiet."

The embassy is about three kilometres from the palace where heavy fighting was reported.

"The embassy has not been shelled, no Iraqi tanks are visible in the area and no embassy staff has seen any Iraqi troops."

Casualties were reported heavy, and the shelling fierce.

The invasion came hours after Iraq abruptly broke off talks on a disputed border oil field. Iraq was demanding billions of dollars for oil they say Kuwait pumped out of the field and the writeoff of billions in loans.

"The Iraqis have occupied all of Kuwait!." a Kuwaiti official shouted in a telephone interview from Kuwait city just hours after thousands of Iraqi troops and hundreds of tanks stormed across the border.

The palace of the country's ruler, Sheik Jaber al-Ahmed al-Sabah, was seized after two hours of heavy artillery and jet fighter attacks.

Iraq's Invasion Condemned

From AP-Reuters-AFP-CP
World powers led by the United States and the Soviet Union condemned Iraq's invasion of Kuwait today as a grave threat to peace and braced for an economic shock of rising oil prices.

Canada also strongly condemned the Iraqi invasion, and Israel's defence minister said his country is ready to respond to any armed threat from Iraq.

In Washington, U.S. President George Bush said the Iraqi move was "naked aggression."

Bush signed an order freezing control of Iraqi assets in the United States.

In Moscow, the Soviet government called for the "urgent and unconditional" withdrawal of Iraqi troops. A Foreign Ministry statement read by spokesman Yuri Gremitskikh said:

"The Soviet Union believes that no contentious issues, no matter how complicated, justify the use of force."

External Affairs Minister Joe Clark said the invasion was "a totally unacceptable aggression."

(CP PHOTO/Hans Deryk)

Canadian Forces M/Cpl. Robert St. Laurent of Rimouski, Que., left, passes a water bottle to Pt. Dominique Benoit as they take a break to watch a hazy sun set while on patrol with their 'Grizzly' APC in Qatar, Friday, Feb. 23, 1991. A black haze filled the sky from fires burning in Kuwait to the north as another deadline passed for an Iraqi pullout during the Gulf War.

1990~1999

Million Soldiers Poised For Battle

The Canadian Press

The deadline for an Iraqi withdrawal from Kuwait has passed, with more than one million soldiers poised for a desert battle and Baghdad warning that "fingers are on the trigger."

Exhausted diplomats said efforts to find a peaceful solution to the gulf crisis were practically dead.

In a move apparently intended to prepare his people for war, President Saddam Hussein took direct command of the Iraqi army today after assuring his troops in a radio broadcast that they were ready for battle.

Later, Baghdad radio gave civil defence instructions for air raids. The speaker of Iraq's legislature said Saddam, already de facto military commander, would "from now on direct the battle."

In Washington, White House press secretary Marlin Fitzwater told reporters today the U.S. remains hopeful that war can be avoided, but added:

"I think, there is a certain feeling of resignation that the sanctions will have to be enforced. There is a growing sense that we

have to carry out the planning for the use of force, with some resignation."

Asked if U.S. President George Bush had decided to use military force, Fitzwater said: "I can't comment on any military decisions at this point."

Bush held meetings today with U.S. State Secretary James Baker and Defence Secretary Dick Chenney.

Shortly after the United Nations set midnight EST deadline for Iraq's withdrawal, the Bush administration gave no indication it intended to attack immediately, leaving the door ajar for Saddam to back down and keeping hidden the timing of any attack.

"Jan. 15 was a day for Iraq to withdraw from Kuwait," said a statement released by the White House just after midnight. "It was not a deadline for UN action. The choice for peace remains with Saddam Hussein."

President George Bush was said to be asleep at zero hour, although about 1,500 anti-war protesters shouted and banged drums outside the White House.

Daylight had already broken

over the Arabian desert, where tense soldiers penned last wills and checked their weapons.

"I just want to get it over with," said Staff Sgt. Brandon Jay, 27, of Pittsburgh, Pa., a transportation crew chief.

The first expected stage of a U.S. led attack would be an aerial bombardment, taking advantage of superior night-fighting technology. The allies' estimated 2,000 military aircraft outnumber Iraq's warplanes 3-to-1.

U.S. soldiers who dominate the 635,000-strong multinational force said they were ready for battle, tired of months of waiting.

The 415,000 American service members in

the region represent the largest U.S. deployment since the Vietnam War. The accompanying American armada, built around six aircraft carriers and their 450 attack jets, is the largest assembled since the Second World War.

No Signs Of Peace

BAGHDAD (CP) —

Iraqi President Saddam Hussein showed no signs of backing down today, taking direct command of the army after telling his troops in a radio broadcast that the country is ready to fight.

In an editorial, the army news-

paper al-Qadissiya proclaimed Saddam's troops poised for "the most honorable war in history," as the UN deadline expired for Iraq to pull out of Kuwait.

"President Saddam Hussein will, from now on, direct the battle, but he will be assisted by his commanders," National

Assembly Speaker Saadi Mahdi Saleh said in an interview.

Saddam holds the rank of field marshal and routinely controls Iraq's highly centralized military machine, even in peacetime, so Saleh's announcement appeared intended for the psychological effect as the country moved to a

war footing.

The speaker said Iraq is still ready for talks with the United States if President George Bush withdraws his forces from the area.

"Bush will not lose anything if he agrees to talk instead of going to war," Saleh said.

Special Report
FRIDAY, SEPTEMBER 28, 1990

The Daily Courier
SERVING THE FOUR SEASONS PLAYGROUND

OKANAGAN CONNECTOR USHERS IN A NEW ERA

OKANAGAN CONNECTOR
·HIGHWAY 97C·

Landmark date in history

October 1, 1990 is destined to rank with July 30,1962 and July 19,1958 as land-marks of Okanagan history.

In three days the opening of the Okanagan Connector will join the Rogers Pass (opened July 30,1962) and the Okanagan Lake Bridge (July 19,1958) as momentous occasions in the transformation of Kelowna from a small agricultural community to a major city.

With the opening of the Rogers Pass many tourists from Eastern Canada poured into the Okanagan, loved what they saw and quickly became permanent residents.

In a few days the Okanagan Connector will do the same for the rapidly-growing Lower Mainland population. The increased access will allow them to see the Central Okanagan as more than a playground, but as a great place to live and work.

Construction has boomed during the past few years in anticipation of the highway opening, but many predict the major impact of the new road link is just beginning.

BRITISH COLUMBIA'S NEWEST HIGHWAY HAS A NICKNAME — THE MISSING LINK

Some 10,000 bumper stickers were printed up to celebrate the opening of the Okanagan Connector highway.

Oct. 1 will encourage British Columbia motorists to "Discover the Missing Link," said MLA Larry Chalmers (SC-Okanagan South).

The bumper stickers - considerably more imaginative than the " I drove the Coquihalla on Opening Day" stickers that greeted the opening of Phase I of the Coquihalla Highway — will be handed out on the connector on opening day and will also be available at local chambers of commerce, said Chalmers.

The connector, the third phase of the Coquihalla Highway, is slated to open to the public 2 p.m. Oct. 1. A series of ceremonies will precede the public opening.

The 84-kilometer, four-lane highway, which travels from Peachland to Merritt, will reduce driving time to the coast by about 1 1/2 hours. It came in on budget - $225 million.

Chalmers is chairman of the official opening committee, which was finalizing opening-day festivities at press time.

Chalmers said the committee consists of representatives from Kamloops to Penticton, indicating that despite concerns the highway may pull traffic and business to Kelowna at the expense of other centres, the entire Valley is behind the project.

1990~1999

Tax As Popular As A Hangover

The Canadian Press

Ringing in the new year brought Canadians their first taste of life in a GST world as the seven per cent goods and services tax kicked in on everything from haircuts to newspapers.

While most businesses across the country were closed for the holiday, some retailers that did open Tuesday found the tax as popular as a New Year's Day hangover.

"Customers are yelling at me," said Roy Cohen, 28-year-old owner of La Maison du Croissant, a downtown Toronto eatery that was doing a brisk business selling sugar-coated baked goods and coffee.

"One guy went crazy. He bought two cups of coffee which used to cost $1.60 but when I told him $1.71 he started yelling, "What happened?"

One person who welcomed the GST's arrival was Revenue Minister Otto Jelinek, who

The G.S.T. is NOT for Me

announced Tuesday the federal government will extend the GST registration deadline.

If they began collecting the GST on Tuesday and register "as soon as possible," they will still be eligible for a federal sales tax rebate, he said.

Under federal legislation, only businesses registered before the new year were to be eligible for the tax break on inventory bought last year.

"I feel somewhat relieved the day is here," he said. "The pressure has finally disappeared," said Jelinek, who spent New Year's Day in Calgary.

He said he hadn't heard of any problems and consumers had not flooded GST phone hotlines to complain. About 90 per cent of businesses have registered, he said.

In Alberta, where there is no provincial sales tax, paying tax at the retail level was something altogether new.

"A few customers didn't like it, saying it's a ripoff. But they paid it," said Helga Graham, a clerk at a Mohawk gas station and food store in Edmonton.

The GST, passed by Parliament last month after bitter debate in the Senate, replaces the 13.5 per cent manufacturers' sales tax. It applies to virtually all goods and services, exempting only a handful of things such as basic groceries, prescriptions and rent.

Manning Pushes National Identity

SASKATOON (CP) —

The Reform party chipped away Friday at sculpting a new image on the eve of its expected move to the national political stage.

Delegates to the party's convention were warned there is no place in their movement for radicals. Leader Preston Manning and top policy aide Stephen Harper tried to pave the way for Reform's expected conversion from a western-based protest movement to a national party.

"We are crossing a threshold," Manning said.

Delegates will decide today

whether all 62,000 members should vote in a referendum on expanding the party into Ontario and Atlantic Canada. Currently, only residents of the four western provinces can be full-fledged members.

It would be a shock if the expansion proposal, which Manning supports, did not get the go-ahead. The more than 1,400 delegates, many of them older than their 48-year-old leader, have clapped obediently on cue and avoided controversy.

In a message that appeared to be aimed east of Manitoba, Harper told delegates extremists are not welcome in the party.

Lowest Food Costs

Canada has the second lowest food prices in the world.
How countries with the lowest prices compare:

Spending on food as a percentage of personal consumption:

United States
Canada
Britain
Netherlands
Australia
Luxembourg
Denmark
Hong kong
France
W. Germany
Austria
Belgium
Sweden
Finland
Japan
Norway

Basic data: The Globe and Mail

1990-1999

New premier for province as old one quits in disgrace

VICTORIA (CP) —

Bill Vander Zalm resigned in disgrace Tuesday and was succeeded as B.C. premier by the first woman in the country to hold the office.

He handed his resignation to Lt. Gov. David Lam hours after conflict-of-interest commissioner Ted Hughes found he mixed politics with the sale of his Fantasy Gardens theme park.

An hour later, Transport Minister Rita Johnston arrived at government house and was sworn in as the province's 29th premier.

Johnston, a year younger than Vander Zalm at 55, made only brief comments after her swearing-in.

"It's been a rough day," she said.

"Bill and (wife) Lillian have been good friends of mine for a number of years and my thoughts are certainly with them this evening."

Earlier, Johnston stood beside an expressionless Vander Zalm as he resigned the job he held since capturing the Social Credit party leadership in July 1986.

Hughes found the premier clearly violated several conflict guidelines related to the sale of Fantasy Gardens to Taiwanese billionaire Tan Yu.

"I am prepared to resign now to

Hughes report highlights

VICTORIA (CP) — Highlights of the report by conflict-of-interest commissioner Ted Hughes on B.C. Premier Bill Vander Zalm's role in the sale of Fantasy Gardens:

• Vander Zalm clearly violates his own conflict-of-interest guidelines in the sale of Fantasy Gardens to Taiwanese billionaire Tan Yu.

• He doesn't draw a line between his private and public life and believes no conflict exists so long as the public isn't aware of what is going on.

• Vander Zalm maintains he didn't tell the lieutenant-governor, his finance minister or even his own principal secretary about his relationship with Tan because he is concerned had those people learned about the relationship they might have been influenced in how they carried out their public duties.

• The premier states charges of conflict arose only when the media became aware of and publicized what was going on.

• Vander Zalm gives the "red carpet" treatment, such as helping Tan set up a trust company in the province, setting up meetings with government officials while the premier's wife was present and arranging a luncheon with the lieutenant-governor.

• Vander Zalm breaches his guidelines by accepting $20,000 in cash from Tan. Hughes finds the circumstances under which the premier accepts the money as bizarre and without reasonable explanation.

• Vander Zalm discusses the sale of property adjacent to Fantasy Gardens withe a top Canadian executive of the owner, Petro-Canada. He denies he spoke to the Petro-Canada executive during his first interview with Hughes, saying in a second session it might have come up in passing over coffee.

• The premier maintains until only recently that he didn't have a controlling interest in Fantasy Gardens.

ensure an orderly transition as quickly as possible," Vander Zalm said in a brief statement. He refused to answer questions.

Last week, Vander Zalm called a sudden news conference Good Friday to announce he planned to call a leadership convention and

resign after his successor was chosen.

Numerous candidates have expressed interest, but sources had said many caucus members wanted Vander Zalm's immediate successor to serve only as an interim leader. A provincial election must

be held this year.

After a few minutes in office, however, Johnston wasn't tipping her hand: "Nothing is ever ruled out."

The Socred party's board of directors met briefly with the new premier, and party president Hope, Rust said. Johnston said the legislature would be reconvened before a leadership convention is held.

Rust said the board would decide today on a date and location for the convention.

Hughes, meanwhile, concludes in a 61-page report that Vander Zalm clearly breached several of the conflict guidelines he introduced in 1987.

"The findings are not what I expected," Vander Zalm said. "in politics there is no court of appeal in these matters. I must live by the guidelines which I initiated."

The report clearly stunned Vander Zalm's caucus. Some were depressed, a few disbelieving and others annoyed.

Longtime Socred Grace McCarthy said British Columbians now will have a different view of politicians.

"I think it's sad for our province," said McCarthy, who quit cabinet in 1988 over differences with Vander Zalm.

Socreds After Vander Zalm

VICTORIA (CP) —

A week after a disgraced Bill Vander Zalm resigned as B.C. premier, Social Credit members say they've got new life while New Democrats insist his spirit lingers.

And their top strategists differ on how his exit will affect strategies in an election, which must be called by fall. Vander Zalm quit after being found in conflict of interest over his business dealings.

"It's been more Bill Vander Zalm and his private affairs, so with Bill Vander Zalm removed

from the formula it takes a lot of that with him."

MLA sees end to bleeding with exit of Vander Zalm

Messmer hopes party will gain in popularity

By TRACEY HYMAS
Penticton Herald Staff

Premier Bill Vander Zalm's resignation will not hurt the Social Credit party says Ivan Messmer, Solicitor General and Boundary-Similkameen Social Credit MLA.

"It certainly hurt it while it was going on, (but) it's clear that the conflict of interest guidelines and that's the reason that it was the reason." Messmer said after a caucus meeting Tuesday.

"As a matter of fact, I think that probably it will help it, because we will have a leadership review, then the decision will be made (on a new leader)," he added.

Vander Zalm resigned Tuesday after a report by conflict-of-interest commissioner Ted Hughes found that he had violated his own conflict guidelines over the sale of the Fantasy Gardens theme park.

Former deputy Premier Rita Johnston was sworn in as party leader, but a date and site for a leadership review will be called announced today...

[See also CANADA]

Britons Ponder Tax On Queen's Riches

LONDON (REUTER) —

A bill to force the Queen, reputed to be the world's richest woman, to pay taxes on her private fortune cleared a symbolic hurdle in Parliament on Wednesday.

The House of Commons gave an unopposed first reading to draft legislation proposed by Simon Hughes, a member of the minority Liberal Democrats.

The bill stands no chance of becoming law because Parliament will not have time to debate it fur-ther. Hughes also is opposed by ardent royalists on the governing Conservative party benches.

But his measure has set off a public discussion on whether the Queen should pay income tax on her private wealth, estimated at the equivalent of up to $12 billion Cdn.

The bill would also change the succession laws, making the monarch's first child, whether a boy or a girl, the automatic heir to the throne. The succession now passes down the male line.

Hughes said his bill is motivated by a desire for justice.

"I cannot justify to people who have incomes just above the poverty line and who pay taxes … that the woman who by common consent is the richest woman in the country is at the same time exempt," he told Parliament.

Hughes said British monarchs used to pay tax but have been exempt since 1910. He said an opinion poll last February showed 79 per cent of Britons think the Queen should pay income tax.

YUGOSLAVIA STEPS BACK FROM BRINK

JULY 4, 1991, BELGRADE (AP) — Yugoslavia's collective presidency today ordered the breakaway republic of Slovenia to turn over control of its international border crossings to federal authorities by Sunday.

There was no immediate response from Slovenia.

Slovenian militia and the federal army have fought bitterly for control of the 27 border posts several times since last week, when Slovenia and the neighboring republic of Croatia declared their independence.

A fragile ceasefire held in Slovenia today, but leaders of the breakaway republic said the fighting might not be over despite a federal army pledge to respect the truce.

G-7 Countries Back Continued Sanctions Against Iraq

LONDON (CP) —

The Group of Seven leading industrial countries united today behind continued UN sanctions against Iraq and urged Israel to stop building Jewish settlements in the occupied territories.

They also patted Soviet President Mikhail Gorbachev on the back and offered him moral support.

But they did not offer him economic aid and told him to solve the problem of his independence-minded Baltic republics.

The G-7 countries – the United States, Canada, Britain, France, Germany, Italy and Japan – said in a communique on the second day of their three-day annual summit:

"We intend to maintain sanctions against Iraq until all the relevant resolutions of the Security Council have been implemented in full."

The sanctions were imposed by the UN Security Council last August after Iraqi forces invaded Kuwait.

The communique said the sanctions should also continue to apply until "the people of Iraq, as well as their neighbours, can live without fear of intimidation, repression or attack."

FAST FACTS

Gene Therapy

Three techniques for treating disease with genetics are being tested.

1. Engineered cells injected to produce lacking chemicals

2. A gene which produces a anticancer enzyme is spliced into a patients blood cell, reproduced and injected in cancer patient

3. Genes directly injected into muscle tissue are soaked up by some cells changing their behaviour

Basic data: Technology Review, U.S. News & World Report, The Economist

1990~1999

Riot Ravages City

Penticton Resembled War Zone In Aftermath Of Rampage

By Tracey Hymas
Penticton Herald Staff

Windows are boarded over and some scattered debris remains today, after a riot tore through the downtown and Lakeshore Drive early Sunday.

The city resembled a war zone early Sunday as smoke filled the air in the early morning after police fired canisters of gas at a 1,000-person crowd rampaging through two concessions and a tourist information building.

The destructive riot is believed to have began when about 20 young people began throwing rocks at an RCMP officer directing traffic shortly after midnight Sunday. Police were also pelted with beer cans and bottles.

One witness said that a crowd gathered downtown near Lakeshore Drive "and they were rocking a police (ghost) car."

"People were running up Main Street saying there was a riot coming up the street," he said. "A few moments later, I saw a guy take a garbage can and chuck it through the Zellers window (on Main Street.)"

Thirty-seven windows on Main Street were smashed and there were reports of looting from some businesses, including a government liquor store, which had almost its entire front window smashed.

Mayor Jake Kimberley read the riot act to the crowd at 12:41 a.m. from a police car, and left when the crowd pelted the car with debris.

Additional extra police officers were called in from throughout the Okanagan, swelling the already reinforced ranks from 55 to 130 officers. This included riot squads from Kelowna and Vernon. Police officers firing tear gas followed the crowd, moving west on Lakeshore Drive.

Witnesses say the crowd kicked holes in the cement peach-shaped concession, then tipped it over onto Okanagan Lake Beach. The crowd ripped out the food and were tossing it around the area. A nearby phone booth was also trashed by the crowd.

A group of about 200 people entered the Jubilee Pavilion tourist information building, and gutted the interior, the witness said.

Police continued to fire tear gas to disperse the crowd.

"I heard a boom and tons of people were running, it was pretty much in a frenzy but no one was getting trampled," said the unidentified witness.

At least one person was directly hit by a canister. "I saw it hit him in the leg and he just came running out of the smoke," a second witness said.

He said many people retreated to the lake when the tear gas exploded on them, trying to clear the pungent gas from their eyes.

The crowd moved west down Lakeshore Drive, ripping out many of the wooden and wrought-iron benches along the walkway. Witnesses say revellers used the wooden planks to destroy the decorative lamps along Lakeshore Drive.

The crowd also swarmed through the Lakawanna refreshment stand and a small clothing kiosk.

Police firing tear gas advanced on the crowd, then there was a 10-minute lull, as "the cops stayed still and the crowd (at Power Street) didn't move" the witness said.

When the crowd began to advance on police, more gas was fired and a line of RCMP officers in gas masks carrying riot shields advanced on them, the witness said. The crowd moved west on Lakeshore, then dispersed when more tear gas was fired.

Police said the main crowd had dispersed after 1 a.m., although the riot squads were kept on alert until 3 a.m.

Hospital officials report about 60 people were treated and released overnight Saturday. One police officer suffered a separated shoulder in the incident.

City crews began clearing up the ransacked area at about 4:30 a.m. Sunday. By 6 a.m., much of the damage was cleared away and the remains of the peach concession had been removed.

City Caught Off-Guard By Riot: Kimberley

Mayor Jake Kimberley admits that the city was caught off-guard by Saturday night's riot in downtown Penticton.

Speaking to reporters following a special closed-door session of city council Sunday afternoon, Kimberley said while preparations had been made to increase security because of the Peach Festival and Saturday night's M.C. Hammer concert, they weren't expecting any major trouble.

"To a degree, we were prepared with a certain amount of extra staffing, but the groups that came in to cause problems caught us a little off-guard," said Kimberley.

"They weren't here to party, they were here to cause trouble."

Kimberley added that he was personally shocked to discover that most of the rioters were between 16 and 20 years old. He said it has been determined that most of the people involved were from "outside the community."

"As to whether the Peach Festival is going to go the same way as the Kelowna Regatta, we don't know. Certainly, we're going to consider it," stated Kimberley.

Following riots during the Kelowna Regatta in 1986 and 1987, the event was cancelled by the the city. A smaller, family-oriented version of the regatta was reinstated this year.

What's Left Of Soviet Union?

Officially Over As Of Jan. 1

MOSCOW (CP) —

Russian President Boris Yeltsin and Soviet President Mikhail Gorbachev have agreed to formally shut down the Soviet Union Jan. 1 - two weeks from today.

They decided after a two-hour meeting Tuesday to symbolically pull down the red hammer-and-sickle flag from the Kremlin walls and to transfer all remaining cen-tral government power and insti-tutions to the new Commonwealth of Independent States set up 10 days ago by Russia, Ukraine and Byelorussia.

The long-anticipated agreement was a great victory for Yeltsin. His Russian government moved quick-ly today to demonstrate its grow-ing power by recognizing the independence of the former Soviet republics of Moldova, Kazakhstan and Armenia. The Soviet news agency Tass, meanwhile, said Gorbachev called on the national Supreme Soviet legislature to hold a final session to "announce a transfer of power to the new inter-state structure."

It said Gorbachev's call came in a letter to leaders of the republics that plan to join the new common-wealth.

The developments came as U.S. State Secretary James Baker visited seeking assurances that the esti-mated 27,000 Soviet nuclear war-heads will remain under tight con-trol and not be sold or transferred to other countries.

Higher Prices, Empty Shelves For Ex-Soviets

MOSCOW (CP) —

Wary shoppers in Russia and Ukraine took their first painful steps into a market econo-my today, finding higher prices with the end of subsidies and price controls but still seeing the same old empty shelves.

"They have said there would appear a lot of goods as soon as the prices were deregulated, but where are they?" asked Galina Kornilova, an office worker who was searching for milk but found only boiled sausages.

The cost of everything from meat to movies went up in Russia and Ukraine today and will rise in Byelorussia on Friday. Even the cost of basic goods such as bread, milk and baby food - although still government-regulated - will rise.

At Food Store No. 2 in Moscow, refrigerated cases were filled with sausage, frankfurters, chickens and spiced bologna, but there was no beef. Despite windows that advertised milk, none was to be found; only displays of cham-pagne for 156 rubles, more than 20 times its state-controlled price just a few days ago.

Among the eye-popping new prices boiled sausages cost five times more; mandarin oranges more than tripled, carrots shot up more than fivefold - as did the cost of a slice of pizza with pepperoni.

Under the old state-set price, sausage cost eight to nine rubles a kilogram. At one store today, the price for the same amount was 45-plus rubles. The average person had to work four to five hours to earn enough to buy the cheaper meat. Now they will have to work about 22 hours.

Although wages also are expect-ed to rise, the average salary last year was about 350 rubles a month.

Warnings of social unrest over increases have come from most officials, including President Boris Yeltsin. His Russian government is leading they way with freed prices and privatization of state property that economists say are needed to boost production and prevent eco-nomic collapse.

Most Russian shops, businesses and plants today set their prices according to supply and demand for the first time after 74 years of communist rule. Soon they will lose the last of their government subsidies.

The abolition of central Soviet power, culminating in the resigna-tion last week of Soviet President Mikhail Gorbachev, has allowed the most determined attempt yet at market reform.

But there was little sign it had also created harmony among the commonwealth members and strife-torn Transcaucasian states used their greater freedom to intensify bloody private battles.

Ukraine and Byelorussia, which initiated the Commonwealth with Yeltsin's Russia, were following his price rises in grudging response to pressure rather than by consensus.

Together with Russia, they make up 70 per cent of the Commonwealth's population.

Other Commonwealth members appear likely to follow their lead as all agreed on price reform at a Commonwealth summit earlier this week.

NEW SOVIET RULERS OFFER ASSURANCES ON NUKES

DECEMBER 17, 1991, MOSCOW (CP) — Three of the most powerful politicians in what is left of the Soviet Union offered their personal assurances Monday that all 27,000 Soviet nuclear weapons will be kept under tight control despite the dis-integration of the former superpow-er.

But U.S. State Secretary James Baker wants more and left Moscow for Kazakhstan to talk with one of the other key players.

Russian President Boris Yeltsin told a news conference Monday after meeting Baker that the nuclear weapons will be placed under "a single authority" when the new Commonwealth of Independent States that Russia set up eight days ago with Ukraine and Byelorussia replaces the former Soviet Union.

Soviet President Mikhail Gorbachev, who latter also met Baker, assured him: "Control over nuclear arms does exist. There is no need to be concerned."

A visibly subdued Gorbachev told Baker he is working to ensure a "smooth and lawful transition" from the Soviet Union to the Commonwealth.

Canada Beats Most With Aid To Ex-Soviets, Says PM

JUNE 20, 1992, OTTAWA (CP) — It's time for other western coun-tries to match Canada's generous assistance to the former Soviet Union, Prime Minister Brian Mulroney suggested Friday.

"Even though we have our own economic difficulties, we've taken this seriously," Mulroney told a joint news conference with Russian President Boris Yeltsin.

"There's already a lot on the table; if everybody else did the same thing, maybe some of the problems would vanish."

Canada has pledged some $2.5 billion in assistance - mostly in credit lines for grain purchases - to the struggling former Soviet republics.

On a per capita basis, that amount is second only to Germany among the Group of Seven leading western industrial democracies, said Mulroney.

If other countries matched Canada's per capita spending, the western aid package would be boosted from the current pledge of $24 billion to $60 billion, he said.

1990~1999

1991 Data Add Weight To Theory Of Greenhouse Effect In Canada

OTTAWA (CP) —

The trend to warmer weather in Canada continued in 1991, with Toronto experiencing its warmest year on record, the Environment Department says.

Some parts of the country, especially Newfoundland and Labrador, experienced temperatures slightly below normal in 1991, but the national trend was generally well above normal, the department said Friday.

The warming trend was most evident in the Arctic, the Prairies, northwestern and southern Ontario, and southern Quebec.

The data are consistent with the theory that pollution is changing the climate, but don't prove conclusively that change is under way, said Donald McKay, director of the department's climate information branch.

"We have seen in the 1980s six of the warmest years, and as well 1990 and 1991 have been warm years, but we still have not got the definitive answer that says, yes, we are in a period of climate change."

The average temperature in Toronto in 1991 was 10.3 C, breaking the previous record of 10.2 C set in 1953, said McKay. Weather records in Toronto go back to the mid 1800s.

Information from other centres has not yet been analyzed in detail.

"In most of southern Canada, except for the Maritimes it has been above normal," said McKay. "What we do not know yet is whether other records were broken."

Scientists say the global climate is likely to grow steadily warmer due to the accumulation of heat-trapping gases such as carbon dioxide in the atmosphere.

The federal government is committed to stabilizing emissions of so-called greenhouse gases but has not yet agreed with the provinces on how this is to be done.

Environmentalists say the best way to fight global warming is to reduce consumption of fossil fuels - such as oil and coal - which release carbon dioxide when burnt, and to protect forests, which absorb carbon dioxide.

The data shows 1991 was the 10th warmest year since 1931, thus continuing the above normal trend of the past several years. During this period of record, the warmest year was 1987 and the coldest was 1972.

Summerland Woman The Last Miss Canada

TORONTO (CP/STAFF) —

Without knowing it, Summerland's Nicole Dunsdon has become the last woman to wear the crown of Miss Canada.

Cleo Productions said today it will no longer present the Miss Canada beauty pageant, first organized in 1946 and broadcast annually on CTV since 1963.

Production of the annual special is being suspended "partly due to changing times and to escalating costs," Randi Abrahamsen, general manager of Cleo Productions, a division of Glen-Warren Productions Ltd., said in a release.

Beauty pageants, most notably Miss Canada, have been the target of feminist groups who for years have pressured organizers to suspend contests that present unrealistic ideals of women.

But it was not immediately known what impact, if any, such protests had on the decision.

The release said the decision followed several meetings with the program's producers and executives of Cleo Productions, owner and operator of the pag-

Miss Canada 1992, Summerland's Nicole Dunsdon poses with pageant hosts Peter Feniak and Liz Grogan.

Photo courtesy of Marcia Dunsdon

eant, and Baton Broadcasting Inc.

"The national pageant was a wonderful experience for young Canadian women and, regretfully, this opportunity will no longer be shared by others," said Abrahamsen.

Dunsdon, crowned last October before a viewing audience of 1.73 million, will be the last Miss Canada, she added.

BANK OF CANADA RATE DROPPED TO ITS LOWEST LEVEL IN FIVE YEARS

By The Canadian Press

JANUARY 3, 1992 — Interest rates are back on the downward path after a drop in the Bank of Canada's bank rate to its lowest level in almost five years. The central bank's key rate fell Thursday by more than a fifth of a percentage point to 7.46 per cent from 7.67 per cent last week.

Mark Chandler, assistant chief economist at the Royal Bank, said the economy has turned the corner and falling interest rates will help produce modest growth in the new year.

"Mostly, the worst is over," said Chandler. "But it's still going to be tough sledding."

The bank rate has been generally declining since May 1990, when it peaked at 14.05 per cent. That decline has dragged down mortgage and many other interest rates to lows unseen since the 1970s.

In announcing a drop in some mortgage rates Thursday of one-quarter of a percentage point, Royal Trust said its rates are the lowest in almost 20 years. The company's five-year rate for a conventional mortgage is now 9.50 per cent.

The dollar rebounded sharply Thursday after the New Year's Day break to close at $86.89 US, up sharply from Tuesday's close of $86.54 US. This morning, the dollar was trading still higher, at $87.13 US.

Canada entered a recession in April 1990 that most economists agree ended in early 1991. But the recovery has been so pitiful, Statistics Canada says there isn't enough evidence yet to officially declare the recession over.

Gorbachev To Resign On Christmas Day

DECEMBER 24, 1992.
MOSCOW (CP) – Soviet President Mikhail Gorbachev will formally resign Christmas Day with a televised address to the country he has led for seven years, Soviet media reported today.

Tass news agency and the Russian Information Agency said he will deliver his final TV speech during the main nightly newscast at 9 p.m. Moscow time (2 p.m. EST).

Tass said Gorbachev told his personal staff and advisers during a farewell meeting in his Kremlin office this morning that he would use the TV address to set out once again his critical views on the creation of the Commonwealth of Independent States set up to replace the Soviet Union.

RIA said he will also "lay out his position on the current situation in the country."

'Roberta Flies High'

CAPE CANAVERAL, FLORIDA. (CP) —

The space shuttle Discovery roared into orbit today with a neurologist, a bug expert, a researcher in the field of blood flow, a hot-air balloonist and a romantic capable of articulating the wonder of heavenly travel.

Her name is Roberta Bondar.

With her academic pedigree and adventurous background, the woman due to become Canada's second astronaut in space seems to have all the bases covered in fulfilling a role where multiple talents are in demand.

During the seven-day mission, she is to work 12-hour shifts pitching in on experiments involving bugs, back pain, leg veins, crystals, bacteria, plants and more.

Marc Garneau, the first Canadian in space, said Tuesday she's so diligent he was worried she would not take the time to go to the flight deck window and look out.

But Bondar, 46, in a pre-recorded statement released later, washed away any thought that it will be all work and no inspiration from 300 kilometres up.

She invoked Flash Gordon and the Northern Lights over her native Ontario as two of the many things that drove her to become an astronaut.

After being chosen one of six Canadian astronauts in 1983, the Sault Ste. Marie native occasionally hit the lecture circuit to keep interest in Canada's space plans alive during delays within NASA that kept her grounded.

"She's a very warm, bright person – an honest, straight up kind of person," said Dr. May Cohen, a colleague at McMaster University in Hamilton, where Bondar is on leave as director of the multiple-sclerosis clinic and assistant professor of medicine.

"There's no wiles about her – she tells it like it is."

Provincial Monies For Fruit Industry's Future

Most orchardists are now getting a share of $15 million of what is called a provincial investment in their future.

Cheques for the first half of $30 million promised by Agriculture, Fisheries and Food minister Bill Barlee in early December are in the mail now, says spokesman Gerald Geen.

"Quite a number received money last week. The minister indicated he wanted to get money into grower's hands by year-end and he essentially did that."

The one-time financial assistance is coming to growers whose average production through 1987, 1988 and 1989 exceeded 20,000 pounds and was sold through recognized shippers. They received 3.9 cents per pound on fancy grade or better apples, most domestic or better soft fruits, and 2.75 cents for other fruit.

Growers are getting cheques averaging about $8,000 per unit, depending on fruit quality. A Vernon orchardist with 30 acres of apples, not all in production, said

he received $20,000.

Growers can still apply up to Feb. 7, but all 1,500 B.C. Fruit Growers Association members are being paid now, said Geen, associate president.

"The priority for most farmers will be to pay down bank loans with this initial money," said Geen.

Growers welcome the help but getting assistance from government means farmers are losing money, he said. "We have lost far more than we get in assistance."

The remaining $15 million promised will come this spring, following presentations to cabinet of a comprehensive revitalization strategy. The minister has not indicated how this aid will be administered to growers, who haven't made production costs for a decade.

Geen said orchardists feel this additional money should also be paid directly to growers, rather than for replanting or industry development.

'It's the greatest feeling'

Alomar wins series MVP as Blue Jays move into first World Series

TORONTO (CP) —

Baseball's showcase event is finally setting foot on Canadian turf, eh.

"Now the rest of the world can see in prime time what Toronto has to offer," said Joe Carter, one of Wednesday's heroes as the Blue Jays clinched the American League pennant by dumping the Oakland Athletics 9-2.

"I'm very happy to represent Canada in the World Series."

Finally, baseball diehards in these parts can let go of past play-off disappointments. Three times in the last eight years, the World Series came and went without the Blue Jays.

That all changed in just over three hours on an October afternoon at the SkyDome. Guys such as Carter, Roberto Alomar, Candy Maldonado and Juan Guzman have found a place in Canadian history.

"It's the greatest feeling I've ever had," said Alomar, the series MVP amid a mob scene of smiles and showers flowing from champagne bottles and beer cans in a boisterous Toronto clubhouse. "We didn't choke this time....the monkey's gone.

"I'm happy the World Series is coming to Canada."

The Blue Jays open the Series on

Torontonians parade down Yonge Street in downtown Toronto early Sunday morning, Oct. 25, 1992, to celebrate the Toronto Blue Jays winning the World Series over the Atlanta Braves. A life size photo of Blue Jays Joe Carter is held above the crowd. An estimated 500,000 people took to Toronto's streets to celebrate the win.

(CP PHOTO - Phill Snel)

Saturday night in Atlanta after the Braves scored three runs in the bottom of the ninth to beat the Pittsburgh Pirates 3-2 in Game 7 of the National League playoffs.

Alomar shifted the momentum of the six game duel with Oakland in the Blue Jays' favor Sunday

with a game-tying two-run homer off A's bullpen savior Dennis Eckersley that capped a comeback from a 6-1 deficit.

The Jays won 7-6 in 11 innings to take a commanding 3-1 lead. Oakland's Dave Stewart pitched a complete-game masterpiece

Monday to force a sixth game. But the East Division-champion Blue Jays, playing before 51,553 patrons who left the dome with reddened palms and worn-out vocal cords, ended any thoughts of a seventh game by grabbing a 6-0 lead by the third inning.

Jay's win toasted across country

TORONTO (CP) —

Hogtown went hog wild with delirious joy early Sunday as the hometown Blue Jays took baseball's ultimate prize, winning the World Series 4-3 over the Atlanta Braves.

More than 500,000 people swarmed onto the key downtown streets of Canada largest city, set off by a victory far away in Atlanta's Fulton County Stadium; Canada's first-ever World Series crown.

"I've never seen anything like this," said police Supt. John Getty, watching with a smile as thousands of cheering, whooping peo-

ple streamed by on Yonge Street, the city's main drag.

At the SkyDome stadium, more than 45,000 fans went crazy as they watched the nail-biting action on Jumbotron, a 10-metre-by-30-metre television screen usually used to give sports fans replays or close-up views of on-field action.

A two-run double by 41-year-old Dave Winfield with two outs in the 11th inning provided the decisive runs in Atlanta.

"It's America's game, now it's coming up to Canada."

A thunderous roar erupted as the Jays won the Series and jubilant fans ran on to the field danc-

ing, screaming and cheering and waving Canadian flags.

In the city's core, strangers high-fived and embraced each other, setting off a roar heard across several city blocks.

"It's a great day for Canada," said John Vares, 27, shouting to make himself heard as he admitted he was indifferent to baseball until the Jays edged close to a World Series win.

"This victory will bring the country together. It excites me to see a Canadian team excelling at what is usually a U.S. sport."

In Atlanta, the triumphant Jays reveled in their team's achieve-

ment.

"This is the oldest man in the room, the one it took the longest to get a World Series championship, but I'm the happiest man in the room," Winfield said as his teammates bathed in champagne and mockingly did the Braves' tomahawk chop. I didn't do a whole lot, but I did it at the right time.

"It's America's game, now it's coming up to Canada."

Prime Minister Brian Mulroney sent a congratulatory message to Cito Gaston in which he said the Blue Jays had "united a nation … captured the imagination of Canadians from coast to coast."

Herald Sports

Wednesday, October 13, 1993 — Page Eight

BRAVO, BLUE JAYS!

Stewart leads Toronto to second American League title

CHICAGO (CP) —

Dave Stewart was talking about being in the right place at the right time. He was being much too modest.

"We tried to seize the moment with Dave going and he came through with a typical Dave Stewart effort," said Paul Molitor after Stewart delivered another post-season gem in the Toronto Blue Jays pennant-clinching 6-3 triumph Tuesday over the Chicago White Sox.

Given the opportunity to shine in the spotlight of October baseball, Stewart has indeed seized the moment. In 10-American League playoff starts, the 36-year-old right-hander is a perfect 8-0.

The staremaster beat Chicago right-hander Alex Fernandez for the second time in the series with 7 1-3 innings of four-hit ball. The two victories, both on enemy territory at Comiskey Park, earned Stewart his second most valuable player award in the AL playoffs. The first came in 1990.

"To pitch four clinchers, you just have to be in the right place at the right time," he said. "To me, this is the best club I've played with."

Stewart missed Monday's workout to serve Thanksgiving dinner at a Salvation Army mission in Toronto. He wiped the smile off his face and brought out the stare for Tuesday's appearance in front of a hostile crowd at Comiskey.

He gave up a pair of runs in the third, including a bases-loaded walk to Frank Thomas. But he only gave up a couple of singles and two walks from that point, giving way to Duane Ward for the final five outs.

"It's been said that through it all, when I started the season with injuries, that what is important is that I be able to pitch at this time of year," said Stewart, who spent most of his career in Oakland.

"I was trying to throw strikes and pitch selectively to the guys I wanted to and pitch around the other guys.

"I threw more fastball tonight, more than normal."

Stewart's effort drew rave reviews from around the Toronto clubhouse.

"Dave Stewart is the greatest pitcher to ever pitch in the playoffs," said Roberto Alomar.

Catcher Pat Borders, who looks out and sees Stewart's intense glare before every pitch, marveled at his batterymate.

"His concentration is amazing," said Borders, who blocked several of Stewart's forkballs in the dirt with runners on base. "You can't break his concentration."

Jays look forward to three-peat

TORONTO (CP) —

Their cheeks sore from all those smiles, maybe a few hangovers after all their parties, the Toronto Blue Jays begin heading home to enjoy their reign as World Series champions.

Some will go fishing for bass, others will go hunting for big-money contracts, all satisfied with a job well done and maybe thinking about winning a third title next year.

"It was a great feeling," Joe Carter told a packed SkyDome on Sunday of his three-run, bottom-of-the-ninth homer that gave Toronto an 8-6 victory Saturday night over the Philadelphia Phillies and a 4-2 win in the best-of-seven series. "You don't know how sweet that made me feel to come through with the world championship on the line.

The only thing better is a three-peat."

A parade through crammed downtown streets led to SkyDome, where the devoted took a chance to worship their heroes who in turn got a chance to say a few words of thanks.

Odds are many of those getting fitted for championship rings will be in other cities next year. Pitcher Jack Morris and left-fielder Rickey Henderson are among those probably on the way out.

But the franchise has shown resilience to withstand change. There were 12 men on the final 1993 roster who weren't on the 92' World Series roster.

Among the additions making big contributions were:

- Designated-hitter Paul Molitor, who set a post-season record by crossing home plate 17 times and then was named most valuable player in the World Series for his 12 for 24 batting;

- Shortstop Tony Fernandez, with a club-leading nine RBIs which was a record for shortstops in a World Series;

- Pitcher Dave Stewart, 0-1 in the World Series but 2-0 in the American League championship series;

But the hero was no ordinary Joe.

Carter provided the defining moment in the bottom of the ninth with one out, two runners on and the Blue Jays trailing 6-5.

His homer over the left-field fence off Mitch Williams made the Blue Jays the first World Series winner to repeat since the 1977-78 New York Yankees, and give its fans something to remember during winter.

"I'm sure people all over are emulating what happened," said Carter, who jumped for joy around the bases. "It's a dream everyone has - bottom of the ninth, two strikes and you hit a home run to win the World Series."

Only once before had the World Series ended on a home run. In 1960, Bill Mazeroski's leadoff homer in the ninth off Ralph Terry lifted Pittsburgh over the Yankees in Game 7.

Crazy about Kim

Tory delegates make Campbell first woman PM

OTTAWA (CP) —

Kim Campbell wants some rest, but it's unlikely she'll get any as she readies herself today to become Canada's first woman prime minister after winning the Progressive Conservative leadership.

Campbell, 46, a lawyer and former academic from Vancouver, must choose a trimmed-down cabinet and discuss transition arrangements with Prime Minister Brian Mulroney before being sworn in, likely around June 25.

She will be the country's 19th prime minister - not only the first woman to hold the post, but also the first baby-boomer and first native of British Columbia.

And she will have just a few short months to put her stamp on the government before deciding when to call a federal election. She indicated a preference for a fall vote during the leadership campaign.

She's expected to meet provincial premiers before making her debut on the world stage - traveling to Tokyo for the annual economic summit of the Group of Seven western industrial nations July 7-9.

Prime Minister designate Kim Campbell waves as she meets with Prime Minister Brian Mulroney at the prime minister's official residence in Ottawa, on Monday, June 14, 1993.

Her biggest tasks will be to win over a country weakened by a lingering recession and an anemic, jobless recovery, two failed constitutional accords and growing voter cynicism about political institutions.

But her first concerns Sunday night were to head to a victory party in downtown Ottawa after a grueling three-month leadership contest.

As she left the scene after the second ballot win and headed across a football field at Lansdowne Park, she said her immediate priorities were to "pull people together and get some rest."

She gave no other indications of what she'll do, except to say she looks forward to working with Jean Charest, whom she narrowly defeated.

Charest said he'll run in the next election and said Conservatives will unite behind Campbell.

"There's a winner tonight, and the party will be behind the winner," he said.

Though Campbell appeared in trouble in the final days of the gaffe-filled campaign, her well-oiled campaign machine gave her an insurmountable lead after the first ballot - 48 per cent to 39 per cent for Charest, 71 votes short of victory.

Charest held on, but Alberta MP Jim Edwards sealed the Quebec cabinet minister's fate with a surprise move to Campbell on the final ballot.

"This unites the party," said Edwards of his move before the second vote. Campbell won by a final count of 1,817 to 1,630 for Charest - a 187-vote edge.

Campbell promised Canadians "good government, with thoughtful policies, honestly presented, openly arrived at , and implemented with competence and with care for every cent of our tax dollar."

Liberals turn to job at hand after sweep

By The Canadian Press

After a stunning electoral victory that crushed the Conservatives, Jean Chretien and his Liberals were turning to their promises of jobs, hope and national unity.

"The work is starting today," Chretien said as he greeted campaign workers at his headquarters in his Quebec riding of St. Maurice.

Chretien, scheduled to return to Ottawa today, said he will give details Wednesday about the transition of power. Government briefing books have been prepared for him.

Sources say Parliament will re-open in the third week of November for a throne speech and an economic statement.

"Prime Minister Kim Campbell said that she will make it easy for us," said Chretien. Campbell, who lost her Vancouver seat as her party was trounced, is expected to give her resignation to the Governor General this week.

Chretien said he spoke to U.S. President Bill Clinton by telephone early today but would not reveal what they discussed.

In Washington, Clinton predicted Chretien's victory won't derail the North American Free-Trade Agreement.

A White House official said Clinton welcomed the Liberal victory, even though the party has promised to renegotiate NAFTA, a deal to link Canada, the United States and Mexico in a giant free-trade zone.

Markets were less sanguine. The Canadian dollar had been trading as high as 76.63 cents US on Asian markets early today but tumbled to 75.44 cents US by mid-morning in Toronto, signalling uneasiness among international investors.

Bloc Quebecois Leader Lucien Bouchard appeared headed for official Opposition with 54 seats.

But Preston Manning, whose party took 52 seats, promised to be the voice of opposition for English Canada.

Sheila Copps, deputy Liberal leader, said the new government will act immediately to deliver its promised job creation program. The program would see federal, provincial and municpal governments each kick in $2 billion over two years to build roads and sewers.

"We have to move very quickly because obviously Candian confidence is one thing that we really have to buld upon," she said on CBC Newsworld.

1990~1999

COMMENT

Depths of Tory defeat a shocker

By Vic Parsons
Thomson News Service

OTTAWA —

Never in the history of federal politics has a ruling party been so utterly crushed as Kim Campbell's Conservatives were in Monday's general election.

In a month where baseball fans marveled over the "worst-to-first Philadelphia Phillies," political junkies can now shake their heads over the first-to-worst Canadian Tories.

It's doubtful that anyone foresaw how low the Tories would go. While pundits fell over themselves predicting the demise of the New Democratic Party, they missed the pending annihilation of the party that had governed Canada with healthy majorities for nine years.

Fifth place and only two seats is an appalling result for a party that only a couple of months ago was led by the most popular political leader in Canada.

In the 1988 election, Brian Mulroney ran up a sturdy majority of 169 seats. That wasn't quite as good as the 178 picked off by Jean Chretien's Liberals this time, but pretty solid for a government that had fought off a vigorous attack on the No. 1 issue of free trade with the United States.

So what happened? The Conservatives rode to power in the last two elections largely on the basis of their popularity in three areas of Canada.

They took the majority of seats in Mulroney's home province of Quebec. They carved out most of Alberta and the British Columbia Interior. And they attracted wide support from Ontario's rural areas and small towns.

The alienation felt by many Canadians in those areas killed the 1993 Conservative team and it's unlikely Campbell could have done much about it. Anger over the GST, the constitutional mess, the inability to stem the deficit, perceived pork barreling by politicians and the lousy economy contributed to the rise of the regional parties that sapped Tory strength.

Those sore points should be placed on the doormat of Mulroney, rather than Campbell's.

But the prime minister contributed with her own gaffes. Her campaign opening remarks that the jobless couldn't hope to see much improvement before the turn of the century may have been rooted in economics, but did little for her popularity among Canadians desperate for work.

And the campaign advertising on her behalf, notably the one depicting Chretien's facial expression, back fired.

All of these errors contributed to the Tory demise.

This could be a distressing situation were it not for the fact that Liberals were elected in each province, a claim once made by Mulroney.

Canada may have a regional opposition, but at least it has a national government.

1990–1999

Lung Cancer Killing More Women

OTTAWA (CP) —

This year, for the first time on record, more women will die of lung cancer than breast cancer, says an authoritative report on Canadian cancer trends.

Lung cancer is now the leading cause of cancer death for both men and women, and 90 per cent of it is due to smoking, says the report distributed by the Canadian Cancer Society.

About 5,600 women are expected to die of lung cancer this year, says the cancer society's report. By comparison, 5,400 deaths are projected from breast cancer, histori-

cally the top killer.

Lung cancer remains more common among men – the male death toll is expected to total 11,000 this year – but rates for men have stabilized while those for women continue to soar.

Lung cancer trends correspond to smoking trends with a lag of about 25 years, reflecting the time it takes for a cancer case to develop, said Michael McFarland of the Canadian Cancer Society.

Women are now suffering the consequences of sharply increased smoking rates in the 1960s, he said. "We're just starting to see the

results now. This is just the beginning."

In other cancer trends, the report says 3,100 new cases of melanoma will be reported this year. The main risk factor is sun exposure.

"The trend is alarming and we are predicting that it will continue in the future," said Elizabeth Kaegi of the cancer society, which is urging people to take precautions.

The prevalence of all cancers combined is expected to increase slightly this year, continuing a trend that has been apparent for years.

Test Pinpoints Gene Causing Alzheimer's

**By The Canadian Press
with Penticton Herald Staff**

A Quebec scientist has developed a blood test to determine a person's chances of developing Alzheimer's disease, an incurable hereditary illness which robs its victims of their ability to remember.

The test, available in Canada since last month, can tell whether someone carries the "bad" gene – apolipoprotein E4 – responsible for killing the neurons in the brain which control memory.

In the past nine months, Dr. Judes Poirier has used 350 brains stored at -80C in the fridges of the Douglas Hospital's brain bank to

develop the test for the debilitating disease which affects about 300,000 Canadians.

A person who has inherited the "bad" gene from both parents has a very high chance of developing Alzheimer's between the ages of 60 or 65. The presence of just one bad gene delays the onset by about 10 years.

Karen Sutton, South Okanagan representative for the Alzheimer Society of B.C., said this morning she has not heard of the test. Both her parents had Alzheimer's and while she is a long way from reaching her mid-sixties, she's not sure she would take the test.

"I think I would really have to

do some deep thinking before I would probably do it," she said, noting that the effect of knowing what will happen in the future could result in numerous other problems including depression.

"If you are going to get cancer, do you really want to know?"

But Poirer said knowing you are at high risk forces you to prepare for it. The test may also help those who up until now face legal nightmare when trying to deal with the assets of an ailing parent.

And he said the information should be strictly controlled.

"The moment someone is tested, we'll know (what genes) the next generation will carry."

Oscar-Winning Mancini Dies At Age 70

The great composer died of complications of liver cancer

BEVERLY HILLS, CAL. (AP) —

Henry Mancini, the four-time Oscar winning composer who produced such evergreen songs as Moon River, Charade and Days of Wine and Roses, died Tuesday, his publicist said. He was 70.

Mancini died of complications of

liver and pancreatic cancer, said publicist Linda Dozeretz. He was at home and his wife, Ginny, was with him.

Late in March, the spokeswoman confirmed that Mancini had been undergoing treatment for an undisclosed cancer for several months and had been in hospital for blood clots.

Still, he continued working in a recording studio with lyricist Leslie Bricusse on a stage version of

Victor-Victoria. They had won the Academy Award for their original score of the 1982 film that starred Julie Andrews and Robert Preston.

In an interview shortly after his cancer was disclosed, he said work was the best therapy he knew.

In April, Mancini was feted for his 70th birthday with a gala performance with such stars as Andy Williams, Julie Andrews, John Williams and Luciano Pavarotti.

Unlike many movie composers,

Mancini wrote scores that were thoroughly hummable. His themes for the Pink Panther comedies and the Peter Gunn and Mr. Lucky TV series became classics.

Nominated for Oscars 18 times, he won statuettes for the songs Moon River (1962) and Days of Wine and Roses (1963) and the scores of Breakfast at Tiffany's (1962) and Victor-Victoria (1982). Johnny Mercer wrote the lyrics for both songs.

BLOOD SHORTAGE PROVINCEWIDE

MAY 19, 1994, VANCOUVER (CP) — The Red Cross says British Columbia has a provincewide blood shortage.

"If the current downward trend of donations continues, we will exhaust our supply over the long weekend," Dr. David Pi, acting medical director for the Red Cross, said Wednesday.

"Our inventory is at a dangerous level, a little over 1,500 units which is a two-day supply."

The Red Cross needs all blood types, but especially O positive and all Rh negative blood types.

"The blood supply is so low that we have been forced to import blood from other provinces," said Pi.

"Elective surgeries may have to be cancelled because we don't have enough blood on our shelves."

The Red Cross needs 700 donors a day to keep up with hospital demand.

Green Light For Downtown Parking Lot

MAY 17, 1994, KELOWNA — Downtown workers could see some relief to their parking woes by the fall of 1995.

Kelowna city council took the first steps Monday to build a $6-million, 500-stall parkade on the corner of Smith Avenue and Ellis Street (just north of Memorial Arena).

Because all reserved parking downtown is spoken for – with a waiting list – council decided to create a specified area with merchants being charged up to $3 per $1,000 of assessed value, if it's required.

That burden will be eased by an $800,000 contribution from the provincial government that makes up for the shortfall in required parking at the courthouse.

"We're trying to alleviate the long-term parking shortfall," city finance director Cliff Kraft said later.

The parkade will be in the area the city refers to as Kelowna Centre, just north of the proposed site for a new library building.

1990~1999

Jails Filled With Hockey Hooligans

South Okanagan Fans Mostly Behave Selves

By The Canadian Press with Penticton Herald Staff

Vancouver jails were filled to overflowing today after hooligans marking the Vancouver Canucks gallant play-off run battled riot police and clouds of tear gas downtown.

As many as 200 people were hurt, including two with serious head injuries, said police spokeswoman Const. Anne Drennan. She said scores were arrested, but had no exact figure.

Drennan said there were no fatalities.

Meanwhile, in Penticton and elsewhere in the South Okanagan police reported a quiet night.

Cpt. Murray Dean, with the Penticton Fire Department, said two garbage bin fires ignited on the 200-300 blocks of Main Street shortly before the game ended.

"It was probably disgruntled fans, but we don't know that for sure," Dean said. "There were just two fires back to back. Nothing serious."

Early today, Drennan described the scene downtown as very quiet. There are glass repair people there, people cleaning up and police on patrol.

Tuesday night's riot will be thoroughly investigated, she said.

"We will be evaluating the entire operation," she said. "We have film, lots on film, and we will be able to assess it directly."

Most of the throng were hockey fans or face-painted teens looking for a party or just to hang out.

The first volley of tear gas came from police about 10:15 p.m. after an officer became trapped in the mob.

Police estimated some 70,000 revellers took to the streets after the New York Rangers defeated the Canucks 3-2 in New York to win the Stanley Cup.

Battered Canucks Gave Their Best Shot

NEW YORK (CP) —

Trevor Linden was wiping blood from a cut on the bridge of his nose with a white towel.

Cliff Ronning was complaining that he'd been unable to shoot with any effectiveness. His right hand was broken. The Vancouver Canucks had given their all.

"It was a battle," said Linden as he sat on a chair against the wall in the Canucks' dressing room, the blood-stained towel hanging over his right shoulder. "I was asked if we got beat by a better team.

"I don't think we got beat by a better team. It could have gone either way."

Linden scored both Vancouver goals in the 3-2 loss to the New York Rangers in the deciding seventh game of the NHL's Stanley Cup final Tuesday night.

Ronning's best scoring chance was ruined when he couldn't get off a proper shot. A Joey Kocur hit in Game 6 had broken a bone in his right hand. He had to have the hand frozen for Game 7.

"I can't shoot," said Ronning, his damaged hand wrapped in bandages. "I just tried to be as effective as I could.

"But I couldn't even feel the end of my stick. I couldn't raise the puck."

"They had to be a good team to beat us," said Canucks centre Murray Craven. "We dug ourselves a hole – no doubt about it.

"It wasn't meant to be, I guess. We made a gallant effort. That's all we can ask of ourselves."

Team owner Arthur Griffiths stood against the corridor wall outside the dressing room trying to cope with the disappointment of defeat.

"These guys didn't quit," said Griffiths. "They forced the issue right to the last minute.

"I guess it wasn't our turn but I think we gained a lot of fans, and rightfully so."

Vancouver Left Feeling Bruised In Wake Of Riot

VANCOUVER (CP) —

The city should have been basking in the glow of the Vancouver Canucks after they came within a hair of winning the Stanley Cup.

Instead, it was left bruised and battered from a downtown riot following the Cup loss Tuesday night.

A 19-year-old North Vancouver man hit by a plastic bullet from a police crowd control weapon lay in a coma in a local hospital, kept alive by life support systems.

Hundreds of other people were injured, a few seriously, after 70,000 people descended on the downtown area following the Canucks lost to the New York Rangers.

"I'm upset about the black eye it has given Vancouver," Premier Mike Harcourt said Wednesday.

He urged Canucks fans to help restore the city's image by turning out today for a fan appreciation party at noon at B.C. Place Stadium, which seats about 60,000 people.

An enthusiastic rally would be "the most appropriate way for us as British Columbians to restore the great reputation the Canucks brought to Vancouver," he said.

Firefighters and ambulance attendants said it was the biggest emergency they had ever handled. At least 21 criminal charges were laid by the police, mainly for assault and mischief and more charges are expected in coming days.

'PACIFIC POPSICLE' SET TO LICK RANGERS

JUNE 14, 1994, NEW YORK (CP) — Call him the Pacific Popsicle.

Kirk McLean, the tall, cool Vancouver Canucks goaltender, says he's not nervous at all as he prepares to face the New York Rangers with the Stanley Cup on the line tonight.

"I don't think there's any room for nervousness now," McLean said before dinner with his teammates Monday night. "We've gone through a tremendous playoff series and we've had our ups and downs."

"I don't think it's going to be a matter of being nervous. It's just a matter of being patient and doing what got us here. We can't think about the end result right now."

The Pacific Popsicle will do just fine.

The spotlight will be on him tonight, and he doesn't intend to melt.

Local Fans Left With Beers, Bets, Barber

By Penticton Herald Staff
JUNE 16, 1994 — Shane Fitzpatrick hid his face in his beloved Vancouver Canucks' towel; Tracy Dionne just stared ahead at the television screen; Darren Geddes had his fingers crossed.

But try as they might, all of the praying, hoping and even cursing Vancouver fans could collectively contribute, couldn't put the puck into the New York Rangers' net as the clock ticked down.

"With 1.6 seconds left, I'm just hoping they slap a shot and it goes in," Geddes said, with the faceoff in the Rangers' end.

But the die-hard Canucks' fan was left with nothing but a mug of beer and bitter disappointment at the end of the seventh game of the Stanley Cup finals, won by the Rangers 3-2.

And while Canucks' fans had visions of celebrating in the streets of Penticton as fans in Vancouver did after their team forced a seventh game with their 4-1 victory Saturday, Tuesday's defeat put those plans on hold for another year, or maybe 12.

"We're proud of them (anyway)," Fitzpatrick said. "They weren't supposed to get past the first round."

1990-1999

Suicidal Simpson Arrested

LOS ANGELES (AP) —

Two bloody gloves. Blood in his driveway. Blood in his car.

Reports of physical evidence mounted daily in the investigation of the slayings of O.J. Simpson's ex-wife and a male companion.

But for several hours Friday, no matter how much evidence authorities were reported to have against him, they didn't have the most important thing of all: Simpson.

Instead of surrendering to police as arranged by his lawyer, the retired football great disappeared. He resurfaced several hours later in a car on Los Angeles freeways, and wasn't arrested until after he returned at nightfall to his estate in the Brentwood section.

Police said a knife was used to kill Nicole Brown Simpson, 35, and Ronald Lyle Goldman, 25. But the weapon hadn't been found as of Friday.

Reports earlier in the week based on police sources had listed the following evidence:

■ A bloody glove found near a side entrance to Simpson's Brentwood estate that was reported to match another glove found at the murder scene.

■ Bloodstains in Simpson's white Ford Bronco.

■ Rust-colored spots in Simpson's driveway determined to be blood.

■ A vehicle resembling Simpson's, spotted by a jogger, parked on Nicole Simpson's street the night she was slain.

"We are very concerned about

the possibility of Mr. Simpson harming himself," Los Angeles police spokesman David Gascon told reporters Friday night after the fugitive sports star was arrested to face charges he murdered his ex-wife and her male companion.

Simpson had left what his lawyer called a suicide note before fleeing earlier Friday and police said he threatened to kill himself during a 90-minute chase across two counties.

Following his arrest, Simpson was booked into the Los Angeles County Jail, where he was placed on a routine of 24-hour surveillance known as "suicide watch," police said.

He was being housed in the high-security wing of the sprawling complex in an individual cell said to contain nothing more than a bunk, a toilet and a sink.

Al Cowling, Simpson's former college football teammate, was jailed on $250,000 bail and charged with aiding and abetting a fugitive. He had fled together with Simpson and was his friend's driver during the chase.

Gascon said crisis negotiators coaxed Simpson out of the vehicle parked in the driveway of his Brentwood mansion with promises of a call to his mother, access to the toilet and a cool drink. He confirmed that officers found a gun inside the Ford Bronco.

"I can't express the fear I had that this matter would not end the way it did," said Simpson's lawyer, Robert Shapiro, who had worried earlier that the former football great would kill himself.

Outside the walls of Simpson's

This is the booking mug for O.J. Simpson, taken Friday, June 17, 1994, after he surrendered to authorities at his Brentwood estate in Los Angeles. Simpson is charged with two counts of murder in connection with the slayings of his ex-wife, Nicole, and acquaintance Ronald Goldman.

(AP Photo/Los Angeles Police Department)

estate, members of his family hugged each other and cried after word of the arrest came out. The crowd of 300 spectators erupted in cheers.

As Simpson arrived at police headquarters, his mother was admitted to hospital in stable condition at California Pacific Medical Centre in San Francisco for an undisclosed reason.

The arrest shortly before 9 p.m. in the slayings of Nicole Simpson, 35, and Ronald Goldman, 25, culminated an incredible drama that unfolded on live national TV.

The district attorney called it "the fall of an American hero," and Los Angeles police, angered that Simpson reneged on a promise to surrender earlier in the day, mounted a manhunt for him.

Trial Became Media Circus

It was hard not to get caught up in the media hype surrounding the O.J. Simpson trial, as it finally drew to a close Tuesday.

Even in "far away" Penticton, crowds of people gathered around television sets to catch the verdict. Was O.J. guilty or not guilty?

With the camera firmly glued to Simpson's face, the drama of the moment hit a high point as the jury's verdict was read. You could almost hear the TV network producers think: "Television just

doesn't get any better than this."

But that's the hitch. This wasn't meant to be a TV show. It was a murder trial.

Irregardless of whether you agree or disagree with the jury's not guilty verdict in the Simpson trial, there can be no denying, what should have been a trial was in reality a media circus.

With some U.S. states now considering banning television cameras from court rooms, we can't help but be thankful such legisla-

tion already exists in Canada.

The experts agree.

"The O.J. case has made us feel very good about our judicial system," said social scientist Seth Feldman of Toronto. Feldman has studied the differences between the Simpson trial and the recently concluded Paul Bernardo sex slaying trial.

"The way we in Canada operate is a system to be envied, to be held out as an example of how dignity and fairness can lead to

better results," added top Toronto defence lawyer Brian Greenspan.

It's hard to argue. We can only shudder at the impact courtroom television cameras would have made in the Bernardo trial. Instead of lawyers grandstanding and reporters falling over each other attempting to get a scoop, the legal proceedings of a gruesome murder case remained first and foremost a trial.

Too bad the same thing didn't happen in the O.J. Simpson case.

O.J. Simpson Acquitted

Simpson May Face More Time In Court

LOS ANGELES (AP) —

A jury has acquitted O.J. Simpson of charges of murdering his ex-wife and her friend, freeing the fallen sports legend to try to rebuild a life thrown into disgrace.

Simpson looked toward the jury and mouthed, "Thank you," after the verdict was announced on Tuesday. He turned to his family and punched a fist into the air. He then hugged his lead defence lawyer, Johnnie Cochran, and his friend and lawyer Robert Kardashian.

"He's going to start his life all over again," Cochran said later.

"It's over from our viewpoint," district attorney Gil Garcetti said.

Police Chief Willie Williams said he has no plans to re-open the murder investigation. "It doesn't mean there's another murderer," Williams said.

However, Simpson still could be back in court – civil lawsuits have been filed by the families of victims Nicole Brown Simpson and Ronald Goldman.

And Simpson said he will ask a court to give him guardianship of his young children, Sydney, 9, and Justin, 7. The Orange County probate court gave Nicole Simpson's parents, Lou and Juditha Brown, guardianship last year.

After hearing nine months of testimony, the majority-black jury took less than four hours Monday to clear Simpson of the June 12, 1994, murders. The verdict was read Tuesday.

As the verdicts were read in court, Goldman's sister Kim broke into sobs. Her father sat back in his seat in disbelief. Prosecutors Marcia Clark and Christopher Darden sat stone-faced.

Simpson's relatives smiled and wiped away tears.

Later, Simpson's lawyers and relatives addressed reporters in the courtroom.

"I was always in prayer," his

A smiling O.J. Simpson reacts to the jury's not guilty verdict in his double-murder trial in a Los Angeles courtroom.

frail mother, Eunice, said. "I knew my son was innocent."

Jason Simpson read a statement from his father:

"I'm relieved that this incredi-

ble part of this nightmare of June 12, 1994, is over. My first obligation is to my young children, who will be raised the way Nicole and I had always planned."

Simpson's Damage Judgments Signed

LOS ANGELES (AP) —

A judge signed three judgments totalling $33.5 million against O.J. Simpson on Monday, starting a 10-day period during which the plaintiffs must wait before trying to collect from Simpson.

In signing the documents, Judge Hiroshi Fujisaki formally entered the jury's February judgments for compensatory and punitive damages in the civil lawsuits against Simpson.

The judge agreed with plaintiff Fred Goldman, father of Ronald

Goldman, the three plaintiffs should each be awarded separate judgments, rather than given a lump-sum award to separate later.

The court order means Fred Goldman is entitled to $13.475 million, his ex-wife – and Ron's mother – Sharon Rufo is entitled to $7.525 million and the estate of Nicole Brown Simpson is entitled to $12.5 million.

None of the plaintiffs can go after Simpson's money yet because the judge previously granted a 10-day stay of the judgment.

The law calls for a complicated procedure for collection of the money, which Simpson said he doesn't have. The process would be complicated further if Simpson files for bankruptcy.

The plaintiffs could, among other things, attach liens to Simpson's property, including his mother's home.

Now that the judgments are entered, Simpson has two weeks to file motions for a new trial and a reduction in the award. He has two months to file a notice to appeal the verdicts.

Simpson Verdict Stuns America

OCTOBER 4, 1995 — The reaction reflected polls that indicated most whites believed Simpson was guilty, most blacks that he was not

Across the continent, everyday life came to a halt for many who stopped whatever they were doing to catch news of Simpson's fate.

President Bill Clinton said the verdict must be respected and Americans should pray for the families of the victims.

At the predominantly black Johnson C. Smith University in Charlotte, N.C., more than 100 students watching on television cheered and whooped when the verdict was read.

Brady Dargan, a 26-year-old white salesman, said: "This is a travesty and I am thinking of the victims and the two children. After today I don't want to see a newspaper again."

1990~1999

JUNE 17, 1994

Rwandan Rebels Rescue 600 In Raid On Refugee Camp

KIGALI, RWANDA (CP) — Rebels broke through government lines early today, rescuing about 600 refugees in central Kigali and shooting their way back out again. UN officials said at least 40 people were killed in the raid.

"It was a daring, successful operation – a real hit-and-run through the government lines," said Canadian UN military spokesman Maj. Jean-Guy Plante.

At least 40 people were killed and 40 others wounded during the raid, mostly due to heavy rebel mortar fire in support of the attack. A platoon-sized rebel unit escorted about 600 civilians through government-held territory, and planned to walk them to rebel-held territory, UN officials said.

More than 3,000 mostly Tutsi refugees have been huddled around the St. Paul and St. Famille Roman Catholic churches in central Kigali for weeks. They have proved easy prey for the militias of extremist Hutus, the majority tribe, who have waged pogroms against Rwanda's Tutsis.

The Red Cross hospital in Kigali, which is operated without blood supplies, reported an influx of more than 200 casualties overnight, many of them refugees wounded in the rebels' shelling. Most were children and women suffering from shrapnel wounds.

France Pushing Mission In Rwanda

PARIS (REUTER) – France has stepped up efforts to win international support for military intervention to stop the bloodshed in Rwanda by canvassing United Nations Security Council members for support.

Foreign Minister Alain Juppe said Thursday that several countries had told France they were ready to join it in a military intervention to halt the slaughter in the central African state.

JULY 4, 1994

Rwandan Capital Taken By Rebels

KIGALI, RWANDA (CP-REUTER) — The Rwandan capital of Kigali fell to the forces of the rebel Rwandan Patriotic Front early today, independent witnesses and rebel commanders said.

The commander of the United Nations force in the capital, Canadian Maj.-Gen. Romeo Dallaire, in an interview with CTV's Canada AM, said reports from UN patrols indicated that most of Kigali is under the control of the Tutsi rebels.

He said Hutu government forces appear to have withdrawn to an area west of the city.

Dallaire said the city is relatively calm, with only occasional rifle fire.

French officers confirmed the fall of Kigali as well, and said the rebels had also seized control of the southern town of Butare after fierce battles with government forces.

The rebel takeover followed two nights of intense bombardments by advancing rebel forces who brushed aside remaining government positions with a dawn ground assault.

Meanwhile, French troops in southwestern Rwanda received the order today to halt the rebels in their advance west.

1990~1999

Axe Likely To Drop On City's Control Tower

The axe will likely fall on the Penticton Airport air traffic control tower next spring, says a Transport Canada official.

But a union spokesman warns such a move will likely cause flight delays and will not save the government as much money as it claims.

Mike Matthews, Transport Canada's regional director-general for aviation, said Tuesday a final decision on the future status of the control tower is expected in September.

"However, we are preparing to close the tower in the spring of 1995," he said.

"It's time for us to really take a look at our levels of service. We have to make sure we put services where we need them."

Matthews emphasized the move will not affect airport safety, noting that the flight service station will continue to operate 24 hours a day.

It's expected one or two more flight service specialists would be hired after Penticton's five controllers are relocated to other airports.

Federal Transport Minister Doug Young announced Tuesday that air traffic control towers in Saint John, Fredericton, and Charlottetown will be closed. The ministry is also considering the closure of several other towers across the country, including Penticton and Kamloops.

Debate Over Same-Sex Bill Continues Despite Its Defeat

By Anne-Marie Tobin
Canadian Press

TORONTO —

Politicians and Ontario residents won't have an easy time forgetting the day the same-sex bill died and pandemonium reigned at the legislature.

Cries of "shame, shame" echoed through the chamber and hallways of the stately old building earlier this month after the 68-59 defeat of legislation that would have extended spousal employment benefits and other rights to gays.

"It was, I think, a bad experience for all 130 people in that legislature, and not one that we'll ever feel good about," says Liberal Greg Sorbara, who voted against the bill.

Ultimately, many of the politicians who voted no said they did so because that's what their constituents wanted.

For weeks, the editorial pages of newspapers and radio hotlines sizzled with the opinions of columnists and citizens.

"If thousands of gays marched to protest the defeat of the same-sex bill, then hundreds of thousands of heterosexual Canadians, including me, should have come out to celebrate," Lou Gelbloom, 34, an electrical estimator wrote in a letter to the Toronto Star.

An Environics poll of 1,000 people taken in March and April found that 55 per cent agreed and 39 per cent disagreed that same-sex couples should have pension, survivor and employee benefits as heterosexual couples do.

Koresh Followers Declare Innocence

SAN ANTONIO, TEX. (CP) —

Followers of doomsday prophet David Koresh declared innocence before a federal judge Thursday but refused to beg for leniency for crimes they committed during a shootout that killed four federal agents.

The eight defendants took turns speaking to U.S. District Judge Walter Smith, who will decide how much time they must spend in prison for their actions during the February 1993 raid at Mount Carmel near Waco, Tex.

Livingstone Fagan was the first defendant to address the judge.

"There is no doubt in our minds that we are innocent," Fagan said.

Fagan said he was not requesting leniency, although others have on his behalf.

Jaime Castillo told the judge "the government should be on trial for its actions.

"We're not following David Koresh, we're following the truth."

Jurors at a trial that ended Feb. 26 acquitted all 11 Branch Davidian defendants of murder and conspiracy charges in the deaths of the agents.

But eight defendants – four Americans, two Britons, a Canadian and an Australian – were convicted of lesser charges ranging from aiding and abetting the voluntary manslaughter of federal officers to carrying a firearm during the commission of a crime.

The biggest issue as the sentencing hearing opened Thursday was whether seven of the eight defendants will face five or 30 years in prison for convictions on a controversial weapons charge.

1990~1999

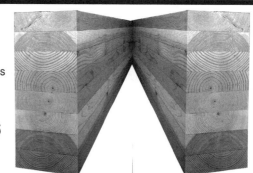

Births a 'medical miracle'

Kelowna triplets delivered 45 days apart

VANCOUVER (CP) —

A British Columbia woman has made medical history by giving birth to the second two babies of triplets 45 days after the first child was born.

The doctor who delivered the babies called it a 'medical miracle' that demonstrates doctors can increase multiple babies' chances of survival and good health by intentionally delaying their births.

It is only the second time on record in the birth of triplets where the babies have survived such a long delay.

In the first case, reported in the United States, there was a gap of

11 days between births. It is also the second time that all three were delivered vaginally rather than by caesarean, where the babies are delivered through an incision in the woman's abdomen.

"You can't generalize to every case but I think what we have learned is that we can attempt delay when it is necessary," Dr. Keith Williams , who headed the medical team at Vancouver's Grace Hospital, told a news conference Tuesday.

"We can attempt to keep fetuses (in the woman's uterus) for longer periods of time."

Joanne March, 29, of Kelowna was admitted to hospital in the Okanagan city March 24, about 22 weeks into her pregnancy.

She had fully dilated cervix, the opening through which the baby

passes from the uterus. The condition is not unusual with triplets, which occur once every 8,000 live births.

March was transferred to Grace Hospital where Dr. Keith Williams and a medical team tried to stitch her cervix to delay the birth.

Her membrane, the sac which holds each baby, ruptured and she was given antibiotics to combat the risk of infection, medication to stop the dilation and ordered to stay in bed.

On April 30, March delivered her first baby- a two-pound one-ounce boy named Clayton - prematurely at 27 weeks, 10 weeks short of a full-term pregnancy. The child has some lung problems as a result of being born early.

Her labor was then stopped

and she resumed her strict bed rest and medication, Williams said . She was monitored carefully over the coming weeks.

Williams said March and the fetuses were watched for possible complication due to infection and possible blood clotting.

"We were also concerned about the growth of the babies (in the uterus) and for a while one baby didn't appear to be growing as well as the other," he said, adding it caught up later.

Doctors decided Monday to deliver the remaining babies, three weeks before full term. The boy was four pounds one ounce and the girl four pounds 13 ounces. The first boy, who remains in a special care nursery has grown to more than three pounds.

Rodriguez appeals to MPs

By The Canadian Press

Mortally ill Sue Rodriguez didn't win the right to have a doctor help her die but she hasn't given up on the hope that euthanasia will become legal in Canada.

"It has been worth it," the 43-year-old Victoria woman said with great difficulty at a news conference Thursday after the Supreme Court of Canada narrowly ruled against her request for an assisted suicide.

Confined to a wheelchair and barely able to move because of a degenerative nerve disorder, the former skier and runner spoke in a broken, barely audible whisper.

"While I may not benefit from the decision today I hope that

Parliament will act and allow those who are in my situation to benefit in the future."

The high court ruled in a 5-4 decision that federal laws against counseling or assisting someone to commit suicide do not contravene the Charter of Rights and Freedoms.

The ruling closed Rodriguez's last avenue of appeal in her fight for a doctor's help to end her life. Her request had earlier been turned down by the B.C. Supreme Court and the B.C. Court of Appeal.

Rodriguez said she hasn't decid-

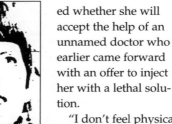

ed whether she will accept the help of an unnamed doctor who earlier came forward with an offer to inject her with a lethal solution.

"I don't feel physical pain - only emotional."

Rodriguez has amyotrophic lateral sclerosis - Lou Gehrig's disease. The affliction causes progressive paralysis, shutting down all bodily functions and eventually causing death, usually through suffocation or choking. There is no known cure.

The former university administrative assistant went to court seeking recourse to euthanasia once her

suffering had become unbearable. Doctors say Rodriguez, who is married with a nine-year-old son, has less than a year to live.

The court was clearly split on the emotional issue.

Chief Justice Antonio Lamer supported Rodriguez's application, writing that laws against assisted suicides prevent "persons who are or will become incapable of committing suicide without assistance from choosing that option."

Justice John Sopinka, writing the majority ruling, provided politicians with a good reason for not acting - Canada's law prohibiting assisted suicides is in line with the law in most other Western democracies.

NBA superstar stuns sports world with decision to retire

CHICAGO (AP) —

Michael Jordan will retire Wednesday after nine seasons, leaving the National Basketball Association without its greatest player and biggest star just days before the start of training camp.

His departure strips the league of its biggest box office attraction, a breath taking acrobat who led the league in scoring the last seven years and carried the Chicago Bulls to three straight NBA titles.

Dateline NBC, the Denver Post and the Chicago Sun-Times reported the news almost simultaneously Tuesday night. A source in the Bulls organization later confirmed the reports.

The Atlanta Journal Constitution quoted NBA deputy commissioner Russell Granik today as saying Jordan informed commissioner David Stern of the decision in a telephone call early Tuesday.

"David called me as soon as he heard," Granik told the newspaper

late Tuesday night. "At first I wondered if he was serious. But David said Michael had made up his mind. Whether it's permanent or not remains to be seen. But it's true."

The story broke as the Chicago Bulls were preparing a bid for a fourth straight NBA championship.

Jordan, NBA scoring champion the last seven years, leader of the three-time champion Chicago Bulls, a two-time Olympic gold-

medal winner and NCAA champion as a freshman at North Carolina, is expected to cite his father's slaying this summer as the reason for his retirement at age 30.

"The thrill is gone. I've done it all. There's nothing left for me to do," Chicago Sun-Times columnist Irv Kupcinet said Jordan told him.

Jordan began his NBA career in 1984 after being named college player of the year at the University of North Carolina in 1983 and 1984.

Red Cross Director Pleads Innocence

Not Our Responsibility To Warn Patients Of Unsafe Blood, Inquiry Told

HALIFAX (CP) —
It was the responsibility of hemophilacs' doctors, not the Red Cross, to warn patients in 1985 they could be receiving unsafe blood products, the medical director of the Red Cross in Nova Scotia testified Friday.

Dr. Max Gorelick came under heavy grilling Friday at the Krever inquiry over why he didn't inform Nova Scotia hemophiliacs in 1985 that the factor 8 they were receiving might be tainted with HIV. Factor 8, made from donated blood, is a blood-clotting agent for hemophiliacs.

The Red Cross did not heat-treat all factor 8, until July 1, 1985. Heat-treating kills the AIDS causing virus.

"It was a well recognized medical consideration: if one treats an individual, one is responsible for his care," Gorelick said under cross-examination by Dawna Ring, lawyer for a group of AIDS-infected hemophiliacs. "If one prescribes he should… know potential dangers of the drug."

People need a prescription to get blood products but Ring said some hemophiliacs, including Randy Conners, didn't regularly see their physicians. They picked up blood products from hospital blood banks on a repeatable prescription.

Connors is a Halifax area hemophiliac who is dying of AIDS contracted from factor 8.

The inquiry was told that the Red Cross distributed non-heat-treated factor 8 during May and June 1985 even though heat-treated product was available.

Dr. Gorelick defended this as being during a phase when there was a limited supply of heat-treated factor 8.

The Red Cross was specifically following treatment guidelines set down by the Canadian Hemophilia Society and other agencies to give new factor 8 users first priority for heat-treated product, he said.

The reasoning was that hemophiliacs who were heavy users of factor 8 stood a greater chance of already being infected with the virus.

Rochelle Pittman, shown in this undated photo, contracted HIV through sex with her husband after their family doctor did not tell him he got tainted blood during heart surgery at Toronto Hospital in 1994. Rochelle Pittman died of AIDS-related complications last year.

Baboon Cells May Repair Damage Caused By AIDS

PITTSBURGH (REUTER) —
Scientists at the University of Pittsburgh said Tuesday they were looking at a radical idea for treating AIDS – using the bone marrow from baboons to help repair the human immune system.

Scientists who have studied acquired immune deficiency syndrome have found that baboons appear to have a natural resistance to the virus that causes AIDS, said Dr. Suzanne Ildstad, a University of Pittsburgh researcher.

Doctors at the university two years ago had transplanted a baboon's bone marrow into an AIDS patient who was dying. The man did die, but doctors were encouraged because he did not suffer any adverse reactions from the transplant.

Ildstad and her colleague at the University of California, Dr. Nancy Ascher, have discovered a cell that makes cross-species bone marrow transplants more possible.

PENTICTON HERALD

THE SOUTH OKANAGAN'S NEWSPAPER

July 26, 1994 — TUESDAY — 50¢ / Fri. & Sat. 75¢

Out of control!

RESIDENTS PUT ON EVACUATION ALERT

Emergency Plan At Ready As Forest Fire Rages Out Of Control Outside Penticton

By Penticton Herald Staff

JULY 21, 1994 — Upper Carmi Avenue residents have been put on evacuation notice while firefighters battle a 150 to 200-hectare fire raging out of control outside Penticton.

The fire broke out around 6:40 p.m. Wednesday and by 8 a.m. today the Penticton Forest District said it had spread to almost 200 hectares on the south side of Ellis Creek Canyon wedged between Carmi and Wiltse Flats, another residential area. One hectare equals 2.47 acres.

"An evacuation plan is in place, but it's not imminent," Laverne Cormier, spokeswoman with the Penticton Forest District said this morning.

"This is a safety precaution – we certainly don't want to alarm people," she said.

This morning Cormier said the head of the fire to the south is starting to pick up and ground crews were placing a handguard close to the Wiltse area to block the fire from moving in that direction.

Meanwhile, 60 firefighters from forest district units in Vernon, Princeton and Kamloops were on the scene early this morning to resume the air attack.

Firefighters are also using helicopters to bucket the area and rapp attack crews were on route at 8 a.m. These crews will rappel into the forest and clear a rough landing place for helicopters.

Last night bright orange flames were visible from throughout the city, as dozens of people stopped at numerous vantage points to watch air tankers attack the blaze.

Blockades were set up on Carmi Road and Wiltse Road limiting traffic to area residents.

The fire broke out beside the creek at the bottom of the canyon, before spreading up the south hillside towards Wiltse Mountain. However, its cause was not immediately known.

Penticton fire chief Brent Hodgins said the city's emergency response program was initiated, but no action has yet been taken.

Evacuation Reaches 4,000

By Penticton Herald Staff

Residents in another dozen homes evacuated early this morning joining thousands of others already pushed out since the Garnet fire escalated Monday afternoon.

Provincial emergency crews evacuated homes in the Smythe Road and Gillies Creek area at 5:15 a.m. near the south end of the fire, which has now scorched 2,200 hectares of land.

About 4,000 people have now registered at the emergency centre based at the Penticton Community Centre.

Estimates are that as many as a dozen homes, all outside Penticton limits, have burnt to the ground.

A provincial emergency team from the Lower Mainland is scheduled to arrive today to help evacuees cope with the stress.

The B.C. Forest Service flew over the area this morning to assess the situation. As of 9 a.m. the fire was tracing its previous path to the south, but also climbing up the Penticton Creek drainage.

"This part of the fire is quite a ways from people's homes, but we're still concerned," forest service spokesman Alan Rasmussen said.

Weather predictions of thunderstorms aren't helping to ease concerns.

"The whole Penticton district is high to extreme (for fires) and with thunderstorms we could have fires starting somewhere else," he said. "We're tapped out now as it is."

Hills east of Penticton burn out of control.

Photo by photo credit

18 Homes Go Up In Flames

Fire Burns Some To Ground And Then Skips Over Others

By Penticton Herald Staff

Weary Penticton homeowners were out sprinkling blackened, ash-covered ground Tuesday afternoon in the wake of the Garnet fire that raced through the upper Carmi area.

Numerous spot fires threatened to flare up amid the smouldering piles of forest debris.

As of this morning, 17 homes had burnt to the ground outside city boundaries and one other had been destroyed inside city limits, city administrator Tim Wood confirmed. Despite that, another 55 homes in the hard-hit upper Carmi area managed to survive the blaze.

"The scene was so grave yesterday we would have lost lives," said Wendy Stewart, spokeswoman for the provincial Ministry of Forests, "This was just wild."

The provincial emergency program, along with forestry and fire personnel, is still trying to determine the damage. Driveways lead to everything from upscale log homes to garages and temporary structures. It's hard to determine exactly what was destroyed.

Forests Minister Andrew Petter viewed the site from the sky Tuesday afternoon along with Okanagan-Penticton MLA Jim Beattie and Penticton Mayor Jake Kimberley.

"These conditions are difficult to operate in," Petter said, referring to the tough terrain. "One can only do everything in one's power and it's very difficult to get equipment on the ground to deal with it."

Petter said he had heard criticism that the forest service didn't move fast enough to stop the fire.

"I understand people are obviously upset, but with everything I have seen, it's clear that everything that could have been done has been done."

The cost of fighting the fire has now climbed over the $1-million mark. While the cost of fighting the fire has soared since it took off earlier this week, Petter said that is simply the price the province has to bear.

"The concern is to protect lives and property and get this fire under control and extinguished as soon as possible."

Naramata Poised To Flee Flames

By Ron Seymour
The Daily Courier

Naramata residents are nervously preparing for possible evacuation today while thousands of long-weekend tourists stream into the Okanagan despite the raging Garnet fire.

The leading edge of the out-of-control 5,000-hectare blaze is less than 10 km from Naramata, a resort and farming community on the east side of Okanagan Lake.

Many homeowners and orchardists are ready to flee with as little as 15 minutes notice if winds push the flames down a heavily-treed slope toward Naramata.

"Everybody's pretty worried because the fire came up again a little last night," said Manuel Araujo, whose family has packed up some of their belongings.

"We're ready to go if we have to. We're just waiting for them (fire officials) to tell us what to do," Araujo said.

"It really is nerve wracking because it seems like there's nothing anyone can do to stop this fire," Carol Shea said early today before she left for work in Penticton.

"I have all the stuff I really need in my car, some clothes, pictures and financial papers," Shea said. "And I'm hanging onto my fire insurance policy pretty tightly."

But others in Naramata seemed to be taking a more skeptical view of the fire threat, saying they hadn't even bothered to prepare for evacuation.

"There's some people that have already picked up and gone, but I'm not panicked," said Duane Bacon. "The fire's still a long way away from the village … it would have to be total pandemonium for it to get this far."

Calm winds overnight and early today have helped the 500 firefighters battling to control the blaze.

Fire information officer Tony Zanotto said the risk to Naramata was considered slight since crews have established fireguards around the western edge of the blaze.

"The fire is basically expanding to the east (away from residential areas)," Zanotto said. "No property or homes are threatened, but a lot depends on what the wind does."

A thick blanket of smoke hung over Penticton this morning, temporarily grounding water bombers and air tankers. But helicopters were able to ferry in equipment to crews working on fire guards, Zanotto said.

This is traditionally the most lucrative weekend for the Okanagan hospitality industry, with thousands of tourists here to soak up the sun and sit on the beaches.

The population of Penticton triples according to some estimates, with visitors pumping millions of dollars into the local economy.

Some motel operators have fretted that news reports of the fire could scare off visitors, but most of those contacted today said they expected their rooms to be full through the weekend.

"We've had between 15 and 20 cancellations, but I think we'll get enough traffic off the street to be full all three nights," said Bruce Weinberg, manger of the 141-room Sandman Hotel Penticton.

The fire could even be something of a tourist attraction for visitors who realize it poses no danger to the city, Weinberg suggested.

"Tourists think it's kind of neat to be near a big fire like this," he said.

Betsy Hogg, manager of the 68-room Best Western Inn, said her staff have fielded dozens of phone calls from people who've made weekend reservations.

"We're reassuring them that the fire isn't a danger to the city," Hogg said. "We've had a few cancellations, but nothing abnormal."

HOMELESS HELPED WITH STRESS

The August long weekend is usually a time to celebrate summer in this lakeside resort community.

But a massive forest fire that continues to grow after destroying 18 homes and threatening hundreds more has brought a more sombre mood to the annual summer blowout.

While there is an increased RCMP presence again to avoid a repeat of the rioting and looting that caused $500,000 damage in 1991, the most prevalent uniform is the day-glo orange fire-retardant coveralls of firefighters.

Many residents will not be in a holiday mood, including 400 from outlying areas who can't return to homes threatened by flames, those who lost property and some 400 on evacuation alert.

Firefighting Hot, Dirty and Frustrating

JULY 30, 1994, PENTICTON — The sun climbs out of smouldering Ellis Creek canyon to bake the burned hillsides and the hundreds of firefighters battling the stubborn, unpredictable forest fire for another day.

They throw on grubby red flame-retardant coveralls and head to the mess trailer for breakfast, looking like beleaguered veterans of a seemingly endless war.

"People are getting burned out and frustrated," says Jayson Charters of Merritt, while waiting for chow. "You get one spot out and then another one flares up."

Despite fatigue and frustration, Charters said morale is still fairly high, largely due to the camaraderie in his 21-member work crew.

Ribbons Showing Support

JULY 30, 1994, PENTICTON (TNS) — Jean Anderson couldn't shake the image of a tired firefighter returning home from another frustrating day in the burning forest outside Penticton.

"I just saw this firefighter in his vehicle. He looked tired and they're working long shifts." Instead of turning away, Anderson decided to do something and has launched a yellow ribbon campaign in support of the hardworking firefighters and volunteers.

"I wanted to let them know that the city appreciates their efforts, regardless of the decisions that were made," she said. "They have been working 12 and 14 hours to protect our homes to the best of their ability and this might boost their spirits."

Recovery Plans Are Set To Roll

By Ted Noonan
The Daily Courier

PENTICTON –

Efforts to repair fire damage in forests above Penticton will begin as soon as the last embers are extinguished.

Some work must be done immediately, but efforts to rejuvenate more than 5,500 hectares will take months and even years of organization and work, said John Wenger of Penticton Friday.

"It will take a long time for that woodland to green out after a fire of this size," said the district manager of the Penticton Forest District.

The fire, which filled Okanagan air with smoke and is estimated will cost $5 million to extinguish, will also mean considerable damage repair costs, he said, although some will be recovered from salvageable timber.

"Natural reforestation will also be considered wherever there's enough natural seed distribution."

Wenger said a rehabilitation team is already being put together to start this work, including ministry, industry and municipal officials.

In that area, about 25 per cent could be private land, with the rest controlled by the Crown.

And about 30 per cent in fire zones was commercial forest of top notch timber value, mostly lodge pole pine, spruce and balsam, he said. Timber was owned mostly by Weyerhauser and Gorman Brothers of Westbank, although the forest service also had some timber.

Comprehensive plans involving everyone must be established, said Wenger.

Those to be involved in planning range from the City of Penticton and water districts to those with guide and trapping licences, along with other ministries such as environment and fish and wildlife.

1990~1999

Where is Mindy?

By Don Plant
The Daily Courier

The mournful cries of a distraught mother heard through an open window signalled a sad truth this morning – Mindy Tran is still missing.

An exhaustive search for the eight-year-old Rutland girl has turned up few clues, despite more than 130 neighbors and search-and-rescue volunteers fanning out from Taylor Road, about a kilometre from Costco, in search of the small girl since she vanished around suppertime Wednesday night.

Police are calling it a "mysterious disappearance," but abduction was on the minds of emergency officials this morning.

"I suspect she's been abducted" said Rex Fitz-Gerald of the Kelowna and District Search and Rescue. "There's no reason for her to wander off – it's just not like her. It leaves us completely in the dark.

"We're grasping at straws trying to get anything we can."

One mother named Sherry, whose daughter is Mindy's friend, spent more than five hours looking for a sign of the youngster on Wednesday night. She and a friend resumed the search in Mission Creek Park Thursday morning.

"What's weird is that everyone who was out (Wednesday) night was calling her name," she said as she hiked through the brambles of the park. "Now, they're just looking."

Mindy had told her older sister Mimi she was going to visit her friend four doors down the street about 6:30 p.m. Wednesday. She rode to the duplex at 360 Taylor Rd., put her bike down on the front lawn and knocked on the door.

One of the last people to see Mindy was the landlady for the duplex, who is staying in a motorhome parked in the driveway outside. She said she was sitting in the motorhome with a friend when Mindy rode her bike along the driveway to see Charmaine, who was out for dinner with her family.

"She walked up the steps to the front door and knocked," said the landlady, who didn't want to give her name. "Then I saw her ride her bike back down the street."

Mindy's mother went looking for her a short time later, but found only the bike, which was on the duplex lawn.

Members of the Tran family stayed inside their home at 385 Taylor for most of Thursday. Friends walked in and out of the two-storey house all day as neighbors handed out soft drinks to volunteers in the street out front.

Neighbors said they were surprised to hear Mindy was missing because her parents are so careful about letting her even run across the street.

"I was so shocked," said Brenda, whose daughter is a friend of Mindy. "I wouldn't say they're overprotective, but they're concerned – as they should be. You never know what's going to happen."

"I know she was never far from home," said another neighbor named Denise. "She was only allowed to go down as far as the bike was found."

Searchers who'd been looking for the small girl for more than 18 straight hours admitted they were tired.

"It's a very frustrating kind of search," Fitz-Gerald said. "Probably the hardest search you can do is an urban search. You're in and out of people's yards, and you have to plow through their out-buildings and overturned boats – every nook and cranny."

Volunteers have expanded their search to as far as Big White Road, the McCulloch Road area in East Kelowna and as far north as Kelowna Airport.

No child has been abducted in Kelowna in recent memory. One senior RCMP member said he'd never heard of one after working nine years at the Kelowna detachment.

Several suspicious vehicles were reported driving up and down Taylor Road all day Wednesday, but police had no substantive leads by this morning.

The ground search was called off for the night but police stayed busy late into the evening, searching door to door and following up tips from residents.

"We've had to turn people away from volunteering to help out," RCMP Staff Sgt. Daryl Graves said Thursday.

The Mounties have set up a phone line (no. 861-1239) dedicated to the Mindy Tran search. If you have a tip or want to volunteer, you can call any time.

WORRIED PARENTS

Worried parents vowed this morning to keep a closer eye on their children as the search for Mindy Tran entered its second full day.

Many people in the Rutland neighborhood where Mindy disappeared say they're keeping their kids indoors, or allowing them only to play in the backyard.

"There's a lot of fear around here," said Al Gingera, a father of two young children. "I kept my own boys in the house all day Thursday."

Gingera, an eight-year resident of Taylor Road who lives next door to the Tran family, said Mindy's disappearance has shocked and upset everyone on the normally tranquil street.

Monica Rhindress, a mother of two who also runs a daycare in her Taylor Road home, said she's not letting the children out of her sight.

"We're always cautious, but now I want to be able to see what the kids are doing all the time," she said

Portrait Of A Missing Eight-Year-Old Girl

The tiny little girl is caring and popular.

"When my mom is sick, she brings a blanket," said her sister Mimi, 18.

"She's going into Grade 3," said Mimi. "She gets a lot of spelling awards and math awards… she excels at reading."

"Whoever has her, let her go," said Mimi. "She doesn't deserve this."

"She's a really good girl; she's never wandered away from home before," said her father John Tran. "She never had any problems with us or with her sister. She's a very happy child."

"She's so tiny and so pretty," said Sherry, a mother whose daughter is friends with Mindy. "She's much smaller than my daughter."

Mindy likes to ride her bike, play store and watch videos with her friends.

Eric, 6, has spent much of the summer playing with the eight-year-old girl in each other's yards and houses and at the children's water park at City Park. Everyone who knows Mindy agrees she's not the type to wander out of eyesight. Neighbors say her parents taught her never to ride her bike beyond where her bike was found Wednesday night, four doors down from her home on Taylor Road in Rutland.

John and Annie Tran moved to Kelowna from Vietnam 14 years ago. They have been living in Rutland for about six years.

Annie Tran was expected to make an appeal for her daughter's safety on television later today.

Mindy is 3'7" tall, weighs 50 pounds, and has black hair and brown eyes. She wore a pink shirt with a Mickey Mouse logo, light-colored shorts and flowered shoes.

Body Confirmed

Mindy's dental records used to identify remains found in Kelowna

Police have confirmed that a body found Tuesday is that of a missing eight-year-old girl.

Mindy Tran disappeared Aug. 17 while on her way to a friend's home.

The body was discovered in a wooded park just blocks from her home.

Dental records were used to make the identification, police said Thursday night.

Cause of death had still not been determined.

Earlier, police downplayed speculation about a possible serial killer on the loose in southern British Columbia.

A Vancouver newspaper said there is a possible link between the slaying of a teenager and the disappearances of a woman hiker at Whistler and a young girl in Kelowna.

"Definitely we in the RCMP have not made any link at this point in time," spokesman Sgt. Peter Montague said Thursday.

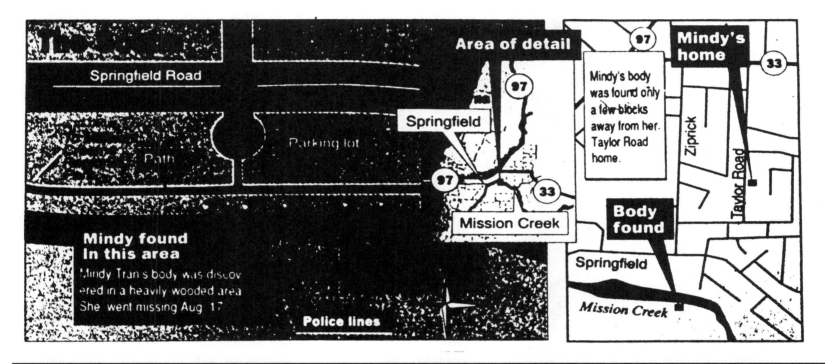

Crown Tight-Lipped On New Murder Evidence

KELOWNA —

A decision on charges in the murder of Mindy Tran will be delayed again, this time because of new evidence.

Regional Crown counsel Geoff Barrow said that "as well as new evidence, police have identified a new avenue of investigation that is now being pursued."

"Given the very serious nature of the events and the complexity of the evidence, the investigation is proceeding carefully and diligently, as is the Crown's review of the evidence," Barrow said in a press release.

When contacted in person yesterday in Kamloops, he would provide no further information.

He also refused comment when asked if the new evidence might point toward someone other than Shannon Murrin, the suspect in the case.

No one in a position to comment was available at Kelowna RCMP headquarters last night.

Mindy Tran, an eight-year-old Rutland girl, disappeared while on a bicycle ride near her home on Taylor Road in August 1994. Her body was found two months later in Mission Creek Regional Park.

Police have accused Murrin, who lived nearby. He is currently in jail in Mission serving out the last few months of a two-year sentence for pointing a gun at a man who beat him up.

Patrick A. Dunn, Robert Holmes and Kenneth Lawrence MacDonald are accused of taking Murrin the night of Jan. 5, 1995 to the spot in Mission Creek Park where Tran's body was found, beating and nearly killing him in the process.

The gateway to your world.

Coming soon.

25th Anniversary
DOES ANYONE CARE?

EARTH DAY

By Greg Lockert
The Okanagan Saturday

While the mantras of reduce, reuse and recycle continue to be chanted by some, environmental issues seem to have lost sway over the masses.

During the heady times of the late 1980s, political parties campaigned as much on environmental issues as economic ones. But the 1993 federal election campaign focused on jobs, the continuation of the social safety net and deficit reduction.

Also, consider Earth Day, being celebrated today. It was only a few years ago that the event fostered huge gatherings and public response. Not anymore.

So far, little evidence has cropped up that any change is ahead. People are more worried about their next paycheque than theories of ozone depletion or global warming. And who can blame them?

But underneath the apparent air of environmental apathy lurks a strong concern with the health of the planet, say those whose life work involves protecting the Earth's ecosystems.

Much of the public uproar regarding the environment in the latter portion of the last decade was fuelled through media hype, said Charlie Hodge, who was in Kelowna this past week helping the local branch of EarthCare plan a clean air program.

"More people are aware than ever before about environmental issues," Hodge said. "Kids study them at school and when they get home they shame their parents into changing their ways."

In sum, most people now live better environmental lifestyles as opposed to engaging in knee-jerk reactions, he said.

One shouldn't gauge environmental interest by media content, Hodge said. Reporters prefer Clayoquot Sound on Vancouver Island where they can get shots of people spiking trees and chaining themselves to cedars. What's more interesting: composting or Clayoquot? he asked.

Day-to-day life of caring for the environment is not glamorous. It's not grist for a front page story or a 15-second soundbyte on television or radio news, Hodge said.

Still, the public can't sit back, he said. "I would say there is what I consider to be a false sense of security about what's happening now."

Multinational corporations and governments have spent millions of dollars reassuring people they're cleaning up after themselves. But that's not always true, he said. "We need to continue to improve our habits and watch corporations and governments."

Dean Trumbley, with his wife, Michele, operate an environmental consulting company in Vernon. He agreed media hype a few years back created an illusion of public environmental concern followed by a false perception of a crash of interest.

People also tired of all the pessimism in the media, Trumbley said. "When you see all the negativity, people lose interest. People

say if it's so bad it's going to keep going that way. It's really sad."

But plenty of work is left to be done, he said. "I think people need to be more involved. People aren't concerned enough. We need an environmental movement."

Roseanne Van Ee, an interpretive naturalist with Outdoor Discoveries in Vernon, said the public is waiting to see what comes next in the environmental movement before responding.

"People were really reacting to a lot of environmental problems in the past," Van Ee said. "I don't think people are becoming less environmentally aware. It's become a way of life."

She said environmental consciousness is becoming part of daily life. For example, regional districts run recycling programs and city governments set limits on household garbage output.

"We have to work together," Van Ee said. "The older I get the more I realize that these changes take a lot longer to develop than I would like to see."

1990~1999

Osoyoos voted Prettiest Town In Canada

Mayor's whoop could be heard all over Parliament Hill after award was announced

By Donna Henningson
Penticton Herald Staff

OTTAWA —

Residents of Osoyoos have something to shout about, after being voted the most beautiful small town in Canada.

Osoyoos Mayor Tom Shields was at the Parliament Hill ceremony in Ottawa Saturday night along with director of development services Brad Elenko and administrator Joe Ukryn.

When the winner of the category for towns under 5,000 population was announced, Shields couldn't contain himself. He flew out of his chair, toppling it over in the process, and let out a whoop "heard all over Parliament Hill."

About 250 people attended the First National Awards of Communities in Bloom, a competition to promote the beautification of towns and cities across the country.

The contest included a category for provincial capitals - with Winnipeg taking honors -as well as three others based on population no greater than 5,000 (Osoyoos); 30,000 (Rosemere, Que.); and 100,000 (Brantford, Ont.).

Four panels of judges toured the country throughout the summer searching for the prettiest

locales in the land, their criteria being beautification, environmental awareness, and level of participation by the community.

Osoyoos itself was judged by Art Drysdale of the Weather Channel, and two others from Nova Scotia and Newfoundland.

The judges were impressed by how Osoyoos has met the unique challenge of straddling two environments - the irrigated orchards of the Okanagan Valley to the north and the desert flora and fauna of the Sonora Desert to the south.

In particular, they were struck by the community's use of "xeroscape" or dryland landscaping, Shields said, and its system of wastewater spray irrigation.

In 1978, Osoyoos became the first community in Canada to use wastewater for irrigation.

Photo by Jo Ann Reynolds

Looking west from Anarchist Mountain onto Osoyoos with the Cathedral Mountains in the background.

Wine Festival Breaks Records

PENTICTON (STAFF) —

The 15th Annual Wine Festival was the biggest and best yet, with records broken for both attendance and for the number of activities.

Wine lovers as well as the curious flocked to 81 events throughout the Okanagan, festival president Rick Thorpe said.

"Our future continues to show promise and 1996 will bring new

and exciting activities to our festival," Thorpe said.

The traditional highlight of the 10-day celebration of the grape, the Consumer Wine Tasting, drew over 2,000 ticket holders to the Penticton Trade and Convention Centre Saturday night.

Jackson-Triggs won in the best red category at the consumer tasting for its 1994 Merlot, while Quails' Gate captured best dessert

wine for a 1994 Late Harvest Optima Botrytis Affected. Meanwhile, Sumac Ridge took best white for a 1994 Gewurztraminer Private Reserve.

A slate of wine experts met for 2 1/2 days last week to choose the best wines, awarding five gold medals, 21 silver and 32 bronze. As well, winemakers gathered Friday to judge their peers.

On top of all the good news

over the success of the festival, Minister of Agriculture David Zirnhelt announced Friday that a $140,000 grant will be made to the Okanagan Similkameen Tourism Association to promote agritourism from the Similkameen to Enderby. The wine industry in particular is expected to benefit as a result.

Next year's wine festival runs Oct. 4 - 13.

1990~1999

Dionne Quint Recalls Her Painful Childhood

MONTREAL (CP) —

The Dionne quintuplets came to hate their father's big black Cadillac.

That's where the world-famous quints, now 61, were fondled and sexually harassed by their father, a surviving quint said Sunday in an interview with The Canadian Press.

The shy Cecile Dionne says it's time she and sisters Annette and Yvonne talk publicly about the abuse by their father, Oliva, even though it's difficult.

"It's part of our lives," she said Sunday in an emotional interview that occasionally brought her to the verge of tears.

"It was a painful time. It really leaves its mark on you."

She was guarded in her comments about their lives and prefers to let a new book do the talking about the abuse – but was open with her advice to other sexual abuse victims.

"Don't keep it inside," she said firmly.

The French-language Family Secrets, by Jean-Yves Soucy, tells how Oliva Dionne frequently fondled the girls during car rides, how he asked to see Emilie's breasts, kissed Cecile passionately and told Yvonne that he would like to sleep with her.

They said they told a school chaplain about the fondling, but were simply told to wear thicker coats.

The three sisters made the allegations – after keeping silent for more than 45 years – as guests on a Radio Canada television program last month. Their estranged brothers and sisters were quick to deny the abuse every took place.

Dionne also said their mother, Elzire, used to beat the quints – but emphasized that was because she was under a lot of stress.

The quints were born during the Great Depression in 1934 in a farmhouse near Corbeil in Northern Ontario. They were the first quintuplets known to have survived infancy. The book is dedicated to their late sisters Emilie and Marie Dionne. Emilie died alone in a convent in 1954 and Marie died in her apartment of an undetermined cause.

The Ontario government took the girls away from their impoverished parents and put them on display at Quintland, a commercial theme park near North Bay, Ont., that attracted thousands of tourists.

The girls, dressed in identical outfits with their hair in ringlets and bows, were also used to endorse hundreds of products.

'REBEL' FANS GATHER TO VIEW GIANT HEAD

OCTOBER 3, 1995, Fairmount, Ind. (AP) — The rebel without a cause is not without fans.

Forty years after this death, they refuse to let his memory fade.

An estimated 250 of them gathered in James Dean's hometown this past weekend to dedicate a park in his name.

Brian McKay, a 33-year old waiter from Perth, Australia, hoarded tips for years to finance his pilgrimage.

"This has been 15 years in the making and I know it's worth it," said McKay.

Dean died in a car wreck in southern California on Sept. 30, 1955. He was 24. His legacy of just three feature films – East of Eden, Rebel Without a Cause and Giant – captured an image of a brooding sex symbol that still draws a world-wide following.

Fairmount, a farm town of 3,200 about 105 kilometres northeast of Indianapolis, has encouraged the legend of the man locals called Jimmy.

The centrepiece of James Dean Memorial Park is a larger-than-life bronze bust that captures the actor's characteristic swooped-back hair, cocked head and mischievous grin. A plaque reads: "This is not a monument to a rebel, those were only roles he played."

At the sunset dedication, actor Frank Mazzola paid tribute with words from a Mayan prayer.

"Jimmy was a light that will shine forever," said Mazzola, who had a knife fight with Dean in Rebel.

"I think essentially that's what he gave us."

Retired Fairmount High School drama teacher Adeline Nall, 89, thought her old student would have approved of the honor.

"I think he would be expecting it by now."

Much of the $25,000 collected for the park's construction was donated by Masao Hayashi, a Japanese businessman, whose son died before realizing his longtime dream of visiting Fairmount.

Hundreds Remember Flyin' Phil Gaglardi

Among those who came to remember Gaglardi was Vancouver multimillionaire Jim Pattison

KAMLOOPS (CP) –

Hundreds of people, including former B.C. premiers Bill Vander Zalm and Rita Johnston, gathered Saturday to remember one of the province's most famous and colorful politicians.

Phil Gaglardi, probably the most famous British Columbian politician after former Social Credit premier W.A.C. Bennett, died a week ago and was remembered Saturday in a memorial service at the Calvary Temple where he preached for years.

Among those who came to remember Gaglardi was Vancouver multimillionaire Jim Pattison, the former Expo 86 chairman who said he was a life-long friend of Gaglardi.

"Phil Gaglardi may have been wrong many times, but he was never in doubt," said Pattison, who played a trumpet solo during the service.

Vander Zalm said Gaglardi might still be working.

"I'm wondering if today Phil isn't preparing to build highways the way he always wanted to build them," said Vander Zalm.

Gaglardi represented Kamloops in the legislature from 1952 to 1972 and was Bennett's controversial highways minister for much of that time.

His nickname Flyin' Phil came from his penchant for using government aircraft, with a record 132 flights in 1955.

It finally cost him his job in 1986 when his son and daughter-in-law were flown on a U.S. vacation in a government jet.

After his retirement from a colorful career in provincial politics, he boasted once in a speech that he had been around the world three times – once at his expense and twice at the taxpayers'.

He returned to politics at age 75 when he was easily elected mayor of Kamloops in 1988. He served one term. He was born in the Fraser Valley community of Mission City, in a canvas-roofed cabin on his father's farm.

1990~1999

A Vote That Was Canadians'

Slim No Resolves Nothing

Sovereigntist leaders say they accept loss but maintain separation is inevitable

MONTREAL (CP) —

Quebecers said No to sovereignty Monday in a paper-thin referendum victory that resolved nothing and doomed Canada to a resurgent nationalist movement that reckons history is on its side.

It was precisely the narrow result – 49.7 per cent versus 48.5 – that few wanted and everyone feared, a messy margin of victory that saw a majority of francophones opt for independence.

Premier Jacques Parizeau shrouded the referendum aftermath with ominous words about Quebec independence being thwarted by non-francophone voters.

"We were beaten it is true, but by what?" asked Parizeau.

"By money and the ethnic vote. All it means is that we were 60 per cent this time; we'll just have to be

63 per cent next time."

Parizeau and Block Quebecois Leader Lucien Bouchard served notice that they believe Quebec separation is just around the corner.

"We will wait a bit, but not for long," said Parizeau in a speech that sounded more like a call to arms than a sovereigntist swansong.

"We won't wait 15 years this time."

In a sombre speech to Yes supporters, Bouchard sounded a similar but more urgent note than former premier Rene Levesque, who promised, "until the next time" after the 1980 separatist referendum defeat.

"Keep hope, keep hope," said Bouchard. "Because the next time it will be it – and the next time could come sooner than we think."

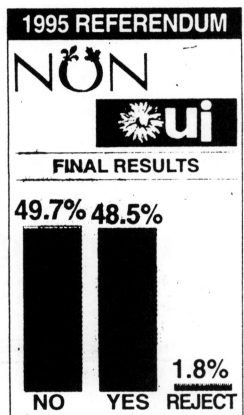

1995 REFERENDUM
NON
Oui
FINAL RESULTS

49.7% 48.5%

1.8%

NO YES REJECT

Nervous Relief - For Now

KELOWNA —

People in Montreal and Ottawa were relieved but anxious about the future after Monday's narrow No victory.

"Everybody here is very antsy," said Lisa Poitras, a first-year science student from Kelowna studying at McGill University in Montreal. "Nobody around here expected it to be this

close."

In Ottawa, Okanagan Centre MP Werner Schmidt said the mood was sombre after the vote.

"At least the country isn't going to break up," Schmidt said. "That is very, very good."

Schmidt interprets the vote as a repudiation by both sides of the status quo.

He said the federal govern-

ment will have to begin negotiating with Quebec and other provinces to decentralize administrative powers and turn more areas of government over to the provinces.

Poitras said up to half the professors at McGill and many students had threatened to leave if the vote was yes. "In the back of my mind it worried me."

She said she probably would have considered leaving after a year, if not right away, if the vote had been for separation.

Saya Patrie, a first-year arts student from Edmonton, said she is worried there could be negative consequences for an English-speaking institution such as McGill because the vote was so close.

1990~1999

Too Close For Comfort

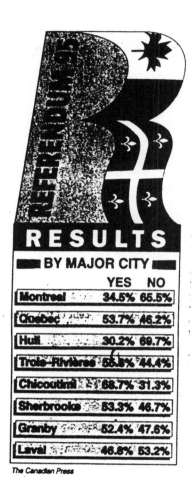

REFERENDUM 1995

RESULTS

BY MAJOR CITY

	YES	NO
Montreal	34.5%	65.5%
Quebec	53.7%	46.2%
Hull	30.2%	69.7%
Trois-Rivieres	55.3%	44.4%
Chicoutimi	68.7%	31.3%
Sherbrooke	53.3%	46.7%
Granby	52.4%	47.6%
Laval	46.8%	53.2%

The Canadian Press

Johnson's office set on fire

MONTREAL (CP) —

Helmeted riot police marched about 300 agitated Yes and No supporters out of the downtown core early today after federalist forces won a narrow referendum victory.

Police officers, cracking batons against their glass shields, used bullhorns to order the crowd to disperse after fights and looting broke out throughout the city's downtown area.

When no one budged, the officers banded together to walk in a straight line across Ste-Catherine Street, forcing the demonstrators into side streets and whittling the crowd down to almost nothing.

Almost 1,000 supporters from both the Yes and No camps massed on Ste-Catherine Street after the result of the referendum was known. They shouted obscenities, threw bottles and pushed and shoved each other.

The two sets of supporters congregated at the corner of St. Laurent Boulevard and Ste-Catherine, the traditional divide between west-end English-speaking Montreal and the French-speaking east-end.

"The idea was to get them apart," said Const. Paul Vidal of the actions by riot police.

The unrest wasn't limited to downtown Montreal.

While Quebec Liberal Leader Daniel Johnson and federalists were celebrating their victory, Johnson's suburban office was set on fire just after midnight.

"We think the fire was deliberately set," Clement Guerin, dispatcher for the Vaudreuil-Dorion fire department west of Montreal.

"There were two broken windows," he said, adding there was no one in the building.

"The inside is pretty well gone. We had to send about 40 men there."

Police said they had no suspects.

The aftermath of the referendum created havoc on downtown streets and resulted in about 50 arrests while police tried to keep both camps apart and away from the downtown shopping district.

Security guards were posted in front of many stores along Ste-Catherine. Many storeowners had already boarded up the windows to their shops in anticipation of trouble.

But windows of a downtown shopping centre were smashed in and looters flooded into the stores to snatch goods. A car was vandalized by No supporters.

A Canadian flag was burned by Oui backers and part of a parking shed was torched.

Few In Penticton Cheer No Win

Victory by federalist forces is too small to keep separatists at bay, say residents

By Erick Ko
Penticton Herald

PENTICTON —

A No victory is no win, according to local residents reacting to Monday night's referendum results.

"They'll do it all again," Gord Paulsen said. "There's going to be another referendum, so what's the point?"

Paulsen shared the opinion of many people polled in Penticton after the referendum ended with a No victory by a slim margin.

Rather than overcome with celebration, people responded matter-of-factly to the news.

If Quebecers want to live and work with the rest of Canadians, then great, Paulsen said. But otherwise, they should just go their own way.

"I kind of wish it was a Yes and they'd get it over with," Paulsen said.

With the results so close, neither side will be willing to give up, Bill Baker said.

"They're going to have another vote. We'll continue to fight another 15 years."

Terror In Oklahoma

(AP Photo/The Daily Oklahoman, Jim Argo)

Nothing has changed Oklahoma City like the April 19, 1995 bombing of the Murrah Federal Building, where 168 people died and scores were injured.

FBI Arrests Bomber Suspect

The blast appears to be the work of domestic terrorists

OKLAHOMA CITY (AP) — A man arrested for speeding just 90 minutes after the deadly bombing of a federal building was identified Friday as a suspect in the explosion.

A second man surrendered to local authorities in Kansas.

At least 65 people died in the worst terrorist attack in U.S. history, the medical examiner's office said.

Timothy McVeigh was arrested in Perry, a town of 5,000 about 100 kilometres north of Oklahoma City. He has been held there since Wednesday.

Late this afternoon, the second suspect, Terry Nichols, surrendered in Herington, Kan., Justice Department spokesman Carl Stern said.

President Bill Clinton said his administration will seek the death penalty for those responsible for the blast.

Attorney General Janet Reno, announcing McVeigh's arrest in Washington, said the 27-year-old man was one of the two "John Does" identified as suspects on Thursday.

Speaking before Nichols turned himself in, she said the

other man was still at large. The attorney general said McVeigh, who was armed when arrested, will be taken into custody by the FBI.

Shortly before McVeigh's arrest was announced, the FBI said it was conducting a raid in a rural section of Michigan in connection with the bombing. Reno declined to comment on that raid, but said searches were being conducted "around the country."

Both Reno and Clinton said the act appeared to be domestic terrorism.

BOMBING LINKED TO HATE GROUPS

OKLAHOMA CITY (CP) — Experts who track hate groups and paramilitary organizations suspected at once a link to the bombing of the federal building here. Now many are repeating calls for a crackdown.

"Americans are dying, and it's time to seriously investigate these movements," said Rick Eaton, a researcher at the Simon Wiesenthal Centre in Los Angeles.

A monitoring group, the Southern Poverty Law Centre, urged Attorney General Janet Reno in a letter last October to investigate unauthorized "militias," saying some of the paramilitary organizations were mixing with white supremacists in a "recipe for disaster."

Reno on Friday announced the arrest of one of two known suspects but refused to answer questions about any possible hate, separatist or militia group connection.

Terry Nichols Found Guilty In Oklahoma City Bombing

Nichols Convicted Of Conspiracy, Manslaughter

DENVER (AP) —

Terry Nichols was convicted Tuesday of conspiracy and involuntary manslaughter in the Oklahoma City bombing, found to be only a junior partner rather than an equal to Timothy McVeigh in the deadliest act of terrorism on U.S. soil.

Nichols, who still faces the death penalty for the conspiracy conviction, was in his Kansas farmhouse more than 300 kilometres away at the time of the blast. His lawyers portrayed him as a family man "building a life, not a bomb."

Jurors deliberated 41 hours over six days to conclude that the circumstantial prosecution case built on fertilizer receipts, phone records and Ryder truck sightings was not enough to make him an equal to McVeigh.

The verdict came six months after McVeigh was convicted and sentenced to death on murder, conspiracy and weapons charges. Jurors in that case did not have the option of considering lesser charges of second-degree murder and involuntary manslaughter.

The Nichols jury will return Monday for a hearing to determine whether Nichols should get life

(AP Photo/Orlin Wagner)

Terry Nichols is led by U.S. marshals from the United States Court House in Wichita, Kan., Wednesday, May10, 1995. Nichols' trial starts Monday, Sept. 29, 1997, in Denver Colo. Defense attorneys are expected to emphasize that Nichols, 42, was home with his family in Herington, Kan., when the bomb went off, killing 168 people at the Oklahoma Federal Building on April 19, 1995.

behind bars or death by injection.

Under the instructions from U.S. District Judge Richard Matsch, the jury was allowed to consider the lesser charges only if they were unable to find premeditation in the eight first-degree murder charges, covering the federal agents who died in the blast.

Second-degree murder is killing "without premeditation and malice." Involuntary manslaughter was defined for the jury as "the unlawful killing of a human being without malice." This would be a "lawful act done without due caution, which might produce death."

Prosecutors contended McVeigh and Nichols worked side by side to acquire the ingredients and build the 1,800-kilogram fuel-and-fertilizer bomb. It destroyed the Alfred Murrah federal building on April 19, 1995, in a plot to avenge the FBI siege at Waco exactly two years earlier.

The blast caused nine floors to collapse into an area the size of

three, crushing the victims, in the words of one rescuer, "like grapes." Among the dead were 19 children, most of whom had just been dropped off at the building's day-care centre.

While McVeigh's trial had heavy doses of survivors describing the ordeal, the streamlined case against Nichols honed in on the "road to destruction" the two took in the seven months leading up to the blast.

Prosecutors traced the trail of low-budget motels, calling card communiques and coded letters that linked Nichols and McVeigh.

They introduced evidence that Nichols used an alias to buy nearly two tonnes of explosive fertilizer at a co-op and helped McVeigh steal explosives from a rock quarry in central Kansas in the fall of 1994.

And they contended he robbed Arkansas gun collector Roger Moore to raise money to live on while they prepared for the Oklahoma City bombing.

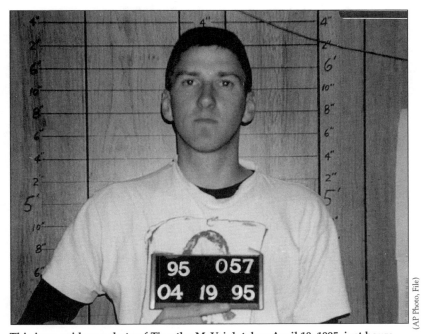

(AP Photo, File)

This is an evidence photo of Timothy McVeigh taken April 19, 1995, just hours after the Oklahoma City bombing. McVeigh, 29, was convicted in June and condemned to death for the bombing of the Alfred P. Murrah Federal Building.

1990~1999

Push never came to shove

New leader needed, says Harcourt

VICTORIA (CP) —

An emotional Mike Harcourt announced his resignation as B.C. premier and NDP leader Wednesday, hours after rumors broke of a back-room plot to sack him over a charity rip-off scandal rocking the party.

With his voice and hands shaking at a hastily called news conference, Harcourt said his two-decade political career had been dragged down by revelations the New Democrats received money stolen from charity.

"I have never shied away from the truth and the consequences that come from the truth being told," he said.

"The task can best be carried on with a new leader who will be free of the baggage that I have been

harnessed with as I have undertaken to clean up some of the problems of the past."

He will stay on as party leader and premier until a successor is chosen, probably in February. The government must call an election next year.

In an evening interview with the Canadian Press, Harcourt said he came close to throwing in the towel last spring when the first in a series of political troubles began dogging his government.

"That was the first time I thought about it," a weary and bitter-sounding Harcourt said.

"I've been in politics 23 years and the only two times I thought about getting out were this year," he said.

Someone had to take the fall

Editorial

Premier Mike Harcourt's announced resignation as NDP leader and premier of B.C. somehow seems a logical conclusion, given the relentless trail of miscues and mayhem that have led up to it.

Simply put, Harcourt has allowed himself to be the fall guy, taking the hit for the shortcomings and weaknesses of those around him.

The NDP proved to be its own worst enemy when it came to maintaining a strong profile, in which the public could have a sense of confidence. Some token move to take a firm hand in resolving any one of several questionable dealings that rocked the government might have restored a measure of faith with the voters. Instead, the public watched as infidelity was overlooked and even rewarded, never mind anyone being punished.

The so-called bingogate was obviously shaping up to be the last straw when Harcourt announced his intention.

Similarities between Harcourt's NDP government and former

Ontario premier Bob Rae's crew of New Democrats are obvious. As with their eastern counterparts, who were ravaged at the polls earlier this year, the westerners haven't been able to sustain their time in the spotlight without the dirty laundry being hauled across the stage.

It may go down as a noble gesture for Harcourt to fall on his sword for the sake of the future of his party. It's certainly a drastic measure to divert at least some of the negative attention that never seems in short supply, when it comes to the provincial NDP - from political colleagues and the party as a whole.

Ultimately, next year's election would probably have been the undoing of Harcourt anyway. Too much history. At least this way, he's giving his party the opportunity, however slight it may be, to try and salvage something in the coming year.

In one respect, perhaps Harcourt deserves a better fate. In the same respect, when it comes down to accountability , there are undoubtedly others from within the same ranks who deserve far worse.

MIKE HARCOURT FINDS A LOOPHOLE

Canadian cup now America's

Baltimore Stallions, U.S. expansion team, beat Calgary Stampeders 37-20 to win Canadian Football League's Grey Cup

REGINA (CP) —

A cold chill blew through the crowd Sunday as an American team made CFL history by winning the most powerful symbol of Canadian football.

Sobered by a bitter north wind and Baltimore's strong play, more than 52,000 fans watched the Stallions beat the Calgary Stampeders 37-20 in the Grey Cup.

The tiny Baltimore cheering section was oblivious to the freezing temperature.

"I feel just terrific; the best team won," said Joe Short of Baltimore, who waved an American flag alongside his Stallions banner.

Short said Canadians should be no more despondent that the Grey Cup is headed to the U.S. than Americans were when baseball's World Series was won by

Toronto in 1992-93.

Somehow, that didn't console Bruce Matthews of Toronto, among the many who were stunned to see a Canadian tradition dashed by the expansion Stallions, in only their second CFL season.

"I'm very upset, I'm terribly disappointed," said Matthews.

Still, many Canadians congratulated the American visitors.

"I could cry I'm so happy,"

cheered Doris Snyder, who traveled from Baltimore with her sister for the game.

Many were blue with cold as fierce winds gusted well beyond 60 km-h and sent trash blowing across the field.

Despite the chill, Calgary fan Tom Marshall toasted his team with a frosty beer.

"It's never too cold for a beer," insisted Marshall. "It's a Canadian tradition."

Compromise CFL? No way!

Editorial

Yesterday marked the close of another Canadian Football League season, with the staging of the time-honored Grey Cup game in Saskatchewan.

Now, some are wondering if this will turn out to be the final game, not only of this season, but of the CFL as we know it.

Amid sagging interest in Canada a few years ago, officials made a bold step by expanding into the United States. What inevitably evolved is a line that has separated the Canadian component from the U.S. component of the league, and that's not just figuratively speaking.

At the onset, the move into the U.S. may have been done with all the best intentions. It was a gamble at the time but one worth taking, given the woeful state of the Canadian game. In hindsight, the Canadian teams may have been their own worst enemies when it came to keeping fans. Loyalty was difficult to build when team locker rooms were fitted with revolving doors and no one could possibly keep up with the com-

ings and goings of players. But that was then, and the league now sits with a whole new set of problems, not the least of which is pressure from south of the border to change the Canadian game.

"The American fans are confused when you say "three-down football," is all too common a complaint from U.S.-based team officials. And make no mistake, their say will unquestionably be the driving force that "Americanizes" the CFL, ultimately bringing an end to the game as we know

it. There's even talk of changing the name of the league.

Canadian league officials try to keep up a brave front, as they have for years, but their over-enthusiastic responses to pointed questions don't mask their fears.

The CFL deserves better than to be simply melded into some grotesque hybrid. If the American team officials think they can turn things around and create a successful league in their markets, by all means, there's the door. Better people

than them have tried and failed. Simply adding a down isn't going to fill those cavernous U.S. stadiums that looked pathetic with a few hundred fans huddled around the mid-field stripe.

If it's the CFL's destiny to meet its end, then so be it. But at least let it be on our terms and not because some johnny-come-latelys think they have a cure-all for what ails our game.

Vernon Times

We're changing with The Times

10 people dead

Wedding-day Tragedy — Vernon In Shock

By Joyce Langerak
The Okanagan Saturday

Instead of a wedding, there will be funerals in the Gakhal family after a horrific killing spree, the second-worst massacre in Canadian history, left 10 people dead Friday.

The victims – including the bride, who was to be married today – were killed in a house in Vernon's Mission Hill district. Some staggered outside, where they collapsed in front of the home at 4104 Okanagan Ave.

The gunman calmly strode from the house after the killings, and returned to a motel room where he killed himself. He left a suicide note apologizing for his terrible rampage, but left no explanation.

Canada's worst single incident of mass murder was in 1989, when Marc Lepine gunned down 14 women before shooting himself at the Polytechnique Engineering School at the University of Montreal.

The victims of Friday's killing spree were identified as Karnail Gakhal, his wife, their five daughters, their son, and a son-in-law. Police said the suspected killer was estranged from the bride's sister, who was found dead at the scene.

Two children were taken from the house unharmed and brought to Vernon Jubilee Hospital, but a wounded six-year-old girl and an elderly woman underwent surgery.

When police arrived about 10:30 a.m., they found one man dead in the driveway of the upper middle class home and other people dead and wounded inside the house.

Five wounded were taken to Vernon Jubilee Hospital where three subsequently died of multiple gunshot wounds.

All nine of the murdered people are adults, the youngest an 18-year-old woman.

While investigating at the scene about a half an hour after the shootings, police were alerted that a shot had been fired at the Globe Motel at 3900 33rd St.

There, in room 45, police found the body of the killer who died of a single gunshot wound. He is believed to be from Burnaby and appeared to be in his mid-20s.

Three weapons believed to have been used in the slayings were found with the body. Two were hand guns and the third was a rifle.

Police are unsure whether all three guns were used, but all the victims died of multiple gunshot wounds.

The owner of the Globe Motel, who would give his name only as Tony, said the suspect had checked in Thursday evening about 4 p.m. and registered under

the name M. Singh.

The bride's fiance was enroute from the Lower Mainland at the time and has been notified of the tragedy. The wedding was to have taken place today at the Sikh Temple in Vernon.

Why? We Can Only Guess

'Anybody can speculate as to what was going on in his mind'

By Joyce Langerak
Thomson News Service

VERNON —

Mark Vijay Chahal chose a time he could inflict the most damage on his estranged wife, says the officer in charge of the team investigating the second-worst mass murder in Canadian history.

"He was not happy with the separation," said RCMP Sgt. Doug Hartl during a press conference Saturday.

"Anybody can speculate as to what was going on in his mind. The motive we're pursuing, and the most logical one, is he chose that time to take revenge on his wife and the entire family."

The attack, systematically carried out in broad daylight, was completely unexpected, said Hartl.

"To our knowledge, there was no prior warning of Mark Chahal showing up." It's unlikely Chahal had been invited to the wedding, he said, or that he would have been welcome at the festivities.

A vehicle registered to Chahal was found in the long-term parking lot of the Kelowna Airport. There, he rented a 1996 dark green Ford Winstar van which he drove to Vernon. The van was recovered outside the Globe Motel following discovery of his body.

At about 4 p.m. on the evening before the killings, the suspect registered at the motel under the name M. Singh.

"It's safe to assume he had planned to come up and commit the murders," said Hartl. But police are unsure whether Chahal had planned suicide following the crime.

"We're still trying to develop this character," said the officer.

The suspect had no criminal record or restraining order against him, but his estranged wife had registered a complaint with police that he had threatened her in Burnaby about a year ago.

The couple, married for about eight months, had been separated for more than a year.

Following the shooting spree, five people were taken to hospital where three died of gunshot wounds. One man died in the driveway outside the home, and five other bodies were found inside.

Dead are Karnail Singh Gakhal, 50, his wife, Darshan Kaur Gakhal, 45, their daughters, Balwinder Kaur Gakhal, 24, Kalwinder Kaur Gakhal, 21, Rajwar Kaur Gakhal, 26, Halvinder Kaur Gakhal, 17, Jasbir Kaur Saran, 30, the couple's son Jaspal Singh Gakhal, 14, and their son-in-law Balgit (Roger) Saran.

A six-year-old girl, Justine Kaur Saran, of Abbotsford, was shot in the leg and is recovering in Vernon Jubilee Hospital.

Gurmail Kaur Saran, 60, was shot in the mouth and transferred to Vancouver Hospital where she is expected to recover.

Two small girls, Brittany and Courtenay Saran, were in the house at the time of the murders. They escaped unharmed and have been taken in by friends.

Police had determined that two types of weapons were used in the killings. They were a Smith & Wesson Model .40 semi-automatic handgun and a Smith & Wesson Model .38 special revolver.

Both weapons, registered to Chahal in 1995, were found in the motel room with his body.

A third weapon, a Mossberg 12 gauge pump shotgun with ammunition, was found in the rented van. It had not been used in the massacre.

Police found two empty clips and 28 shell casings inside the residence.

A third clip was found in a gun at the motel room.

Autopsy results are expected late Sunday.

City's Saddest Day

By Patrick Brennan
Thomson News Service

VERNON —

Friends and relatives of the Gakhal family struggled with their emotions Saturday as they bid farewell during an emotional public funeral.

About 1,500 people filled the Vernon Recreation Centre with others standing in the foyer.

The funeral was an emotional outpouring of grief for many, who sobbed uncontrollably as they walked past the seven open caskets.

"Friday, April 5 was a black day for the Gakhal family and all God-fearing people of the human race," said Satwant Dhindsa, a spokesman for the local Sikh community.

Dhindsa reminded the audience children in the family who survived the attack Good Friday were forced to watch.

"Even the gods wept by pouring cold rain down to show their anger," he said, referring to showers which poured down on a huge crowd at a candlelight vigil three days ago in Vernon.

The funeral, conducted in both English and Punjabi, was for the seven members of the Gakhal family. Another service is planned in Abbotsford for two members of the Saran family who were also killed.

Speakers included representatives from the Kelowna and Vancouver Sikh temples, representatives of the federal and provincial governments, co-workers and friends of the victims.

Mourners file past the seven open caskets Saturday during a public funeral service in Vernon. Seven of nine members of the family were remembered following their April 5 murder by the estranged husband of one of the family's daughters.

They expressed a variety of emotions from subdued anger to a plea for understanding that would help the family and community begin to heal.

The family was remembered as model citizens by many speakers. Dhindsa described the parents as exemplary while others said the Gakhal children were gifted.

"We will have to search our souls today to ask what positive actions we should be adopting so such an event will not be repeated," said Jaswant Singh, a friend of the family.

After the service, family and friends left for a private cremation ceremony. A private prayer service is planned for the Vernon Sikh Temple today at 4 p.m.

POLICE DEFEND NOT INVESTIGATING KILLER

VANCOUVER (CP) — The RCMP say they merely followed the law in not investigating violence-related complaints from the wife of a man who murdered her and eight other people before killing himself.

Rajwar Gakhal told the RCMP in January 1995 and again this January that her estranged husband, Mark Chahal, had threatened her. One threat apparently came during their divorce proceedings.

A woman officer tried to persuade Gakhal to press charges but Gakhal told authorities not to pursue the matter, RCMP Sgt. Peter Montague said Monday. "What kind of a police force would we be if we didn't abide by a complainant's wishes?" Montague said.

"If you extrapolate that and just picture the RCMP ignoring the wishes of a complainant … and the husband then resorts to violence, then we are going to be blamed for causing that."

Montague said the Gakhal case is not the same as a domestic dispute where there is overwhelming evidence of an assault.

Then, police have no choice but to arrest the spouse and charge him, even over the woman's objections.

B.C. To Tighten Rules On Guns

VANCOUVER (CP) —

British Columbia's top law officer promised Wednesday to put tougher restrictions on people applying for a restricted weapon because of the mass murder-suicide of 10 people in the Okanagan Valley last weekend.

"We can add to existing guidelines and my ministry will be speaking to police as well as federal government," Ujjal Dosanjh said Wednesday in an interview.

A potential gun owner is asked tough questions before getting a firearms acquisition certificate. But police should ask questions of marital status and personal history again if a person later applies for a restricted weapon, the attorney general said.

Mark Chahal was single in 1993 when he got a firearms acquisition certificate, which allowed him to buy guns that aren't restricted.

He was in the midst of a stormy marriage breakup when he got permission to buy two handguns he later used to gun down his estranged wife and eight members of her family in Vernon, B.C., before killing himself.

Dosanjh said if he doesn't have the power to tighten up the application process, he'll lobby Ottawa to do it.

The RCMP have been criticized for issuing restricted gun permits to Chahal when they knew he had threatened his wife, Rajwar Gakhal, and her sister.

The Mounties received four complaints starting in January 1994 when Gakhal reported that her husband had assaulted her over the previous eight months. But she asked them not to conduct a formal investigation.

In the midst of those complaints Chahal got his permit to own the restricted handguns – a .40-calibre pistol and a .38-calibre revolver.

Dosanjh also said police must use more discretion in approving gun permits when there have been complaints against a potential gun owner. "I want them to be able to revoke the (gun) permits or the firearms acquisition certificates upon learning of even the slightest hint of a potential danger to a spouse," he said.

Sgt. Don Brown of Burnaby RCMP, which gave Chahal the permits, said police are obliged to issue them once a person has a firearms acquisition certificate.

"If we don't want to give him the permit, we have to take the FAC away as well and all his guns," Brown said. "He can challenge that in court and we have to give reasons why.

"That would be revealing that his wife had made complaints."

Support Grows For New Bridge

Calls to the Ministry of Highways favor the new bridge proposal by a 20-1 margin

By John Keery
The Daily Courier

KELOWNA –

The Highways Ministry should decide within two weeks if it will seriously consider replacing Okanagan Lake Bridge with a new one.

This would mean a report scheduled to go to Highways Minister Corky Evans on bridge improvement options will be delayed, but it wouldn't necessarily delay the project, said Sue Thomas, project communications manager.

"It would be quicker to construct a new bridge," she said.

The plan for a new bridge that would parallel the existing one on the north side and have an elevated section over City Park came up a month ago in a value engineering study.

The ministry commissioned a private consulting group in Washington state with experience in floating bridges to look into the options for Okanagan Lake.

A community focus group that looked into the bridge recommended the ministry add a fourth lane to the existing bridge or consider building a new one.

Glenn Thomsen, chairman of the focus group, said the new bridge proposal, known as Option 6, was not given to the group in time for it to poll members of neighborhood associations.

"It wasn't in our mandate," Thomsen said. "But we feel it deserves serious consideration and study."

The focus group, which released its report Tuesday, also supported the concept of a north/south couplet in Kelowna.

This would make streets such as Pandosy and Richter one-way to improve traffic flow.

Councillors Robert Hobson and Henry Markgraf say Option 6 is worth looking at.

"Option 6 has some technical appeal," Hobson said. "It could allow us to restore the beach area along Mill Creek."

Thomas said it will take about three months to have a good preliminary look at the proposal, if the ministry decides to go that route.

City council and the Central Okanagan Regional District's transportation committee have suggested the ministry look at Option 6.

Calls the ministry has received favor the new bridge option 20-1, Thomas said.

The ministry will have to determine if it is technically possible to build adequate footings and what the costs, including property acquisition for related road improvements, would be.

"A cost-benefit analysis will be a big part of it," Thomas said.

Internet Can Be Frustrating, But Liberating For Some

TORONTO (CP) –

For a lot of people, using the Internet is more like drowning than surfacing. Busy signals. Long delays. Outdated web sites. Too many ads.

The Internet is still in its infancy, just learning how to walk.

It has exploded in the last six months, hooking 22 new users per minute into the global electronic system that links millions of computer users. In Canada, 2.3 million people are registered users and businesses are linking in at a record speed, said Janice Murray, a spokeswoman for the Canadian Internet Show.

"So many people are trying to sample the Internet and find their local providers are overwhelmed with new subscribers," said Daniel Pittsford of Compuserve USA.

Many people log on with high expectations only to be disappointed, said Ilene Lang of Digital Equipment Corp., a big U.S.-based computer company.

"Right now, it's not as robust as it should be, and it's frustrating."

But Lang and other Internet faithful believe the kinks in the system will soon be worked out.

"It's really important for the future," said one 10-year-old girl whose Toronto Grade 5 class set up a web site about their favorite things to do in the city.

"It's important for the jobs we want," she said.

"And the graphics are cool," quipped a classmate, explaining why in fluent techno-speak.

But the younger generation's enthusiasm is making their parents panic, said Jaellayna Palmer, who visited the Canadian Internet Show for tips to teach her Internet classes in Kitchener, Ont.

"I don't think it's a fad," said Palmer. "But I don't think what's got people excited is what's important."

Right now, businesses are rushing to the Internet like panhandlers to gold, flooding the system with high-tech graphics and advertising gimmicks.

"Everybody wants to be the biggest and the best," Palmer said, glancing around at the towering booths and lines of computer terminals at the show.

"It's fuelled by an advertising frenzy, but that's what it takes to get it going."

Some facts about the Internet:

Sites: As of December 1995, there were 150,000 web sites.

November: In November alone, there were 17,000 new sites or 772 a day.

Canadians: 2.3 million people are registered Internet users in Canada.

News Groups: The Internet carries about 15,000 news groups.

Zines: About 18,000 electronic magazines are on the Net.

100TH WIN FOR JACK

APRIL 8, 1996, SCOTTSDALE, ARIZ. (AP) – Jack Nicklaus was already one for the ages.

So his victory on Sunday in the Tradition – enough to start a legend for many – would have taken its place on the shelf of other storied triumphs except that it was Nicklaus's 100th pro victory.

The total includes foreign tournaments, and Nicklaus said he wasn't as sure about it as Larry O'Brien, his administrative assistant.

"Let's call it 100," said Nicklaus, who won his fourth Tradition title, becoming the first to win a Senior PGA tournament four times. "After I won (Feb. 18) in Tampa, I went to see Larry O'Brien, and he said, 'Jack, your next win will be your 100th.' And I said, "Great. Now I have a monkey on my back."

Nicklaus has won 70 titles on the regular tour, 10 as a senior, and 20 others around the world. He was the defending champion in the eight-year-old tournament. He also won on his first attempt, in 1990, and in 1991.

He vaulted past Hale Irwin with a three-shot swing on the 12th hole and stayed ahead, finishing with a 15-foot birdie putt on the last hole to put the finishing touch on a second straight round of 7-under-par 65 for a 16-under 272.

Bifocals Equal Big Business

As Canada's baby boomers hit 50, marketers are rethinking products and approaches

APRIL 8, 1996. TORONTO (CP) – As an entire generation pushes 50, products from bifocals to antacids are being retooled to entice consumer spending well into the next century.

Marketing changes are meant to tap into the greying of North America's population – particularly the postwar baby boomers whose numbers are projected to push Canada's population of seniors to 8.3 million by 2031.

More than one in five Canadians will be 65 or older.

Companies as diverse as book publishers and cell-phone marketers are adapting or repositioning products with an eye on the commercial potential of those numbers.

"Smart marketers are beginning to be aware of the aging trend," said David Foot, a University of Toronto economist specializing in demographics. The recent success of invisible bifocals are one example of a product that mirrors this, he said.

Paul Faibish, a Toronto lens maker, said seamless bifocals have been available since the late 1970s but became commercially successful only five years ago – about the time the oldest boomers turned 45.

The music business is also getting into the act. After a few rock artists such as Eric Clapton scored successes among baby boomers with "unplugged" (acoustic) albums, others have capitalized on that age group's interest in softer sounds.

Pesticide Tied To Mad Cow Epidemic: Farmer

EDINBURGH (REUTER) —

Excessive use of an organo-phosphate pesticide some 10 years ago could have caused the epidemic of Mad Cow disease, a farmer-researcher told the International Science Festival Saturday.

Organo-phosphate chemicals are widely used as pesticides in agriculture, horticulture, fish farming, forestry and veterinary medicine and in the home for medicated shampoos, fly-sprays and flame retardant clothing or bedding, Mark Purdey said.

He said farmers were forced to use phosnet – a blend of organo-phosphates and base of the drug thalidomide – in the 1980s to combat warble fly infestation.

Massaging it into a beast's rump to ensure it penetrated hide, flesh and muscle and reached deep-burrowing larvae meant OP toxins affected the animal's nerv-

ous system.

Scientists announced last month they had found a likely link between Mad Cow disease and a lethal human equivalent, causing worldwide consumer panic and a European Union imposed global ban on British beef.

Purdey says it was significant that Switzerland, the only other

European country to insist on the use of phosnet is the only other European country with large-scale BSE (bovine spongiform encephalopathy) outbreaks.

He maintains OPs, derived from military nerve gases, have permeated the food chain and water supplies to present potential health hazards throughout the eco-system.

RCMP Came Close To Calling In Army

Documents show army takeover considered at natives' standoff

VANCOUVER (CP) —

Senior RCMP officers considered asking the army to take over its role containing the Gustafsen Lake armed standoff with aboriginal renegades last year after a furious gun battle.

Emergency discussions took place immediately after a Sept. 11 fight with heavily armed militants at the besieged camp near 100 Mile House, B.C., about 320 kilometres northeast of Vancouver. Thousands of rounds of ammunition were fired but no one was seriously hurt.

At that point, senior RCMP officers indicated to the military they did not know if police could con-

trol events any longer. The information is contained in secret documents released by the Department of National Defence under an access to information request by the Vancouver Sun.

The month-long standoff was triggered in August after about 20 native Indians and white supporters refused to leave private, ranchland. They claimed the spot was a sacred site on unceded aboriginal territory.

Despite initial strong reservations about helping the RCMP, the military agreed to take an early role. It had an operational plan in place a week before police blocked access roads to the militants' camp on Aug. 26.

The plan to provide armored escort services to the RCMP was kept secret for nearly two weeks after Attorney General Ujjal

Dosanjh officially requested help the day the police blockade went up.

It was not until Sept. 5, when four armored personnel carriers drove through the roadblock following another serious gunfight, that the military's presence was acknowledged.

But it was the Sept. 11 incident, when rebels waged a fierce battle with the RCMP that resulted in one personnel carrier being disabled, that nearly led to the military assuming complete control.

A memo obtained by the Sun reported a telephone conference between Col. Bill Sutherland, senior operations officer at the army's western headquarters in Edmonton and an unidentified officer at national defence headquarters.

It described how the RCMP felt the situation was out of control.

UNABOMBER SUSPECT TURNED IN BY OWN FAMILY

APRIL 9, 1996, WASHINGTON (REUTER) — Hoping to stop the Unabomber from striking again, the brother of suspect Theodore Kaczynski made his own investigation into his suspicions before putting the FBI on the trail, a family lawyer said Monday.

The brother, David Kaczynski, hid his fears from his aging mother Wanda until two weeks ago.

At that time, the FBI's evidence had mounted and the arrest of brother Theodore as the main suspect in the bombings was imminent.

"She expressed her sincere belief that Ted could not be the Unabomber but if he was, he had to be stopped," lawyer Anthony Bisceglie said in Washington.

No one in the family has any idea of what turned a loving brother and brilliant scholar into a recluse and possibly a bomber, Bisceglie said, adding: "We may never know."

In Washington, Justice Department officials met federal prosecutors from at least seven states around the country to consider how to proceed as FBI agents build a case.

Officials said issues include pressing more charges, where to hold the trial and whether to seek the death penalty.

Theodore Kaczynski, 53, is a Harvard-trained mathematician who jettisoned an academic career for a life as a hermit in a shack in Montana.

He is being held in jail in Helena, Mont., on a charge of possessing bomb-making components.

David Kaczynski provided the FBI the materials that led them to his brother.

He called federal investigators because of his "very sincere desire to make sure that no further lives were lost if indeed his brother was involved."

Bisceglie said David spent months examining incriminating letters and documents of his brother's on his own, with a private investigator, with his lawyer and then the FBI.

The Kaczynski family is in isolation and through Bisceglie sent their condolences to the Unabomber's victims.

1990~1999

More than a century of publishing comes to an end

Newspaper's colorful history grew with the community it served

On the day that Angus K. Stuart and W.J. Harber first hung a shingle outside the office of the newly-created Vernon News, the partners probably would have been surprised to hear the prediction that their newspaper would last a year, let alone a century.

Like most successful business ventures, the Vernon Daily News grew with its community. In keeping with the Vernon of the 1890s, the early years of the Okanagan's first newspaper were small, humble, but ultimately hopeful.

The newspaper was founded on May 14, 1890, pre-dating the formal incorporation of the City of Vernon by half a year.

The end of an era

Bill MacIntyre
Vernon Daily News

While most of the city slept, an institution that has been part of Vernon for 105 years, quietly melted away into history.

This final edition of the Vernon Daily News marks the end of one of the oldest newspapers in the province.

While the death of a newspaper does not alter history, or create shock waves around the world, it nonetheless represents the passing of something that has touched the lives, at one time or another, of almost every person in the community.

One hundred and five years is a long time. The Vernon News was here to record the dying days of the great cattle empires. It saw motor vehicles replace wagons and carriages on the city's streets.

The Vernon News mourned the loss of the city's young men as they marched off to war and rejoiced with those whose family members came home.

It recorded the births, marriages and deaths of countless Vernon citizens. It also recorded their accomplishments in school, sport and business.

Politicians of all stripes were lambasted or praised for their efforts in public office and tracked while they sought re-election.

We covered Vernon's transition from a small town to a bustling city. We have suffered with its citizens through the Great Depression, fires, drought and storms. All faithfully recorded for posterity. And we benefited from the good times as well.

There are many reasons the Vernon Daily News could not continue to publish. Yes, advertising revenues were not there. Circulation dropped and it was clear there was little hope of regaining the paper's position it once held in the community.

But there are other reasons as well and perhaps we were so caught up in the day-to-day pressure of deadlines that none of us could see it coming.

Perhaps we just didn't see the incredible changes coming to our society over the last 40 years. We stood by and watched our sisters, daughters and mothers head into the paid workforce and didn't understand how far reaching the effects would be.

We were puzzled by the shrinking family and changes of societal values. We didn't see the impact of the time crunch on people's reading habits. And, as crime, violence and moral decay crept into our community, perhaps too much time was spent on negative things.

While we will no longer be part of the excitement of reporting on our community, we are not leaving with any sense of bitterness. Instead, we feel we produced the best newspaper we could given our resources and financial position.

We feel we were fair in our treatment of the news and did not buckle under to pressure groups who would manipulate the content of the newspaper for political or financial gain. We were not always right, but we always kept our subscribers in mind. Of that we are proud.

Certainly none of us wanted to be the last managing editor, salesperson, circulation rep, reporter or customer service clerk of the Vernon Daily News. But that's life.

It will now be up to others to carry on the craft of newspapering in Vernon and the North Okanagan. We wish them well.

We also thank our subscribers who stuck with us to the end. It was a pleasure, privilege and challenge to serve you.

As you read this, desks are being emptied, memories being rehashed and farewells are being expressed among the 22 people who will turn off the lights, lock the doors and get on with their lives.

Thanks again, and goodbye.

Bill McIntyre has now gone fishing.

1990~1999

Bennett and buddy guilty

With files from CP

Former premier Bill Bennett, his brother and another man were found guilty yesterday by the B.C. Securities Commission of insider trading.

The former premier, his brother Russell and lumberman Herb Doman were each handed 10-year prohibitions from trading securities, or being directors or officers of public companies.

"This is a case about insider trading," said the commission in its 186-page report. "Insider trading is often characterized by deceit and greed and sometimes by conspiracy. All these elements were present in this case involving R. J. Bennett, W. R. Bennett and Doman."

A Doman spokesman said the lumberman was "extremely disappointed with the decision and intends to appeal the decision vigorously."

In Kelowna, Bill Bennett also criticized the decision. "I have to deal with it and quite frankly I'm horrified at the decision," he said. Bennett said he had not decided whether to appeal.

The commission concluded the Bennetts and Doman contravened

section 68 (1) of the Securities Act, which prohibits tipping and trading on the basis of undisclosed information about a publicly traded company.

The commission said the order against Doman allows him to return as a director or officer of Doman Industries after one year, provided certain conditions related to the corporate governance of Doman Industries are met.

The Bennetts and Doman were also ordered to pay costs of the commission hearing - estimated by a Doman lawyer to now stand at approximately $1.5 million.

The hearing - the longest and most expensive insider trading hearing in B.C. history - began in August, 1994 and concluded April, 1996.

The province's superintendent of brokers alleged lumberman Doman tipped the Bennetts that a proposed takeover of his company by forest products giant Louisiana-Pacific had collapsed in November, 1988.

The Bennetts sold their 500,000 shares, for a profit of almost $2 million.

The Bennetts and Doman were acquitted in provincial court in

1989 on criminal charges of insider trading.

"Quite frankly, most of the public will believe (the court decision) than will believe a four-person provincial panel who have, in my view, a vested interest in recovering the money, their legal expenses ... it's a very tough forum that I have to face." said Bennett.

In closing arguments in April, Lawyer Joseph Array said the crux of the case is what time Harry Merle; president of Louisiana-Pacific Corp. called Doman to tell him Louisiana-Pacific's proposed takeover had fallen through.

Both Bill and Russell live on the

(CP Photo)

Former B.C. premier Bill Bennett ponders a question during testimony at the B.C. Securities Commission. Bennett and two other men were found guilty of insider trading, radio station CKNW reported.

Westside - Bill on Pritchard Drive and Russell on Gellatly Road where he has a prominent horse farm.

When Bill was premier, he was also Kelowna's MLA.

Gamble By World's Biggest Mall Pays Off

By Tamsin Carlisle
The Wall Street Journal

The world's largest mall, in Edmonton, Alta., was in disarray three years ago. Many of its biggest tenants were leaving, including Ikea, the Swedish home store; Woodwards department store and the fancy Bretons women's store. Meanwhile, its largest lender had unexpectedly decided to call in its loans.

Similar scenarios have played themselves out at many North American malls in the last five years, a period of takeovers, clos-

ings and disappointments in the retail real estate business.

Malls that once appeared to have bright futures lost tenants and closed, and some were even razed.

But instead of collapsing, the roughly $800 billion West Edmonton Mall has resurrected itself by betting heavily on gambling and entertainment, a strategy that other huge malls may follow.

Triple Five Corp - is slashing available retail space to 60 per cent from 80 per cent and doubling the amount of space for entertainment to 40 per cent from 20 per cent.

The change is startling. At two in the afternoon on a recent overcast Wednesday, all seats were taken at the banks of gleaming slot machines arrayed on the lower level of the new Palace Casino.

Upstairs, a poker game was in progress, while a group of smartly dressed thirty-somethings clustered eagerly around the blackjack tables.

Not too far away, artificial sunshine beamed down on a group of teenagers in swimming trunks who were bopping around in the artificial waves that were crashing

on a concrete shore. The temperature outside: nearly zero.

Sprawled across 110 acres, West Edmonton Mall, which received 20 million visits last year, has more than 800 retail stores and three cinema complexes.

It also has a hotel with "theme rooms," where one can soak under a mock waterfall.

And its more than 100 restaurants range from McDonalds to the ultra-chic Modern Art Cafe, where shoppers can pay up to $5,000 for a painting or sculpture to complement their meal.

1990~1999

Diana's Death

(AP Photo)

SEPTEMBER 2, 1997

Authorities Say Driver Was Drunk

PARIS (AP) –

The driver in Princess Diana's fatal car crash was legally drunk and apparently driving over 150 kilometres an hour, French authorities said Monday.

The revelations introduced a major new element in an investigation that had seemed focused on the role played by paparazzi who pursued Diana's vehicle.

Police extended the detention of seven photographers taken into custody after the crash. They were expected to be placed under formal investigation Tuesday – a step short of being formally charged. The precise charges they might face were not known.

Other new details emerged about the tragedy, including reports that the driver had been trying to weave around a slower-moving vehicle, and that photographers who snapped photos of Diana and boyfriend Dodi Fayed after the crash tried to push police and rescuers away.

Police said the speedometer on the wrecked Mercedes-Benz sedan was found frozen at 196 kilometres an hour after Sunday's accident, which also killed Diana's millionaire boyfriend and driver Henri Paul.

In a statement, prosecutors said blood tests on Paul showed he had an illegal blood-alcohol level. They did not give the level, but a judicial source said it was 1.75 grams of alcohol per litre of blood or 0.175 per cent, which would be more than double the 0.08-per cent level which determines impairment in Canada.

Under French law, exceeding 0.5 grams is considered a misdemeanor, while a 0.8 level is considered a greater offence. France's law is one of the strictest in Europe.

Stuns World
Photographers Declared Suspects

PARIS (CP) —

A French judge declared seven paparazzi to be manslaughter suspects Tuesday in the death of Diana, Princess of Wales – including one photographer said to have reached into the wreck car and took the dying princess's pulse.

Judge Herve Stephan placed all seven photographers under formal investigation for involuntary homicide – the French equivalent of manslaughter – and failing to come to the aid of Diana and three others as they lay trapped in the wreckage.

The court order means the photographers, arrested at the scene early Sunday, will be further investigated concerning their roles in the crash. It does not mean that they will necessarily be charged with any crimes.

Diana, her millionaire boyfriend Dodi Al Fayed and the driver were killed in the crash. A bodyguard, Trevor Rees-Jones, survived.

Rees-Jones was reported out of danger Tuesday, but his face was crushed and it could be weeks

21:50:34 24H
30-8-97

(AP Photo/APTV)

Britain's Diana, Princess of Wales, arrives at the Ritz Hotel in Paris Saturday, Aug. 30, 1997 in this picture made from a security video. Just hours later, the Princess along with her boyfriend Dodi Al Fayed and their chauffeur died from injuries sustained in a car crash in Paris in the early hours of Sunday morning Aug. 31. Princess Diana's funeral will take place at London's Westminster Abbey on Saturday.

before he could speak to investigators, said Georges Kiejman, a lawyer for the Al Fayed family.

Fresh disclosures pointed at a combination of deadly factors in the accident, including the apparently drunken condition of the car's driver – a Fayed employee.

A Paris newspaper reported

chauffeur Henri Paul's blood alcohol level may have been almost four times the legal limit at the time of the crash – higher than originally believed.

Five of the seven arrested photographers – Nikola Arsov, of the Sipa agency; Jacques Langevin, of the Sygma agency; Laslo Veres, a

freelancer; Stephane Darmon, of the Gamma agency; and Serge Arnal, of the Stills agency – were freed on their own recognizance.

The others – Romuald Rat, of Gamma, and Christian Martinzez, of the Angeli agency – were released on $16,000 bail and forbidden to work as photojournalists while the case is pending.

Police accuse Rat of obstructing the first officers on the scene.

Rat's lawyer, Philippe Benamou, argued that his client merely checked Diana's pulse when he was taking pictures of the wreckage.

"He took Diana's pulse. He wanted to see if she was dead or alive," the lawyer said. "He saw that she was alive, and police were arriving at the same time. It happened so quickly."

A U.S. tourist who passed by the accident scene in a taxi, however, contradicted that claim. Jack Firestone, a 42-year-old tourist from Hewlett Harbor, N.Y., said photographers swarmed the wreckage and snapped pictures like "sharks after raw meat" as Paris police stood by.

PRINCES MAKE FINAL TRIP HOME WITH THEIR MOTHER

SEPTEMBER 6, 1997, LONDON (CP) – The poise and poignancy of Diana's sons briefly lifted the pall over Britain, while the Queen urged mourners to use the Princess of Wales' funeral to unite behind the memory of her former daughter-in-law.

Prince Harry, all of 12 years old, found himself spontaneously clutched in an embrace by a teary admirer outside his mother's home.

"We love you," the woman said, as Harry returned the embrace with on arm and clasped the gift of a white lily in the other.

"Thank you so much for coming," he told her.

Harry, his brother Prince William, 15, and their father Prince Charles went straight to Diana's residence at Kensington Palace upon arrival from Balmoral, Scotland.

Flood of calls prompts City Hall to make provision for people wanting to honor memory of princess killed in weekend crash

PENTICTON — That Diana, Princess of Wales, touched the lives of many in Penticton was made clear by an avalanche of calls to City Hall Tuesday.

"We just had so many inquiries right off the bat Tuesday morning for people wanting to know where they could put flowers," said Cathy Ingram, clerk-secretary at Penticton City Hall.

"People are leaving flowers, candles, cards, etc. at the base of the Canadian flag outside City Hall," said Ingram.

"We've got candles, cards and flowers out there right now." Receptionist Denise Kurtz, fielded calls throughout the day from people wanting to know how to pay their respects to the royal family.

In response, the city has set up a desk and a book of condolences in the foyer at City Hall where Pentictonites can sign their names and add a short message. By ____ Tuesday, almost 60 names appeared in the small book.

The book ____ ____ ____ ____ til Sept. 12, will be sent to th ____

Vernon Remembers A Princess

VERNON – It was a scene that has been played out throughout Europe.

People gathering to bid farewell to a princess through flowers, notes and private thoughts.

Even though Vernon is on the other side of the globe from England, people still came to the steps of City Hall to pay tribute to Princess Diana during an hour-long ceremony Friday.

The memorial service was organized by local residents Eileen Foster and Peter Hill. Mourners left flowers and notes and gave their speeches at the open microphone.

"The murmur has been going on since she died," said Foster. "People have wanted a place to go. It shows she was loved not just in Britain."

Goodbye Diana

KELOWNA — A memorial service for Diana, Princess of Wales, will be held today in the same Kelowna park where she first won the city's heart.

The 10 a.m. tribute at the cenotaph in City Park provides a chance for Kelowna residents to join together and publicly express their sorrow over Diana's death, organizers say.

"There seems to be a lot of grassroots, heartfelt emotion out there. People feel like they've lost a friend, but they haven't had any way to show what they're feeling," Jim Shackleton, president of the Kelowna branch of the Royal Canadian Legion, said yesterday.

"We thought that holding a service like this would give people the opportunity to pay their respect, and maybe begin to come to terms with the death of such a great public figure," Shackleton said.

While British embassies and consulates in bigger cities have been besieged with mourners dropping off flowers and cards, there isn't that kind of outlet for residents of the Okanagan, Shackleton noted.

As a result, some people here have felt themselves at a loss, wondering how they could share in the worldwide outpouring of grief at the Princess' death in a Paris car crash last Saturday.

Leafs Unload More Salaries

Veteran players change uniforms at NHL trade deadline

By The Canadian Press

The Toronto Maple Leafs dumped two veterans with big salaries at the NHL trading deadline Tuesday, trading away Kirk Muller and Larry Murphy as part of their rebuilding.

Muller was sent to Florida for young right-winger Jason Podollan while Murphy, who had fallen out of favor with the fans, was traded to Detroit for future considerations.

"As far as we're concerned, this is the start of the 1997-98 season for us tomorrow," said Toronto GM Cliff Fletcher. "We're going to prepare and get the team ready so next year there's no repeat of our start this year."

Canadian teams were among the busiest at the deadline, with salaries playing a part in some of the moves. Edmonton and Calgary both traded away hefty contracts, with the Oilers dealing veteran defenceman Jeff Norton to Tampa Bay and the Flames sending centre Robert Reichel to the New York Islanders.

In all, there were 18 trades (one less than the 1995 record) involving a record-tying 35 players (the same as 1994).

Some of the top teams weren't involved. Colorado, Dallas, and New Jersey were all silent on the day. And Philadelphia only managed to pick up defenceman Frantisek Kucera from Vancouver for future considerations.

The Montreal Canadiens were also active, shipping defenceman Murray Baron and tough guy Chris Murray to the Phoenix Coyotes for rugged defenceman Dave Manson. Phoenix promptly sent Murray to Hartford for defenceman Gerald Diduck.

"I was happy with the team before, but with Dave Manson we're even happier," Montreal GM Rejean Houle said.

At $2 million US this season, Reichel was Calgary's second-most expensive player after Theo Fleury. But he only ranked fifth in team scoring with 16 goals and 27 assists.

In exchange, the Flames got left-winger Marty McInnis, who at 20 goals and 22 assists has just one point less than Reichel but makes only $550,000. Calgary also got junior goaltender Tyrone Garner (Oshawa, OHL) and a sixth-round pick. Having picked up Reichel, the Isles then sent Derek King, their second-leading scorer with 23 goals and 30 assists, to Hartford for a fifth-round draft pick this year.

Toronto didn't pull the trigger on a deal involving goalie Felix Potvin. And the Leafs elected to keep fan favorite Wendel Clark, turning down a first-round draft pick for the 30-year-old former captain.

"Wendel's a marquee player," Fletcher said. "This is the National Hockey League. You have to have marquee players."

But Fletcher has had no problem dumping marquee salaries. The Leafs, who traded captain Doug Gilmour to New Jersey late last month, have now unloaded three of their top five salaries.

Amelia Earhart's Flight Re-Enacted

Texas business woman sets out to fly around the world commemorating Amelia Earhart's famous last flight

OAKLAND, CALIF.
(REUTER) –

Sixty years after legendary aviator Amelia Earhart disappeared while flying around the world, a Texas business woman set out Monday to complete the journey in an almost identical plane.

Hundreds of schoolchildren and well-wishers waved and cheered as Linda Finch's gleaming 1935 Lockheed Electra 10E lifted off from the same Oakland airfield where Earhart took off 60 years earlier on her first attempt to fly around the world.

The plane, painstakingly restored to resemble Earhart's slowly circled the airport in the clear blue skies and several times flew low over the crowd before Finch steered the plane south on the short first leg to Burbank, Calif.

After that, Finch will pilot the Electra across the United States, South America, Africa, Europe and Asia before her scheduled return to Oakland on May 22. She will make more than 30 stops during the 50,000-kilometre trip which follows a route similar to the one planned for Earhart.

"I'm having a great day. This is wonderfully exciting," said Finch, a 46-year-old businesswoman from San Antonio.

Finch's $4.5-million World Flight 1997 project coincides with the centenary of the birth of Earhart, who became a household name with her daring aviation feats, including becoming the first woman to fly solo across the Atlantic in 1932 and many other record flights.

Earhart's first around-the-world flight attempt, begun March 17, 1937, was abandoned after the plane was damaged at the start of the second leg.

On May 20, 1937, Earhart left Oakland again. She and navigator Fred Noonan disappeared July 2, 1937 on the leg from Lae, New Guinea, to Howland Island in the Pacific Ocean.

No trace of her plane was found, despite a long search. What happened to her is an enduring mystery and spawned numerous theories.

Despite the tragic end of Earhart's flight, Finch said she had no fear about her journey. Several different navigators will fly with her on different legs of the journey.

"World Flight will remind the world of Amelia's life and her values, that you do not have to live a small life, that limitations come from within and we alone have the power to release ourselves from the limitations that we set," Finch told the crowd before takeoff.

The Electra 10E is one of only two in existence. When Finch bought it, it was in boxes with many parts missing. She and her team worked painstakingly to rebuild it. The Electra was powered by two Pratt and Whitney Wasp engines, which were the same type used by Earhart.

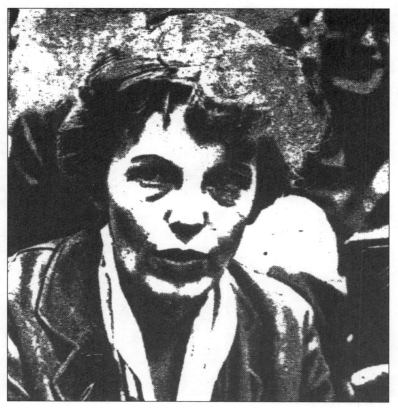

Amelia Earhart

Mother Teresa Dies

CALCUTTA, INDIA (CP) — Mother Teresa, a Roman Catholic nun whose name became synonymous with charity for her work with "the poorest of the poor," died Friday. She was 98.

Her successor, Sister Nirmala, said Mother Teresa died of a heart attack Friday evening at her convent in Calcutta.

Mother Teresa's doctor in Rome, Vincenzo Bilotta, said nuns in Calcutta telephoned him with the news.

"Her heart, which held up for all those years, suddenly gave way," Bilotta said.

She will be buried Wednesday in her religious order's headquarters

in Calcutta, Indian authorities said.

"Mother will be buried in Mother's House on September 10," a senior police officer said today. Mother Teresa said on September 10, 1946, while travelling to the Himalayan region Darjeeling, she received a message from God to devote herself to the poor. Her order celebrates the "inspiration" every year on September 10.

Her body will be kept at St. Thomas Church of Loreto Day School in Middleton Row in southern Calcutta from Sunday to September 10, for public viewing, City Police commissioner Dinesh Bajpai said.

Outside the nun's home at her Missionaries of Charity headquar-

ters in a poor central Calcutta neighborhood, hundreds of people gathered in the rain as news of the death of Calcutta's most famous personality spread. Many of them were weeping.

"I cannot breathe," Mother Teresa told a doctor before slumping in her bed, said Sunita Kumar, a close friend of the nun.

Mother Teresa complained of pain in her back early in the evening after she had eaten soup and toast for dinner and finished her prayers. A doctor was called from a nearby hospital.

When many poor people living on the streets outside the charity saw the doctor, they began to mill outside the building.

Mother Teresa

Trans Canada Trail More Than Just Trestles

By Rob Munro
Daily Courier Staff

Restoring the trestles in Myra Canyon was just the start of trail building for Murray Swan.

The Kelowna man was recently elected chairman of the Okanagan Regional Council for Trails B.C. in its efforts to create the Trans Canada Trail by June 21, 2000.

"It's like any volunteer effort - you get a little bit interested then, all of a sudden, you're very involved," Swan said. "You get pulled right into it."

About three months ago, he was asked to join the council as a representative of the Myra Canyon Trestle Restoration Society and ended up becoming chairman of the new group.

The trestle society was formed in 1993 to repair the 18 trestles on the old Kettle Valley railbed in the hills south of Kelowna.

They had deteriorated to the point they were considered a danger to the public.

Decking was replaced and railings installed because a number of people have fallen off and been killed or seriously injured. In 1994, Carol Faye Fingler died in a fall from one of the trestles.

Work on the trestle project wrapped up in the fall of 1995.

"We had great success in getting people interested and using their skills very quickly," Swan said. "But we have to be careful here (with the Trans Canada Trail). We don't want to get peo-

ple stirred up too early."

The Okanagan council has just been formed and will spend the next few months getting organized and setting priorities.

The Trans Canada Trail is being developed from St. Johns, Nfld. to Victoria as a recreational corridor, not strictly a hiking trail.

That means parts will be wheelchair accessible, suitable for cycling, horseback riding and snowmobiling in the winter.

"I had to adjust my own notions of things for the Trans Canada Trail," Swan said, noting he likes mountain biking and wilderness hiking.

His region stretches from Midway to Brookmere (near the Coquihalla Highway).

The trail will be along the old KVR railbed that was completed in 1906 but abandoned a few decades later because of the high cost of operation through dangerous mountain passes.

The rails were removed in the 1980s and vandals ripped up parts of the wooden trestles over gaping canyons.

Parts of the rail line, like Myra Canyon, are complete and have been dedicated as part of the trail. But there's a tremendous amount of work to do on other parts of the line. Although the provincial government owns much of the rail line, most of it still hasn't been designated for a trail and parts are used as roadways or farms.

1990–1999

New Test Could Detect HIV Almost Immediately

TORONTO (CP) —

Researchers have found a revolutionary new way to detect HIV infection which they say could dramatically speed up diagnosis of the killer disease.

"This is very exciting news," said Dr. David Phipps, a post-doctoral fellow at the Toronto Hospital, who made the discovery along with Dr. Donald Branch, staff scientist at the hospital and at the Canadian Red Cross.

Results of their research were published in the November issue of the medical journal Blood.

In a development that could significantly improve the safety of donated blood, they found that an enzyme called fyn kinase is switched on in HIV-infected patients in as little as 30 minutes following infection.

"We expect that this marker could lead to new, early-diagnostic methods for HIV," said Phipps.

With current HIV tests, there's a substantial lag-time between infection and the time when the virus is detected in the blood.

This lag-time, lasting between six weeks and six months, means someone unknowingly infected with HIV could become a blood donor and the virus would escape detection.

It's estimated that one unit of blood out of every 913,000 taken in Canada is tainted with HIV because of that window period.

"We are currently conducting more studies, but our early work shows that this test could actually replace current testing for HIV," said Branch.

Y2K Bug May Cause Crisis For Canadian Hospitals

By Jane Coutts
The Globe and Mail

Imagine this scenario: It's midnight, Dec. 31, 1999.

But in hospitals across the country, it's not the sound of New Year's bells that rings out; it's a clamor of competing alarms as medical equipment, from respirators to heart monitors.

All go flat line at once.

Not much of a New Year's celebration for the patients depending on that equipment to stay alive, but some people feel Canadian hospitals are so far behind in dealing with the so-called year-2000 problem that a crisis, instead of a party, could be looming.

The problem lies deep in the bowels of modern medical equipment. Almost all those pulsing, beeping, flashing pieces of machinery that hospitals and patients depend on use microchips.

This embedded technology may have any number of functions in the machine, but if, as is usually the case, it also has a built-in calendar, then hospitals run the risk of the equipment pooping the party on New Year's, 1999.

That's because for years, to save precious memory space, computers were designed to show the date with just the last two numbers of the year.

"If the chip is there to prompt regular maintenance, then what it's going to read at one minute after midnight on Jan. 1, 2000, is that this machine hasn't had maintenance since 1900 and it's going to shut it down," said Scott Rowand, president and CEO of the Hamilton Hospital Corp.

While the newest equipment is built with calenders that can handle the turn of the century, many hospitals are still using older machines.

Ice Storm Aftermath

OPRAH ON HOT SEAT

AMARILLO, TEXAS (AP) —
Oprah Winfrey is on the spot in cattle country, accused of taking a bite out of beef by falsely spreading the word that American meat could cause mad cow disease in the United States.

Jury selection in the federal defamation trial was to begin today in Amarillo, home to majestic ranches, pungent feedyards and real cowboys.

Cattle producers who sued Winfrey would appear to have a definite home-field advantage in a town whose largest private employer is a slaughterhouse..

But the queen of television talk has the advantage of celebrity.

"There's push and pull on both sides," said Bobby Lee, co-owner of the Big Texan Steak Ranch in Amarillo. Cattle feeder Paul Engler is suing Winfrey and vegetarian activist Howard Lyman over comments they made about beef safety on her April 16, 1996, show.

During the show, Lyman said feeding ground-up animal parts to cattle, a practice that was banned in the United States last summer, could spread mad cow disease to humans in the United States. To applause from the studio audience, Winfrey exclaimed: "It has just stopped me from eating another burger!"

After the broadcast, already slumping cattle prices fell to some of their lowest levels in a decade, and Engler claimed he lost $6.7 million. He and other plaintiffs who later joined the suit are seeking to recoup total losses of more than $12 million, plus other, unspecified damages.

MONTREAL (CP) —

Hydro-Quebec is recommending that $650 million be spent to bolster its battered power distribution network after it was crippled by a vicious ice storm almost three weeks ago.

"I presume that people in the last years thought that the network as it stands was perfectly secure," Premier Lucien Bouchard said at a briefing on the situation Wednesday evening.

Hydro said it wants to add several high-powered links whose new lines would create loops to transmit a supply of continuous power to areas that were hit by outages in the current crisis.

It also wants to strengthen its transmission towers by using tubular pylons which would make them less susceptible to collapse. About 900 pylons went down in this month's storm along with 128 transmission lines.

Bouchard said the utility would like to get the work done by next winter but because of environmental impact studies and technical considerations, it could take 18 months.

About 1.4 million households – about three million people – were blacked out at the peak of the crisis, which began on the night of

(CP PHOTO)

A volunteer holding a chain saw watches a truck unload wood to be cut and piled in Quebec City, before it is sent to the Montreal region. Last week's ice storm which cut power to over three million people has led a cable television station, Telemag 24, to organize the delivery of one thousand cords of wood.

Jan. 5 with a vicious storm that coated trees and power lines with ice, causing them to crash to the ground.

About 190,000 of those households – 450,000 people – remained without power on Wednesday.

There will still be about 70,000 households without power when the bulk of Hydro-Quebec's repair work to its battered network is done next Sunday.

The fragility of the public utility's power network was emphasized Wednesday when 12,000

households lost their electricity again.

The outage occurred in four south-shore communities because of problems at a power-distribution centre.

Hydro officials acknowledged Wednesday that despite all the work that's been done, the utility's network is still fragile.

More than 14,000 Canadian Forces troops were mobilized to help relief efforts in Quebec and eastern Ontario that were hit by the storms, which also blasted parts of the Maritimes.

New Beetle Bugged

Volkswagen eases pain with cash

DETROIT (AP) —

The Bugs have a bug, but cash and a courtesy phone call could ease the bother of a recall of 10,100 New Beetle buyers in Canada and the United States. Volkswagen said Friday it needs to fix a wiring problem that could cause engine fires in all the New Beetles it has sold since March, when it reintroduced the car to the North American market for

the first time in 19 years. VW said no accidents or injuries have resulted from the problem.

The German automaker said it will give dealers up to $100 for New Beetle owners for car washes, gas, a flower in the new Beetle bud vase or other perks - all in an effort to sat-

isfy inconvenienced owners and help the new Bug avoid the old Beetle's reputation as a tin can.

It has sold 8,500 of the cars in the United States and an addi-

tional 1,600 in Canada. A company spokesman said the steps are needed because the New Beetle has received more attention and created more excitement than any car in years in the the U.S. market, as drivers wait for months on lists that are dozens of people deep to get their shot at buying the car.

"It's a real emotional purchase for these people," VW spokesman Steve Keyes said. "It's almost like a member of the family for them."

1990~1999

Tributes Pour In For The Man Who Always Did It 'His Way'

LOS ANGELES (REUTERS) — Presidents, prime ministers, entertainers and friends paid homage to Frank Sinatra Friday along with others moved by his ballads and the idea of doing it "my way."

Sinatra died of a heart attack Thursday night in Los Angeles. He was 82.

One of the most heartfelt tributes came from his third wife, Mia Farrow, who said in a statement: "Frank was the first love of my life and he remained a true friend, always there when I needed him. I will miss him more than words

can say."

French actress Jeanne Moreau said Sinatra would now "sing with the angels."

U.S. President Bill Clinton, who's attending the economic summit in Birmingham, England, praised Sinatra.

"I had the opportunity after I became president to get to know him a little, to have dinner with him, to appreciate on a personal level what hundreds of millions of people around the world, including me, had appreciated from afar. I think every American would have to smile and say he really

did do it his way."

Actor Ernest Borgnine, filming on location in Shamrock, Tex., said he learned of Sinatra's death in a telephone call from his wife Tova, who told him, "Your friend has died."

"It's pretty hard because, you know, we loved each other … The world has lost a hell of a man," Borgnine said.

Sinatra won an Oscar as best supporting actor for From Here to Eternity.

The area near Genoa, on Italy's north-western riviera where Sinatra's mother, Natalina

Garaventa, was born, sent its condolences to his family.

Fans honored Sinatra's memory by placing flowers on his three stars on the Hollywood Walk of Fame – one each for music, film and television – and lighting candles.

Frank Sinatra

Sinatra's Style

NEW YORK (AP) — Never yawn in front of a lady. Top your martini with two olives and give one to a friend. Make sure your trousers break just above the shoes.

Like the rock stars who knocked him temporarily off the charts, Frank Sinatra didn't just perform his songs, he lived them. Around swinging standards and lonely ballads, he arranged a brash philosophy and an intricate set of codes and rituals.

"He believed in lecturing to others about how things should be done," said Bill Zehme, author of The Way You Wear Your Hat, an informal biography and compilation of stories about Sinatra and his way of life. "He wanted people to live up to his standards of class and elegance."

The Sinatra style was in the details.

Some examples:

– Cock your hat – angles are attitudes.

– Don't put on a brown suit at night – wear dark grey. Better yet, wear black.

– If black tie is optional, wear it. Except on Sunday. Never wear a tux on Sunday.

"I am," Sinatra once said, "a thing of beauty." He owned more than a hundred suits and didn't want anyone ruining them, like the old man who grabbed his arm at the 1956 Democratic national convention.

"Take your hand off the suit, creep!" the singer is reported to have snapped, not realizing (or caring) he was talking to Sam Rayburn, Speaker of the House of Representatives.

Sinatra had it all thought out: Tip big and tip quietly – fold the bills three times into small squares and pass them in a handshake; let the ice sink in your glass so the flavors will blend; never drink a drink immediately after it's poured; better a carton of milk than a serving of warm vodka.

Women: When Sinatra dies, Dean Martin once joked, they're going to leave his zipper with the Smithsonian Institution. The Chairman liked sex, but he also cared

about style. No miniskirts. Forget about topless. He admired poise, restraint, class. He hated chain smokers and too much perfume. He couldn't stand being nagged.

"Fun with everything" was one of his mottos, like in 1955 when he and his pals – Humphrey Bogart and Lauren Bacall, Judy Garland and David Niven – spent four days in Las Vegas, where they did just about everything but sleep. On Day 5, with all but Sinatra feeling like they had fallen out of an airplane, Bacall checked out the survivors and a gang was born: "You look like a … rat pack!"

The Rat Pack was Bogart's, but when he died Frank took over. Frank brought in Dean, Joey, Sammy and whoever else might drop by the steam room at the Sands Hotel. They wore monogrammed robes – FAS (Sinatra), DAG (Martin), SON OF A GUN (Bishop) – and spoke their own language. Endsville. Scramsville. A "bunter" was a drag. A "gasser" wasn't. Don't even ask what it meant to lose your "bird."

Of all the Rat Pack stories, the best ones usually involved Martin, the laid-back "Abruzzese" Sinatra always wanted to be, the guy who could tell Frank where to go and live to tell about it.

There was the night in the mid-1960s when the Martins had everyone over for their anniversary. They had an orchestra and white-coated bartenders. By 11 o'clock, however, DAG was missing and the cops had arrived, say-

ing there had been a complaint about the noise. Sinatra couldn't figure it out. All the neighbors where at the party. Who could have done it?

The call, he was told, came from inside the house.

Sinatra headed straight for the master bedroom.

"Did you call the cops on your own party?" he said to Martin, whom he found lying in bed, holding a golf club, watching television.

Martin: "Hey, they ate, they drank. Let them go home. I gotta get up in the morning."

"You," answered Sinatra, paying the ultimate compliment, "are one crazy bastard."

Sinatra believed in God. But death, the Big Casino, left him speechless. For days, Sinatra couldn't talk after the death of his mother, killed when the plane he hired for her crashed into a mountain. On the phone with a dying Sammy Davis Jr., the two old friends simply held onto their receivers, grieving beyond words.

He thought you should live every moment as if it were your last, that too much thinking wasn't good for a man. He fought for his privacy, but he hated being alone. Anything but boredom, especially after hours.

"You only live once," he liked to say, "and the way I live once is enough."

Sinatra with Grace Kelly and Bing Crosby

Supreme Court Orders New Trial In AIDS Case

OTTAWA (CP) —

Henry Cuerrier's failure to tell his lovers that he had the AIDS virus amounts to fraud, the Supreme Court of Canada ruled Thursday as it overturned his acquittal and ordered a new trial.

The decision sets a legal precedent for how AIDS cases should be dealt with under the Criminal Code.

The court found that Cuerrier, of Squamish, B.C., acted not only reprehensibly, but criminally as well.

Cuerrier will now go to trial for a second time on charges of aggravated assault after the court found his failure to disclose his condition nullified sexual consent.

"Without disclosure of HIV stats, there cannot be true consent," wrote Justice Peter Cory.

The court overturned the rulings of two B.C. courts that found no assault took place because the women had consented to having sex.

"In my view, it should now be taken that for the accused to conceal or fail to disclose that he is HIV positive can constitute fraud which might vitiate consent to sexual intercourse," said Cory, writing for the majority of judges.

Discoverers Of Viagra Principle Win Nobel Prize

Trio of American scientists to share $978,000 U.S. prize

STOCKHOLM (REUTERS) —

Three U.S. scientists whose discoveries led to the use of the Viagra anti-impotence drug won the 1998 Nobel Prize for Medicine on Monday.

Robert Furchgott, Ferid Murad and Louis Ignarro were awarded the $978,000 US prize jointly for their discoveries about the role of nitric oxide – long considered just an air pollutant – as a single molecule in the cardiovascular system.

The discovery has applications for the treatment of cardiovascular disease, shock and possibly cancer, as well as impotence, said Sweden's Karolinski Institute, which awards the annual prize, one of the most prestigious in medicine.

Joint winner Furchgott, 82, said in New York he was "somewhat surprised" and had no plans yet on what to do with his share of the prize money.

Nitric oxide is a gas that transmits signals in an organism, allowing messages to be sent from one part of the body to another, and regulates blood pressure and blood flow.

Furchgott, 82, a pharmacologist at the State University of New York (SUNY) in Brooklyn, established in 1980 that blood vessels dilate, or become wider, because their surface cells – the endothelium – produce an unknown signal molecule that makes their smooth muscle cells relax.

Furchgott's "ingenious experiment" led to a quest to identify the factor, the institute said.

Murad, 62, now a pharmacologist at the University of Texas Medical School in Houston, analyzed how nitroglycerin and similar substances affect vessels, and discovered in 1977 that they release nitric oxide, which relaxes smooth muscle cells.

Ignarro, 57, and now a pharmacologist at the University of California Los Angeles (UCLA) School of Medicine, participated in the quest for the unknown signal molecule posited by Furchgott, and in a brilliant series of analyses, independently and with Furchgott, concluded it was nitric oxide.

"He (Ignarro) discovered the principle which led to the use of Viagra as an anti-impotence drug," said Sten Orrenius, professor of toxicology at the Karolinska Institute.

Viagra, the product of research into cardiovascular disease, counters impotence by dilating the blood vessels in the penis.

ATLANTA BOMBINGS

Public help sought to track down fugitive blamed for three blasts

OCTOBER 15, 1998. Washington (AP) — Police asked for the public's help Wednesday in tracking down Eric Robert Rudolph, a fugitive who now has been charged with the 1996 bombing at the Olympics as well as two other Atlanta attacks.

U.S. Attorney General Janet Reno told a news conference the complaint charging Rudolph with the Olympic blast and the 1997 bombings of a gay bar and an abortion clinic in Atlanta had been filed with a federal court.

New evidence against him was kept sealed to protect "the safety of witnesses who have come forward," she said.

Two people died and scores were injured by the six bombs Rudolph is charged with planting.

"Eric Rudolph is on the run" from earlier charges that he bombed a Birmingham, Ala., abortion clinic Jan. 29, Reno said. "We're not going to rest until we bring him to justice."

"We hope anyone who sees this man will contact us immediately," Reno said.

For nine months, hundreds of FBI and state and local agents have futilely searched rugged, mountainous wilderness in western North Carolina where the 31-year-old carpenter and experienced woodsman grew up.

U.S. Border Crackdown Pushed Back 30 Months

OCTOBER 8, 1998. Washington (CP) — Canadians won't have to worry about a crackdown along the American border until 2001 after the U.S. Congress agreed Wednesday to delay a tough new law for 30 months.

"I think many western New Yorkers and businesses are breathing a collective sigh of relief," congressman Jack Quinn said Wednesday.

His district includes Buffalo, which would have become one of several cross-border bottlenecks had the law, known as Section 110, been implemented.

Repeal of Section 110 has been the top item on the Canadian agenda of bilateral relations for more than two years.

"We're very confident we will get a permanent delay in the implementation of the bill," said Canadian Embassy spokesman Rodney Moore.

Canadian Ambassador Raymond Chretien has spent much of his time over the last several months lobbying members of Congress and working with business groups with operations on both sides of the border.

Opponents of the law have predicted border chaos if it ever is enforced.

1990~1999

SwissAir Jetliner Crashes Into Sea Off Nova Scotia

BLANDFORD, N.S. (CP) — Rescue crews were searching the ocean early today for a SwissAir jet carrying 227 passengers and crew that crashed near this tiny fishing village.

The MD11 jet, en route from New York to Zurich, was attempting an emergency landing at Halifax airport but did not make it that far, said Andre Ereau of search and rescue in Halifax.

The pilot of Swiss Air Flight 111 reported smoke from the cabin shortly before losing contact with the air traffic control tower in Moncton, N.B. The plane disappeared off the radar screen about 10:30 p.m. ADT Wednesday.

An airport worker said the pilot dumped 108 tonnes of fuel over nearby St. Margaret's Bay.

There was no immediate word on survivors, though there were unconfirmed reports of debris and an oil slick in the water.

Five searchlights, from helicopters and vessels on the water, could be seen from shore. Rescue crews were scouring an area about seven nautical miles off Peggy's Cove on Nova Scotia's South Shore.

Dozens of ambulances and fire trucks were gathered along the coastline while hundreds of residents crowded the shore road. A Hercules aircraft and two Labrador helicopters were leading the search.

Witnesses reported hearing sputtering sounds before a thunderous crash.

"It wasn't the smooth sound of an airplane," said Alberta Martin. "I heard the crash (and) a clap of thunder shook the house."

"The motors were still going when the plane flew over, but it was the worst-sounding deep groan that I've ever heard," said Claudia Zinck-Gilroy.

The weather was overcast, with a light sprinkle of rain and calm seas.

Transport Canada was setting up an emergency centre at Halifax International Airport.

"They are mobilizing fishing boats and anything to head out," said Eleanor McMahon, vacationing in the Blandford area.

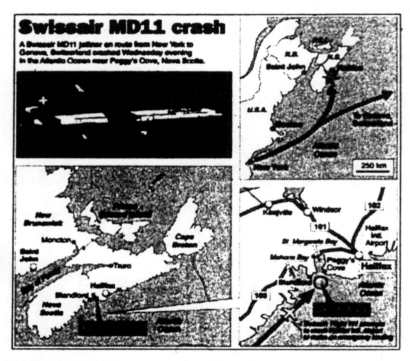

A SwissAir MD11 jetliner en route from New York to Geneva, Switzerland crashed Wednesday evening in the Atlantic Ocean near Peggy's Cove, Nova Scotia.

Police Sift Through Debris For Clues

PEGGY'S COVE, N.S. — The visitors from Europe and the United States who will journey to Peggy's Cove today will not take home the care-free memories of thousands of tourists who are typically drawn to this picturesque fishing village.

These new arrivals will be family and friends whose lives are intertwined with the 229 passengers and crew members who died in the crash of SwissAir Flight 111 on Wednesday night.

Rescue efforts continued throughout the night with officials stubbornly clinging to the hope that there still could be survivors in the fairly warm and calm seas.

"Our assessment with the weather and sea temperature is that people could actually survive," said Lt.-Cmdr. Jacques Fauteux of the Halifax rescue co-ordination centre.

"You know and I know that time is running out … but there's probably one thing you're probably not factoring and it's called sheer will power. Sometimes scientific figures don't work when you have will power."

But the harsh reality as searchers moved through the second night since the crash was there's virtually no chance of finding anyone alive among the small bits of debris floating on the surface.

A low-pressure system ahead of Hurricane Earl is expected to bring showers, then steady rain today.

Benoit Bouchard, chairman of the National Transportation Safety Board, flew over the crash site Thursday and was struck by the devastation.

In addition to bits of the fuselage, sad remnants of lost lives floated by. Children's toys, baby bottles, wallets, pieces of clothing and shoes hung quietly in the debris field.

Officials were refusing to give a body count on Thursday night, although it was known that at least 36 bodies had been recovered by the afternoon. There were also reports that officials had dozens of body bags.

One RCMP official indicated as many as 60 bodies had been recovered.

"It's impossible to be accurate about the number of bodies recovered at this time. I refuse to be more graphic," said Lt.-Cmdr. Glenn Chamberlain.

"It's a very grisly scene out there."

The difficulty in getting an exact number on the body count was hampered by the many body parts rescuers were picking up.

Keith Anderson, the maritime regional director of the Canadian Air Traffic Assoc., said Thursday the pilot of the doomed jetliner communicated several times with the control centre in Moncton, N.B., before the crash.

"The initial call was to report smoke in the cockpit and the captain indicated an abnormal situation," Anderson said of the centre that handles transatlantic flights in the region.

"He used the term PAN which implies an emergency situation, but not a desperate situation."

Anderson said the SwissAir captain asked for and was given clearance to Boston. However, he was advised that Halifax was closer and decided to go there instead.

There were unanswered questions why an airport in Yarmouth, N.S., which is closer to the site of the crash, was not recommended.

The pilot swung out over the ocean and began emptying his tanks because he was too heavy to land at the Halifax airport. Moments later, the plane went down in 20 metres of water over Inner Rock Shoal with an impact heard by locals along the south shore.

Search For Survivors Is Over

SwissAir Flight 111 Rescuers give up hope, crash investigation moves into gear

PEGGY'S COVE, N.S. (CP) —

The pilot heading the investigation into the Flight 111 disaster defended the actions of the cockpit crew Friday, saying the conversation with air traffic controllers was professional in the final moments before the jetliner plunged into the ocean.

Vic Gerden, lead investigator from the National Transportation Safety Board, began his remarks on the probe into Wednesday's crash that killed 229 people by chastising the media for what he called inaccurate reports of the pilot's last words.

Contrary to some reports "promulgated in the media," Gerden said the conversation was professional at all times. Until a transcript is released today, he urged people not to manufacture remarks.

He told a testy news conference crowd he would not speculate on what happened in the jet's final moments.

"I don't deal in maybes, could haves and would haves," he said in careful, controlled tones.

"The crew indicated there was smoke in the cockpit. We don't have further indication of specific problems."

Investigators still don't have the telltale flight and voice recorders. Constant searching has turned up little more than fragments of the plane – the largest piece pulled out so far about the size of a kitchen tabletop.

Sonar probes beneath the choppy surface turned up no hints of where, or if, larger pieces of the Boeing MD-11 aircraft lie hidden on the bottom.

Gerden said the pilot reported a problem, suggested turning back to Boston, then accepted the controllers' alternative of Halifax. The plan descended, apparently made a turn to dump fuel. Then it crashed. Why? How? Where exactly? There were no answers.

Meanwhile, Nova Scotia's chief medical examiner told a news conference that many of the victims were killed on impact.

Dr. John Butt said the process of identifying the victims is slow, and no one has yet been identified. It will take X-rays and dental charts.

The rescue operation which criss-crossed the sea for 36 hours was officially abandoned as a vain effort. Rear Admiral Dusty Miller, head of the search and rescue operation, expressed regret over the failure to find anyone alive.

HMCS OKANAGAN AIDS IN SEARCH FOR PLANE'S BLACK BOX

SEPTEMBER 5, 1998. — The Canadian Forces submarine HMCS Okanagan put its retirement on hold to help search for SwissAir Flight 111's black box.

The sub - a source of pride in the valley for which it was named in 1968 - was one of three British Oberon class submarines commissioned.

The sub was supposed to conclude its service with a final sail-past Sept. 8 in the St. John's harbour.

Instead, it spent Friday using its sensitive sonar ears to listen fruitlessly for the telltale pingers attached to the flight and voice recorders of the aircraft.

The navy vowed to find the black boxes, which are key in any crash investigation.

Chain Of Errors May Have Led To Crash

SwissAir Flight 111

HALIFAX (CP) —

A chain of errors, rather than a single technical malfunction, likely caused the crash of SwissAir Flight 111, says an aviation safety expert.

Though the media and others focus on "the safety fix of the day" after air crashes, many things contribute to a disaster, says Roger Rozelle of the Flight Safety Federation in Alexandria, Va.

"Generally, the crew is overwhelmed by a series of events that finally lead them to a situation where they are unable to cope," Rozelle, the federation's director of publications, said in an interview.

The federation, established about 50 years ago to disseminate safety knowledge, calls itself the only group in the world committed totally to commercial aviation safety. Its members include most of the world's airlines and aircraft manufacturers.

Rozelle said aromatic polyimide wiring insulation that has come into question in the wake of the Sept. 2 crash off Peggy's Cove, N.S., deserves a look as the probe continues.

Observers have also fingered other pieces of equipment as unsafe, including the Mylar insulation blankets used on the SwissAir MD-11.

The pilots smelled and saw smoke in the cockpit in the minutes preceding the crash, and the main flight instruments were also affected.

"There obviously was a fire in a portion of the radio bay of the aircraft, and as a result of that fire, systems were shut down," Rozelle said.

1990~1999

Home Run History on Deck

McGwire could set new home run mark tonight against Cubs

ST. LOUIS (AP) —

No. 61 flew off Mark McGwire's bat Monday, matching Roger Maris' home run record and leaving just one question: How soon will it be his alone?

History came quickly. McGwire launched Mike Morgan's pitch 430 feet to left field in the first inning, tying the hallowed mark that has stood for 37 years.

McGwire immediately threw his hands in the air after connecting and then, with a fist thrust high, began his triumphant trip around the bases.

Big Mac got a high five from Cubs' first baseman Mark Grace as he rounded the bag and got another high five from former St. Louis teammate Gary Gaetti as he approached third.

The 50,530 roaring fans at Busch Stadium stood all the while, except for those in the midst of a wild scramble for the ball. Chicago's Sammy Sosa, whose 58 home runs have pushed McGwire down the stretch, joined the celebration by applauding his rival from right field.

McGwire's 10-year-old batboy son, Matt, was waiting at home plate where the Cardinals' slugger ended his trek with a two-footed hop. McGwire hoisted his boy in a big hug, while groundskeepers rushed onto the field to replace the bases - no doubt headed to the Hall of Fame.

The Cardinals spilled out of the dugout to mob McGwire and it took him a few moments to make it to the bench. But he didn't stay there long, springing back out to salute Sosa and the Maris family, watching from seats on the first-base side.

In a touching tribute to the man he matched, McGwire acknowledged Maris' children by pointing his right index finger to the sky, tapping his heart three times and blowing a kiss.

"He tapped his heart, like dad was in his heart," said Kevin Maris, a son of the former New York Yankees' slugger.

McGwire homered in the Cardinals' 144th game and now has 19 left to become the home run champion. And when he does, certainly no asterisk will be needed.

Maris hit No. 61 on the last day of a 162-game schedule in 1961. Toward the end of that season, Commissioner Ford Frick declared that any record would have to carry a "distinctive mark" if it did not beat Babe Ruth's mark of 60 in 154 games. In all, McGwire has

St. Louis Cardinals' Mark McGwire reacts to his 61st home run of the season to tie Roger Maris.

homered 15 times in the last 20 days. This latest one came at 2:22 p.m. EDT, with Canadians getting live updates from TSN and CBC.

McGwire finished 2444 in adding a later ground single - he has 53 singles this season, compared to 61 homers - while Sosa went 1-for-5 with a single. Sosa struck out with a runner on the third to end the game.

The landmark shot provided a nice present to McGwire's father, John. He was sitting in the stands celebrating his birthday - No. 61, naturally.

It also made it a nice day for Mike Davidson, a 28-year-old fan from St. Louis who wound up with the historic souvenir, which he planned to give to McGwire.

The Cardinals won 3-2, blunting the Cubs' bid to increase their lead in the NL wild-card race. Fittingly, all but one of the runs scored on homers, with Eli Marrero and Delino DeShields connecting for the Cardinals and Gaetti doing it for Chicago.

The two teams play again tonight, giving McGwire and Sosa another chance to highlight the greatest homer chase ever, topping even the race between Maris and Mickey Mantle in 1961. McGwire and Sosa have homered on the same day 20 times this year, twice connecting in the same game.

St. Louis Cardinals' Mark McGwire gets a hug from Chicago Cubs' Sammy Sosa, right, after Sosa reached first base on a single Monday in St. Louis. Earlier, McGwire tied Roger Maris' major league home run record of 61 homeruns.

Sosa slams pair, gets even with McGwire

CHICAGO (AP) —

Sammy Sosa passed Babe Ruth and Roger Maris, then caught up to Mark McGwire.

Sosa homered twice Sunday, tying McGwire at 62 and touching off one of Wrigley Field's most raucous celebrations ever.

Standing in the on-deck circle in the 10th with a chance for No. 63, Sosa watched Mark Grace hit a game-winning solo homer that gave the Cubs an 11-10 victory over Milwaukee, keeping Chicago one game ahead of the New York Mets in the National League wild-card race.

In a wild series, the Brewers won 13-11 Friday and the Cubs won 15-12 Saturday by scoring five runs in the ninth.

In this one, Chicago trailed 10-8 in the ninth before Sosa's long homer off Eric Plunk and Gary Gaetti's RBI single.

Sosa homered in all three games of the series. As Grace was mobbed by his teammates as he hit the plate with the winning run, the Cubs then turned and carried Sosa off the field on their shoulders.

McGwire answers back

ST LOUIS (AP) —

This time, Sammy Sosa's lead in the home run derby lasted only 45 minutes.

Mark McGwire answered Sosa's 66th homer with his 66th Friday night, a two-run shot in the fifth inning off Shayne Bennett in St.Louis's 6-5 victory over Montreal.

McGwire and Sosa have homered on the same day 21 times, and as usual, McGwire said it was just a coincidence.

"We don't have any control over it," McGwire said. "We get in the box and he has to battle, I have to battle. It's one of those things that's unexplainable, so let's leave it unexplainable."

Also as usual, McGwire reiterated that he didn't care who won the home run derby.

"What he and I have done, whoever's on top nobody should be disappointed," McGwire said. "How can you walk away disappointed if you walk away one below? You can't. It's impossible."

Rookie J.D. Drew had a pair of two-run homers for the Cardinals, who have won 10 of 12 to guarantee a winning record. But the focus was all on McGwire and the deadlocked home run derby, which has two games to go.

Manager Tony La Russa has stressed team performance all year, even after McGwire broke Roger Maris' record on Sept. 8.

Not any more.

"As far as I'm concerned, Mark McGwire's home run chase is the most important thing the next

two days," La Russa said. "It's like heresy for me to say it, but he deserves everything we've got behind him and he's going to get every little bit we do."

When Sosa took the lead in the home run derby for only the second time all season leading off the fourth at Houston, it prompted a collective groan from a sell-out crowd at Busch Stadium and booing when Sosa's home run number was changed on the scoreboard.

McGwire said he doesn't watch the scoreboard, but he was aware of it.

"Of course, how can you not?", McGwire said. "It's pretty obvious."

With a runner on first, two outs and the fans on their feet, McGwire brought back the cheers

when he hit a 1-2 pitch an estimated 375 feet into the left-field stands. It was McGwire's second homer this year against Montreal.

HOUSTON (AP) —

Neither Sammy Sosa or the Chicago Cubs wound up with the lead Friday night.

Sosa took a short-lived lead in the home run race by hitting No. 66, but Mark McGwire tied him less than an hour later. And Sosa's Chicago Cubs blew a chance to take the lead in the NL wildcard race by losing to the Houston Astros 6-2.

The loss left the Cubs tied with the New York Mets, who were beaten by Atlanta 6-4. San Francisco, which began the day one game behind Chicago and New York, playing later at Colorado.

McGwire ends record-smashing season at 70

ST. LOUIS (AP) -

An incredible 70 home runs! Even Mark McGwire couldn't believe it.

"I've, never even thought about it, dreamed about it," he said. "It's absolutely amazing! It blows me away!"

The St. Louis Cardinals' slugger ended his record-smashing season as mightily as he started it. He hit his 69th and 70th homers on the season's last day, - a fitting finale for a year he began with a grand slam on opening day.

"This is a season I will never, ever forget, and I hope everybody in baseball never forgets," McGwire told the cheering crowd after the game.

Big Mac, who hit five homers on the final weekend, connected against Montreal rookie Mike Thurman in the third inning Sunday, then homered off Carl Pavano for No. 70 in the seventh. McGwire moved four ahead of Sammy Sosa and ended nine- nine! - in front of Roger Maris's old record.

Sosa went 2-5 with no homers as the Cubs lost to Houston, 4-3, in 11 innings, but his season is not done.

The Cubs face San Francisco at Wrigley Field tonight in a one-game playoff for the wild-card spot.

"I wish him the best of luck, along with the Giants," McGwire said.

McGwire, who has 10 multi-homer games this year and 53 in his career, left many in awe.

McGwire hit a 1-1 fastball 377 feet into the left-field seats for No. 69. After stomping on home plate, he took a few slow steps, then made several salutes to the sellout crowd.

Kerry Woodson, a 22-year-old bodyshop worker from Maryland Heights, Mo., wound up with the ball and said he didn't know what he would do with it.

"I reached up, closed my eyes, and it landed in my glove," Woodson said.

With two on and two outs in the seventh, and the score 3-3, he connected off Pavano (6-9), lining a first-pitch fastball 370 feet over the left-field wall, sending the Cardinals on to a 6-3 win over the Expos.

This time, even a curtain call

from McGwire didn't quiet the 46,110 fans, who remained on their feet, cheering even as Brian Jordan took a called third strike for the third out of the inning.

McGwire said No. 70 felt almost like No. 62, the homer that broke Maris' record, with the crowd at fever pitch and Expos infielders shaking his hand as he rounded, the bases.

"What can I say?" McGwire said. "I'm speechless."

The second home-run ball landed in a party box and was snared by Phil Ozersky of Olivette, Mo., attending the game with a group of Washington University research lab scientists. He said he didn't know what he'd do with the ball, which is worth a lot of money on the collectibles' market.

Across town, the homer cost the Rams a five-yard penalty. A huge cheer spread through the Trans World Dome late in the third quar-

St. Louis Cardinals' slugger Mark McGwire acknowledges the crowd at Busch Stadium in St. Louis Sunday during a post-game ceremony where he received the St. Louis Award from the City of St. Louis. McGwire hit two home runs during the Cardinals' final game to set a new major league single-season homerun record with 70 homeruns.

ter as the Rams faced a third down just inside Arizona territory. The sudden uproar seemed to disrupt the play calling, leading to an illegal motion penalty.

McGwire drew his NL record 162nd walk, tying Ted Williams (1947 and 1949) for the second-highest total in major league history, on a pitch that nearly beaned him in the fifth. Thurman threw the last three balls way inside and was booed vociferously after ball four.

McGwire has 180 homers the last three seasons. In 206 career games with the Cardinals, he has 94 homers, 189 RBIs and 205 walks. At Busch Stadium, he has 51 homers and 102 RBIs in 106 games.

1990-1999

Russians Protest, Demand President Yeltsin To Quit

Up to one million people gather for anti-government rallies

MOSCOW (REUTERS) —
Red flags fluttered beneath the walls of the Kremlin on Wednesday as hundreds of thousands of people took to the streets of Russia to protest against unpaid wages and to call on President Boris Yeltsin to quit.

But apathy again won out over the apocalyptic visions of the Communist party and labour leaders, and the turnout fell far short of the many millions they had forecast.

Boris, Get Lost! read one banner above a crowd of about 70,000 people gathered just off Red Square as Yeltsin, more isolated than at any time in his seven years in power, got on with what his spokesman called a "normal working day" inside the Kremlin.

The red flags of the Communist opposition were the order of the day, from Vladivostok on the Pacific to the Winter Palace in St. Petersburg, where tens of thousands rallied at the flashpoint of the Bolsheviks' October Revolution of 1917.

Some elderly protesters carried portraits of dictator Josef Stalin.

"They (in the Kremlin) have poisoned the Russian people with the two greatest evils – private property and religion," said construction worker Yuri, 59.

But this was a broad-based outpouring of anger at the way post-Soviet market reforms have left most Russians worse off, as well as a call for a new start not a return to the old days.

Exhibit Traces Czar's Story

NEW YORK (AP) —
In the first Russian census in 1887, the year after he was crowned in one of the most opulent pageants the world had ever seen, Czar Nicholas II listed his occupation as "owner of all Russia."

Twenty years later, the Bolshevik guards who would soon execute Russia's last czar and his entire family, described him in a ration coupon book as simply "ex-emperor."

Both documents will be on display for the first time this summer in a new exhibit of 700 items, mostly from the Hermitage Museum in St. Petersburg.

Organizers say Nicholas and Alexandra is the biggest exhibit ever to come out of Russia. It opens in Wilmington, Del., on Aug. 1

The exhibit tells the story of the end of the 300-year-old Romanov dynasty and the events that changed the course of history: the love story between a Russian prince who did not want to rule and his bossy German wife, his abdication and their execution, the discovery of the family's remains more than 70 years later, and maybe even their burial, which is to take place two weeks before the exhibit opens.

"It's a large story, we think, of the 20th century and of world history," says Jim Broughton, the American whose company is organizing the exhibit.

"We think that these events surrounding Nicholas and Alexandra and their demise and the advent of communism defined our lives pretty much around the world, and particularly here in the United States, for the better part of this century."

Most of the objects in the exhibit are from the Hermitage Museum, the czar's former palace, and many have never before left Russia.

The Hermitage will be paid $500,000 US, plus a percentage of profits, money that can go to badly needed repairs to the majestic but crumbling building and the display of its three million objects.

One of the highlights of the exhibit has been rolled up in a box in the basement – a 58-metre panoramic mural of Moscow painted at the time of Nicholas' coronation and never displayed in its entirety since 1900.

Other treasures being loaned by the Hermitage include a gilded coronation carriage, a throne, costumes and icons.

The Forbes museum in New York is loaning the Faberge egg that opens to reveal a miniature of the carriage.

And from the State Archives in Moscow come a treasure trove of documents, some only recently acquired from a private collector.

Besides the census form and ration coupon book, the exhibit will feature Nicholas's abdication letter, and family photographs including pictures of Rasputin, the reputed faith healer who Alexandra hoped would cure her hemophiliac son.

Broughton said plans for the exhibit were almost complete when the Russian government announced that the remains of the czar and his family would finally be buried in St. Petersburg on July 17, 80 years to the day after their deaths and only two weeks before the exhibit was to open.

He hopes to include some elements from the funeral, possibly film footage.

The exhibit will travel to two other U.S. cities, which have not yet been announced.

LOONIE LIFTS OFF, BOOSTING TSE

Canadian dollar closes up more than a cent on news that Japan is moving to ease banking crisis

OCTOBER 8, 1998. Toronto (CP) — The Canadian dollar recorded its largest intraday gain in nearly 30 years Wednesday amid fresh hope that Japan's banking industry will soon be on its way out of a deepening financial morass.

News that the Japanese government had submitted a bill to allow the use of public money to ease the country's banking crisis hammered the U.S. dollar Wednesday and hoisted the loonie 2.24 cents to 66.84 cents US in early European trading.

However, the increase – the loonie's largest since 1970 – faded somewhat by the time the currency opened a full cent higher on North American markets.

The dollar still managed to impress, closing up 1.06 cents at 65.66 cents US.

What was stunning about Wednesday's events was not so much the Canadian dollar as the U.S. greenback, which lost a punishing 2.51 cents to finish the day at $1.5229 Cdn.

The U.S. currency, which also lost substantial ground to both the Japanese yen and the German mark, has shed 10 per cent of its value after months of reaping the rewards of an international tide of investment in the American money markets.

"These are financial market moves of unprecedented proportions," said Aron Gampel, economist with the Bank of Nova Scotia.

"We have never seen this in the history of markets, to see such violent moves day in and day out," he said. "Even the mighty U.S. is not immune to the Asian contagion."

1990–1999

Glenn Gets His Space In History

Successful launch for shuttle Discovery

CAPE CANAVERAL, FLA. (AP-CP) —

Still the hero and still making history, John Glenn roared back into space Thursday, retracing the trail he blazed for U.S. astronauts 36 years ago.

"Enjoying the show," Glenn said as Discovery soared 547 kilometres over Hawaii three hours into the flight.

"This is beautiful. It's still a trite old statement: zero-g and I feel fine," he added, repeating the words of his first flight.

His commander, Curtis Brown, said: "Let the record show that John has a smile on his face and it goes from one ear to the other and we haven't been able to remove it yet."

Glenn, the first U.S. astronaut in orbit on Feb. 20, 1962, became at age 77 the world's oldest space traveller when he and six crewmates lifted off aboard the shuttle Discovery at 2:19 p.m. EST.

(AP Photo)

John Glenn poses prior to his first space mssion on Feb. 20, 1962

It was a space sequel with all the right stuff. Discovery's departure a mere 19 minutes late was practically routine compared with Glenn's oft-postponed, pioneering flight. The launch was marred by a panel that fell from the shuttle and struck an engine moments before liftoff. But NASA said it posed no risk to the crew.

In taking the second spaceflight of his life, Glenn realized a dream he never thought possible. His return to space as the first orbiting geriatric test subject captured the imagination, so much so hundreds of thousands of people jammed the area to see the retiring U.S. senator off.

Bill Clinton, the first U.S. president to witness a shuttle liftoff, pronounced Glenn's flight "a great day for America and a great day for our senior citizens."

Soon after reaching orbit, Glenn – a Payload Specialist No. 2 who will carry out Canadian scientific experiments on board the shuttle – unstrapped himself and for the first time ever floated free and weightless. He never left the seat of his cramped Friendship 7 Mercury capsule during his five-hour, triple spin around the planet in 1962.

Scott Carpenter, watching with the two other surviving Mercury astronauts from the press site, sent his best wishes to the crew and reprised his immortal benediction from 1962: "Good luck, have a safe flight and … once again, Godspeed, John Glenn."

HISTORIC BUILDING TO ONCE AGAIN OPERATE AS A HOTEL

By John Moorhouse
The Okanagan Saturday
OCTOBER 10, 1998. — They started breathing new life into the historic Naramata Hotel Friday.

A new concrete slab was poured in the basement of the landmark building, almost 90 years after it was opened by developer J.M. Robinson. By late next summer, it should be ready for business as an active hotel for the first time in decades.

The million-dollar renovation project is being undertaken by former South Okanagan residents Keith Leach and Hugh Rennie, who purchased the hotel last summer from Renee and Jen Roy. Leach's sister, Janette and brother-in-law Norm Davies have also become partners.

Plans call for the original 19 rooms to be reduced to 11, each with its own bathroom and an old-style radiator, as hot water heating will be featured throughout. There will also be a full dining room, a wine bar featuring locally grown vintages, plus a basement spa facility.

Meanwhile, as the renovation work continues, they've already discovered one dusty, hidden momento from the past – a 1909 McGill University yearbook belonging to Bill Robinson, J.M.'s nephew, who lived in the building until his death almost 10 years ago.

Kelowna Tunnel Idea Nixed For Time Being

By Rob Munro
The Okanagan Saturday

There won't be a tunnel built to replace Okanagan Lake Bridge.

But a floating tunnel isn't out of the question for a proposed second crossing that's expected in the next 10-12 years.

"On a per-metre cost, a four-lane SFT (submerged floating tunnel), as compared to a four-lane floating structure, the SFT is cheaper," said Mayor Walter Gray.

Earlier this week, he met with consultants hired by the provincial Transportation Finance Authority to study the construction process patented by Kelowna inventor Gordon Jennens.

While it may be cheaper when compared to a new bridge, it would be more expensive than the $64 million earmarked to add a fourth lane to the bridge.

The difference in the current bridge proposal is to retrofit an existing structure rather than start from scratch.

The review determined that Jennen's technology is feasible and cheaper than conventional floating bridges. The cost savings would increase the longer the structure and could be ideal for a 50-km crossing proposed for Japan.

Suggestions were made at the meeting that the federal government be approached to help develop the technology for export.

Gray, however, said it would be great if the first application of this "made-in-Kelowna" technology is a second crossing in Kelowna.

Four sites for that crossing have been proposed north of the existing bridge.

He expects them to go to the public for review in February.

1990~1999

House Approves Clinton Impeachment Inquiry

WASHINGTON (CP) —

The U.S. House of Representatives voted Thursday for a wide-ranging impeachment inquiry of Bill Clinton, making him only the third U.S. president in history to face the threat of being removed from office.

The investigation was approved by a 258 - 176 vote, with 31 Democrats joining the majority Republicans.

"We want to get this behind us and behind the country and move on," said judiciary committee chairman Henry Hyde. "It's an onerous, miserable, rotten duty, but we have to do it or we break faith with the people who sent us here."

Republicans touted their Watergate-style inquiry in a debate that stretched far beyond the planned two hours.

Democrats argued in vain to limit the investigation to the Monica Lewinsky affair and finish it by year's end.

"(The controversy) has hurt our nation and it has hurt our children," House Democrat leader Dick Gephardt declared in a final plea for limits. "We must not compound the hurt."

But Democrats were resigned to the idea that conservatives in their party and those with tough election races only a month away were defecting to the Republican side.

In this image taken from video, Monica Lewinsky embraces President Clinton as he greeted well-wishers at a White House lawn party in Washington Nov. 6, 1996. Laying her love life bare for Independent Counsel Ken Starr's inquiry, Lewinsky described not just sex with President Clinton but long talks about their childhoods. Shared jokes, frequent hugs, the way the president 'always used to push the hair out of my face.' ``I never expected to fall in love with the president. I was surprised that I did," she said.

(AP Photo/APTV)

Clinton appealed, after the vote for a timely investigation.

"Beyond that, I have nothing to say. It's not in my hands. It is in the hands of God. There is nothing I can do."

Republicans rejected Democratic arguments that Clinton's attempts to conceal an affair with Lewinsky was not impeachable conduct, saying the issue was not sexual conduct but lying under oath.

Impeachment vote delayed over attack

By The Associated Press

WASHINGTON —

Republicans in the House of Representative agreed Wednesday night to a delay an impeachment proceeding against President Bill Clinton because of U.S. air strikes against Iraq.

The delay came even though many Republicans questioned whether the military attacks were politically motivated.

"We're going to defer action tomorrow," Representative Bob Livingston (R-La.), the House speaker-designate, told reporters Wednesday without using the word impeachment.

He added that he was asking all legislators - already in Washington in anticipation of a momentous impeachment debate - to remain in town pending "further action, possibly Friday, possibly Saturday, but within the near future."

Clinton's prospects for avoiding impeachment flickered ominously during the day, as a fresh batch of Republicans announced plans to support at least one of the four articles of impeachment the House Judiciary Committee approved last week.

The four articles of impeachment cover perjury, obstruction of justice and abuse of power in connection with Clinton's efforts to conceal his sexual relationship with Monica Lewinsky.

Passage of any of them would send the issue to the Senate for a trial, the likes of which hasn't occurred since Andrew Johnson sat in the White House in 1868.

1990~1999

Impeachment effort is dead

Clinton tells Americans he's sorry for burden he put on public for a year

WASHINGTON (CP) —

No removal from office, not even a meaningless reprimand.

Bill Clinton will have history's mark of Cain upon him as just the second U.S. president ever to have been impeached, but his remarkable ability to survive crises that would end the careers of lesser politicians remained intact Friday with his acquittal.

Clinton's Republican prosecutors failed to convince even a simple majority of 100 senators - let alone the two-thirds majority required for conviction - that the president committed perjury and obstruction of justice in trying to conceal his affair with Monica Lewinsky.

The Senate votes leave Clinton in office for the remaining 21 months of his final term and ends a tawdry drama that Americans found alternately riveting, revolting and irrelevant.

Clinton did not watch the votes on television, but received word of the results by telephone while exercising in the White House.

He walked out of the residence and into the Oval Office to write a statement free of both gloating and rancor. There was also no fudging his responsibility for the crisis that ate up an entire year of his second term.

"I want to say again to the American people how profoundly sorry I am for what I said and did to trigger these events and the great burden they have imposed on the Congress and the American people," Clinton said, pausing to bite his lip.

The president turned to leave the Rose Garden when he was stopped in his tracks by someone asking if he could forgive his pursuers.

"Anybody who asks for forgiveness has to be prepared to give it," he said.

He later sent a private apology to each White House employee, expressing his regret for forcing them to endure a year of exhausting tumult.

The five-week trial ended swiftly and with few surprises.

Chief Justice William Rehnquist asked a hushed chamber, "Senators, how say you? Is respondent William Jefferson Clinton guilty or not guilty?"

One-by-one, senators voted 55-46 to reject the charge of perjury and 50-50 on the impeachment article. Ten Republicans joined the Democrats to vote against the perjury acquittal.

"It is therefore ordered and adjudged that the said William Jefferson Clinton be, and he hereby is, acquitted of the charges in the said articles," Chief Justice William Rehnquist intoned.

The votes, coming several months after the dismissal of Paula Jones' sexual harassment lawsuit, marked the second consecutive major legal and political victory for Clinton. He still faces the threat of an indictment from special prosecutor Kenneth Starr, either before or after he leaves office.

Clinton polls

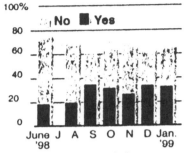

IMPEACHMENT

Do you think President Clinton should be impeached and removed from office?

Source: CNN/USAToday/Gallup

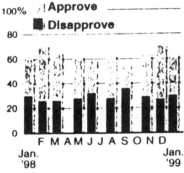

JOB APPROVAL

Do you approve or disapprove of the way Bill Clinton is handling his job as president?

Source: Pew Research Center

Judge cites Clinton for civil contempt

WASHINGTON (CP) —

President Bill Clinton was found in contempt of court Monday for repeatedly lying under oath about his affair with Monica Lewinsky.

The sharp legal rebuke came scant hours after the president's nemesis, Kenneth Starr, suffered an embarrassing setback in his attempt to send one of Clinton's former business partners to jail.

Judge Susan Webber Wright's decision to cite Clinton for civil contempt could lead to his being

disbarred and prevented from practising law in his home state of Arkansas after he leaves office.

It will also cost Clinton, who already has millions of dollars in legal bills, thousands of additional dollars in penalties.

The decision comes at a time when Clinton is counting on erasing public skepticism about his moral fitness to lead the country as he struggles to convince the populace of the need to risk U.S. lives in Yugoslavia.

The judge made the ruling

based on Clinton's "Willful failure" to obey her repeated orders to testify truthfully Jan. 17, 1998 in the Paula Jones' sexual harassment case.

"The court takes no pleasure whatsoever in holding this nation's president in contempt of court," the judge said in her order, released in Little Rock.

"The record demonstrates by clear and convincing evidence that the president responded to plaintiffs' questions by giving false, misleading and evasive answers that

were designed to obstruct the judicial process."

Wright ruled Jones was deprived of significant information, when Clinton denied having had sex with any state or federal employee.

He was asked specifically about Lewinsky by Jones' lawyers during the deposition.

"I have never had sexual relations with Monica Lewinsky," he said.

Clinton changed his story after his DNA was found on a dress belonging to Lewinsky.

Canada's Celine tops sales in '98

Singer Celine Dion belts out "The Prayer" during the 1999 Grammy Award rehearsals at the Shrine Auditorium in Los Angeles, Monday, Feb. 22, 1999. Dion is up for several Grammys including Record of the Year and Best Female Pop Vocal Performance.

(AP Photo/ Victoria Arocho)

LOS ANGELES (CP) — Celine Dion has nabbed honours as the top-selling artist of 1998, according to the Recording Industry Association of America.

The Canadian singer, appeared on two of the year's best-selling albums, including Let's Talk About Love, which was certified at eight million units by the trade organization.

Dion's recently released holiday-themed disc, These Are Special Times, was certified at triple platinum.

The association certified 354 gold albums (shipments of 500,000 copies each) in the U.S. in 1998, an increase of 11 albums over 1997. Platinum albums (one million units) topped 209, a five-album increase over the previous year.

Dion was also responsible for leading the Sony Classical/Sony Music Soundtrax disc Titanic to the top of the soundtrack and score certifications. The disc's only vocal track, My Heart will Go On, helped the album log over 10 million U.S. sales for '98 and become the industry's best-selling score with a worldwide tally topping 26 million units.

Garth Brooks maintained his title as the best-selling solo artist in domestic recording industry history with the 12-million unit certification of his recently released Double Live disc.

Shania Twain's sophomore Mercury Records Nashville disc Come On Over earned honours as the second-best-selling country album of the year with a quintuple certification adding to the disc's double-platinum tally earned in 1997.

Shania Twain accepts the entertainer of the year award at the Country Music Association Awards show in Nashville, Tenn., Wednesday, Sept. 22, 1999.

(AP Photo/Michael S. Green)

Centre focuses on agri-tourism

Revamped Laurel building links Valley's past with future of tourism industry

By J.P. Squire
The Daily Courier

The historic Laurel packing-house has been transformed into a unique agri-tourism centre, the first in Canada and possibly the world.

"In the past, we've focused on smaller individual projects like the Wine Museum and Orchard Industry Museum," notes Wayne

Wilson, curator for both and assistant director of the Kelowna Museum.

"This marks the emergence of The Laurel as a historic site. We wanted to invite people down to view the upgrading and updating."

During the past six months, $125,000 was spent to open up meeting and performance space as well as highlight the building's beautiful red brick, wood beams and vaulted ceilings.

"The project was made possible by corporate and community donations and through the assis-

tance of Human Resources Development Canada, which provided the labour through a job creation grant," said Wilson.

The most striking change when you enter the building is new pine flooring, thanks to the generous donation of 5,000 board feet of one-by-10s from Gorman Bros. Lumber.

"They got their start in the tree fruit industry by cutting shooks (wooden pieces) for apple boxes," said Wilson.

Calona Vineyards purchased new glass doors for the entrance to the Wine Museum.

Design Consultant Peter Wiebe selected vibrant colours for the walls and designed a series of large display panels on the cattle industry, grain/mixed farming, tobacco and the history of The Laurel.

Future panels will focus on the wine and fruit industries as part of the development of the agri-tourism centre.

"Agri-tourism is our future in the Okanagan," says Wilson.

"We need to market our industry, its historic past and its continuing progress as we approach the new millennium."

Broadcaster Jack Webster dies at 80

Gruff, unabashed exterior hid a man who was troubled about putting his career before his family

VANCOUVER (CP) —

Legendary broadcaster Jack Webster, known for his acerbic wit, thick Scottish brogue and his blast-furnace interviews, has died. He was 80.

"It was very peaceful," said his son, Jack Webster Jr. "He had good humour and a sparkle in his eye. He just stopped breathing."

Webster died at 10:15 a.m. Tuesday of heart disease, congestive heart failure and Alzheimer's, his son said.

He was surrounded by his son and three daughters, including Joan from Scotland whom Webster and his wife gave up for adoption in Great Britain in 1936 and were reunited with 36 years later.

Anyone who ever heard Webster on radio or watched him on TV remembers the inimitable style -

Legendary broadcaster Jack Webster, shown in an Oct. 3,1990, file photo, has died. He was 81.

(CP PHOTO/Vancouver Sun-Ian Lindsay)

part showbiz, part newsman, all at full throttle.

"He wouldn't let people lie, cheat and steal when they were being interviewed," said his son.

He honed his belligerent exterior while working as a print reporter for the Vancouver Sun in the early '50s.

After 16 years as a newspaper and radio reporter, he began his

talk radio show in 1963.

But his biggest success was on television where he did a live morning show at BCTV.

After his retirement, he sat as a regular panelist on CBC's Front Page Challenge and established the Webster Awards for Excellence in Journalism.

He received the Order of Canada in 1988.

NEW, 'EASY' AIDS DRUG UNVEILED

MARCH 26, 1999, TORONTO (CP) — To keep HIV in check, Kevin Tomlinson used to swallow 30 pills each day. Now, he needs only seven pills a day as new, easier-to-take drugs reach the market.

The latest HIV-fighting drug to be approved by Health Canada is called efavirenz.

Sold under the brand name Sustiva, it's the first one-a-day pill for HIV and AIDS, making it easy to take in combinations, called "cocktails," with other drugs.

"I'm very positive about this," Tomlinson told a news conference sponsored by the pill's maker, DuPont Pharma.

"But it doesn't mean the war is over. We're still fighting this disease."

Although efavirenz was approved just last week, more than 1,500 Canadian are already taking it under an expanded-access program.

It's in a family of drugs used as an alternative when widely used protease inhibitors start to fail, or when patients have bad side effects from this common treatment.

While protease inhibitors have saved many lives, "they're not the answer for everybody," said Dr. Sharon Walmsley, assistant director of the Toronto Hospital immunodeficiency clinic.

" A number of patients in our clinics are starting to fail their therapies." That's where new drugs, like efavirenz are useful, Walmsley said.

Photo by photo credit

Viagra to heat up Kelowna bedrooms

By Chuck Poulsen
The Daily Courier

The foreplay is over.

The anti-impotence pill Viagra is expected to be in Kelowna drug stores this morning with, no doubt, further developments tonight.

"I've had an e-mail saying it will be in Thursday morning," said London Drugs pharmacist Shirley Taylor. "We've had a lot of people phoning - six or seven yesterday."

Dyck's Pharmacy also reported the phone lines had heated up as customers counted the days.

Health Canada approved

Viagra, or sildenafil citrate, earlier this month. Pfizer Canada initially projected that the drug wouldn't be able to be shipped from its manufacturing facility in Arnprior, Ont., for at least another week.

But high demand from pharmacists and doctors calling a special Pfizer phone line kick-started the company to get things moving, said spokesman Don Sancton.

The amount of Viagra initially produced for Canada has been based on Pfizer's American experience. Using statistics from the first nine months of availability in the U.S. , where Viagra was approved

a year ago, it's estimated about 300,000 Canadian men with impotence - or erectile dysfunction- may seek treatment over the same period here.

Viagra is the first in a new class of medications, known as phosphodiesterase type 5 inhibitors, that improve blood flow to the penis.

Cost in Canada is $12 to $13 a pill plus the pharmacy's dispensing fee. Viagra is sold in blister packs of four for now, but will later be available in eight-packs.

Fears about Viagra knock-offs, which have been a problem in the

U.S., resulted in Canadian packaging with a special hologram printed on the outside of the box.

There have also been worries about Viagra abuse in Canada. There have been cases in some countries where men have used the pill indiscriminately.

In Canada, pill packs will also contain information sheets "so that patients and their partners directly receive information on the proper and responsible use of Viagra," Pfizer says.

Clinical trials around the world have found Viagra is effective in seven out of 10 men.

1990~1999

Finished with talking, NATO starts bombing

Air defence, communication facilities the target of first attacks

BELGRADE (AP-CP-Reuters) —
Waves of NATO planes and missiles struck Yugoslavia on Wednesday, blasting army barracks, power plants and air defence batteries in an attempt to force the country's defiant leader to cease his onslaught against separatist Albanians.

The NATO attack came after months of diplomacy failed to end fighting that has killed more than 2,000 people in Kosovo and left over 400,000 homeless in the last year.

In a speech from the White House late Wednesday, U.S. President Bill Clinton said NATO had "a moral imperative" to save thousands of defenceless people from Serb aggression.

"We've seen innocent people taken from their homes, forced to kneel in the dirt and sprayed by bullets," Clinton said. "By acting now, we are upholding our values, protecting our interests and advancing the cause of peace."

Using a full-colour map with arrows pointing throughout central Europe, Clinton also claimed the attack was in America's national security interest. "Let a fire burn in this ear and the flame will spread," he said. "We act to prevent a wider war."

The Yugoslav army declared a state of war shortly after the first wave of attacks. It said more than 20 targets were hit in the first hour but insisted none of its air-defence units were damaged.

Explosions resounded in Pristina, capital of Serbia's Kosovo province, starting at 7:55 p.m. local time, and the city of 280,000 was plunged into darkness when the electricity failed. Yugoslavia's Tanjug news agency reported four heavy blasts in the city, including three from the area of Slatina airport.

The U.S. and allied forces pounded Yugoslavia with a heavy missile barrage that gave the bat-winged B-2 stealth bomber its first taste of battle and engaged Yugoslav pilots in dogfights that knocked at least two Soviet-made MIGs out of the sky.

U.S. Defence Secretary William Cohen announced all allied planes returned safely in the initial strikes. He said NATO forces would continue hitting the Yugoslav military, until President Slobodan Milosevic calls off his campaign against the majority Albanian people of Kosovo, a Serbian province.

"We are attacking the military infrastructure that President Milosevic and his forces are using to repress and kill innocent people," Cohen said.

In addition to hitting Yugoslavia's extensive air defence, including communications and command sites, NATO air strikes targetted at least one factory that makes parts for air-defence systems, a U.S. official said. The president's national-security adviser, Sandy Berger, said NATO would not let up. "It's not a one-night operation," Berger said.

YELTSIN WON'T RULE OUT MILITARY ACTION

Calls air strikes 'deeply troubling'

MARCH 25, 1999, MOSCOW (AP) — President Boris Yeltsin pulled Russia out of its partnership with NATO on Wednesday and warned of possible further steps to protest against air strikes on Yugoslavia - attacks he called deeply troubling.

If the conflict grows, Russian reserves the right to take "adequate measures, including of a military character, to ensure its own and general European security," Yeltsin said after air strikes began.

His statement did not elaborate.

"Russia is deeply upset by NATO's military action against sovereign Yugoslavia, which is nothing more than open aggression," Yeltsin said.

NATO strikes began a few hours after Yeltsin spoke with President Bill Clinton for more than half an hour by phone, urging him not to take the "tragic step" of bombing.

Russia has vehemently opposed the use of force against its ally Yugoslavia for a military crackdown on separatist Albanians in the Serbian province Kosovo.

Despite Russia's opposition to NATO strikes, its options appear limited.

It is desperately seeking new loans from the U.S.-dominated International Monetary Fund to revive an economy that's been in deep recession.

Local Serb church leader worries for his relatives

No war is a good war, says Kelowna man unafraid to admit he's a proud Serb

By Don Plant
The Daily Courier

Dragi Djordjevich was actually relieved when NATO warplanes began pounding military positions in his Serbian homeland Wednesday.

As president of the Serbian Orthodox parish in the Okanagan, Djordjevich has expected the bombs to fall on Belgrade and Kosovo for several months. The Kelowna grape grower is deeply worried about his relatives in Yugoslavia, but admitted he feels "more comfortable" than he did before NATO launched its air attack.

"At least they started bombing, and I don't have to think, 'will they or won't they?'" he said Wednesday at his South Kelowna home. "My wish is that it never came to this. I wish the Americans didn't get involved."

About 100 Serbian families live in the Okanagan, most of them in the Kelowna area. There many be others, but Djordjevich believes they're afraid to admit they're Serbian.

He has two brothers in Yugoslavia - one of them in the city of Novisad, which was bombed Wednesday. He spoke to his niece Tuesday in Pirot, who lives 500 metres from an armoury. He couldn't get through to any relatives last night.

"I guess all the lines are burned, " he said. "Where to go? The Serbs don't have another country to go to. The Hungarians can go to Hungary. The Serbs have got no other country, except to beg someone to accept them as refugees."

Djordjevich, 69, says his Serbian nationality has become the victim of one-sided media coverage, and he accuses the NATO allies of hypocrisy.

Since the bloodshed in his homeland, Djordjevich has experienced animosity from people in Kelowna who found out he was Serbian.

He fears the civil war could spark unrest in the neighbouring country of Macedonia, where one third of the people are ethnic Albanian, and in northern Greece.

"Their aspirations are greater than Albania," he said. "I wish it never started. No war is a good war, no matter what side you're on."

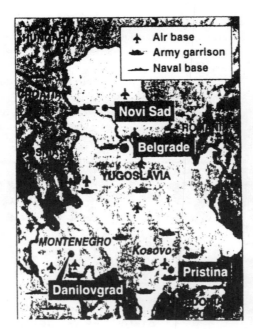

Legend:
- Air base
- Army garrison
- Naval base

Novi Sad
Belgrade
YUGOSLAVIA
MONTENEGRO
Kosovo
Danilovgrad
Pristina

Canada opens doors to Kosovar refugees

Federal government plans airlift to bring 5,000 refugees out of war-torn region

OTTAWA (CP) —

Five thousand refugees from the ethnic terror of war-ravaged Kosovo will soon be en route to a safe haven in Canada.

Defence officials said Sunday the military is ready to start the airlift as early as today but other government departments cau-

tioned that making necessary arrangements will take time.

"We're ready for action virtually now," said Lt.-Gen. Ray Henault, deputy chief of defence staff.

Canada has a military Airbus jetliner at the NATO based in Aviano, Italy, and "it's ready to plug in to this mission virtually as soon as we give it the order to do that."

The government plans to use a combination of military and chartered aircraft and may consider ships if the refugees are healthy enough to endure the long transat-

lantic voyage from the Balkans.

Four federal ministries — Defence, Foreign Affairs, Immigration and International Co-operation — and the Canadian International Development Agency will co-ordinate the effort.

Officials said one option would be to house the refugees at military installations such as the mothballed Downsview base near Toronto or militia or cadet training camps.

"The prime minister felt it was very important that Canada do its part to relieve suffering," Foreign

Affairs Minister Lloyd Axworthy said at a Sunday briefing at Defence headquarters.

"It's an emergency rush situation but we believe we can provide some relief of the pressure that has been built up."

Axworthy stressed that the exodus to Canada is not a resettlement program but a way to ease the strain on countries bordering Kosovo that are being overwhelmed by the tide of refugees.

Most of the refugees would favour returning to Kosovo, he said.

Generals sign deal to withdraw Serbs, end air strikes

Yugoslav Col. Gen. Svetozar Marjanovic declares, "The war has ended'"

KUMANOVO, MACEDONIA (CP) —

After 77 days of intense NATO air strikes, Yugoslav and Western generals signed a pact Wednesday clearing the way for a Kosovo peace plan to end the bombings, pull Yugoslav troops out of the troubled province and allow hundreds of thousands of refugees to return home.

"The war has ended," Yugoslav Col. Gen. Svetozar Marjanovic told reporters in Macedonia, after lengthy negotiations at this French military base near the Kosovo border.

President Clinton tempered his remarks, calling the agreement "another important step toward achieving our objectives in Kosovo."

He also warned that NATO will

A resident of Belgrade kisses the Serbian flag as he celebrates the Kosovo peace agreement early today. Britain's Lt. Gen. Michael Jackson announced Wednesday that NATO and Yugoslavian generals had signed an agreement providing for the withdrawal of Serb forces from Kosovo, suspension of the NATO air campaign and the return of hundreds of thousands of refugees. In Belgrade and the Kosovo capital Pristina, people welcomed the news by firing weapons in the air in celebration and honking horns.

"watch carefully" to make sure the forces leave Kosovo peacefully according to the agreed timetable.

Canadian Prime Minister Jean Chretien, speaking to CTV Broadcast News, sounded relieved that a settlement had

been reached, adding that he was "impressed at the way the 19 countries (in the NATO alliance) stuck together throughout the bombing campaign. It was a real collective effort ...we got the results that we were hoping for."

In Belgrade and the Kosovo capital Pristina, people celebrated by firing weapons in the air and honking horns. Refugees in northern Albania embraced one another when they heard news of the agreement.`

A Serbian official said Belgrade would begin withdrawing its forces Thursday.

Details of the agreement were not released. But Lt.-Gen. Michael Jackson, commander of NATO troops in Macedonia, said it detailed how all Serbian forces would conduct a "phased, verifiable and orderly withdrawal from Kosovo."

NATO's bombing campaign, which began March 24, is to stop once a Serb pullout has been verified.

1990-1999

A new territory born: Nunavut

Today marks first day of self-government for Inuit people in their own part of Canada

IQALUIT, NUNAVUT (CP) — With games, feats, pride and hope, people across the eastern Arctic said goodbye to the old Northwest Territories on Wednesday and took their place as residents of Nunavut, Canada's new territory.

"Let the rest of the world know that we have our own culture, and they're going to get to know us," a beaming Sila Kelly said as the celebrations began.

In Iqaluit, the Nunavut capital, about 150 people braved bitter winds that chilled the air to -42 C as they gathered outdoors for traditional Arctic games such as harpoon tossing and nusuuraut, a four-way tug of war.

Smiles may have been a bit forced in the teeth of north winds gusting up to 60 kilometres an hour. But there was nothing forced about the joy.

The formation of Nunavut is the first redrawing of the Canadian map since the entry of Newfoundland - which is celebrating its 50th anniversary the same day.

The new territory, formed from the eastern half of the old Northwest Territories, will cover 2.2 million square kilometres of tundra, ice cap and rock, frozen coast - more than twice the area of Ontario.

The vast expanse is populated by only about 25,000 people - not even enough to fill a football stadium. About 85 per cent are Inuit and they face unemployment, poverty, low education and substance abuse.

Jobs and better housing are two things many Nunavut residents say they want from their new government.

Millennium Madness Oh, Baby!

It's time to get in the mood if you're hoping to have a baby for the turn of the millennium, doctors advise

By Chuck Poulsen
The Daily Courier

This is the week to put the plan into action for couples who want to have their baby born on Jan. 1, 2000.

Then again, masterminding a birth date is as much a roll of the dice as it is science.

"This would be the week, with ovulation and conception on April 8, to be exact," said Dr. Louise Graham, a Kelowna family physician.

However, adds Graham, there is nothing exact about it, starting with the female's chances of ovulating at the right time.

Ovulation usually occurs 14 days before the onset of a woman's next menstrual cycle, and that can range anywhere from 20 to 40 days, with 28 being the average.

"The egg will last 48 hours at the most and sperm about the same," said Graham. "So we usually say 24 hours either side."

Women can buy home ovulation tests to detect a surge of luteinizing hormone in their urine, which occurs 24 to 36 hours before an egg is released.

Even if that part of the planning is right, gestation periods can vary by two weeks on either side of the 265 day target and still be considered normal.

The next date to keep in mind for would-be millennimoms is about April 22. That would be the ideal day for a woman to use a home pregnancy test to confirm she is pregnant.

You may try all of this at home, although women thinking of becoming pregnant should consult their doctors ahead of time.

There are an average of 1,000 births a day in Canada. But that number has been in the 700s for more recent New Year's days.

There is some evidence that oysters may help in the conception process. They are rich in zinc, which plays a role in ovulation and fertility.

For the man, one study has indicated that coffee improves sperm mobility. However, the more caffeine a women consumes, the less likely she is to get pregnant.

The odds against hitting the target date aren't as long as winning a lottery, but they're not very good either.

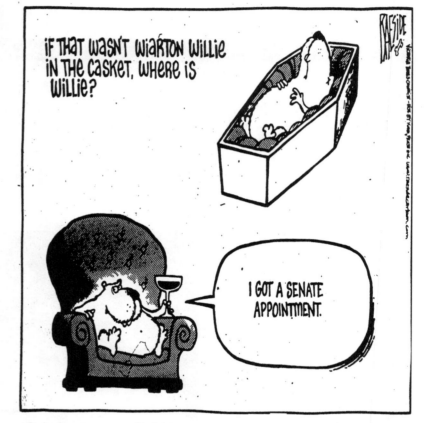

Only five per cent of babies arrive on their due date.

Confide In Us

What will the most popular name of the new millennium be?

We need your help to find out.

If you're hoping to have a millennium baby, let us know your first choices for boys' and girls' names and we'll list the names in order of popularity in an upcoming issue of The Daily Courier.

Let the rest of the community share in your anticipation and joy.

As we close in on 2000, we're looking for couples that are trying to get pregnant in time for a New Year's delivery.

We want to know your hopes and dreams for raising a family in the 21st century.

Drop off your list of names at our office at 550 Doyle Avenue downtown, or call us at 470-0739. You can also fax the newsroom at 762-3866 or send e-mail to remote@ok.bc.ca

EUTHANASIA

Kevorkian sentenced to 10-25 years in jail

APRIL 14, 1999,PONTIAC, MICH. (AP) — A judge sentenced Dr. Jack Kevorkian to 10 to 25 years in prison for the videotaped death of a Lou Gehrig's disease patient, lecturing the euthanasia crusader: "No one, sir, is above the law. No one."

On Tuesday, Judge Jessica Cooper also sentenced the 70-year-old Kevorkian to three to seven years for delivery of a controlled substance. The sentences will run concurrently.

Kevorkian will be eligible for parole after serving two-third of the sentence.

Kevorkian, who could have been sentenced to life in prison, was convicted of murder in the death of 52-year-old Thomas Youk.

As during his trial last month, Kevorkian sat stone-faced while Cooper handed down her sentence.

After being sentenced, Kevorkian smiled as he was handcuffed and led away by deputies.

Airport clash averted

By MAURICE SMITH
Penticton Herald
© Copyright

The city of Penticton won a last minute extension of airport transfer talks Wednesday, just as Penticton Indian Band members were preparing for a 10 a.m. protest at the airport.

The protest, which prompted three flight cancellations, was getting under way when Mayor Beth Campbell emerged to announce the six-week reprieve.

Campbell said city council requested the extension due to the "serious confrontation brewing at the airport" between the Penticton Indian Band, the city and Transport Canada.

"Gustafsen Lake cost the federal and provincial governments millions of dollars, and a small city like Penticton cannot afford such an expense," Campbell said.

A proposed deal that would have seen the airport land, expropriated from the band, returned if and when the airport closes fell

Protesters from the Penticton Indian Band banged drums, carried protest signs and chanted a traditional Okanagan Indian song during a two-hour occupation of the Penticton Airport Wednesday

apart recently, prompting the band's protest.

Campbell said city council feels the city was being held hostage by the federal government and the band.

"Either council could proceed with airport transfer and catalyze a major confrontation with Okanagan First Nations that would potentially shut down airport operations, or council could decline to proceed with the transfer and watch the federal government close down the airport under the National Airports Policy."

Either way, the city would lose the airport, she said.

Council passed a resolution Tuesday to request the extension, and to ask that Transport Canada consider a lease option and a management/operating agreement as a means of addressing band concerns.

In a conference call with transport and Indian affairs ministry officials Wednesday morning, Transport Canada agreed to consider a lease of the land to the city, something Campbell called a breakthrough.

"This is something we have been after for years. All this could have been avoided if we had agreed to this earlier."

Transport Canada spokesman Rod Nelson said the city's options will be looked at, but he noted there is no other regional airport in Canada he is aware of that has a lease agreement extending beyond March 2000, the ministry's target date to divest itself of all such airports.

Increasingly hard line taken by Indian Band

By GARY SYMONS
Penticton Herald

Penticton is facing what could prove to be the worst economic crisis in its history, as a rapidly escalating conflict with the Penticton Indian Band threatens the survival of the city's airport.

This week things went from bad to worse as the band's membership voted to withdraw their own council's mandate to negotiate any deal involving transfer of the airport lands to the city. In fact, Penticton Indian Band (PIB) leaders say the band is currently leaning toward a takeover of the airport lands, either by negotiation or force.

To make matters worse, they say the band members have not yet decided whether they want the airport to continue operating, even though the future of their own casino/resort project may depend on it.

Faced with economic disaster, Penticton city council has been huddled in almost constant meetings for weeks, and still the situation has worsened day by day, culminating in the two-hour occupation of the airport by the Penticton Indian Band.

Wednesday, Mayor Beth

Campbell's reaction was to blame Transport Canada for three years of inflexibility, and to a lesser extent, the media.

But the view from the other side of the Okanagan River Channel is quite different.

While Chief Stewart Phillip stopped short of laying blame directly at the feet of city council, he did say negotiations fell apart over two city demands. One was that the airport lands would only revert to the reserve if aircraft flight movements fell below 1,000. The other was that the city wanted the reverter clause removed from the airport transfer agreement entirely, if the band council did not sign the agreement.

According to Phillip, when that news hit his community, the effect was politically devastating. At two band meetings this week, band members voted to withdraw the council's mandate to negotiate any kind of airport transfer agreement that involves the City of Penticton and the National Airports Policy.

"We are no longer authorized to participate in discussions within that framework," Phillip said, adding that the band may settle for nothing less than a transfer of

the land back to native jurisdiction. To that end, they have hired the high-profile law firm of Mandell-Pinder to investigate a new land claim on the airport itself. Mandell-Pinder was also involved in the landmark Delgamuukw decision from the Supreme Court of Canada.

Ironically, the band's new hard line comes at the same time Transport Canada is showing new flexibility in negotiating a transfer agreement.

Transport Canada spokesman Rod Nelson confirmed the ministry will consider suggestions that the city could merely lease the land, or even operate the airport under a management agreement, something that was not an option before this week.

Unfortunately, the band's position has become rigid since Monday, and the band council is already rejecting offers they would have jumped at a week ago.

Elders with the Penticton Indian Band added a human element to the protest, recalling in detail what occurred during a long-ago meeting with federal officials when the airport lands were expropriated.

Louise Gabriel, 89, recalled that during World War II, the government convinced the band to sign over the land, but promised to return it five years after the war was over.

"When they did come and give us money (for compensation), I think they gave $200 an acre, and the land was still coming back to us. They even said they would take all that tar off and reseed it with the hay for our stock."

1990~1999

JEEZ... WHAT A DAY!
MORE FAST FERRY
DISASTERS, THE DEFICIT
IS OUT OF CONTROL...
IT'S SO GOOD TO BE
HOME.

THE CLARKS

Growers Make Plea For Bailout

By Don Plant
The Daily Courier

B.C.'s apple industry will be little more than a cottage industry if the government rejects a new plan to save it from bankruptcy, warns a leading packinghouse director.

Representatives of the B.C. Fruit Growers Association are scheduled to meet Agriculture Minister Corky Evans in Victoria late this afternoon with a list of suggestions to keep more than 1,000 apple growers operating.

If Evans dismisses their proposals, Okanagan growers may stop supplying countries around the world and distribute fruit only to the Western provinces, said John Duncan, president of the B.C. Fruit Packers Cooperative. That would slash the $80 million the industry pumps into the Valley's economy every year.

"We're in big trouble. It's up to the provincial and federal government to decide what sort of an industry they want in this Valley," said Duncan, who helped hammer out the financial plan with

other packinghouse directors last month.

"The future of the industry as we know it is at stake. The last two years have been disastrous."

The Okanagan's fruit industry supplies Mexico, the U.S., the Philippines and other Far Eastern countries with apples almost year-round. But hail damage in 1997, sunscald in '98 and a world glut of apples have driven down prices to record lows, pushing many producers to the financial brink.

Directors of the Valley's four main packinghouses have outlined the dollar losses growers have sustained over the last six years, and argued for a government bailout to ensure a crop this season.

The package is similar to one the BCFGA presented to growers two weeks ago, said association vice-president Penny Gambell. The directors added how much packinghouses have lost recently and the losses facing more than 80 per cent of the Valley growers.

"They make a very good case for the increasing debt load that a

lot of growers are facing this year," said Gambell. "It's definitely a very substantial loss. It could get worse."

Evans rejected a bailout package presented by the BCFGA executive in February, but the current plan contains more research and makes a more solid argument, said Gambell.

Evans' push to revitalize the industry's replant program falls short of what growers need, said Duncan, because producers in Washington state are growing the same new varieties. Most can't afford to invest in new trees like Fujis and royal galas. Without new money for growers to reinvest in their operations, the industry will eventually die, he said.

"Morale in this industry is so low right now the replant program would be meaningless. Growers won't invest. If the government is involved only in a replant program, forget it. Growers have used up most of their resources they have just getting into this year."

Details of the latest package haven't been disclosed.

NDP speeding up Nisga'a treaty process

Premier anticipates long-awaited treaty to be ready in two weeks

VICTORIA (CP) —

The Nisga'a aboriginals waited more than a century for their treaty, but British Columbia's government is only prepared to wait another two to four weeks to pass the deal.

Moves to ensure debate on the historic land-claim deal is wrapped up before the end of the month are in the works, says Premier Glen Clark.

He says the treaty could be ready in two weeks.

"Actually, when we come back from the (Easter) long weekend, I'm hoping we can sit down with the Opposition and say what's a reasonable time period. How many hours would you like?"

But Liberal leader Gordon Campbell says the NDP government mishandled the Nisga'a debate and the Opposition is not about to adhere to any time line.

The government called a special session of the legislature last November to debate the treaty.

But that session was adjourned in February when it became

(CP PHOTO/Nick Procaylo-str)

B.C. Premier Glen Clark and Nisga'a Tribal Council President Joe Gosnell shake hands before signing the Nisga'a Final Agreement in Terrace, B.C. April 27, 1999. The historic ratification of the Nisga'a Treaty and Nisga'a Constitution won a majority vote by the Nisga'a Nation on November 6, 1998 after 113 years of negotiations.

apparent the government was being battered by a scandal involving massive cost over-runs on its fast ferry construction project.

Aboriginal Affairs Minister Gordon Wilson ruled out invoking closure to end the Nisga'a debate, but suggested politicians may start debating well into the night to speed passage of the treaty.

"It's really important that we drop the rhetoric and get down to the substance and detail of the discussion," he said.

The agreement reached last August between Ottawa, Victoria and the Nisga'a resulted after more than 25 years of negotiations.

The deal gives the Nisga'a ownership of almost 2,000 square kilometres of land, self-government rights and about $500 million in cash, grants and government program money.

The Nisga'a, who approved the treaty in a tribal referendum, gave up their tax-exempt status and rights to make future claims.

TREATY LEGISLATION GIVEN ROYAL ASSENT

APRIL 27, 1999, VICTORIA (CP) — The Nisga'a treaty was given royal assent in the B.C. legislature Monday (26th), allowing Premier Glen Clark to triumphantly attend a Nisga'a convention today. Chief Justice Alan McEachern, acting on behalf of the vacationing lieutenant-governor, gave royal assent Monday despite being urged by some critics to refuse.

Late last week, B.C. Reform party president Bill Vander Zalm wrote the Lieutenant-Governor Garde Gardom asking that he refer the "damaging and deceitful document" back to the legislature for a full debate.

"The people of British Columbia have not had a proper say on this treaty...since the government has invoked closure before the bill has been fully debated," said Vander Zalm.

The treaty legislation was passed last week in the legislature and the royal assent came one day before Nisga'a band members meet in Terrace to discuss their future.

There is likely to be some dissent expressed at the meeting. Frank Barton, a member of the Nisga'a's Kincolith band who opposes the treaty, said many grassroots Nisga'a have not been heard.

NDP tactics could delay passage of Nisga'a treaty

NDP attempt to force treaty debate closure may backfire

VICTORIA (CP) —

Extraordinary measures used by the B.C. government to pass the Nisga'a treaty could actually force band members to wait even longer before it becomes law.

That's because the federal government is being pressured to give the treaty the full hearing critics say was denied in British Columbia by the NDP government's decision to chop off debate on the treaty.

The treaty was pushed through

the legislature Thursday (22nd). The Nisga'a have already ratified it. Ottawa has yet to hear the deal.

Premier Glen Clark called the passage "wonderful," despite the heavy criticism he's faced for the methods his government has used.

Clark said the treaty has been debated in the legislature for more than 100 hours, longer than any other piece of legislation.

"The length of time is extraordinary and I just feel quite strongly...that it would have taken another several months of filibustering by the Liberals."

The NDP used a so-called guil-

lotine motion to clear the way for the treaty to be passed through the legislature by the end of Thursday.

The motion has never been used in this way in Canada or in other parts of the British Commonwealth, the Opposition Liberals say.

The B.C. government had to rely on precedents from the British parliament in using the motion to force the treaty through.

Liberals called the motion "draconian and sinister" and walked out of question period in protest.

"This is how the NDP would like the legislature to work: No questions, no answers, no debate, no information and that means no

democracy," Opposition leader Gordon Campbell said.

The Liberals have accused Clark of ramming the treaty into law so the beleaguered premier can attend the Nisga'a annual meeting next week and present the signed document.

Frank Calder, a Nisga'a elder who sat in the B.C. legislature from 1949 to 1977, said the provincial government has tainted the treaty and the future of the treaty process.

"I wonder how the politicians in the House of Commons will look upon this treaty knowing that one of their provinces delivered it to them on the basis of closure."

1990~1999

What Can We Say, But Thank You, Wayne

Hockey's greatest player gets ready to leave the stage

NEW YORK —

Wayne Gretzky made it official Friday, confirming his storied hockey career is over.

"It's obvious today that I have officially retired. Sunday will be my last game," said the 38-year-old, his voice breaking.

The New York Rangers star made the announcement at a packed news conference at Madison Square Garden, less than a day after an emotional farewell game on Canadian soil at the Corel Centre in Kanata, Ont.

"You could not be a better competitor on the ice," said NHL commissioner Gary Bettman. "No person in sports has done as much for their sport as you have been able to do for ours.

"You have been the consummate ambassador for sports everywhere. On and off the ice, you have always composed yourself better than anyone could ever imagine."

"And for that we are grateful. Thank you and we will miss you."

Gretzky, who was joined by wife Janet and sons Ty and Trevor, smiled as Bettman paid tribute to him. But he was red-eyed as he watched a video tribute to the sounds of Natalie Merchant and Green Day.

Former NHL player John Davidson introduced Gretzky as "the greatest player who ever played."

"For the last couple of weeks people have been asking me why this is the time," Gretzky said. "It's a gut feel, something I really believe is right."

"I love the game and I love to play. Gordie Howe told me the other day that he still loves to play and he's playing in charity games and he's 70 years old."

"Whether it's now or the next year or 20 years from now I'm always going to miss the National Hockey League and the game of hockey."

Wearing a dark suit, Gretzky seemed subdued. At times, it seemed like he was just trying to stay in control of his emotions. His voice broke several times as he thanked a long list of friends, fellow players and associates.

His wife Janet looked on, also seemingly fighting her emotions. His daughter Paulina did not attend, because Gretzky said she was worried she would cry too much.

Gretzky, who holds more than 60 NHL records, emphasized that he wanted people to look at his retirement as a celebration, not a cause for sadness.

Gretzky's career stats

Regular season

YEAR	TEAM	GP	G	A	PTS.
1979-80	Edm	79	51	86	137
1980-81	Edm	80	55	109	164
1981-82	Edm	80	92	120	212
1982-83	Edm	80	71	125	196
1983-84	Edm	74	87	118	205
1984-85	Edm	80	73	135	208
1985-86	Edm	80	52	163	215
1986-87	Edm	79	62	121	183
1987-88	Edm	64	40	109	149
1988-89	LA	78	54	114	168
1989-90	LA	73	40	102	142
1990-91	LA	78	41	122	163
1991-92	LA	74	31	90	121
1992-93	LA	45	16	49	65
1993-94	LA	81	38	92	130
1994-95	LA	48	11	37	48
1995-96	LA-StL	80	23	79	102
1996-97	NYR	82	25	72	97
1997-98	NYR	82	23	67	90
1998-99	NYR	69	9	52	61
TOTALS		1,486	894	1,962	2,856

Playoffs

YEAR	TEAM	GP	G	A	PTS.
1979-80	Edm	3	2	1	3
1980-81	Edm	9	7	14	21
1981-82	Edm	5	5	7	12
1982-83	Edm	16	12	26	38
1983-84	Edm	19	13	22	35
1984-85	Edm	18	17	30	47
1985-86	Edm	10	8	11	19
1986-87	Edm	21	5	29	34
1987-88	Edm	19	12	31	43
1988-89	LA	11	5	17	22
1989-90	LA	7	3	7	10
1990-91	LA	12	4	11	15
1991-92	LA	6	2	5	7
1992-93	LA	24	15	25	40
1995-96	StL	13	2	14	16
1996-97	NYR	15	10	10	20
TOTALS		208	122	260	382

No re-Gretz for Wayne

NEW YORK (CP) —

Flashing a wan smile through a veil of tears, a weary Wayne Gretzky glided nobly out of the game he revolutionized Sunday. Gretzky took his final bow on Broadway, surrounded by stars, starlets and a slow-footed New York Ranger supporting cast, far from Brantford, Ont., where he spent endless hours learning the game as a prodigiously talented tot.

"I'm devastated I will no longer be a hockey player," Gretzky said, following the Rangers 2-1 overtime loss to the Pittsburgh Penguins. "I will miss every part of the game, because I loved every part of the game.

"But I've made the right decision."

Gretzky set up the Rangers' lone goal, collecting assist No. 1,963 and point No. 2,857 in his brilliant 20-year National Hockey League career.

It was, in truth, a dull game, lifted above the mundane only by the pre and post-game festivities.

The 38-year-old star centre had billed his final curtain call as a celebration. But Madison Square Garden was rife with melancholia and emotion. The sight of former teammates Mark Messier and Paul Coffey on the other side of the glass moistened his eyes during the game. The finality of it all came flooding out of him when a time-out was called with seconds left on his career's clock.

"That's when it really hit me that I was done," he said afterward. "I looked up and I said, 'My goodness, I've got 30 seconds to go.' That's when it hit me."

He insisted there were no regrets. He even found it fitting that the game's winning goal was scored by Jaromir Jagr, who has inherited his place as the most prolific scorer in the game.

"Everyone always talks about passing the torch. He caught it."

The event was awash in nostalgia. Leather-lunged New Yorkers applauded aplenty during a pre-game ceremony, but they reserved their loudest ovation for Messier, the former Ranger who brought them a Stanley Cup in 1994.

There would be no last playoff waltz for Gretzky. His dreary team had already been banished from the playoffs.

There were unmistakable flashes of his old game. Labouring from behind the net, twisting goalie Tom Barrasso's neck into a Windsor knot, he must have slid a half-dozen of perfect passes to his teammates Sunday before they finally mustered the wit to propel one of them into the Pittsburgh net.

National Hockey League commissioner Gary Bettman announced before the game that the league will retire Gretzky's number.

"Words can't describe (it)," Gretzky said when asked about it after the game. "When this gentleman (Soo GM Muzz MacPherson) in 1977 told me to wear the sweater, I didn't expect one day that they wouldn't let anyone else wear it again. It's a great honour."

So there will never be another No. 99.

"He did some incredible things on the ice that nobody is ever going to be able to repeat in the future," said Mario Lemieux, who was at the game. "I can say that his records are pretty safe.

"Jagr is Jagr. Gretzky is the greatest of all time and there's never going to be another Gretzky."

Lemieux, the man who was supposed to inherit his crown left not just because of, ill health, but also because he was tired of being stifled by referees looking the other way as a league bloated by expansion strives for mediocrity.

Gretzky's legacy is immense. He holds or shares 61 records and his name is engraved four times on the Stanley Cup.

After Sunday's game, he took a lonely series of slow, languorous turns around the ice at Madison Square Garden, waved at the paying customers cheering and extinguished an era in the National Hockey League.

Gretzky by the numbers

A look at some of Wayne Gretzky's accomplishments:

4 Stanley Cup victories with the Edmonton Oilers.

92 goals in the 1981-82 season, an NHL single season record.

163 assists and **215** points in the 1985-86 season, both single season NHL records.

894 regular season and **122** playoff goals totaling **1,016** goals for his career.

1,962 regular season and **260** playoff assists totaling **2,222** assists for his career.

9 Hart Memorial Trophies for regular season MVP.

10 Art Ross Trophies for regular season scoring champion

Clark says he's quitting with clear conscience

VICTORIA (CP) —

Glen Clark resigned as B.C. premier Saturday, a day after a politically fatal court document was released alleging he used his influence to help a friend get a lucrative casino licence.

He becomes the third consecutive elected B.C. premier to be forced from office by scandal.

Clark said he visited Lt.-Gov. Garde Gardom earlier Saturday and tendered his resignation, something he said he knew he'd have to do in March after RCMP raided his home.

But Clark maintained he has done nothing wrong, despite an ongoing criminal investigation.

"I'm completely confident I will be exonerated and cleared," said Clark, who appeared tanned and relaxed.

"No premier should be driven from office by the existence of an investigation that remains incomplete and much of which has already been disproven."

But he added: "I've concluded it would be wrong of me to continue."

Deputy premier Dan Miller was named interim premier. Miller challenged Clark for the NDP leadership in 1996, but said he will not run for the job again.

The three MLAs most likely to run to succeed Clark include Finance Minister Gordon Wilson, Attorney General Ujjal Dosanjh and Joy MacPhail, who resigned from the Finance portfolio last month.

Clark has been under fire since the police raid. Debacles such as the massive cost overruns on the fast ferry project, a scandal surrounding fudged budgets and a faltering economy have contributed to his woes.

But release of the information to obtain the warrant for the March search was explosive.

"I like being the underdog, but this is getting ridiculous," Clark said.

(CP PHOTO/Victoria Times-Colonist - Sean White)

B.C. Premier Glenn Clark gestures during his resignation announcement at the Legislature, on Saturday, August 21, 1999. Clark resigned as premier Saturday, a day after a politically fatal court document was released alleging he used his influence to help a friend get a lucrative casino licence.

1990~1999

Olympic sponsor pulls out

SALT LAKE CITY (AP) —
Johnson & Johnson became the first sponsor to pull out of the scandal-ridden Olympics, backing off an estimated $30 million deal for the 2002 Winter Games.

The company on Sunday blamed the decision on internal disagreements about how to link the company's many brands under a sponsorship umbrella in time for the Salt Lake City Games. But Olympic bribery was a factor.

"We can't say that it didn't have anything to do with it," company spokesman John McKeegan said. "It was certainly in the background."

The Salt Lake scandal sparked several investigations after it was revealed the city's bid committee offered $1.2 million in cash, scholarships and other gifts to International Olympic Committee members and their relatives during the successful campaign to win the games.

Ten IOC members have been removed or have resigned after being linked to the cash payments and other vote-buying inducements.

Ten others have been censured or warned about their actions in the worst ethics scandal in the history of the modern Olympics.

Johnson & Johnson, a health care product company in New Brunswick, N.J., had just signed a letter of intent to increase financial support when the bribery accusations surfaced late last year.

Public buying into future of historic sternwheeler

Sales of shares raise funds toward restoration of SS Sicamous

By Dave Duncan
Penticton Herald

Restoration efforts on board the SS Sicamous have been shored up by the Skaha Rotary Club's Save Our Sicamous fundraising campaign.

And the historic vessel, moored on Okanagan Beach, is again open to the public, 9 a.m. to 4 p.m. daily, following a winter closure.

Incoming Skaha Rotary Club president Paul Glen said about 500 limited edition shares have already been sold for $10 each, with a goal to sell 10,000 over the next several months.

"Our ultimate goal is to have the funds in place for the folks at the (SS Sicamous) Restoration Society to do their work by the end of June 2000," said Glen.

Money collected from share sales will be put into trust for the society, to be used as need.

None of the funds will go toward operating costs. They go directly into the sternwheeler's restoration.

"There's a tremendous amount of work to do up there (second and third levels). It's fine detailed work that takes a lot of skill," said Wayne Dods, restoration society vice-chair.

Money generated through share sales will pay for painting, woodwork restoration, flooring and setting up a display in the purser's office, among other things.

"This gives us a chance to return that part of the vessel to its original splendour," said society president Don Vass.

Canada Trust has purchased 25 shares and challenged other financial institutions to match its donation.

Goepel McDermid Inc. has also purchased 25 shares and issued a similar challenge to other investment brokers. "Folks have been really supportive. This has been an easy sell," said Glen.

Vass said the society has received a $20,000 operating grant from the City of Penticton and the boarding fee of $3 per person, coupled with donations and fundraising activities, should keep the Sicamous open to visitors through late fall.

It costs about $74,000 per year for volunteers to operate the beached vessel.

Photo courtesy of Penticton Museum

1990~1999

Slaughter at school

Two gunmen on apparent suicide mission kill as many as 25 in suburb of Denver, Colo.

LITTLETON, COLO. (AP-REUTERS) —

Two young men with shotguns, handguns and homemade grenades opened fire at a suburban Denver high school Tuesday, killing as many as 25 people in what police called a suicide mission.

"They were going around, they were laughing about it," said Joshua Lapp, who was in the library of Columbine High School when the gunmen approached.

"They'd shoot somebody, they'd laugh, they'd giggle....you'd hear a shot go off, you'd hear somebody yell and scream, another shot go off and they'd yell and scream, another shot and there would be silence."

The local sheriff said the gunmen killed up to 25 people and injured 23 others before turning their weapons on themselves.

Sheriff's department spokesman Steve Davis said there was still no accurate count of the victims late Tuesday, but said there were "at least 25 victims...It may end up at 20 or 21, or it could be higher."

Police said the dead included students and teachers alike, but nearly 12 hours after the shooting, officers had yet to remove any bodies because of the danger of explosives and the need to preserve evidence. FBI agents and police SWAT teams were slowly making their way through the building.

"There's a possibility we may find additional victims," said Davis.

Several students said the killers appeared to be gunning for minorities and athletes.

One female student, her arms spattered with the blood of her fellow students, sobbed as she spoke to a local television station. "He was shooting people right in front of me. He was shooting people of colour and people who play sports," she said.

"He put the gun right in my face and started laughing and said it was because people were mean to him last year."

Most of the wounded were taken to hospital with gunshot wounds. One girl suffered nine shrapnel wounds. At least 11 were in critical or serious condition; one was in guarded condition.

Shots ricocheted off lockers as the gunmen walked calmly through the sprawling high school, which has 1,800 students.

Many students dived to the floors or sprinted for the exits.

Dozens of students hid in classrooms before escaping with the help of police in an armoured car. Others were trapped for hours while SWAT teams searched the school.

Police sweep school for bombs among dead

Officers check for booby traps before clearing bodies

LITTLETON, COLO. (AP) —

Working around bodies still lying where they fell more than a day earlier, bomb-squad officers checked lockers and backpacks for booby traps Wednesday as investigators tried to piece toether one of the deadliest school massacres in U.S. history.

Fourteen students and one teacher were killed at Columbine High School, most of them in the library. They included the two teenaged gunmen who laughed as they opened fire on their schoolmates Tuesday.

The gunmen, Eric Harris, 18, and Dyland Kiebold, 17, apparently shot themselves in the head.

Officials were trying to determine if others were involved and they questioned other members of the boys' group of outcasts, the "Trench Coat Mafia."

Authorities on Wednesday removed the bodies of two victims who died outside the building. Also, more than 24 hours after the attack, parents finally received official word of their children's fate. Police hoped to remove the other bodies later in the day.

Investigators left the corpses in place overnight so they could check for explosives and record the details of the crime scene, which SWAT members described as something from "Dante's Inferno."

Many bodies were sprawled on the floor, slumped in desks or crouched beneath tables, boxes and cubicles where they apparently tried to hide. Police found a handgun under one of the killers and a semi-automatic rifle and two sawed-off shotguns elsewhere.

"It was a different sort of chaos inside," SWAT Sgt. George Hinkle said.

"There were fire alarms going off, strobe lights, four inches of water in the cafeteria. We had been told there were bombs in backpacks and there were backpacks everywhere.

"It was the toughest tactical problem I've ever seen."

Sheriff's spokesman Steve Davis said 30 explosive devices were found at Columbine, in the killers' vehicles and at their homes. Late Tuesday, more than 10 hours after the shootings, a time bomb blew up but no one was hurt.

"Some of these devices are on timing devices, some are incendiary devices and some are pipe bombs," Sheriff John Stone told ABC's Good Morning America.

"Some are like hand grenades that have got shrapnel in them wrapped around butane containers."

Eleven of the victims were male and four were female. District Attorney Dave Thomas said there was no evidence the killers targeted minorities, as some students claimed. Only one of the 13 victims was black.

"I've only seen the photographs but it appears to me that most of the victims were victims because of where they were at a particular time, not that they were sought out," Davis said.

Sixteen people remained in hospital, 11 in critical or serious condition.

70,000 attend memorial

LITTLETON, COLO. (AP) —

As rays of sunshine burst through a slate grey sky, more than 70,000 mourners clutched flowers, blue-and-silver balloons and Bibles on Sunday as they wept for victims of the Littleton high school massacre and wondered why it happened.

Authorities delayed opening the service by 30 minutes, as twice as many mourners as expected had arrived.

Beneath a fluttering awning of blue and white, the Columbine High School colours, Vice-President Al Gore and retired U.S. army Gen. Colin Powell led an array of dignitaries surrounding the makeshift stage stretching across a movie theatre's concrete steps.

Roman Catholic Archbishop Charles Chaput of Denver opened the services with a prayer.

"Surely the past week is about as much suffering as any community can bear," Chaput said.

"Love is stronger than death. I believe that.

"Perhaps beyond all this suffering, something good can be achieved."

Mourners of all ages began arriving four hours before the service. For some, it was the second or third vigil they had attended since Tuesday's rampage.

Student killed in school shooting

Boy shoots one teen dead, injures another at Alberta high school

TABER, ALTA. (CP) — Students at W.R. Myers High School were just settling down after lunch Wednesday when a 14-year-old boy walked in and shot two students, killing one, just a week after a school massacre in Colorado.

"At first everybody thought it was a joke because we didn't think it could happen in our school in such a small town," said Raeanne Kunz, one of the 400 students at W.R. Myers.

"When we found out it was real, everyone was pretty much hysterical. There was a lot of crying and scared kids."

Police confirmed the gunman shot two boys, both 17, before he was taken into custody by the school resource officer, who is also a member of the Taber Police

Friends of Jason Lang hug outside a memorial service for the slain teenager at W.R. Myers high school in Taber, Alta., Monday, May 3, 1999.

(CP PHOTO/Lethbridge Herald-David Rossiter)

Service.

The dead teenager was identified as Jason Lang. The other victim was in Lethbridge Regional Hospital after emergency surgery.

One student was threatened by the shooter but was let go.

"I met him downstairs," said Colby Cannady, 15, a Grade 9 student. "He pointed the gun at me from about one foot away, at my head, and then at my stomach and said, 'Get out of here.'"

Cannady ran toward the school office only to find Lang pleading for help.

"Jason was lying in blood. He was on his hands and knees crawling and saying 'Help me.' There was blood all over him."

Several students called gym teacher Cheyno Finney a hero because he stopped the youth before he shot anyone else.

"The shooter was tackled straight away and the gun was taken out of his hand before anyone else was hurt," said student Jordan Bareman.

Police would not release any details, but talk of a copycat killing ran wild after some students told one reporter the shooter was a "real loser-type" who walked in with a blue trenchcoat and a sawed-off .22 -calibre rifle.

Later, after evacuating single file much like a fire drill, coatless students huddled together for comfort and warmth as a late spring storm dropped heavy, wet snow

around them.

Classes were canceled for the rest of the week. At least 15 counsellors were immediately made available.

The emotional aftermath of the first fatal Canadian high school shooting in 20 years produced conflicting reports over exactly what happened.

Bruce Bell said his schoolteacher wife told him classes were in session when the boy walked in with a rifle and threatened a teacher.

"The kid just turned around and walked out, heading for the front door," Bell said.

"There were two other kids there, two kids who were late. He just shot them and kept walking."

The suspect was said to be a Grade 9 student who had quit W.R. Myers and was being taught at home. It was not clear whether he knew his victims.

The identities of the accused and the survivor are protected under the Young Offenders Act.

School gunman described as smart with few friends

TABER, ALTA. (CP) — Years of bullying may have led a shy, smart, computer-loving teenager from a solid Mormon family to gun down two students at a southern Alberta high school, says a former classmate.

Andrew Gervals said the 14-year-old boy accused in the shooting appeared to have few friends - not unlike two teenagers who went on a shooting rampage last week at Columbine High School in Littleton, Colo.

"I wasn't surprised to hear it was him," Gervals, 15, said. "I guess he was going to break down sooner or later, fight back, but people didn't know how.

"People had the wrong impression of him - he wanted more friends."

The slight, dark-haired teenager showed no emotion Thursday as

he stood quietly in Lethbridge youth court listening to charges of first-degree and attempted murder being read out against him.

He was charged after Jason Lang, 17, was fatally shot Wednesday in a hallway of W.R. Myers high school in the predominantly Mormon town of Taber, about 300 kilometres southeast of Calgary.

Shane Christmas, who was wounded in the attack, was in fair to serious condition at a Lethbridge hospital.

The suspect's Lethbridge lawyers, Greg Maxwell and Timothy Jervis, reserved his plea. He was remanded into custody and will be back in Lethbridge court May 6.

The accused, wearing a white dress shirt buttoned to the neck, dark grey pants and silver wire-

rimmed glasses, peered at Judge Gerald Debow through a plastic shield surrounding the court's prisoner box.

The accused - who could see the school from the backyard of the modest brick and beige-sided bungalow he lived in - did not speak during the 15-minute session. He did not glance at his mother and stepfather who sat huddled together in the courtroom.

The identity of the boy is protected under the Young Offenders Act. Students say he didn't know his victims.

Neighbour Thomas Gejdos said they often saw the accused playing basketball in his driveway.

"I was shocked and surprised to hear it was him," he said. "He's never been a problem kid."

Another neighbour, who

requested anonymity, began crying as she described a "normal" kid from a good family.

Shawn Mezei, 14, also said the accused - who came to Taber from Ontario after his mother's marriage to his stepfather - was "one of those kids who was picked on.

"Nobody knew a lot about him, but he was a really smart kid. He must have just flipped out.

"He suffered a lot of verbal and physical abuse."

Mezei said the accused had apparently made threats against some kids last year about putting bombs at their houses.

But John Loeppky, who was a Boy Scout with the accused, said he never heard him talk about seeking revenge against his tormentors.

Others described him as a polite teenager from a loving family.

1990-1999

Parents see meeting on threats as failure

OK Falls parents say issues surrounding school district's handling of incident remain unresolved

By Gary Symons
Penticton Herald

Parents of Okanagan Falls Elementary School students were not impressed by School District 53's handling of threats made by a student to shoot fellow students.

But they were even less impressed with the school district's handling of the meeting held Tuesday to discuss the issue.

The school was virtually emptied Friday when angry parents brought their children home, complaining the school refused to answer any questions about the alleged threats.

A special meeting was held at the school at 4 p.m. Tuesday, but none of the parents' concerns appeared to be resolved.

Several parents said superintend-ent Brian Fox and school board chair June Harrington were arro-gant, rude and failed to accept any responsibility.

"I think the whole purpose of the meeting was to find out what went wrong, and I don't think that got resolved," said Kristina Gardner.

"I don't think they were listening at all, especially the superintendent. My impression is they feel they did everything right, and they feel that was the only way it could have been handled."

Gardner is among the hundreds of parents who beg to disagree. Considering parents already know a threat had been made, she believes the school should have been more forthcoming, and then left the decision about a child's safety up to the parent.

"They should be apologizing for perhaps lying to parents when they called and asked about the safety of their children," Gardner said. In fact, she says it was the school that caused a panic, because parents didn't have the information they

Mad mom Lori Glaseman blasts School District 53 officials at a meeting in Okanagan Falls over the handling of a threat to shoot students at the elementary school. Parents say the school is a long way from solving its problems because district officials refuse to deal with their own role in creating a mass panic.

needed to make an informed deci-sion.

"They were blaming everybody else instead of taking a little bit of accountability, and I don't see why

they can't admit everything wasn't handled the best it could be.

"I think they created a panic; I don't think the parents did, I think they did."

School district to review plan for emergencies in wake of crisis

By Gary Symons
Penticton Herald

School District 53 superin-tendent Brian Fox says he still believes officials acted properly in their handling of threats allegedly made last week to shoot students at Okanagan Falls Elementary School.

But Fox does concede the dis-trict's policy regarding communi-cation with parents during "criti-cal incidents" needs to be improved.

"Considering the circumstances and looking at the situation... I think the district still did the right things," Fox said. "But in terms of releasing information, that's going to be an interesting debate. The question is how do you deal with a crisis involving parents and keep it from catching fire, passing from the students to

the parents?

"We have to review that whole issue of communication within the school."

Fox says the district followed their critical incidents plan in this case, but he admits that plan needs some serious updating.

"There is a critical incident plan, but it doesn't take into con-sideration the kinds of events that happened here," Fox said.

The events leading up to the crisis last Friday reportedly began Wednesday evening. An Okanagan Falls student was involved in an altercation with some other students in the same grade. He was subsequently sus-pended from school.

A friend of his later reported to her parents that the boy had made threats to bring a gun to school to kill the vice-principal

and some fellow students.

Penticton RCMP Const. Pete Gibbenhuck began investigating the allegations Thursday, and says he was able to ascertain the threats were not likely to be car-ried out.

The boy and his mother agreed he would come to the Penticton detachment on Friday to discuss a plan to deal with the threats and the boy's problems at school.

But Staff Sgt. Henk Wamsteeker said the plan "went off the rails" on Friday because the boy and his mother did not come to the detachment as planned. Instead the boy and his mother were seen walking by the school Friday morning.

At the same time, parents in the community were learning of the threat allegations and some decided to keep their kids at

home Friday morning. Others became concerned throughout the day and called the school, but when they didn't get any expla-nations there, decided to take their children out of classes for the day.

The majority of parents inter-viewed said their concerns have shifted from the threats that were made to the way school officials handled their request for infor-mation. At a Parents' Advisory Council meeting Tuesday night Lori Glaseman said, as a parent, she has the right to be informed of potential threats to her child's safety, and the school district took away that right.

Fox now admits the school dis-trict has to take a hard look at when and how parents should be informed of any threat to student safety.

Pot ruling offers hope for OK Falls man

Federal government grants exemptions from drug laws to two people with fatal illness

By John Moorhouse
Penticton Herald
With The Canadian Press

The federal government's decision to allow two people to legally smoke pot for medical purposes may have opened the door for similar use by an Okanagan Falls man.

However, Gerald Hopcraft isn't jumping for joy just yet.

The government has given permission for the cultivation and use of marijuana for medical purposes for the first time in Canadian history. Health Minister Allan Rock announced he has granted special exemptions from federal drug law to Jim Wakeford of Toronto and Jean-Charles Pariseau of Vanier, Ont., both of whom have AIDS.

"This is about showing compassion to people, often dying, suffering from grave debilitating illness," Rock told the Commons.

To date, Health Canada has received indications of interest for exemption from some 30 potential applicants for exemption. Further applications to possess and cultivate pot for personal medical use will be considered as well.

Hopcraft, 53, reacted cautiously to the announcement Thursday.

"It's not a solution," he said. "For me to grow it here is ridiculous. We'd have to grow it outside where it becomes a safety issue."

Hopcraft fears passersby would be tempted to steal the plants, coming right up to his house and putting his family at risk. Although the marijuana could be grown indoors, that would require the use of expensive grow lights. Instead, he said, the drug should be made available at pharmacies.

But Hopcraft said he plans to make further inquires into the government's exemption mechanism and will likely make an application within the next couple of weeks.

The Okanagan Falls man suffered severe cranial nerve damage from a series of farming and motor vehicle accidents dating back to when he was a teenager. He must smoke marijuana to increase the fluid in his eyes and brain, and claims he could die within days without it.

His plight was brought to national attention in November 1997 by Okanagan-Coquihalla MP Jim Hart, who presented a private member's motion in the Commons calling for the legalization of marijuana for medical purposes only.

People with illnesses such as cancer and AIDS have claimed for years that marijuana helps relieve pain and stimulate appetite. So far there is little solid scientific data to support those claims.

However, Rock this week unveiled a federal research plan, first announced in March, in which the health department will soon invite bids from firms interested in supplying marijuana for use in upcoming clinical trials.

The Church of the Universe, a Hamilton-based religious group that practises nudity and uses marijuana as a sacrament, has already applied to supply researchers with medical-grade pot. The group proposes turning the Guelph Correctional Centre, which is slated to close, into a secure site for growing marijuana, the National Post reports.

Health Canada is also negotiating with a British firm to test a non-smoked form of marijuana, which is ingested using an inhaler.

JFK Jr. Missing

Kennedys prepare for another funeral

HYANNISPORT, MASS. (CP) — They held out hope and prayed for a miracle long beyond the dictates of reason, but the Kennedy family was prepared for yet another funeral after being told Sunday that John F. Kennedy Jr., his wife and sister-in-law could not have survived the crash of their airplane.

After two days of scouring the cool, flat ocean floor off the resort island of Martha's Vineyard, there was still no sign of the only son of slain president John F. Kennedy.

His wife, Carolyn Bessette Kennedy, 33, and her sister Lauren Bessette, 35, were also on board the Piper Saratoga he was piloting when it disappeared Friday about 20 kilometres off Martha's Vineyard.

"With water temperature of 68 degrees (20 C), survivability in those waters has been exceeded," said Rear Admiral Richard Larrabee, of the U.S. Coast Guard.

He said later Coast Guard efforts would "shift very purposely, from our focus on search and rescue to search and recovery."

The announcement, not unexpected, put an official signature on the death of JFK Jr.

Larrabee told an evening press

John F. Kennedy Jr. and his wife Carolyn Bessette Kennedy leave a party in New York in 1996. With "a lot of tears and hugs," the Kennedy family spent a second anguished day Sunday, July 18, 1999 awaiting any sign of John F. Kennedy Jr., his wife and her sister.

(AP Photo/Douglas Healey)

conference he had offered his condolences to the families by telephone.

A single ping emitted from an emergency transponder Sunday afternoon was picked up by the

Coast Guard, and offered some hope for several hours that the aircraft would be found. However, Larrabee said later at a 9:30 p.m. news conference that the ping was not from Kennedy's plane and

could have been from a beacon placed as part of the search effort.

A pair of headrests, chunks of foam insulation, the wheel and strut section of landing gear and Lauren Bessette's luggage was all that had been recovered.

Caroline Kennedy, who was exceedingly close to her brother, remained in seclusion at her Long Island home. His death would make her the only surviving member of what was once America's glittering first family.

The Bessette family spent Sunday in seclusion at their home in Greenwich, Conn., waiting to hear if they had lost two daughters and a son-in-law in a plane crash.

A mass was held at the Kennedy compound here. Senator Kennedy, surrounded by his nieces and nephews, sat near the front of the veranda of the main house while the family sought solace in the faith that had sustained them through the assassination of two Kennedy brothers and the deaths of two other siblings in air crashes.

No one among them spoke publicly Sunday but much was going on behind the whitewashed walls and crisp green shutters.

A lot of tears and hugs was the way Mary Medeiros, a family babysitter, described the scene inside the compound.

Kennedy to be buried at sea today

OTIS AIR FORCE BASE, MASS. (CP) — The agonizing vigil for the Kennedy family ended Wednesday after navy divers located the body of John F. Kennedy Jr. in a shattered section of his single engine plane.

Several hours later, the bodies of his wife, Carolyn Bessette Kennedy, and her sister, Lauren Bessette, were also found nearby in about 30 metres of water.

The wings, tail and engine compartment of the Piper Saratoga were torn away from the passenger compartment during the crash.

John Kennedy will be buried at sea this morning with the assistance of the U.S. navy, a Clinton

administration official said Wednesday night.

"He will be buried tomorrow

A handwritten memorial message to John F. Kennedy Jr. is attached to a fence at Essex County Airport in Fairfield, New Jersey where Kennedy, his wife Carolyn Bessett Kennedy and her sister Lauren Bessette, departed on their ill-fated flight to Martha's Vineyard.

morning," the official said.

The official had no other details about the burial but con-

firmed it would be at sea.

The USS Briscoe was in the area and could be used in the event of any burial or funeral ceremony, a Pentagon spokesman said.

Kennedy, his wife and sister-in-law died Friday after the single engine plane piloted by Kennedy went into a nosedive and slammed into the Atlantic.

Senator Edward Kennedy made a slow 10-kilometre trip to a U.S. navy recovery ship after searchers found the body of his nephew in the tranquil waters off Martha's Vineyard.

The Kennedy family patriarch and his two sons were aboard the USS Grasp when the three bodies were brought to the surface.

Losing the lake

INSPECTOR WARNED US

Fred Alcock took a little dip in Okanagan Lake almost a quarter of a century ago, and he's never gone in since.

As Chief Public Health Inspector for 30 years, from 1948 to 1978, Alcock disagreed with the government's decision to use the herbicide Killex to battle milfoil in the lake.

"I didn't agree with dosing the lake with chlorinated hydrocarbons," recalls Alcock.

It was enough to keep him from swimming in the "pristine" lake he loved.

Alcock, now 83 years old, along with David Clarke, the Medical Health Officer for the Southern Okanagan at the time, fought city council tooth-and-nail to keep sewage and chemicals out of the lake, with little success.

Twenty-five years ago, The Daily Courier quoted Clarke's plea to municipal officials:

"I have spent the better part of my professional life trying to save that great lake out there and I am not going to sit idle and see it ruined forever by this council."

Okanagan's gem may be losing its lustre

By SHELLEY WOOD
Special to The Okanagan Saturday

They come for the lake. Flatter than the Eiffel Tower, less predictable than the Taj Mahal, Okanagan Lake can still take its place proudly beside premier tourist magnets the world over.

Summer visitors flood to the Okanagan to taste the wines, gorge in the orchards, savour the sun, or ski the waves. The lake, directly or indirectly, is the reason they come. If it disappeared, the tourists would too.

Of course, lakes don't just vanish. But listen to the banter between citizens, industry, scientists and environmentalists over the quality and quantity of water in the Valley, and you begin to wonder whether we will always be able to use and enjoy the lake as much as we do now.

How do you assess the long-term health of a lake? Check its pulse, some blood tests, prescribe a diet that will keep it hearty and pure as the day it was born?

The proof is in the puddles.

"The lake is fine," says Ken Cooper, Kelowna's deputy chief public health inspector. He is interested primarily in the bugs - mostly bacteria and parasites - that live in the lake.

Cooper says the lake is "in pretty good shape" and easily meets federal guidelines for Canadian recreational water quality. When water quality falls below levels set by the guidelines, the health inspectors move in.

It's a strategy that doesn't hold water for Leonard Fraser, who mans the ship at the Canadian EarthCare offices in Kelowna. He would like city planners and healthboard officials to act proactively to prevent contaminants from entering the lake in the first place, rather than reacting only after problems arise.

Working in the Penticton branch of the Ministry of the Environment, Vic Jensen oversees sampling programs that test twice yearly for nutrients such as nitrogen and phosphorus in the lake.

Okanagan Lake, explains Jensen, is historically a low-nutrient lake and it has remained relatively low in nutrients.

"We haven't seen large changes in nutrients status since the 1970s," says Jensen.

"And that's a good thing."

A 1996 B.C. water quality status report fingered agriculture, municipal waste, storm water drainage, forestry and inputs from upstream lakes as the major sources of phosphorus and other nutrients.

Jensen says treated waste water discharged directly into the lake has been treated better over the past decade and that treatment facilities have kept pace with the growth of the population.

Fraser is not convinced. He agrees that some of the unwelcome agricultural nutrients entering the lake have declined over the past few decades, ever since farmers made the switch from surface ditches to sprinkler irrigation.

The problem, says Fraser, is that there just isn't the money or political will to figure out exactly what chemicals, in what quantities, are coming from where.

In fact, the last comprehensive study to trace lake contaminants back to their primary sources was conducted in the early 1970s and many of the decisions made today about water use and sewage treatment in the Okanagan basin are based on information almost three decades old.

In Fraser's opinion, Okanagan Lake still gets treated like a toilet.

Fraser speaks passionately about the filtering role of the wetlands and associated creeks and rivers that feed into Okanagan Lake, many of which have been dammed, re-routed or forcibly tunnelled beneath the ground.

He claims that of the 30 some-odd creeks that used to flow into the lake from the Kelowna flood plain, only six still flow and function normally.

His figures don't match those of the 1998 City of Kelowna environment report, which states there are 27 tributary streams that flow through the city.

According to Fraser, it's a question of terminology, since most of these so-called streams do not support the diversity of life seen in a wild creek.

"To me a ditch is not really a stream. It's a conduit for water," says Fraser.

He believes that unless government, individuals and industry get together to decide upon long-term strategies for reducing pollution, especially via the remaining waterways, Okanagan Lake will die "a death of a thousand cuts."

Kevin Ade, who founded the Friends of Brandt's Creek in Kelowna, believes that how both locals and Okanagan visitors treat their natural surroundings will ultimately decide the fate of the lake.

"We've got all this water and all this sunshine, but we abuse what we have," says Ade.

"People want to come to the Okanagan to retire or to party: it's a place where people come to take advantage, and opportunism is frequently abusive."

But just how much longer can we abuse the lake and still enjoy it as much as we do?

"That's the million-dollar question," says Jeff Curtis, a professor in fresh water science at Okanagan University College.

He explains there are "finite supplies of water in the Valley" - water of a high enough quality that it can be used for all the things we use it for now. He has attempted to pin down when the taps will run dry.

Basing his calculations on a population growth rate of around three per cent, Curtis believes we only have 25 to 30 years left before we can no longer draw water from the lake.

1990-1999

Five killed in mid-air crash

**By John Moorhouse
and Joyce Langerak
The Okanagan Saturday**

PENTICTON —

Five people were killed in a mid-air collision over Penticton Friday.

Witnesses say the two light planes crashed into each other just north of the Penticton Airport at about 11:30 a.m. Both aircraft spiralled while crashing to the ground — one smashing into the parking lot at Okanagan University College where it burst into flames. The other crashed into the work yard of a nearby metal working shop. Although no fire occurred, the bodies of the four occupants, believed to be two men, a woman and a child, were strewn about.

No one on the ground was injured, although two employees of Steelworks Inc. were working in the yard when the crash occurred. The body of the fifth victim, the lone occupant of the second plane, was still inside the burnt remains of the aircraft while firefighters doused the flames.

Witness say it appeared one plane had just taken off from the airport when it collided with the descending plane 200 or 300 feet in the air. Air traffic controllers were eliminated from the Penticton Airport in a cost-cutting move by Transport Canada in 1995.

Elin Bigler and her husband, Ken of the Seattle, Wash. area were

Photo by photo credit

This Mooney 20, one of two planes downed after a mid-air collision over Penticton Friday, broke apart on impact in the Steelworks Inc. yard, claiming the lives of all four occupants. The collision broke one wing off the aircraft, causing it to spiral to the ground. Though there were two workers in the yard at the time, no one on the ground was injured.

cycling along Fairview Road when Elin looked up and saw the planes come together.

I said, "'Ken, there's an air show!' They made a boom when they hit, but I thought they were just practising something. They hit and I thought they were practising an air show at first. It was so incredible."

To her horror, the planes began to break apart in mid-air.

"Then all of a sudden, the debris started falling out of the sky from where they hit. You could see red and white parts. I said, 'Ken, they hit!' There was all this stuff falling out of the sky. I saw it. Then that one spiraled right to the ground."

Bigler was referring to one plane that came down in the parking lot at the Penticton campus of Okanagan University College.

"Black smoke just plummeted up from where it hit the ground. We just stopped at the fence at the college. It was engulfed in flames. There wasn't much left when they were through putting it out."

Transport Canada investigators were scheduled to arrive at the crash scene late Friday afternoon. No names have yet been released.

Three with local ties among crash victims

**By JOYCE LANGERAK
Penticton Herald**

Two Penticton men and a former Summerland man were among five who perished in a mid-air collision between two small planes over the city Friday.

Douglas Riley, 59 and Stuart Anderson, 61, both of Penticton, were a among four who died aboard a 1962 Mooney M20C aircraft which spiraled into the ground behind Steelworks Inc. on Waterloo Avenue off Fairview Road.

The wreckage narrowly missed a fork-lift driver who was only metres from the point of impact. No one on the ground was injured.

Three members of one family

died in the crash of the Mooney. Dead at the scene were pilot, Thorsten Watterodt, 33, of Beaumont, Alta., his son, four-year-old Auston and Douglas Riley, the pilot's father-in-law. Anderson, who also died in the

Mooney, was a family friend.

Pilot Terrance J. Sabourin, 56, of Valemount, B.C., was the sole occupant of the second plane, a Cessna 177 RG, that plunged into the parking lot of Okanagan University College, about 300 metres north of the Mooney crash site.

Sabourin, formerly of Summerland, was manager of the Canadian Imperial Bank of Commerce there for about 10 years.

Preliminary investigation suggests Sabourin had just taken off from the Penticton Airport and was headed north when the collision occurred in the air over the Channel Parkway.

Investigators from the

Transportation Safety Board of Canada out of Richmond, B.C., were on site at both crashes Saturday and Sunday. They were joined by RCMP member, RCMP forensic investigators, insurance investigators and personnel from the Penticton Fire Department.

By Sunday the wreckage had been cleared away and there was nothing left at that crash scene but a depression in the blackened pavement. There, someone had laid rocks in the shape of a cross and a bouquet of flowers.

Though witnesses reported hearing a loud "pop" when the planes collided, there was no mid-air explosion, said Penticton coroner Gary Davidson who is assisting in the investigation.

1990-1999

Marketing Skyreach

Kelowna's much-anticipated and much-hyped 6,000-seat Skyreach Place opens its doors for the first time tonight for a Moist concert.

By STEVE MacNAULL
The Okanagan Saturday

Everybody seems to want a piece of Skyreach. The public can't wait to get in for concerts. The city's Western Hockey League team gets in on Sunday and business interests can't wait to see their sponsorship signs up and products on sale in the $20-million, 6,000-seat arena.

"It's a privately-owned-run-and-managed building (RG Properties of Vancouver)," says Skyreach Place manager Dave Dakers.

"That means we can be much more business oriented than a municipality that owns an arena. We can go out and get the sponsorships and make those deals."

So far, alliances have been formed with more than 50 companies covering everything from beer (it's a Molson house) and soft drinks (Pepsi's the name) to the name that's on the building (Skyreach, of course) and who will supply the food to the on-site restaurant and concessions (HRI).

"We feel this venue will be one of those places people will naturally be drawn to," says Alan Baldwin, regional manager of Shaw Cable, the official cable, Internet, computer hook-up and phone system supplier for Skyreach.

"We want to be there and let people know we are a TV station and a provider of cable and Internet."

Everything about Skyreach Place is new and exciting for Kelowna.

For starters, there is its sheer size and the promise of a large, dynamic venue for both Western

Hockey League action with Kelowna Rockets and big-name concerts - including Moist tonight, Alice Cooper announced in September and Tom Jones in November.

Corporations and advertisers naturally want to be part of this excitement and market to the

500,000 people who will attend events at Skyreach annually.

"An arena is an entirely different advertising format than, say, a mall, a billboard or TV," explains Dakers.

"At the arena, you're in a dynamic entertainment environment and you are there for three

hours."

Sponsorship is the wave of the future for most major sports and concert venues - just look at Air Canada Centre in Toronto, GM Place in Vancouver, Canadian Airlines Saddledome in Calgary, Molson Centre in Montreal and Corel Centre in Ottawa.

1990~1999

OGO Believe

SEPTEMBER 9, 1993

Ogopogo spotted near Kelowna

KELOWNA — Ogopogo has reared its ugly back again.

Okanagan Lake's legendary sea serpent is the prime suspect after three women spotted a strange object swimming in Okanagan Lake near Bear Creek Park about 3 p.m. Monday.

Lidia Allen, Trudy Towers and Debbie Nielsen were sitting in the picnic area of the park looking over the calm water when a black streak appeared in the water about 60 metres off-shore.

"It almost looked like a wave, but it was so long and it stood there - really dark black," said Allen, 21.

"Then it move and went under. IT was a thick black line and it started to go up and down... It looked like a serpent."

The three women, all from Kelowna, watched the object for close to 10 minutes as it swam like a snake south along the Westside shore. They did not have a camera with them.

"We saw this black streak coming out of the water. It was really thick, like a big black snake," Allen recalled. "It went up and down, slithering.

"The part above the water was 10-15 feet long. It was really dark. We couldn't see a head. Its back was coming up and then going down."

The women watched object disappear around a point, then reappear in the distance minutes later.

This is the third reported sighting in less than three week. Last Thursday, a Kelowna woman and her two adult grandchildren spotted two humps and a wake.

The two humps were blackish, bluey and smooth, said Brenda Massey, 23. She described it as a large water snake coming up out of the water and down.

On Aug. 11, two couples were motoring in a speedboat across Okanagan Lake just north of Rattlesnake Island when the two women sitting in the bow noticed a strong fish smell.

"My sister-in-law said to me, 'It stinks,'" said Chris Barile, a Kelowna resident. "it was gross - strong and smelly."

Moments later there was a strange churning in the water about six metres from the boat. A large object then appeared above the surface. It looked like the back of a snake, but it was huge," said Barile. "It had a hump coming out of the water and then went down. IT didn't come up again."

Barile described the hump as greenish-gray, but stopped short of identifying it as that of Ogopogo.

"I believe there's something big in there, but I don't think there's a sea monster... The thing that really made us thing (though) was that awful fishy smell."

There have been five sightings of Ogopogo- or a distant relative who looks just like him - so far this summer.

APRIL 9, 1996

12-storey Okanagan ambassador takes to the air in June

KELOWNA — After centuries of lurking in the murky depths of Okanagan Lake, Ogopogo is taking to the air.

A 12-storey (38-metre) high "Oggy" will officially surface at the Olds Balloon Classic in Danville, Ill. June 6 - 9. (An earlier appearance is possible.)

Oggy will also pop up over Idaho, Michigan, Missouri and Reno, Nevada during a summer long series of hot air balloon exhibitions.

However, his crowning achievement will be the Albuquerque Balloon Festival, known simply as The Big One, Oct. 5 - 13.

Oggy will join 650 balloons at the most photographed event in the world on its 25th anniversary.

Winfield balloonist Ron Martin can't wait for his $75,000 US creation to be completed by Aerostar balloon manufacturers of Sioux Falls, S.D.

The 53-year-old Central Okanagan flyer has dreamed of an Ogopogo balloon for upwards of five years.

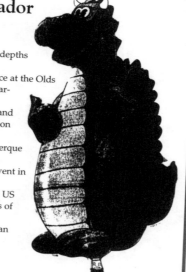

POGO
it or not!

APRIL 23, 1997

Serpent in the spotlight

KELOWNA— Ogopogo's popularity is soaring.

The mysterious Okanagan Lake monster has not only resurfaced this spring but is attracting increasing attention from TV producers.

"They're coming out of the woodwork," said Arlene Gaal, Kelowna's Ogopogo expert. "I just got a call from Omni-Films in Vancouver and, last Friday, got a call from London on a British production."

The Discovery Channel has sent her a contract, a German films team is expected in mid-May and a FoxTV film crew just spent two days filming.

Each crew tends to spend time with Gaal, interviewing her and going over some of the more spectacular sightings and film footage.

The legendary lake creature has never been confirmed to exist and has been variously described as a beaver or sturgeon.

Last year, there were four or five sightings, down from the average of five to seven a year, Gaal said.

This year, there has already been one reported off City Park, on April 3 by a boy named Bill, who was embarrassed to admit the incident.

"He said it was mirror calm, which is the best time for sightings," Gaal recalled. "He claimed it was at least 50 feet long."

He watched it swimming around for an hour, apparently feeding, and described the skin as similar to a halibut's.

It was near the concession stand in City Park, about the same place a photograph was taken in 1990, Gaal said.

MARCH 15, 1996

Lake creature startles strollers

PENTICTON (Staff) — A spring walk may have provided the event of a lifetime for two residents.

Frank Serio said he and his girlfriend were out for a stroll near the dock between where the SS Sicamous and SS Naramata are moored, when they came upon a large creature swimming rapidly in the water.

"As we were walking, we heard two large splashes and when we turned towards them, we saw a large head swimming southward," said Serio.

"The head was moving faster than anything I've ever seen swimming in my life," he said.

Serio followed the movement, running along the shore maintaining a distance of about 25 feet, before being forced to stop by a fence.

The mysterious creature stayed afloat for a few more minutes, then disappeared into the night.

Speculation on what the creature was abounds. However, that area is known to be home to an amiable beaver that created a bit of chaos in the Penticton Rose Garden area, several months ago.

PREMIERE EDITION

The Okanagan SUNDAY

93¢ +7¢ GST = $1.00
COIN BOX $1.00

SEPTEMBER 12, 1999

New Sunday paper only the beginning

By TODD VOGT
Publisher

Welcome to The Okanagan Sunday
I am very pleased and honoured to
introduce you to your new Sunday
newspaper. I want to emphasize th
this is your newspaper; without th
support and dem
from you, our re
ers, The Okanar
Sunday would r
have been laun
The Okanaga
Sunday repre:
the first of se
new publicat
from The Ok
Valley New:
Group, which publishes The
Courier, The Penticton Hera

Todd Vogt

INSIDE

OKANAGAN
Daily Courier steps in to sponsor tourney

The Daily Courier and its affiliated Okanagan Valley Newspaper Group publications have added a local flavour to the Kelowna International Midget AAA Hockey Tournament by agreeing to sponsor the event for the next five years.

Formerly sponsored by Tim Hortons, the tournament, which is gearing up for its 21st year, is one of the marquee events of its kind in B.C.

In addition to The Daily Courier, Skyreach Equipment, the company which lent its name to Kelowna's new arena, has also jumped on board as a major sponsor.

Skyreach Place general manager Dave Dakers confirmed Friday that the tournament final will be played

New Sunday paper only the beginning

By TODD VOGT
Publisher

Welcome to The Okanagan Sunday'

I am very pleased and honoured to introduce you to your new Sunday newspaper. I want to emphasize that this is your newspaper; without the support and demand from you, our readers, The Okanagan Sunday would never have been launched. The Okanagan Sunday represents the first of several new publications from The Okanagan Valley Newspaper Group, which publishes The Daily Courier, The Penticton Herald, Southern

Exposure, Westside Weekly and the rest of your local newspapers.

The Okanagan Sunday also represents the second regional newspaper that we publish for the Okanagan. We hope The Okanagan Sunday will mirror the success of The Okanagan Saturday, recognized as one of the best regional papers in North America.

Regardless of the success of your two regional newspapers, they will be contained to Saturday and Sunday. We have absolutely no intention of creating a single regional paper to serve the Okanagan Monday through

Friday. Each community, will keep its respective newspaper for now and the foreseeable future.

The decision to launch The Okanagan Sunday was an obvious one: the success of The Okanagan Saturday, the continued regionalization of the economy and community of the Okanagan and, most notably, the demand for a Sunday newspaper for the entire Valley.

Kelowna, you're still special, but no longer extra special on Sundays.

We believe we have put together the beginnings of what will become a great Sunday newspa-

per. We listened to our readers and the result is what you now hold in your hands. The Okanagan Sunday will feature great new writers, interesting columns and all the news from the Okanagan Valley and around the world.

We'll make some changes and tweak a few things as we evolve into the great Sunday newspaper we've promised.

So, enjoy your new Sunday newspaper, The Okanagan Sunday. And, please, let us know what you think.

As I've said before, we are listening.

1990~1999

What a difference a daily makes

It's already become a daily habit for hundreds of Vernon residents and it's only the first day.

Vernon Times owner Todd Vogt says he's astounded by the positive response to the city's newest daily newspaper.

"Everywhere you go in town people are talking about us and it's great," said Vogt, who owns 45 newspapers, including The Daily Courier and Penticton Herald.

Virtually every home in Greater Vernon will receive a copy of today's inaugural edition and the sampling will continue for the rest of the month.

But even without seeing a copy of the paper, hundreds of local residents and businesses have paid for subscriptions.

"That's a strong endorsement for the team we've put together and our belief in the need for a daily newspaper in Vernon," said Vogt.

Today's paper is a fair representation of what subscribers can expect on a daily basis, said Managing Editor Russ Niles.

"We have to cover the major issues affecting the area and we have the most comprehensive package to date for Vernon readers on the native logging issue," he said.

But life isn't all turmoil and conflict.

"You'll see a big winner, people enjoying themselves and people helping others," said Niles. "It's just another day in Vernon."

Look inside and you'll find us to be your window on the nation and the world with stories from Canadian Press, Reuters and Associated Press, plus sports, entertainment and business news.

As we grow, we'll expand coverage in all areas and improve the paper every way we can.

Now we want to know what you think about us and the issues of the day.

In fact, we've already had some suggestions. Mrs. Cunningham, we have already committed to cover all high school sports. Mrs. Crozman, we'll do our best for bowling.

Before we'd published a paper, we already had letters to the editor. Keep them coming.

And if there's something we're missing, let us know.

"This is your newspaper, Vernon, and we want it to reflect your Community," said Vogt.